1 MONTH OF
FREE
READING

at

www.ForgottenBooks.com

By purchasing this book you are eligible for one month membership to ForgottenBooks.com, giving you unlimited access to our entire collection of over 1,000,000 titles via our web site and mobile apps.

To claim your free month visit:

www.forgottenbooks.com/free168806

ISBN 978-1-5283-9045-3
PIBN 10168806

THE EQUITY DECISIONS

F(

THE HON. JOHN W. RITCHIE,

JUDGE IN EQUITY

OF THE

PROVINCE OF NOVA SCOTIA.

1873-1882.

EDITED BY

BENJAMIN RUSSELL, M. A.,

BARRISTER-AT-LAW,

Official Reporter to the Supreme Court of Nova Scotia.

Parts 1. 02 wm spud as
Chesley & this is what wa
all Nub ~~teed~~ 2f Russell & Che

HALIFAX, N. S.:
PUBLISHED BY A. & W. MACKINLAY.
1883.

EDITOR'S PREFACE.

THIS volume is supposed to contain all the decisions delivered by Mr. Justice Ritchie, as Judge in Equity for the Province of Nova Scotia. It may well be that some of his decisions have never come into the hands of the Editor, as there was no regular record kept of the proceedings of the Equity Court, and no set time for the delivery of judgments. A decision has been included in the present volume which does not come strictly within its scope, as it was delivered by His Lordship as a member of the Supreme Court *in banco*, but the importance of the question discussed, its intimate connection with the subjects treated in a class of cases coming strictly within the scope of this volume, and the fact that the case does not appear in print elsewhere, seemed to warrant its being included in the present collection. The hope is indulged that the volume now presented may do something to perpetuate the fame of a tribunal to which, in His Lordship's time, the words of the late Chancellor Kent were pre-eminently suitable, a tribunal "presenting the image of the sanctity of a temple where truth and justice seemed to be enthroned and to be personified in their decrees."

LIST OF CASES.

CASES

SUPREME COURT OF NOVA SCOTIA,

IN EQUITY.

FROM JULY, 1873, TO DECEMBER, 1877.

ALMON ET AL., ADMINISTRATORS OF COGSWELL, v. FOOT.

Defendant obtained a loan of £200 on mortgage from Cogswell, through a Solicitor doing business at Wolfville, who made a charge of £10 for conveyancing and commissions, and a further charge of £10 for guaranteeing the defendant from loss, in case the principal was called for within five years. The mortgagee did not authorize the taking of anything beyond the legal rate of interest, was not cognizant of it, and did not participate in it; the rate of interest stipulated for was six per cent., which was all that the mortgagee received. The Solicitor stated, in evidence, that when the defendant applied to him for money he wrote to the mortgagee, who agreed to lend it on the security offered, and sent a sum which, together with an amount already in his hands, made up the £200; that he was not the agent of the mortgagee in any case to invest his money, and that in remitting the interest he deducted nothing for commissions. But defendant swore that on the first occasion when he applied to the Solicitor the latter told him he had £200 to lend, that he had advertized it, and that it was the mortgagee's money.

Held, that the wrong done to defendant was not done by the mortgagee, but by the Solicitor, not as mortgagee's agent but while acting on his own behalf, and further, that assuming him to be the agent of the mortgagee, as he was not a *general* agent, but a particular agent, defendant could not assume that he had been authorized to do an illegal act.

RITCHIE, E. J., delivered the judgment of the Court:—

This suit was brought to foreclose a mortgage made by the defendant to James C. Cogswell, now deceased, by his administrators. The only defence relied upon is usury, by which it is contended the mortgage is invalidated. It is admitted that Cogswell himself neither authorized the taking of anything beyond the legal rate of interest, nor was cognizant of it or sanctioned or participated in it; but it is contended that Mr. Webster, by whom the loan was negotiated, and who made the deduction from the amount loaned for his own benefit, was the agent of Cogswell, and that he was responsible for the act of his agent. On the other hand, the plaintiffs contended that Webster was the agent of the defendant, and that the estate of Cogswell is not to be held accountable or responsible for any agreement which may have been entered into between them.

The account of the transaction given by Webster is that he is an attorney residing at Wolfville, and has been in the habit of obtaining loans of money on mortgage for parties applying to him from persons residing in Halifax and elsewhere, and for such services he always charges the borrower; that in this case he was employed by the defendant to obtain the loan, and was not employed by Cogswell as his agent to invest it. On receiving the application, he wrote to him to ascertain if he would lend to him the sum required on the security offered, which was described to him; this he consented to do, and sent him a sum of money which, together with an amount in his hands, made up the £200. He goes on to say that, when defendant applied to him for the money, he told him he should make the usual charge, being five per cent., which was his charge in all cases when he got money from Halifax; he had to search title, conduct correspondence, and risk the money coming through the post-office, prepare papers and pay recording fees,—for all which he charged five per cent.; he considered he was employed by defendant in this case professionally to procure the money for him, and he seemed perfectly satisfied with the terms proposed, and assented to them. The mortgage was executed and recorded, the principal being payable in one year and the rate of interest six per cent. The defendant intimated to him that he would not be in a position to pay the principal before the expiration of five years, and he, Webster, agreed to guarantee him against being required to pay the amount sooner for one per cent.,—that is, two pounds;—a year, for five years; and at defendant's request he made this memorandum: "In case Mr. Isaac N. Foot shall be called upon for payment of the two hundred pounds secured by mortgage to James C. Cogswell, Esq., within five years from this date, I hereby engage to raise said money for him free of any commission or take an assignment of the mortgage, he paying the interest yearly when it becomes due. April 15th, 1861. Henry B. Webster." The full sum of £200 was placed in Webster's hands by Cogswell, out of which he retained £10 for the services above stated and £10 on account of the guarantee. This sum of £20 was retained by Webster for his own use, and he gave the guarantee on his own personal responsibility; the defendant paid the interest punctually for six years, and it was remitted to Cogswell by him and at his risk, the defendant paying for registering the letter. On his cross-examination, Webster says that when he paid the £180 to the defendant, he asked him if he was not going to give him any more money, when he explained his charges, with which he was satisfied; his usual charge for preparing a bond and mortgage, without procuring the money, he said, was $7.50. He further said that Cogswell would not employ him as his agent, because he would not pay a commission. He said he must have his interest every year in full, and he, Webster, was not his agent in any case to invest money.

The only statement of the defendant in which he materially differs from Webster, is that he says on the first occasion he went to Webster for money he asked him if he had £100 to let on mortgage; he replied he had £200, but would not divide it. Defendant then said he was not prepared to give security for that sum until he got another deed. Before he left it was arranged that he should take the £200. He was told then that it was Mr. Cogswell's money; that he, Webster, had advertised it to lend, and that he must go and take down the advertisement. In all other respects he confirms Webster's statements, as to what took place between them, as does the evidence of the defendants' wife, as to what took place when the money was paid to her husband.

The terms of our statute of usury, in force when this money was loaned, were these: "No person shall take, directly or indirectly, for the loan of moneys or goods, above the rate of six per cent. per annum; all contracts whereby a greater rate of interest is reserved shall be void, and all persons taking or receiving upon any contract or security a greater rate, shall forfeit treble the value of the moneys or goods in such contract or security contracted for or secured."

It is difficult to see how the provisions of this statute can be construed so as to render void the mortgage in question. The lender did not take either directly or indirectly for the loan of his money more than the lawful rate of interest, and this the borrower knew to be the case when he effected the loan and gave the security; and the charge made, however exorbitant it may have been, was made against him by Webster for services rendered to him, and for a guarantee given to him which Cogswell neither directly nor indirectly sanctioned, and of which indeed he knew nothing, the defendant making his agreement with Webster, well knowing that it was made by the latter, not on behalf of Cogswell, but on behalf of and for the benefit of himself personally.

If Webster had been lending his own money and had exacted such charges as he did in this case, the Court would have little hesitation in arriving at the conclusion that he had violated the statute, for it would look at the real nature of the transaction and not merely at its form and terms, and not allow illegal interest to be taken, though under another name.

The evidence shows that the defendant went to Webster to employ him to get a loan for him. This he himself admits, and though he says that Webster subsequently told him he had advertised money to lend, he does not pretend that he was aware of any advertisement or went to him in consequence of it. Webster and he agree upon the terms on which the former is to obtain the money and prepare the necessary documents, and when these have been completed and executed they enter into another agreement unconnected altogether with Cogswell, whereby Webster for a consideration arranged between them guarantees that the defendant shall not sustain loss or inconvenience by his being called upon for the money when it should become due under the mortgage, or within a period of five years, and not that Cogswell shall not call upon him for it.

If this mortgage is to be held void it can only be because Cogswell, through himself or an agent, has made a corrupt agreement, whereby he has exacted usurious interest from the defendant, but it appears to me that the wrong done to the defendant has not been done by Cogswell, but by Webster, not as the agent of Cogswell, but while acting for and on behalf of the defendant himself, and the agreement, the terms of which are complained of, was entered into by the defendant with Webster, personally, and not as Cogswell's agent. It would be most unreasonable if, under these circumstances, a person wholly innocent in the transaction is to lose the security for his money.

Assuming that Webster had been authorized by Cogswell to invest this money for him, and he had thereby become his agent for this special purpose, which is the most that the defendant can contend, it does not, it appears to me, seem necessarily to follow that the security taken by him would be void because the person so employed had, without his knowledge or consent, made unreasonable charges for his services; the borrower knowing at the time that the lender neither knew of them nor participated in them; suppose that we had it in evidence that Cogswell had expressly forbidden Webster to take more than the legal interest or to exact more than the usual charges for preparing the mortgage, etc., and this was known to the borrower, could it still be contended that the lender had taken directly or indirectly illegal interest. To arrive at such a conclusion, a most forced and unnatural construction must be put upon the statute. The defendant had every reason to believe that the authority given to Webster was to make the investment legally, and he had no right to draw any other inference, and it is the duty of a party dealing with a particular agent employed in a single transaction to ascertain the extent of his authority, for in this respect there is a difference between such a one and a *general* agent, and one dealing with him is not to assume that he is authorized by his employer to do an illegal act.

Mr. Weatherbe in the course of the argument called my attention to two American cases on the subject (no English cases bearing directly on the point were cited by the counsel on either side,) *Coudit* v. *Baldwin*, 21 N. Y., 219, and *Bell et. al.* v. *Day et. al.*, 32 N. Y., 165. The court there held that, where a principal delivers money to his agent to be loaned, and he, without the authority or knowledge of his principal, in lending it, besides the lawful interest takes a bonus or charge for himself, the loan is not thereby rendered usurious. If these decisions had taken place in a British court, and we were bound by them, they would be conclusive in favor of the plaintiff; but though they are the decisions of a court,—the Appeal Court of the State of New York,—entitled to every consideration and respect, they do not, under the circumstances, carry as much weight as they otherwise would, for, though the first mentioned of them decided the question broadly, the second was decided on the authority of the other on the principle of *stare decisis* rather than on the soundness of the doctrine propounded in it. Though I am not prepared to say that those decisions are not sound, my judgment is based on the ground that what is complained of as a usurious contract was a contract entered into between the defendant and Webster personally, and not as the agent of Cogswell, and that the validity of the mortgage is not affected by it, so that the plaintiffs are entitled to a foreclosure with costs.

ALMON et al. *v.* GRAY et al.

Writs of attachment against the mortgagor, as an absconding debtor, were issued, and delivered to the Sheriff on May 20. An appraisement of the mortgaged premises was made, and copies of the writ, with the appraisement and description of the land, were registered on May 21. On the same day a writ of attachment, under the Insolvent Act of 1869, was taken out against the mortgagor, but was not delivered to the Sheriff until after he had registered the documents connected with the proceedings under the Absconding Debtor's Act.

Held, that the claims of the Assignee of the estate, to the surplus proceeds, must prevail over that of the attaching creditors.

Section 24 of Chap. 79, R. S., is controlled by the Insolvent Act.

RITCHIE, E. J., delivered the judgment of the Court :—

On the foreclosure and sale of the mortgaged premises in this case, and the payment of the amount due the mortgagees, there remains a balance of $2,345.58, which is held by the Receiver-General of this Court, subject to its order. This amount Creighton, the defendant, claims, as the Assignee of

Gray, the mortgagor, and 'his claim is contested by certain creditors of Gray, who have taken proceedings against him under the Absconding Debtors' Act.

On the 20th May last, these creditors, six in number, took out attachments against Gray as an absconding debtor, which were the same day delivered to the Sheriff to be executed. An appraisement of the mortgaged premises was then made, and the next morning copies of the writ with the appraisement and description of the land were registered in the office of the Registrar of Deeds. On that day a writ of attachment under the Insolvent Act of 1869, was taken out against Gray, under which the Sheriff attached all the estate and effects of the insolvent; but this writ was not delivered to the Sheriff until after he had registered the documents connected with the writs under the Absconding Debtors' Act. The foreclosure was commenced on the 29th May, 1875, and the sale under it took place on the 21st August.

The spirit as well as the language of the Insolvent Act seems to be opposed to the claimants under the attachments taken out against Gray as an absconding debtor. They are simply creditors, who have initiated proceedings to recover debts claimed to be due to them by the insolvent; or in other words, have commenced actions against him by *mesne* process, and until that is followed by proof of their debts and the entry of judgments, and the issue and the levy of an execution on the property attached, it cannot be made available to satisfy the creditors' debts, and the defendant in the meantime is permitted to appear and relieve his property by putting in and perfecting special bail to respond the judgment.

It never could have been intended that creditors should by this means gain a priority, which is not accorded to those who have acquired an absolute and unconditional lien or property by the issue and levy of their executions upon it.

It was argued that a difference existed between a levy on real and personal property, but the Insolvent Act, it appears to me, places them in the same category. It is true our Registry Act declares that lands levied on under writs of attachment against absconding debtors shall be bound thereby from the time that a copy of the writ and a description and appraisement of the lands shall be lodged for registry, and shall continue to be bound until thirty days after final judgment, signed in the cause, but so with respect to a lien acquired on goods of the debtor, which are as much bound by a levy on them under execution as the land is by the recording of the attachment. There is, therefore, no distinction in principle, and the language of the Insolvent Act seems to me to be clear and explicit on the subject, and its provisions in relation to insolvency must be held to control the pre-existing provincial legislation.

By the 10th section of the Insolvent Act all the real estate of the insolvent and all his personal estate are made to vest in his assignee, the only exception being such articles as are exempted from seizure and sale under execution, and the rights of a pledgee of any of the effects of the insolvent. And by the 29th section all his real and personal property is vested in the assignee in case of compulsory liquidation. And section 116 specially declares to what assets these two sections shall apply, making no distinction between real and personal property. Its terms are, " the operation of sections 10 and 29 of this Act shall extend to all the assets of the Insolvent of every kind and description, although they are actually under seizure under any ordinary writ of attachment or under any writ of execution, so long as they are not actually sold by the Sheriff under such writ; but in Nova Scotia and New Brunswick, (where such an Act had not previously been in operation, as it had been in Ontario and Quebec,) "this section shall not apply to any writ of execution in the hands of the Sheriff at the time of the coming into force of this Act;" after which the section goes on to protect the seizing or attaching creditor for the costs he may have incurred. It is only necessary to turn to the 59th section to see that it was never contemplated that all liens on either real or personal property should be protected, and a distinction is there made between those liens there re. ferred to which existed at the time of the passing of the Act, and those subsequently acquired. I think, therefore, that the claim of Creighton, the assignee of Gray, must prevail, and that he is entitled to have the surplus proceeds paid to him.

AMERO *v.* AMERO.

Plaintiff and defendant agreed orally that defendant should advance the consideration money and take a deed of certain lands for plaintiff, who should have fourteen months to repay the consideration money, defendant occupying the lands meanwhile, in lieu of interest for the money advanced, and that defendant should execute a bond to reconvey the premises to plaintiff, on payment of the consideration money. Defendant took the deed, but did not execute the bond, went into possession of the land, and made improvements upon it; and when plaintiff, within the time stipulated, tendered the consideration money and demanded a reconveyance of the premises, refused to execute a conveyance, claiming the premises as his own, under his deed.

Held, that the Statute of Frauds could not be set up as a defence, to aid the defendant in the perpetration of a fraud, but that the plaintiff was entitled to a reconveyance of the premises.

RITCHIE, E. J., delivered the judgment of the Court :—

The jury in this case have found that the plaintiff, in the year 1870, was in possession of the land and premises described in his writ, under an agreement made by him with Charles Everett and Edward Everett, to purchase them for the sum of £19 15s; that it was agreed between the plaintiff and defendant that the latter should advance the sum of £19 15s. to Charles and Edward Everett for the plaintiff, to be repaid in fourteen months by him, and that they should give a deed of the land and premises to the defendant, to be held by him as security for the repayment of the £19 15s., and that the latter should execute a bond to the former, with a condition that he would reconvey the land and premises to the plaintiff, upon being paid the said sum at the time agreed upon ; that a deed of the land was executed and delivered to the defendant, under the agreement that the defendant should execute a bond to reconvey them, which he fraudulently refused to do, and though the plaintiff, within the period agreed upon, tendered and offered to pay to the defendant the sum of £19 15s. and demanded a conveyance of the said land and premises, the defendant fraudulently refused to convey the same to him under the agreement entered into between them. The jury also found that a bond was not prepared and tendered to defendant for execution, and that improvements have been made on the premises by the defendant since he purchased and obtained the deed, and that he has since then exercised ownership over them exclusively, and that the property has increased in value, and also that no note or memorandum in relation to the said land, or the agreement between the plaintiff and defendant was signed by the defendant or by any person on his behalf.

The evidence well justifies the jury in the conclusions at which they have arrived on the issues submitted to them. For the defendant it was contended on the argument, that no bond having been tendered for execution by the defendant, he had a right to presume that the plaintiff did not intend to treat the deed otherwise than as an absolute conveyance. That the agreement was void under the Statute of Frauds; it was not to be performed within a year. And the possession of the land having followed the deed, parol evidence could not be admitted to affect it, and should the plaintiff be entitled to a conveyance, the defendant would be entitled to be paid for his improvements, and the plaintiff, under the circumstances, was not in a position to ask for costs.

I can see nothing to warrant the presumption sought to be raised in the first point taken by the defendant, for, on turning to the evidence, it appears that the bond to the plaintiff and the deed to the defendant were to have been executed simultaneously, and the bond was not then prepared, because the person who drew the deed had not then time to write it, and the defendant having promised to return on a day named to execute it, the deed was executed and delivered to him on the faith of that promise, which promise was not fulfilled, as he did not return on the day appointed or on any other day to execute the bond, and when the bond was subsequently demanded of him he refused to give it, not on the ground that it had not been prepared for his execution, but because he had bought the land, had received a deed of it, and intended to keep it; after which and before the expiration of the fourteen months the stipulated money was tendered to him. It is only necessary to refer to this evidence to dispose of this objection.

The evidence I have referred to has a bearing on the next contention raised on the part of the defendant, for if a defense so fraught with fraud were allowed to avail him, the statute of Frauds, instead of preventing, would enable parties to practice fraud and reap the fruits of it; and Courts of Equity have held by a series of decisions, from an early date to the present time, that an instrument which purports to be an absolute conveyance may, notwithstanding that statute, be shown by parol evidence to have been made by way of security for the payment of money. See *Maxwell* v. *Mountacute,* Prec. in Ch'y. 526. Passing over a number of intermediate cases, I would refer to two or three of a late date. *Lincoln* v. *Wright,* 4 De G. & J., 16, very much resembles that under consideration. L. J. TURNER there says, " If the real agreement was that, as between the plaintiff and Wright, the transaction should be a mortgage transaction, it is in the eye of this court a fraud to insist on a conveyance as being absolute, and parol evidence must be admissible to prove the fraud; here is an absolute conveyance, when it was agreed there should be a mortgage, and the conveyance is insisted upon in fraud of the agreement;" and in *Booth* v. *Turle,* L. R., 16 Eq., 187, MALINS, V. C., said " The conduct of the defendant in attempting to avail himself of the legal assignment of the whole property is fraudulent, and he cannot protect himself by the Statute of Frauds in the commission of such a fraud. That statute was passed, as has been often said, to prevent, and not to protect or cover, fraud." See, also, *Haigh* v. *Kaye,* L. R., 7 Ch., App. 474, to the same effect. In this view of the case the possession of the property by the defendant does not affect the question; indeed that possession is quite consistent with the plaintiff's claim, for the evidence shows that he was to have the use and produce of the land in lieu of interest.

There is in this case also a part performance of the agreement which takes it out of the statute, for the deed was executed by the Everett's and delivered to the defendant on the promise of the latter to execute a bond to convey the land to the plaintiff on payment of the sum specified, which promise he failed to fulfill, and this court will not allow a party to adopt one part of an agreement and repudiate the other. See *Pain* v. *Coombs,* 1 De. G. & J., 34, and where a man makes a promise to another with a view and as a consideration of his doing a certain act, which, relying on such promise, he 'does, equity will compel him to make good the promise. *Loxly* v. *Heath*, 27 Beav., 532; *Laver* v. *Fielder*, 32 Beav., 1, 12.

Lord WESTBURY, speaking of the Statute of Frauds and the course adopted in equity in respect to it, expresses himself thus: " The Court of Equity has, from a very early period, decided that even an Act of Parliament shall not be used as an instrument of fraud, and if in the machinery of perpetrating a fraud an Act of Parliament intervenes, the Court of Equity, it is true, does not set aside the Act of Parliament, but it fastens on the individual who gets a title under that Act and imposes on him a personal obligation because he applies the Act as an instrument for accomplishing a fraud." *McCormack* v. *Grogen*, L. R., 4 H. of L., 97. The plaintiff is entitled to the relief he seeks, and if ever there was a case where a defendant ought to be made liable for costs it is such as this, based, as the defense is, on an attempt on his part to defraud the plaintiff, and he has no right to expect an allowance to be made for improvements on the land which he wrongfully withheld from the plaintiff and unjustly laid claim to.

BANK OF B. N. AMERICA *v.* WORRALL,
ASSIGNEE OF J. T. FRASER & CO.

J. T. F. & Co., being indebted to the plaintiff, gave, as collateral security, a mortgage which they were to receive on a vessel, being built by McK. & V., debtors of theirs in Prince Edward Island. The arrangement was made October 19, 1875, and on the same day J. T. F. & Co. wrote to plaintiffs, enclosing a draft on H. & Co., Liverpool, at ninety days, for £1,000, stating that the same was drawn against proceeds of the vessel, which was to be sold in Liverpool, G. B., by H. & Co., and concluding : " The above vessel is bere. with pledged to you for the due payment of said Bill of Exchange, as well as for payment of the obligations of McK. & V." J. T. F. & Co. then proceed. ed to Prince Edward Island, to obtain the mortgage ; but previous to its being delivered to plaintiffs, they had, on the 12th November, caused a demand of assignment to be served on J. T. F. & Co., and the plaintiff's manager, when the mortgage was afterwards tendered to him, said it should have been made to the Bank, instead of to J. T. F. & Co., and handed it back to J. T. F. who gave it to the Assignee. On the 15th November, J. T. F. & Co. made an assignment, under the Insolvent Act, and on the 27th November, the Bill of Exchange, for £1,000, was presented and dishonored. The vessel was sold for more than £1,000, by the Assignee, who retained the proceeds. Plaintiffs claiming to have an equitable lien on the mortgage for the amount of the Bill of Exchange, and of an unpaid note of McK. & V., endorsed by J. T. F. & Co.

Held, that, although, if the proceedings were between the plaintiffs and J. T. F. & Co., alone, the latter might be estopped from resisting the claim of the plaintiffs, on the ground that they had no title to the vessel at the time they pledged her; yet, under the provisions of the Insolvent Act of 1875, Sec. 118, the pledge or lien, if it could otherwise have been effective, was rendered null and void, a demand of assignment, followed by an assignment, having been served within thirty days after the pledge was given, and the plaintiffs, (upon whom the burden of proof lay under that section,) not having shown that the pledge had not been made in contemplation of insolvency.

The Bank of British North America claim to have had an equitable lien on a mortgage given McKeen & Vickerson, debtors of the insolvent, on a vessel then being built by them in Prince Edward Island, to the extent of £1000 sterling, the amount of a bill of exchange drawn by the insolvents in favor of the Bank, and of an unpaid note of McKeen & Vickerson, endorsed by the insolvent; this claim is contested on the part of the assignee, who, having received the mortgage with the other assets of the estate, on the sale of the vessel received over £1000 sterling, the price she brought, which the Bank assert a right to.

I need only refer to such of the facts stated in the case as will convey an idea of the nature of the transaction.

John T. Fraser & Co. were indebted to the Bank in the sum of twenty thousand dollars and upwards, which they were unable to pay, but in order to meet their liabilities they proposed to put in and have discounted notes to the extent of $9000, and to give a draft on their agent at Liverpool, G. B., for £1000 sterling, which would leave about $8000 overdue and unprovided for, and they agreed to deposit with the Bank a mortgage which they were to obtain from McKeen & Vickerson for $12,000 on a vessel called the " Charlotte Grant," that amount being about the amount of their indebtedness to J. T. Fraser & Co., and their liabilities on which they were endorsers, the Bank to hold the mortgage when deposited with them as collateral security. This arrangement was assented to by the Bank, and accordingly notes to the amount of about

$9000 were discounted, and the bill for £1000 was given, which yielded $4,765; these sums, amounting to $13,694, were passed to the credit of the insolvents, and the whole, with the exception of $600, was applied in discharging their liabilities to the Bank.

This arrangement was made on the 19th Oct., 1875, when the following letter was addressed to Mr. Penfold, the Manager of the Bank at Halifax :—

"Dear Sir,—Our Draft on Messrs. John Hawes & Co., Liverpool (90 days) for £1000 stg., enclosed herewith, be good enough to pass to credit of our account. The same is drawn against proceeds of vessel built by Messrs. McKeen & Vickerson, of Georgetown, P. E. Island, proceeding to Liverpool to be sold by Messrs. Hawes & Co. Be good enough to forward said Bill of Exchange by next regular mail steamer, by which date the necessary papers will be completed and handed you. The above vessel is herewith pledged to you as collateral security, for the due payment of said Bill of Exchange, as well as for the payment of the obligations of Messrs. McKeen & Vickerson."

Mr. John T. Fraser proceeded to P. E. Island to obtain the mortgage, which, after some little delay, arising from the vessel not having been launched, was duly executed and delivered to him; but previous to its having been obtained, on the 12th November, the Bank caused a demand and notice of insolvency under the Insolvency Act, to be served, after which, the mortgage having been received, it was handed to the manager of the Bank, who said it ought not to have been made out to Fraser, being the property of the Bank. Fraser then said that he would hand it to their assignee, with the other papers and assets. The manager then handed it back, and it was given to the assignee.

The members of the firm of J. T. Fraser & Co., both individually and as a firm, made assignments, under the Insolvent Act, on the 15th November.

The case stated that at the time of the writing of the letter of the 19th October, John T. Fraser & Co. were insolvent, of which fact the Bank was not aware, but believed them to be solvent, although they had not met their notes promptly, as they became due at the Bank, from the previous July.

The Bill of Exchange, for £1,000 sterling, was presented on the 27th November, and dishonored.

The mortgaged vessel was sold by the assignee, for a sum over £1,000 stirling, who received the price. When the letter of the 19th October was writter, J. T. Fraser & Co. had no title to the vessel, nor any legal right to pledge her to the Bank; but having reason to believe, or to know, that their debtors, McKeen & Vickerson, would give them a security on her for the advances they had made, and liabilities they had incurred on their account, in order to reduce their liabilities to the Bank, they undertook to pledge the vessel as specified in the letter, and it is contended, on the part of the Bank, that J. T. Fraser having succeeded in obtaining the mortgage of the vessel, the benefit of it enured to the Bank, under their letter, which thereby acquired an equitable lien on the vessel, and, on its sale, became entitled to the proceeds.

Had this been a question between the Bank and J. T. Fraser & Co., the latter might well be estopped from resisting the claim, on the ground that, though they subsequently acquired a right to the vessel, they had none when they pledged her to the Bank; but I do not see how the difficulty can be overcome, which rises from the provisions of the Insolvent Act, and the question has become one between the Bank and the Assignee.

The whole object of the proposed arrangement was to give the Bank security for the liabilities of the insolvents, and not for an advance to enable them to pay their liabilities, generally; no advance, indeed, was contemplated at the time. The case states that J. T. Fraser & Co. were then insolvent, and while it is alleged that their insolvency was not known to the Bank, there is no intimation whatever that it was not known to the members of the firm themselves; the inference is, that it was; if otherwise, it should have been so stated in the case. The proposal to give the security was first made on the 19th October, and within thirty days; that is to say, on the 12th November the Bank caused a demand and notice of insolvency to be served on J. T. Fraser & Co. If, therefore, a lien on the vessel, either legal or equitable, had been acquired, it would

have been invalidated by the provisions of Sec. 113 of the
Insolvent Act of 1875, which enacts that a pledge given to
secure payment to a creditor within thirty days, next before
demand of an assignment, when it shall be followed by an
assignment, shall be presumed to have been given in contemplation of insolvency: the presumption of law being, that the
security was given in contemplation of insolvency, in order to
establish the validity of the pledge, it was for the Bank to
shew the contrary.

Mr. McCoy relied much on the mode in which the Bank had
made their claim on the insolvent estate, as of itself preventing them from recovery, if no other objection existed; and
seemed to think that a decision of this Court had been given
to that effect, in *Sherlock* v. *McLellan* ;* but there is no similarity or analogy between the two cases. There the party held
a judgment against the insolvent, and, instead of claiming on his
judgment, and putting a value on it, as the law required him
to do, he ignored it, claimed for his whole debt, and voted as a
creditor for the full amount, and ranked on the estate for it;
there the Court held, and held correctly, as I still think, that
the creditor had forfeited his right, subsequently to set up a
claim on his judgment. But the Bank have done nothing to
indicate that they did not intend to rely on their supposed
lien; they stated in their claim on the estate, the nature and
amount of the security. The security itself was in the hands
of the assignee, who had disposed of it, and ascertained its
value, which he claimed to hold, as of right. The other provisions of the section, 84, have no application to such a case
as this, which simply involved the question whether or not the
Bank was entitled to the proceeds of the sale, and the amount
to be received by the Bank from the assignee would be greater
or less, as the Court should decide in favor of the one or the
other, and the Bank has presented its claim against the
estate, as I think, in an unobjectionable manner. Being of
opinion that under the provisions of the Insolvent Act, the
pledge or lien, if it could otherwise have been effective, was
rendered null and void, the judgment must be in favor of the
assignee, and I think he is entitled to his costs.

---

* Reported *post.*

BEGGS *v.* McDONALD ET AL.

Defendant, D. McD., being part owner, with plaintiff and the other defendants, of a barque, was authorized by the other owners to sell her, and did so, depositing plaintiff's share of the proceeds to his own credit, in the Pictou Bank. Plaintiff wrote to one S. C. in these terms : "I want you to put my share of the money in the bank, to my credit. I have written D., (meaning D. McD.,) stating that I have authorized you to do so." S. C. had, before this letter came to him, drawn the money from the Bank, the manager having advanced it to him on his own check; but defendant, D. McD., upon the letter being shown to him by S. C., signed a release to the Bank from any claim on account of the payment of the money to S. C.

Held, that D. McD., was not justified in releasing the Bank; that in doing so, he assumed the liability which the bank had incurred by the unwarrantable payment to S. C. of the money placed to his (McD.'s) credit and that plaintiff was entitled to a decree for the amount of his share, deposited in the Bank.

RITCHIE, E. J., delivered the judgment of the Court :—

The plaintiff, in his writ, alleges that the defendants were joint owners, with himself, of the Barque *Scarnichia,* the defendant, Daniel McDonald, being the registered owner of twenty-eight shares, Smith Copeland of thirty, John S. Mc-Donald of two, and the plaintiff of four shares. Daniel McDonald was authorized, by the other owners, to sell the vessel, and he sold her and received the price, the precise amount of which was not known to plaintiff; and he also received the freight which she earned on the last voyage she made previous to the sale. This he is charged with having appropriated to his own use and refusing to account for to the plaintiff, who prays that he may render a true account of the amount received for the sale of the vessel and her freight, and of the sums disbursed by him, and that he may be decreed to pay what is due the plaintiff.

Daniel McDonald, in his answer, admits the sale of the vessel, and the receipt of the purchase money; and of the freight earned on the last voyage, and alleges that he has been always willing to give an account of it, and of the disbursements of the vessel, and every other information in regard to her, and has never refused to do so. He has annexed to his answer a full account of all moneys received by him, or disbursed by him, and he never appropriated any part to his own use; but,

2

after the money had been received by him, he had it remitted to the Pictou Bank, in Pictou, to be placed to his credit, and the plaintiff authorized Smith Copeland, the defendant, to draw out of the said Bank the plaintiff's share of the amount of the proceeds of the sale of the vessel and her earnings, and to invest and dispose of the same on his behalf; and Smith Copeland, acting on the plaintiff's authority, and as his agent, drew from the Bank the amount there; and he says that after he had deposited the said moneys in the Pictou Bank, he did not receive or interfere with any part to which the plaintiff was entitled,—the amount to which he was so entitled being $1,560.34.

There are, I think, no grounds for the allegations in the plaintiff's writ, that Daniel McDonald refused, or showed any indisposition to account to the plaintiff for the moneys received by him on account of the vessel, or that he appropriated any part thereof to his own use. He has admitted that the money to which the plaintiff was entitled was received by him, and deposited in a bank at Pictou, to his credit; and the evidence shews, as stated by him, that it was paid by the Bank to Copeland, Daniel McDonald says, by the authority of the plaintiff, which is denied by him, who in his evidence states positively that he never gave Copeland any such authority. The account given by Daniel McDonald, in his evidence, is that he himself never drew or received any part of the money from the Bank; that, having heard that Copeland had received it, he asked the manager of the Bank why he had given the money to him, without his authority; that he was unable to get it from the Bank, though he had applied for it, and that he never gave any authority to Copeland to receive it. He goes on to say that he subsequently saw a letter from the plaintiff to Copeland, which the latter produced to him as an authority to receive it, and that, on seeing that letter, he, McDonald, signed a release to the Bank from any claim on account of the payment of the money to Copeland. The contents of the letter were as follows : "I want you to put my share of the money of the vessel in the Bank, to my credit, as I cannot come till March. I have written Dan, (meaning Daniel McDonald,) stating that I have authorized you to do so."

Smith Copeland, in his evidence, says that he received this letter about November, and drew out the money in different drafts,—he thinks that there was not any of the money left in the Bank when he got it,—all the money deposited in the Bank was drawn out by him,—he had no special authority to draw it,—he drew it on his own cheques, and had drawn it all before the letter came to him.

Passing by the fact that the letter had not been received when Copeland drew the money from the Bank, at which time he unquestionably had no right to take it, if he had produced it when he applied for the money, it would have conferred on him no authority to draw it, and no bank official, having any knowledge of his business, would, on such a document, have paid him money, deposited to the credit of a third party. It could only have been paid on the cheque of the depositor or of some one authorized by him. To have paid it on any authority from the plaintiff would have been irregular, but to have paid it as it was paid to Copeland, without any authority from any person, was most unaccountable conduct on the part of the Bank, and if the money has been lost to any party by the insolvency of Copeland, the loss should fall on the Bank. The letter did not authorize Copeland to take the money from the Bank, the authority conferred on him was confined to depositing it there, if it came to his hands from Daniel Mc-Donald; but, having fraudulently and without authority obtained the money, and appropriated it to his own use, before he received the letter, Daniel McDonald was not justified, on the subsequent receipt of such a letter, in releasing the Bank; and, by so doing, he assumed the liability which the Bank had incurred by the unwarrantable payment to another person of money which had been lodged to his credit. It is very unfortunate that he should have acted so injudiciously, especially after the caution he received not to do so, for no fault is to be found in any other respect with the course which he has pursued in the business; and he seems himself to have been a loser of his own share of the money deposited by him, as Copeland, not content with the plaintiff's share, appears to have drawn out that of the other owners, without the pretence of any authority.

The plaintiff is entitled to a decree for the amount of his share of the money deposited in the Pictou Bank by Daniel McDonald, and costs.

BELL, ASSIGNEE, &c., *v.* BROWN ET AL, EXOR'S. OF JENNINGS.

D. made a mortgage to defendants' testator, to secure the payment of three promissory notes. The notes were paid, and handed over to D., upwards of twenty years before this action was brought by D., to compel defendants to execute a release of the mortgage. During the subsequent period no payments were made by D. or demanded of him, and the Estate of testator was settled without any reference to the mortgage as an outstanding debt due the Estate. After bringing the action, D. became insolvent, and made an assignment under the Insolvent Act, and his Assignee intervening, under an order of the Court, became plaintiff in the suit.

Held, that defendants must be decreed to execute a release of the mortgage, though without costs, they not having opposed the proceedings of plaintiff.

Held, also, that D., not being a party to the suit when evidence was taken, was not prevented by Section 41 of Chap. 96, R. S., from giving evidence of transactions with defendant's testator, deceased.

RITCHIE, E. J., delivered the judgment of the Court:—

This suit was instituted to obtain from the defendants the release of a mortgage made by Durney to Jennings, in his lifetime, the amount of ' which, it is alleged, was paid to him, but no release given.

The suit was commenced by Durney, but he having become solvent, Bell, his assignee under the Insolvent Act, intervened, and by the order of the Court became plaintiff in his stead.

It appears that the mortgage was given on or about the 28th May, 1853, to secure the payment of £250 in two years and six months, with interest, as the same was expressed and made payable by three promissory notes, one of which was payable in one year, one in two years, and the remaining one in two and a half years.

On the first of June, 1854, according to Durney's evidence, he paid £115, being the amount of the first note, and the interest on the three. On the 28th May, 1855, he paid £109, being the amount of the second note, and interest on that and the remaining note ; and on the 28th November, 1855, he paid the amount of the last note and interest, £51 10s. These payments were all entered by Durney at the time, and the book containing them was produced at the hearing. The notes were delivered up to Durney by Jennings, but no release was asked for or given.

Jennings died several years ago, but during his lifetime he never treated the mortgage as a subsisting and unsatisfied security, by calling for principal or interest, and after his death, though the defendants were aware of the existence of the instrument, which was among his papers, they never called upon Durney for payments, nor inserted it in the inventory of the estate, nor otherwise treated it as an asset, but had the estate finally settled and distributed under a decree of the Court of Probate, without any reference to it.

Application was made to the defendants, as executors of Jennings, for a release, and a release was tendered to them for execution, with an offer to furnish them with proof of the payment. This application was refused, and in their answer they say that they do not think they would be warranted, or had the legal or equitable power to release the mortgage ; but on behalf of themselves and all others interested in the estate of Jennings, they submit to the Court, and will abide and carry out any instructions, decision, or decree which may be made herein. Though the defendants have appeared and answered, they have taken no further part in the suit, neither they nor their solicitor or counsel having attended the examination before the master, nor did any one appear on their behalf at the hearing.

Considering the time which has elapsed, both before and since the death of Jennings, during which the mortgage was allowed to remain a dead letter, and the fact that the notes referred to in the instrument were not to be found among the papers of the deceased, the executors ought, when called upon for the release, to have been satisfied with the evidence of payment offered to them, especially as the estate had then been finally settled by a decree of the Probate Court. I cannot but regard as very unsatisfactory the statement in the defendants' answer, that it was an unintentional oversight that they did not place the amount of the mortgage in the inventory of the estate, nor call upon Durney for payment, nor include it in their final account on the settlement of the estate in the Court of Probate.

If the amount of this mortgage appeared on the books of Jennings as a debt due by Durney, and the instrument was found, as they say it was, among his papers, so as to lead to the inference that it was an outstanding and subsisting security, the ignoring of its existence by the executors can, I think, be considered in no other light than negligence, for which they would be accountable to the heirs if it was, in fact, a subsisting security for a debt actually due to the estate.

The evidence of Durney corroborated, as I think it is, leaves no doubt on my mind but that the money due on the mortgage was paid as it fell due, and that on the 28th November, 1855, when the last payment was made, Durney was entitled to a release.

Though no counsel appeared for the defendant at the hearing, and no defence was then made, or objection taken, some doubt existed in my mind whether Durney was a competent witness, as having been originally a party to the suit; but whatever doubt existed on that subject has been removed, and I am of opinion that no valid objection could have been taken to his testimony.

There is no provision in any English statute similar to ours on this point, and we cannot therefore look for authorities on the subject in that quarter, but in the State of Massachusetts they have; and in their statute which makes parties in civil actions and proceedings competent witnesses, there is a provision that when one of the parties to a contract or cause of action is dead, the other party shall not be permitted to testify in his own favor. In *Jones* v. *Wolcott*, 15 Gray 541, the action was commenced by a party who subsequently became insolvent, when Jones, as his assignee, was admitted to prosecute. The Judge, in giving his decision, remarked: " Interest in the event of the suit does not operate as a disqualification. The witness was not a party to this suit; although it was originally commenced by him, yet upon his becoming insolvent, the present plaintiff was admitted to prosecute the action in his own name, "(for the benefit of his creditors,)" and consequently the insolvent was no longer a party." The view there taken is, I think, sound ; the facts in that case and the one before me are identical, and the provisions are in effect the same.

These defendants, whether intentionally or from unintentional oversight, have allowed upwards of twenty years to elapse without any payment having in the meantime been made on account of the mortgage, or any acknowledgment made by the mortgagor, and during that time have taken no proceedings to enforce payment by foreclosure or otherwise. It is too late now to make it available, as a valid and subsisting security, to the estate, and by granting the release, the right of no persons can be injuriously affected, and I think the plaintiff is entitled to a decree requiring the defendants to execute the release which has been tendered to them.

The plaintiff has asked for costs against the defendants, but although I cannot approve in all respects of the course pursued by them, I am not disposed to make them liable to costs, acting as they are on behalf of others, especially as they have done nothing in the conduct of the defence, nor raised any objections calculated to increase the expense of the litigation, but have merely left the plaintiff to the proof of his case.

BIGELOW v. BLAIKLOCK.

Defendant, a mortgagor, claimed a re-sale of premises sold by the Sheriff under foreclosure process and bought in by the plaintiff (the mortgagee,) on the ground of a misunderstanding at the sale, arising out of the fact that the properties were described differently in the advertisement, from the way in which they were described in the mortgage and writ. In the latter documents only three parcels were enumerated, two on the peninsula and one on Queen street ; in the advertisement they were described as four lots, the Queen street property being divided into two lots, each separately described, so that when purchasers were told that the last lot was excluded from the sale they would naturally infer that the whole Queen street lot was excluded, and there was clear evidence that such an understanding had prejudicially affected the sale.

Held, that the defendant was entitled to a re-sale, and that the fact of plaintiff having, after the purchase, agreed to sell one of the lots, did not affect that right, as he had obtained no deed, and the sale had not been confirmed by the Court.*

RITCHIE, E. J., delivered the judgment of the Court :—

On the sale of the mortgaged premises, forclosed in this suit, the plaintiff became the purchaser of certain portions, and this application is for a re-sale, on the ground that a misunderstanding existed at the Sheriff's sale as to what portions of the mortgaged premises were set up.

It is obvious that a misunderstanding did exist, and it probably arose from the course pursued on the part of the plaintiff in having the several parcels described differently in the advertisement from the way they were described in the mortgage and in the writ. In the latter documents *three* parcels only are enumerated, two on the peninsula of Halifax, and one on Queen Street, in the City of Halifax ; while in the advertisement, under which the Sheriff sold, they are described as *four* lots, the lot on Queen Street being divided into two and each separately described, so that those conversant with the mortgage and the writ, or who might have searched the registry of deeds in relation to the title, would very naturally infer, when told that the last lot was excluded from the sale, that the two lots on the peninsula alone were set up together ; and they would the more readily be led to this inference from the fact that the premises on Queen Street were wholly unconnected with and far apart from them. And I cannot help saying that setting up together different properties of a different character in different localities was calculated injuriously to affect the sale by destroying competition. The effect of such a course would be to throw the property into the hands of a plaintiff at a low price, or otherwise to occasion a sacrifice, as few persons would be likely to desire to purchase both classes of properties, while many might desire to compete for them separately. I am convinced no owner of property would pursue such a course who desired to obtain the best price for his land.

---

*Although the same result might follow if a stranger, possessed of the same knowledge, had been the purchaser, yet there is a distinction between the plaintiff in the suit and a stranger ; and the Court did not wish it to be inferred that where the plaintiff himself had bid, and the amount of principal, interest and costs was tendered to him before the deed was given and the sale confirmed, he would not be required to take it and give up the purchase.

I assume that the Sheriff did, as he states he did, put up the three first mentioned lots,—that is the two peninsula lots and a part of the lot on Queen Street,—yet, I think, he could not have pointed this out quite clearly to the bidders, as, with the exception of the plaintiff, under whose instructions it was so sold, all persons interested in the sale or who bid or had any intention of bidding, believed and acted on the belief that the lots on the peninsula alone were set up for sale; and Alexr. Forsyth, one of those present, who gave the bid before the last bid of the plaintiff, of $3,260, says, in his affidavit, that his bid was $3,250, and that if the property had been knocked down to him he would have expected to have received a deed of the two peninsula lots only; and he goes on to say that, if he had supposed that the lot in Queen Street had been included, he would have bid as high as the amount due on the mortgage. Under these circumstances, the plaintiff himself having been the purchaser, it would be most unjust to refuse a re-sale. The plaintiff filed his bill to obtain the amount due on his mortgage, and the sale was ordered to effect that object, and if that object is attained he has no reason to complain that he has not, in addition to the payment of the amount due him on the mortgage, made a profit by a sacrifice of the mortgagor's property.

As to the plaintiff having agreed to sell one of the lots, I take no account of it. He had no right to do so, as he had obtained no deed, and the sale had not been confirmed by the Court as required by its practice; and I must assume that he or his solicitor was aware of the alleged misunderstanding, and the protest against the sale, made to the Sheriff at the sale or immediately after. As regards this protest, referred to in the affidavits in support of this motion, the Sheriff, the plaintiff and his attorney are all silent. I think it would have been better if some reference had been made to it in their affidavits.

There must be a re-sale.

Though I have in this case ordered a re-sale on the grounds I have stated, the plaintiff being the purchaser, and under similar circumstances the result might have been the same *if a stranger, possessed of the same knowledge, had been the pur-*

chaser, yet there is a manifest distinction between the plaintiff in a suit and a stranger; and I do not wish it to be inferred from what I have said, that in a case where the plaintiff himself has bid on the mortgaged property, and the amount of principal, interest and costs is tendered to him before the deed is given and the sale confirmed, he would not be required to take it and give up the purchase. This point, however, is not before me at present.

CHIPMAN, EXECUTOR, *v.* GAVAZA ET AL.

The practice of the Supreme Court on the common law side, in relation to setting aside verdicts and granting new trials, is peculiarly applicable to the trial of issues in Equity, on circuit, and a party dissatisfied with a verdict in an equity suit, tried on circuit, should apply to the Judge before whom it was tried for a rule *nisi*, or, in the event of his refusing a rule, should take it out under the statute, and cannot, having ignored that practice, move the Equity Court at Halifax to set aside the verdict.

RITCHIE, E. J., now, (Oct. 8th, 1877,) delivered the judgment of the Court :—

This suit was brought at Annapolis, and the issues were tried there by a Jury at the last Spring circuit, before Mr. Justice WILKINS. All the issues were found in favour of the plaintiff, and no application was then made to set aside the verdict, but some time after a motion was made with that object in the Equity Court at Halifax, on the ground of the improper reception of evidence, and that the evidence adduced did not warrant the findings.

The question now raised is, whether that motion can be sustained in this Court, and ought not to have been made at Annapolis during the sitting of the Court there, to the Judge before whom the case was tried, and a rule *nisi* obtained from him, or, in case of his refusal to grant one, a rule taken under the Statute, (the 212th Sec. of the Com. Law. Practice Act,) on his giving security to respond the judgment to be finally given, and specifying the objections raised to the verdict.

It is quite clear that if this had been an action at common law, and no motion had been made to the Judge who tried it during the sitting of the Court, no application could afterwards be made to set aside the verdict on the ground that evidence had been improperly received or rejected, or that it was insufficient to sustain the finding of the Jury. But it is contended on the part of the defendant that this Court is not guided by the same rules and practice, with regard to granting new trials, which prevail at common law.

There is a distinction made in the statute regulating the procedure in equity, between suits brought in Halifax and those brought in the country. In the former they are to be tried by the Judge, unless he shall direct issues to be submitted to a Jury; in the latter they are to be tried by a Jury, unless the parti:s otherwise agree, or the Judge otherwise order, and the c_use is entered with the other causes for trial on the circuit docket. In Halifax the trial of issues takes place before the Judge in Equity himself, and there are no statutory directions as to the course to be pursued in applying to set aside a verdict and obtain a new trial. But this is not the case in respect to trials in country causes; the enactments of the statute clearly indicate the course to be pursued, and point out that the same practice is to prevail as in actions at common law. The 31st Sec. of the Equity Act provides that country causes shall continue to be tried before a Jury, to whom issues of fact shall be submitted; and the next section provides that when the verdict on such issues shall determine all the matters in dispute and further directions are not required, and a rule *nisi* for a new trial shall not be obtained from the Judge or taken under the statute, (that is under the Com. Law Practice Act,) final judgment may forthwith be entered on the verdict as the Judge who tried the issues may direct; and the following section enacts that the rule *nisi* for new trial in such cases shall be returned before the Judge in Equity.

It is quite clear to me that the Legislature intended that a party dissatisfied with a verdict in an Equity suit, tried on circuit, should, on applying for a new trial, adopt the common law practice, and apply in the first instance to the Judge before whom the cause was tried. If the contention of the

defendants' counsel is sustained, all the statutory provisions I
have referred to are ignored, and a party dissatisfied with a
verdict is left at liberty to pass by the Judge who heard the
evidence, and subsequently apply to the Equity Court at Halifax,
without having given any security whatever. I do not see
that the course to be pursued could have been more clearly
indicated than it is by the statute, and the defendants in this
case, having disregarded its provisions, cannot afterwards
move this Court to set aside the verdict. I may add that the
7th section of the Equity Act has a bearing on the question, which enacts that in all cases now conducted in this Court,
the practice of the Supreme Court then or thereafter to be
established, as far as it is applicable, shall be observed, except
in so far as altered or modified by statute or by rules, and the
practice of the Supreme Court on the common law side, in
relation to setting aside verdicts and granting new trials, is
peculiarly applicable to the trial of issues in Equity suits on
circuit, and should therefore have been pursued, even without
the special statutory directions.

CHIPMAN, EXECUTOR, *v.* GAVAZA ET AL.

The original plaintiff died after writ issued and before answer, and the suit was
revived by her executor. Defendants, in their answer, did not call in question the death of the original plaintiff, or the appointment of the present plaintiff as her executor, and raised no objection to his not being the proper person to
revive the suit. But after the issues raised by their answer were found against
them, the objection was taken at the hearing that other parties should have been
before the Court as plaintiffs.

Held, that the objection should have been raised by demurrer or plea, or defendants should have insisted on it in their answer, and that, although such an objection might be taken at the hearing, if it were made to appear that the rights of
other parties not before the Court would be prejudiced by the decree sought for,
yet, if the Court could make a decree which would do justice to all parties, it
would not allow the objection then to prevail.

RITCHIE, E. J., now, (October 15, 1877,) delivered the judgment of the Court :—

Mrs. Levery Chipman was the sole plaintiff when the writ issued, the prayer of which was that the defendants might be declared to be trustees for her of the real estate in question, and that they should be decreed to convey it absolutely to her.

After the issue of the writ, and before answer, she died, and the suit was revived by Edward W. Chipman, her son, who suggested her death, and his appointment as the executor of her last will and testament.

The defendants, in their answer, did not call in question the death of Levery Chipman, or the appointment of Edward W. Chipman as her executor, and raised no objection as to his not being the proper person to revive the suit; but they denied that the property was held by them in trust for Mr. Chipman, and claimed to hold it as their own property.

Issues bearing on this question alone were raised and submitted to a jury—that is, whether the property had been purchased for Levery Chipman and paid for with her money, and conveyed to Thomas Gavaza, to be held in trust for her, or had been purchased by Gavaza on his own account and paid for out of his own funds, and it was not till after these issues had been all found against the defendants that the objection was raised at the hearing that other parties should have been before the Court as plaintiffs, viz., other children of Levery Chipman.

If the defendants desired to object to the want of parties, they should have raised the objections by demurrer or plea, or should have insisted upon it in their answer. It is true that such an objection may be taken at the hearing, if it is made to appear that the rights of other parties, not before the Court, will be prejudiced by the decree sought for. In such a case the Court itself will require them to be made parties at any stage of the proceedings; but if the Court can make a decree which will do entire justice to all parties, and not prejudice the rights of any, it will not allow the objection then to prevail. This can be done in the present case, and the interests of all parties can be fully protected, if indeed there are any other persons interested in the subject matter of the suit, which at present has not been made to appear; and it was for the defendants, if they wished to raise the objection, to show that there were other parties interested in the controversy, otherwise than under the will of Mr. Chipman, of which the present plaintiff is the executor. If this had been made distinctly to appear, such parties would have been called in; the Court is now called upon to act on a mere surmise.

The decree will be in accordance with the findings of the jury, that the defendants, at the time of the issuing of the writ, were trustees of the property, and held it in trust for Levery Chipman, in her lifetime, and that they do forthwith convey it to Edward W. Chipman, to be held by him in trust for such person or persons as shall be entitled thereto, under the last will and testament of Levery Chipman, or as her heirs-at-law, if undisposed of by her will,—the terms of the deed to be settled by the Court.

COGSWELL *v.* GRAHAM.

Mitchell, who had been the owner of three lots upon which the plaintiff held mortgages foreclosed in the present suit, conveyed one of the lots, known as the Chebucto Foundry lot, to Montgomery and Budd, by deed registered in 1866. In 1871, Budd became insolvent, and his assignee conveyed his interest in the lot to Montgomery, by deed registered in 1871, after which, in October, 1872, a mortgage was made by Montgomery to Stairs, which was recorded in November, 1872. Previous to Budd's failure, Montgomery and Budd had entered into an agreement with Mitchell, reciting that plaintiff held mortgages on certain property of Mitchell, on which there was due $16,000, that Montgomery and Budd had purchased part of said property, and as part of the consideration therefor agreed to assume the said mortgages and relieve Mitchell therefrom, and the instrument contained covenants to indemnify Mitchell, his heirs, &c., from all actions which might arise in consequence of the said mortgages covering more land than that purchased from him, or in consequence of the bonds given with the said mortgages. This agreement was registered, previously to the mortgage to Stairs, but was unknown to him and to Wylde, Hart & Co., who were interested with him in the mortgage, until after the mortgage was recorded. The Master, reporting as to the disposal of the surplus proceeds, treated Stairs as the first encumbrancer, after the plaintiff, on the property over which his mortgage extended, and exception was taken to the report on the ground that effect had not been given to the agreement registered previously.

Held, that,—although Montgomery, if he had not given the mortgage, and those claiming under him with a knowledge of the existence of the agreement when they took conveyance from him, would have been deprived of any right to the surplus funds,—the agreement in question was not an instrument, the registration of which was contemplated by the Registry Act, and therefore the registration of it could not be deemed to be notice of its existence and contents to a party claiming under a deed or mortgage for valuable consideration, and that Stairs and those claiming with him, not having received actual or constructive notice of its existence when the mortgage was taken, were to be considered as *bonafide* mortgagees, unaffected by it.

RITCHIE, E. J., delivered the judgment of the Court :—

An application having been made for the surplus proceeds of the sale of lands under foreclosure in this suit, it was referred to Mr. William Twining, a Master of this Court, to report on the respective priorities of the subsequent incumbrancers or parties claiming the amount paid to the Accountant-General in this cause, after payment of the plaintiff's claim and costs, and what they are severally entitled to receive thereout ; who reported that the mortgaged premises foreclosed in this suit, and sold under the order of this Court, consisted of three lots of land, one known as the "Chebucto Foundry and Brewery," near Freshwater Bridge, on the western side of Pleasant Street, in the City of Halifax, and the other two situate nearly opposite, on the eastern side of that street ; that the lots were sold separately, the first-mentioned lot having produced $18,200.00, and the two other lots having produced $3,200.00, making in all the sum of $21,400.00, and that there remained a surplus of $3,964.37 after paying the plaintiff the amount of her mortgage and costs ; that the next encumbrance on the first-mentioned lot, ("The Chebucto Foundry and Brewery Property,") was a mortgage made by William Montgomery to John Stairs for the sum of $16,000 ; and the next encumbrance on the two other lots was a mortgage made by Thomas Mitchell to Robert Davis for $8,000.00, which was afterwards assigned to David Sterling.

The Master further reported that the amount paid to the plaintiff on account of the mortgages foreclosed in this cause should be charged against the properties situate respectively on the eastern and western sides of Pleasant Street, in the proportion that the amounts respectively produced by the sales of the lots on the western and eastern sides of the said street bear to the whole amount of the said sale,—*i. e.*, the western property to be charged with $14,828.63, and the eastern properties with $2,607, thus leaving a balance on the sale of the "Chebucto Foundry and Brewery Property" of $3,371.37, and a balance on the sale of the other two lots of $593; and he reported that John Stairs, as the first encumbrancer of the former property after the mortgages of the plaintiff foreclosed in this cause, was entitled to the said sum of $3,371.37, and that David Sterling, as the first encumbrancer upon the two other properties, was entitled to the said sum of $593.

Assuming that no other facts were in proof before the Master, all parties would be prepared to acquiesce in the correctness of the conclusion at which he has arrived, and no exception would have been taken to the report; but it appears from the evidence taken before him and returned to the Court, that the mortgages foreclosed in this cause were made by Thomas Mitchell, the then owner of the three lots, who subsequently sold the "Chebucto Foundry and Brewery" lot to William Montgomery and Thomas G. Budd, by deed, dated the 9th August, 1866, which was registered on the 23rd of the same month.

Thomas G. Budd, having become insolvent, his assignee, John H. Harvey, conveyed all his estate and interest in the said lot to William Montgomery, by deed, dated 27th January, 1871, which was registered on the 20th February, 1871, after which the mortgage by William Montgomery to John Stairs, above referred to, was made, bearing date the 30th October, 1872, which was recorded on the 4th of November following; but previous to this date and before Budd's failure, an agreement had been entered into between Montgomery and Budd of the one part, and Mitchell of the other, whereby, after reciting that the plaintiff held mortgages on certain property of Mitchell, on which there was due $16,000, and that Budd and Montgomery had purchased a portion of the said property from Mitchell, and as part of the consideration therefor, had agreed to assume the said mortgages, and relieve him and the remainder of the said property from the payment thereof; it was agreed between the said parties that a previous agreement entered in between them on the 9th of August, 1866, with reference to the purchase of said land, should be cancell.

ed ; and Budd and Montgomery for themselves, their heirs, executors, or administrators thereby covenanted, promised, and agreed, to and with Mitchell, his heirs, executors, and administrators, that they would assume the said mortgages, and pay off the same within seven years, with all subsequent interest accruing thereon, and save and keep harmless and indemnified the said Mitchell, his heirs, executors, and administrators, and his and their lands, tenements, goods, and chattels, of and from all actions, etc., which might arise in consequence of the said mortgages covering more land than that purchased from him, or in consequence of the bonds given by him in connection with the said mortgages.

This agreement, though recorded previously to the mortgage made by Montgomery to Stairs, was unknown to the latter and to Wylde, Hart & Co., who were interested with him in the mortgage, till long after that mortgage was recorded.

The exception taken to the report is, that due effect was not given to the agreement, which, it is contended, deprived Stairs of any right to the funds in question. It is quite clear that Montgomery himself, if he had not given the mortgage, would have been debarred, by his agreement, from any claim to them ; and those claiming under him, *with a knowledge of its existence when they took the conveyance from him*, would have been equally deprived of any right to them, for one who purchases an estate, though for valuable consideration, after notice of a prior equitable right, makes himself a *mala fide* purchaser, and will not be enabled, by getting the legal estate, to defeat such prior equitable interest: Lord HARDWICKE in *LeNeve* v. *LeNeve*, 1 Amb. 436.

No actual knowledge existed in this case, nor was there anything which could be deemed constructive notice, unless the registration of the agreement is to be considered such ; but the Courts have held that neither under the English nor Irish Registration Acts is the registry of an instrument constructive notice to a subsequent purchaser ; but if the instrument be such as the law contemplates the registry of, such registry may bind his title though not his conscience, which actual notice would do. See *Wrightson* v. *Hudson*, 2 Eq.

3

Ab. 498; *Bedford* v. *Backhouse*, Ib., 615 ; *Morecock* v. *Dickens et al.*, Amb., 680, on the English Act; and *Bushell* v. *Bushell*, 1 Scho. and Lef. 98, and *Mill* v. *Hill*, 3 House of Lords cases, 828, on the Irish Act. See also *Wiseman* v. *Westland*, 1 Y. and J., 120; *Spence's Eq.*, 762; and *Sudgen on Vendors and Purchasers*, 730; *Fisher on Mortgages*, 701, &c.

On referring to those acts, and to ours on the same subject, it will appear that there is nothing in the latter to induce a different decision by our Courts; and in New Brunswick registration alone has been held not to amount to notice, the Judges there having recognized the English decisions as binding on them. See *Doe e. d. Hubbard* v. *Power*, 1 Allen, 272.

By the statute of 7 Anne, Chap. 20, referring to registry in England, it is enacted that a memorial of all deeds and *conveyances*, which, after the time therein mentioned, shall be made and executed, and of all wills and devises in writing, whereby any honors, manors, land, etc., in the County of Middlesex, *may be in any way affected in Law or Equity*, may be registered in such manner as is there directed, and that every such deed or conveyance that shall thereafter be made and executed shall be adjudged fraudulent and void against any subsequent purchaser or mortgagee for valuable consideration, unless such memorial be registered as by the Act directed before the registry of the memorial of the deed or conveyance under which such subsequent purchaser or mortgagee shall claim.

By the Irish Registry Act, 6 Anne, Chapter 2, an absolute priority is expressly given to the instrument first registered. In the United States, though it is recognized as the English law that registration of a deed does not amount to constructive notice, their Courts have not adopted that view, and they have decided that a deed duly recorded is constructive notice of its existence and contents; see *Story's Eq. Jur.*, Sec. 401; but registration even there is not deemed to be constructive notice if the instrument on record is one which was not required by law to be recorded. See *2 Wash. Real Property*, (1st edition,) 592.

On referring to our Registry Act, it will be apparent that the classes of instruments to be registered under it are particularly specified. The 9th Section enacts that all *deeds, judgments* and *attachments* affecting lands shall be registered, &c., and directions are given as to the mode by which these are to be placed on record. Grants, leases and mortgages are mentioned in subsequent sections, but no other instruments are referred to. By the 19th Sec. it is enacted, that *deeds* or *mortgages* duly executed, but not registered, shall be void against any subsequent purchaser or mortgagee for valuable consideration, who shall first register his *deed* or *mortgage*; and the only section in which any general words are used is that to prevent the tacking of mortgages, which provides that no mortgage, judgment, or *other encumbrance* affecting lands shall have any priority or effect, by reason of being held by or vested in the same person with another mortgage or encumbrance of prior date or registry, which can have no bearing on the point under consideration.

We have thus the classes of instruments to be recorded, specifically defined, and in this respect our act differs much from the English, the Irish, and the New Brunswick registry acts. Ours also contains directions for recording, which are applicable alone to the classes specified, and not to such agreements as this, or to any other document which a party might be disposed to enter on the registry.

The 7th Section enacts that a double index shall be made and kept in the case of deeds, including the names of all the grantors and grantees, and in the case of *judgments and attachments*, the names of all the plaintiffs and defendants; and again by the 15th Section, where a *deed* shall be duly proved and lodged, or a *docket of a judgment,* or a *copy of an attachment* with the description and appraisement duly lodged as above for registry, the time when the same shall have been so proved and lodged shall be accounted the date of the registry of such *deed, judgment* or *attachment* respectively, and the same shall be registered in the same order in which they were so lodged or proved; and in the 18th Section, the *certificate* of *registry* endorsed on any *deed, docket of judgment* or *attachment,* and signed by the Registrar, shall be taken and allowed in all Courts as evidence of registry. The 22nd and

23rd sections refer exclusively to judgments, and the 24th to attachments.

From the language used by the Legislature, I can arrive at no other conclusion than that registration of the documents enumerated, *and of these alone*, was contemplated; and if so, the registration of instruments not within the purview of the statute cannot be deemed to be notice of their existence and contents to a party claiming under a deed or mortgage for valuable consideration, whereby such a presumption of knowledge is raised that the Court will not allow it to be rebutted by evidence to the contrary.

The parties claiming under the mortgage to Stairs have all been examined, and have denied any knowledge of the agreement; they were not asked whether they had employed a solicitor to search the records to ascertain the state of the title to the land before taking the mortgage, for if that had been done it might have had an important bearing on the question; but I presume, from the absence of any evidence on the point, no such search did in fact take place, and it was for the party resisting their claim to have shown it, for the *onus* lies upon the party who claims priority over another on the ground that he took with notice, expressed or implied, to prove such notice.

The terms used in the English Registry Act are so different from the language of ours, as regards the instruments to be recorded, that on this point decisions under it are not in all cases a guide for us; for while, as I have shown, our act particularizes the documents, the English act embraces in general terms all "*deeds and conveyances whereby lands may be in any way affected at law or in equity.*" It also contemplates the registry of wills and devises affecting land, &c., which with us need not be registered, however much they may affect the title to lands, and on reference to *Moore* v. *Culverhouse*, 27 Beav. 639, it will be seen that great stress is laid on the word, "*conveyances*," a word not used in our act in connection with registration, but to be found in that of New Brunswick; the words there being, "*conveyances* and other instruments by which lands may be affected in law or equity."

On the subject of constructive notice, Vice Chancellor WIG-RAM in *Jones* v. *Smith*, 1 Hare, 55, says: "I believe I may, without danger, assert that the cases in which constructive notice can be established, resolve themselves into two classes; first, cases in which the party charged has had actual notice that the property in dispute was in some way charged, encumbered, or affected,—the Court has there bound him with constructive notice of facts and instruments to a knowledge of which he would have been led by enquiring, after the charge, etc., of which he had notice ; and secondly, cases in which the Court is satisfied from the evidence that he has designedly abstained from enquiry to avoid notice." And again, "if mere want of caution, as distinguished from fraudulent and wilful blindness, is all that can be imputed to the purchaser, the doctrine of constructive notice will not apply ; there the purchaser will be considered, as in fact he is, a *bona fide* purchaser without notice."

The conclusion at which I have arrived, after the best consideration I can give the subject, is, that under our Registry Act the order of priority of all deeds, etc., which the Legislature contemplated should be recorded, is the order, in point of time, in which they are recorded, that the agreement in evidence is not an instrument embraced within the terms of the act, and that Stairs and those claiming with him under Montgomery's mortgage, not having received actual or constructive notice of its existence when the mortgage was taken, are to be considered *bona fide* mortgagees unaffected by it, and therefore that the exceptions to the Master's report must be over-ruled and the report confirmed.

COOK *v.* DAVIDSON ET AL.

Plaintiff brought action against the defendants for a mandamus to compel them to provide for a debt due him by the trustees of a school section. The writ was against the defendants personally, but contained a statement that they were trustees, &c., and that defendant, D., was secretary. Evidence was taken as to the existence of the debt, and the case came on for hearing under the pleadings and evidence.

Held, that the trustees could only be sued in their corporate name; and that the amendment to that effect, asked for by plaintiff at the hearing, could not be permitted.

RITCHIE, E. J., delivered the judgment of the Court:—

This suit was brought against the defendants under the provisions of the chapter of the Revised Statutes, "Of Procedure in Equity," for a mandamus to require them to provide for the payment of a debt due the plaintiff by the Trustees of the Port-a-Pique School Section, Number Nine, in the County of Colchester, by the collection of an assessment already made and not yet collected, or, otherwise, by a new assessment and rate, to be levied and collected from the rate-payers of that section, to the amount of the debt due him by the section.

An answer has been put in by the defendants, in which they deny that the debt claimed by the plaintiff is justly due by the section, and also object to the mode in which they have been sued, as the trustees of school sections are corporate bodies, and the proceedings should have been against the corporation. Evidence having been taken on both sides, the case was fully heard on the pleadings and evidence, both on the merits and also on the objection I have referred to.

Though the writ is against the three defendants personally, there is a statement in it that they are School Trustees of Port-a-Pique School Section, Number Nine, in the County of Colchester, and that the defendant, Davidson, is their secretary, and the defendants, in their answer, admit that they were Trustees of School Section Number Nine, in the District of Port-a-Pique, at the time the writ was served upon them.

By the Chapter of the Revised Statutes, "Of Public Instruction," it is provided that each section shall have a board of three Trustees, and at each annual meeting of the section one of them shall go out of office, and a new one shall be elected in his place. The Trustees are made a body corporate for the prosecution and defence of all actions relating to the school and its affairs and other necessary purposes, under the title of "The Trustees of School Section Number —, in the District of ——," and they are empowered, when authorized by the school meeting, to borrow money for the school purposes, and among other things, for building school-houses, which is to be assessed on the section, and is made a charge thereon. The money, the subject of the debt claimed to be due the plaintiff, was borrowed for the purpose of erecting a school-house in the section; but the money was borrowed and the school-house erected before the present defendants came into office as Trustees.

The defendants have, I think, failed in supporting that part of their answer in which they deny that the debt in question is due the plaintiff by the section. In this respect the plaintiff has established his case and shewn that the amount is a charge on the section and should have been assessed and levied thereon by the Trustees; but the proceedings should, in my opinion, have been brought against the corporation, and not against the individuals who happened to be trustees at the time the suit was commenced, and I did not feel myself justified, in a case like this, in making an amendment to that effect at the hearing, as requested by Mr. Rigby.

I know of no exception to the rule that a corporation aggregate must be sued by its corporate name. *Attorney General* v. *Corporation of Worcester*, 2 Phill. R., 3, has decided that the Court will not permit it to be sued by any other. In the case before us the name is given by statute, by which, and by which alone, I think, the Trustees can sue or be sued. (*Tapping on Mandamus*, 314.) Cases may occur where officers or individual members may be made parties to a suit, where they are charged with illegal or unauthorized acts, and sometimes they may be joined where discovery is sought, for the purpose of obtaining it under oath, but never in proceedings of this character.

The inconvenience which would result from a different course of proceedings is very apparent. The debt was not contracted by the persons sued, and when the decision is given they may be out of office, so that if a mandamus should be granted agreeably to the prayer of the writ, it may not be in their power, however willing they may be, to obey it. It would not be reasonable to punish them for their disobedience, and their successors would not be liable to punishment for disobedience to the writ, so that there would be no means of carrying out the judgment of the Court in favor of the plaintiff; and it is to be borne in mind that the suit is based, not on the liability of the Trustees for the debt, but of the section on which the debt is made a charge, and the object of the plaintiff is to compel the section to pay it, and the corporation, as such, is alone vested with the power of assessing and levying the amount on the section. If the suit is brought against the corporation, it matters not who may happen then to compose it, and if a writ of mandamus is subsequently granted, it must be obeyed by the corporation, and whoever then may compose it must be responsible for disobedience to it.

I cannot do otherwise than refuse the relief prayed for, which I do on this ground alone, and as much expense might have been saved by having this question raised preliminary to that by which the evidence was taken, as it might, and, I think, should have been, I will make no order at present with respect to costs.

ANDREW Y. CORBETT *v.* JOSHUA L. CORBETT.

W. J. C., being indebted to plaintiff, was sued November, 1867, and judgment recovered for $298.52, a docket of which was registered October, 1868. Execution was issued on the judgment, and land of the said W. J. C. was bought in by plaintiff, under Sheriff's sale. In May 1866, W. J. C., being so indebted, conveyed all his real estate, (found to have been then worth $850,) to his son, the present defendant, the consideration named in the deed being $300, and this suit was brought to set aside the deed as fraudulent. The jury found that W. J. C. was in possession of the land at the time he gave the deed to defendant, and continued so for four years afterwards, to May 1870; that he was in possession at the time of the Sheriff's sale to plaintiff, and at that time resided in the old homestead; that defendant was in possession, exclusive of W. J. C., from May 1870, under title of the conveyance from W. J. C.; that there was no money paid by the defendant at the time the deed was given, except two fifty dollar notes o hand; that defendant knew, at the time he got the deed, that W. J. C., was indebted to plaintiff; and that the deed was given by W. J. C. and received by defendant to prevent or impede plaintiff and other creditors of W. J. C. in obtaining payment of their debts.

Held, that under the findings of the jury, which the Court considered warranted by the evidence, the deed from W. J. C. to defendant must be set aside as fraudulent.

RITCHIE, E. J., delivered the judgment of the Court :—

This suit is brought for the purpose for setting aside a deed made by William J. Corbett to his son, the defendant, as having been made in fraud of the plaintiff, a creditor of William J. Corbett, in order to prevent his obtaining payment of his debt.

The writ sets forth that William J. Corbett was indebted to the plaintiff, and the latter, after exhausting every means to obtain payment, and just before the debt was liable to become barred by the Statute of Limitations, on the 15th November, 1867, commenced an action for its recovery against him, to which he pleaded, in order to occasion delay, and when the cause was about to be tried, the pleas were withdrawn, and the plaintiff obtained judgment for $293.52, which was duly registered on the 12th October, 1868. On this judgment the plaintiff caused an execution to be levied on the lands described in the writ, which, being sold by the Sheriff under it, were purchased by the plaintiff. The writ goes on to state that William J. Corbett, being so indebted to the plaintiff, on the 15th May, 1866, conveyed the said lands to the defendant, the consideration money mentioned in the deed being $300, and on the 11th August, 1866, the defendant appointed William J. Corbett, his attorney, among other things, to occupy the said lands, and to sell and dispose of them ; that William J. Corbett remained in possession of the lands till May 1870; that the lands were of much greater value than $300, having been at the time of the giving of the deed and now being of the value of $950 and upwards; that the consideration mentioned in the deed was a fraudulent consideration, and that no money was paid by defendant to William J. Corbett on account of the said lands; that the defendant knew at the time the deed was given to him, that William J. Corbett was indebted to plaintiff for the amount of his claim, and that the deed was given and received for the purpose of defrauding plaintiff and other creditors of Wm. J. Corbett.

The defendant, in his answer, admits the indebtedness of William J. Corbett to plaintiff, the issue of the process to recover the debt, the judgment obtained thereon, and the sale

and purchase of the lands described in the writ, by the plaintiff, and his having obtained a deed thereof, as alleged therein ;
but he denies all the other material allegations of the plaintiff
contained in the writ.

Issues on the controverted facts having been prepared and
submitted to a jury ; they found as follows :—

1. That William J. Corbett was in possession of the lands
   described in the writ at the time the deed was given
   to defendant by him.
2. That William J. Corbett had been in possession since the
   said deed was given to defendant, and was in posession four years, from May 1866, to April or May
   1870.
3. That defendant has been in possession of said lands,
   exclusive of William J. Corbett, since said deed was
   given, for two and a half years, since May 1870,
   under the title of deed from William J. Corbett.
4. William J. Corbett was in possession of said lands at the
   time of Sheriff's sale to plaintiff.
5. William J. Corbett resided in the old homestead at the
   time of said sale.
6. There was not any money paid to William J. Corbett by
   the defendant, in consideration for the land, before or
   since the deed was given, except two fifty-dollar
   notes of hand at the time the deed was given.
7. There was paid as consideration money, by the defendant, two fifty-dollar notes and one hundred and forty-
   eight dollars, previous to the deed, for the Brown
   Lots.
8. Eight hundred and fifty dollars was the value of the
   lands at the time the deed was given to defendant,
   and one thousand dollars was the value of them at
   the time of the issuing of the writ in this cause.
9. The defendant did know that William J. Corbett was
   indebted to the plaintiff at the time the defendant
   got the deed from William J. Corbett, and defendant
   acknowledged that William J. Corbett owed other
   parties small amounts at that time.

10. Previous to the commencement of the trial, this issue was added: Was the deed of conveyance given by William J. Corbett, and received by the defendant, Joshua Corbett, for the purpose of preventing or impeding the plaintiff, Andrew Y. Corbett, or other creditors of William J. Corbett, in obtaining payment of their debts? On which the jury found that the deed was given and received for that purpose.

Assuming that the jury were justified by the evidence in finding, as they have done, it can hardly be contended that the deed can stand; the finding on the last issue would be enough to establish the plaintiff's right to relief, and the contest on the hearing rather was that the evidence did not warrant the conclusion at which the jury had arrived, and that though the deed was given by the father, for the purpose of defeating the plaintiff's claim, there was nothing to lead to the inference that the son participated in the fraudulent intent of the father.

At the trial of the issues, I felt satisfied with the findings of the jury, as I thought the evidence justified them; and I have since carefully read my notes, and see nothing in them to induce me to change the opinion I then formed.

There is evidence that the son knew of the indebtedness of the father to the plaintiff. The sale was not of one particular lot of land, but of all the real estate owned by the father. The father continued in possession, and occupied the properties after he had made the deed, just as he had previously done. The deed was prepared by the father, and executed in the presence of a daughter, and its existence not communicated to any one out of the household. The father retained possession of the deed from May to August, unrecorded, and did not then record it till he had obtained from his son a power of attorney, authorizing him to occupy the lands and to sell them; in fact, to exercise the same control and authority over them as if he had never given the deed, and then he recorded both instruments simultaneously. The son, in his evidence, said he purchased the lands to accumulate property; and yet he gives power to his father to sell them, and nothing

appears to have been said by the son as to price or terms on
any such sale.   There is also the great inadequacy of price, the
consideration money mentioned in the deed being much less
than the actual value, while the evidence in relation to the
pre-existing debt, said to form part even of that, is of the
most unsatisfactory character.

Under these circumstances, can it be said that there is no
evidence to justify the jury in finding as they have done ?
Inadequacy of price, as between vendor and vendee, would not
of itself make a sale and conveyance invalid; yet it would be
an element affecting the case, if connected with other suspicious circumstances; *a fortiori* would it be so, where the
rights of creditors were concerned; for a conveyance will be
liable to be avoided, if given on full and valuable consideration, if it is made and taken with the intention of defeating
creditors. *Mala fides* supersedes all enquiry into the consideration, and though, as against creditors, inadequacy of price
alone might not in general make a conveyance void, yet it
might be so great as to lead to the inference of a fraudulent
intent between the parties; but where inadequacy of price is
coupled with all the suspicious circumstances connected with
this case, comprising, as they do, almost all the badges of fraud
referred to in the cases on this subject, I see no grounds for
saying that the jury came to an erroneous conclusion.

Where parties combine to defeat creditors, we can hardly
expect to have it proved otherwise than by evidence of fraudulent circumstances leading to that conclusion ; it is not to be
supposed that, where two persons combine to defraud a third,
other evidence can generally be obtained, for it is only by concealment of their object that they can hope to escape; *fraus est
celare fraudem.*

In *Cadogan* v. *Kennett,** Lord MANSFIELD said: " The principles and rules of the common law, as now universally known
and understood, are so strong against fraud in every shape, that
the common law would have attained every end proposed by
the Statutes 13 Eliz., c. 5, and 27 Eliz., c. 4.   The former
relates to creditors only, the latter to purchasers.   These
statutes cannot receive too liberal a construction or be too
much extended in suppression of fraud."

* Cowper 482.

"The Statute 13 Eliz., c. 5, does not militate against any transaction *bona fide*, and where there is no imagination of fraud, and so is the common law; but if the transaction be not *bona fide*, the circumstance of its being done for valuable consideration will not alone take it out of the statute. I, have known several cases where persons have given fair and full prices for goods, and where the possession was actually changed, yet, being done for the purpose of defeating creditors, the transaction has been held fraudulent, and therefore void." And again: "The question in every case is whether the act done is a *bona fide* transaction, or whether it is a trick and contrivance to defeat creditors."

In *Taylor on Evidence*, 6th Ed., 160, Sect. 128, *a.*: "Although Courts of Law are in general bound to presume *prima facie* in favor of deeds which appear to have been duly executed, an exception to this rule is recognized where sales are sought to be set aside by the creditors of the vendor as fraudulent, within the 13th Eliz., c. 5. This excellent act enacts in substance that all conveyances of lands or chattels, which are not made for a valuable consideration and *bona fide*, shall be void, as against any person whose claims on the original owner of the property shall be thereby delayed or disturbed; whenever, therefore, any transaction is sought to be invalidated, by virtue of this act, it becomes necessary for the vendor to establish the justice of his title, and to show affirmatively, not only that the deed under which he claims was duly executed, but that it was made in perfect good faith, and also for valuable consideration. In determining the question of *bona fides*, the jury will take into consideration all the circumstances connected with the transfer, always bearing in mind that if the conveyance is absolute,—that is, if it passes to the vendee an immediate right of possession,—the fact of the vendor being allowed to continue as the apparent owner of the property, must necessarily raise a very strong presumption of fraud."

Acting upon the verdict of the jury, as I think I am bound to do, justified as I believe it to be by the evidence, I have no alternative but to make a decree in favor of the plaintiff, with costs.

DANIEL et al. v. VEITH et al.

J. W., by his last will, among other things, devised all his real estate to trustees, to let it during the natural life of his wife, or, in case she should die before his youngest surviving child should attain the age of twenty-one years, then until such child should attain that age, to receive the rents and, after paying a certain annuity and charges, to divide all balances equally among *all his before mentioned children*, and such further child or children as might be born. The testator, in another part of his will clearly indicated his intention that upon the decease of his wife or upon his youngest surviving child attaining the age of twenty-one years, whichever event should last happen, the real estate should be sold and the proceeds divided equally among his *surviving* children.

During the life of the widow a daughter died, leaving children, who claimed the daughter's share of the rents.

Held, that they were entitled to such share.

RITCHIE, E. J., delivered the judgment of the Court :—

John Withan, by his last will, made the 5th June, 1834, among other things, devised all his real estate to trustees, to let it during the natural life of his wife, or in case she should die before his youngest surviving child should attain the age of twenty-one years, then until such child should attain that age, and receive the rents thereof and thereout, to pay to his wife during her natural life the annual sum of one hundred pounds, Nova Scotia currency, and keep the houses insured and in good repair, and all annual balances of rents which might remain, and as they should from time to time accumulate, to divide equally among *all* his *before-mentioned children*, and such further child or children as might be born, to be paid to or invested for them in the same way or manner, and subject to the same matters and things as the several bequests were before made to them, in the division of his personal estate, and upon further trust, upon the decease of his wife, in case she should live until after the youngest surviving child should attain the age of twenty-one years, or in case she should die during the minority of his said child, then, upon such youngest surviving child attaining the said age, to cause the whole of his said real estate to be sold to the best advantage, in three months thereafter, and to cause the proceeds thereof to be equally divided among and paid to such of his children as might be living at the time of such sale, and in case all of his said children should be dead at the time of such sale, then to cause the proceeds to be equally divided among the lawful representatives of his said children.

The testator's widow is still alive; his daughter Catherine has died, leaving children, the plaintiffs in this suit, who claim a portion of the rents,—their mother's share; their right is contested by George Withan, a surviving child of the testator.

The testator has clearly indicated that on the sale and division of the real estate, those of his children who are then alive shall take, to the exclusion of the issue of those who may have died, and that the representatives of his children generally shall only take in case all of them shall be dead at the time of the sale.

This being the declared intention of the testator in respect to the distribution of the proceeds of the sale of the real estate, I was at first inclined to think that in disposing of the rents in the meantime, he had carried out the same intention; that till the sale should take place they should be paid to his children alone, and not to their representatives, so long as any of them should survive; but after a careful consideration of the subject, I am led to the conclusion that as the testator directed that the rents should be divided equally among *all his before-mentioned children*, whom he had particularized in a previous part of his will, and to each of whom he had bequeathed one-ninth of the proceeds of his personal property, the gift must be considered as made to them individually, and not as a class—see *Bain* v. *Lescher,* 11 Sim., 400; for while he alludes to *all* his children, as it were, by name, he gives no intimation that on the death of one, the survivors should take, as he had done in the case of the death of his four younger children before arriving at the age of twenty-one years, where he provided that the share of the child so dying should go to such of his other children as might then be alive, and as in the case of the share of his personal property, which he directed to be invested for his grand-children, the children of his daughter, Mrs. LePousie, and to be paid to them, or the survivor of them, on their attaining the age of twenty-one. As a gift to a class implies an intention to benefit those who com-

pose it, and to exclude others, so a gift to individuals described by several names, though they may happen to constitute a
class, implies an intention to benefit the individuals named.
That intention is to be implied here; and, as in the case of the
gift, by will, of a rent charge or annuity to one person till the
death of another, such gift would be valid; see *Co. Lit.*, 111,
a, and *Taylor* v. *Martindale*, 12 Sim., 158, *Kerr* v. *Middlesex Hospital*, 2 De. G., M. & G., 583; and on the death of the
donee before the death of the other, his representatives would
take; so, assuming this gift to be to each individual child of
the testator, it would enure to the benefit of his representatives till the sale of the real estate, on the death of the testator's wife.

In this view of the case, which I have adopted, the plaintiffs
are entitled to the relief sought by them in this suit.

EATON v. WEATHERBE.

Where the demurrer is to the whole writ, if there is any part of it which entitles
the plaintiff to relief, the demurrer must be over-ruled.

Plaintiff in his writ, set out among other things that defendant and himself were
engaged in a co-partnership as Attorneys, &c., from September 1866, to December 1871, that in 1867 one Kirby informed them that a certain coal area would be
vacant, and asked them to join with him in applying for it, as he anticipated
trouble in getting it, and wanted assistance, to which they agreed, the license
to search being taken in the name of defendant, who held it for the benefit of said
Kirby and the said firm (the respective proportions being set out in the writ):
that afterwards defendant obtained, with the same consent, and for the benefit of
the same parties, a license to work, the fee therefor being paid out of the partnership funds; that a renewal of the license to work was afterwards obtained by
defendant, and before the expiration of the renewal, and after the dissolution of
the co-partnership, defendant, without consulting plaintiff, and without his
knowledge, obtained a lease of the area in conjunction with said Kirby, and refused
to recognize plaintiff's claim to any interest therein.

Held, on demurrer, that it was not necessary that the agreement in respect to
said area be alleged in the writ to have been in writing; that Kirby mentioned in the writ was not a necessary party, as no complaint had been made
against him, no relief was sought from him, and no decree could be made against
him; and that the facts set out constituted a good ground for the relief sought
for by plaintiff, as, assuming the statements in the writ to be true, the defendant
was a trustee for the plaintiff to the extent of plaintiff's interest in the area.

On the trial of issues of fact, an account book was produced, kept by plaintiff, and the attention of the Court was turned to certain entries.

Held, that, although in going into an accounting, every portion of the book could be referred to by both parties, yet on the trial of the issues, only those portions of the book could be commented on to the jury which had been referred to and read.

Where the trial took place at Halifax before the Judge in Equity, and the verdict was found on September 25th, and the rule, having been refused by the Judge, was not taken out until October 30th. *Held*, that, assuming the plaintiff to have had a right to take out a rule under the Statute, he had allowed too much time to to elapse, and had by the delay lost his right to do so.

The writ in this case set out that plaintiff and defendant entered into a co-partnership in the business of Barristers, Attorneys, &c., by agreement in writing, dated September 1st, 1866, which co-partnership continued until December 31st, 1871 when it was dissolved by mutual consent, plaintiff's interest in the assets and profits of the business being one-third, and defendant's two-thirds; that the affairs and accounts of the partnership had never been settled; that a large amount of debts was due the firm, and that they were owners, among other things, of a valuable coal-mine, and of certain lots of land in the City of Halifax; that in or about October, 1867, one Kirby had informed plaintiff and defendant that he knew of a coal-mine that would shortly be vacant, and asked them to join with him in applying for it, as he anticipated great difficulty in getting it, and wanted assistance, to which they agreed, the license to search being taken in the name of the defendant, who held it for said Kirby and the said firm, and that it was afterwards agreed between the parties that Kirby should own half the property, and the said firm of plaintiff and defendant the other half; that in October 1869, the defendant, with the consent of Kirby and of the plaintiff, and for their benefit and his own, obtained a license to work over the same area, for which fifty dollars were paid out of the said firm, whereof one-half was afterwards re-paid to them by Kirby; that when the license to work was about to expire, in October 1871, the plaintiff, at defendant's request, prepared the papers to obtain a renewal, which was obtained for one year; that before the said renewal expired, and after the dis-

4

solution of the co-partnership, the defendant, without consulting plaintiff, and without his knowledge, applied for and obtained a lease of the said area, to be granted to him and said Kirby; and although the plaintiff was interested ·therein to the extent of one-third of defendant's share, or one-sixth of the whole, the said defendant had refused to recognize his claim, or assign the same to him; that the said mine was very valuable, and defendant and said Kirby were about to sell it, whereby plaintiff would lose his interest therein, unless defendant was prevented from disposing of it; that the said firm had also owned six lots of land, which had been conveyed by deed to defendant, and which he held for the benefit of himself and the plaintiff, who had contributed one-third of the purchase money, the whole having been paid out of the assets of the firm; but defendant had refused to recognize, in any way, the plaintiff's right thereto; and plaintiff therefore prayed that defendant might be required to answer, etc., and that an account of said partnership dealings should be taken, and defendant should be decreed to pay to the plaintiff such amount as should be found due, and to convey to the plaintiff one-third of his interest in the said properties, the plaintiff being ready and offering to pay any amount found to be due from him on the account, as well as his share of expenses incurred in obtaining said lease; and plaintiff also prayed for an injunction to restrain defendant from disposing of said property, and for such other relief, &c.

To this writ or bill, defendant demurred, for the following among other causes:—

First—That plaintiff had not made such a case as entitled him to any relief in a Court of Equity, against the defendant, and that the said bill did not contain any matter of Equity on which the Court could ground a decree, or give any relief to the plaintiff.

Secondly—That it appeared by the bill in respect to the claim for a conveyance of the mining area referred to, that Kirby should be represented, and had not been made a party to the writ; that the promise or contract alleged in relation to said area was not, nor was any memorandum thereof alleged to have been reduced to writing, signed by the defendant or any person authorized by him; and that the said bill contained several distinct matters which in no manner depended upon each other.

After argument of the questions raised by the demurrer—
RITCHIE, E. J., delivered the judgment of the Court:—

The defendant has demurred to the plaintiff's writ, and the first question that arises is as to the principles and practice which are to prevail in respect to demurrers in an Equity suit. This, I think, is settled by the chapter of the Revised Statutes " Of Proceedings in Equity," (124,) which provides that in such suits the practice of the Supreme Court shall be observed as far as applicable, and as regards demurrers the Statute is more explicit; it states that either party may demur to the pleading of the adverse party, on the same grounds, and such demurrers shall be heard and determined on the same principles as obtain in the Supreme Court; we must therefore be guided by both the principles and practice of the Supreme Court in considering this demurrer. By the chapter of the Revised Statutes regulating the practice and pleadings in the Supreme Court, except in certain cases particularly mentioned, special demurrers are not allowed, and the form of the demurrer is given, which is, that the pleading is bad in substance, for the following reasons, viz., &c.: This demurrer is not in the form prescribed, and does not state that the writ is bad in substance, and many of the grounds assigned as such are only applicable to special demurrers. I shall, however, proceed to consider whether, if the demurrer had been in the prescribed form, the writ is, in fact, bad in substance on the ground taken at the argument, and inasmuch as this demurrer is to the whole writ, if there is any part of it which entitles the plaintiff to relief, the demurrer must be over-ruled. See *Daniel, Ch. Pr.,* 5 Ed., 500, and cases there referred to.

To the objection that there are several causes of action, unconnected with each other, united in this suit, the answer is obvious that both at Common Law and in Equity such a course is sanctioned by Statute. It was also objected that the plaintiff in his writ had not stated that the agreement with respect to the coal mine mentioned therein was in writing, and that therefore it was invalid under the Statute of Frauds; this objection would avail if it appeared by the writ that the agreement which the Statute required to be in writing was oral; but it is not necessary that it should be alleged to be in writing, either in pleadings at Law or in Equity. This has been decided in numerous cases. See *Young* v. *Austen*, L. R., 4 C. P., 553, and in *Davies* v. *Otty*, 33 Beavan 540, it was held that a trust need not be alleged to be in writing, but it is sufficient if the trust be proved by writing.

It was contended that Kirby, mentioned in the writ, should have been made a party. If he were shown to have been a necessary party, it could only apply to a part of the plaintiff's case, leaving still grounds for relief untouched: and then, if the demurrer had been confined to that part of the writ, it might have been sustained, as in that case the causes of action would not have affected all the defendants, and therefore they ought not to have been joined in the same writ; but I do not think he is a necessary party, no complaint is made against him in the writ, and no relief sought from him, and if he had been joined, no decree could be made against him; and a decree against the defendant will give him all he can be entitled to.

But assuming, as we must do, that, as the demurrer is to the whole writ, if there are any good grounds for relief there stated, it must be overruled, there seems little difficulty in this case.

The writ sets out the existence of a partnership between plaintiff and defendant, as Attorneys, &c., &c., which commenced in 1866 and terminated in 1871, the affairs of which have not yet been settled; that the interest of the plaintiff in the partnership was one-third, and that of the defendant two-thirds; that a large amount of debts are due the firm, and that they are the owners, among other things, of the half of a valuable coal mine, and some lots of land in the City of Halifax, and goes on to shew how their interest in the coal mine was acquired; that one Kirby informed plaintiff and defendant that he knew of a coal mine that would shortly be vacant, and asked them to join with him in applying for it, as he anticipated great difficulty in obtaining it and wanted assistance, which they agreed to do, and the license to search was applied for and taken out in the name of the defendant, who held it for the said Kirby, and for the firm of Weatherbe & Eaton, the plaintiff and defendant; and it was afterwards agreed between the parties that the said Kirby should own one-half and the said firm the other half; that subsequently the defendant, with the consent and approval of Kirby and the plaintiff, and for their benefit and his own, obtained a license to work over a portion of the same area, for which the sum of fifty dollars was paid out of the money of the said firm, and of which one-half was afterwards repaid them by the said Kirby; that when the license to work was about to expire, plaintiff, at defendant's request, prepared the papers to obtain a renewal, which was obtained for a year, and the writ goes on to state that, before the renewal of the license to work expired, and after the co-partnership had been dissolved, the defendant, without consulting plaintiff, and without his knowledge, applied for and obtained a lease of the area described in the license to work, to be granted to him and the said Kirby, and although the plaintiff is interested therein to the extent of one-third of defendant's share, or one-sixth of the whole, the defendant now refuses to recognize his claim or to assign the same to him.

If these statements be true in every respect, and for our present purpose they must be considered as having been confessed to be so by the defendant, is there any room for doubt that the plaintiff would be entitled to relief?

Constructive trusts or trusts arising by operation of law, embrace, not only cases where property has been acquired by fraud or improper means, but also where it has been fairly acquired, but it is contrary to principles of Equity that it should be retained by the party in whom it is vested, for his own benefit. See *Spence's Equity*, 511; *Hill on Trustees*, 116; *Lewin on Trusts*, 199-200; and a trust will result to one for whom a purchase is in whole or in part made, whose money contributes to the purchase, though the conveyance may have been taken in the name of another. See *Dyer* v. *Dyer*, 2 Cox, 92; and, if in this case the original agreement for the license to

search, which is stated to have been paid for out of the joint
funds of the plaintiff and defendant, is established so as to
raise a trust in favour of plaintiff, then all the subsequent acts
whereby the right to the mine in question was perfected, must
be held to have been taken for the benefit of those interested
in the license first taken out; they were, in fact, the carrying
out of what must have been contemplated by the parties in
making application for it; and if therefore the defendant, in
taking the lease, embraced in his share what should have been
given to the plaintiff, he must be held a trustee for him to that
extent.   If the plaintiff has shewn a right to relief as regards
the coal mine, he has done so more clearly and distinctly in
respect to the lots of land in Halifax, for the writ sets out
that these lots were purchased by the plaintiff and defendant;
that the plaintiff has contributed one-third of the purchase
money, the whole of which was paid out of the assets of the
firm; that the defendant took the deeds in his own name, and
holds them for the benefit of himself and the plaintiff; and
that the defendant refuses to recognize in any way the plaintiff's right thereto.   Being of opinion that a case for relief has
been shewn by the plaintiff, in his writ, with respect to both
these properties, it is unnecessary, at this stage of the case, to
refer to the only other matter referred to in the bill, viz., the
settlement of the affairs of the partnership.   I cannot do
otherwise than overrule the demurrer with costs.

The demurrer having been overruled, the defendant filed his
answer to the plaintiff's bill, the Court directed certain issues of
fact to be tried by a jury, and a trial took place before the
Judge in Equity, at Halifax, on the 25th of September, 1875,
when a verdict was found for the defendant.   Plaintiff applied
to the Judge for a rule to set the verdict aside, which was
refused, and plaintiff, on the 30th October, 1875, took out a
rule under the Statute to set aside the findings of the jury.
Objections were taken to this rule on the part of the defendant, the nature of which appears in the following judgment:—

RITCHIE, E. J., delivered the judgment of the Court:

A rule *nisi* was taken out under the Statute in this case, to set aside the findings of the jury, a rule to that effect having been refused the plaintiff by the Judge. Objection was taken on the part of the defendant, that the rule was irregularly and improperly taken out, as no such rule could be taken under the Statute where the issues have been tried before the Judge in Equity himself, on his refusal to grant it; that the rule *nisi* not having been granted by the Court, nor taken out under the terms of the Statute, assuming that it could be so taken, it ought not to have been signed by the Prothonotary, and that plaintiff was guilty of *laches*, in allowing too great delay to take place before applying to the Court. These objections were urged at the argument, in addition to answering the rule *nisi* on its merits. The grounds chiefly relied on in support of the rule were, that the evidence did not justify the findings of the jury, and that the weight of evidence so preponderated in favour of the plaintiff that the issues ought to have been found in his favor; and that certain evidence which ought to have been submitted to them was withheld by the Judge.

The evidence of the plaintiff and defendant, the only witnesses examined, conflicted in very many particulars, and the case was submitted to the jury, to find on it as they should think right, and when application was made for a rule to set aside their findings, I refused it, because the questions involved were matters of fact, and I failed to see that there was such a preponderance of evidence in favor of the plaintiff, as made it incumbent on them to find the issues in his favour; and I may add that the jury, who had been drawn from the special jury list, were very intelligent, and gave great attention to the case. I have since read and carefully considered the evidence, and I remain of the same opinion, so that, in case the same evidence were given on another trial, I should feel obliged to leave the question open to the jury, and should not feel justified in telling them that it was their duty to find for one or other of the parties.

In the course of the trial, an account-book was produced, kept by the plaintiff for the firm of Weatherbe & Eaton, and in the course of his examination, the attention of the Court was turned to certain entries in relation to the questions involved in the issues, which were read to the jury. Mr. Henry, in his general reply for the plaintiff, proposed to refer to and read other entries in the book, different from those referred to and read in evidence to the jury, and relating to matters not connected with the subject of the issues, on the ground that the contents of the whole book were in evidence. This I ruled he could not do on the trial of the issues, which, on the argument, was urged as a ground for a new trial ; but I think now, as I did then, that, though this book was a partnership book, and in going into an accounting between the partners, every portion of it could be referred to by either of them ; yet, on the trial of the issues, only those portions could be commented on to the jury, which had been referred to and read ; if otherwise, there would be, in fact, an introduction of new evidence, to which the attention of the defendant's counsel had never been called, and which he would have no opportunity of explaining or commenting on.

Assuming that the plaintiff had the right to take the rule under the Statute, and, in doing so, had complied in all respects with its terms, I should feel obliged to discharge it, and perhaps it would be unnecessary for me to say more ; but, as the plaintiff may be desirous of appealing from my decision, to enable him to do so on all the points involved, if he should be so disposed, I will shortly advert to the other questions which have been raised.

The reason for allowing the rule for a new trial to be taken out under the Statute, in cases tried on the Common Law side of the Court, when the Judge refuses it, does not seem to apply to cases tried before the Judge in Equity ; he hears the application for the rule, and, if, on application so made and unopposed, he thinks that no sufficient grounds are shewn to induce him to grant it, I do not see any good reason why he should be called upon to hear the same arguments again addressed to him, with the only difference that then the other party would be heard in opposition, and at Common Law the Statute gives an appeal from the ruling of the Judge who tries the cause, to the Court in banc, where the rule is made returnable ; but in Equity the rule is made returnable before the Judge in Equity himself.

The right to take the rule at Common Law, where the

Judge has refused it, is strictly statutory, and the terms of the Statute must be strictly complied with, which, it appears to me, can only be done at the sittings or on Circuit in Common Law or Equity cases tried there. See Sect. 212 of the Pract. Act, as to the time and mode of taking out the rule. There are no terms or sittings, so called, in the Equity Court, which is always open, and if, in this case, we overlook the letter of the Statute, which requires that the rule should be taken out the last day of the term or sittings, or such extended time as the Judge shall allow, and as far as possible act upon its spirit, we must come to the conclusion that the plaintiff allowed too much time to elapse before he did so. The issues were tried and the verdict found on the 25th September, 1875, and the rule was not taken out till the 30th October following. I think, therefore, that if the plaintiff had the right of taking the rule under the Statute, he has lost it by the delay.

I may observe that a party in this Court is not without redress when he is dissatisfied with the ruling of the Judge in Equity, for, except in relation to matters of practice and costs, he has an appeal from every decision, order, judgment, and decree, made by him, and on the rule for the new trial being refused the plaintiff here, he could have asserted an appeal and obtained the opinion of the Court in banc.

The rule must be discharged with costs.

FORREST v. MUIR ET AL.

One R. T. Muir, who died 4th September, 1871, by his will, bequeathed his business, including stock in trade, &c., to A. F. Muir, on certain conditions, among which was the payment or guaranteeing to defendants as trustees for his two sisters, the sum of $4000 each, for which they were to take security upon the stock in trade if they saw necessary, within a convenient time after the death of the testator; and it was also provided by the will that a sum of $2000 should be paid or secured to the defendants personally. A. F. Muir continued trading, collecting the debts of the concern, and disposing of the stock, the money payable to the defendants on their own account and as trustees being left in the business without any security being taken. On the 5th April 1875, A. F. Muir conveyed his stock, then worth about $60,000, to the defendants as security for the payment of the said sums together with a further sum alleged to be due to one of the defendants from the estate of R. T. Muir, and on the 15th of June, 1875, defendants took possession of the stock and proceeded to sell it, shortly after which, on the 30th June, A. F. Muir made an assignment under the Insolvent Act. Plaintiff as assignee brought this action to set aside the conveyance to defendants, alleging in his writ that the conveyance had been made to give the defendants a preference over other creditors, and that the defendants knew or had reasonable cause to know and believe that A. F. Muir was unable to meet his liabilities. Defendants in their answer denied that A. F. Muir was insolvent when he made the conveyance to them and asserted that when they received it they believed him to be solvent. They denied all fraud on their part in the transaction, and asserted that they demanded the security in pursuance of the directions of the will of R. T. Muir.

The jury found that, at the time of the conveyance being made, A. F. Muir was embarrassed and unable to meet his engagements, that defendants did not then know and had not reasonable cause to know that such inability existed, that the conveyance was not made by A. F. Muir with intent fraudulently to delay or impede his creditors, and that the original stock had been all disposed of except about $1600 worth of machinery.

Held, that under the findings of the jury the conveyance must stand, and that it was not competent for the plaintiff to contend that, even in the absence of knowledge on the part of the defendants, the conveyance should be set aside, as made by A. F. Muir in contemplation of insolvency and in violation of section 89 of Insolvent Act, that being a different cause of action from any set out in the writ.

Plaintiff having obtained an injunction to restrain the defendants from disposing of the stock, the Court directed that the amount for which defendants claimed a lien, with $160 for possible costs, should be deposited with the Receiver General to respond the judgment if favorable to the defendants, in which case the injunction should continue, otherwise to be dissolved.

The facts of this case are set out in the above head-note, and more fully in the judgment given below. A motion having been made to dissolve the injunction obtained by plaintiff to restrain the defendants from disposing of the goods in their possession under the conveyance above referred to ;

RITCHIE, E. J., delivered the following judgment :—

From the writ and answer and the affidavits which have been produced, it appears that the late Robt. T. Muir, who carried on business as a Book-seller and Stationer in Halifax, died on or about the 4th September 1871, having on or about the 3rd August in the same year made his will, whereby, among other things, he directed that his brother Allan F. Muir should carry on the business which he had conducted in his lifetime, and bequeathed to him all his interest therein, including the stock in trade, book, and other debts, shop, shop furniture, &c., and every other thing connected therewith, on the following condi_ tions : first, the payment or guaranteeing to William Muir and John Muir, the defendants, as trustees for his two sisters Agnes and Euphemia Muir, $4000 each, to be secured at a convenient time after his death, if the said trustees should see necessary, by a first lien upon the stock in the business, or, if it should be found inconvenient to pay the said money they were au- thorized to let it remain in the business, the said Allan F. Muir paying to each of his said sisters the sum of $400 during her life, with liberty to pay off the principal at any time if he should find it convenient to do so ; and if the money should re- main in the business it should be the duty of the trustees to examine the books and take such steps as would effectually secure the interest of his said sisters in the sum of $8000 in the said business.

On the death of the testator, Allan F. Muir took possession of the stock in trade &c., and carried on the business of Book- seller and Stationer under the name of R. T. Muir & Co., and it is stated by the plaintiff, and not denied by the defendants or the said Allan F. Muir, that he sold and disposed of the whole of the stock so bequeathed to him, and collected the debts and purchased and acquired new stock and assets, and no security was taken from him for the said $8000, nor for the sum of $2,- 000 which was bequeathed to the defendant William Muir, to be paid by Allan F. Muir at a convenient time after the testator's death, but which the testator directed might remain on pay- ment of six per cent. interest secured next after the bequest to his sisters ; nor was any security demanded till between three and four years after, when, by indenture bearing date 5th April 1875, Allan F. Muir conveyed to the defendants all his stock in trade, goods, chattels, debts and personal effects con- nected with the business carried on by him in trust to hold the same as a lien and security for the payment of the $8000 to Agnes and Euphemia Muir or the annual payment to each of them of $400, and as a lien and security for the payment of $2000, and the annual interest thereon to the defendant Wm. Muir, and as a lien and security for the sum of $549.79, and interest, being an amount in the said indenture stated to be due

him from the estate of Robert Thomas Muir deceased; and it
was further agreed in and by the said indenture that if any
of the stock in trade should be separated from the possession
of Allan F. Muir, and other stock and goods be substituted in
their stead, or if any stock should be added, the same should
be held to be included and conveyed by those presents; it was
provided nevertheless that in case Allan F. Muir should pay
the said sums and all interest thereon the indenture should
become void, and until default should be made in the payment
Allan F. Muir should hold, make use of and possess the said
stock, goods &c.; and he did continue in possession, and carried
on the business until the 15th June 1875, when the defendants
obtained possession of all his stock in trade, debts, and assets,
and have remained in possession ever since, and have since
then been disposing of the goods, collecting the debts and continuing business under the same name.

On the 30th June, 1875, Allan F. Muir made an assignment
of his property under the Insolvent Act, and this suit is
brought by the Assignee to set aside the Indenture of assignment made by Allan F. Muir to the defendants, and he asks that
the defendants may be decreed to deliver up to him the assets
and stock mentioned therein &c., &c., and in the meantime that
an injunction may issue to restrain the defendants from disposing of any more of the stock or collecting the debts, and
that a receiver be appointed, or that the property be delivered
to him on his giving security to the satisfaction of the Court
for the payment to the defendant of any amount which may
be decreed to be due under and by virtue of the said indenture. The grounds on which this relief is sought are that Allan
F. Muir was insolvent and unable to pay his debts when he
made the indenture of assignment to the defendants, and that it
was made by him for the purpose of giving the defendants and
Agnes and Euphemia Muir an unjust preference over his other
creditors, and impeding and delaying them in their remedies
against him, and that the same was made fraudulently and
illegally, and contrary to the provisions of the Insolvent Act of
1869, the defendants well knowing, or having reasonable cause
for knowing and believing, that he was unable to meet his
liabilities.

The insolvency of Allan F. Muir at the time he made the assignment to the defendants is denied, and they assert that when they received it they believed him to have been solvent, and they deny all fraud on their part and now seek that the injunction obtained by the plaintiff should be dissolved.

In general, if the allegations on which an injunction has been obtained are falsified by the affidavits on the other side it will be dissolved, but not necessarily so; it will be continued or dissolved according to the merits as disclosed by the pleadings and the preponderance of the evidence. See *Kerr on Injunctions,* 627 (American Edition), and again page 631 note, " Whether or not to dissolve an injunction, even upon a full denial of the equity of the bill, is a matter within the discretion of the Court." And see *Magnay* v. *Mines Royal Company,* 3 Drew 133-4, and *High on Injunctions,* Section 899. To the general rule that a preliminary injunction will be dissolved on the coming in of the answer, fully denying the equities of the bill, there are numerous exceptions based on recognized principles of equity; it is largely a matter of judicial discretion to be determined by the nature of the particular case under consideration, and the Court may, in the exercise of a sound discretion, on the coming in of the answer denying the material allegations of the bill, refuse the dissolution and continue the injunction when the circumstances of the case seem to demand that course."

In granting an interlocutory injunction the court does not profess to anticipate the determination of the right in controversy, but acts on the assumption that there is a substantial question to be tried, and that, until the decision upon it, the defendant shall not interfere with the property involved to the prejudice of the claimant; but while the rights of the Plaintiff are thus protected, care must be taken that those of the defendant are not jeopardized.

The defendants in this case have obtained a security for their debt, which we are to assume, till the contrary be made to appear by the evidence to be produced, is in all respects valid, and, in the meantime that security should be preserved; but the plaintiff contests the validity of that instrument, and it appears to me that a course may be pursued by which the

rights of both plaintiff and defendants can be respected and no
injury arise to either party till the judgment of the Court is
obtained.

The value of the assets assigned to the defendants is stated to
be $60,000 or thereabout, and the amount secured to the defend-
ants by the assignment is $10,549. The debt of the defendants
is therefore fully secured by the goods &c., in their hands however disposed of, but it is of importance to the creditors of Allan
F. Muir, represented by the plaintiff, that every available means
be resorted to so as to dispose of them advantageously. The
defendants, therefore, claiming only to have a lien on them for a
certain sum, can be placed at least in as good a position as they
now are if the whole amount of their claim be paid into Court
to abide the judgment. In this way their interests are protected independently of the property, while leaving it at the disposal of the defendants might be greatly to the injury of the
plaintiff whatever the final decision of the case might be. Indeed the defendants in their answer say that they are willing
to give the plaintiff possession of all the property in question,
except enough to satisfy their claim, but while the matter is in
controversy all they can reasonably require is that the amount
due them should be deposited for them should the judgment of
the Court be in their favour. In *High on Injunctions*, Section
902, it is laid down that if the continuance of the injunction,
even admitting the defendants' answer to be true, cannot prejudice or imperil his right, and on the other hand its dissolution
might seriously impair the right of the complainants, the
motion to dissolve on the coming in of the answer would not
be allowed ; thus in case of an injunction, in aid of a creditor's
bill the answer of the defendants denying the ownership of any
property or interest in property of any nature whatever, does
not necessarily entitle him to a dissolution of an injunction
restraining him from disposing of the property; in such case if
the answer be true the injunction can work no injury to
defendant, and if, notwithstanding his answer, he is possessed of property the injunction should be continued for the
protection of creditors; so where the fact is disclosed by defendants' answer, that they have no substantial interest in the
subject matter of the action, such interest being in a third per-

son not a party to the bill, and that the interest of the defendants cannot be prejudiced by continuing the injunction while
the complainant's right may be seriously jeopardized, the writ
will not be dissolved on such answer.

The injunction in this case will be dissolved if the full
amount for which the defendants claim a lien on the property
in dispute, with $160 to meet any costs which may be decreed
against the plaintiff, be not deposited with the Receiver General of the Court to respond the judgment of the Court if in
favor of the defendants. That this course is not without
authority, see *Taft* v. *Harrison* 10 Hare, 489 ; *Kensington* v.
White, 3 Price, 164 ; *Solly* v. *Moore*, 8 Price, 631 ; and if such
deposit be made, the injunction will continue, as in that case
the amount having been paid into Court, for which defendants
hold a lien on the property there is no good reason why they
should further hold or dispose, or otherwise interfere with it.

The costs of this application will be subject to the further
order of the Court.

I have avoided expressing any opinion on the questions
likely to arise at the hearing; all that I feel it necessary for me
to say is that there is a question involved which the plaintiff
has a right to bring before the Court for adjudication, and that
as the equities of the plaintiff's writ have been denied by the
defendants, they should not be enjoined from pursuing their
remedy under their assignment for the amount secured by it,
unless that amount is paid into Court.

The case was then submitted to a jury, whose findings upon
the several points submitted to them are given in the following judgment of the Court, delivered by RITCHIE, E. J. :—

The writ set out that one Robert T. Muir, since deceased,
carried on business at Halifax as a Bookseller and Stationer,
and at the time of his death was possessed of a large stock
and had debts due to him. In his last will he, among other
things, directed that his brother, Allan F. Muir, who is now
insolvent, and of whose estate the plaintiff is assignee, should
carry on the business, which he bequeathed to him, including
all the stock, debts, furniture, and fixtures connected with

it, on the following conditions :—*First*—The payment or
guaranteeing to the defendants, as trustees for the testator's two sisters, Agnes and Euphemia Muir, four thous-
and dollars each, to be secured at a convenient time after
testator's death, if the trustees should see necessary, by a
first lien on the stock, or if it should be found incon-
venient to pay the said sum, the trustees were authorized to
let the money remain in the business, Allan F. Muir paying
to each of the sisters four hundred dollars during the life of
each. The testator also gave to the defendants two thousand
dollars each, to be paid by Allan F. Muir from the business, at
a convenient time after the death of the testator, but which
might also remain upon payment of six per cent. interest,
secured, second to the bequest to his sisters ; that, on the
death of the testator, which took place in September, 1871,
Allan F. Muir took possession of the business, and the defendants allowed the $8,000, devised to his sisters, to remain in the
business, and also the $2,000 devised to the defendant, William
Muir, and no security was taken for either of these sums upon
the stock of the said business. Allan F. Muir continued the
business under the name of R. T. Muir & Co., and sold and
disposed of the whole of the stock so bequeathed to him, and
collected the debts and purchased new stock ; that in the
Spring of 1875, he became in insolvent and embarrassed circumstances and unable to pay his debts in full, and for the
purpose of giving the defendants and Agnes and Euphemia
Muir an unjust preference over his other creditors, and with
intent to defraud them, and impede and delay them in their
remedies against him, he, on or about the 5th April, 1875, by
indenture of that date, fraudulently and illegally, and contrary to the provisions of the Insolvent Act of 1869, conveyed
to the defendants, who then knew, or had reasonable cause to
know and believe, that he was unable to meet his liabilities,
all the stock-in-trade, goods, chattels, debts, and personal
effects then belonging to him, upon trust, first, to hold the
same as a lien and security for the payment to the said Agnes
and Euphemia Muir, of the said sum of $4,000 each, or
the annual payment of $400 each in lieu thereof, as pro-
vided for in the will of Robert T. Muir ; second, to hold the

same as a lien and security for the payment of the sum of
$2,000, and the annual interest thereof, to William Muir, as
provided for in the said will; third, to hold the same as a
lien and security for the sum of $549.79 and interest,
being an amount due to William Muir from the estate of
Robert T. Muir; which indenture contained a proviso that
it should be of no effect, in case Allan F. Muir should pay to
Agnes and Euphemia Muir the said sum of $4,000 each, or
should continue to pay them annually $400 each, and should
pay William Muir the said sum of $2,000, with interest, and
should pay to him on demand the said sum of $594.79,
with interest; and it was further provided that if default
should be made by Allan F. Muir in these payments, or the
defendants should become dissatisfied with that security, and
he should neglect or refuse to furnish to their satisfaction
other security in lieu thereof, after notice as therein specified,
it should be lawful for the defendants to take possession of
the property so conveyed to them and to sell and dispose of
the same, and out of the proceeds to pay or secure the said
amounts; that Allan F. Muir continued his business, knowing of his insolvency, from the time of the assignment so
made till on or about the 15th June, 1875, when, with intent
to defraud his creditors and impede and prevent them in
their remedies against him, he voluntarily gave up the
whole of his stock, debts, and assets to the defendants, who
have remained in possession thereof and have been and are
disposing thereof; that as soon as the defendants took possession of the stock, Allan F. Muir called a meeting of his
creditors, and afterwards, on or about the 30th June, 1875, he
made an assignment, under the provisions of the Insolvent Act
of 1869, to the official assignee, and on the 15th July, 1875,
the plaintiff was duly appointed the assignee of his estate,
who, on behalf of the creditors of the estate, prayed that the
said indenture might be set aside and cancelled, as fraudulent
and void.

In their answer, the defendants deny that prior to and at
the time of the making of the indenture of assignment, they
had any knowledge of the insolvency or embarrassment

5

of Allan F. Muir, but believed the contrary to be the
fact, and they deny that it was made to give Agnes and
Euphemia Muir and the defendants an unjust preference
over his other creditors, and with intent to defraud them,
and impede and delay them in their remedies against him;
and they say that being advised that it was necessary for
them as Executors, to have their accounts passed upon in
the Court of Probate, they believed it to be necessary in
order to a settlement of the Estate, that the direction in the
will of Robert T. Muir should be obeyed, and they demanded
from Allan F. Muir security for the said sums, and thereupon
obtained from him the said indenture of assignment; that they
had from time to time after the the death of Robert T. Muir
made enquiries into the condition of the business of Allan F.
Muir from himself and otherwise, and were led to believe and
did believe that he was solvent and able to meet his engagements in full, and they deny that he voluntarily gave up to
them the possession of his stock, &c., but on the contrary say
that they took possession in accordance with the terms of the
assignment, without his concurrence, and proceeded to sell it
for the purpose of paying and satisfying the amounts payable
under the provisions of it with the intention of transferring any
suplus that might remain to Allan F. Muir, or other person
lawfully entitled to it; that they were led to take possession
of the assets of Allan F. Muir from having discovered, for the
first time, about the first of June, that suits had been commenced against him, and they demanded other security, which
was not given them. The defendants deny that the assignment was given fraudulently, illegally, and contrary to the
provisions of the Insolvent Act of 1869; and say that Allan F.
Muir gave it as he was in duty bound, and the defendants in
the discharge of their duty under the will of Robert T. Muir,
demanded and took it *bona fide* and without any fraud whatever on their part.

An order having been obtained to have the case submitted
to a jury, they found that at the time the mortgage referred to in the plaintiff's writ was made, Allan F. Muir was
in embarrassed circumstances, and unable to meet his engagements; that the defendants did not then know that he was

unable to meet his liabilities in full, and had not reasonable cause to know and believe that such inability existed; that the said mortgage was not made by Allan F. Muir with intent fraudulently to impede, obstruct or delay his creditors in their remedies against him, or with intent to defraud his creditors, and was not so made with the knowledge of the defendants; that Allan F. Muir had sold and disposed of the stock, and collected the available debts bequeathed to him by Robert T. Muir before the making of the mortgage, with the exception of about $1,600 worth of machinery; that Allan F. Muir did not voluntarily give up the whole of the stock, debts, and assets to the defendants with intent fraudulently to impede, obstruct, or delay his creditors in their remedies against him, nor was it so done with the knowledge of the defendants.

Objection was taken to the finding of the jury, on the ground that the evidence shewed that the defendants knew of Allan F. Muir's insolvency, or had reasonable cause to know and believe it, and that they knew that the assignment to them was made by Allan F. Muir, with intent, fraudulently to impede or delay his creditors, or with intent to defraud them. It was agreed that the objection to the finding should be considered at the hearing. That Allan F. Muir was unable to meet his engagements when the assignment was made, was shown, but there is no evidence that the defendants then knew it, and they positively assert in their evidence that they then believed him to be able to meet all his liabilities in full, and there is no evidence to lead to the necessary conclusion that they must have known or believed it. The plaintiff contends that it is to be inferred from the evidence, but the jury have not drawn that inference. I cannot, under these circumstances, say that the jury were bound to disbelieve the defendants' evidence.

The ground on which the plaintiff, in his writ, seeks to set aside the assignment, is that it was with intent, fraudulently, to impede, obstruct, or delay creditors, or with intent to defraud them, and was so made and intended with the knowledge of the defendants that it was so made in violation of the 88th sec. of the Insolvent Act of 1869. If, therefore, the findings are sustained, as I think they must be, the plaintiff's case fails.

At the hearing, it was contended that even if the findings were allowed to stand, the plaintiff was entitled to have the assignment set aside, notwithstanding any want of knowledge on the part of the defendants of Allan F. Muir's insolvency or fraudulent intent, on the ground that it was made by him in contemplation of insolvency as made in violation of the 89th section of the Act. This objection is, in my opinion, not open to the plaintiff; if he had intended to rely on it he should have set it out in his writ, when the defendants could have answered it and had the issue submitted to the jury. It forms a separate ground of complaint; in fact, a new and different cause of action from that contained in the writ, and the plaintiff, if he succeeds in the suit, must do so not only *secundum probata* but also *secundum allegata*.

In the view I have taken of the case, it is not necessary for me to pass any opinion as to whether the assignment was valid, as having been made in pursuance of a previous agreement, or obligation, on the part of Allan F. Muir, or whether it was or was not made by him in contemplation of insolvency, and I do not wish it to be understood that if the allegations in the writ had raised that question, and it had been submitted to the jury, the plaintiff, under the evidence, would necessarily have been entitled to a verdict in his favor.

The defendants are entitled to a decree, with costs.

In re FRASER & PAINT.

Fraser and Paint, having terminated their partnership business, referred all their disputes of every description to the award of two arbitrators and such umpire as they should select before entering upon their duties as arbitrators. Authority was given to the arbitrators or any two of them to enlarge the time for making the award, and the two originally appointed extended the time, and after doing so, selected an umpire and entered upon the inquiry. Desiring to obtain all the information possible, the arbitrators, without the request of either party, called before them certain persons, neither of the parties being present, but it appeared that the persons so called had no evidence to give about the matters in controversy, and no objection was taken by the party moving to set aside the award, who knew that the arbitrators had called such persons before them, but yet continued to attend and conduct the reference on his own behalf. The partnership was indebted to Fraser in the sum of $52,840, and there was due to it by Paint $2624, and the award directed that the assets should he held and managed by Fraser under the inspection of the Umpire, and that the sale of the partnership property should be made by him at such times and places as the Umpire should approve. The award was made 28th September 1875, and no motion was made to set it aside until March 1876, the objecting party having in the meantime, with knowledge of the facts upon which he based his objections, proceeded with the arbitration, attended the sale of the property, and, at the request of the auctioneer, furnished information as to the boundaries of the land.

Held, that the provision in the award as to the sale of the property by Fraser, under the approval of the Umpire, was not such a delegation of authority as should invalidate the award; that although the arbitrators had acted unadvisedly in calling persons before them in the absence of the parties, yet as Paint had made no objection, but had afterwards proceeded with the reference, the objection was not, in view of the lapse of time, entitled to much favor; that the two arbitrators, in extending the time, before appointing an umpire, had not "entered upon their duties as arbitrators" within the meaning of the clause of the submission providing for the selection of an umpire before so entering upon their duties; that the policy of the Legislature and the practice of the Court required a party desirous of setting aside an award, to move promptly, and that Paint by his delay in moving as well as by his tacit and active acquiescence in the award, had waived irregularities in the conducting of the arbitration.

RITCHIE, E. J., delivered the judgment of the Court.

An application was made by Fraser to make the submission and award in this matter a rule of Court on the 17th January last, and on the 13th March a rule *nisi* was taken on the part of Paint to set aside the award which had been made on the 28th September last. The grounds on which the rule *nisi* was taken are set out in it. Those relied on at the argument were:

1. That the award does not follow the submission.
2. That the arbitrators have delegated their authority.
3. That the award contains directions to a stranger unauthorized.
4. That the award was not signed simultaneously.
5. That examination of witnesses took place in the absence of parties.
6. That the umpire should have been appointed before proceeding with the arbitration.

These in fact embrace all the grounds contained in the rule.

The two parties to the submission, Fraser and Paint had been partners in business. The partnership had terminated, and differences and disputes having arisen between them in relation to the settlement of it and other matters, they mutually agreed to refer *all* their disputes of every description to the award of two arbitrators and such umpire as they should select before entering upon their duty as arbitrators. Paint in his affidavit states that he saw the award in the possession of Hart, one of the arbitrators, which was then signed by the two other arbitrators, but not by him, who informed him he would not sign it; that during the investigation he on one occasion saw Lewis P. Fairbanks at the office of White, one of the arbitrators, and that Fairbanks and Hart informed him that he had been examined after he left; and that he, Paint, had been requested to retire and had no opportunity of cross-examining him, and that Hart also informed him that Augustus West had been examined in his, (Paint's) absence and that he never knew of it till his examination was over.

There are no affidavits from Fairbanks or West, or from Hart, but that of Fraser states that neither Fairbanks nor West was produced by him as a witness, nor did he request that either of them should be examined, nor was he present when they or either of them were examined. White and Taylor, the other arbitrators, state that being desirous of obtaining all information possible on the questions in controversy, and having heard that Fairbanks and West knew something about them, they requested them to attend before them, but when they did so they found they could give no information which in any way affected the matters in dispute; that neither Fraser nor Paint was present when they appeared before them; that Paint never objected to the examination of them, or either of them, taking place in his absence, though he was aware of it, and attended several meetings of the arbitrators, and conducted the reference on his own behalf after he knew they had been examined; that after the evidence had been concluded and the parties had been heard, the three arbitrators met and agreed upon the award, but Hart wished some modification made with respect to the interest, which was in favour of

Paint, to which the other arbitrators assented, and the award was signed by all the arbitrators who fully concurred therein.

Fraser in his affidavit also stated that after the award was published, he advertized the property of the late firm of Fraser, Paint & Co., for sale at public auction as therein directed, and the same was sold at public auction by Edward Lawson on the 12th day of November last; that Paint was present and made no objection thereto, but at the request of the auctioneer gave some information as to the size or boundaries of one of the lots offered; that Paint never to his knowledge made any objections to the award, and he did not know that he disputed the same, until a week or ten days after the said sale, when he made some difficulty about executing a deed to the purchaser of one of the lots sold thereat.

In reference to the first three objections it was contended that the arbitrators had exceeded their authority, and had deviated from the submission in having awarded that the assets of the firm should be held and managed by Fraser under the inspection and direction of the umpire Taylor, and that the sale of the partnership property should be made by Fraser at such times and places as Taylor should approve of; that they had no right to confer this privilege on Fraser to the exclusion of Paint, and that they had delegated a power to Taylor which they were not authorized to confer on a stranger, whereby the award was invalidated, and that the submission did not authorize the settlement of the partnership or sale of the real estate.

It appears to me that the settlement of the partnership was the main object of the reference, and the disposal of the partnership property, real as well as personal, was within its scope; and I can see no principle violated, nor anything unreasonable in the arbitrators having given the control and disposal of the property to Fraser. The firm had, it seems, made a compromise with its creditors for seventy-five cents on the dollar, for the payment of which the assets were liable; it was indebted to Fraser in the sum of $52,840, and there was due to it by Paint $2,624. Under these circumstances it might well be deemed proper that Fraser should hold and dispose of the assets in liquidation of the liabilities of the firm. The arbitrators would, I think, have been justified in vesting that power in him without restriction, and I can see no good reason why their award should be invalidated at the instance of Paint, because for Paint's protection and benefit they have made his acts subject to approval of a third party, the umpire. It is quite true that an award may be invalidated by the arbitrators delegating to a stranger a power entrusted by the submission to themselves, but it appears to me there has been no delegation of that character ; provision is merely made for the carrying into effect of the award fairly as between the two parties. A delegated power is not neccessarily unauthorized; the arbitrators here could certainly have directed that the property should be sold by auction, and that necessarily involved the intervention of an auctioneer, and in case there should be a difference of opinion between the parties as to who should act as such, I do not see why the arbitrators could not settle that question by naming one.

As to the objection that the award was not signed simultaneously by the three arbitrators, the inference from the affidavit of White and Taylor is that it was so signed. There is no doubt as to the full concurrence of all of them in the award, which concurrence took place at their last meeting when Hart signed it, but if we are to assume that it was first signed by White and Taylor, and subsequently by Hart, yet as the award by two of them is made valid by the submission, the signature simultaneously put to it by them would be sufficient under the decision of our Court, in *Purdy* v. *Burbridge*, Thomson's Reports, 154.

The next objection, if it had been established, that the arbitrators had examined witnesses in the absence of the parties without their knowledge and consent, and there had been no waiver of the objection, would be fatal to the award, for no principle is more clearly established than that evidence cannot be received by arbitrators without the knowledge of the parties to the reference, and these arbitrators in my opinion acted unadvisedly in having Fairbanks and West before them in the absence of the parties to the submission, even to ascertain whether any knowledge they possessed would or would not affect the case. But inasmuch as it appears from the affidavit of Taylor and White that when they appeared, it was ascertained that they possessed none, and that Paint made no objection to the course pursued, and, though aware of the fact, subsequently attended the arbitration, and conducted the reference on his own behalf, the objection taken at this late day is not entitled to much favor.

The only remaining objection is that the umpire was not appointed before proceeding with the arbitration as directed by the submission. Authority was given to the arbitrators or any two of them to enlarge the time for making their award ; on the 30th July, White and Hart duly extended the time, and on the 2nd August, before they otherwise acted, they appointed John Taylor as umpire.

I cannot think that extending the time can be considered as entering upon their duties as arbitrators, which I take to be their judicial duties of hearing and arbitrating on the case, to which the extention of the time was merely incidental; and the object of the provision doubtless was, that the umpire should not merely be called on in case the two arbitrators should ultimately disagree, but that he should hear the whole case, and act with them throughout: In *Baker* v. *Stephens*, L. R., 2 Q. B., 523, it was held that the arbitrator entered on the reference, not when he accepted the office and took upon himself the functions of it by giving notice to proceed, but when he entered into the matter of the reference either with the parties before him, or under such an appointment as enabled him to proceed *ex parte.* Paint does not say that this was not known to him while the reference was in progress, and he cannot be allowed to keep such an objection in reserve to use or not as he should be satisfied or otherwise with the award.

In opposition to the rule it was urged that the application to set aside the award was too late. By the Statute 9 & 10, Wm. III, cap. 15, which in the absence of any legislation of our own on the subject governs our practice, the motion must be made before the last day of the next term after the making and publishing of the award, and the English courts have held in numerous instances that they are bound by this statute, and have no discretion in cases within its terms. To refer to one of the older cases, in *Lowndes* v. *Lowndes*, 1 East, 276, it was decided that the application to set aside an award must be made within the time limited, though the objection to it appeared on its face, and in one of the later cases, *in re North British Railway Co. and Trowsdale*, L. R., 1 C. P., 401, the Court refused a rule, even though the motion was made with the consent of both parties, the Chief Justice saying, "all motions to set aside an award must be made within one term after the award is published," and it matters not that the submission is not made a rule of court until a subsequent term. The cases of *Moore* v. *Darley*, 1 C. B., 445, and *in re Smith* v. *Blake*, 8 Dowl., 133, show how strictly the rule is enforced, and the Court in cases not within terms of the Statute, that is where the submission does not contain a stipulation that it may be made a rule of court, requires that the motion must be made within the time allowed for moving for a new trial. *Rawsthorn* v. *Arnold*, 6 B. & C., 629; *Reynolds* v. *Askew*, 5 Dowl., 682.

In cases of compulsory references under our statute the application must be made within a month of the making of the award, so that it is apparent that the policy of the Legislature as well as the practice of the Court requires a party dissatisfied with an award to act promptly if he desires to have it set aside, and I may add that the Court of Chancery in England acts upon the same rules as the courts of Common Law.

Quite independently of the statutory limitation, the party making this application must be deemed to have waived all objection to this award, as well by his conduct since it was made, as by the time he has allowed to elapse, for not only does he, with a knowledge of all the facts, take no steps to set it aside from the 28th September 1875, when the award was made till March 1876, thus tacitly acquiescing in it, but he does so actively by attending the sale of the land six weeks after the making of the award, which had been advertised to take place at public auction in accordance with its terms, and showing his assent so far as, at the request of the auctioneer, to give information in relation to the property then on sale.

There is nothing to lead to the inference that any injustice has been done to the applicant by the award, or that the arbitrators have not acted honestly and to the best of their judgment, or that they have not arrived at a correct result, and courts are disposed to sustain awards under these circumstances where it can be legally done; and even in a case where the conduct of the arbitrators did not commend itself to the Court, *in re Hopper*, L. R., 2 Q. B., 375, the award was sustained, and COCKBURN C. J. said, " we must not be over ready to set aside awards where the parties have agreed to abide by the decision of a tribunal of their own selection, unless we see that there is something radically wrong and vicious in the proceedings," and MALINS V. C. in *Mosely* v. *Simpson*, L. R., 16 Eq., 232, quoted these observations of the Chief Justice, and said he entirely subscribed to them; and in that case it was held that irregularities in the mode of conducting an arbitration might be waived by continuing the arbitration after they had been discovered.

I am of opinion that the rule *nisi* to set aside this award should be discharged with costs.

GODET *v.* LeBLANC.

Where plaintiff prayed for an account on the dissolution of co-partnership between himself and defendant, alleging that a balance was due him, but the Master's report, showing a large balance to be due to defendant, was sustained, except as to a comparatively small item; *Held* that the defendant was not entitled to a decree *with costs* as the plaintiff had succeeded in establishing his right to one half interest in a mill, which was disputed.

RITCHIE, E. J., delivered the judgment of the Court:—

The plaintiff in his writ sets out that he and the defendant in 1871 entered into co-partnership for the purpose of manufacturing shingles, and for the erection of the necessary building, frame, and the obtaining the machinery, and that he largely contributed by furnishing logs, lumber, labor and money, and also furnished one half of the mill site and one half of the mill dam; he alleges that some of the money supplied by him was appropriated by the defendant to his own use; that each party was to be interested in the mill to the extent of one half; that the work at the mill commenced in the summer of 1874, and continued till February 1876, during which period the defendant managed the business and kept the accounts, and the plaintiff derived little or no benefit from it, as the proceeds of the work done were received by the defendant and retained by him, of which he refused to account with the plaintiff. On the 23rd February 1876 the plaintiff put an end to the partnership, and he seeks in this suit an account and settlement of all matters connected with the partnership.

The defendant alleges that the outlays and expenses were almost exclusively made and borne by him, the amount contributed by him being upwards of $6000, while that contributed by the plaintiff was about $300; he alleges that the share or interest of each party in the mill was to be equivalent to the amount contributed by each, he denies that any money furnished for the mill was appropriated by him to his own use, or otherwise than in furnishing machinery &c., for the mill, he denies that he ever refused to account with the plaintiff, or to give him access to the books of account which were always open to the inspection of him or his agent.

In June term, 1876, of the Supreme Court at Digby, it was ordered by consent of the attorneys of the plaintiff and defendant, that the cause be referred to Wm. B. Stuart, Esq., a master of the Court, to hear and examine under oath the evidence and witnesses on the part of the plaintiff and defendant on the several matters contained in the writ and answer, and to report the same for the adjudication of the Judge in Equity, and to return to him the evidence with the report. In pursuance of this order the master took the evidence and returned it to this court, and on the cause coming on for a hearing on motion of Mr. Harrington on behalf of the plaintiff, it was ordered that the matter be referred back to the master to report the amounts due, if any, by either and which of the parties, with any furthere vidence which might be adduced, who reported that the plaintiff was indebted to the defendant in the sum of $3612.34. The master in making this report adopted the plaintiff's view of the terms of the partnership, that each of the partners was to be equally interested in the mill, and to contribute equally in the outlay, in which view of the case the defendant's counsel had acquiesced previous to the last reference.

The plaintiff, on the case again coming on for a hearing, excepted to the report of the master as to the amount due by him, on the ground that it was not justified by the evidence. At the references before the master the plaintiff and defendant attended with their counsel, and all the witnesses produced on both sides were examined and cross-examined by them, and there does not appear much conflict in the testimony. The whole of the plaintiff's account is allowed without any deduction, though the testimony in regard to it is very vague. He can neither read nor write, and kept no accounts, and as regards some of his charges he does not undertake to speak with exactness, especially those for boarding the men employed at the mill the amounts of which are large, of which he admits he kept no account. Assuming the evidence of the defendant to be true, and it is not contradicted, nor is doubt thrown upon it on the cross-examination, he has established the correctness of his account. He has testified to the correctness of every charge, and on his cross-examination he produced his books and exhibited them to the plaintiff's counsel, when his accounts produced in evidence were compared with the books and vouchers. No attempt was made to rebut this evidence or to show that the charges were improperly made or were unreasonable. I do not see under these circumstances how the master could have reported otherwise than he has done, with the exception of one of the charges, which I think ought not to have been allowed, the $300 for commission. This would not have been an unreasonable charge if the parties had contemplated that commission should be charged at all, but of this there is no evidence. This sum must be deducted, so that the amount for which the defendant is entitled to credit is $3312.34.

Though there is this balance found to be due by the plaintiff, I do not think the defendant is entitled to a decree with costs, as the plaintiff succeeded in establishing his right to one half interest in the mill, which was disputed, and was entitled to an account on that basis.

HAMILTON *v.* HAMILTON ET AL.

Plaintiff and defendants entered into a co-partnership to work certain mining areas, a lease being taken out in the name of the defendants, but for the benefit of all the parties. Plaintiff's share of the expenses of working the mine, as they became due from month to month, were paid by the defendant, George Hamilton, and, only a small portion being refunded, the latter wrote to plaintiff that if his indebtedness was not paid by a day named, he would consider that he intended to withdraw from the adventure. Receiving no reply, he afterwards wrote to plaintiff, enclosing the amount received from him on account of his contributions, to which plaintiff replied, accepting the money, and concluding, " now that I am no participator with you in the tribute, let your mind rest quiet, and let the past *requiescat in pace.*" ¦The mine having subsequently turned out well, plaintiff, claiming to be a partner, brought action for an account, &c., which was dismissed with costs.

Distinction between mining, and ordinary trading partnerships as to *delectus personae.*

RITCHIE, E. J., delivered the judgment of the Court:—

The writ sets out that plaintiff and defendants, in July 1782 agreed to become partners in the business of gold mining quartz crushing, amalgamating and smelting gold, and other business connected therewith in certain gold mining areas belonging to the Meridian Gold Mining Company, with the crushing mill and appurtenances thereon at Goldenville, each of whom were to participate equally in the profits and losses of the business, the accounts of which were to be made up monthly, and the losses or profits then due by or to each adjusted and paid; that the defendant George Hamilton should negotiate for a lease of the said property for the benefit of the co-partnership, which he did, and procured, on the terms of paying a certain percentage on the gross product of the areas, but in doing so omitted to have the name of plaintiff included with those of the defendants as a party; that on his remonstrating with them at this omission he was assured that there was no intention of excluding him from the benefit of it; that in July operations were commenced, from which time till January following, monthly accounts were regularly made up and submitted to plaintiff by the defendant, George Hamilton, who managed the co-partnership business, in which and in the correspondence with whom the plaintiff's rights as a partner were recognized, and payments received from him by the said George Hamilton on account of calls required to carry on the undertaking, and when the amounts so paid were insufficient to meet the calls due by him, the said George Hamilton agreed to pay the same and charge the amounts to plaintiff who was to re-pay them with interest; that in January 1873, when the partnership property for the first time yielded a large profit, the defendants sought to exclude plaintiff from the co-partnership, and from a share of the profits thereof, and though the business is still being carried on, and the profits divided monthly, and though plaintiff has always been ready and willing to carry out the provisions of the partnership agreement, and to perform all the conditions and stipulations on his part, and never withdrew therefrom, or agreed to a dissolution thereof, and has frequently demanded an account and settlement for each month, the defendants have refused to give it or to recognize him as a partner; and he prayed that an account might be taken and the defendants be decreed to pay him what should be found to be due to him. The writ also prayed for an injunction and a receiver, and that directions should be given for the management of the partnership in future, for the joint and equal benefit of plaintiff and defendants.

The defendants by their answer, (which is not prepared in accordance with the practice of this Court, which requires that the facts relied on as a defence should be briefly and distinctly stated, and should be consistent with each other,) sets out, in the first instance, that they did not enter into the partnership on the terms alleged, and that the lease referred to was not held in trust for plaintiff as stated in the writ; and yet in subsequent parts of the answer the statements contained in the writ as to the terms of the co-partnership, and the obtaining of the lease for the benefit of the partners including the plaintiff, are admitted, and they say that the lease was taken in the name of the defendants with the consent of the plaintiff, and that they did not seek to exclude him from the partnership until after repeated breaches on his part of the partnership agreement, and repeated and continued failure on his part to pay his proportion of the monthly expenses and disbursements incurred in working the mine, nor until after he had withdrawn therefrom.

The defendants deny that George Hamilton agreed to pay the deficiency and arrears of calls due by plaintiff as alleged, and, though monthly accounts were made up and regularly rendered to him by defendants, shewing the amount which he was required to contribute, and though payment was demanded from month to month, plaintiff did not pay any part thereof, and declared his inability to do so, and offered to retire and did retire from the said business, since which time defendants have conducted it at their own risk and expense and on their own account, and so long as the mine was not paying its working expenses the plaintiff left all the expenses to be borne by the defendants and abandoned all connection with it, and only when it began to yield a reasonable profit upon the amount expended by defendants, and the skill and labor employed by them in developing it, was a claim made by plaintiff to participate in it.

Though Robert McNaughton and Alexander Fraser have been made defendants, the question involved does not much affect them; the real controversy in this suit is between the plaintiff and his brother George Hamilton, who, on the non-payment of the assessment required from the plaintiff, and his alleged withdrawal from the business, assumed the plaintiff's interest, the two other defendants retaining only their original share of one-fourth each, so that if the plaintiff were to recover in this suit, he would recover from his brother George one-half of the interest which he now claims to have in the business.

There appears from the evidence to be no difference of opinion as to the original agreement between the parties, and I think it has been satisfactorily shown that the lease of the mine was taken in the name of the defendants alone, with the plaintiff's assent. Yet it was the understanding of all concern-ed, that he, as a partner in the business, should have an equal interest in it with the other partners. It is not denied that in fact the plaintiff contributed nothing whatever to the carrying on of the business from its inception till the time it is alleged he ceased to be a partner.

It was contemplated that each party should furnish his proportion of the funds necessary for the prosecution of the work. This the plaintiff was unable to do, and as these funds were indispensable, and without them the undertaking must be abandoned, it is obvious he had no alternative but to withdraw, or make over his interest to some one who was able and willing to make the necessary advances, unless he could induce another to make them for him. The plaintiff contends that the defendant, George Hamilton, engaged to do this for him, and that there was want of good faith on his part in his not doing it, and thereby attempting to forfeit the plaintiff's interest in the undertaking. This George denies, and he alleges that, finding it impossible to obtain the necessary advances from the plaintiff, he was notified that his interest in the adventure must cease unless the funds were forthcoming, and the latter, admitting his inability to furnish them, consented to and did withdraw from the concern. The evidence on the subject is principally contained in written correspondence which took place between the plaintiff and George Hamilton, from the 10th April 1872, to 7th March 1873. George in a letter of the 19th October to the plaintiff, says, "I have paid our assessments and I send a memorandum of account. We intend sinking another shaft, &c." In a letter of the 24th October, he gives an account of what was doing at the mine, informs him that they had commenced to start a new shaft on the lead and speaks favourably of their prospects; and in a postscript he says, "there will be some more assessment on the work now doing before we are able to get a crushing, and as we intend having a settlement every month, you had better let me know what I am to do as regards your share. I feel quite certain we have a big thing, and intend risking $200 or $300 in it before I give it up. Robert and Alexander, (i.e., McNaughton and Fraser, the other defendants,) say that they will risk a winter's work, and Robert leaves $100 with me to pay up for him when he leaves; so you can imagine what confidence they have in it. McLean told me that the 24.12 all came out of the three barrels, &c." In a letter of the 1st November, George gives plaintiff an account of what was doing, and continues to express a favour-

6

able opinion of their prospects. On the 3rd November plaintiff writes to him, " I am delighted to hear such good news of the lead. I sincerely hope your anticipations of success will be fully realized. Will you kindly *put up* for me for the present, as the funds have not commenced to come in, and I do not care about drawing on Canada. I shall have considerable in a short time." On the 10th November, George, after describing what had been done, says, " the assessment last month was $19.25 per share; this did not include timber, $12,40, or hauling, $3, which will go into this month's expenses;" and he says, " I enclose Mr. Stairs' bill, which you will please pay, also for my ale; send back account receipted and I will credit the amounts to you against assessment; (tobacco same.) If our lead gives us 15 dwt. it will pay first rate, and I hope it will, as this month's work will be a heavy bill and I do not expect we will have many tons when we commence to drive the tunnels. Alexander said last night he would go all his winter's work in it and money besides. How much are you willing to go if it would be required? and what arrangements are you going to make for the assessments which I have already paid for you, and for others which may come? for we can hardly expect the lead to pay all the dead work unless it turns out extra. I am asking these questions now and I ask you to answer them, so that there cannot be any misunderstanding in the matter. I've made up my mind to stick to it as long as Alexander does and no longer." On the 20th November he writes plaintiff that they had 20 tons from 9 feet sinking, which showed gold pretty well, &c. On the 23rd November he informs him that the 20 tons produced 7 dwts. per ton, and adds, " not bad, as more than half was suckers and cross leads; our next stripping will give a better return &c.; the assessment for the month will be about $40 per share. McLean paid $1.50 which I have given you credit for. I paid Alexander 50 cents for road work, my share, and also your assessment for this month." On the 2nd December the plaintiff writes to his brother; "Am glad you are getting on so satisfactorily, and I sincerely trust it will turn out fully equal to your expectations. I hardly see how I can liquidate those accounts you requested me to, as I really have not the funds on hand; nearly •

all my sales are at three months, so that I do not get much cash in, and the notes I forward to Wilson. What cash I do receive is barely sufficient to meet current expenses &c., &c., I am very sorry indeed, George, that I cannot gratify your requests." On the 5th December George writes plaintiff, "Your letter I received yesterday, and I beg to tell you that I was very much disappointed in not receiving money from you to settle up your three month's assessment to the Meridian Tribune, and also the bills which I asked you to settle. You will now be kind enough to send same to me so that I may pay them. Your account stands thus :

Oct. 18th.—Amount paid Meridian ass't					....	$63.90.
Nov. 2nd.—	"	"	"	"	....	$19.05.
Dec. 1st.—	"	"	Twist		....	3.25.
"	"	"	"	"	Meridian	35.40.
						———
Cr.						$121.60
Cash from C. McLean						1.50.
						———
Balance due.						$120.10.

" Let me know at once when you can settle this amount, as I cannot afford to be out of pocket so large an amount. There will be an assessment of probably $25 per share this month, and which you must provide for, as I shall not pay any more for you until the three last assessments are paid. If you do not think it worth the risk which we are now running you had better make your arrangements for same at once. I intend to go pretty heavy into this lead before giving it up, and so does Alexander and Robert.   *   *   *   Let me hear from you at once as I must have everything settled before next pay day, 1st January."

To this letter the plaintiff replied; "Yours dated 5th instant reached me last night. I am very sorry indeed that my inability to meet the assessments has caused you any annoy-. ance. I am still unable to remit as you desire, and of course if you desire it, I will retire immediately from the Tribune.   *   * I will endeavour to be in Goldenville before the first *proximo*, when we can settle the indebtedness you refer to. In the interim, as I said before, you must use your own judgment in the matter of allowing me to share in the tribute."

The correspondence thus far clearly shews that the plaintiff had failed to produce any funds to meet his liability as a co-adventurer with the others, and that he was unable to do so, and to my mind as clearly indicates that no agreement had been entered into between the plaintiff and George Hamilton, that the latter would make the necessary advances for him, or was under any obligation to that effect, and up to this time, certainly, there was no attempt made to induce the plaintiff to withdraw by a depreciation of the mine by his brother. So far from any endeavour on his part to deceive him in respect to the undertaking, he urges him to come down *at once* to the mine that he might be able the better to judge of the prospects of the company. In the letter of the 10th December to plaintiff, he says; "Your letter I received this morning; in reply I must tell you I decline to accept the position in which you want to place me, that is, to use my own judgment in regard to your retiring from the tribute. You know your position better than I do, and I would advise you to come down at once, instead of delaying it to the first, and see the state the mine is in. We are now taking off lead and by the time you arrive the quartz will be through. You will then be better able to judge if it is advisable to remain in or not. * * * If you can manage to settle up the assessment when you come I shall be better pleased, as I require the money."

It appears that the plaintiff did not go down as he had proposed to do, and George addressed this letter to him :— "Your non-arrival to settle all indebtedness as you promised in your last letter, and not having heard from you since in answer to mine, I shall consider you intend withdrawing from the tribute unless the balance of account is paid on or before the 20th." No communication is received in reply till after the 20th. The plaintiff on the 23nd writes : "Your statement came to hand a few days ago, I am sorry there is so much owing by me, and I think you hard and severe on your brother by making such peremptory demands to pay up by a certain date or be ejected, but probably you think I have no more claims on your generosity and affection than on the merest stranger. I think the least you could have done would have been to tell me of the prospects and advise me what to do, as you are thoroughly acquainted with my circumstances in life. I will see you next month, D. V., as I intend visiting Sherbrooke and Goldenville."

It appears to me that when the alternative was given to the plaintiff to pay up the assessment or to retire, the fullest information had been afforded him by his brother, and so far from depreciating the adventure every letter was encouraging as to its results, and the best evidence that he thought the prospects good was the intimation he gave the plaintiff that he should himself persevere with it.

On the 29th January George writes; "Your not having paid up your assessment disbursed by me at the time specified in my note and memorandum of account sent you the first of the month, I now enclose you the money I have received here for you, and which you paid out in Halifax for me;" to which on the 4th February, plaintiff replied; "Your letter dated 29th *ult.*, to hand. Enclosed I found $27.40 for which you will please accept my thanks and this receipt. Though quite unexpected, was most opportune and acceptable. I consider it very honorable and kind of you." In this letter, though he complains of being ejected from the adventure, he in the course of it says; " Now that I am no participator with you in the tribute, let your mind rest quiet, and let the past *requiescat in pace.*"

The receipt of this money by the plaintiff, and the terms in which the receipt is acknowledged, accompanied by the statement that he is no longer a participator in the adventure, show clearly that he had found it necessary to abandon his share in it from inability on his part to meet his engagements with his co-adventurers.

It was urged at the hearing that, these parties having entered into a partnership, the plaintiff could not be excluded by the others in consequence of his not having paid up the assessment required by him. From the evidence, it appears to me, that he withdrew, reluctantly, it is true, but unequivocally, and he certainly was reasonably required to do so, for he had no right to have the mine developed for his benefit at the expense of others. But if he had not consented, I think he could have been compelled to retire on his failure to produce the funds required from him under his agreement with his co-partners. The distinction between partnerships in relation to the working of mines and trading partnerships is recognized. The former are not held to be founded on the *delectus personæ*, as is the case in ordinary trading partnerships, and the mining partner has a right to transfer or relinquish his share without the consent of his co-partners; *Collyer on Partnership,* 90; and shares may be forfeited by the failure of parties to furnish the funds required for prosecuting the undertaking . according to agreement, as the non-payment of early calls may be destructive of the whole adventure, to the great loss of those willing to make the payments required of them, and it would be most inequitable for one to leave to the others the whole labor and expense of developing a mine, and when they had thus made the adventure profitable, seek to participate. *See Prendergast* v. *Turton,* 1 Yo. & Col. C. C. 98, and *Norway* v. *Rowe,* 19 Ves. 143. In *Clark et al.* v. *Hart,* 6 H. L. C. 656, Lord CHELMSFORD said; "the case of mines has always been considered by a court of Equity as a peculiar one. The property is of a very precarious description, fluctuating continually, sudden emergencies arising which require an instant supply of capital, and in which the faithful performance of engagements is absolutely necessary for the prosperity and even existence of the concern; and therefore, where parties under these circumstances stand by and watch the progress of the adventure to see whether it is prosperous or not, determining that they will intervene in case the affairs of the mine turn out prosperous, but determining to hold off if a different state of things should exist, courts of Equity have said that those are parties who are to receive no encouragement, and if they come to this Court for relief its doors will be shut against them." And Lord WENSLEYDALE, (page 667,) "it appears to me that the principle to be deduced from *Prendergast* v. *Turton,* and *Norway* v. *Rowe,* is that, if a party lies by and by his conduct intimates to the other parties that he has abandoned his share, they may deal with it as they please.

I should have been disposed to view this case in a different light, if there was evidence to justify me in coming to the conclusion that George Hamilton, at the time he refused to make further advances for his brother, had withheld important information in regard to the undertaking, which he then possessed, or had in any way deceived or misled him with a view of excluding him or inducing him to withdraw from it, but I see no evidence to lead to such an inference.

The suit must be dismissed with costs.

HENDERSON v. COMEAU.

Defendant took a conveyance of land from A. F. LeBlanc in the form of an absolute deed, dated 26th July, 1864, and at the same time executed a bond to re-convey upon re-payment of the consideration money of the deed within two years. At the expiration of that period, defendant asked LeBlanc whether the money would be repaid or he should keep the land, to which LeBlanc replied that he would prefer that defendant should keep the land. The bond was given up to defendant and he took the land, allowing LeBlanc to live on it, but no rent was paid, and neither the principal nor the interest of the money advanced by defendant, who afterwards sold the land for a larger sum than the amount of his advances. LeBlanc afterwards became insolvent, but at the time of his giving up the property he was not indebted to any of the creditors who had claims against him when he went into insolvency. His assignee sought in this action to have the deed decreed to be a mortgage. Decree for defendant with costs.

RITCHIE, E. J., delivered the judgment of the Court:—

The plaintiff, as assignee of Augustus F. LeBlanc under the Insolvent Act of 1869, seeks in this suit that a deed made by the insolvent to the defendant may be decreed by this Court to be and operate as a mortgage security, and not be deemed an absolute conveyance in accordance with its terms, and that the defendant may be held to be a trustee for the creditors of the insolvent for the amount which may be shown to have been received by him beyond the amount due to him on the security of the indenture, the land having been sold by the defendant for a sum greater than that loaned him by the insolvent.

It appears from the evidence that the deed, which in its terms is an absolute conveyance from the insolvent to the defendant, was given on the 26th July 1864,—the consideration expressed in it is $312,—and at the same time a bond was executed by the defendant to the insolvent in the penal sum of $1200, with a condition therein that, if the insolvent should pay the defend-ant the sum of $312 with interest in two years from the date thereof, then the defendant should return the deed that day executed by the insolvent and the obligation should be void, otherwise to remain in full force.

The consideration money mentioned in the deed was paid and the deed was delivered to the defendant, and the bond, after having been executed by him, was left with Anselm Comeau, who had prepared the papers and was the subscribing witness to the bond. The insolvent, who is the only witness produced on the part of the plaintiff, says that, being indebted to Messrs. Heustis & Moulton of Yarmouth in the sum of $140 or $150, and to Urbane Doucette in the sum of $40 or there-abouts, the defendant at his request paid those debts in addition to the $312 mentioned in the deed. It appeared sub-sequently that the first mentioned debt amounted to $172.79 and the second to $49.80. He goes on to say that some time after the expiration of the two years he had a conversation with the defendant, who asked him if he intended to pay him. He said he could not, and that defendant could take the place and do with it what he pleased; the defendant said he could live on it provided he paid some rent. He never did pay rent but at the request of defendant, he kept up the place and the fences, &c., and this he understood he was to do for the rent. He occupied the place four years. After he gave up the place Peter LeBlanc had the crops two years from the defendant. He further says that after he left the place he told the defend-ant to get the bond from Anselm Comeau and do what he liked with it, and he never saw it till he saw it handed by Peter J. Godet to Philip Comeau in the Court House and by him hand-ed to Mr. Chesley. The insolvent also said that he considered the $312 received from the defendant and the debts paid for him by the defendant as much as the place was worth; if he could have got any more for it he would himself have sold it and paid the defendant; that when he gave the place up he was not indebted to any of the creditors who afterwards had claims against him when he went into insolvency; that he never paid defendant anything either for principal or interest or rent, and he does not know of defendant ever getting anything from the place except what he may have got from P. LeBlanc. Godet, the purchaser from defendant, says that the first he knew of the existence of the bond was that Philip Comeau, the son of Anselm, who is now dead, gave it to him to deliver to defendant, which he did, and after defendant had given him his deed he gave him also the bond and told him to keep it, which he did, till Philip Comeau asked him for it to show to Mr. Chesley; that he gave it to him thinking he would return it, but Mr. Chesley did not do so.

The evidence of the defendant is to the same effect as is that of the insolvent. He says, that in addition to the consideration money mentioned in the deed, he paid to Heustis & Moulton, $172 and some cents for the insolvent, and Urbane Doucette nearly $50; that he left the bond with Anselm Comeau, to be given to LeBlanc, the insolvent, if the money was paid within two years; that he asked LeBlanc after the expiration of that time, if he intended to pay him the money he had advanced, or must he take the land, who replied that he preferred that the defendant should take the land rather than that he should pay the money. The defendant alleges that he thought he should lose by doing so, as the land was not of much value, and he would have preferred receiving the money. They spoke, he said, about the bond, and the insolvent told him to go and get it; that Godet subsequently brought the bond to him, and he gave it back to him and told him to keep it.

That this Court will treat a transaction as a mortgage, although it was made to bear the appearance of an absolute sale, if it appears that the parties intended it to be a mortgage, is unquestionable; but it is equally clear that if the parties intended an absolute sale, a contemporaneous agreement for a re-purchase and re-conveyance, the terms of which have not been carried out, will not entitle the vendor to redeem. In order to ascertain whether such such a transaction is to be deemed a mortgage, we must see whether the rights of the grantor and grantee are reciprocal. There must have been a debt due by the former if a mortgagor, which the latter could have sued for, and in the case of a sale of land by him, if it produced more than his debt, he must account for the surplus, so if it had produced less, he would have a right to recover from the mortgagor the balance of his debt. See *Goodman* v. *Grierson,* 2 Ba. & Be., 274, and the judgment of Lord COTTEN-HAM, in *Williams* v. *Owens,* 5 My. and Cr., 303, overruling the judgment of Sir LANCELET SHADWELL in 10 Sim., 386. In the case before us, LeBlanc conveys to the defendant, by an absolute deed, certain lands. He takes no acknowledgment from the vendor to indicate the existence of a debt, or create an obligation to pay back the amount received by him, but he himself executes a bond, conditioned to return the deed, that is, to re-convey the land, if LeBlanc shall pay the amount of the consideration money mentioned in the deed in two years. This bond is not delivered to the obligee, but is placed in the hands of a third person, to be held by him till the expiration of the two years, and then to be delivered to LeBlanc, if he shall have paid the money, and to be returned to defendant if he shall have failed to do so. He did fail to do so, and the bond was re-delivered to the defendant with his assent. There is no conflicting evidence in the case, and this explicit agreement has been carried out by the parties to the letter, and in its spirit, and to the mutual satisfaction of both parties,—and this where no rights of creditors or third persons were involved. Both parties seem to have acted with entire good faith, and before LeBlanc had become insolvent he had recognized the defendant as the absolute owner of the property under the legal title which he had given him, and had authorized him to receive from Comeau the bond which had been deposited with him on which alone he could have founded any claim against him.

If after what thus took place between the parties, LeBlanc on the one hand had insisted on the defendant accounting to him for any profits which he might make on a subsequent sale of the land, or on the other hand, if the defendant had insisted on having any deficiency made good to him by LeBlanc, in either case the claim would be made in violation of good faith and of the agreement which existed between them.

The legal title to the land in question being vested in the

defendant and LeBlanc having abandoned all claim, legal or
equitable, and recognized the defendant's title previous to his
becoming insolvent, nothing passed to his assignee under his
assignment under the Insolvent Act, for he had nothing to
assign, and there is no pretence for saying that anything was
done by either of the parties in violation of the provisions of
that act.

I cannot think that the plaintiff has exercised a sound discretion in instituting this suit. The evidence he himself produced would have deprived him of any right to recover,
independently of that produced on the part of the defendant,
and, if he had not evidence which would very clearly have
established his claim, it was not the interest of the creditors to
enter into a contest when the amount was so small in case the
suit were successful. The defendant in that case would beyond
question be entitled to receive out of the proceeds of the sale
of the land all his advances to LeBlanc with interest up to the
time of the sale to Godet. These advances with interest
amount to $762, less the amount received from Peter LeBlanc,
$100, leaving a balance of $662, the amount received from
Godet for the land being $700, thus leaving but $38, to be
further reduced by any expenses there may have been connected with the sale and conveyance. The decree will be for
the defendant with costs.

CHARLES D. HUNTER, Trustee, &c. v. THE PEOPLE'S BANK OF HALIFAX & RHINDRESS, Assignee OF DONALD MATHESON, Insolvent.

G. E. Bisset, by his will, bequeathed to his daughter Maria Matheson £2000
"for herself and her children, issue of her marriage, now or hereafter living, to be
exempt from any debts or liabilities of her husband, Donald Matheson, should he
from accident or misfortune hereafter become embarrassed, with power in his
executors to invest the same at her desire in good securities with interest for her
and her children's benefit," subject to a deduction of £870 due the testator by
Donald Matheson. The plaintiff, together with Matheson, testator's widow, and
another were appointed executors. Testator died in 1861, there being at that time
and at the time of the making of the will, children of his daughter living, but the

estate was not settled until September 1871, when Matheson deposited in the People's Bank $6000, being the balance of the bequest due his wife after deducting the amount due by him to the estate, with interest to the date of the deposit. In the same month he made an assignment under the Insolvent Act of 1869. During the ten intervening years the amount had been used by him in his business, and for his family, though without the knowledge or sanction of his wife, and entries were made by him from time to time in accounts rendered to the widow (who with himself chiefly managed the business of the estate,) of sums received as interest on his wife's legacy, amounting in all to the whole interest that would be due thereon. This was not authorized by his wife, but she did not object to it, or apply for the interest herself. Defendant Rhindress, as assignee, having claimed the fund deposited in the People's Bank.

Held, that the children took an interest under the will, but that independently of their interest, as there was no evidence that Mrs. Matheson had sanctioned the use of the money by her husband, plaintiff, as trustee for her and her children, was entitled to an amount equal to the balance of the legacy after deducting the debt due by Matheson, but that the assignee was entitled to the amount deposited for interest thereon, as the Court must presume the acquiescence of the wife in the husband's receipt of the interest from year to year in the absence of very clear evidence to the contrary.

RITCHIE, E. J., delivered the judgment of the Court :—

The will of the late George E. Bissett contained among others the following bequest: " I bequeath to my beloved daughter, Maria Matheson, £2000 currency, for herself and her children, issue of her marriage, now or hereafter living, to be exempt from any debts or liability of her husband, Donald Matheson, should he from accident or misfortune hereafter become embarrassed in his affairs, with power in my executors to invest the same at her desire in good securities, with interest, for her and her children's benefit, subject to a deduction of the sum of £870 or thereabouts now due to me by her husband, Donald Matheson, should he not think proper to re-pay the same to my executors within twelve months; and should he not repay the said debt, I hereby direct that my executors shall give him a release of the same, on being deducted from the above £2000."

The testator also bequeathed £200 to Donald Matheson. This sum he has received, and the debt due by him to the estate was never paid. Donald Matheson, the Revd. Peter G. McGregor, the plaintiff, and Mrs. Bissett, the widow of testator, were appointed executors of Mr. Bissett's will, and all of them took probate of it. The testator died 31st March, 1861, and then and at the time of the making of the will there were several children born and living, the issue of Mrs. Matheson's marriage with her husband, Donald Matheson.

At the hearing, the question raised before me was whether the sum of $6000, deposited in the People's Bank of Halifax, was the property of Maria Matheson and her children, as contended for by the plaintiff, who was their trustee, and claimed on their behalf, or that of the creditors of Donald Matheson, on whose behalf it was claimed by John Rhindress, his assignee under the Insolvent Act of 1869.

This $6000 was paid into the Bank as the balance of the £2000 legacy to Mrs. Matheson, after deducting the debt due by her husband to the estate, and interest thereon from the death of testator till the deposit was made, about ten years.

On the part of the creditors of Donald Matheson, it was contended that the whole legacy having in fact been received and spent by Donald Matheson, his wife could have no claim on this sum, her husband being authorized by law to receive and appropriate it, and that even if he were not entitled to the principal, no claim now could be made for interest, as he had, from year to year, from 1861 to 1870, credited the estate, on account of his wife, with various sums which he had received, amounting in all to the interest on the balance of her legacy after deducting his debt.

Mr. Rigby's contention was that the bequest to Mrs. Matheson for herself and her children would, if the subject of it had been real estate, have given an estate in special tail, and being personal, she took the legacy absolutely independent of any right in her children; and even if it should be held that the bequest was to her separate use, which her husband would not have been entitled to claim, the employment of the money by him in his business and for his family, with the knowledge of his wife, would amount to a gift to him; but he contended that until her husband's insolvency or embarrassment, Mrs. Matheson's rights were the same as if the amount had simply been bequeathed to her, which he could receive and use as he had done, and that only on his becoming embarrassed in his business was the legacy, or what then remained unpaid, to be placed out of the reach of his creditors, if she so desired.

I cannot adopt this view of the case. The objects of the testator's bounty were the children of his daughter as well as herself, and they took an interest under the will, and he clearly indicated that he intended that the amount bequeathed should be protected from the husband's creditors for the benefit of both, in case at any time he should become insolvent. *Wild's case*, 6 Rep. 17, was much relied on for the defendant, but that case turned on the fact that at the time of the devise there were no children in existence to take under it, which is not so here. In *Roper* v. *Roper*, L. R., 3 C. P., 35, KELLY C. B. said, "If the words of this will had devised the estate in question to Mary Roper and her children, and she had two or more children in existence at the date of the will, we might have been compelled to hold that they gave a joint tenancy to the mother and her children." And again, "the rule of construction, now commonly called the rule in *Wild's case*, is to this effect,—where lands are devised to a person and his children and he has no child at the time of the devise the parent takes an estate tail, for it is said the intent of the devise is manifest and certain, that the children or issue should take, and as immediate devisees they cannot take, because they are not in *rerum natura*, and by way of remainder they cannot take, for that was not the devisor's intent, for the gift is immediate, and therefore such words shall be taken as words of limitation." See also V. Ch. MALINS' observation on the rule in *Grieve* v. *Grieve*, L. R., 4 Eq., 180.

In *Armstrong* v. *Armstrong*, L. R., 7 Eq., 518, the testator gave all his estate, being personalty or of that nature, to his wife, her heirs, executors, administrators, and assigns, absolutely for ever, &c., for the benefit of herself and her children; he left a wife and six children. The question arose after the mother's death and JAMES, V. C., held that the children took under the will as joint tenants. He said that, "though it was not necessary to determine whether it was a gift to the wife for life with remainder to the children, or a gift to the wife and children equally, the strong inclination of his opinion was in favour of the former view." In *Newill* v. *Newill*, L. R., 12

Eq., 432, a testator gave all his real and personal estate to his wife for the use and benefit of herself and all his children, whether born of his former wife, or such as might be born of his then present wife. V. Ch. MALINS, in his judgment, after referring to numerous cases of this class, expressed his opinion that the current of authorities now ran in the direction which effectuates the intention of the testator, viz., that, when a man gives to his wife, for the benefit of herself and her children, he does not mean to put her on a mere equality with her children, but that she is to take for life, with remainder to her children.

These cases clearly indicate, that in such a bequest as this, the children take an interest under the will, and the attempt on the part of the husband's creditors to obtain possession of the whole *corpus*, if successful, would frustrate the testator's intention with regard to them. But independent of the interest of the children in the fund as regards the principal sum, I see no evidence that Mrs. Matheson sanctioned the use of it by her husband in his business or in the support of the family, or indeed that she knew of its being so used, and she may have supposed that it was secure in the hands of the executors.

I think therefore that she is entitled to have that amount paid to the plaintiff, as the trustee of herself and her children, out of the amount now in the bank. But, as the sum there includes interest as well as principal, the question remains whether she is entitled to have the whole amount paid to her. The testator died in 1861, and the estate was not settled in the Court of Probate till September, 1871, when the money was paid into the Bank, in which month Donald Matheson made his assignment under the Insolvent Act of 1869. If therefore any of that money belonged to him, it passed to Rhindress, his assignee. It appears from the evidence of Matheson and the accounts produced by him, which were the same he had exhibited at the Probate Court, that payments had been made from time to time to all the legatees, and, though no entry appeared of any payment to Mrs. Matheson on account of the principal sum, the following sums were charged against her by Matheson in his account with the executors, which he had received from the assets of the estate, viz :—

Cash £25.

1863, Dec. 31	"	£67	15 -	5.
1864, Apl. 5	"	£160	7	11.
' Dec. 31	"	£125 - 16 -,	6.
1865, " "	"	£46	14	5.
1870, " "	"	£250 - 0 -	0.

making in all the sum of £675 14 - 3.

The principal sum was £1148-3-3, being £2000 currency, less £851 16 - 9, that being the amount to be deducted on account of Donald Matheson's debt. The interest on this principal sum for ten years would be about the amount received by Matheson; The accounts in which these sums appeared as received by him for his wife were rendered by him yearly to Mrs. Bissett, the widow, who with him principally managed the business of the estate, Mr McGregor and the plaintiff taking little part in it. Mr. Matheson, however, states that he had no authority or consent from his wife for what he did; but though she may not have given any direct authority or consent to his receiving the money, it is not pretended that she dissented or objected or made herself any application for the interest during those years. The inference is, I think, inevitable that she knew he received it. At any rate under these circumstances the court will presume the acquiescence of the wife in the husband's receipt from year to year. *Lewin on Trusts*, 3rd Ed'n., 643. "If the husband receives the wife's income, though there was a clause against anticipation, and the wife survives, it is clear that she, or her personal representatives cannot claim against his estate more than one year's arrears, but it is still *sub judice* whether even so much can be claimed." After referring to several authorities, the author goes on; "the principle upon which the relief is thus limited is, that the Court presumes acquiescence of the wife in the husband's receipt *de anno in annum*. If therefore the wife did not in fact consent, but remonstrated and required that the separate income should be paid to herself, which was promised, the Court will carry back the account of arrears to the time of the wife's assertion of her claim. But the Court requires very clear evidence that the demand was seriously pressed by the wife and will not charge the husband's estate from any idle complaints against its receipt which she may have occasionally made. See also to the same effect, *Hill on Trustees*, 612, 641. [*See* Lib. Ed., 666.] And it is to be borne in mind that the testator indicated no intention or desire that the income should be protected for Mrs. Matheson's separate use as against her husband, but only that she and her children should be protected in the enjoyment of the bequest as against his creditors.

As regards the indenture of assignment made by Donald Matheson to his co-executors referred to in the answer of the defendant and in the replication of the plaintiff, and produced by Matheson in his evidence, it is not necessary for me to say more than that it can only be deemed a security to the estate for the amount due by him as contended for by the plaintiff, and not as an investment of the fund to be secured for Mrs. Matheson in accordance with the terms of the will, to which she could alone have recourse for her legacy. The recitals shew that Matheson had received funds of the estate which he was unable to refund so as to secure the legacy to his wife and children according to the will of her father, otherwise than as therein mentioned, and he then proceeded to convey to them certain real estates therein described and his personal property, apparently all he possessed, to his household furniture, which were to be sold, and out of the proceeds his co-executors were to appropriate enough to satisfy the bequest to his wife and children, and, as far as the same would extend, to discharge the amount for which he was accountable to the estate, to pay the legacies contained in Bissett's will and to pay the balance if any, to him.

In the view I have taken of this case the plaintiff is entitled to a decree in his favor for £1148   3 - 3, N. S. currency, with interest upon it* out of the money deposited in the Bank, and the defendant Rhindress is entitled to the balance, and as neither party has succeeded wholly in his contention, the costs of each to be paid out of the portion to which he becomes entitled under the decree.

---

* Presumably from the time the deposit was made.—REP.

7

JOHNSON ET AL. *v.* PARR.

The imitation of labels and wrappers whereby the public are misled and the plaintiff injured will be restrained as a fraud upon him, and though an imitation will be deemed colorable if it be such that a careful inspection is required to distinguish it, yet a court will not interfere when ordinary attention would enable a purchaser to discriminate. It is not enough that a careless, inattentive or illiterate purchaser might be deceived by the resemblance.

RITCHIE, E. J., delivered the Judgment of the Court :—

On the argument of the rule *nisi* to show cause why an injunction should not issue against defendant to restrain him from using the trade mark or label of the plaintiff, the question resolved itself into whether the defendant had or had not adopted and used trade-marks or labels similar to that of the plaintiffs, or so closely resembling it as to mislead the public, and to induce persons to purchase the article manufactured and vended by the defendant, supposing it to be that for which the plaintiffs had acquired a reputation in trade.

A trade-mark is any sign by which an object of commerce may be distinguished, and the name of a manufacturer or trader written or stamped in a mode peculiar to itself may constitute it, but a mere label, as such, composed of words only, is not in itself a trade-mark, though the imitation of labels and wrappers whereby the public are misled and the plaintiff injured, will be restrained as a fraud upon him.

In *Holloway* v. *Hollaway*, 13 Beav., 209, the plaintiff, Thomas Holloway complained that his brother Henry Holloway had commenced selling pills and ointment at No. 210 Strand, under the description of Holloway's Pills and Ointment in boxes and pots, similar to and with labels and wrappers copied from those used by the plaintiff at No. 244 Strand, and he asked for an injunction.

The Master of the Rolls held that, while the defendant had a right to sell Holloway's Pills and Ointment, his name being Holloway, he had no right to do so in such a way as to deceive the public and make people believe that he was selling the plaintiff's goods. And in *Burgess* v. *Burgess*, 17 Jurist, 292, the decision was to the same effect. These cases, and there are others to the same effect, show that a party will be

restrained from attempting to deceive the public and lead purchasers to believe that they are buying the plaintiff's article
though there may not be technically a trade-mark simulated.
The case of *Wotherspoon et al.* v. *Currie*, L. R., 5 H. L., 508,
had reference to the imitation of a label and it was held that
the name "Glenfield Starch," which had been adopted by the
plaintiffs, who had manufactured a particular article which they
designated by that name, could not be usurped by the defendant, though in other respects the labels were dissimilar. And in
Cocks v. *Chandler** the defendant was enjoined because he used
the word *original* Reading Sauce. It was admitted that the
only thing to which exception could be taken was the use of
that word, as the defendant's wrappers, labels and bottles differed from those of the plaintiff and were wholly unobjectionable.
So in *Hirst* v. *Denham*, L. R., 14 Equity, 542, where the imitation was that of a ticket affixed to cloth of a particular kind
manufactured by the plaintiff.

Lord CHELMSFORD, in giving judgment in *Holloway* v. *Holloway*, said, "where the trade mark is not actually copied,
fraud is a necessary element, that is, the party accused must
be proved to have done the act complained of with the fraudulent design of passing off his own goods as those of the party
entitled to the exclusive use of the trade mark. It is not
necessary to shew that there has been the use of a mark in
all respects corresponding with that which another person has
acquired an exclusive right to use, if the resemblance be such
as not only to show an intention to deceive, but also such as
to be likely to make unwary purchasers suppose that they
were purchasing the article sold by the party entitled to the
trade mark." And in *Seixo* v. *Provezende*, L.R., 1 Ch.App., 195,
Lord CRANWORTH said, "if the question turned on the enquiry whether a person having a cask of the plaintiff's and
a cask of the defendant's placed before his eye could mistake
the one for the other, there could be no doubt of the result, for
they are altogether different. But that is not the question;
the principle on which relief is given in these cases is that
one man cannot offer his goods for sale, representing them to
be the manufacture of a rival trader.

---

* L. R., 11 Eq., 446.

Now in the case before us, any one looking at the labels *A* and *B*, referred to in the affidavit of the plaintiff Isaac S. Johnson, and annexed to it, even side by side, would assume them to be identical. It is true that some of the wording is different, but there is much that is exactly alike, especially in what would catch the eye of a casual observer, the form, size, heading and color of the label, the name "Johnson's Anodyne Liniment," the cures to be effected, most of them in the identical order, and three lines copied verbatim.

From the similarity between the two, which could not be accidental, I can come to no other conclusion than that the defendant prepared and used this label for the purpose of enabling him to sell his preparation as that known in the trade as "Johnson's Anodyne Liniment," and inducing purchasers to believe that it was such. The defendant does not deny using this label, and he gives no reason for doing so, and shews no justification for using the name of *Johnson*, or affixing an apparent *fac simile* of the signature of a person of that name. If the article was not prepared by a person of that name, it could only be used to deceive and mislead the public.

Having arrived at this conclusion with respect to the label marked *B*, I cannot but look at the other label annexed to plaintiff's affidavit, marked *C*, with much suspicion, which also resembles the plaintiff's label in many particulars in general appearance, and some part of the printed matter is an exact transcript of that in the plaintiff's. But at the same time there are very material differences between the two, and though an imitation will be deemed colorable if it be such that a careful inspection is required to distinguish it, yet a court will not interfere when ordinary attention would enable a purchaser to discriminate. It is not enough that a careless, inattentive or illiterate purchaser might be deceived by the resemblance, but the Court would enquire whether a person paying ordinary attention would be likely to be deceived. When "Johnson's Anodyne Liniment" was used by the defendant, there was a specific article offered for sale which would be asked for *eo nomine*, and when the plaintiff's article was so asked for, the defendant would furnish him with his manufacture so labelled, but it would be otherwise with an article not so designated.

I can see no objection to the use of the words, "Anodyne Liniment," by the defendant; no person could I think have a right to appropriate exclusively to himself such a designation. The plaintiffs assert that the words, "Johnson's American Anodyne Liniment," are the essential parts of their mark or label. Now the defendant has in this label of his made a very important alteration, he has omitted from it the very important word "Johnson's", and has affixed his own signature—a *fac simile* of it—clearly and distinctly, in place of that of Johnson, and has used a wrapper different from that of the plaintiff, the directions in which are dated Yarmouth, and refer to the short time the liniment has been in the market. It is, indeed, somewhat remarkable that while the defendant claims to hold a patent for his preparation by the name of "Parr's North American Anodyne Liniment," in his label he leaves out the word "Parr's," a very material word, if he wished to describe the patented article, and to distinguish his manufacture from that of others, yet I cannot say that this label bears so close a resemblance to that of the plaintiffs as to make it manifest that the defendant intended to deceive, or that a purchaser of average intelligence would be deceived. An injunction will go to restrain the defendant from the use of the label I have first referred to, and that alone.

KINNEAR *v.* SILVER.

Plaintiff brought suit to foreclose a mortgage made by defendant, who alleged in her answer that she had been induced to sign it by the fraud of Thos. S. Fowler. Her testimony as to the imposition alleged to have been practised upon her was contradicted by Fowler, and it was in proof that she had re-executed the instrument in the presence of the clerk of plaintiff's solicitor, who had deferred paying over the money in order to assure himself that defendant understood the transaction. There was also evidence that defendant was aware of the nature of the instrument shortly after signing it, and did not repudiate it, but entered into negotiations to obtain security from Fowler who had retained the money advanced on the security of the mortgage. The Court, in view of the vidence, concluded that defendant when she signed the instrument must have understood its nature, and held that whether she did or did not understand it, she was estopped, as against plaintiff, from saying that she was not aware of its contents.

RITCHIE, E. J., delivered the judgment of the Court :—

This suit is brought to foreclose a mortgage made by the defendant to the plaintiff for $5000. In her answer the defendant does not deny having executed the instrument, but states that when she signed it, she was not aware of its purport; that she never borrowed or authorized the borrowing of the money and never received it; that she is an aged woman and was not in a fit state bodily or mentally to transact business, and that not knowing the contents of the instrument, which was not read to her, she was induced to sign it by fraud, deceipt, and misrepresentation of Thos. S. Fowler.

It appears from the evidence that Fowler is a relative of the defendant and lived with her at the time the mortgage was signed, that he made an application to Mr. Shannon on her behalf for a loan of $5,000 on mortgage in the month of January, 1872. Mr. Shannon procured the money from the plaintiff and prepared a mortgage and bond which were handed over to Fowler for the purpose of obtaining the defendant's signature. Both of the papers were returned to Mr. Shannon, executed by her, Fowler being the subscribing witness, who then did not give the money to Fowler but requested him to call again, and, in the meantime, sent his clerk, Mr. Allison, to the defendant with a note addressed to her to the effect that he had received the papers which she had executed, and that as he wished to have another witness to them she would oblige him by acknowledging her signature before Mr. Allison. After handing the note to her, Mr. Allison exhibited to her the mortgage, which she looked at and said that the signature to it was hers, and that she understood all about it. Mr. Allison thereupon witnessed the mortgage and returned it to Mr. Shannon.

After Fowler had brought the mortgage and bond, executed by defendant, to Mr. Shannon, he told him he required to have the policy of insurance, which was brought to him with an endorsement on it, signed by the defendant, assigning it to the plaintiff as mortgagee. Fowler received the $5000, out of which he paid Mr. Shannon his charge for obtaining the money and preparing the papers. This policy having expired, the plaintiff applied to Mr. John Silver, who is admitted by the defendant to have been her general agent, relative to the removal of the insurance, who gave him to understand that he did not intend to insure again. But, as the plaintiff insisted, as mortgagee, on having the property insured, Mr. Silver acquiesced and agreed to insure again, and shortly after effected insurance and the policy was sent to the plaintiff, in which it was stipulated that in case of loss payment should be made to the plaintiff as mortgagee. This took place in April 1873. Sometime after this the plaintiff called on Mr. Silver and intimated to him, that as the mortgage money was a trust fund, he desired to get seven per cent. interest which the law then allowed to be taken. To this Mr. Silver objected as he thought he could obtain a loan of the money at six per cent. The plaintiff then agreed to take the money.

The interest on the mortgage was paid by Fowler who handed the receipts to Mr. Silver as the several payments were made. The first bears date, July 1st, 1872, and is in these words: "Received from Mrs. Diana Silver one hundred and fifty dollars for six months interest on mortgage to this date. T. C. Kinnear, per J. H. Sweet." Two other receipts for the same amount are dated respectively, 31st Dec., 1872 and 1st July, 1873. It was not until some time after these payments had been made that the plaintiff was made aware that the validity of the mortgage was questioned, though Mr. Silver, who says he is the stepson of the defendant and has attended to her business ever since her husband's death, and had all her business in his hands, knew of the existence of the mortgage in the summer of 1872, knew of the receipts having been left at his office, that the defendant had in her possession a note of Fowler for the $5000, and Fowler had offered him, as defendant's agent, security on certain lands of his as a security to her for the re-payment of the money, which offer he had communicated to the defendant who left the matter in his hands to do as he liked, and that he had applied to Fowler again and again for the necessary documents to enable him to make out the security to the defendant. Yet, notwithstanding all this, he treated with the plaintiff as the holder of a valid mortgage, recognised the payment of interest to him for a period of eighteen months, insured the property at his request and for his benefit as mortgagee, and as late as July 1873, or thereabout, while he objected to have the rate of interest increased, gave him to understand that he would pay off the principal and obtain a loan of the money from another source. The existence of the mortgage and its purport and effect were known to the defendant herself, as well as to her business agent, as far back as 1872, that is, three or four months after its execution, if unknown before. For her son, Henry Silver, says that he at that date returned to Halifax, and was then told of the existence of Fowler's note to his mother for the $5000. This his mother showed to him, and he explained the matter to her.

The statements of the defendant and Fowler are at variance with each other as to what took place between them previous to and at the time of the execution of the mortgage. The account given by Fowler is that the defendant received his application favorably and agreed to raise money on her property in Tobin Street; a portion of the loan she wanted for her own use to assist her son Gay, and she authorized him to obtain a loan of $5000, and in consequence he made the application to Mr. Shannon; that after the mortgage and bond were prepared, he took them to her and told her what they were, that one was a mortgage and the other a bond; he stated the amount, the person who was lending the money, and upon what property it was loaned, and she signed the papers fully understanding their contents; that Mr. Shannon on his handing him the bond and mortgage asked him for the policy of Insurance; this he got and wrote the endorsement on it, which the defendant signed, and Mr. Shannon then told him to call the next day for the money. This was about the 22nd, or 23rd January, 1872.

Fowler goes on to say that the defendant had in the meantime consented to let him have the whole of the $5000 and he gave her a note for that amount, and in May he first heard of any dissatisfaction on the part of the defendant; that he proposed to give security for the payment of it, and mentioned several properties which he specified, with which she was satisfied, and consented to any arrangements he should make with Mr. John Silver, whom he saw on the subject; that the security was not given from dilatoriness on his, (Fowler's,) part, and because he had hopes of realizing the amount from some mining properties he owned.

The defendant, on the contrary, in her evidence states that she never authorized Fowler to borrow the money from the plaintiff, and never signed a mortgage of her property knowing it to be such. She remembers his bringing her a paper to sign, and if she put her name to it she must have known what it was; did not know it was a mortgage, had no idea of mortgaging her place. In one part of her examination she said Fowler was always asking her for money,—that was the way she came to lend him this; in another, that he asked her for a loan of money, but was a long while getting about it; he said he had a quantity of marsh land. She did not receive his proposals favourably, did not agree to raise money on her place, never dreamt of such a thing. She admits Fowler brought her a policy of Insurance to sign, and said something about the plaintiff which she does not recollect; she did not understand it.

Though the defendant is an aged woman, seventy-four years of age, and her memory defective, there is not sufficient evidence to lead to the inference that she was so incapable of transacting business as to render her acts invalid, while it is natural to suppose that she would be more liable to be influenced by those around than a younger person of more vigorous intellect would be. I am induced, however, to think, on a review of the whole evidence, that she did authorize the borrowing of the money by Fowler, partly on her own account and partly on his, as he has testified, though it is quite possible she may not subsequently have authorized him to retain it. Yet the possession by her of his note for the amount would seem to indicate that she eventually acquiesced in it. Speaking of having lost confidence in Fowler, she says she did so when she found he had taken the money and appropriated it

to his own use, and though she says she was induced to sign
the mortgage by the fraud and through the misrepresentation
of Fowler, she does not say what he represented to be the
contents or the purport or effect of the paper submitted to her
by him for her signature. We are not to view this case as
one between the defendant and Fowler, but between her and
one who is an innocent party and has parted with his money
on receiving as his security for its re-payment a mortgage
unquestionably executed by her. And assuming that there
was fraud on the part of Fowler, it was the defendant, who
by her misplaced confidence in not reading the document or
requiring it to be read to her, put it in his power to mislead
the plaintiff; for it is a recognized principle that when one
of two innocent persons must suffer by the fraud of a third,
he must be the sufferer who, by his conduct, has, however
innocently, put it in the power of a third person to commit
the fraud.

On the part of the plaintiff there was no disposition to put
especial confidence in Fowler, and therefore his solicitor placed
himself in communication with the defendant herself in order to
ascertain if the instrument had been duly executed by her, and
it was only after she had assured him that it was and that she
knew all about it, that the money was advanced. Surely, after
this, so far as the plaintiff is concerned, she is estopped from saying that she was not aware of its contents; for though in general
it is competent for a party to prove that a statement was made
under a mistake, yet he is estopped from doing so to the
injury of another who has been induced to act upon it. In the
present case, however, there was a re-execution of the mortgage
in the presence of a subscribing witness and in the absence of
the party who is alleged to have misled the defendant. It
would be most dangerous in its results to allow a deed to be
invalidated under such circumstances as these, and that too,
on the sole evidence of the defendant who alleges herself to
have been deceived, which is contradicted by that of the party
who she alleges has deceived her.

But if the defendant really had grounds for impeaching the
validity of the mortgage, or thought she had, she was bound to
have communicated them to the plaintiff as soon as she dis-

covered that a fraud had been practiced upon her, especially in a case like this where the rights of an innocent person are involved, so as to enable him, without loss of time, to seek redress, by security or otherwise, from the party through whom he had been misled. So far from doing this, though she and her agent are made aware of all the facts shortly after the making of the mortgage, they not only do not communicate this to the plaintiff but for a year or upwards they allow him to believe the mortgage to be a valid security, and recognise it as such by their own acts, and themselves negotiate with Fowler for security to the defendant for the amount of the mortgage. It is not necessary in order to render a transaction unimpeachable, that any positive acts of confirmation should take place ; it is enough if proof can be given of a recognition of its validity and a determination not to impeach it.

In every view that I can take of this case it appears to me that the defence has failed, and I therefore think that the plaintiff is entitled to a decree of foreclosure and costs.

LAWSON ET AL. *v.* BELLONI.

Plaintiffs having amended their writ, served it on defendant, with a notice, endorsed, requiring him to answer within fourteen days, otherwise, plaintiffs to be at liberty to sign final judgment by default, and have the writ taken *pro confesso*. Defendant, who had duly put in his answer to the original writ, did not within the time limited in the notice, answer the amendment, and plaintiffs obtained a rule *nisi*, calling upon him to shew cause why the writ should not be taken *pro confesso*, etc., before the argument of which rule defendant put in an answer, not denying the statements in the amendment, but leaving the proof of them to the plaintiffs.

Held, that the rule *nisi* must be discharged with costs, defendant having a right to put in his answer at any time before the marking of a default.

RITCHIE, E. J., delivered the judgment of the Court :—

A rule *nisi* was obtained by the plaintiffs, calling on the defendant to show cause why the writ should not be taken *pro confesso*, and why the plaintiffs, Henry Lawson, Cathcart Thompson, and John Taylor should not be authorized to sell at

public auction all the real and personal properties specified in
the writ, which are in fact the subject matter of the suit, and
why, out of the proceeds of such sale, after paying the costs of
this application and all expenses incident to the sale, they
should not pay certain amounts to themselves and other plaintiffs and the balance to the Accountant General of the Court.

Unless there has been a judgment by default or an order
obtained for taking the writ *pro confesso*, I am at a loss
to understand upon what ground an application can be made
by the plaintiffs for a sale of the property in dispute and disposal of the proceeds in the present stage of the proceedings,
which would practically be deciding the case on the allegations
of the plaintiffs alone.

It appears from the affidavits on which the rule *nisi* was
obtained that the writ was issued on the 19th of May last, to
which an answer was put in on the 17th of June; and on the
12th July the plaintiffs obtained leave to amend their writ,
which was done by inserting a statement to the effect that the
amount of certain advances made by the plaintiffs and referred to in the writ was still due and unpaid. No answer
was put in to this amendment previous to the obtaining of the
rule *nisi*, but, before it came on for argument, an answer was
put in, not denying the statement so made but leaving to the
plaintiffs the proof of it.

No special order of the Court was taken and served on the defendant requiring him to answer the amendment within a limited time, but the following notice was endorsed on the amended
writ : " Notice is hereby given that if the defendant does not
appear and answer within fourteen days from the service here-
of, the plaintiffs shall be at liberty to sign final judgment by
default and have their writ taken *pro confesso*." This notice is
in accordance with the common law practice, and a notice of
a similar character has always been endorsed on writs taken
out on the equity side of the Court. The 18th sec. of Cap. 95 of
the Revised Statutes, "of Proceedings in Equity," provides that
in case of default for want of appearance and answer, the Court
may make thereupon such order as the right and justice of the
case shall require both as regards the relief prayed for and
the costs of the suit.

But in this case there has been no judgment by default, and until such a judgment has been entered, agreeably to the notice the defendant is at liberty to file and serve his answer notwithstanding the time for answering may have elapsed. This is done every day at common law, and the 7th sec. of the chapter of the Revised Statutes to which I have referred provides that in this Court the practice of the Supreme Court, that is the Common Law practice, shall be adopted as far as it is applicable, except as altered or modified by statute or by rules made by this Court. In other cases the practice of the English Chancery shall be adopted.

The course pursued by the plaintiffs in following the common law practice and not that of the English Chancery, was in my opinion quite correct, and following out that practice the defendant had a right to put in his answer at any time before a default had been marked.

But supposing the plaintiffs to have been justified in adopting the practice of the Court of Chancery, the application would be irregular, for according to that practice the plaintiffs could not, because the defendant had not within the time limited answered the plaintiff's amendment, apply at once and by the same motion for an order to take the writ *pro confesso*, and also for an order for the disposal of the subject matter in dispute in the suit. The notice in the first instance should simply be for an order to take the bill *pro confesso*, of which the defendant should be entitled to notice, and the usual order, when obtained, is to show cause why the bill should not be taken *pro confesso*, unless in the meantime the defendant shall have put in his answer, and it is only after this order has been made absolute that any motion can be made in regard to the merits of the case based on the assumption that there is no defence.

Where the defendant, as in this case, has substantially answered the plaintiffs' writ and has omitted to answer a single statement, not eventually affecting the issues raised in the suit, whether such omission arose from inadvertence, or, as was alleged, from the belief that the statement did not require to be answered, the Court in the exercise of a discretion which it possesses in such cases, would refuse to shut out a party from his defence to the suit when he had, previously to the argument of the rule *nisi*, actually answered or was prepared to do so.

It was contended on the part of the plaintiffs that the defendant should not merely answer the amendment but should have answered the writ *de novo*, but such is not the case. *Daniel* in his *Chancery Pr.* 632, 5 Ed. says : "In answering an amended bill the defendant, if he has answered the original bill, should answer those matters only which have been introduced by the amendments. In fact the answer to an amended bill constitutes together with the answer to the original bill but one record, in the same manner as an original and an amended bill; hence it is impertinent to repeat in the answer to the amended bill what appears upon the answer to the original bill, unless by the repetition the defence is materially varied." And again, p. 677, " if a defendant repeats anything contained in a former answer he will be ordered to pay the costs occasioned by the introduction of such impertinent matters." It is quite true, however, that where, after an answer, a bill has been amended and the amendments are not answered and the defendant is in contempt for not answering them an order may be obtained to have the bill taken *pro confesso*, but according to the English practice, if the plaintiff requires an answer to his amendment he obtains an order on the defendant requiring him to answer.

As the plaintiffs in this case have not shewn themselves entitled to the order asked for, either under the practice of the English Chancery or that of the Supreme Court, the rule must be discharged with costs. I wish it, however, to be distinctly understood that the plaintiffs were right in giving notice in accordance with the Supreme Court practice, and if a default had been marked the defendant could only have been allowed to answer after having had the default removed, if on his application the Court should order its removal.

I have avoided going into the merits of the case. The introduction of them was premature on the motion, which should have been confined to the question as to whether or not the bill should be taken *pro confesso*, for unless such an order was obtained or a default had been signed the plaintiffs were not in a position to bring them under the consideration of the Court.

LAWSON *v.* TOBIN.

Hon. James Tobin, by his will, devised land to his executors to their use during the natural life of his son, Michael Tobin, upon trust, to permit his said son to occupy the said premises and receive the rents, after certain deductions, for his own use and benefit, and from and immediately after the decease of his said son Michael, in trust to convey and assure said premises unto the child or children of his said son Michael, living at the time of the decease of his said son Michael, and to their issue. Defendant, a son of said Michael Tobin, mortgaged his interest to plaintiff, and in answer to the writ of foreclosure, set out the above facts, adding that said Michael Tobin was still living, and that some of his children were married and had lawful issue.

Held, that defendant, having mortgaged his interest to plaintiff, could not repudiate the transaction, and ask to have the mortgage declared inoperative, while retaining the amount received as consideration for it; and further that plaintiff was not bound to wait until the title of the mortgagor became complete, before foreclosing.

RITCHIE, E. J., delivered the judgment of the Court :—

The plaintiff, in his writ, seeks the foreclosure and sale of all the estate, right, title, and interest of the defendant and his wife, or of either of them, in and to certain real estate therein described, and the defendant in his answer states that the land in question was formerly owned by the Hon. James Tobin, deceased, who by his will devised it, with other lands and premises, to his executors, to their use during the natural life of his son, Michael Tobin, upon the trust to permit his said son to occupy the said premises, and to receive the rents, etc., after deductions for repairs and premiums of insurance, for his own use and benefit, and from and immediately after the decease of his said son Michael, in trust to convey and assure the said premises, with the appurtenances, unto the child or children of his said son, Michael, living at the time of the decease of his said son, Michael, and to their issue ; that the said Michael Tobin is the father of the defendant, and is still living; that some of the children of the said Michael Tobin, including the defendant, are married, and have lawful issue ; and the defendant alleges that the interest sought to be foreclosed in this suit is not such a mortgageable interest as can or ought to be foreclosed.

I see no difficulty whatever in this case. The defendant has, according to the view taken by his counsel, a contingent remainder in the property mortgaged. This he has conveyed to the plaintiff, in the amplest terms, for a valuable consideration, with covenants that he has good title and right to convey. Can he now repudiate the transaction so far as to have the mortgage declared inoperative, while he retains the large sum he has received as the consideration for making it? That such a result would be most unjust to the plaintiff cannot be questioned, and it is in my opinion unquestionable that such a defence as that set up by the defendant can not, as it ought not, to prevail.

At one time a contingent remainder was not supposed to be the subject of alienation at law, because it was deemed rather a possibility that an estate, like the possibility of an heir at law; but it has been settled that where the contingency upon which the remainder is to vest, is not in respect of the person, but the event, where the person is ascertained who is to take, the remainder may be granted, and the grantee shall occupy the place of the grantor, with his chance of having the estate.

Though at law, a mere expectancy was not assignable, courts of Equity give effect to assignments for valuable consideration of possibilities, and even of expectancies of heirs at law. *Spence* in his *Equitable Jurisdiction*, Vol. 2, p. 852, after referring to the rule at law, says: " But Courts of Chancery from the earliest times, thought the doctrine on which the Common Law proceeded in these cases, as too absurd for it to adopt. The Court of Chancery, acting upon principles of general jurisprudence, held that a man may bind himself to do anything which is not in itself impossible, and that he ought to perform his obligations; it has given effect to assignments of every kind of future and contingent interest, and possibilities in real and personal property, if made for valuable consideration." And on page 896, "a mere expectancy may be the subject of contract for valuable consideration, though whether anything shall be obtained under such contract or not, must, from the nature of the subject-matter, depend upon chance." See 2 *Washb. Real Prop.*, 238, 367; *Story's Eq.*, sec. 1040, b.

It was suggested at the argument that the right to mortgage might exist in the defendant, and yet the plaintiffs have no right to foreclose and sell till the title of the mortgagor to the land had become complete ; but if the defendant in this case could have conveyed his right to the property, whatever it was, to the plaintiff, so as to deprive himself of all claim or interest therein by an absolute deed, upon what principle can it be contended that if he does so by way of mortgage he has any other right than that reserved to him to redeem on payment of the amount due ? Of course a contingent interest will not in any case produce on a sale as much as a vested and absolute interest, and it might be for the mortgagor's benefit to postpone the sale, but it might have the effect of rendering the mortgagee's security worthless. If the mortgagor desired to have the right of doing this, he should have stipulated for it when he applied for the loan, in which case it is not improbable the plaintiff would not have advanced his money on the security.

To refuse the plaintiff the right to foreclose and sell, would do a manifest injustice to him, not merely by depriving him of his money, which, by his agreement with the defendant, he is now entitled to receive, but also, by putting in jeopardy the whole security, which would become valueless if the defendant should die before the happening of the contingency upon which the vesting of the estate depended.

LORDLY, Assignee of Pryor, *v.* YEOMANS.

The Messrs. Pryor, in December 1873, of their own accord, signed and sealed a mortgage, whereby defendant was to be secured from loss on endorsements of their paper; but defendant did not become aware that such a mortgage had been made until some time in 1874, and his information then was not derived from Messrs. Pryor, or any person authorized by them. The mortgage was not recorded until March 20, 1875, when the Messrs. Pryor knew they would have to go into bankruptcy, and on March 22, 1875, they made an assignment under the Insolvent Act of 1869. *Held*, that the mortgage was void, being made in contemplation of insolvency.

8

RITCHIE, E. J., delivered the judgment of the Court:—

The plaintiff seeks to set aside a mortgage, made by the Insolvents to the defendant, as having been made in violation of the Insolvent Act of 1869.

The mortgage in question bears date 17th December, 1873, and was recorded 20th March, 1875. The instrument, from the evidence, appears to have been signed and sealed by the Messrs. Pryor at the time of its date, but no intimation was ever given or authorized to be given by them to the defendant of its existence until after it had been put on record, which took place two days before they made their assignment under the Insolvent Act, which was made 22nd March, 1875; though he became aware that a mortgage, whereby he was to be secured, had been made by them, in the course of the year 1874, but that information was not communicated to him by a person who was authorized by the Insolvents to do so, and he neither applied for the instrument nor sought from any one information respecting it, which may be accounted for from the implicit confidence which he seems to have had in their solvency up to the time of their assignment.

The account which Mr. William Pryor gives of the mortgage is explicit and candid. He says their firm had been in the habit of receiving accommodation from Mr. Yeomans, by indorsements of their paper for eight or ten years before, and when the mortgage was made in December 1873, they were indebted to him for indorsements on notes matured or then running, and there might have been five or six thousand dollars overdue at that time; he was on their paper for about eighteen or twenty thousand dollars, but he did not have to take up any of that paper; it was all taken up or renewed as it became due. Mr. Yeomans, he says, did not ask them to give a mortgage; he was induced to make it so that he, Yeomans, should be protected if anything went wrong with them; as he had always been their friend and had helped them he was anxious to secure him, looking at the doubtful state of affairs and business at that time, and if anything unexpected should arise it was right he should be protected, as he had no remuneration whatever for helping them; business looked pretty bad here at that time; he did not make Mr. Yeomans aware that they had executed the mortgage until their failure, as they had always intended he should be secured, and the mortgage was in his possession, (witness's,) up to the time it was recorded; if he had thought there was any necessity for it, he should have recorded it before. When the mortgage was recorded he knew they should have to stop. In his cross-examination, in answer to the question why he did not think it necessary to record it, he replied that from the general view of their business he thought they could get through, and therefore there was no occasion to do so.

It is obvious that Mr. Pryor had some fears as to the stability of his firm when the mortgage was made, and though he says he thought they could get on, and had assets to meet their liabilities, at the value he put upon them, it is impossible, I think, in looking at the evidence and statements of accounts, to come to any other conclusion than that at the time the firm was insolvent, and its assets insufficient to meet its liabilities. It matters little, however, as I view this case, whether the firm was or was not actually insolvent in December 1873; it was so unquestionably on the 20th March, 1875, and being so, the mortgage is in my opinion void, as having been made in contemplation of insolvency. It is obvious, that if it were in the power of a merchant, though at the time solvent, to make a mortgage of his property, whereby one of his creditors was secured for existing and accruing liabilities, and retain it in his possession, unknown even to the creditor to be secured, only to be used in case of insolvency, to give him in that event a preference over other creditors, the Insolvent Act could be rendered inoperative. Unless the recording of this mortgage is to be considered a delivery of it to the defendant, there has been no delivery; and as delivery is essential to give operation to it as a deed, the mortgage had no operation as such till then. In the meantime, Mr. Yeomans had no rights under it, and if the Messrs. Pryor had destroyed it instead of recording it he would have been entitled to no redress. The most favorable view that can be taken for the defendant is that the recording was tantamount to a delivery, in which case we must consider that the conveyance of the property was then made, and then he, for the first time, acquired any rights under it. And being so made, it most assuredly was made in contemplation of insolvency, whereby Mr. Yeomans would obtain, what, under the Insolvent Act, is deemed an unjust preference over other creditors.

I felt no doubt on the subject at the time of the argument, and only reserved my judgment to look into the authorities Mr. Gray cited, as he seemed impressed with the idea that they bore strongly in favor of the defence, but they are manifestly distinguishable from this case. Had the statements in the defendant's answer been substantiated by the evidence they would have had more application.

Though Mr. Yeomans is wholly innocent in the transaction and suffers from his good nature in affording gratuitous accommodation to the Messrs. Pryor, by indorsing their notes, it is obvious that, but for this accommodation, they must have stopped before, perhaps years before they did. The firm was thereby enabled to acquire credit to which its state of affairs did not entitle it, and if a preference were allowed to Mr. Yeomans by giving effect to this mortgage, it would be at the expense of those who, by this fictitious credit, were led to give property to the firm. It is the policy of the Insolvent Act to deprive debtors of the power of giving such preferences when insolvency is imminent, in order that in the disposal of the assets of an insolvent, all creditors may share alike.

MARSHALL v. STEEL.

Defendant, in March 22, 1861, conveyed to J. J. Marshall certain real estate, by an instrument in the form of an absolute deed, but which defendant contended was given as a mortgage to secure a debt due Marshall. On January 1, 1861, Marshall signed a memorandum acknowledging the receipt of £78 - 18 - 4 from defendant on account of the property, " leaving a balance of £171 - 12 - 11— " which when paid to me, and the interest thereon, I bind myself to reconvey the " said property, &c.;" and there were other memoranda showing that Marshall had treated the conveyance as a mortgage. In January, 1868, defendant having continued in possession of the land ever since the execution of the conveyance, became the tenant of Marshall under a lease then entered into. After the death

of J. J. Marshall, plaintiff, claiming under his will, brought an action of ejectment against the defendant. *Held*, (an equitable plea having been pleaded), that
the conveyance from defendant was a mortgage, and that the relation of mortgagor and mortgagee was not altered by the fact of the lease being made in 1868.

RITCHIE, E. J., delivered the Judgment of the Court :—

This suit was commenced at Common Law by writ of ejectment issued 17th January, 1872, to which the defendant put
in an equitable defence, the purport of which is, that, though
the property sought to be recovered was conveyed by the
defendant to the late John J. Marshall, deceased, under whose
will the plaintiff claims, the deed so given was not intended to
operate as an absolute conveyance, but as a mortgage only,
and that this is evidenced by a receipt or memorandum, bearing date 1st January, 1861, in the following terms : " Received
of John A. Steel, Esq., the sum of £78 - 18 - 4, on account of
farms and store at Boyleston, leaving a balance due me on the
said farm and establishment of one hundred and seventy-one
pounds twelve shillings and eleven pence, which, when paid
to me, and the interest thereon, I bind myself to reconvey the
said property to the said John A. Steel. (Signed) John J.
Marshall." The deed bears date the 22nd March, 1861.

In considering this case, I shall have reference to and be
guided rather by documents under the hand of the late Mr.
Marshall and the accounts kept by him, than by conversations
alleged by the defendant to have taken place between himself
and the deceased Mr. Marshall ; for, even if the view taken by
the defendant's counsel be correct, that Cap. 7 of the Acts of
1869 does not prevent the reception of such testimony, yet independently of the provisions of that Act, such evidence is open
to grave objections, especially in cases such as this where an
attempt is made to affect and control the operation of a deed.
Sir W. M. JAMES, L. J., in *Hill* v. *Wilson*, L. R., 8 Cha. App., 900,
said, " conversations alleged to have taken place with a dead
man in his lifetime by a party interested, unless corroborated,
should be wholly disregarded in the interest of justice and the
interest of mankind." See also *Gray* v. *Warner*, L. R., 16 Eq.
580, to the same effect.

On the part of the plaintiff it is contended that the parties

contemplated an actual sale and purchase of the land in question, that the deed was intended to be what it purports, an
absolute conveyance of the property to Mr. Marshall, and that
the memorandum given by him should not have the effect of
turning it into a mortgage, but merely amounted to an agreement for re-purchase and re-conveyance.

The question, therefore, is whether, at the time the deed was
given, a *bona fide* sale of the land was intended, or whether it
was given and intended as a security for the re-payment of
money due. If, having regard to the nature of the receipt or
memorandum given by Marshall and the concomitant circumstances, it appears that the parties intended a mortgage, there
will be a right to redeem; for though there may be an absolute
bona fide sale and conveyance with a collateral agreement for
repurchase and reconveyance, yet, wherever a conveyance of an
estate is originally intended as a security for money, however
this intention appears, it will ever after be considered in
equity as a mortgage, and, therefore, redeemable on the usual
terms, even though at the time of the loan or as part of the
same transaction, there may have been an express agreement
that it should not be redeemable, or not so before a particular
time; *2 Spence's Equity,* 618; *Smith's Manual of Equity,* 296.

With the exception of the form of the deed given by the
defendant to Marshall, I see nothing to lead to the inference
that the parties contemplated an absolute sale of the land, but
there is very much to show that a debt was due by the defendant and that the conveyance was made to secure the payment
of it. No money passed from Marshall to the defendant as the
consideration of the deed, and the memorandum already referred to shows that the defendant then owed about £250, on
account of which £78 18 - 4 was paid; and it appears by a
memorandum in evidence in the handwriting of Mr. Marshall
that the sum, the receipt of which was then acknowledged,
had been paid, the most of it at least, several years before, and
at the foot of this memorandum, Mr. Marshall added, "which
sums, [amounting in all to £78 18 4,] have been credited
on account of the mortgage on his farm to John H. Anderson,
assigned to me;" so that we have here on the 2nd of January,
1861, an acknowledgment that this £78 - 18 4 is to be credit-

ed on a mortgage held by him. The next account produced in evidence, also coming from Mr. Marshall, contains under date, January 1st, 1865,—"interest to date due on your farm £41"; the next, under date December 31st, 1865,—"interest on your mortgage for the year 1865 to date, £10 - 6 4," being the interest on the amount remaining due after the payment above referred to. There is then a letter from Mr. Marshall, the date of which is 16th October, 1869. This date it is contended has been altered from 1859, but whether written in the one year or the other it seems to me to recognize the existence of a debt due by defendant to Mr. Marshall, secured on this property, which he recommends should be paid, that he might deed it to another, but of course, in that case, for defendant's benefit; and the terms in which Mr. Marshall expresses himself would lead to the inference that at the time the legal title was in him, and if so, it must have been written after 1859, and has an important bearing on the case.

But not only does Mr. Marshall treat the conveyance he held as a mortgage to secure a debt due by the defendant to him by charging interest on the debt, and referring to it as a mortgage, but the defendant is allowed to remain in possession of the property for several years after the deed was given, which was consistent with his character of a mortgagor, and not with that of a vendor, who had made a *bona fide* sale of it. I refer to the period which elapsed from the time the deed was given to the taking of the lease, six or seven years; so that if the written document given to the defendant by Mr. Marshall, had not of itself clearly established that the deed was given as a security for a debt, the way in which both parties acted can lead to no other conclusion than that it was so intended; and if at the time the deed was given that was the object for which it was given and received, has anything occurred since so to alter the rights of the parties as to turn that which was originally a mortgage into an absolute conveyance? Courts of Equity hold that when once the character of a mortgagor is established, the right of redemption and other incidents of a mortgage follow, the rule being, where once a mortgage always a mortgage. *Newcomb* v. *Bonham,* 1 Vern., 8.

Inadequacy of consideration is another important element in this case. The only money that appears ever to have been advanced by Mr. Marshall to the defendant on account of the land was £250. Of this, £78 - 18 - 4 was paid by defendant before the deed was given, so that if the deed is held to be absolute, the defendant will have parted with his property for £170, or thereabouts. But the consideration in the deed is £400, and the evidence shows that its value was even greater than that.

The plaintiff relies, as shewing that Marshall was the actual owner of the property under his deed, on the fact that in Jan. 1868, the defendant became his tenant under a lease entered into between them, which was produced, as was also an account certified by the defendant to be correct, in which he was charged by Mr. Marshall with rent of farm, 1868, £12. I can see nothing in this inconsistent with the character of mortgagor and mortgagee. Surely if in this case there had been an ordinary mortgage, with the usual proviso for redemption, the right to redeem would not be lost by such a lease; the mortgagee had a right to insist on the possession, and if he took it he would be obliged to account to the mortgagor for the rents and profits; why could the mortgagor not accept a lease without forfeiting his right to redeem? The rent would go to pay the interest, and if it exceeded it, to reduce the principal.

A mortgagor may by a subsequent act extinguish his equity of redemption, and the mortgagee may purchase it from him, but courts view such a transaction with jealousy, and they require clear evidence that the mortgagor, by his deliberate act, has parted with his interest. In *Ford* v. *Olden*, L. R., 3 Eq., 463, Sir JOHN STUART, V. C., said, "It has been laid down by the editor of a valuable text book, (*Powell on Mortgage*), without sufficent qualification, that a mortgagee may purchase from the mortgagor his equity of redemption." Lord REDESDALE in *Webb* v. *Rorke*, 2 Sch. and Lefr. 661, says that courts view transactions between mortgagor and mortgagee with considerable jealousy, and will set aside the sale of an equity of redemption, where, by the influence of his position, the mortgagor has purchased for less than others would have given, and where there are circumstances of misconduct in obtaining the purchase. In *Hicks* v. *Cook*, 4 Dow., 16, it was held that the taking of a lease from the mortgagor to the mortgagee is objectionable ; a mortgagor may be a man of wealth and in a situation to make any contract he pleases with the mortgagee. But the principle upon which the courts act is, not that the mortgagor is unable to enter into a contract of this kind, but that the transaction ought to be looked upon with jealousy, especially when the mortgagor is a needy man, and when there is pressure and inequality of position and the sale has been at an under value.

In the case before us, there is no evidence to show that the defendant ever released his equity of redemption, or contemplated doing so, and the evidence having clearly established that Mr. Marshall and himself stood in relation to each other of mortgagee and mortgagor, the defendant is now entitled to redeem on paying the amount of principal and interest.

McKEEN *v.* McKAY.

Allan McKay conveyed property to plaintiff by a deed, absolute in its terms, but admitted to have been given as a security for a debt. Nothing was paid on account of principal or interest by the mortgagor or his heirs, for a period of over twenty years before suit to foreclose, but within that period an action of ejectment had been brought to recover possession, in which a judgment was obtained, a record filed and a writ of *hab. fac. pos.* issued but not executed. *Held*, that these proceedings prevented the statute of limitations from operating except from the judgment.

RITCHIE, E. J., delivered the judgment of the Court :—

This suit is brought to foreclose the equity of redemption in a lot of land conveyed by Allan McKay to William McKeen, dated 8th October, 1849, by a deed absolute in its terms, but admitted to have been given as a security for a debt due by McKay.

It was contended on the part of the defendant that as nothing had ever been paid for principal or interest by the mortgagor in his life time, and his heirs since his death, from

the date of the deed to the present time, the plaintiff is precluded after a lapse of upwards of twenty years, from disturbing
them in their possession, or setting up the mortgage as a subsisting valid encumbrance on the land comprised in it, of which
he can avail himself by foreclosure. The answer to this is, that
within twenty years a payment had been made by the mortgagor to the mortgagee.. The payment relied on was not made
in money, but a small quantity of hay was supplied by McKay,
which was to go to his credit on account. In the receipt the
mortgage was not referred to. The Jury to whom the issue
was submitted were not satisfied that this was to go as a payment on the mortgage, and they found that no payment had
been made on it, to which finding no objection was taken by
motion for a new trial previous to the hearing; and I cannot .
say, if the objection was now open to the defendant, that the
evidence was such as made it incumbent on them to find
otherwise than they have done.

There is, however, a difficulty in the defendant's way, which
I think he cannot get over. From the evidence it appears that
in 1862 McKeen the mortgagee brought an action of ejectment
against McKay to recover possession of the land conveyed by
by the deed, in which a judgment was obtained and record filed,
31 May, 1862, and on the same day a writ of *hab. fac. poss.* was
issued but not executed. These proceedings in my opinion
prevent the Statute of Limitations from operating except from
the date of the judgment, and McKay and those claiming
under him, are estopped from now setting it up as a defense.
A judgment in ejectment not only destroys the right of
possession of the defendant but gives to the adverse party a
right of possession. His having a right to enter and sue out a
hab. fac. poss. infers that. Suppose this defence to succeed
and that the Court should hold that the statute prevented
the plaintiff from succeeding in this foreclosure, what benefit
would the defendant derive from it? The plaintiff could still
have the judgment revived, on which a *hab. fac. poss.* would
issue, and the defendant be turned out of possession; and, at
most, all that the defendant would then ask for would be to
be allowed to redeem on paying the amount due.

The plaintiff is entitled to a decree of foreclosure with costs.

MILNER v. RINGWOOD.

Plaintiff brought action of ejectment, claiming under a deed from one Purdy, but it appeared from uncontradicted parol evidence that Purdy had purchased the land for the benefit of defendant's father, who had paid considerable sums on account of the purchase money. After the death of defendant's father, Purdy agreed to convey the land to plaintiff; and it was in evidence that plaintiff held the land for the benefit of defendant, then in possession of the property, that he was to give him a deed of it when he paid him what he owed him, and that plaintiff was to have the hay and half the pasture for interest; but no writings passed between the parties. Plaintiff received part of the hay and had pasturage on the property, and before action brought, defendant tendered to him the principal money. *Held*, that the equitable defence, based upon the above facts, must prevail.

RITCHIE, E. J., delivered the judgment of the Court:—

This is an action of ejectment to which the defendant has set up an equitable defence. There was a trial at common law, and, after the evidence had been taken, the learned Judge before whom the trial took place suggested, and his suggestion was adopted, that a verdict should pass for the plaintiff, subject to the equities of the defendant as they appeared from the evidence, and the whole subject matter was transferred to this Court, under Sec. 6 of Cap. 89, Revised Statutes. The plaintiff produced a deed of the property in question from John K. Purdy. The land had been originally owned by Isaiah Ringwood, and a deed was produced from him to Margaret McCarthy, who conveyed it to Purdy, so that the legal title was shewn to be in the plaintiff; but it appears from the evidence on the part of the defendant, and that evidence is uncontradicted, that Purdy made the purchase from Margaret McCarthy, not for himself, but for the benefit of Peter Ringwood, who paid considerable sums on account of the purchase money. Peter subsequently died, and after his death Purdy agreed to convey it to the plaintiff, who was to take a mortgage or give a bond to the defendant, Abraham Ringwood, a son of Peter, he being then in possession of the property, to convey it to him on payment of the amount due him, and, under this arrangement between plaintiff, defendant and himself, Purdy gave the deed to plaintiff. The Ringwoods have never been out of possession, and have improved the land and built a house upon it. The plaintiff has repeatedly admitted to Purdy and others that he was to give the defendant a deed of the land when he paid him what he owed him, and all he claimed was that he should pay him interest on the amount due. The defendant testifies that before going to Purdy in relation to the property, the plaintiff agreed with him that he was to have half the hay and pasture for interest till the debt was paid. This statement is not denied by the plaintiff, and plaintiff gave him as a reason for not getting Purdy to write the bond when the deed was given, that if he wrote it, he would have to be paid for it; that he, plaintiff, would get a person to write it, and said that he would give it to him at any time.

Henry D. Crouse, one of the witnesses, testifies that he had a conversation with plaintiff four years ago, when he told him that he took the place *on conditions that he bought it for Ringwood*, who was to pay him the principal money back in a certain time, and he was to have the hay and half the pasture for his interest, and no doubt rests on my mind that this was the actual agreement between the parties. The plaintiff has been in the receipt of part of the hay, and has had pasturage on the property, and a tender of the principal money was made previous to the commencement of the action, but as no writings have passed between the parties, it is contended on the part of the plaintiff, that no effect is to be given to such a verbal agreement.

The question thus raised is in effect the same as that which was before this Court very lately in *Amero* v. *Amero*, (Ante, p. 9), in which it was held that though an absolute conveyance be made, it might be shown by parol evidence to have been made by way of security for the payment of money. The evidence clearly shews the existence of a debt between the parties, for which interest is demanded, which has been received by the plaintiff in hay and pasture, from time to time, the defendant retaining the possession of the land notwithstanding the deed; and Purdy says that plaintiff was to take a mortgage or give a bond to convey the land to defendant on payment of the amount due, that is, the security he was to have for his money was to be a mortgage on the property; or if he took an absolute deed of it, he was to give a bond. Now this Court will always treat a transaction as a mortgage if the parties intended that it should be such, though the instrument given be an absolute deed; and if the transaction be such at its inception, it will always be deemed so,—once a mortgage always a mortgage—and the authorities are numerous which recognize the principle that where a question arises whether an absolute conveyance is intended as a mortgage or not, parol evidence will be admitted to shew that what appears on its face to be absolute, was intended to be a conveyance by way of mortgage. As I referred to the more important of these cases at large in *Amero* v. *Amero*, it is unnecessary for me to do more at present than name them, viz: *Maxwell* v. *Montecute*, Prec. in Ch., 526; *Lincoln* v. *Wright*, 4 DeG. & J., 16; *Booth* v. *Turle*, L. R., 16 Eq., 187; *Haigh* v. *Kaye*, L. R., 7 Ch. App., 474; *Pain* v. *Coombes*, 1 DeG. & J., 34; *Loxly* v. *Heath*, 27 Bea. 532; *Laver* v. *Fielden*, 32 Bea., 1–12; *McCormack* v. *Grogan*, L. R., 4 H. of L., 97, and there are others to the same effect.

Viewing the deed held by the plaintiff to be so held as a security for the payment of a debt due by the defendant, and the amount of that debt having been tendered to him before this action was brought, it was his duty to have accepted the amount and conveyed the property to the defendant as he had undertaken to do, and, as under our Statute an equitable defence is allowed in ejectment, he cannot in violation of equity insist on his legal right to possession of the property under his deed, and the defendant will be entitled to his costs.

MISENER *v.* GASTON.

Plaintiff and defendant in settling their affairs on dissolution of their co-partnership, entered into an accounting by which it was shown that plaintiff had drawn $318.86 from the partnership funds in excess of the sum drawn by defendant, which defendant contended was due from plaintiff to him, but which plaintiff insisted was due to the partnership, so that only half the amount was due to defendant. Plaintiff finally yielded to defendant's contention, and paid over the money. Becoming satisfied afterwards that his own view was correct, he brought action, after the lapse of about a year, to recover the amount improperly paid over. *Held*, that having paid over the money with full knowledge of the facts, the very point now in controversy having been discussed at the settlement, the plaintiff could not, after the lapse of a year, during which he had carried out in all respects the settlement agreed upon, apply to have the mistake corrected.

RITCHIE, E. J., delivered the judgment of the Court :—

The plaintiff in this suit asks the Court to decree that the defendant should re-pay him a sum of money, which he alleges was paid to him under a mistake that occurred on an accounting which took place between them.

They had been partners in business, and when about to close the partnership, they had a settlement, and in his writ, plaintiff alleges that it was agreed between them that the plaintiff should purchase from the partnership the assets and credits at a valuation settled and agreed upon, amounting to $351.13, and assume the liabilities of the business. From the sum of $351.13 was to be deducted $47.36 and $59.51 for unfinished work, which the plaintiff was to perform, leaving a balance of $244.26, which it was agreed should represent the value of stock, assets and credits, at which they should be purchased by the plaintiff. It was also settled that the amount drawn by him from funds of the partnership was $695.87, and the amount drawn by the defendant was $377.01; that the defendant contended and insisted, at the settlement, that the amount due him by the plaintiff for the assets and credits of the partnership was to be ascertained by subtracting the amount drawn by defendant from the amount drawn by plaintiff—less $20, which it was agreed plaintiff should receive for his trouble and risk in collecting the accounts. This the plaintiff objected to at the time as erroneous, as it treated the $318.86, being the excess of the amount drawn by the plaintiff from the partnership fund, as being wholly due to the defendant; whereas in fact it was due to the partnership, and therefore only one-half due to the defendant; but though he so contended and insisted, he says he allowed himself to be persuaded of the correctness of the defendant's contention, and yielded, and paid the defendant the balance so erroneously made up, being

$318.86, when in fact he should only have paid him $159.43; that subsequently he became satisfied that the calculation had been erroneously made, and he now prays that the mistake may be rectified, and that the defendant should be decreed to pay to him the said sum so overpaid. The evidence, in my opinion, sustains the case set out in the plaintiff's writ, and the only defence which, it appears to me, can avail the defendant, is that the money now sought to be recovered from him was paid by the plaintiff with a full knowledge of all the facts and after the question now in controversy had been raised by him and discussed, and he had yielded to the contention of the defendant, for the plaintiff was right in the view he took of the accounting; but I think this defence must prevail, and that it is too late now for the plaintiff to seek to have the mistake rectified and the money refunded, especially as he not only consented to pay the amount, knowing all the circumstances of the case, but having done so, allowed a year to elapse before any attempt was made to have the mistake rectified, and in the meantime not only paid the money to Gaston, but in all other respects carried out the settlement as agreed upon.

The cases are numerous which establish the principle that money voluntarily paid, with full knowledge of the facts, is not recoverable. In that of *Bilbie* v. *Lumley*, 2 East, 469, where an underwriter had paid a loss which he sought to recover back; on the ground that a material letter had been concealed, it was held that he could not, as he knew of the letter at the time of the adjustment. Lord ELLENBOROUGH asked the plaintiff's counsel if he could state any case, where, if a party paid money to another voluntarily, with full knowledge of the facts of the case, he could recover it back again on account of his ignorance of the law. And *Brown* v. *McKinally*, Esp., 279, is directly in point. There the plaintiff and defendant entered into an agreement, whereby the defendant agreed to sell the plaintiff all his old iron, except bushell iron, which was of an inferior quality, at £9 a ton. The iron delivered was of inferior quality, part being bushell iron, and the full value of the best sort was charged. The plaintiff objected to the amount charged, and defendant sued him, when he paid him the full demand, telling him at the same time that he did so without prejudice, and meant to bring an action to recover back the overcharge. Lord KENYON held that such an action could not be maintained, that money paid by mistake was recoverable in assumpsit, but here it was paid voluntarily, with full knowledge.

Brisbane v. *Dacres*, 5 Taunt., 153; *Dew* v. *Parsons*, 2 B. & Ald., 562; *Steele* v. *Williams*, 8 Exch., 625, recognize the same doctrine, though they make a distinction between such a case as this, where the payment is voluntary, and cases where money is paid under an extortionate demand, made *colore officii*, which cannot be considered voluntary, it being *contra equum et bonum* for a public officer to retain what he has acquired by taking undue advantage of his situation. *Skyring* v. *Greenwood*, 6 D. & R., 401, is a strong case in support of the defendant's contention. There the defendant's army agents had given credit to the plaintiff, a Major in the army, in certain sums of 1/1 and 2/ *per diem* in a running account between him and themselves; they delivered him a statement, shewing a balance of £116   9   7 in his favor. It turned out that 1/1 and 2/ *per diem* were not payable to officers in Major Skyring's situation, and that the defendants had received an intimation to that effect, which they did not communicate to him, otherwise than by ceasing to credit him with the 1/1 *per diem,* and by writing him requiring the re-payment of the sum they had paid him. In an action by the admistrators of Major Skyrings for the balance due at the time of his death, they were not permitted to retain the sums with which they had by mistake credited him. And in *Bramston* v. *Robins,* 4 Bing. 11, BEST, C. J., said that if money be paid with a full knowledge of the circumstances at the time of the payment, it cannot be recovered by the payer; and Lord ELDON said the same in *Bromley* v. *Holland,* 7 Ves., 23, quoting the judgment of Lord KENYON in *Beauchamp* v. *Borret,* Peakes N. P. cases, 109. The language of HEATH, J., is applicable to this case. "He, the plaintiff, has acted as judge in his own cause, and has decided against himself, and he cannot be heard to repeal his own judgment."

MOODY, ET AL. *v.* BANK OF NOVA SCOTIA, ET AL.

Sanderson, one of the defendants, had been obtaining discounts from the Bank of Nova Scotia on paper endorsed by one or more persons, and the Agent of the Bank becoming dissatisfied on account of the numerous renewals, and referring to the possibility of the endorsers being called upon to take up the notes, Sanderson, in July 1859, gave the Bank a judgment for the exact amount then due on the notes. In September 1860, the plaintiffs recovered judgments against Sanderson, and a number of other judgments were entered up against him by parties who were made defendants in the present suit. Sanderson continued to get notes discounted until 1874, when his affairs became embarrassed, and the Bank ceased to discount his paper. The notes then at the Bank were taken up by the endorsers, and Sanderson ceased to be indebted to the Bank. In 1874 the parties who were then endorsers on Sanderson's paper discounted at the Bank took proceedings to revive the judgment, and issued and delivered to the Sheriff an execution, with instructions to levy on Sanderson's real estate. *Held*, that, the judgment having been taken for a specified sum ascertained at the time to be due the Bank and which had been long since paid, neither the Bank nor the endorsers of Sanderson's paper could make it available for any subsequent liabilities.

Simultaneously with the issuing of the execution at the suit of the Bank, the other defendants whose judgments were subsequent to those of the plaintiff's, had executions placed in the Sheriff's hands by Mr. Grantham, who was the attorney by whom all the executions were issued, with instructions to levy for the amount of them on Sanderson's real estate, and the land was advertised by the Sheriff as one sale, the advertisement being headed in all the causes of the several defendants, including the Bank. *Held*, that under the circumstances, the sale being under the direction of Grantham, the attorney in all the causes, the plaintiffs were justified in making the encumbrancers subsequent to the Bank defendants in this suit. Otherwise, possibly, if these subsequent incumbrancers had not connected themselves with the Bank, but had advertised sales under their respective judgments, subject to prior encumbrances.

Injunction to stay the sale until the validity, or otherwise, of the judgment at the suit of the Bank was settled, continued, but only on the condition that the plaintiffs should give an undertaking to bring on the case for trial at the next term of the Supreme Court in the County, or that their bill be dismissed.

Costs decreed against the Bank, but not as against the other defendants.

The following judgment was delivered by RITCHIE, E. J., on the motion to dissolve the injunction :—

This is not a case where the statements of the bill and the affidavits on the part of the plaintiffs are contradicted by the answer and the affidavits on the part of the defendants, but it is apparent that there is a case submitted to the Court requir-

9

ing investigation. The injunction granted is not, therefore, necessarily to be dissolved. The effect of a sale of the land in question at the suit of the parties who hold judgments obtained after that now in controversy, though made subject to the prior judgment, must, I think, be prejudicial to the interests of all concerned. If no question had arisen as to the validity of the prior judgment, no objection would necessarily exist to such a sale; but, where the validity and efficiency of the judgment to bind the land are in controversy in this suit, to sell subject to such a judgment would preclude prudent persons from bidding, or, if they did bid, they could only safely do so by assuming the prior judgment to be a valid and available security, and if this were not case and the prior judgment should be decreed to be inoperative to bind the land they would get the property for much less than its value,—would in fact profit to the extent of that judgment at the expense of the debtors or encumbrancers subsequent to them. If the whole property had been shewn to have been going to decay from the delay in bringing on the cause to a hearing, I should, under the circumstances, have ordered a sale of it, and directed the proceeds to have been paid into Court subject to the rights of the parties claiming them, as the Court should ultimately decree; and as regards a part of the property both parties agree that it is desirable that a sale should at once take place. Let a sale of this portion take place, the proceeds to be paid into the Court to abide its further decree. The injunction will for the present be continued, but only on condition that the plaintiffs give an undertaking to bring the case on for trial at the next term of the Supreme Court in the County of Yarmouth, or that their bill be dismissed.

After trial and argument, RITCHIE, E. J., delivered the following judgment of the Court:—

The defendant, Gilbert Sanderson, commenced to do business with the Bank of Nova Scotia at Yarmouth about thirty-five years ago, obtaining from time to time as his business required it loans of money on notes at three months, indorsed by one or more persons. In July 1859, Mr. Murray, the agent of the Bank, not being satisfied with his account, intimated to Sanderson that the notes discounted were renewed from time to time, and referred to the possibility of his indorsers being called upon to pay those then in the Bank, whereupon he said perhaps he had better give a judgment. He went away and had a judgment entered for the exact sum then due on the notes which had been discounted, a memorandum of which Mr. Murray gave him; this was all that took place between Mr. Murray and Sanderson in relation to the judgment given to the Bank. In September 1860, Messrs. Moody, Brown & Co. recovered judgment against Sanderson for $1990.90, on which there is due a small balance, and in May 1864, the plaintiff, J. W. Moody, as administrator of the estate of E. W. B. Moody, recovered judgment against him for $1754.30. All of these judgments were duly recorded shortly after they were entered. Subsequently judgments were entered against him and recorded by James W. Shatford, Sydney D. Jenkins, and Messrs. Young, Watson and Drysdale.

Sanderson after giving the judgment to the Bank, continued to get notes discounted from time to time, till September 1874, when his pecuniary affairs became embarrassed, and the Bank ceased to discount his paper; the notes then at the Bank have been taken up by the indorsers, and he has ceased to be indebted to the Bank.

The judgment was allowed to lie dormant for about fifteen years, but in 1874 the parties who were then indorsers on Sanderson's paper, which had been discounted at the Bank, took proceedings to revive the judgment, and, after having done so, they had an execution issued and delivered to the Sheriff, with instructions to levy upon the real estate of the defendant. Mr. Murray, the agent of the Bank, testifies that when this was done the indorsers had taken up Sanderson's notes, and that no debt was then due by him to the Bank; that in this suit the directors are but nominal defendants, the indorsers having assumed the defence and indemnified the Bank against all costs which may be incurred. Notwithstanding this, in their answer, the directors contend that the judgment has never been paid, satisfied or released, and that they have a just, legal and equitable right to hold and retain the same as a continuing security upon Sanderson's real estate, as well for the amount of their own claim, as for the indemnification and protection of the indorsers of Sanderson's paper to them, that having been its original purpose or intention; and they claim priority over the judgments of the plaintiffs, and assert a right to levy on the real estate of Sanderson to recover the amount due to the bank by him, and thus to protect, reimburse and indemnify his indorsers and sureties to the Bank.

There is no evidence that any agreement or arrangement was made between Sanderson and the bank, or with those who had indorsed or were about to indorse his paper, previous to or at the time of the giving of the judgment, that it was to operate otherwise than as a security to the bank for the amount of his then liability to the bank; it is, therefore, needless to remark on the character of the defence set up, or to consider whether, if the statements in the answer of the directors had been sustained by proof, it would have availed those on whose behalf the defence is conducted. The evidence adduced leads to no other inference than that the judgment was taken for a specific sum, being the amount ascertained at the time to be due to the bank, which amount has long since been paid, and neither the bank nor the indorsers of Sanderson's paper could make it available for any subsequent liabilities.

Simultaneously with the issuing of the execution at the suit of the bank, the other defendants I have referred to, who have judgments subsequent to those of the plaintiffs, had executions issued and placed in the hands of the Sheriff by Mr. Grantham, who was the attorney by whom all the executions were issued, with instructions to levy for the amount of them on Sanderson's real estate. This the sheriff did, and he advertised it as one sale, heading the advertisement in all the causes, including that of the bank. These defendants do not claim priority over the plaintiffs' judgments, but they, in their answer, assert that they gave instructions to the Sheriff to sell the land subject to all prior encumbrances. This, however, they have failed to prove. The only question with respect to them is one of costs, whether the plaintiffs were justified in making them defendants, and seeking to stay the sale of the land at their suits. I think that, under the circumstances, they were; the sale being under the direction of Mr. Grantham the attorney in all the causes, and there being but one sale about to take place, the plaintiffs were entitled to have it stayed till they should have an opportunity of asserting their rights as the first encumbrancers. If these subsequent encumbrancers had not connected themselves with the Bank of Nova Scotia, and had advertised a sale under their respective judgments, *subject to prior encumbrances*, it might have been otherwise. The case of *Smith et al.* v. *Smith et al.*, 2 Oldright, 308, was cited to shew that a judgment creditor could sell notwithstanding the existence of a prior judgment without notice to the prior encumbrancer. The question there was not between encumbrancers; all that the Court held was that a second or subsequent judgment creditor might sell the lands of the defendant whose interest would pass, "subject to prior encumbrances."

Without calling in question the authority of that case, the plaintiffs were I think in this case well justified in asking to have this sale stayed, advertised as it was in conjunction with a judgment, the validity of which they controverted. At the same time I may remark that the practice of a subsequent judgment creditor selling without reference to the prior judgment or notice of its existence might not infrequently be attended with injury or inconvenience, especially to purchasers. In this Court, in foreclosures, a second or subsequent mortgagee or encumbrancer cannot obtain a sale of the mortgaged premises without the consent of the first mortgagee, except upon such terms as the Court may think proper, and in the interest of intending purchasers as well as of the mortgagor, there is good reason for the provision. But, while I think these defendants are not entitled to have the suits as regards them dismissed with costs, they should not be made to pay costs, as the whole litigation had been occasioned by the course pursued by the Bank of Nova Scotia, against whom the plaintiffs are entitled to a decree with costs.

MOREN *v.* SHELBURNE LUMBER CO., ET AL.

Plaintiff applied for an injunction to restrain defendant from selling or otherwise disposing of lumber of which he claimed to be owner under an alleged purchase from the Company, the validity of which was disputed. The injunction
was refused, plaintiff having an adequate legal remedy at Common Law by actions
for damages.

RITCHIE, E. J., delivered the Judgment of the Court:—

A rule *nisi* for an injunction was obtained by the plaintiff to restrain the defendants from selling or otherwise disposing of a quantity of lumber &c., of which he claims to be
the owner under an alleged purchase from the company. The
validity of the purchase is disputed and his title to the property is denied by the defendants. The court is not called
upon at this stage of the case to decide the question thus at
issue between the parties. What we have to consider is
whether an injunction should be granted to protect the property and prevent the disposal of it pending the litigation.
It seemed to be assumed by the plaintiff's counsel that if the
plaintiff shewed a right to the property the injunction would
be granted of course, but that is by no means necessarily the
case. Before granting an injunction the Court must be satisfied
that its interference is necessary to protect him from what is
termed irreparable injury until the legal title can be determined, that is such an injury as is not adequately reparable by
damages in an action at law, for if one has a full and complete
remedy at law he cannot assert that the damage is irreparable.

In the case before us damages in an action at common law
will afford a full and complete remedy and the plaintiff has
had recourse to such an action. He has brought trover against
Stewart Freeman *et al.* for taking a portion of the property
the subject of this suit, which is defended and is now pending.
He has also taken out a writ of replevin for a portion of it
against the same parties which is defended and pending, the
defendants retaining the property having given the security
required by law. In addition to which the said Stewart
Freeman *et al.* have taken out a writ of replevin against the

plaintiff for a portion of the property after giving security, and this suit also is pending.

In these actions is embraced all the property in dispute except that portion levied on by the defendant John A. Purney the Sheriff of Shelburne, against whom an action for damages can be maintained if the property belonged to the plaintiff. I can, therefore, see no grounds for the interference of this Court by injunction where a court of common law is quite competent to deal with the question involved and to give full relief, and there is the less reason for the interference that in both the actions of replevin the plaintiff has security to abide their result. If an injunction were granted in this case the writ could never be refused in any case where the title to personal property was in controversy and trover or trespass was the ordinary remedy.

The rule *nisi* for an injunction must be discharged.

MOTT *v.* BURNS.

Where the defendant had no drain leading from his premises to the common sewer on the street, and the plaintiff prevented all access to a drain on his own property through which the water might flow to the sewer from defendant's property, but defendant proved no title or right to use such drain, the Court granted an injunction to restrain defendant not only from permitting his waste water to flow on plaintiff's property, but from receiving water from the city water works until a suitable drain was constructed, the evidence shewing that the introduction of such supply, in the absence of a suitable drain, occasioned an overflow on plaintiff's premises.

RITCHIE, E. J., delivered the judgment of the Court:—

The writ sets out that the defendant obtains water from the City water works and has no drain or other means by which the waste or other water from his premises can be carried off, which, therefore, flows into and upon the plaintiff's property adjoining, whereby the kitchen, the cellar and lower parts of the house are overflowed, thereby endangering the health of his family and occasioning serious inconvenience; and he prays;

that the defendant may be restrained from permitting any
waste or other water to flow from his premises into the plaintiff's, and that he may be ordered to construct a suitable under-
ground drain from his dwelling house to the common sewer in
the street on which the house is situate.

The defendant, in his answer, states that he has a drain
suitable for carrying away the waste and other water from
his premises, which would have that effect if it had not been
choked and obstructed by the plaintiff, and that any water
which flows into the plaintiff's property does so because of such
obstruction.

It is provided by the 310th Section of Chapter 81 of the
Acts of 1864, that every dwelling house shall be furnished with
a suitable drain for carrying out the waste water &c., and, by
the 314th section, that all waste water shall be conveyed
through drains under ground to a common sewer or such
reservoir as a health inspector shall appoint; and, by Chapter
14 of the acts of 1873, power is given to the Commissioner of
Streets, where there is a common sewer, to cause the owner of
the land adjoining to make a sufficient drain from his house
to it, when, in the opinion of the Board, the same shall be
necessary, and in case the owner shall neglect to make it, the
Board shall cause it to be done at the expense of the owner,
such drain to be laid as pointed out by the City Engineer
under the direction of the Board; and no person is authorized
to make any such drain and connect it with the sewer without the permission of the Board.

From the evidence it appears that there is a common sewer
in the street on which the defendant's house is situate, but
there is no drain leading into it from his premises. There is
a drain from the plaintiff's land which connects with the sewer
and all access to this drain from the defendant's premises the
plaintiff has prevented, as he asserts he has a right to do, as
it is entirely on his own land, and was constructed by those
under whom he claims. This he has established by the
evidence, and the defendant has failed to show any title to
it or any right to have the waste water from his premises
pass into it or through the plaintiff's land.

Courts of Equity will not in general undertake to decide

whether a nuisance exists or not, when the fact is in controversy, but will in that case require the party seeking the interference of the Court to establish in the first instance his right
at law; but here it is not contended that the plaintiff has sustained no injury by the overflow of the defendant's waste water,
and it must be conceded that the injury has been such as from
its continuance must occasion a constantly recurring grievance,
impairing the just enjoyment of his property, the only defence
set up being the existence of a drain of the plaintiff, sufficient to carry off all the defendant's waste water, which drain
the defendant has obstructed, thereby himself creating the
nuisance. The defence, has, I think, entirely failed, and the
plaintiff is entitled to an injunction, to restrain the defendant
from permitting waste water to flow from his premises into
those of the plaintiff; and as the evidence shews that the introduction of water by pipes from the city water works without
such a drain occasions an overflow on the plaintiff's premises,
the injunction should extend to restrain him from so receiving
that water till a suitable drain be constructed to the common
sewer in accordance with the terms of the statute I have
referred to.

MURDOCH v. WINDSOR & ANNAPOLIS RAILWAY COMPANY.

Plaintiffs had security on the undertaking of the defendant company, future
calls on shares and all tolls and money arising from the undertaking, for £200,
000 as a first lien. Messrs. Roberts, Lubbuck & Co., an English firm, had a lien
on the rolling stock for £25,000, and there were about £70,000 due to unsecured
creditors. Defendants, under Chapter 104 of the Acts of 1874 of the Legislature
of Nova Scotia, entitled "An Act to facilitate arrangements between Railway
Companies and their creditors,"* filed a scheme, whereby preferential stock to
the extent of £75,000 was to be created, to be a first charge on both the undertaking, calls, tolls, &c., and the rolling-stock, and this, or the money coming from
it, was to be applied to the payment in full of Messrs. Roberts, Lubbuck & Co.
and certain unsecured debts specified; stock to the extent of £350,000 was then
to be created, to be a subsequent charge on the undertaking, &c. and rolling-
stock, and was to be issued at par to the existing debenture holders in lieu of the

---

* See page 1 of the Acts of 1875.

debentures they then held, which were to be delivered up to be cancelled. Plaintiffs obtained an order for the appointment of a receiver, which defendants obtained a *rule nisi* to rescind. The Court, considering that the Act was *ultra vires*, as it dealt with the subject of insolvency, and further, that the scheme filed was unreasonable, as its object was to secure other creditors at the expense of debenture holders having a first lien, discharged the last rule *nisi*, but, in view of the possible reversal of the judgment on appeal, offered to modify the order appointing the receiver, by directing him to pay the amount to be received to the Receiver General, to abide the further order of the Court.

RITCHIE, E. J., delivered the judgment of the Court :—

The plaintiff, on the 16th November last, obtained an order *nisi* for the appointment of a receiver, which was on the 28th December last, after argument, made absolute, and on the 2nd February last William Twining was appointed receiver to collect and receive the tolls and sums of money arising from the Windsor and Annapolis Railway Company, and to pay them over to the plaintiff till the amount due him by the Company on the mortgage debentures, the subject of the suit, and his costs should be fully paid, with leave to apply to the Court for further directions, who, after having given the required security, entered upon the duties of the office. On the 15th of March last an application was made by Mr. Henry, on behalf of the Company, to rescind the order appointing Mr. Twining receiver, and to annul his appointment, and he obtained a rule *nisi* to that effect which was argued on the 29th March. The rule *nisi* was obtained on the affidavit of Mr. Henry that a scheme of arrangement between the Company and their creditors had been filed in the Supreme Court at Halifax on the 12th day of February last, notice of which had been duly published under and in compliance with the provisions of an act of the Province of Nova Scotia entitled "an Act to facilitate arrangements between railway companies and their creditors,* and it was further stated that he, Mr. Henry, had been informed by the Secretary of the Company in London, and fully believed, that the scheme had been assented to by three-fourths in value of the creditors of the Company.

* See page 1 of the Acts of 1875, where this Act is placed as Cap. 104 of the Acts of 1874, having been reserved for the assent of the Governor General.

In shewing cause it was contended on the part of the plaintiff that the Legislature had exceeded its power in passing the act referred to, as it dealt with a subject over which the British North America Act conferred on the Parliament of Canada exclusive power of legislation, Bankruptcy and Insolvency being among the enumerated classes of subjects with which that Parliament alone can deal; and that this act could be considered in no other light that as an insolvent act. It was also contended that if the Local Legislature had authority to pass the act the scheme proposed was so unreasonable in its provisions, that by merely filing it the Plaintiff should not be restrained from obtaining the benefit of the judgment he had obtained and from his remedy for the recovery of the debt due him by the Company. It was also urged that the application, if made at all, should have been made sooner.

The following sections of the Act bear more particularly on the question involved, viz: the 2nd, 3rd, 4th and 5th; Sec. 2nd, "A company may propose a scheme of arrangement between the company and their creditors (with or without provisions for settling and defining any rights of shareholders of the company as among themselves, and for raising if necessary additional share and loan of capital or either of them,) and may file the same in the Court;"—Sec. 3rd, "After the filing of the scheme, the Court may, on the application of the company on summons or motion, in a summary way, restrain any action against the company on such terms as the Court thinks fit;"—Sec. 4th, "Notice of filing of the scheme shall be published in the Gazette, and in two other newspapers published in the City of Halifax";—Sec. 5th, "After such publication of notice, no execution, attachment or other process against the property of the company shall be available or be enforced, without the leave of the Court, to be obtained on summons or motion in a summary way."

These provisions, as well as the other provisions of the Act, have been transcribed from sections of the Imperial Statute, 30 and 31 Vict., Cap. 127, but in transcribing the second section of the Nova Scotia Act, from the sixth of the Imperial Act, with which in other respects it is identical, these words at the commencement of the section are omitted; "where a company are unable to meet their engagements," and at the close of it the company is required to file a declaration in writing that it is unable to meet its engagements, with an affidavit of the truth of such declaration.

Had these words been transcribed into the Act in question, it would have appeared on the face of it that it treated of a subject over which the Provincial Parliament had no power of legislation, and it would doubtless have been rejected as *ultra vires.* It is of little importance, however, whether an act does or does not profess in terms to deal with insolvency; the question is, does it in fact deal with that subject. If power is taken from creditors to pursue their ordinary legal remedies for the recovery of debts due them, whether by companies or firms or individuals, or they are compelled, without their consent, to give time to their debtors, or to forego securities which they hold, and postpone a priority of lien which they possess to parties who may be willing to advance money to their debtors to meet pressing necessities, surely such legislation can only be predicated upon such debtors being unable to meet their liabilities, or, in other words, being insolvent. That a company having become insolvent, in order to settle with all its creditors alike, should have the power of declaring itself such, and on such declaration the remedies of creditors should be suspended, is not unreasonable, but that the Legislature should give to a company solvent and able to meet all its liabilities, the power of staying all proceedings against their creditors by merely proposing and filing a scheme of arrangement with them would be incomprehensible. The legislation must have been based upon the assumption of the insolvency of the company; the whole of the provisions of the Act can lead to no other conclusion; and the company itself has so regarded it, for the scheme which they have filed is preceded by this recital, "and whereas the company are unable to meet their engagements with their creditors."

But, assuming that validity is to be given to the Act, yet, where an application is made to the Court to stay the proceedings of creditors, reference must be had to the terms of the scheme; for it could hardly have been contended that the application must necessarily be successful because a scheme, however unreasonable in its character, had been filed. In any such scheme, the various classes of creditors must be fairly treated, and it should shew a reasonable prospect of providing for the ultimate payment of their claims.

The present debenture holders, of whom the plaintiff is one, have security on the undertaking of the Company, future calls on shares, and all tolls and money arising from the undertaking for £200,000, as a first lien ; Messrs. Roberts, Lubbuck & Co., an English firm, have a lien on the rolling-stock for £25,000, and there are about £70,000 due to unsecured creditors. By the scheme, preferential stock to the extent of £75,000 is to be created to be a first charge on both the undertaking, calls, tolls &c., and the rolling stock, and this, or the money coming from it, is to be applied to the payment in full of Messrs Roberts, Lubbuck & Company, and certain unsecured debts specified ; then stock to the extent of £350,000 is to be created, which is to be a subsequent charge on the undertaking &c. and rolling stock, which is to be issued at par to the present debenture holders, in lieu of the debentures which they now hold and which are now due. These latter are to be cancelled and the remainder of the newly created stock is to be issued to all the creditors of the Company now unsecured, or who shall not be entitled to preferential stock or cash ; so that, not only are certain creditors given a first lien on what the present debenture holders now have a first lien on, but even that over which the scheme gives them a secondary security is extended to a large body of creditors who have now no lien on it, and those creditors who have become such without security are to be placed on the same footing with those who originally advanced their money on the lien, whereby, after their debts so secured have become due, their security is to that extent lessened and payment indefinitely postponed. The object of the proposed scheme seems to me to be to secure, as far as possible, the other creditors of the company at the expense of the present debenture holders.

Entertaining as I do a strong opinion that the Local Legislature, in passing the Act, exceeded its powers, and that the scheme does not deal fairly with the present debenture holders, I cannot comply with the application which has been made on behalf of the Company, and must discharge the rule *nisi* with costs; but as both the questions I have been considering will properly come before the whole Court in term, when it is possible a different view may be taken of them, I am disposed so far to modify the order appointing the receiver, as to direct him to pay the amount to be received by him to the Receiver General of the Court, there to abide the further order of this Court, if this course should be desired on the part of the company.*

MURRAY *v.* McDONALD, ET AL., ADMINISTRATORS OF FINDLAY McDONALD.

F. McDonald, deceased, made a mortgage to plaintiff which plaintiff brought suit to foreclose, defendants set out an agreement by which plaintiff agreed to release the mortgage on receiving three promissory notes made by one McKinnon, to whom part of the land had been sold by the mortgagor. Plaintiff, replied that the notes were only taken as collateral security, to be credited to the mortgagor when paid, and that nothing had been paid on account of them. On the trial of the issue, plaintiff proved the mortgage, and defendants produced no evidence whatever. The jury found for defendants. *Held*, that the burden of proof of the issue raised was on the defendants, and that as they had proved nothing, the finding must be set aside.

RITCHIE, E. J., delivered the judgment of the Court:—

The issue settled in this case was submitted to the Jury by Judge DesBarres, who, after having explained it to them, told them in his charge that, as the defendants had offered no evidence, their defence had failed, and the issue ought to be found in favor of the plaintiff. They, nevertheless, found in favor of the defendants, whereupon a rule *nisi* was taken to set aside the finding and for a new trial. The proceedings in the suit were taken to foreclose a morgage made by Findlay McDonald to the plaintiff. On the part of the defendants it was not denied that the mortgage had been given, but it was alleged that after it had been given the plaintiff and the mortgagor agreed to sell, and did sell one hundred acres, a part of the

---

* The decision was not appealed from, but the subject came before the full Court on application for the confirmation of the scheme.

mortgaged premises, to one Hector McKinnon, and the mortgagor thereupon, at the request of the plaintiff, gave up the
possession of the part so sold to McKinnon,—it is not asserted
that he ever received any deed of the land so sold,—and the
plaintiff received three promissory notes of McKinnon, whereupon the plaintiff agreed to relinquish, discharge and release to
the said Findlay McDonald all claim, right and interest which
he had in and to the residue of the said mortgaged premises;
that the amount of the three notes, with the exception of eight
dollars, which they paid into Court, was sufficient to satisfy
the mortgage, and the plaintiff agreed to accept, and did accept
the said notes in full payment and satisfaction of his claim on
the said mortgage, except the said sum of eight dollars.   To
this the plaintiff has replied that the land was sold to McKinnon
by the mortgagor who took the notes, payable to the plaintiff
and gave them to him, that when paid they should be credited
to him on the mortgage, and he held them merely as collateral
security; McKinnon shortly after left the Province without
having paid any part of the notes, and the plaintiff denied that
he accepted or agreed to take the notes as payment or to relin-
guish his claim under the mortgage.   On the trial before, Mr.
Justice DesBarres, the plaintiff produced and proved the mortgage, and the defendant produced no evidence whatever.   The
only ground upon which it appears to me the verdict could be
sustained would be that the proof of the issue was on the plaintiff, and as he had failed to adduce the proof, the defendant was
entitled to have the issue found in his favor.   The defendants
have been deprived of the evidence of the mortgagor by his
death, and on account of his death, the plaintiff could not be
examined in support of his case, though the defendants might
have examined him if they had thought fit.   The sole question
now is, on whom the onus of proof lay.

The plaintiff, having proved his mortgage, and the defendants contending that the benefit of his security has been
waived by the acceptance of the notes, it is for them to shew
to the Court that his lien has been discharged, and not for the
plaintiff to disprove the substitution of the new security for
the old.   See *Fisher on Mortgage*, p. 811, sec. 1469.   The same
author, on page 817, says: "If a bill be taken on account of

a debt, and it turn out worthless, a lien is not affected by it unless proved to have been taken in discharge of a debt;" and even a lien for unpaid purchase money, where there is no mortgage, is not necessarily destroyed by the receiving of a promissory note for the amount. No English authorities in support of their contention were cited on the part of the defendants, and the American authorities referred to cannot avail them, as from them, it appears that the Courts there have adopted a rule on the subject different from that in force in the English Courts. In *Fowler* v. *Bush*, 21 Pickering's R. 230, Shaw C. J., said: "The rule of the common law differs from that of this commonwealth; here from the fact of giving and accepting a negotiable note for a simple contract debt, we, without further evidence, construe it to be payment, but the common law deems it collateral security." The *onus probandi* of the issue being on the defendant by the English law, the learned Judge's charge was in my opinion correct. The rule *nisi* must be made absolute. As the counsel for the plaintiff did not desire it, I have abstained from considering any other question than that raised by the rule, which I have therefore made absolute in its terms. I cannot help thinking it would have been more for his interest to have had a hearing on the case at the same time, as thereby a reference to another jury might possibly have been rendered unnecessary, a course the defendants were willing to acquiesce in. The question of costs on this rule will be reserved for the present.

McNEIL *v.* BEATON, et al.

Plaintiff brought suit against defendants as administrators of the estate of John Beaton to recover an amount due on an account stated and interest, and obtained judgment by default, no answer having been put in; after which it was referred to a master to ascertain the amount due. At the investigation all the partie were represented by their respective attorneys, and the master reported a sum due by defendant. Some of the defendants having objected to the report, on the ground that many of the charges comprised in the settlement had been originally entered against another party, and that no right of action existed against John Beaton's estate; *Held*, that the objection was not now open, but should have been taken in an answer to the writ.

RITCHIE, E. J., delivered the judgment of the Court :—

This suit was brought by Malcolm McNeil against Donald Beaton, and John McDonnell and Mary Beaton, administrators and administratrix of the estate of John Beaton, to recover an amount alleged to be due him on an account stated and settled by Donald and John Beaton and interest. The defendants have not put in answers denying their liability and defaults have been marked against them. In the absence of any defence by answer or demurrer, the only question to be settled is the amount now due. To ascertain this, there has been a reference to a master, and after an investigation before him at which all the parties, plaintiff and defendants were represented by their respective attorneys, he has reported that there was due the plaintiff by the defendants £111 - 15 - 5; equal to $447.08, with interest from the 8th October, 1872, amounting in the whole to $581.88 at the date of the report. No objection is taken to the report by Donald Beaton, but Mr. Thompson, on behalf of the other defendants, contends that though John Beaton was present at, and acquiesced in the settlement, his administrators should not be held liable, as from the plaintiff's books it appeared that many of the charges comprised in the settlement had been originally entered against Donald, and that no right of action existed against the estate of John Beaton. From the evidence returned by the master, it appears that John was the son of Donald, and that they lived together up to the time of the settlement, John being part of the time a married man. The plaintiff and Donald commenced dealings as far back as 1847, and the account continued in his name up to a comparatively late period, when it was transferred to the name of "Donald Beaton & Son." When the settlement took place, accounts, whether entered against John or Donald, were transferred to this account, and after giving them the credits to which they were entitled, the balance was ascertained and entered thus :—" To balance due at settlement £111 - 15 - 5;" signed by Donald and John Beaton and witnessed by Daniel McNeil.

If the representatives of John Beaton considered that he

10

was not liable for this debt though he concurred in the settlement, and intended to resist the payment, they should have
put in an answer and therein set up their defence, and it is not
now open to them.   But if such a defence had been put in, it
does not at all follow that it could prevail.   The plaintiff's
account was for work done by him as a blacksmith, and for
goods sold to the family; and living together as they did, we
might not unreasonably conclude that both father and son
participated in the benefit derived from both the work done
and the goods furnished, and in the absence of all evidence to
the contrary, this is to be inferred from their both of them
joining in the settlement, each thereby recognizing his liability;
and both of them have recognized their liability to pay interest.
Their agreement to pay interest is specially set out in the
writ, and there is not only no denial of their liability to pay
interest by an answer, but Donald does not deny it before the
master.

The plaintiff is entitled to a decree for the amount reported
due by the master with costs.

McDOUGAL, ET AL. *v.* HAWES, ET AL.

Thos. S. Crow, an ordained Presbyterian minister, and David and Jacob Frieze
Presbyterians and members of his congregation, purchased a lot of land in 1853
for the purpose of building a house of worship, and for a burial place for that
part of the congregation residing in its neighborhood, and having erected at their
own cost a place of worship, and fenced in the land, conveyed the land and build-
in 1854 to W. McDonald and other persons, thirty in number, by deed in which
it was stated that the land had been purchased for a Presbyterian church and
cemetery, and that the grantors had agreed to sell the land and church on the
same terms and for the same use as they held them.   The deed proceeded to convey to the said thirty persons in fee simple thirty-eight forty-fifths of the land
and buildings (reserving seven forty-fifths to the grantors) to be held in common
by the grantees, but as separate and sole owners of the pews on which their names
were recorded on a plan annexed.   The persons to whom the deed was given
were then Presbyterians, and Mr. Crow was a minister of that Church, and after
he ceased to officiate, a Mr. McLellan, who had been his colleague and succeeded
him, officiated there until 1871.   He was a regularly ordained minister of the
Presbyterian Church, but about that time charges were preferred against him by
his congregation.   He first appealed to the Synod at Truro, but afterwards inti-

mated that he had joined the Congregationalists and was thereupon deposed, some of the congregation seceding with him. The plaintiffs, (as Presbyterians,) and the defendants, (as Congregationalists,) each party claiming the exclusive right to the lot of land and building,—*Held* that the intention of the parties being clear and unequivocal, that the house of worship was to be for the use of Presbyterians, the court must carry out that intention and could not recognize the right of the defendants, even if comprising a majority of the congregation to defeat such intention, though it might be otherwise if the congregation were unanimous.

DOUGLAS, ET AL. *v.* HAWES, ET AL.

Caleb Putnam conveyed a lot of land to the persons named in the deed for the purpose of building a Presbyterian Church and for a burial ground, to hold to the said grantees for the aforesaid purpose only. *Held*, that even should the grantees unanimously concur in changing the use of the property from that of a Presbyterian Church, &c., such change could not be effected, but the property on being applied to other uses than those for which it had been conveyed, would revert.

Objection having been taken that the proceedings should have been by information in the name of the Attorney General,—*Held*, that the plaintiffs had rightly proceeded by the writ substituted in this Court by statute for the bill in Chancery, and that although the writ stated that plaintiffs were acting on behalf of all the Presbyterian members of the congregation, even that was not necessary, as they might under R. S. Cap. 95, Sec. 19, have maintained the suit on their own behalf alone.

The statement was made in both writs that by certain legislation the title to the lands in question was vested in the Presbyterian Church of Canada, but the legislation referred to did not affect the title to the property in question in these suits. Defendants not having demurred to the writ.—*Held*, that they could not reasonably ask to have plaintiffs turned out of Court because the Presbyterian Church was not a party to the suits when the Court was satisfied that it could not be made a party, and that the proper parties were before the Court.

RITCHIE, E. J., delivered the judgment of the Court :—

These cases being in many respects similar were argued together, but as they differ in some particulars I will consider them separately. The facts upon which both of the cases depend are few and simple, and in my view very much of the evidence which has been taken is irrelevant.

The first named suit relates to a place of worship and cemetery at a place called "Five Mile River," and from the evidence it appears that on the 1st August, 1853, George Dow and wife, by deed of that date, conveyed to Thos. S. Crow, David Frieze and Jacob Frieze, their heirs and assigns, a lot of land about six miles from the village of Maitland, Thos. S. Crow being then an ordained Minister of the Presbyterian Church at Maitland and David and Jacob Frieze being Presbyterians and members of his congregation. The lot was purchased by them for the purpose of building a place of worship and for a burial place for the use of that part of the congregation residing in its neighborhood. The grantees subsequently erected at their own cost a place of worship and caused the land to be fenced and thereafter, on the 24th August 1854, Thos. S. Crow and David and Jacob Frieze conveyed the lot with the building erected thereon to Wm. McDougal and certain other persons, thirty in number. In the deed which they gave it was stated that they had purchased the lot as a site for a Presbyterian Church and Cemetery and had erected a church thereon and pewed it and finished it fit for occupation as a place of Public Worship, that it contained thirty-eight pews on the ground floor, with a desk and pulpit and seven pews in the front gallery, agreeably to a plan annexed, that the land and church had cost them £246, that the land had been purchased and the house erected thereon to meet the wishes of the inhabitants of the vicinity and they had agreed to sell said lands and church, or so much as might be required, in lots or pews on the same terms and for the same use as they held said land and church, that is as a Presbyterian Church and Cemetery, each purchaser to be sole owner of the pew or pews on which his name was written on the annexed plan with a fee simple title as tenant in common to the whole premises in proportion to the relative first cost of each pew as marked on the said plan as compared with the cost of the whole premises. The deed then went on as follows: —" Now, know all men by these presents, that we Thomas S. Crow, David Frieze and Jacob Frieze, for and in consideration of £226 lawful money of Nova Scotia to us in hand well and truly paid the receipt whereof is hereby acknowledged, have, for ourselves, our heirs and assigns, bargained, sold, enfeoffed, released and confirmed, and by these presents do bargain, &c. unto William McDougal, Jr.," and twenty-nine other persons named, "and their heirs and assigns forever, thirty-eight forty-fifth parts of the foregoing described Lot and Church thereon erected as tenants in common of said thirty-eight forty-fifth parts of said lot of land and with us in the remaining seven forty-fifth parts, together with thirty-eight forty-fifth parts of said Church but as separate and sole owners of the pews, nevertheless, on which their names are respectively recorded on the aforesaid annexed plan; to Have and to Hold the said lot of land and premises, &c., unto the afore-mentioned persons their heirs and assigns forever;" after which follow a covenant that the grantors had a good right to sell, and a warranty of the title to the grantees.

Mr. Crow officiated as Minster at Five Mile River as well as at Maitland, previous to 1853, and afterwards officiated in the Church in question which continued to be used by Presbyterian Ministers without interference till the third day of September last, when, for the first time, the right to do so was resisted. After Mr. Crow ceased to officiate a Mr. McLellan, who had been his colleague and succeeded him, officiated there and continued to do so till 1871. He was a regularly ordained Minister of the Presbyterian Church, but about that time he had some difference with his congregation, and charges were preferred against him. He first appealed to the Synod at Truro but afterwards intimated that he had joined another denomination, (the Congregationalists), and he was deposed; some of his congregation seceded with him. Though Mr. McLellan does not appear to have been ordained a Minister of the denomination he then joined, he continued for some time after to preach in the church, and, after he left, Congregationalist Ministers preached there as well as Presbyterian, but no conflict took place, as they used the building at different times of the day. This continued till September last, when the difficulty arose which led to this suit in which the plaintiffs, as Presbyterians, and on the behalf of the rest of the Presbyterians interested, and the defendants, as Congregationalists, each claim the exclusive right to the lot of land and building.

The evidence clearly shews that when the deed was given the congregation and the persons to whom the deed was given were Presbyterians, and that Mr. Crow was a Minister of that Church; the attempt to prove the contrary entirely failed. All the persons who claimed a right to officiate there were Presbyterians till the secession of Mr. McLellan and some of his congregation. If by the deed the church and lot of land were held for and on behalf of Presbyterians alone, no possession or anything that has occured since can have affected their right to them. The contention that Congregationalists and Presbyterians are so identical in doctrine that they cannot be deemed different denominations, is out of the question; it is more relied upon in the answer of the defendants than it was by their counsel at the hearing. There is obviously no foundation for such a contention, and the introduction of evidence to show the intention of the parties to the deed, in opposition to the terms of it, cannot be of any avail; the instrument must speak for itself, and the whole question turns on the construction to be put upon its language and the effect to be given to it.

The deed is so unusual that it would be vain to look for precedents of decisions on instruments couched in similar terms, so that in interpreting it we must be guided by general principles applicable to it.

The grantors convey to thirty persons in fee simple thirty-eight forty-fifths of the land and buildings, reserving seven forty-fifths to themselves, to be held in common by the grantees, but as separate and sole owners of the pews on which their names are recorded on the annexed plan. The intention of the parties to the deed and the purposes for which it was to be held and used are clearly expressed. It is therein stated that the land had been purchased and the building erected by three individuals, (all of whom it is in proof were Presbyterians, and one of them a Minister of that denomination). They agreed to sell an interest in it to the grantees, who were their co-religionists, not absolutely so that it could be used by them for any purpose, or so that they could insist upon a partition, and hold their shares in severalty, but for one only purpose, for a Presbyterian Church and Cemetery, the only several ownership being in the particular pew or pews indicated to each of the grantees on the plan; but that ownership could only have been intended to have been a limited one, for it never could have been contemplated that the owner could put the pew to any use he pleased, or occupy it otherwise than as a pew in a church which had been designated as Presbyterian, or to confer on him a right to authorize the use of the pulpit by Ministers of other denomination of Christians against the will of the other pew-holders.

The intention of the parties to this deed as to the use of the House of Worship being for Presbyterians, and for them exclusively, is clear and unequivocal, and I know of no principle of law or equity to prevent effect being given to that intention; and this Court must carry it out, and cannot recognize the right of the parties, even though they should compose a majority of the congregation, to disregard such intention, and to say, "we have joined another denomination, and the place of worship hereafter shall be for the use of that denomination, and you, the minority, must join it or find a place of worship elsewhere." The grantees accepted the deed on condition that the house of worship should be used as and for a Presbyterian Church, and the grantors conveyed the property on that condition, reserving to themselves a certain interest. To exclude the grantors and such of the grantees as remain Presbyterians from the use of the building as a Presbyterian house of worship, because some of the grantees have changed their opinions in church government, would be great injustice. If all parties interested, grantors and grantees, had been unanimous on the subject, and had all concurred in the change, no injustice would be done, and I see no reason why, in that case, such a change in the trust, could not legally be made; but that is not the question now before the Court.

In the *Atty. Gen.,* v. *Munro,* 2 DeG, & S., 122, money had been subscribed for the purchase of land, and for the erection of a Presbyterian church and schoolhouse, which was settled upon trust for the the worship and service of God, according to the rites and usages of the Established Church of Scotland, the service to be conducted by a minister belonging to, and in full communion with the same church. Such a minister was appointed, who afterwards seceded to the Free Church. It was contended that there was no difference in doctrine between the two churches, and a large majority of the congregation concurred in the views of the minister and seceded with him. The court held that he was no longer competent to fill the office. The Lord Chancellor, in giving judgment confirming that of the Vice Chancellor, said: "The trusts of the deed are clear and explicit. Those who were interested in the establishment of the church had an undoubted right to stipulate as between themselves, and so long as there are any persons claiming the benefit of such trusts the Court is bound to secure and enforce the performance of them;" and in *Broom* v. *Summers*, 11 Sim., 353, land was held in trust for the trustees and the rest of the congregation of Protestant dissenters of the Presbyterian persuasion and the minister and some of the congregation severed themselves from the Presbyterian mode of government. It was urged that a very large majority adhered to the minister and that the doctrines, principles and form of worship were the same. The Vice Chancellor said, "it is not admitted that the congregation has the same church government and discipline, which are matters of great importance with Presbyterians; the minister and the persons who adhered to him have altogether seceded from that church, and consequently do not answer the description of the congregation for whose benefit the land was granted." The cases of *Foley* v. *Wontner*, 2 Jac. & W., 247, and *Attorney General* v. *Pearson*, 3 Merivale, 400, and 7 Sim., 290, are to the same effect, and support the view I have taken of this case.

The suit of *Douglas et al.* v. *Hawes et al.*, also depends on the effect to be given to the deed under which the land in question is held, and on that alone. The deed is from Caleb Putnam to the persons therein named, of a lot of land for the purpose of building a Presbyterian Church and for a burial yard, to hold to them for the aforesaid purpose *only*. These words are explicit, and their meaning unmistakable. The grantor reserved no interest to himself in the Church, as the grantors did in the other case, but he annexed a condition to his grant, that the land conveyed should only be used as a site for a Presbyterian Church and a burial place. If, therefore, in this case, the congregation, including the whole of the grantees, should unanimously concur in changing the use of the building from that of Presbyterian to Congregational, Church of England, or Roman Catholic, or any other religious body, they could not confer on such denomination a title or right to the property;—it might, on its being applied to other uses than those for which it was conveyed, be claimed by the heirs of the grantor as reverting to them.

It was objected that the proceedings should have been by information in the name of the Attorney General, but this is not a case where that officer need be, or ought to be, a party. The Crown had no interest in the matter in litigation, nor the public at large; both the cases depend on the construction of deeds and the parties interested in the questions involved are the proper parties, and the proceedings should be by the writ which we have substituted for the Bill in Chancery and not by information. In *Milligan* v. *Mitchell*, 3 Myl. & Cr., 72, the pewholders and members of the congregation for whose use a chapel was held in trust for religous services were permitted to maintain a suit on behalf of themselves and all others of the congregation, because the object of the suit was for the common benefit of all the members except the offending trustees. There the objection that the Attorney General ought to have been a party, and that the proceedings should have been by information was taken, but was overruled; and there are many other cases to the same effect. In *Davis* v. *Jenkins*, 3 V. & B., 154, the Lord Chancellor said: "The question, what is that species of suit which must be maintained by information and cannot proceed by bill is a point of great difficulty. It is not true, as has been contended, that when the subject is a public right the suit must be by information." If the proper parties are not brought before the Court in the suit the course for the defendant to pursue is to take advantage of it by demurrer if the want of the proper parties appear on the writ, and if it does not, by plea, and not to suffer all the expense of taking evidence and preparing for the hearing and then raise the question,—that will only be allowed when the defect is of such a character that a decree could not be given or complete justice could not be done without other parties whose rights might be prejudiced, which is not the case here. The writs in both suits state that the plaintiffs are acting not only for themselves but also for all the Presbyterian members of the congregations. It does not follow that the suit might not be maintained if brought by the plaintiffs on their own behalf alone. Cap. 95 of the Revised Satutes, Sec. 19, enacts that no defendant in any suit shall be permitted to object for want of parties in any case to which the following rules extend;—the 4th rule is, "any one of several persons for whom a trust is held under any deed or instrument may without including any other of such persons have judgment for the execution of the trusts of the deed or instrument;" but quite independently of this enactment the parties interested in the subject of the suits are sufficiently before the Court.

There is a statement in both of the writs which would probably have sustained a demurrer, to the effect that by certain legislation which had taken place the title to the lands in question had been vested in "the Presbyterian Church of Canada," but on being referred to the acts alluded to, it appeared that they had no such effect but left the title to these properties in their original owners. The effect of a demurrer if such a course had been pursued would have resulted in an amendment by striking out the statement in the writ. At the close of the argument Mr. Rigby, in his reply, asked leave to strike it out. I declined to allow the amendment then as the defendants' counsel had retired, but at his request made a note of his motion. The defendants not having resorted to a demurrer, cannot reasonably ask to have the plaintiffs turned out of Court because the Presbyterian Church in Canada is not the party bringing the suits when the Court is satisfied it could not properly be made a party and the parties actually bringing the suits are the proper parties.

In re MONTGOMERY, An Insolvent.

The Insolvent conveyed certain property to Wylde, Hart & Co. by an instrument, reciting that he had agreed to give them security on all his real estate, *plant and machinery*, in the City of Halifax, and after conveying certain lands he conveyed " all that and those the *machinery, implements and things* specified in the schedule hereto annexed, which schedule was headed, "Plant in the Machine Shop," and was found to contain, not stock on hand or articles manufactured, but only such articles as would come under the designation of machinery, implements and *things of that sort.* A subsequent part of the instrument, provided that all the *machinery, implements and things* which, during the continuance of the security, should be fixed or placed in or about the land described in addition to or substitution of the said machinery, implements and things describ-ed in the schedule annexed, should be subject to the trusts, &c. expressed in the instrument. *Held*, that under the instrument, only the things enumerated in the schedule annexed, or those added to or substituted for them, passed to Wylde, Hart & Co., and that the word "things," could not be held to embrace the general stock in trade, but must be limited to property *ejusdem generis* with that described in the words preceding and connected with it.

The word "plant," defined as applied to a manufactory.

RITCHIE, E. J., delivered the judgment of the Court:—

The question involved in the case which has been submitted to the Court depends on the construction to be put upon the words used in the conveyance made by the Insolvent to Messrs. Wylde, Hart & Co. the claimants; the assignee of the insolvent contending that the articles enumerated in a schedule annexed to the conveyance, headed " Plant in the Machine Shop," only, passed to them, while Messrs. Wylde, Hart & Co. contend that, in addition to these, a large amount of property consisting of stock in trade and other articles, which the insolvent had on hand at the time of his insolvency, a schedule of which is produced, also passed to them under the terms of the conveyance.

The instrument recited that the insolvent had agreed to give them security on all his real estate, *plant and machinery* in the city of Halifax, and, after conveying certain land described therein, he conveyed "all that and those the *machinery, implements* and *things specified in the schedule* hereunto annexed," to Have and to Hold them to the said machinery implements and things. In a subsequent part of the instrument these words are used: "It is further declared and provided, that all the *machinery, implements and things* which during the continuance of the security shall be fixed or placed in or about the lots of land herein before described, in addition to and in substitution of the said machinery, implements and things described in the schedule hereto annexed, shall be subject to the trust, powers, provisos, and declarations in these presents expressed and contained," after which follows a provision that if any of the *machinery, implements or things assigned* should be removed without the leave of

the claimant, or if legal proceedings should be taken or judgment entered against the insolvent, or any application should
be made to make him an insolvent, or if he should die, or become incapable of conducting his business, or in case payments
should not be made at the times specified, it should be lawful
for them to enter and take possession of the said plant, machinery, implements and things or any other plant, machinery,
implements and things which have been added thereto or
substituted therefor.

It appears to me very obvious from the terms of the
instrument what the parties intended should pass under it.
The recital says that the insolvent intended to give the
claimaints security on all his *plant and machinery*, and he
then proceeds to convey to them all the *machinery, implements and things specified in the schedule* thereto annexed,
which schedule is headed, "Plant in the Machine Shop;" and
on turning to it we find it to contain, not stock on hand or
articles manufactured, or in the course of manufacture, which,
in the course of business would come and go, but only such
articles as would come under the designation of machinery,
implements and things *of that sort*, which would be expected
to remain on the premises for the carrying on of the business,
and without which it could not be conducted; and provision
is made that if additional machinery, &c. should be brought in
or other things substituted for those in the schedule, they
should become subject to the conveyance.

At the argument, much stress was laid on the comprehensiveness of the word "things," as embracing all personal
property of every description, but if we should be justified in
disconnecting that word from those which precede it, we find
it expressly connected with those that follow, "*things specified
in the schedule annexed.*" We are, however, not at liberty to
consider them unconnected with what goes before, for it is a
well understood rule of construction that where general words
such as "*goods*" or "*chattels*" or "*effects*" or "*things*" are preceded, and connected with words of narrower import they
will be confined to property *ejusdem generis* with those previously described. Mr. McDonald, to meet this difficulty, contended that the word 'plant' used in the conveyance included

stock in trade and goods manufactured or in the course of manufacture on the premises. I cannot concur with him. 'Plant', when used in reference to a manufactory was probably applied in the first instance only to such apparatus or machinery as was affixed to the premises, but a more extended meaning seems now to be given to the word, and the plant of a manufactory embraces all the apparatus or machinery, whether fixtures or otherwise, by means of which the business is carried on. I am therefore of opinion that the articles in the printed schedule annexed to the case did not pass to the claimants under the insolvent's conveyance to them.

In re O'MULLIN & JOHNSTONE.

H. & M. McDonald made a bill of sale of personal property, dated July 5th, 1876, conditioned for the payment of $400 on the 5th July, 1877, and became insolvent 24th April, 1877. On the 8th June, 1877, to avoid leaving the property on the premises as a lien for rent, which accrued on the 12th of June, the insolvent's assignee and the holder of the bill of sale, after each advertising a sale of the property to which the other objected, agreed that it should be sold, reserving the proceeds for the adjudication of the Court.

Held, that the holder of the bill of sale was entitled to the proceeds, which were less than the amount due him, but that the decree should be without costs as the controversy had arisen out of an asserted right to sell which did not exist in either party.

RITCHIE, E. J., delivered the judgment of the Court :—

This is a case submitted without pleadings. The case states that Johnstone obtained from H. & M. McDonald, hotel-keepers, a mortgage of all their household furniture for an advance of money to enable them to purchase it. The mortgage contained a proviso that it should become void on their paying him $400 with interest, in one year from its date, which was the 5th July, 1876.

On the 25th April, 1877, H. & M. McDonald became insolvent and on the 18th May following, O'Mullin having been appointed creditors' assignee, the assets of the insolvents were duly transferred to him. At the time of their insolvency they had a lease of the Hotel which contained the furniture, for one year, from the 12th June, 1876, at a rent of $450, payable half-

yearly; no rent was then in arrear and none would become
due till the end of the year.   On the 1st June, 1877, Johnston,
advertised the furniture for sale, claiming a right to do so
under his mortgage, and on the 3rd June O'Mullin advertised
it, claiming a right to sell it as the assignee of the McDonalds.
Each party protested against a sale by the other, when it was
mutually agreed between them that the property should be
sold on the 8th June, each reserving his right to claim the
proceeds of the sale, and none of it was removed from the
Hotel till about the time of the sale.   The proceeds of the sale
were $240.60 and the claims of the parties to this amount are
submitted for adjudication.

The mortgage conferred on Johnstone the title to the property in question subject to the McDonalds' right to redeem
by paying him the amount due, and his title was in no
respects affected by their insolvency, the assignee merely
acquiring the right to redeem ; and he had no more right
to dispose of the property than McDonalds would have had if
they had not become insolvent.   But, until the lapse of a year
from the date of the mortgage Johnstone had no right to sell.
If the McDonalds had sold the property before the insolvency
or O'Mullin had done so after it, Johnstone could at once have
brought an action for the recovery of the property or the proceeds of the sale; for by thus disposing of the property they
would have forfeited their right to the possession of it, which
they were otherwise entitled to under the mortgage.   O'Mullin
was bound to respect Johnstone's rights, and should either have
redeemed the property by paying the amount due on it, or
have sold the equity of redemption merely ; or he might have
allowed the matter to remain in in *statu quo* till the time
specified for its redemption.

It was argued that if neither Johnstone nor O'Mullin had
interfered with the property till the rent became due, and it
had remained in the hotel, the landlord could have distrained
for his rent.   It is enough to say that it did not so remain,
and until the rent fell due the landlord could have no lien
whatever on it.   Johnstone and the McDonalds, before the
insolvency of the latter, could have agreed that a sale of it
should take place, and subsequently to the insolvency Johnstone

and O'Mullin could do so, and on the sale and removal of the furniture, the landlord could not look to it for payment of rent which subsequently accrued. The only right which the landlord has is to distrain on whatever property is found on the premises at the time the rent falls due. There was no obligation on any of the parties to keep the property there till then to enable him to distrain upon it. I fail to see any ground whatever for the contention that under the insolvent act a *lien* is created in favor of the landlord for rent not due at the time of the insolvency; the controversy, however, in this case is not between the landlord or O'Mullin, acting on his behalf, and Johnstone, but between O'Mullin on behalf of the creditors of the McDonalds, generally, and Johnstone the latter is entitled to the proceeds of the property of which he was the owner. The decree will, however be without costs, as the controversy in the first instance arose out of the claim of a right to sell by each of the claimants, when at the time no right to sell existed in either, but the concurrence of both was then required to make a valid sale. Had there been a surplus after the payment of Johnstone's claim, O'Mullin would of course have been entitled to it.

THE QUEEN *v.* CUTLER AND OTHERS.

Matthew Walsh, by his will, directed that his real estate, after the death of his widow, should be sold, and the proceeds placed at interest, to remain and be a perpetual fund, and that when the principal and interest together with other donations which might happen should amount to £1000, the annual interest of said £1000 should be applied "for the purpose of aiding the inhabitants of the township of Guysboro' to maintain a free Grammar and English school in said township, or establish the same into an academy at the discretion of his trustees, for the benefit of said township." The testator died in 1822, his widow surviving him, after whose death the property was sold by the trustees, and an information was filed at the instance of the trustees of School Section No. 1, (which embraced the whole town of Guysboro, but constituted only one of nineteen school sections included in the township,) to obtain a decree requiring the defendants to pay the proceeds of the real estate to the relators to aid in the support of the County Academy and free Grammar and English School established in the town of Guysboro under the free school law. The court directed that the fund should be held

till it accumulated to the amount specified, and that the interest arising from it
should then be applied to the support of the County Academy, assuming that it
should continue, as it then was, free to all the inhabitants of the township.

The object of the Information filed in this case by the
Attorney General at the instance of Thomas Condon and others,
trustees of School Section No. One, of the county of Guysboro'
is to obtain the decree of this Court requiring the defendants,
as trustees under the will of Matthew Walsh, deceased, to pay
the proceeds of certain real estate in their hands or under their
control to the relators to aid in the support of the County
Academy and free Grammar and English School now established and in operation in the town of Guysboro.   The testator,
who fomerly resided in the township of Guysboro', by his last
will, bearing date the 26th May, 1818, disposed of his real
estate after the death of his widow to whom he had given the
use of it during her life, in these terms : that it should " be
sold at public auction, and the means arising from such sale "
after payment of his debts, " be placed at interest in some good
public fund and remain and continue forever at interest, and
be a perpetual fund, and when the principal and interest
together with other donations which might happen, should
amount to the sum of one thousand pounds, that then and not
till then the annual interest of the said thousand pounds
should be applied annually for the purpose of aiding the inhabitants of the township of Guysboro' to maintain a free
Grammar and English School in the said township, or establish
the same into an Academy, at the discretion of his said
trustees for the benefit and advantage of the rising generation
of said township."*

The testator died in the year 1822 and his widow has since
died, and, the real estate having been sold, the proceeds are
now held by Messrs Cutler & Hartshorne two of the respondents, the amount of which with an accumulation of interest is
about sixteen hundred dollars.   The relators contend that as
provision is now made by law for the maintenance of free

---

*These provisions are quoted not from the will, which the Reporters were unable
to obtain, but from deeds of the property in which they are recited.   As cited here
they seem to embody the terms of the codicil referred to in a subsequent para.
graph of the judgment.

schools throughout the province which may prevent the respondents from strictly and literally carrying out the testator's intentions in a manner they otherwise might have done, yet his wishes could be practically fulfilled by their applying the fund in maintaining and supporting the Academy, Grammar and English School in Guysboro'. The evidence shows that the township of Guysboro' includes within its limits eighteen school sections in addition to No. One, which, though it embraces the whole of the town of Guysboro', forms but a small portion of that township; that the Academy referred to has been in operation ten years, and was built with money assessed on Sec. No. One; admission to it is free to all the children of the county, sufficiently advanced to enter. There are preparatory and elementary schools connected with it, and there is no other institution of a like character in the county.

Though free schools are now established by law throughout the province, which was not the case when the testator made his will, it does not appear to me that this change would necessarily prevent the trustees from fulfilling the trusts of the will in accordance with the testator's intention, for his object was to assist the inhabitants of the township of Guysboro' in obtaining a higher class of school for their children; and as only a portion of the funds for the support of the public free schools is supplied from the provincial treasury, the remainder being payable by the inhabitants, which would be greater or less, according to the character of the school and the attainments of the teachers, a better school could be secured at less expense to the inhabitants by the application of these funds to that object.

By the codicil, the testator authorizes the application of the interest to the support of an academy, if the trustees should think fit; if, therefore, a difficulty exists as to applying it to the support of a school exclusively confined to the town of Guysboro', on account of the gift being made for the benefit of the whole township, the trustees should contribute the amount to the support of the academy which is open to all those whom the testator has designated as the objects of his bounty.

If this is not literally within the terms of the will, and the

10 a

doctrine of *c'y pres* is to be resorted to, that course must
be adopted as that which will as nearly as possible meet the
testator's views and carry out his wishes. It appears to me,
however, that in whatever way the fund is to be applied, there
is nothing to prevent the trustees from keeping it invested till
the amount shall reach £1000, either by the accumulation of
interest or other donations for the same object. This clearly
expressed intention of the testator must be respected, and
when the specified amount shall be attained, the interest and
profits arising therefrom will thereafter be applied by the
trustees towards the support of the Academy at Guysboro',
assuming that it shall continue free to all the inhabitants of
the township.

In re THE ESTATE OF JAMES W. ROOP.

The granting of administration *de bonis non* to the widow of the deceased was
appealed from by his daughter, on the ground that the administratrix had been
guilty of waste on the lands set off to her as dower. It appeared from Respondent's affidavit that, whether her acts amounted to waste or not, she considered
herself justified in the course she had pursued. *Held*, that as there was nothing
to indicate such dishonesty on the part of the widow as should preclude her from
all right to the administration, the Court could not control the discretion conferred by the act on the Judge of Probate.

The Court will not consider other grounds of appeal than those contained in the
statement filed in the registry of the Probate Court.

RITCHIE, E. J., delivered the judgment of the Court :—

The question involved in this case, which is an appeal from
the decision of the Judge of Probate at Digby, is, whether the
granting of administration *de bonis non* to the respondent as
the widow of the deceased, in preference to the appellant, his
daughter, was justifiable under the circumstances. The ground
of appeal is that the respondent was not entitled to administration inasmuch as she had been guilty of waste on the lands
set off to her as dower. There are indeed six grounds set out;
they all, however, resolve themselves into this one. Several

other objections were taken at the argument, but as, by the statute regulating appeals from the Probate Court, the appellant is required to file in the registry of that Court a statement of the grounds on which the appeal is sought, I am of opinion that I am precluded from considering any other. It appears from the evidence that James W. Roop, the husband of the respondent, died intestate in the year 1869, possessed of real and personal property of considerable amount, leaving the respondent, his widow, and two children, Christopher Roop and Catherine, wife of Timothy Titus. Administration was granted to Christopher who entered upon the duties of the office and took possession of the estate and effects of the deceased and collected debts due to him. After the real estate had been divided and the dower set off to the widow, Christopher died in June 1872, leaving the estate unsettled. At present the interest of the appellant and the respondent in the estate unadministered is equal, as Christopher left children, each being entitled to one third. The waste complained of as committed by the respondent consisted in taking away wood and timber from the dower lands beyond what was necessary for the use and consumption of the widow on the premises. The acts alleged against the respondent are more distinctly admitted by herself in her affidavit than testified to by any of the appellant's witnesses, who mostly speak from hearsay; and while she fully admits all the acts charged against her as waste, the inference to be drawn from her statement is that, though they should amount to waste and the heirs may be entitled to redress against her in consequence, she thought herself justified in the course she pursued. We have now to consider whether this conduct on the part of the respondent precluded the Judge of Probate from granting administration to her.

Our statute regulating the granting of administration of intestate estates, like that in force in England, declares that it shall be granted to the widow, or next of kin, or both as the Judge shall think fit. From the words of the act it would seem, to be left to the Judge's discretion to grant administration either to the wife or next of kin, but, under ordinary circumstances, a preference has always been given to the widow. See *Williams on Exrs.*, 414; *Dodd and Brooks' Practice of Court of Probate,*

409; *Stapleton* v. *Sherrard*, 1 Vern., 315; *Crooke et al.* v. *Watt*, 2 Vern., 125; and Sir John Nicholl, in *Webb* v. *Needham*, 1 Addams, 494, said, "administration may be granted to the wife or next of kin; at the same time it is well known that in practice, at least in modern times, the wife is preferred in this matter under ordinary circumstances." For good reasons she may unquestionably be passed over, and several such are given in the books. See *Dodd and Brooks*, 409; and independently of the reasons there assigned, if in this case the respondent had no interest in the unadministered estate, or her conduct had been so dishonest as to lead to the inference that the administration of the estate could not safely be entrusted to her, the Judge ought, in my opinion, to have given a preference to the next of kin; but, as the law has given a discretion to him in cases like the present, on appeal, it must I think be made clearly to appear that he has exercised it improperly before his decision is reversed.

Assuming that she had committed or permitted waste on the dower lands the heirs-at-law have their redress against her, and that, as well whether she be administratrix or not, for those lands are in no way affected by the administration; but it was contended that her conduct indicated such dishonesty on her part as to preclude her from all right to the administration and to require the judge to pass her by in favour of the appellant.

From her affidavit, however erroneous in law the view taken by her may have been, she seems honestly to have thought herself justified in the course she pursued. In the very sentence in which she says she has not committed waste on the dower lands, she says that she has merely disposed of sufficient wood thereon to aid in her support and to secure to her the daily necessaries of life, and that what wood was so cut, was cut with the sanction of Christopher Roop one of the heirs at law.

Under these circumstances I cannot say that the Judge of Probate was wrong in coming to the conclusion that such dishonesty has been manifested on the part of the respondent as to make it unsafe to entrust her with the administration, especially when it is borne in mind that she is required to give security for the faithful performance of her duties, and I think I cannot, therefore, in this case control the discretion conferred on him by the act and reverse his decree, but must discharge the appeal with costs.

SHERLOCK v. McLELLAN.

Crowe, as judgment creditor of the insolvent McLellan, filed a claim for the full amount of his judgment, stating that he held such judgment as security but could give no estimate of its value, and ranked on the insolvent estate for the full amount of the judgment. Previous to the insolvency he had assigned the judgment to McDonald & Witt, who acted as his solicitors in the filing of the claim. *Held*, that by claiming for the whole amount of the judgment without putting a value upon it as required by Section 60 of the Act, Crowe had practically abandoned his security, and McD. & W. could not succeed in the present application, which was for surplus proceeds on foreclosure and sale.

RITCHIE, E. J., delivered the judgment of the Court :—

McDonald & Witt, as assignees of a judgment of Jonathan Crowe against the defendant McLellan, ask for the proceeds of the sale of land under foreclosure in this suit remaining in the hands of the Receiver General of the Court, after paying the mortgagor his claim and a prior incumbrance held by one Fultz, whose application was unopposed. Johnstone & Bligh who hold a judgment subsequent to that of Crowe, resist the application on the ground that Crowe had forfeited his right and that of McDonald & Witt, by having filed a claim against the estate of McLellan, who became insolvent and made an assignment under the Insolvent Act of 1869, for the full amount due him on the judgment, without any deduction for or on account of it, and ranked on the estate as if he had no security whatever for the debt, and did not put a specific value on his judgment as the law required him to do if he intended to retain the security. The claim so filed set forth that the insolvent was indebted to the claimant in the sum of $580.18 for a judgment duly entered up against the insolvent, and that the claimant held as security the said judgment, of the value of which he could not give any estimate. The claim so made was sworn to and filed 25th March last. In making the claim the present applicants acted as the Solicitors of Crowe, though the assignment to them was made on the 1st March, and the assignment of McLellan under the Insolvent Act was made on the 9th of that month.

Under these circumstances can the present applicants succeed? Had Crowe himself been the applicant, and had no assignment of the judgment been made by him, there are facts stated in the affidavits which, independently of the question now before us, would have precluded him from succeeding.

If the judgment was, as the present applicants allege, assigned to them before the insolvency of McLellan, it is very remarkable that they should have recognized Crowe as the debtor and allowed him to swear that the insolvent was indebted to him in the amount of the judgment, whereby he was enabled to appear at the meeting of the creditors as a creditor of the estate and take part in their proceedings and vote and obtain the appointment of assignee, when, in truth and in fact, he was not a creditor at all,—in which capacity of assignee he possessed himself of certain property of the estate with which he subsequently absconded. If the assignment to the present applicants was made *bona fide*, and for a valuable consideration, the claim of Crowe on the estate of the insolvent must have been made on their account. But I cannot, in any aspect in which the case can be viewed, approve of the course which was pursued, and if, by that course, their rights have been compromised, they have themselves to blame, as what was done by Crowe was sanctioned by them, and we must conclude was done at their instance and for their benefit.

By the 60th section of the Insolvent Act of 1869 a creditor who holds a security for his debt is required in his claim to put a specified value on his security under oath, and the assignee, under the authority of the creditors, may either consent to his right to rank for such liability or to the retention of the lien by the creditor at such specified value, or he may require from him an assignment of such security at an advance of ten per cent. on the specified value, and in either of such cases the difference between the value at which the security is assumed and the amount of the claim shall be the amount for which the creditor shall rank and vote. This provision has been disregarded in the present case, for Crowe not only put no value on the judgment but he claimed for the whole debt and voted on it, and has treated the security as of no value. If such a course could be adopted and the creditor retain his lien it would always be pursued. If the creditor desires to retain the benefit of his security he has no alternative but to estimate and put a value on it and he practically abandons it by claiming for the whole amount of his debt independently of it. This has been done in the present case. I am of opinion, therefore, that the applicants for these surplus proceeds are not entitled to them, and I may add that the English Bankrupt Law does not allow a creditor who has a security for his debt to participate with the other creditors until he places himself on an equality by giving up his security for the benefit of the estate generally or allows for it by deducting the value from the amount of his debt, and a creditor who has a lien on property of the bankrupt, if he prove his debt and vote in the choice of assignee, &c., is concluded thereby and will be ordered to give up the property on which he has a lien. *Doria on Bankruptcy*, 752, citing *ex parte Solomon*. And in *Robson on Bankruptcy*, 313, it is laid down that a creditor shall not be allowed to prove his whole debt unless he gives up any security held by him.

The Rule *nisi* must be discharged with costs.

SIBLEY *v.* CHISHOLM, ET AL.

Matthew Chisholm mortgaged land to Archibald and James Chisholm, the former of whom assigned his interest to plaintiff, who brought suit to foreclose the mortgage against Matthew Chisholm alone. Subsequently the writ was amended by making Archibald and James Chisholm and John T. Smith defendants, the latter having taken an assignment of the mortgage from Archibald and James Chisholm subsequent to the assignment by Archibald Chisholm to plaintiff. *Held*, that Archibald Chisholm, having a separate interest, had a right to assign it to plaintiff; that although plaintiff could not sustain his suit as originally brought against the mortgagor alone, the writ, as amended, brought all the parties interested before the Court, and that although the ordinary course would have been to make Smith a co-plaintiff, yet as he denied plaintiff's rights under the assignment, he had been properly made a defendant.

RITCHIE, E. J., delivered the judgment of the Court:—

The plaintiff on the 6th February, 1873, commenced this suit, in the first instance against Matthew Chisholm alone, to foreclose his interest in a mortgage made by him to Archibald Chisholm and James Chisholm of the land described in the writ, conditioned for the repayment of the sum of $200 in five years, Archibald Chisholm having assigned to him his interest in the said mortgage for $100. Subsequently the writ was amended and Archibald and James Chisholm and John T. Smith were made defendants, Smith having taken an assignment of the mortgage from both the mortgagees subsequent to the assignment to the plaintiff by Archibald of his interest therein.

Smith denies the right of plaintiff to claim under an assignment from one of the mortgagees, and contends that nothing passed to him under it, that even if any right had been acquired by him under it, he was not in a position to institute a suit for the foreclosure of the mortgage, and that his only mode of asserting any claim is by allowing the foreclosure to take place at the instance of himself, and applying for a portion of the proceeds of the sale, if he can shew himself entitled to it. Mr. Smith, after the plaintiff had taken out the writ in this case, commenced proceedings to foreclose the mortgage under the assignment made to him by the two mortgagees. The present application is to set aside the plaintiff's writ and all proceedings under it.

There is nothing before me to indicate that the two mortgagees were not equally interested in the mortgage, and I can see no objection to one of them assigning his interest in it any more than there would be to any conveyance by a tenant in common of his estate. The case of *Richardson* v. *Younge*, L. R., 6 Ch. App., 481, recognizes the distinction between mortgagees who are co-trustees, and jointly interested as such, and mortgagees who have a several interest. Sir G. MELLISH, L. J., said: "Had the mortgagees not been trustees the case would have stood very differently, for they must almost of necessity have been entitled to some distinct interest in the mortgage moneys." In that case it was considered that the two mortgagees represented but one interest; here Archibald Chisholm, having a separate and individual interest, had a right to assign it. It might well be contended that the plaintiff could not sustain his suit as he originally brought it against Matthew Chisholm alone, without making Smith a party, but having brought him in with the two original mortgagees, all parties interested are now before the Court. Under ordinary circumstances the suit should have been brought by the plaintiff and Smith as co-plaintiff, but Smith denies the plaintiff's right to claim anything under his assignment, which he contends is inoperative. They could not on that account join as plaintiffs, being contesting parties, so that the plaintiff, in order to obtain payment of the amount due him had no alternative but to make him a defendant, and in this Court it is immaterial in which character he appears. All that the Court requires is that all persons materially interested in the matter of controversy should be made parties to the suit, either as plaintiffs or defendants; and, such being the case, there are no grounds for the application to set aside the writ and proceedings of the plaintiff, and I see no difficulty in so dealing with the case as to do justice to all the parties interested.

SILVER v. SILVER.

Plaintiff, the widow of Chas. S. Silver, was entitled to certain property, placed in trust among other things, for the payment of rents, &c. free from the control of her husband and not subject to his debts. She directed her trustees to pay over to her husband the income for certain years. Her husband was at that time in partnership with Wm. C. Silver, carrying on a business in Halifax which was conducted by Chas. S. Silver alone, Wm. C. Silver having withdrawn from the management of it, and taking no oversight of its affairs. When plaintiff directed the money to be paid to her husband she knew he was in embarrassed circumstances, and he had then and long before exhausted his capital and become indebted to the firm, his family being meanwhile supported from the funds of the firm. In those circumstances he had ordered the money paid over to him by his wife's trustees to be paid to creditors of the firm, and opened an account on the firm books, charging the firm and crediting Mrs. Silver with the money so paid. Chas. S. Silver died insolvent in 1870, when Wm. C. Silver first became aware of the course pursued by his co-partner. Plaintiff in this suit claimed from Wm. C. Silver, as surviving partner, the re-payment of the moneys so received by the firm and credited to her. *Held*, that Chas. S. Silver was not justified in crediting such moneys to plaintiff without her concurrence or that of Wm. C. Silver, and that the latter was not liable.

RITCHIE, E. J., delivered the judgment of the Court:—

This suit has been instituted by Elizabeth Silver, the widow of Charles S. Silver, against William C. Silver as the surviving partner of the firm of W. & C. Silver of which her husband was a partner. A case has been agreed upon, from which it appears that Mrs. Silver was entitled to certain property in her own right which was, previous to her marriage, placed in trust, among other things, for the payment to her during her lifetime of all the rents, issues and profits thereof. These were made payable to her on her own receipt alone without the concurrence of her intended husband, and exclusive of his *jus mariti*, and were declared to be so payable to her as an alimentary provision and not subject to her husband's debts.

Out of the annual profits of the trust fund so payable to her, she directed her trustees, by writing, to pay over certain sums to her husband or to his order, which sums, being the income for the years 1868 and 1869, were paid by her trustees under such directions into the Fore Street Warehouse Co. in London, and to Messrs Campbell in Glasgow, to the credit of Charles S. Silver. Charles S. Silver and William C. Silver carried on business in Halifax, under the style of "W. & C. Silver," which was conducted by the former alone, Wm. C. Silver having withdrawn from the mannagement of it, taking no oversight and possessing no knowledge of the transactions of the firm. At the time she directed the money to be paid to her husband, Mrs. Silver was aware that he was in embarrass-ed circumstances, and then, amd for a long time before, he had, without the consent of his co-partner, and in breach of their partnership agreement, exhausted his capital and become heavily indebted to the firm, his family and establishment being in the meanwhile entirely supported out of funds drawn from the firm. Having thus drawn upon the capital of his partner and being unable in consequence to remit money to Great Britain to pay accounts due by the firm, he ordered the money paid to him by his wife's trustees, to be paid over to the credit of the firm towards payment of such accounts, and at the same time entered in the books of the firm an account in the name of Mrs. C. S. Silver, charging the firm and crediting her with the money so paid. Besides these trust funds Mrs. Silver had stock in her own name in the Glace Bay Coal Mining Company, the dividends on which she was in the habit of ordering to be paid to her husband; two of these dividends so paid to him he charged the firm with in the same way.

Charles S. Silver died insolvent in the early part of the year 1870, when Wm. C. Silver, for the first time, became aware of the course which had been pursued by his co-partner, and of his want of good faith in the management of the business. Mrs. Chas. S. Silver in this suit claims from Wm. C. Silver re-payment of the monies so received by her late husband under her orders which have been by him paid into the firm. When Mrs. Silver directed the payment of the money to her husband no instructions were given to him, nor was there any understanding between them as to its application or use by him, and he received it in such a way as to give him the absolute control of it, and to make it his property to all intents and purposes, so that but for the entry made by him in the books of the firm, which entry was made without the direction, consent or knowledge of his wife, there could be no grounds whatever for her present claim. Chas. S. Silver could with propriety have applied this money to replace the funds which he had wrongfully taken from the business, and, inasmuch as those funds so taken were employed in the maintenance of his family, his wife, who was aware of his embarrassments, could have had no just grounds of complaint at that course having been adopted. In my view of the case, the money when paid to her husband by Mrs. Silver's directions without any condition or restriction, became his as much as if he had received it from a stranger who had been indebted to him, and he was but performing his duty by replacing with it the money he had taken from his co-partner, and he had no right to make his wife a creditor of the firm for the amount, especially without her knowledge or concurrence. Where money has been borrowed by one of several partners, the mere fact that it has been *bona fide* applied to the partnership purposes is not sufficient to render the firm liable to re-pay it where there has been no actual or implied authority to borrow, and there has been no ratification of the loan; *1 Lindley on Partnership*, 286. A firm can only be made liable for what is done by one of its members on the supposition that the act in question was authorized by the other members. *1 Lindley on Partnership*, 286. This money was not required for the general conduct of the business, but to make good a deficiency caused by Charles S. Silver, and he, as a partner, had no implied authority to borrow on the credit of the firm money which he should obtain on his own individual credit, to pay his own debt, or to raise or make good his own portion of the capital. See *Fisher* v. *Taylor*, 2 Hare, 218, and *Loyd* v. *Freshfield*, 2 C. & P., 333.

To make Wm. C. Silver liable to repay this money, we must arrive at the conclusion that it was a loan to the firm by Mrs. Silver, but we have no evidence whatever and no reason to suppose that she ever contemplated a loan when she authorized her husband to receive the money. Nothing of the kind is intimated, and the only inference to be drawn is that when she gave him the order to receive it she intended to put it at his sole disposal, and she has not, in my opinion, any right, legal or equitable, to claim money from Wm. C. Silver which she never lent or contemplated lending to the firm of W. & C. Silver, or in fact lending to any one, but which she gave to her husband to be at his own disposal, and he was not justified under these circumstances in crediting the money to her in the books of the firm without her concurrence, or that of Wm. C. Silver. See *Beresford* v. *Archbishop of Armagh*, 13 Sim., 643; *Carter* v. *Anderson*, 3 Sim., 370, and *Caton* v. *Rideout*, 1 Mac. & G., 603.

STEPHENS ET AL. *v.* WIER, ET AL.

Mitchell sold property to Dodge for $16,000, which plaintiffs purchased from Dodge for $20,000. The property was subject to a mortgage made by Mitchell to Davis, who assigned it to Sterling, and it was agreed between Dodge, Mitchell and the plaintiffs that Mitchell should take up the mortgage, and that plaintiffs should pay Dodge $5000, give him notes for $2000, and make a mortgage to Mitchell for the balance of $13,000, payable in instalments, for which notes were also given to Mitchell. In the mortgage made by plaintiff to Mitchell it was provided that the latter should pay off the mortgage made by him and assigned to Sterling, and that until it was paid off Mitchell should only receive from plaintiffs the difference between the interest due on their mortgage to him and the interest on Mitchell's mortgage assigned to Sterling, and that until Sterling's mortgage was paid plaintiffs should not be liable for anything but the difference between that mortgage and their mortgage to Mitchell. Defendants Wier and White obtained from Mitchell an assignment of plaintiffs' mortgage and notes as security for a debt, after which Mitchell became insolvent, defendant Graham becoming his assignee, and Sterling's mortgage was foreclosed, and the property sold. Wier and White obtained a resale on giving a bond to the assignee to bid the property up to $11,800. Wier and White purchased the property for $8520, and an action was brought on the bond, to which they pleaded that the balance had been credited to Mitchell, by agreement, on an account due White. Plaintiffs paid on the mortgage to Mitchell $2250 besides interest, and took up three notes for $750 each, when Wier and White commenced action against them to recover the amount of two other notes for $750 and $500 respectively. *Held*, that Wier and White should be restrained from further proceeding in the action to recover the amount of the notes, and from transferring the remaining notes, the difference between plaintiff's mortgage and the mortgage assigned to Sterling being more than covered by the amount paid by plaintiffs and the amount credited by Wier and White to Mitchell on the purchase at the Sheriff's sale under foreclosure.

RITCHIE, E. J., delivered the judgment of the Court:

This suit is brought by the plaintiffs, Alexander Stephens and Alexander Stephens the younger, against Joseph Wier and James White, James R. Graham assignee of the insolvent estate of Thomas Mitchell, and Wm. H. Neal, and Thomas M. Neal. The facts, as they at present appear, are that Mitchell sold certain property to one Dodge for $16,000 which Dodge subsequently sold to the plaintiff for $20,000, that the property was subject to a mortgage made by Mitchell to Davis, which mortgage it was agreed between Dodge, Mitchell and plaintiffs that Mitchell should pay and take up, (it was then held by Sterling to whom it had been assigned by Davis,) and it was also agreed between them that the $20,000, the price of the property, should be paid thus: that the plaintiffs should pay Dodge $5000 and give him notes for $2000, and should give Mitchell a mortgage for the balance, $13,000, the payment of the $13,000 to be made by instalments extending over a period of ten or twelve years. The amount was also secured by the plaintiffs' promissory notes for the amount of the several instalments and interest. Mitchell never did pay off the mortgage held by Sterling, but it was allowed to remain with plaintiffs' consent on his engaging to keep the interest paid, which he did not do.

The mortgage to Mitchell provided that he should obtain a release of Sterling's mortgage, and that, while any interest should remain due thereon, Mitchell should only be entitled to receive from the plaintiffs the difference between the amount so due for interest on that mortgage, and the amount due for interest on their mortgage to him, and that until the mortgage to Sterling should be paid and a release thereof obtained and recorded, the plaintiff should not be called upon or liable to pay any more than the difference between the amount due on the mortgage to Mitchell, and that due on the mortgage to Sterling. The defendants Wier and White obtained from Mitchell an assignment of the plaintiffs' mortgage and notes as collateral security for a debt due them.

Mitchell became insolvent and the defendant Graham became his assignee; neither Mitchell nor his assignee, nor Wier and White, paid the amount of Sterling's mortgage, nor did they keep down the interest, and in consequence he foreclosed. On a sale by the Sheriff under the order of foreclosure the property was knocked down to the defendant Graham for $8,300, but a resale was subsequently ordered on condition that the said Wier and White should undertake to bid the property up to $11,300 and give a bond to Graham to that effect. The bond was given, and the property was resold, when it was purchased by Wier and White for $8,520, being $2780 less than they had undertaken to bid.

An action has been brought on this bond at the instance of the plaintiffs in the name of Graham, and the defendants have pleaded that Mitchell owed White and that it had been arrang-ed between Graham, Wier and White, that the estate of

Mitchell should be credited in account with White, with the full amount for which they undertook to bid in the property, less the amount due on Sterling's Mortgage. The plaintiffs have paid on their mortgage to Mitchell the sum of $2,250 principal and $1102.50 interest, and have taken up three of the notes given by them to Mitchell for $750 each, and Wier and White have commenced an action against the plaintiffs for the recovery of two of the remaining notes, one for $750 and the other for $500. The plaintiffs have obtained a rule *nisi*, calling on the defendants Wier and White to show cause why they should not be restrained from further proceedings in the action at common law, brought by them for the recovery of the amount of the two notes, and why they should not be enjoined from assigning and transferring the other promissory notes of the plaintiffs, now held by them. The only question at present before the Court is whether, under the circumstances above detailed, the defendants Wier and White should be enjoined from proceeding at law for the recovery of the two notes now in suit, and from assigning or transferring the remainder of the notes in their possession; and this involves the question, whether the plaintiffs have or have not already paid the amount due by them on their mortgage to Mitchell. As between the plaintiffs and Mitchell, and Wier and White, the assignees of of his mortgage, the matter stands thus :

Amount due by plaintiff on his purchase	$13,000
Less the amount of Sterling's mortgage	8,000
	$5,000
Plaintiffs have paid, in addition to interest, on principal	2,250
	$2,750

The property sold under foreclosure brought, beyond the amount due on Sterling's mortgage, $2,800, so that, assuming the estate of Mitchell to be entitled to credit for that amount as the defendants Wier and White claim, the plaintiffs have overpaid their mortgage to the extent of $50 and that, too, long before the instalments became due under the terms of the mortgage, and I have not taken into account the discount to which they may be entitled by such anticipated payments.

Without expressing an opinion in this stage of the case, whether the plaintiffs or Wier and White are entitled to the surplus proceeds of the land sold under foreclosure, as the latter claim them and assert that they have received credit for them from Graham, the assignee of Mitchell, it is against equity and good conscience that they should insist on retaining them and also persevere in the suit on the notes, and that they should assign or transfer the notes now held by them. I think, therefore, that the injunction should issue as prayed for.

As regards the notes in suit I do not see how there can be anything due on them. The holders of them stand in no better position with respect to them than Mitchell would if he were still the holder of them. The plaintiffs have been forced to pay the amount due Sterling, or rather their property has been taken to pay what should have been paid by Mitchell or Wier and White, and surely they are entitled to credit on their mortgage and notes, and of course on those notes first falling due, including those in suit, for what has been so paid. The question of costs is reserved.

STEPHENS *v.* TWINING ET AL.

Thomas and John Archibald mortgaged to plaintiff two third parts of several lots of ungranted crown lands applied for and paid for by Ellershausen and others the right to receive which was by them transferred to the St. Croix Manufacturing Company, (said Archibalds having become interested therein to the extent of two third parts.) Before the grants were taken out the Archibalds became insolvent, and defendants, as trustees for the creditors, procured said grants of land based on the original application, but they selected the lots in localities somewhat different from those indicated in such application. *Held*, that plaintiff had a lien on two-thirds of the land comprised in the grants for the debt intended to be secured by the mortgage, and that an order must pass that the amount thereof should be paid to him, otherwise said two thirds of the land to be sold to satisfy plaintiff's claim.

RITCHIE, E. J., delivered the judgment of the Court :—

The claim of the plaintiff in this suit is founded on a mortgage made to him by Thomas Archibald and John Archibald, dated 15th February, 1867, whereby, among other property, they conveyed to him what is now in controversy, in these words : " two third parts of all those several lots of ungrant- ed lands applied for and paid for at the Crown Land Office by Stephen Krackenweizer, Adolph Guzman, and Francis Ellers- hausen, amounting to 4000 acres on or near the St. Croix River and Panuke Lakes; the right or title to receive grants of such lands having been secured by the said Francis Ellers- hausen from the Crown and from the said Stephen Kracken- weizer and Adolph Guzman, and by said Francis Ellershausen transferred to the St. Croix Manufacturing Company, (the said Archibalds having become interested therein to the extent. of two third parts,) which mortgage was subject to a proviso. that it should become void on payment of $3,101.25 and interest by two equal instalments at nine and fifteen months. after the date thereof."

The applications of Krackenweizer, Guzman and Ellershausen had been made in July and August, 1865, and $1320, the price of the land, was then paid by them under Chap. 26, Revised Statutes, (3rd Ser.,) whereby it is enacted, " that the Governor in Council may settle the price of Crown Land, and the mode of making application therefor, and that any person, upon due application to the Commissioner of Crown Lands, may become the purchaser upon making immediate payment therefor to the Receiver General."

On or about the 4th of October, 1867, the Messrs. Archibald became insolvent, and assigned all their real and personal estate to E. C. Twining, Chas. J. Wylde, and J. B. Campbell, in trust for the benefit of their creditors, all of whom accepted the trust, but Campbell has departed this life since the com- mencement of the suit.

At the time of the insolvency and assignment the grant which had been applied for had not been taken out, and the assignees assumed the right, under the general assignment made to them, to have the lands granted to them, and they applied for and obtained four grants, dated severally the 19th. October, 1868, comprising 2278 acres, they having, with the permission of the Commissioner of Crown Lands, selected the

10 b

lands to be comprised in the grants, two lots in the County of
Hants, one in the County of Halifax, and one in the County
of Lunenburg. These lots were selected in somewhat different
localities from those indicated in the original applications, but
the application of the assignees for the grants and the selection of the lands were based on the original applications, and
the money paid for the lands so granted was the money paid
in on such original applications, and the defendants, E. C.
Twining and C. J. Wylde, now claim that the money so paid
passed to them under their assignment as well as the right to
obtain the grants on account of which it was paid and to hold
the land, &c., granted, for the benefit of the creditors of the
Archibalds, unaffected and unencumbered by the mortgage
held by the plaintiff. The portion of the money so appropriated was $1002.32.

The plaintiff by his writ claims to have been interested in
two-thirds of the money so appropriated by the assignees, as
well as in two-thirds of the balance of the $1320; and he
claims that the lands comprised in the grants obtained by
them should be held subject to the mortgage. He prays that
the assignees may be declared to hold two-thirds thereof as
trustees for him, to the extent of the amount due on his mortgage, and that they do pay him the amount of principal and
interest due thereon, and, in default thereof, that a decree of
foreclosure do pass, and the lands be sold and the proceeds
applied to the payment of the mortgage and costs; and that
the balance of the money paid to the Commissioner of Crown
Lands, amounting to $317.68, and the right of pre-emption of
land secured thereby be declared subject to the plaintiff's
mortgage.

The defendants Twining and Wylde, by their pleas, admit
that their application for the grants in question was made by
them, not in their own interest, but as assignees, and acting
for the benefit of the creditors of T. & J. Archibald, in the
belief that the money which had been originally paid for the
purpose of obtaining grants of land belonged to the estate of
the Archibalds, and they appropriated a portion of it in payment for *the lands applied for by them which they caused to be
surveyed and run out and granted to them in different localities*

*from those specified by the original applicants in their appli-
cations,* and in ignorance of the claim of the plaintiff under
his mortgage. The other statements in the pleas are either
irrelevant or unsubstantiated by proof.

These defendants, according to their own shewing, occupy
the position which the Archibalds would have done but for
the assignment. They do not pretend that they made the
application for the grants independently of those which had
been previously made; and Twining, one of defendants, says
truly in his affidavit, "that they would not have been justified in speculating with the funds of the creditors in purchasing lands from the Government, and that they had in fact no
funds for that purpose, but they felt themselves authorized to
apply and take out grants for the benefit of the creditors,
which had been paid for by the insolvents."

That they had the right of doing so cannot, I think, be
questioned, for the plaintiff could only claim a right to a lien
on the lands as a security for his debts; and as it would not
have been in contravention of his rights for the Archibalds to
have taken out grants in their own name before the assignment, so, after it, their assignees would have the right to
have the land surveyed and granted to them, and the money
deposited in payment applied to that purpose, but whether
this was done by the one or the other it could only be done
subject to the rights of the plaintiff under his mortgage.

For the Archibalds to have attempted to evade the effect of
their mortgage by applying to the Commissioner of Crown
Lands for permission to take up lands in other localities than
those indicated in the original applications and appropriate
the money in payment of those, and then contend that the
mortgage did not apply to such lands, would have been a fraud
on the plaintiff, and as I think the Archibalds could not do
this, so I think their assignees could not without violating the
rights of the plaintiff.

Under an application to the Commissioner of Crown Lands
for a grant of lands, and on the payment of the price required
by the Government, the applicant does, in my opinion, acquire
rights under the act I have referred to, not that he would
thereby be necessarily entitled to a grant, for there might be

good reasons which would justify the Government in with-
holding it, but I cannot bring myself to the conclusion that, as
contended in the argument, he has no right, legal or equitable,
and that after a due application and payment of the purchase
money, the Commissioner of Crown Lands can arbitrarily
prefer a subsequent applicant. The whole scope and terms of
the act lead me to the inference that the Legislature intended
that, as between subject and subject, a right of pre-emption
should be acquired by the first applicant who had fulfilled all
the requirements of the law; and, in the present case, whatever
the rights of the Archibalds were to the grants, or to the
money paid in as the price of the lands, those rights were
pledged to the plaintiffs before their assignment to defendant.

Passing for a moment from the claim of the plaintiff under
his mortgage, what is the nature of that set up by the defendants to these funds and to the lands purchased with them ?
They hold a general assignment from the Archibalds, having
no special reference either to the money or the lands. Upon
what principle can they seek to take those from another party
to whom they had been previously and specifically assigned,
certainly more specifically than to them, as a security for a
debt, the justness of which is not called in question, nor is the
bona fides of the mortgage. How is theirs a preferable title ?
They could take no more than the Archibalds had to give them,
and if the latter would have been estopped from denying the
rights of the plaintiff under his mortgage, so are their assignees.

If it were necessary to refer to any authority to show that
the assignees under a general assignment can only take such
rights as the assignor or debtor held at the time of the assignment, and subject to all previously existing rights and leins,
see *Smith's Equity,* 570' (Eng. Ed.) ; *Story on Equity,* §1038.

The plaintiff having a lien on two thirds of the lands comprised in the said grants for the debt due him and intended to
be secured by the said mortgage, an order will pass in case
the amount thereof is not paid to him by the said defendants,
E. C. Twining and C. J. Wylde, the assignees of T. & J.
Archibald, that the said two thirds of the said lands be sold,

and that out of the proceeds the amount due the plaintiff for principal, interest and costs be paid to the said defendants.

In case there should be any dispute as to the amount due on the mortgage reference will be made to a Master to settle the amount.

THOMSON v. LONGARD.

Plaintiff brought suit to compel the performance by defendant of a contract in writing for the purchase of a house. During the negotiations defendant asked expressly as to the drainage, which plaintiff assured him was perfect, but which in fact was seriously defective. It appeared that the representations had been made by the plaintiff in good faith and in ignorance of the facts, and the house being occupied defendant could not inspect it for himself. Nothing was said about the matter in the written contract. *Held*, that in the suit for specific performance the verbal representations made previous to the written contract must be taken into consideration, and that, being material representations on the faith of which defendant entered into the contract, they constituted a defence, although plaintiff did not know them to be untrue.

RITCHIE, E. J., delivered the judgment of the Court :—

The plaintiff seeks the specific performance of a contract in writing entered into by the defendant on the 1st Feb'y, 1873, who thereby agreed to purchase from him a house and premises on the south side of Victoria Road in this city, for the sum of $4,085, of which $50 was then paid on account, possession to be given on the delivery of the deed. The defendant admits that he entered into the contract, but he alleges that he was induced to do so by the assurances of the plaintiff that the drainage of the house and premises was good and in perfect order, that the water-closet and cesspool were perfect and complete in every respect, and the house itself in a healthy condition; that he plainly and distinctly gave the plaintiff to understand that he would not entertain any proposition for the purchase of the house except on that basis, and that, having received this assurance from the plaintiff, and relying thereon, he agreed to become the purchaser; that when the agreement was entered into, the house was occupied, and the defendant was, on that account, unable to

make for himself a personal examination of the premises, and
subsequently when it became unoccupied, on his examination
of it, he found that there was no drainage, that the cesspool
was overflowing, and underneath the floors of the house a mass
of filth and dirt from the water closet had accumulated, from
which a most pestiferous stench arose, whereby the house was
rendered unhealthy and unfit for habitation, and finding this
to be the case he abandoned the purchase and gave the plaintiff
notice that he rescinded the contract in consequence, and he
goes on to allege that he was induced to enter into the said
agreement through fraud, misrepresentation and deceit on the
part of the plaintiff.

The evidence, I think, establishes all that the defendant
alleges with respect to the state of the house and drains, from
whatever cause it may have been occasioned. Testimony of
the most unexceptionable character shows this to have been the
case, and that the house in its then state could not have been
inhabited without great discomfort and risk of health, and if
the stipulations alleged to have been made had been contained in the written contract the plaintiff would have had no right
to the relief he seeks. But he contends in the first place, that
he never made the representations attributed to him and that
the contract was not made on the faith of any such representations, and, in the next, that, even if they had been made, the
defendant is now confined to his written agreement and cannot insist on anything not contained in it. It is, I think,
sufficiently apparent from the evidence that no fraudulent or
wilfully false representation was made by the plaintiff to the
defendant in respect to the state of the house or the drainage,—
they may have been in the state described without his knowledge. He testifies himself to his ignorance on the subject,
and none of the evidence adduced leads to a contrary conclusion.
Yet though the written contract is silent on this subject, the
court will not decree a specific performance of it if the defendant was induced to enter into it on the representations of
the plaintiff which turned out to be false, though he may not
have known them to be so, if so material that the defendant
would not otherwise have made the purchase.

It is evident from the testimony of both plaintiff and defendant that the latter considered the state of the drains and the drainage of the house a very important element in the negotiation, on which subject he was ignorant and was not in a position to acquire full and satisfactory information for himself before the making of the contract, and it was a subject on which the plaintiff would be supposed by the defendant to be possessed of the requisite knowledge.

To support the defendant's case the representations of the plaintiff must not only have been material and such as induced him to enter into the contract, but must have been explicit and distinct, and not vague and uncertain or merely expressing an opinion which he really entertained, though erroneously.

The only evidence we have on this point is that of the plaintiff and defendant, and the father of the latter. The defendant states that the plaintiff, in reply to particular enquiries, guaranteed the house to be in a perfect state of repair and condition, that he asked him particularly in reference to the drains and he said they were perfect, and there never had been any trouble; that on a second occasion on the day he visited the house with his father, the plaintiff repeated the same thing in the presence of his father, who asked him particularly with regard to the drains. He then replied, they were perfect, there could be no trouble, every thing was in perfect working order, and there could be no trouble, or words to that effect; that defendant saw no way of examining the drains, and did not do so because the house was occupied, that he was induced to purchase on these representations, and that, but for them, he would have had nothing to do with the house, and that as soon as he discovered the state of the house and drain, he refused to carry out the agreement and notified the plaintiff to that effect, and it was not till the 14th May that plaintiff tendered him a deed of the property. On his cross-examination he said, with reference to what he had before stated, that "there never had been any trouble or could be any trouble", or words to that effect, and again, "the plaintiff did not decline giving me every opportunity of seeing the house but spoke of the tenants being there as an excuse; I understood I could not have a full examination then, but at the same time he gave me his word it was all right for what I could not see; I asked the plaintiff what the drainage was like, he said it was perfect. I did not ask him further."

Mr. John Longard confirms in all essential particulars the evidence of his son as to the plaintiff's representations respecting the drains.

The plaintiff was examined both before the testimony on the part of the defendant had been taken and after, so that a full opportunity was afforded him of contradicting the statements made by the defendant, but after the most careful perusal of his testimony I can see no material contradiction. His testimony leads to the inference that he knew of no defect in the drains &c., he admits he was asked about the drainage but he does not deny that he made the statements attributed to him by the defendant and his father. He said he knew of no defect about the premises or drainage whatever; had he known of them he would have told him. The effect of his testimony is not so much a denial of the statements made by the defendant as a statement on his part that, believing the drains, &c. to be in good order, what he did say he believed to be true, and it was said in good faith and with no intention of misleading the defendant. On his first examination his words on this subject are, "I gave the defendant all the information I possessed with regard to the premises;" "as far as I knew the house was in good habitable condition when I agreed to sell it to the defendant;" "defendant and his father were with me when the premises were examined, we did not at that time examine the drains, we might have examined them, we must have taken up the floors to do so." "About a fortnight after the agreement the defendant complained about the drainage; he said he would rather not have anything more to do with the property, and asked me if I knew there was anything the matter with the drain; I said I did not know." On his examination after the evidence on the part of the defendant had been taken, when the object of again calling him must have been to give him an opportunity of contradicting or explaining the defendant's evidence, he said, "the defendant did not give me to understand that he would not purchase without a garantee as to the drains; I knew of no defects about the drainage, cesspool, pipes or water closets; had I known of them I would have told him; I knew of no defect in the premises whatever; and at the time the house was sold I did not know in what state the cesspool was; I was asked about the drainage by the defendant and his father, also where the cesspool was; I shewed where it was; I concealed nothing and gave them all the information I could; I did not know at the time that there was a bad smell in the house. It was not till after the auction," (of the furniture, about 10th February), "that I discovered the state the house was in; somewhere about the middle of February I had the house cleaned out."

There was in this evidence no denial of the representations said to have been made by him, and if they could have been denied it should have been given distinctly and unequivocally; but nothing is more probable than that the plaintiff, believing, as he says he did, every thing connected with the drainage to be in perfect order, should have said so. If then we are to assume, as I think we must from the evidence of the defendant, uncontradicted by the plaintiff, that he did make material representations on which the former was induced to enter into the contract, and those representations turned out to be untrue, the only questions are whether they can be taken into consideration, having been made verbally previous to the execution of the contract and not alluded to in it, and whether the representations, having been made by the plaintiff in the belief at the time that they were true, deprive him of the relief he seeks, of having the contract specifically performed.

On the first point no doubt, I think, can be entertained, and the principle is so clearly established that this Court will refuse to interfere in enforcing specific performance of a contract where a misrepresentation is made by one of the parties to the other at the instance of the party by whom the representation is made, that I need only refer to *Fry on Specific Performance*, Sec. 425, &c., and the numerous cases referred to in that and the succeeding sections. As regards the second, I think the law is equally well established in *Fry on Specific Performance*, Sec. 431. In equity it furnishes a good defence to a suit for a specific performance that the plaintiff made a representation which was not true, though without a knowledge of its untruthfulness and though the mistake be inno-

cent, for a man before making a representation ought not
only not to know it to be untrue but he ought to know it to
be true, and in *Smith's Manual of Equity Jurisprudence,* 59,
speaking of setting aside contracts, (and something less will
suffice to prevent the Court interfering in the case of specific
performance,—see *Fry*, Sec. 427,) it is laid down that misrepresentation is a ground of relief whether the party who made
the assertion or intimation knew it to be false, or made it
without knowing whether it was true or false.   See *Story*, Sec.
193; *Pulsford* v. *Richards* 17, Bea., 95 ; *Rawlins* v. *Wickham,*
1 Giffard, 355 ; *Reese River Silver Mining Company* v. *Smith,*
L. R.; 4 H. L., 64.   In the last mentioned case Lord CAIRNS
said : " I apprehend it to be the rule of law that if persons
take upon themselves to make assertions as to which they are
ignorant, whether they are true or untrue they must, in a civil
point of view be held to be responsible as if they had asserted
that which they knew to be untrue."   And I know of no case
where the rule would with more propriety be applied than this,
where the the owner of the house, who would be assumed by
the intending purchaser to know the state of the premises,
makes representations to him regarding important particulars
concealed from view and of which the purchaser professes
himself to be and is ignorant, on the faith of which he enters
into the contract.   I think therefore that the plaintiff has not
made out a case for specific performance, and his suit must
therefore be dismissed with costs.

TROOP *v.* BONNETT et al.

Plaintiff, as assignee of E. W. Chipman, under the Insolvent Act, obtained an
order to restrain the Sheriff of Annapolis from selling under execution personal
property of the insolvent, which he claimed had passed to him under the assignment, said property having been allowed by the assignee to remain in the hands
of the insolvent, who had removed it to Annapolis, where it was levied upon.
Held, that as the remedy of the assignee by action at law, assuming the levy and
proposed sale to be unjustifiable, was complete, the restraining order must be
discharged.

RITCHIE, E. J., delivered the judgment of the Court:—

The plaintiff in this suit is the assignee of Edward W. Chipman, an Insolvent, and has obtained an order restraining the defendants from selling certain property which he claims to belong to him under Chipman's Assignment; this property has been levied on and was advertised for sale by Bonnett, the Sheriff of Annapolis, one of the defendants, at the suits of Vose and Campbell, the other defendants, against Chipman, in whose possession the plaintiff has allowed it to remain from the time of the assignment in March 1874, to the present time. The defendants seek to have this order discharged, contending that the writ discloses no equitable ground for relief to entitle the plaintiff to resort to this court; that the plaintiff, if he ever had any right to claim the property, has waived or forfeited it by abandoning it to the insolvent, that an injunction will not in any case be granted to stop a sale under an execution, and that under no circumstances will this Court interfere by injunction unless to prevent irreparable injury.

In cases of injunction the jurisdiction of this Court is not confined to the protection of equitable rights, but extends to the protection of legal rights to property from loss or damage pending litigation. The Court does not in such cases profess to determine the legal rights, yet the suitor, to entitle himself to the writ, must shew not only a right to the property but also that he needs the aid of the Court for its protection till the right is established. The plaintiff here has shown a sufficient *prima facie* right to the property in question, but has, I think, failed to make it appear that if this Court should not interfere serious if not irreparable loss or injury will be sustained by him. The property in dispute consists principally of household furniture of the estimated value of $685; this the assignee, instead of taking possession of and selling as he should have done, allowed to remain in the insolvent's possession and use, and to be removed from Halifax, where he resided when the insolvency took place, to Annapolis where he now resides. In this a wrong would seem to have been done to the creditors, who, under the Insolvent Act, have a right to expect the assignee *at once* to take possession of the

Insolvent's property and to proceed *promptly* to render it available for the payment of their debts; and the plaintiff, not having done this, may have been guilty of a dereliction of duty, but he is not thereby deprived of his legal right to the property, which would in effect be depriving the creditors generally of their rights to have it applied to the payment of their debts. If the assignee has failed in the performance of his duty and the creditors are thereby injured they have ample means of redress, but, as a sale must take place whether the property belongs to the assignee or is liable to seizure under the defendants' executions, it is not very material by which of the parties the sale is effected, the Assignee or the Sheriff; the important matter is, who will be entitled to the proceeds. If therefore this suit had not been brought and the sale had taken place the remedy would have been by an action at law, in which the full value of the property would be recoverable. The assignee had therefore a full and complete remedy at law if his rights had been improperly invaded by the levy and sale, and therefore all claim to the interference of this Court by injunction on the ground of irreparable or serious injury or loss to the plaintiff by the defendants' act fails.

It must not, however, be inferred that under certain circumstances this Court might not interfere to prevent the sale of of property by the Sheriff, though the party seeking its interference might have a right of action at law, as, for instance, where household furniture of " A " is improperly levied on and taken by the Sheriff under an execution against " B." There the suddenly depriving a party of the whole of his furniture might inflict such an injury and occasion such suffering to his family as that damages in an action at law would afford a very inadequate compensation. It is not necessary that the injury should be actually irreparable to entitle a party to this remedy but it must be of a serious character, and if it be so, though he may have a remedy at law, he may, notwithstanding, obtain an injunction if he can shew that the remedy is not full and complete. A full and complete remedy at law did exist by replevin where goods other than those of the defendant against whom the execution issued had been levied, but that remedy has been taken away by a late act, the policy of which may well be doubted.

That this Court has power, on a proper case being made, to stay a sale under an execution is unquestionable and it is con. stantly exercised, and there can be no reason why it should not be exercised to enjoin parties from interfering with the property of an insolvent estate; but an assignee must estab. lish his right to have it exercised on his behalf on the same principles as any other suitor.

It is not for me to express any opinion on the respective claims of the parties to this property; my province is merely to say whether the plaintiff is entitled to maintain the restrain. ing order or not. I think he is not, on the ground that he had a full and complete remedy at law. The order must therefore be discharged and I see no reason why the defendants should not have their costs.

TROOP v. MOSIER ET AL.

Plaintiff, a member of the firm of Black Bros. & Co., took a mortgage of a vessel which was given by defendants for outfits supplied by that firm, and a policy of insurance was effected to secure the payment for the outfits. The vessel was lost and plaintiff received the insurance, which he credited in account with one Mal. colm, to whom he had agreed to sell 35/64 shares in the vessel. *Held*, that the amount received from the insurers must go to the credit of the mortgage.

RITCHIE, E. J., delivered the judgment of the Court:—

This action is brought on a covenant in a mortgage of a vessel, and on the part of the defendants it is contended that the mortgage was given by them and others, the then owners of the vessel, to the plaintiff, a member of the firm of Black Bros. & Co., for advances made by them for her outfit, and that to secure them in case of her loss she was insured, and by the policy the loss was made payable to them; this course was adopted as soon as the outfits were obtained. The vessel was subsequently lost and the plaintiff received the amount insured on her, and he contends that he was not obliged to credit the amount so received in the account for outfits and he has credited it in account with Thomas A. Malcolm.

It appears that after the giving of the mortgage the plaintiff purchased from one of the owners 36 / 64 shares in the vessel; these he subsequently agreed to sell to Malcolm. The price was not paid and no title was given to him, but he entered into possession and sailed her with the other owners, and acted as ship's husband. The evidence clearly establishes that the mortgage was given for outfits and that the insurance was effected to secure them, and this course was adopted as soon as that debt was contracted; and there is no evidence whatever to lead to the inference that the insurance was solely for the benefit of Malcolm and on his interest in the vessel, in which case alone could the amount received be placed to his credit in his individual account with the plaintiff.

The insurance was effected with one object from the first; it was upon the whole vessel for the benefit of all the owners, and the object of all of them was to secure Black Bros. & Co. in case of the loss of the vessel before the mortgage was paid. Under these circumstances the amount received from the Insurers must go to the credit of the mortgage, and it must be referred to a master to ascertain what amount, if any, is still due on that account.

VERNON ET AL. *v.* SEAMAN.

Provision in a will that defendant should hold land, &c. in trust to cultivate, demise, let and manage the same to the best advantage for testator's daughter, without impeachment of waste, held not to exonerate the trustee from responsibility for wasting the trust property, but simply to empower him to do "such acts as he could do if a tenant who was not accountable for waste."

Held, further, that the trustee under such devise was not obliged to work a mill on the trust property; and that if the trustee was unable to procure a suitable tenant, he ought not to be held answerable for the unproductiveness of the property.

Held, further, that the defendant, in selling the grass uncut at auction, instead of making it into hay and storing or disposing of it as such, had pursued a course which, he was, under the circumstances, at liberty to adopt.

RITCHIE, E. J., delivered the judgment of the Court:—

The writ in this case sets out that a share in the estate of the late Amos Seaman had been devised to the defendant in trust for his daughter Mary Vernon, one of the plaintiffs, to enter upon the several premises in such share, and to work, cultivate, demise, let and manage the same to the best advantage, without impeachment of waste, and the rents, issues, products, profits, and emoluments thereon arising, to collect and receive, and, after reimbursing himself for any necessary charges, and deducting therefrom an adequate allowance for his own time and oversight, to apply the remainder of such rents, &c., and to pay the same to the plaintiff for the use of the said Mary Vernon during their joint lives, and for the survivor during his or her life, which trust he accepted and entered upon, and undertook the management and control of the trust property, but did not faithfully fulfil the trusts reposed in him, having received large sums of money in respect thereof which he failed to pay to the plaintiffs or to account for, and so mismanaged the business of the trust that large sums of money were lost by his negligence and mismanagement, and that he wilfully allowed the lands and tenements to remain unoccupied and unproductive, and wilfully allowed a valuable mill and buildings and a shipyard and other valueable property embraced within the trust to be dismantled and go to ruin, and certain of the lands to lie waste and unenclosed, and in other respects abused the trust reposed in him; and the writ prayed that the defendant might be removed from the trust and a proper person appointed in his place, and that he should account for the amounts which had been received under the trust, and what, but for his wilful and negligent default, might have been received, and that an account might be taken of the waste, conversion and destruction which the defendant had committed or allowed on the trust estate, and that he might be decreed to make reparation and compensation.

The defendant in his answer has denied all the allegations and charges made by the plaintiffs of negligence, conversion, waste and improper conduct, or breach of trust while the property was under his control and management, and has asserted that he used and managed it and took the same care and control of it as a careful owner would have done of his own property, and was guilty of no wilful default in respect of any of the matters alleged. He relied also on a clause of the testator's will which exonerated him from responsibility for any loss or damage which might arise in or about the execution of the trust without his wilful default. He also asserted that he accepted the trust on the stipulation made by him, and agreed upon by the plaintiffs, that he should not be liable or held accountable for any negligence in the execution of the trust, the duties of which they undertook themselves to perform, and that for a large portion of the time which has elapsed since the death of Mr. Seaman, the property has been in their possession and under their sole management and control. The defendant also alleges that he has always been ready and willing to account with the plaintiffs, and is willing and anxious to be relieved from the trust.

Before considering the question whether there has been a breach of the trust in this case, it is proper to advert to some of the positions taken by the defendant, whereby he seeks to relieve himself from responsibility, even if the trusts have not been carried out.

With respect to the alleged agreement that the defendant accepted the trust on the express stipulation and agreement that the plaintiffs themselves were to manage the trust property, and the defendant was to have no trouble or responsibility in connection with it, I need only say that if such an agreement had been entered into, and effect were to be given to it as contended for by the defendant, there would practically be no acceptance of the trust. But without passing any opinion upon the effect of such an agreement, the defendant, though he allowed the plaintiffs in the first instance to manage the trust property as they saw fit, asserted his right as trustee to assume the management and control of it, and did so in opposition to the wishes of the plaintiffs, and it is only for alleged acts of misfeasance and nonfeasance during the period that he had possession that they now seek to make him liable.

The defendant also contends that, though waste may have been committed or permitted by him, he cannot be made chargeable with it, as the will provides that he is to work and cultivate the trust property without impeachment of waste, which he claims exonerates him from any waste caused by him during the trust term. This, I think, is an entirely erroneous view of the provision. It was never the intention of the testator that the trustee was to be allowed to waste the trust property, but that in the management of it he was to do such acts in behalf of and for the benefit of the *cestui que trust* as he could do if a tenant who was not accountable for waste, so as to enable him to cut or allow to be cut wood for the supply of the saw mill on the premises or for sale, and do other acts of that character which an owner might do to make the property as productive as possible to the plaintiffs, without being liable to be made accountable by those entitled to the property in remainder or reversion.

Before referring to the evidence, I cannot help remarking on the very inartificial manner in which the examination of the witnesses has been conducted; needless repetitions abound in it, and much irrelevant matter has been introduced which ought not to have been offered, whereby much unnecessary expense has been incurred, while the evidence bearing on the real points in issue is presented in a very confused and unsatisfactory manner.

Mr. Seaman died in September, 1864, and it appears that from that time to the year 1866, when a division of the property took place, the plaintiffs, with the exception of the mill property, the rents of which were received by them, received their proportion of the proceeds of the whole estate; and as to this, as it has been the subject of a reference, it must be considered out of the question in this suit. The plaintiffs then went into possession of the trust property under a power of attorney from the defendant, as trustee, and they managed it as they saw fit till about the 1st May, 1869, when the defendant revoked the power of attorney and resumed the possession and management of the property, which he retained till the month of November, 1871, after this suit had been commenced, when the plaintiffs resumed the possession and management of it, which they have ever since retained; and it is the

10 c

defendant's management of the estate during the period that he assumed control of it which is now in controversy. I cannot perceive from the evidence that the defendant failed to collect the rents, or that any portion of them was lost through his negligence or misconduct. It was urged at the argument that the defendant had not taken the best mode of disposing of the grass on the several lots of land comprised in the trust estate, the plaintiffs contending that it should have been made into hay by him, and stored and disposed of by him, as such, instead of his selling it on the ground uncut at auction. The course pursued by the defendant, if not the best, as I am disposed to think it was, is one which under the circumstances he was at liberty to adopt, and the plaintiffs seem to have made no objection at the time, and would seem to have acquiesced in it. Objection was taken to the mode in which the sales were conducted, the advertisements, &c., but I can see nothing in the evidence to lead to the inference that there is any ground for such objection.

The defendant is charged with having dismantled the saw and grist mill on the premises and allowed them to go to destruction, and with not having taken proper means to make them available. As regards the grist mill it seems to be admitted that there is no ground of complaint, and if dismantled it was done by the plaintiff Vernon. The saw mill had been leased to Tabor previous to the death of the testator Seaman, and there is nothing to show that the defendant had anything to do with his leaving; the only reason assigned for it is that while Vernon had control of the property, he seized for rent the logs and deals he had at the mill and Tabor shortly after left. The question then arises, was it in the defendant's power to have procured another tenant; if he could not, he ought not in my opinion to be held answerable for the unproductiveness of the property. But the contention of the plaintiff is that he was bound to work the mill, to employ men to cut timber, to manufacture it and to ship it to the United States or elsewhere to a market. That I think he was not bound to do as trustee; as well might it be contended that, if he could not otherwise make available the shipyard, he was bound to build vessels for the benefit of the *cestui que trust*, and, indeed, from some of the evidence adduced it would appear that the plaintiffs or their counsel had some such idea. Now, assuming that the defendant was unable to get a tenant for the mill, and that he was not bound himself to work it, he appears to have done the next best thing by removing for preservation and safe keeping such of the gear as was likely to sustain injury by being left in the mill. I may here refer to a complaint of the loss of a lot of logs purchased by Vernon at Sheriff's sale, which loss he considered the defendant should bear, though it is difficult to see on what principles. He, at the time he purchased the logs, had the control of the trust estate; he had distrained on Tabor's property who remained the tenant, till the power of attorney was revoked or very shortly before; the loss arose from Tabor refusing to saw the logs on any terms, and it does not appear that he ever applied to any one else to saw them. No evidence was adduced to shew that the shipyard and fishery could have been made productive, and this the plaintiff is required to do before he can expect to throw any liablility on the defendant. The shipyard indeed was in the possession of Fitz Gibbon, who had built upon it and refused to leave it, and was only at last ejected by an action at law, which did not terminate till the property was out of the defendant's control.

A question remains upon which I felt much difficulty, whether the defendant has been guilty of a breach of trust in not having repaired the saw mill, and upon the best consideration I can give the subject, I have arrived at the conclusion that he has not. What he did to the mill, assuming that he could not get a tenant for it and it was to lie idle, the plaintiff's own witnesses admit not to have been injudicious. It was unquestionably out of repair when Tabor left, if not in a state of decay. What it would take to put it in thorough repair we are not told, but the inference from the evidence is that it would take a large sum; and to put it in even temporary repair would require a considerable outlay. Under these circumstances, considering the state of the timber lands connected with it, the outlay would not have been judicious unless there had been a prospect of getting a suitable tenant.

The defendant says that the mill was greatly dilapidated, that he looked at it with Greeno with a view of repairing it and, after doing so, concluded to let it remain there as it was, that immediately after resuming the trust in 1868, he looked round with a view of getting some person as a tenant, sent advertisements to the "*Amherst Gazette*" and enquired for one; and Mr. Hibbert, in his testimony says, he tried to rent it for defendant, and finally defendant got Greeno for a tenant and an agreement was made whereby he was to pay $3 a thousand for all the timber he sawed; defendant told him he thought he could get the logs to saw which Vernon had there, and he sent him to Vernon to endeavour to make a bargain with him for the sawing of them. Greeno then left him and afterwards told him that he could not succeed, and he then gave up taking the mill. Mr. Vernon says he never spoke to him on the subject, but it is unimportant whether he attempted to make the bargain or not; the important point is, that he declined to take the mill, and it is quite possible, having determined to do so, that he merely made the excuse of Vernon's alleged refusal to agree with him. The defendant went on to say that he thought it not advisable to repair the mill till he got some person to whom he was sure of letting it; he left Greeno, who lived near, in charge of the mill, and said that if the property had been his own he could have done nothing else to protect it, and that in the management of that property he exercised his best skill and judgment under the circumstances, and, speaking generally of the whole property, he had taken greater care of it than he had of his own; and there are other witnesses from whose testimony the inference to be drawn is that this was the case, particularly Dr. Mitchell a witness for plaintiffs. Greeno's son, also a witness for plaintiffs, says that his father would have taken the mill if it had been repaired, but that the defendant seemed doubtful whether it would be advisable to expend the money upon it, as it would cost $200; and, again, he says after his father went there he and the defendant conversed about the condition of the the mill, and the result was that the defendant concluded not to repair,—he thought his father gave him an estimate of what the cost of repairs would be. This witness, in his cross-examination said that nothing could have been done to protect the mill more than was done. On this latter point I may remark that there is not the slightest evidence that the defendant intended wilfully to injure the property by what is termed dismantling it, for we have the evidence of the man who was sent to perform the work, Hunter, and he says he was sent to take off the belts, &c., to preserve them, and that what he did would have that effect, and that defendant's instructions to him were to put everything in order about the mill to preserve it.

The contention of the plaintiffs is that the defendant, wilfully and with the intention of wasting the trust property, dismantled and allowed the mill to go to ruin, while the defendant asserts that he exercised what he thought a sound discretion in regard to it, and acted as he would have done if the mill had been his own. There is very little to lead to the former conclusion, and it is no small confirmation of the defendant's assertion that not a word of remonstrance or objection as to the course he was pursuing came from the plaintiffs; indeed it is worthy of remark that with respect to none of his acts was a suggestion made to the defendant that any dissatisfaction existed on the part of either of the plaintiffs.

The plaintiffs have, in my opinion, failed to establish their case against the defendant of having wasted the trust property or been guilty of such negligence in the management of it as to make him chargeable with deterioration or loss which may have occurred. As regards the state of accounts between the *cestui que trust* and the trustee as to the receipts and disbursements or charges of the latter, that will be the subject of an accounting if dissatisfaction on those points exists.

WATERMAN *v.* WILL.

Plaintiff brought action in 1878 to enforce payment of $400 and interest for land alleged to have been purchased by defendant, the deed being made out to defendant's brother and left with a third party, to be delivered to defendant on his handing him a note for the purchase money signed by himself and his brother.

Defendant, in his answer, contradicted all the statements in the writ, and set out that the sale was made directly to his brother, though he admitted that he would have assisted him by joining in a note for the purchase money. The evidence was conflicting, but the alleged agreement having been made in 1866, the Court held that the delay in sueing was itself a bar to the action, if, as plaintiff contended, the agreement was to be considered as the original undertaking of the defendant, while on the other hand if it was to be viewed as a guarantee, the statute of frauds prevented a recovery.

RITCHIE, E. J., delivered the judgment of the Court :—

The plaintiff seeks in this suit to enforce against the defendant the payment of $400 and interest, on the ground that he purchased from him a lot of land for that sum and has never paid him. He sets out in his writ that he agreed with him for the purchase, and, the title of the land being in John N. Hebb, it was agreed, to save the expense of two deeds, that the conveyance should be made direct from him, and at the request of defendant, it was made to his brother Zera Will. It was, he says, further agreed between the plaintiff and the defendant and one Thomas K. Cragg that the deed should remain in the hands of Cragg, to be held by him and only to be delivered to the defendant on his handing to him a promissory note, signed by himself and Zera Will for $400 and interest payable in three years, but that after it had remained some months in his custody he delivered it to Zera Will on a promise from defendant that he would call and give the note, which he failed to do.

The defendant in his answer denies that he made the purchase from the plaintiff; he denies that the deed was prepared at his request, or that he was a party to an agreement that the deed should be placed in the hands of Cragg, or that it was ever so left for his benefit or at his desire; he denies that it was delivered to Zera Will by Cragg at his request, and he asserts that he had no interest in the lands conveyed, and that he did not promise to give his own note for the consideration money, but that the purchase was made by Zera Will for his own benefit, though he admits that in order to assist his brother he would join him in a note for the amount of the purchase money payable on demand or in three months, and if plaintiff would prepare the note and obtain his brother's signature and produce it to him he would sign it; that this was never done, and if it had been done he would have signed the note and would have secured himself against loss by taking from his brother security on the land; and, after having in fact denied every important statement contained in the plaintiff's writ, he concludes with relying on the Statutes of Frauds and Limitations as answers to the plaintiff's claim.

The plaintiff, in the evidence which he has given, has sustained all the statements contained in his writ, and the defendant, in his evidence, all those contained in his answer, and if there had been no other testimony adduced in corroboration of one or other of the statements I do not see how it would be possible to grant the plaintiff the relief he prays, the evidence of plaintiff and defendant being so diametrically opposed to each other. The only other evidence of any importance is that of Cragg, Zera Will and Mr. DesBrisay. Cragg testifies that he wrote the deed at the request of plaintiff, who came to him with the defendant,—he knows nothing of the bargain between plaintiff and defendant; that he understood the consideration money, £100, was to be paid in three years, for which the plaintiff was to receive the joint note of defendant and Zera Will; he does not corroborate the plaintiff's statement that it was agreed between himself and plaintiff and defendant that the deed was to be left in his hands, only to be delivered on the note being handed to him; he says the deed was left in his hands after its execution, and defendant told him Zera Will would get it, and some time after he did get it. Zera Will, in his testimony, declares that the purchase of the land was made by himself and for himself, that the bargain was made by him with the plaintiff, and the deed was executed to him as the result; that defendant had no interest in the purchase, and he had no knowledge that defendant had agreed with plaintiff to join him in a note for the purchase money, and that he had no understanding to that effect with plaintiff; that when the bargain was closed between himself and plaintiff the latter was to look to him for payment, and that defendant had nothing to do with the purchase. He goes on to say that he did not get the deed from Cragg at the request of any person, but that, having asked plaintiff about the deed, he told him he could get it at Cragg's office; that he was and is liable to the plaintiff for the purchase money, part of which he has paid to him. Mr. DesBrisay knows nothing of the transaction further than that in September, 1871, the plaintiff applied to him as an attorney to collect $400, which he said was the amount of a note which was to have been given by the defendant for land conveyed by Hebb to Zera Will; that he did apply to him for it but he set up a counter claim for a much larger amount, and, admitting his indebtedness, he said he was willing to settle, provided plaintiff would settle his claim.

The evidence of Mr. DesBrisay would have had much effect on the question if the defendant had admitted to him that he had himself been the real purchaser of the land from the plaintiff, and that, though the deed had been made to his brother, it had been so made at his request in carrying out his bargain with plaintiff; but he does not go that length, he only spoke in relation to a note which defendant was to have given, and he does not now deny that by the arrangement he was to have become a party to the note to be given for the purchase money.

If the plaintiff really considered himself entitled to the redress he now seeks, he has been most unaccountably remiss in pursuing his claim. He had a right under the agreement as stated by himself to have had the note for the land in 1866; he allows the time for payment to expire, and Zera Will, who at the time of the purchase seems to have been solvent, to become insolvent and leave the province, and to remain absent ever since, and though in 1871, Mr. DesBrisay makes application to the defendant on his behalf unsuccessfully, no steps are taken to enforce the claim till two years after, when this suit was commenced, upwards of seven years from the time the plaintiff's cause of action, if any existed, first accrued. This delay would of itself be a bar to the plaintiff's claim if we are to consider the agreement as the original undertaking of the defendant, and on the other hand if we are to consider the agreement between plaintiff and defendant in the light of a guarantee for the price of the land conveyed to Zera Will, that undertaking not having been in writing the Statute of

Frauds as well as the Statute of Limitations would preclude
him from succeeding in this suit; and I think I have no alternative in every view that can be taken of this case but to
dismiss the plaintiff's writ with costs.

WOOD ET AL. *v.* HARE ET AL.

Where trustees, having power to sell a mining property conveyed to them by
way of mortgage to secure the payment of interest on bonds issued by the Mining
Company, the principal of which was not yet due, advertised the property for
sale, instead of proceeding by way of foreclosure, and the plaintiffs, who had the
equity of redemption, although aware of the intention to sell, delayed seeking the
information necessary to enable them to prevent a sale to their injury, and applied
for an injunction only two days before the day of sale, the Court granted the injunction upon payment by the mortgagors of the interest on the outstanding bonds,
and their undertaking to pay the expenses incurred in preparing for the sale.

The Block House Mining Company by indenture, dated
September 15, 1868, conveyed certain mining properties by
way of mortgage to Daniel P. Ingraham, Christopher Meyer,
and William Hare, to secure the payment of certain bonds to
be issued by the Company, to the amount of $125,000, the
interest on which was to be payable half-yearly, but the principal not to become due until 1883. By the indenture, it was
agreed that in case the interest on the bonds should remain
unpaid for ninety days after it became due, and the holders of
five or more of said bonds should, by writing, request the
trustees to foreclose the said mortgage, then the said trustees
should forthwith take possession of said property, and cause
the same to be advertised and sold after notice specified in
the mortgage. The mortgage also contained a provision that
in case the trustees should so determine they might, instead of
selling the property, apply to the Supreme Court for a foreclosure and sale of the premises; and it was further therein
agreed that in case the Company should pay or cause to be
paid the money due on the bonds, then said indenture and
everything therein contained should cease and be of no effect.

Default was made in the payment of the interest on the

bonds, and, more than ninety days having elapsed, the trustees took possession of the property and advertised it for sale. The plaintiffs obtained a rule *nisi* for an injunction to stop the sale, which was argued by Weatherbe for plaintiffs, and McDonald, Q. C., for defendants.

RITCHIE, E. J., delivered the judgment of the Court:—

I cannot arrive at the conclusion, from the facts stated in the affidavits on the part of the plaintiffs, or the arguments of their counsel, that the mortgage under which the defendants have advertised the property in question is invalid, or that the trustees have not a right to sell under its terms; but, as they have resorted to this course instead of foreclosure, it became incumbent on them to furnish parties interested in the equity of redemption with every information necessary to enable them, if so disposed, to pay what was due and prevent a sale to their injury. Information of that character was sought for from Mr. Hare, the only trustee in the province, which it would appear he was not able to give, and which, as a trustee who had advertised the property for sale, he should have possessed.

The plaintiffs were late in seeking this information. Being aware of the intention of the trustees to sell, they should not have waited till a day or two before the time appointed for selling, and then apply for an injunction to stop the sale, and that too without any offer on their part to pay the arrears of interest. Under these circumstances, I do not think that they are in a position to ask for an injunction without being required to pay these arrears.

I intimated after the argument that I should probably grant the injunction on these terms, to which Mr. McDonald seemed much opposed, but I then thought and still think without good reason. He is acting for the trustees, and in the interest of the bond holders. To the former the mortgage was given to secure the payment of the bonds, with interest as the same should become payable, *i. e.*, half yearly, on the first days of January and July in each year, the principal not being payable till the 1st January, 1883. The interest appears to have been paid up to July, 1874. Power is given to the trustees to enter upon the property and sell it if it should remain unpaid upwards of ninety days, and the mortgage contains a proviso making it void in case the mortgagor should pay or caused to be paid the moneys due or owing on the respective bonds, according to the true intent and meaning thereof. The proviso in this mortgage is that which is usually introduced into mortgages, that the instrument shall be of no force or effect if the principal and interest are paid according to its terms, but where the principal is not payable till a distant day, and the interest happens not to paid on the very day it fell due, surely a mortgagor should be able to prevent an immediate foreclosure and sale of his estate, by paying the interest due, and should not be required to pay the principal not made payable by the instrument till a lapse, as in this case, of some ten or twelve years. This court does not so deal with mortgages.

The trustees have no personal interest in the matter; all that they can require is to be able to carry out the trust reposed in them, that is, to pay the interest half-yearly and the principal when it falls due; and the bond holders can ask no more than that they shall receive their interest and retain their security on the property for the ultimate payment of the principal, according to the terms of their bonds. If, therefore, the parties who ask for the injunction now pay the interest due on the outstanding bonds and undertake to pay the expenses which have been incurred in preparing for the sale, if the Court should so order, then the rule *nisi* for an injunction to be made absolute, otherwise to be discharged.

WYLDE ET AL. *v.* UNION MARINE INSURANCE CO.

Plaintiff filled up an application for a policy of marine insurance, describing the risk thus: "Voyage at and from Block House Mines to Montreal; vessel arrived at Sydney 2nd August; on chartered freight $3000." The defendants being authorized to effect the insurance, inserted in the policy without plaintiffs' privity the words, "beginning the adventure upon the said freight from and immediately following the loading thereof on board." The vessel was lost at Block House Mines before she commenced taking her cargo on board, and plaintiff first became aware of the insertion of the last recited words in the policy on being informed that the Company did not hold themselves liable. *Held*, an action having been brought to reform the policy, that the plaintiffs had a right to assume that the Company in preparing the policy would strictly adhere to the terms in the memorandum, that had the policy been so prepared, the plaintiff would have had a right to recover under it, and that it must therefore be reformed accordingly.*

RITCHIE, E. J., delivered the judgment of the Court :—

The plaintiffs seek in this suit to have a policy of Insurance rectified, so as to make. it conform to the terms on which the insurance was agreed to be effected by the defendants, the policy which was prepared and delivered to them not being, as they allege, in accordance with the agreement. There is no dispute as to what took place when the terms were offered and accepted. The plaintiffs made their application in writing, by filling up one of the forms of application in use by the company, thus,—"What premium will be demanded on the following risk ; Vessel's name and designation, Barque *Fanny M. Carvell ;* Master, Watkins ; Voyage at and from Block House Mines to Montreal ; Where vessel is at present,—arrived at Sydney 2. August ; on chartered freight, $3000 ;"—which having been submitted to the directors, the rate one per cent. was filled in and initialled by them, after which the plaintiffs signed the memo. at the foot; " effect the above, 5 August, 1873." Nothing further took place between them on the subject, and a policy was subsequently made out and handed. to the plaintiffs. The vessel was subsequently lost on her arrival at the Block House Mines and before she had commenced to take on board her cargo. On notifying the loss to the defendants at their office, the plaintiffs were informed by the Secretary that the Company did not hold themselves liable for the loss under the policy, as the cargo had not been put on board, and then, for the first time, it came to their knowledge that in making out the policy these words had been inserted in it without their privity,—" beginning the adventure upon the said freight, from and immediately following the loading thereof on board," which they contend materially alters the contract which had been mutually agreed upon.

---

* The above decision was sustained on appeal to the Court in *banc.* See 1 R. & C., 205.

At the hearing, the defendants' counsel contested the right of the plaintiffs to have the policy reformed, inasmuch as that instrument evidenced the agreement of the parties, and, having been received by them without objection, it cannot be impeached, though in its terms it should differ from the application for insurance as made and accepted. This position is, I think, wholly untenable. If the plaintiffs had been made aware of the alteration and had after that received the policy without objection they could not subsequently object to it on a loss taking place, but if an agreement has been entered into between two parties, and one of them, whose province it is to prepare the instrument to evidence it, inserts in it, without the knowledge or consent of the other, terms which materially vary the contract, surely a Court of Equity ought to and would give redress. It would have been more prudent for the plaintiff to have inspected the policy, and to have ascertained that the defendants had faithfully embodied in it the terms which had been mutually agreed upon, and this they would probably have done if, as in most contracts, they, as parties, had been required to execute it; but they had every right to presume that in preparing the document the Company would strictly adhere to the terms contained in the memorandum of agreement in their possession.

Though it is a principle of law that a written instrument purporting to contain the agreement of the parties is to be considered and treated as *alone* expressing their intention, and in a court of law such intention cannot be controverted, yet, if it be made clearly to appear that it does not, in fact, express the real intention of the parties to it, a Court of Equity will reform it, so as to make it conform to such intent. Numerous decisions to this effect are to be found, and it is not long since this court reformed a policy of insurance, not only after a loss had occurred, but after an action had been tried on the policy at common law; and the decision then given, was affirmed on appeal. I refer to the case of *Banks et al.* v. *Wilson.*

This Court, however, will not interfere in such cases unless the evidence adduced is clear and satisfactory, and though the mistake may be established by parol testimony when it is clear and satisfactory, yet less difficulty is felt in reforming an instrument when it can be shewn, as in this case, by a preliminary written document. And, where the existence of a mistake is thus corroborated, and there is nothing to shew that the terms were altered between the time the two documents were made, the Court will not hesitate to rectify the mistake. Here there is no contradictory evidence. The proposal was made and accepted in writing, and it became the duty of the defendant to prepare a policy in accordance with the terms then arranged between the parties. This is admitted on both sides. The real question before us is, have they done so, or have they inserted in the policy other and different terms. Before considering the question it may be well to see in what light the plaintiff's application and the defendants' acceptance of it are to be viewed. In England such a document, initialled as this was by the directors of an Insurance Company, is called a slip or label, and is there held to be in itself a contract of insurance, though no action can be maintained upon it in consequence of the Stat. 30 and 31 Vict., Chap. 23, Sec. 7, which enacts that no contract of marine insurance is to have validity if not expressed in a policy, which must also be stamped. We have no such statute, and I know no reason why here, as in the United States, (see *1 Duer on Insurance*, 107), an action could not be brought on such an instrument, if no policy had been contemplated, or the insurers had refused to execute one.

Two English cases decided within the past year shew how they are viewed there, and what effect would be given to them but for the legislation on the subject. In *Fisher* v. *Liverpool Marine Insurance Company*, L. R., 9 Q. B., 424, in Exchequer Chamber on appeal, the Court held that a slip initialled was a contract for insurance, and as such came within the words of the Statute, and was thereby made absolutely void and incapable of being enforced, though binding in honor. And in *Cory et al.* v. *Patton*, L. R., 7 Q. B., 304, BLACKBURN, J., who delivered the judgment of the Court, recognised the slip as in practice the complete and final contract between the parties, fixing the terms of the insurance and the premiums, and that neither party could without the assent of the other deviate from the terms thus agreed upon without a breach of faith; and he adopted language to that effect used in *Ionides*

v. *Pacific Insurance Company*, L. R., 6 Q. B., 674. And he added, "though for fiscal purposes the legislature has enacted that this contract shall not be enforceable at law or in equity." See the same case in L. R., 9 Q. B., 580. So much was the initialling of a slip in that case considered as constituting a complete and final contract binding on the insurers in honor and good faith that, notwithstanding the Statute, it was held that the insured need not communicate to the insurers material facts affecting the risk which came to his knowledge between the initialling of the slip and the signing of the policy. These cases recognise the correctness of the view of this subject taken by Lord HARDWICKE in *Motteaux* v. *Gov. and Co'y. of London Assurance*, 1 Atk. [545] 631, which in more respects than one has a strong bearing on the case before us. That eminent Judge held that if a policy of insurance differs from the label, which is the memo. of agreement, it should be reformed and made agreeable to it, and, there as here, the question arose, what was the real agreement. In the label the words were *at and from* the port of loading, Fort St. George. This, the Lord CHANCELLOR said, certainly included the continuance there; and there, as here, in the first part of the policy the same words were used as in the label, but in subsequently describing the risk the adventure was confined to the departure from St. George, as here it was confined to the cargo being laden on board. And the learned Judge went on to say, "it is pretty difficult to reconcile the first part of the policy and the latter, but the label makes it very clear, for that considers the voyage and the risk as the same, and therefore it was only the mistake of the clerk, and it ought to be rectified agreeably to the label; and as to the question regarding the loss, that is not properly determinable in equity." I cannot but think that in preparing this policy the difference between insurance on chartered freight and on cargo was not adverted to, for, had the insurance been on goods, the words introduced in the policy would have been properly there, even though not in the slip, as in that case the goods must have been on board to entitle the insured to recover.

In the case I have just referred to it was also held that the taking away the policy without having compared it with the label did not preclude the assured from afterwards objecting when he discovered the mistake. This case, it appears to me, touches every point raised in that now under consideration. I think I may assume that this loss would never have been contested by the defendant, at least on the ground of the risk not attaching on the arrival of the vessel at the port of lading, if the directors had not believed that the policy was made out in accordance with the terms agreed on, and that they had embodied in the policy the effect of the previous agreement; for, had they intentionally altered the terms, and inserted a different risk, without the concurrence of the plaintiffs or any intimation to them, there would have been a violation of the confidence reposed in them, and I cannot for a moment entertain the belief that the directors would have sanctioned such a course. In this respect I think they have been in error.

According to the evidence a contract, though a verbal one, had been made for the freight of the *Fanny M. Carvell*, from Block House Mines to Montreal, the vessel being as was represented to the underwriters at Sydney. It cannot be contended that expected freight is not a lawful subject of insurance; all that the insured is required to have is an inchoate right to it, that is, he must be in such a position in respect to it, that nothing can prevent him from obtaining it but the intervention of the perils insured against, and this inchoate right, the shipowner has as soon as the vessel under charter has commenced to perform it. This right the plaintiffs had, as soon as the vessel left Sydney for the port of loading, but no risk attached under the defendants' agreement, till her arrival there, as their liability was only to attach *at and from* that place. Immediately, however, on her arrival there, it did attach under the terms of the slip, but not under the terms of the policy. In *Barber* v. *Fleming*, L. R., 5 Q. B., 59, the plaintiffs had chartered a ship then lying, as in this case, at the specified port, Bombay, for a voyage from Howland's Island to a port in the United Kingdom. He effected insurance on freight, at and from Bombay to Howland's Island, while there, and thence to any port in United Kingdom. She sailed from Bombay in ballast, to go to Howland's Island to earn freight under the charter, but did not reach it, and it was decided that the plaintiffs were entitled to recover the insurance, as the interest in the chartered freight had commenced. COCKBURN, C. J., in giving judgment, said: "from the moment a vessel is chartered to go from port A to port B, to take a cargo to port C for freight, the ship-owner, having got such a contract, has an interest unquestionably in earning the freight secured to him by the charter, and, having such an interest, it is manifest that it is insurable, and he loses the freight and the benefit of the charter just as much by the ship's being disabled on her voyage to this port, at which the cargo is to be loaded, as he would by a disaster between the port of loading and discharge;" and BLACKBURN, J. said: "the law seems perfectly settled by a variety of cases, as I find it laid down by *Phillips on Insurance*, sec. 328, thus: 'In regard to the commencement of this interest in freight, it is a general rule that it commences, not only with the vessel sailing with the cargo on board, but also when the owner or hirer, having goods ready to ship on a contract with another person for freight, has commenced the voyage or incurred expense, and taken steps towards earning the freight.' This I think is the accurate rule." *Foley* v. *United Fire and Marine Insurance Company of Sydney*, in the Exchequer Chamber, L.R., 5 C.P., 155, is very like this case. There KELLY, C. B., said; "The plaintiff has insured certain chartered freight at and from Mauritius to Rice Ports, and at and thence to a port in the United Kingdom; a total loss has occurred, the ship having been by a peril of the sea destroyed some little time after her arrival at Mauritius, but before the cargo which she had brought from Calcutta was completely discharged. It is now insisted on the part of the insurers that the loss is not within the policy. The question turns on the construction of the words *at and from*. It requires no argument to shew that where freight is insured at and from a given port, it is insured as long as the ship is at the port. It is insisted that the risk could not commence before the cargo was discharged. If that argument be correct it amounts to this, that there never can be an effective insurance on freight to be earned on a voyage from a given port until the ship is in a condition to receive

10 *d*

goods on board. But we find a long series of decisions, from *Thompson* v. *Taylor*, 6 T. R., 478, to *Barber* v. *Fleming*, L. R., 5 Q. B., 59, which conclusively establish the contrary." It was admitted in that case that if the entire cargo had been discharged the loss would have been within the terms of the policy. I have no hesitation in arriving at the conclusion that the policy in the case before me differs, in its effect as well as in its terms, from the preliminary agreement, and that, if it had conformed to that agreement, as it ought to have done, the risk would have attached under it on the arrival of the vessel at the Block House Mines, and this certainly would not have been the case under the language of the policy. The decree will be that the latter instrument be reformed by making it conformable to the application as accepted and agreed upon.

I have not adverted to what was said at the hearing as to the precise locality of the vessel at the time of her loss; that question does not properly come before me, but if thought of any weight, it can be relied on as a defence to an action on the reformed policy.

The plaintiffs should have their costs.

BANKS ET AL. *v.* WILSON.*

Joseph Banks, one of the plaintiffs, applied for a policy of insurance on the Brigantine *Sophia* by filling up a printed form. " J. Banks and others" were entered as owners, and the "hull and materials" filled in as what was to be insured; and the application, after the printed words "effect the above on account of," was signed, "Joseph Banks." The policy issued by the Company purported that Joseph Banks did make assurance, &c., but the words, "or whom it may concern," were not inserted in the policy. The vessel being lost, the plaintiffs, as owners, brought action on the policy, the claim being resisted on the ground that there was not a total loss, but on the trial, the objection was raised for the first time by the defendant's counsel, that the policy covered only the interest of Joseph Banks. Plaintiffs then brought suit in the Equity Court to have the policy

---

* This is the case referred to in the decision of RITCHIE, E. J., in *Wylde* v. *Union Marine Insurance Co'y.* See *Ante*, p. 205. It is inserted here, although delivered some three or four years before the appointment of the present reporters, as it is not at all probable, judging from appearances, that it will ever be published in any other way.

reformed on the ground of mistake, and issues were settled by the Equity Judge and tried by a jury, who found that there was a mutual understanding between the parties which the policy, as executed, did not carry out, and that to do so it would require to be altered by inserting the names of the other registered owners; which finding there was evidence to justify. *Held*, that the policy must be reformed so as to cover the interests of all the owners.

The following decision of the Equity Court was pronounced by JOHNSTONE, E. J., sometime previous to the December term 1871–72 :—

The plaintiffs seek to reform a Marine Policy of Insurance on the Brigantine *Sophia*, by making it cover the interest of all the Plaintiffs, instead of the interest only of Joseph Banks, on the ground of mistake. The defendant denies the mistake, and alleges that at the time of the insurance, as it was not known that Joseph Banks was not the sole owner, as represented by him, the words " or whom it may concern " were not inserted in the policy, and that the policy was made agreeably to the instructions. The cause was tried on issues settled by me before His Lordship the Chief Justice at Shelburne in the September term 1869, when the Jury found that there was a mutual understanding between the parties which the policy as executed does not carry out, and that to do so it would require to be altered by inserting the names of the other registered owners.

The plaintiffs' counsel claims the judgment of the Court for reforming the policy; the defendant's counsel asks judgment dismissing the bill, or otherwise a new trial on the ground that the finding is against the evidence.

Joseph Banks applied for the insurance by an application in the printed form used by the Barrington Marine Insurance Association, of which the defendant was a member and Gabriel Robertson was the broker. Where it is not printed, it is in the hand-writing of Mr. Robertson excepting only the plaintiff Joseph Banks' signature at the foot. It is in the form of questions in print and answers in writing. "J. Banks and others" are entered as the owners and "the Hull and materials" are filled in as "what was to be insured." The vessel was valued at £1000 and £750 is stated to be the sum to be insured on the "vessel," and after the rate of premium and average the instrument concludes: "effect the above on account of Joseph Banks;" the words, "effect the above on account of," being in print, and the signature in the plaintiff Joseph Banks' writing. On the back is an endorsement signed by the defendant and three other persons, who it appears were with him directors of the Barrington Marine Insurance Association. The dates of the application and endorsement are 26 Dec. 1866. A policy of that date was executed by the different members of the association by Gabriel Robertson, their attorney, for various sums, among others by the defendant for £12 - 10. It purports that Joseph Banks of Barrington, Mariner, do make assurance and cause himself to be insured, lost or not lost, the sum of £750 on the hull and materials of the Brigantine *Sophia* for six months &c. Joseph Banks took up the policy and gave the broker a note for £45 for the premium, signed by himself and a surety. The policy is in the printed form used by the association which omits the words " or whom it may concern," words which, or some equivalent terms, are so universally inserted in marine policies. Out of this omission the present controversy grows.

The vessel, within the period, was wrecked in Barrington harbour, and notice of abandonment was given under the policy, and also under a policy effected by Nathaniel Banks on the *Sophia* for $1000 at Halifax. The Barrington office having refused to accept the abandonment on the ground that the loss was not total, an action was brought and tried at Barrington in May term, 1868.

On the trial the register showed that the vessel was owned in the following proportions, viz: Joseph Banks 20-64th. parts, Stephen Banks 8, Benjamin L. Banks 16, William Banks 8, Nehemiah Banks 12; and the defendant's counsel took the objection that the policy only covered Joseph Banks' interest who could only recover to the amount of his interest, and that the other plaintiffs could not recover at all. In consequence of this objection the present suit was instituted for reforming the policy on the ground that it was the intention of the parties that it should cover the interest of all the owners.

Of the law regulating this case there is no question. It

cannot be doubted that a Court of Equity has power to reform a contract of insurance according to the true intention of both parties, and it is also clear that this power will only be exer. cised in cases of undoubted mistake. As regards the present enquiry the mistake must be mutual. The instances in which the mistake of one of the parties only will be ground of relief depend on the power of placing the other party in his original position, (*Harris* v. *Pepperell*, L. R., Eq., vol. 5, p. 4,) and therefore have no relation to the subject under consideration in the present action, where it is impossible to do so. Although the principle of law be defined, its application may not be without difficulty, and it is here that whatever embarrassment there may be in deciding this cause arises.

Mr. McDonald for the defendant strongly urged the language of Mr. Justice STORY, that a Court of Equity " ought to be extremely cautious in the exercise of such an authority, and ought to withhold its aid when the mistake is not made out by the clearest evidence, according to the understanding of both parties and upon testimony entirely exact and satisfactory." Mr. Arnould, however, appears to go even further, if his language is to be taken as requiring the testimony of both parties to the mistake. He says, p. 51, " a Court of Equity will in very strong cases disregard the language of the policy and interpret it according to that which by the concurrent testimony of the parties concerned appears to have been their real meaning." The opinion of Lord HARDWICKE which he cites, *1 Ves. Sr.*, 318, does not go this length. He says, " No doubt but this Court has jurisdiction to relieve in respect of a plain mistake in contracts in writing as well as against frauds in contracts, so that, if reduced to writing contrary to intent of the parties, on proper proof that would be rectified." He proceeds,—and his remark is applicable to the present case, —" but the plaintiff comes to do this in the harshest case that can happen,—of a policy after the event and loss happened,— to vary the contract so as to turn the loss on the insurer who otherwise it is admitted cannot be charged; however, if the case is so strong as to require it, the Court ought to do it." And he adds, " that to come to that there ought to be the strongest proof possible." Arnould refers to *Motteux* v. *London As-*

surance Company, 1 Atk. p. 545, decided by Lord HARDWICKE ten years previously, as " the only well authenticated instance in which the Court has actually exercised this power ;" and I may add that certainly in this last named case the mistake in the policy was manifest, as appeared from the label and the admission of the assurers.

This is a case in which in an especial manner the statements of a defendant are to be looked to. The question is what did he intend. His clear denial of the intention charged by the plaintiff must be entitled to great weight. He can hardly fail to know what his own mind was, and, knowing it, his testimony is conclusive unless wilfully untrue. Hence the evidence to rebut the denial of a defendant in such a case must be strong—almost irresistible. Some modification is necessary however. There may be incidents to a transaction to which a party to it may not have given his attention,—collateral points to which he gave no thought, and when the retrospect is called for he cannot recall what his intention was respecting these incidents; he cannot, because he had no intention. For instance, in this case the defendant knew that he had contracted with Joseph Banks, on his application, to insure the *Sophia* to the extent of £750, and he knew there were other owners, but the thought may never have occurred to him, whether his liability was confined to Joseph Banks' interest, although less than that amount, or was to cover the interest of all the owners up to that extent.

Will this neutral condition of mind satisfy the exigency of the case ? Will it fulfil the obligation imposed on the plaintiff to establish a mutual intention and a mutual mistake ? The defendant, indeed, cannot absolutely deny, and ought not to attempt it. But if he can truly say that he had no thought, and therefore no intention on that particular point, can there be said to have been a mutual intention, which the instrument has by mistake failed to carry out? I think not. The inquiry is difficult and delicate. It searches the mind and seeks to ascertain whether a particular act was done with a purpose different from that which the act indicates. The burden is on the plaintiff of shewing that the defendant did intend and understand something additional to or different from that

which the paper he executed expressed. The first consideration, therefore, is naturally directed to what the defendant
says on a point so peculiarly relating to himself. The defendant was examined on written interrogatories, and also on the
trial at which he offered himself in his own defence. The
interrogatories are full, explicit and searching; the answers
fall far short of meeting them with the explicitness the case
demanded.

The 6th interrogatory enquires whether the defendant or
the broker did not know that Joseph Banks was not the sole
owner, and that the application for insurance was made on
behalf of the plaintiff, or on behalf of others beside himself.
The answer is that he did not know that Joseph Banks was
not the sole owner, nor who were the real owners. "I took
the application as the application of Joseph Banks only."

With the application before him, in which the vessel is
stated to be owned by Joseph Banks and others, and with a
multitude of facts in the case, it is not easy to understand
what the defendant meant by saying he did not know that
Joseph Banks was not sole owner. If he meant to give the
word "know" a very strict meaning, the answer was uncan-
did, and in no other way can I reconcile this answer with the
facts. But in the material point of the interrogatory, the
answer is most unsatisfactory. The enquiry whether the
defendant did not know that Joseph Banks' application was
made on behalf of others beside himself was capable of, and
should have received a distinct reply, and not one by inference.
It touched the essence of the case which the statement, I
took the application as the application of Joseph Banks only",
did not meet. In one sense he and any one else might say
that he took the application to be the application of Joseph
Banks and his only, for apparently it was so. But when the
very object, the sole object of the suit was to distinguish
between the real and the apparent, it is difficult to comprehend.
how the defendant or his solicitor could be satisfied with any
thing short of a distinct, "I did not know that the application
was made on behalf of any others besides himself," if the truth.
would have warranted such a denial.

The 8th interrogatory put it to the defendant to say whether

"he did not know that the insurance was required on the
whole vessel, and not on a part thereof, or a partial interest
therein." No answer is given to what was the essence of the
enquiry, viz; his knowledge that insurance was not required
on a partial interest; and otherwise also the answer has a
significant bearing. The defendant says, " I considered the
insurance as on a part of the vessel, the vessel being valued
at £1000, and £750 only insured. Elsewhere he says—what
is known to be the case—that it is not customary to insure to
the full value; and hence the answer coupled with the question, appears to amount to this, that not a partial interest was
insured, but the whole vessel up to her insurable value.

The evasion of the 13th interrogatory is entire; nothing whatever receives reply;—1st. The defendant is asked whether all
the plaintiffs or which of them were recognised and treated as
parties to and interested in the insurance; 2ndly., whether any
objection was made at the time before the (first) trial, to the
claim of the plaintiffs, that the insurance had not been made
for their benefit; 3rdly., when such objection was raised, and
by whom. The answer is, " I have already stated that I did
not know who were the owners of the vessel at the time the
insurance was effected. I know no person in the transaction
but Joseph Banks. I presume when he ordered the insurance
to be effected on his account he so meant. As soon as we
apprehended any difficulty, and before I was sued, we employed an attorney and were guided by his advice, and have acted
upon it, as we were not very conversant on legal matters."
There was nothing in the question to justify the defendant
in thus limiting any part of his answer to the particular time
when the insurance was effected, and by shutting out information of subsequent transactions, he defeated the just aim of the
interrogatory.

The pertinency of the enquiries and the unfairness of the
evasion are understood, when it is ascertained from the evidence in the cause, that, in point of fact, from the time of the
loss, up to the time of the first trial the owners of the *Sophia*
and not Joseph Banks alone, were treated by the directors as
the persons interested in the insurance, that the objection
taken was, not that Joseph Banks' interest alone was insured,

but that the loss was not total as it was claimed to be, and that this new objection was first started at the first trial, and was raised not by the defendant, but by the counsel.

In the last two interrogatories, the plaintiff's counsel endeavoured to bring the defendant to the very point in issue, with however but small success.

By the 16th interrogatory, the defendant is asked whether "in order to carry out the intention of the parties, insurers as well as insured, the policy ought not to have been made out for the benefit of all the owners, or of whom it might concern." The answer was; "The policy was made out in conformity to the application for insurance, and the printed part of the policy is the same in all cases. If Joseph Banks at the time had wished to have other names inserted in the policy, perhaps no objection would have been made, if the parties were known, but we supposed we were insuring his interest. I knew nobody but him." The object of the action was to discover the intention, and this interrogatory was directed to that point. I cannot think that the assertion of a supposition that they were insuring Joseph's interest necessarily, in this particular case, negatived the fact that other interests were contemplated, and the defendant ought not to have been so unacquainted with the law and practice of underwriting as to imagine that knowing nobody but one excluded the covering of the interests of others under the words, "and whom it may concern." The defendant's answer was short and simple, if denial could fairly be given; "such a form of policy as the interrogatory suggests would not have carried out my intention;" and the roundabout and inferential answer given is not entitled to be accepted as an equivalent.

"Was it not intended by the parties who applied for insurance as well as those who accepted the application that the whole interest in the *Sophia* should be insured and that the policy should cover the interest of all the owners whosoever they might be?" The answer is; "I have already answered this question as fully as I can." Where the defendant had done so I know not, and it would have been impossible for the defendant to have so treated this last question if he had not so fixed his mind on the intention apparent from the paper as to exclude his giving a fair consideration to the enquiry whether there not had been in fact a different intention in the minds of the parties at the time of the insurance which the peculiar form of the company's policies had kept out of sight.

The defendant's evidence on the trial is more conclusive than his answers to the interrogatories.

In the direct examination he says; "We accepted the insurance as covering the interest of Joseph Banks only;" but the cross-examination introduced some uncertainty. He there says, "I think I saw the answer that the vessel was owned by Joseph Banks and others; we intended to cover three-fourths of the value. I supposed that some of his boys owned a share with Joseph Banks, but that he was the principal owner; I was satisfied some of his sons were owners. I also heard that Capt. Sterling owned a part. We intended to indemnify the assured to the extent of £750. We seldom insure vessels to their full value. I intended to cover Joseph Banks to the extent of £750 and he ordered insurance accordingly. I did not know what share Joseph Banks possessed and had no belief as to his share." These qualifying and uncertain statements in the cross-examination may be made consistent with the defence on the supposition that the defendant believed that Joseph Banks owned the chief part of the vessel and that £750 would not exceed his proportion of interest. In that view the intention to indemnify the insured to the extent of £750, or to cover three-fourths of the value might not militate against the statement that the insurance was accepted as covering the interest of Joseph Banks only. Nevertheless, as the defendant declined to meet the interrogatories of the plaintiffs as to intention in the same explicit manner as they were put, I cannot think his statements on the whole entitled to be placed in the category of a distinct denial.

The other witnesses examined for the defence were the broker and Mr. Warren Doane, a director. Their testimony does not materially strengthen the defence. Mr. Robertson did not know the names or proportions of the owners. The risk, he says, was taken for three-fourths of the value; that in May, '67' after the loss, Nehemiah claimed as part owner, and it was in May, '68' that he "first learnt from Mr.

Creighton the objection now taken." Mr. Doane was at the board when the application came in. "I supposed," he says, "that Nehemiah, being the master, had an interest in the vessel; I had no other knowledge of the ownership." "We supposed we were insuring Joseph Banks' interest." In cross-examination he says;—"Had always understood that Joseph Banks was owner to a considerable extent of these vessels, I supposed that Nehemiah Banks was the other owner." He does not negative an intention to cover the vessel by whomsoever owned to the extent of the sum insured, and does not carry this essential part of the case further than the defendant did.

In view of the absence of any distinct denial by the defendant of the intention which the writ charges him to have had when the policy was made, the terms in which the pleas are drawn in this particular become the more entitled to notice, and they were commented on by the plaintiffs' counsel at the argument.

It is pleaded that the words, "or whom it may concern," were not inserted in the policy, because it was not known that Joseph Banks was not the sole owner as represented by him. The meaning of this is, that it was believed that Joseph Banks was sole owner, and therefore, the policy covering the whole interest in the vessel, the words, "or whom it may concern," were unnecessary. But it follows, that had it been known that he was not the sole owner, those words would have been inserted. It is true that Joseph Banks did not represent himself to be sole owner, and the defendant did know that he was not; but the plea must be taken as it stands, and it is surely strange that where the defendant's pleas dilate on this, the vital point of the case, there is not only not an assertion that the policy was intended to cover a partial, and not the whole interest, but that there should be an indirect admission that the policy was believed to cover the whole interest, or otherwise the words would have been inserted which would have given it that operation, being that which the plaintiffs contend for.

Having examined the statements of the defendant and the testimony of his witnesses, with a view of ascertaining whether or not the burden was laid on the plaintiffs of meeting an unqualified denial of the supposed intention on which their claim depends, I proceed to the testimony given in support of their case. It may be distinguished as acts previous to the policy in question, the application and policy, and acts after the loss.

Joseph Banks, it was shown, for a number of years—not less than seventeen—owned various vessels with sons, and other near relatives, and during that time continuously insured with this Barrington Company, of which at one time he was a director, and he did so for the account of all the owners, as he and his son Nehemiah testified. To establish this fact a great number of policies, more than thirty were given in evidence, extending over many years, in all of which Joseph Banks is the person insured in precisely the form and manner that was adopted in this case, and the applications, where these accompany the policies, are similar to the present one, in stating the owners to be Joseph Banks and others, and in desiring the insurance to be effected on the account of Joseph Banks.

It is sufficiently clear that it was understood in the community that Joseph Banks' sons, or some of them, were part owners with him; but there is no ground for believing that the defendant or the other underwriters knew the proportions in which they held respectively. For this reason I do not perceive that the fact of these insurances necessarily brings home to the defendant a knowledge that Joseph Banks was in the habit of insuring beyond his own interest. It is true it might be presumed that he would not probably leave his sons' interest unprotected, but this was an inference the defendant was not bound to make, and may not have made. There are, however, circumstances connected with these insurances which may have more bearing. There were losses, I think four, one total, the others partial. In all these cases the underwriters acted as they would have acted had the insurances covered the interests of all the owners, and they paid for the total loss of the *Sea Lark* under a policy identical with the present policy. They thus gave to the former the effect of an insurance of all the owners' interests, while they now limit the latter to an insurance of the interest of Joseph Banks.

No explanation has been offered of this inconsistency, and none can be required, except as the former instances may be regarded as evidence of the understanding with which the underwriters accepted Joseph Banks' orders for insurance, and the intended operation and effect of the policies in the mind of both parties. So far and no farther this fact goes; and whatever consideration in this aspect it may be entitled to is strengthened by the conduct of the underwriters in not raising the objection that the policy on the *Sophia* covered only the interest of Joseph Banks, until it was taken by their counsel on the trial which was brought on to determine what was till then the only controversy, viz:—whether the loss was total or not. It is impossible that the enquiry should not suggest itself, whether in this case had the loss been an unquestioned total loss, the whole sum insured would not have been paid without controversy, as was done in the case of the *Sea Lark.*

The application and policy form the next class of evidence by which the defendant is attempted to be implicated in the intention charged by the plaintiffs. It was contended by Mr. Ritchie that as the application described "the hull and materials" as "what was to be insured" and £750 to be the amount to be insured on "the vessel" instead of describing the subject of insurance to be the shares of the applicant, and as the paper shewed there were other owners, the language imported that the insurance of the whole vessel and not of a partial interest was designed, and that this sense controlled the document, and therefore that the policy should be reformed by the application read with this construction. To give application to this argument, it must be understood that the other owners were cognizant of the transaction and designed to be insured, for without this no change in the form of policy would include them. Even then I cannot go to this length. I think the order to insure a vessel given by a part owner, as on his own account, read in its own light, must be construed to mean insurance on his own interest.

The remaining evidence is of acts that occurred after the loss, and this can be introduced not to create a new contract, but only to elucidate the intent and object the parties had in their original agreement, in the nature of admissions, in fact.

Nehemiah Banks describes negotiations which he had with
the directors for adjusting the disputed claim, and which, he
says, they held with him as one owner and on behalf of the
others.   He says, (line 134,) " They, (the directors,) said they
wanted me to see the other owners and we must abate our
claim or expect war." He consulted the other owners, and
again met the directors as it would appear on May 28th, at
which time the vessel which went on shore on the 2nd of that
month had been got off, and was lying at anchor in Barrington
harbour.   On this occasion, he says, he told them : "We considered our claim good, but as we were not men of war, but men
of peace, we would deduct $100.   Defendant then said they
estimated our loss at $900 which they would raise to $1000.
I rejected this at once.   Defendant then handed me the protest of 27th May, which he read ; he said he handed it to me
as managing owner and ship's husband.   Defendant finally
offered me $1200."

This testimony is corroborated by several papers.   A letter
dated 27th May, 1867, signed by Gabriel Robertson, the broker,
is addressed to "Captain Nehemiah Banks and owners of the
Brigantine *Sophia*," and in it Mr. Robertson says he is instructed by the directors to ask a conference with them relative
to the affairs of the *Sophia*.   The protest which Nehemiah
Banks stated the defendant read to and gave him, is dated
27th May, 1867, is addressed " To the owners of the
Brigantine *Sophia*," and is signed by the defendant and six
other persons.   They, on behalf of the underwriters on the
Brigantine *Sophia*, forbid her sale, as they consider her capable of being repaired at a cost much below her value, and
give notice that they are ready to undertake the repairs, or to
allow the owners to repair her at the underwriters' expense.

A letter dated 8th August, 1867, is signed by the defendant
as the President of the Company, and by Nehemiah Banks for
" owners *Sophia*."   It is addressed to Messrs. William Rogers
and Amasa Durkee, Yarmouth, and is to this effect ;—" A
difference of opinion having arisen between the owners of the
Brigantine *Sophia* and the directors of the Barrington Marine
Insurance Company, in whose office the vessel was insured,
regarding a compromise, we have mutually agreed to leave

the matter to your decision, as arbitrators, and we would be glad to know if you could attend at Barrington. We think if you could name a time when you could attend, matters might be brought to a position that your decision could soon be made. We shall be glad to hear from you at your earliest leisure. Yours respectfully, Thomas W. Wilson, President. Nehemiah Banks, for owners *Sophia*." Of this letter Nehemiah in his evidence said that it was mutually signed, and was written by Mr. Robertson, and that the referees would not act.

It cannot be denied that these papers are entitled to great weight in the particular enquiry before me, and as to these also no explanation is found in the minutes, or was offered on the argument.

It may be said that the directors had a right to seek an adjustment with their neighbours, and to deal with the owners if by doing so an adjustment might be facilitated, and, failing to effect a compromise, they had a right to revert to their original position. There would be some reason in such an argument if the evidence was designed to establish a new contract,—not where it appears that the owners claimed, as the parties entitled as a matter of course, and the directors met them in the same manner, and not a shade of doubt appeared on either side, as to the right of the owners to claim under the policy, but the only question was, how much they were entitled to receive as the parties insured. Then the question fairly arises whether such a coincidence, apparent in the views and conduct of the two parties, on this particular point, is not pregnant evidence of the conviction entertained by both that the policy had been designed to cover the interests of all the owners. It is not conclusive but it is entitled to serious consideration.

I have said little of the evidence which goes to establish what was the intention of Joseph Banks in effecting the insurance in question. He and his son Nehemiah have sworn to it positively, and from this and the forcible presumptions growing out of the current of the transactions between him and the Company, there is no just reason to doubt that Joseph Banks, when he applied in December 1866, for the insurance of the *Sophia*, intended to cover the interests of all the owners and that he took out the policy believing that it had this operation. Indeed, otherwise, his conduct would have been irrational, for he would have paid through a long series of years premiums sufficient to effect the insurance of himself and his sons and relatives, co-owners with him in the various vessels they owned together, and yet without any reason, have left their interests uninsured.

I think, however, that the plaintiffs were defective in not going farther and proving by facts as well as assertions that the several owners were interested in the insurances, by showing the mode in which the premiums and the moneys received on losses had been distributed among the different owners.

It will be seen that the evidence offered by the plaintiffs to prove that the directors, when they made the policy in question, intended that it should cover to the extent of £750 the interests of all the owners is purely presumptive,—inferences drawn from their conduct before and after the policy was effected, and the loss had occured, and in this I do not fail to include the fact that when distinctly questioned, the defendant shrank from an explicit denial of such intention. The question is whether evidence of this character, in general, and whether the evidence in this case, in particular, is sufficient to meet the severe obligation of proof imposed on the plaintiffs by the task they have undertaken in this cause. I know, however, of no rule which requires or which excludes any particular class of testimony in cases of this nature more than in cases of any other.

In *Barstow* v. *Kilvington*, 5 Ves., 601-3, a settlement was reformed on a letter of a mother stating the intention, and the Lord Chancellor thought it the stronger that it was after the settlement, and therefore entitled to more weight than a letter of instruction prior to a settlement. Evidence was also admitted of declarations by the mother in her life time; likewise, accounts of rent and letters showing the understanding of the parties interested after the death of the mother. In 2 Ves. Sr., 377, the Master of the the Rolls cited the case of the *South Sea Company* v. *D'Oliff*, where Lord KING sent it to an issue, to try whether in a written agreement it should have been two months notice instead of six, as expressed in the agreement, and on a verdict finding the mistake, relief was granted.

For the character of the proof required I may refer to 1 Story's Eq. Jur., 162; *Fowler* v. *Fowler*, 4 DeG. & J., 265; *Harris* v. *Pepperell*, Law Rep., Eq., 1867, p. 2; 17 Johnson's Rep., 373; *Malmesbury* v. *Malmesbury*, 31 Beavan, 417. But in whatever form the proof may be it must be strong. Lord HARDWICKE has said it must be the strongest proof possible; Judge STORY, that it must be entirely exact and satisfactory. We must not however press these emphatic expressions too far; reason applied to each case must govern. I have however no disposition to relax; I see great danger in rendering easy the alteration of solemn written contracts on pretence of mistake supported by parol testimony or by uncertain inferences. Yet great injustice would arise were mistakes to be held incapable of correction, or, what would amount to nearly the same thing, were correction rendered next to impossible by the extravagant amount and nature of the proof required.

I am happy that the responsibility of deciding does not entirely or even mainly rest with me. I might have found it difficult to bring my judical opinion into conformity with my individual belief. In this case there is the verdict of a Jury which now demands consideration. In several cases the Chancellors have referred the question of mistake to a jury and have been guided by their verdict. Under the practice in this country in Country Causes, the facts in Equity cases are presented to a jury for their decision before the case comes before this Court for judgment, and it only comes up when a new trial is sought, or something is required to be done for which the authority of this Court is necessary. In England, on issues from Chancery, the verdict, although not conclusive on the conscience of the judge, yet receives great consideration, and is not set aside except on very adequate grounds. So here, while I should not hold myself bound by the verdict in all cases, still, equally, if not more than in England, owing to the constitution of our Court, am I bound to regard the finding of a jury. I have already in more cases than one been governed by the verdict. In the case of *Brown* v. *Chesley*, I felt myself

10 *e*

constrained to yield the tendency of my own opinion on the facts to the finding of the jury, because the case was within their province, and there was not wanting some evidence on which to sustain their verdict, although in their place I might have found differently.

In the present case the jury have not exceeded their province, and there was evidence before them to justify their finding. They have said that the defendant intended that the policy should extend to the whole vessel, and that there was a mutual understanding between the two parties which the policy, as it was executed, does not carry out; to do so it would require to be altered by inserting the names of the other registered owners.

I cannot direct a new trial, when I see no reason to believe that another jury would find a different verdict. I cannot pass by the verdict and dismiss the bill on the ground that there is nothing in the evidence which adequately required the consideration of a Jury. I am therefore of opinion that the prayer of the plaintiffs' writ should be granted, and that it should be declared that the policy is not conformable to the contract between the parties, so far as it is limited to the insurance of Joseph Banks' shares, but that it ought to have expressed that Joseph Banks did make assurance, and cause himself and the other owners of the Brigantine *Sophia* to be insured; that the policy should be reformed so as to cover the interest of all the owners of the *Sophia;* that the defendant should be enjoined from setting up as a defence to an action or claim on the policy by the plaintiffs or any of them that the insurance applied only to the share and interest of Joseph Banks, and that the other plaintiffs were not insured thereby; that the policy should be held and acted upon as if so reformed, and that the plaintiffs should have their costs.

This judgment was appealed from and argued before the Court, in banc.

Sir Wm. Young, C. J., now, (Jan'y 15th, 1872,) delivered the judgment of the Court:

This is an appeal from a judgment delivered by His Lordship the Equity Judge in favor of the plaintiffs, permitting them to reform a policy of insurance, so as to cover their united interest in a brigantine called the *Sophia*, which had been insured by the defendant and his associates in the name of Joseph Banks, owning only 20/64th parts thereof. The policy is in the printed form used by the Association which, for some reason that remains unexplained, omits the usual words, " or whom it may concern," and has led to the present protracted litigation. The real dispute between the parties was the character of the loss, whether a constructive total loss involving a payment of $3000, less an inconsiderable salvage of $600 or $700, or a partial loss of $900 to $1200, which last was the utmost amount offered to the plaintiffs by way of compromise. This was rejected, and the defendants having learned from their counsel that they had a defence arising out of the form of the policy, the plaintiffs were obliged to come into this Court on its Equity side to have the policy reformed. Should they succeed in this, they have still to encounter the main question, and a third trial will probably be held at common law. Between parties of undoubted respectability, near neighbors and friends until now, this long delay and very heavy expenditure are surely to be regretted.

The action at common law was first tried at Barrington, in May term, before Mr. Justice DODD, and, issues having been settled in the Equity suit, these were tried before me at Shelburne in September 1869, and on the finding of the jury at that trial the judgment mainly proceeded. It contains a most searching and elaborate review of the facts and law of the case, occupying seven closely printed pages, the greater part of which it would be superfluous in this judgment to repeat. With the legal conclusions drawn from the cases, the defendants counsel on the hearing of the appeal professed themselves satisfied, and two or three of the more recent decisions appear to me to confirm them. It is admitted that it is not enough that the plaintiffs or either of them really and *bona fide* intended to cover their whole interest in the vessel, and that they or one of them paid the premium with that view. Nor is it enough that the defendants intended to cover the whole value of the ship if the party insuring did not own it. The question is, what was the understanding of both parties, the real contract which ought to have been, but by mistake, or error, has not been set out in the policy. The Court of Equity is not to make a new contract according to its conceptions of what is right and just, but to find out by means of legal evidence what the contract really and truly was, and reform the policy so as to give it effect.

The leading case in the American Courts, so much relied on by the defendant's counsel, that of *Lyman* v. *The United Insurance Company*, 2 Johnson's Chancery Reports 630, and 631, 17 Johnson, 373, in the New York Court of Errors, recognises these principles. SPENCER, C. J., says, in his very able opinion; "Before a written contract can be amended or altered on the pretence of mistake, the proof must be entirely clear, first, that a mistake has occurred, and, secondly, that the amendment sought would conform the contract to the ·intention of both parties. The proof of the mistake must be clear and decisive, for the written contract, executed by the one party and accepted by the other, affords very high evidence that it speaks the agreement and intention of the parties. It is not enough, in cases of this kind, to shew the sense and intention of one of the parties to the contract; it must be shown incontrovertibly that the sense and intention of the other party concurred in it; in other words it must be proved that they both understood the contract as it is alleged it ought to have been, and as in fact it was but for the mistake. There must be a material mistake in the policy to be reformed."

The Court of Errors, in this case, upheld the policy as it was drawn, and stated the principle on which they proceeded, as we have seen, in very emphatic terms. PLATT, J. said; "There is no evidence of any agreement between the parties, different from that expressed in the policy; on the contrary, the allegations of the bill on that point are fully and expressly denied in the answers and those denials are strongly fortified by the testimony of the only witness who was present at the negotiations."

In one of the latest English cases, cited. also by the defendant's counsel, that of *Fowler* v. *Fowler*, 4 DeG. & J., 250, decided in 1859, the judgment of the Lord Chancellor CHELMSFORD, delivered just before his resignation of the office then transferred to Lord CAMPBELL, modifies somewhat the extreme rigor, while affirming the general principle of the previous cases. It still insists on a common intention and a mutual mistake, but takes exception to the very strong language used by Lord THURLOW, (*1 Bro. Ch. Ca.*, 341.) that the evidence to establish the intention must be irrefragable evidence. "If," said Lord CHELMSFORD, "this word was used in its ordinary meaning to describe evidence which cannot be refuted or overthrown, the language of Lord THURLOW would require some modification; but it is probable that he only meant that the mistake must be proved by something more than the highest degree of probability, and that it must be such as to leave no fair and reasonable doubt upon the mind that the deed or instrument does not embody the final intention of the parties. It is clear that a person who seeks to rectify a deed upon the ground of mistake must be required to establish in the clearest and most satisfactory manner, that the alleged intention to which he desires it to be made conformable continued concurrently in the mind of all parties down to the time of its execution, and also must be able to shew, exactly and precisely, the form to which the deed ought to be brought."

These last sentences seem to me to contain the essence of the rule, and I find this case cited accordingly in the modern text books. *Sugden on Vendors and Purchasers*, Lib. Ed., 171; *Smith's Manual of Equity*, 47, &c. The evidence must be such as to leave no fair and reasonable doubt of the intention of both parties, and the mistake must be established in the clearest and most satisfactory manner. The same principles, I see, have been extended to the reforming of ante-nuptial settlements. They are laid down by the present Lord Chancellor, (then Vice-Chancellor WOOD,) in the case of *Rooke* v. *Lord Kensington*, 2 K. & J., 764, and by Vice Chancellor KINDERSLEY, in *Sells* v. *Sells*, 3 L. T. R., N. S., 229. We are to look then to the evidence; but this, for the reason already given, I have no intention of doing in detail. We have a facility and advantage in Equity cases in this Court which they do not enjoy in England. Although the Chancery Courts.

there, under recent enactments, in the years 1858 and 1863, may call in the aid of a jury to settle disputed facts, it is rarely resorted to, because it is alien to the habits of thought and the prepossessions both of Bench and Bar.   But here it is the familiar practice, and I must take occasion to reiterate my strong conviction and desire in the interest of suitors, that the practice of the English Courts of Chancery should never be introduced into this Court, except by legislative enactment, where our own common law practice will avail.   Under the *Rev. Stat.* ch. 124, and the Acts of 1866, ch. 11, Equity causes "shall continue to be tried before a jury to whom issues of fact shall be submitted."   How is their verdict when rendered to be treated, and on what principle is a new trial to be granted or withheld ?   In my opinion, precisely on the same principle as on the common law side of this Court.   We hear it asserted sometimes in argument that the verdict in an Equity suit does not bind the conscience of the Equity Judge as a verdict binds our consciences here.   But, for my part, I repudiate any such distinction.   I think the conscience should be bound, or in other words, the rights of parties determined, equally by a verdict resting on sufficient evidence in both Courts; and I am not aware that the Equity Judge dissents from this view, although he may not be disposed perhaps to go quite so far.

To what conclusions, let us ask, would any other rule conduct us ?   It will be found from *2 Daniell's Chancery Practice,* 753, that the Court of Chancery will frequently direct new trials of the issues as to the title of land, even in cases in which the issue has been properly tried and the verdict is satisfactory upon the evidence, the practice of the Court being adverse to making a decree to bind the inheritance where there has been but one trial at law.   Where the object is to establish a will against an heir, the Court will not bind him by one trial only, but will direct a second; even after two trials, in both of which the verdict is in favor of the will, the Court, where it was not satisfied with the manner in which the last trial was conducted, has directed a third, and that, even though it did not appear from Judge's report that there was any reason to disturb the verdict.   It seems, also, that even after three trials, the Court, if it sees reason to be dissatisfied with the verdict, will grant a fourth. These rules I take from the library edition of *Daniell's Practice*, published in 1840, and I find them repeated in the edition of 1871, where the rule is laid down thus: (*Daniell's Chancery Practice, 5th Ed. 988;*) "When issues are directed to be tried at law, if the verdict is not such as to satisfy the Court that it ought to found a decree upon it, there are several cases in which this Court has directed a new trial for further satisfaction, notwithstanding it would not be granted in a Court of Common Law, because it is *diverso intuitu*, and because the Court proceeds on different grounds." This practice we must assume to be fitted for an old country where enormous sums have accumulated and a large fortune, as in the Tichborne case, may be spent upon a suit. But in our humble sphere we cannot afford such costly experiments. These successive trials of the same facts are totally unfitted to our condition, and I take them to be expressly repudiated by our Legislature.

In this case the findings of the Jury were substantially in favor of the plaintiffs. They found that the application for the insurance, as is apparent on the face of it, gave information to the defendant that the vessel was owned by Joseph Banks and others; that the defendant and his broker believed Joseph Banks to be principal owner, but admitted his sons, (the present plaintiffs,) were owners with him; that both parties intended the insurance to cover the whole vessel; and, above all, they found in answer to the ninth issue, that when the policy was executed there was a mutual understanding between the two parties as respected the extent of the indemnification. The jury added that the policy, as it was executed, does not carry out that understanding; to do so it would require to be altered by inserting the names of the other registered owners. Those issues, as I have said, were tried before me, and I was entirely satisfied with the verdict. The Equity Judge attached great importance to it, as he has to other verdicts in his Court, even against the tendency of his own opinion. For my part, I deem such a verdict, till set aside on sufficient grounds, as conclusive evidence of the facts. The ninth finding was said at the argument to be inconsistent with the third, and it is not easy to reconcile them. But the findings as a whole and the evidence in the Judge's minutes remain intact, and as they bring this case completely within the principles recognised on both sides, I am of opinion that this appeal should be dismissed with costs.

DALEY *v.* FARRELL.

Plaintiff purchased a house from the defendant, the consideration stated in the deed being £250. Defendant had mortgaged the property to the Building Society and there was a balance due the Society on the mortgage of £210 - 16, which plaintiff agreed to assume. The other conditions of the bargain were in controversy, and defendant contended that plaintiff was to pay him all the sums that he had·paid to the Society for dues, in addition to the bonus and entrance fee, and the difference between the consideration and the amount due the Building Society on the mortgage, while plaintiff stated that he was only to make good to the defendant the payments he had made in obtaining the loan. The evidence was conflicting, but the plaintiff's statement was corroborated by his wife. *Held,* that plaintiff could not be charged with the amounts paid by defendant to the Society as dues.

RITCHIE, E. J., delivered the judgment of the Court : —

The question in controversy between these parties is the amount due by the plaintiff to the defendant on the purchase of a property made from the latter by the former.

The consideration named in the deed is £250. There was a mortgage on the property at the time of the sale, held by the Building Society, on which there was due £210 - 16, which the plaintiff says he agreed to assume the payment of, and to pay, in addition, to defendant the sums which he had paid to the Society. He paid at the time £10 on account, and was to pay the balance of the £250 with interest. The statement of the transactions, as the plaintiff makes it, stands thus ;—

Amount of purchase money............	£250	0 - 0		
"　　　　　　Building Soc..........	19	4 - 0		
	269	4 - 0		
"　　due Building Society on mort　..	210	16 - 0		
	58	- 8 - 0		
"　　Cash paid at time of purchase....	10	- 0　0		
Balance due by pltff. to defdt. payable with int.,	48	- 8 - 0		

This sum of £48 - 8 the plaintiff has always been willing to pay, and he tendered £50 to defendant's solicitor to cover this balance, which, subsequent to the commencement of this suit, has been paid to the defendant, and he has, he says, now overpaid the defendant.

The defendant alleges that though the price agreed upon for the land was £250, yet, by the agreement between himself and the plaintiff, the defendant on taking his shares in the Building Society was to repay him all the money he had paid the Society on account of them, which he has ascertained to have been £76 8 - 4, made up of monthly dues, entrance fee and bonus. The defendant became security to the Society for the plaintiff, and took from him a confession of judgment for $1084, as a security. His statement of the transaction is:—

Amt. due on mortgage to Building Society, to be assumed by plaintiff £210	16 - 0	
Payments made to Society on account of mortgage by defendant .... 55 -	4' - 4	
Bonus paid on loan by Society................ 19	4 - 0	
Entrance fee.... 2	0 - 0	
Amount payable by plaintiff for this land 277	4 - 4	
Paid on account .... 10 -	0 - 0	
267	4	4

Thus leaving £66 - 8 4 payable to the plaintiff in addition to the amount remaining on mortgage, or, since the receipt of the £50 - 0 - 0, £16 - 8 - 4.

The evidence of what the contract really was is contradictory, but, from the vague terms in which it was expressed, it is quite probable that it was understood differently by the contracting parties, each believing the agreement to have been as he now states it. There was certainly no definite amount settled upon at the time to be paid by the plaintiff beyond the amount of the mortgage, and this the defendant admits he never ascertained till lately, in fact till the dispute arose, when he, for the first time, furnished plaintiff with a statement of it, which he says he obtained from the Secretary of the Building

Society. Without either party knowing the exact balance, the plaintiff, assuming it to be £50, tendered that sum, which the defendant refused, requiring interest on £60.

By the defendant's statement it will be perceived that the consideration named in the deed, £250, is not introduced. His account of the agreement is as follows: " I said my price was £250. Plaintiff said he had not the money to pay for it,—he had a little money and he thought he could get the money from the Building Society. I told him there was no necessity for that,—it was already in the Building Society, and I could make a transfer of the shares to him provided he would repay me the amounts I had paid on these shares; he asked me the amount, I said I did not know, that I thought I had been in the Society about two years; there was no specific sum mentioned except the £250, and no figures were mentioned except the £250. I recollect of nothing further being said except that he said it was a bargain." The sale took place in 1865, and he says the first time he ascertained the exact amount plaintiff was to pay him for the land was in 1870, and he further says he could not say how much money he received on the shares from the Society in 1863.

Taking this account of the transaction given by the defendant, I find it difficult to adopt the construction he has put upon it. He distinctly admits that the price of the land was £250, and the only modification of it was by the plaintiff's taking his place in the Building Society, and it was quite reasonable that he should be repaid by the plaintiff the bonus which he had paid for the money when he effected the loan from the Society, as that was deducted from the money loaned, and the plaintiff, if he had made a new loan from the Society, would have been liable to have paid a bonus for it. But why he should repay to the defendant the sums which he had paid from time to time on account of interest, and the reduction of the capital, is what I cannot understand. It is only with the balance as reduced that he has to do; the defendant received from the Society a larger sum than the plaintiff was to assume, but it is not that sum, but the reduced sum, that is deducted from the amount of the purchase money, £250. The defendant therefore gets all the benefit of his payments on account of principal, and why should the plaintiff repay him the interest he had paid in the two preceding years? He had himself enjoyed the benefit of the loan, and this in his view he could do without interest, while he was in possession of and enjoying the rent of the property mortgaged.

I confess I do not see how the defendant, on his own account of the transaction, can hope to succeed in his claim, and if there had been no counter statements and the plaintiff had acquiesced in the correctness of the account of the defendant, he might well have inferred that while he might be called upon to make good to the defendant all payments he had made in connection with his obtaining the loan, he could not be called upon to repay him what he had paid in reduction of the principal and back interest, and probably a large amount of fines. That is the inference, I think, I should have drawn. The plaintiff however does most distinctly assert that such was the express agreement, and his wife corroborates his evidence; and as this evidence is in accordance with the deed which states the consideration to have been £250, the plaintiff is entitled to the relief he seeks by his writ.

FRASER, Assignee, *v.* ADAMS et al.

Howell and Stewart, in June 1871, entered into co-partnership as founders, &c., the former to give his skill and ability to the business, and the latter, who was a minor, to supply capital and purchase stock to the extent of $4000. At the time of the agreement, a lot of land was purchased for $10,000 on which to erect buildings for the business, but nothing was paid on account of the purchase money, which was secured by a mortgage. The deed was taken in the name of Howell and Mrs. Adams, the mother of Stewart, who advanced the $4000 to start the business. Although plaintiff contended that this advance was simply made by Mrs. Adams to her son, there was some evidence to show that it was to be repaid by the partnership. Stewart became of age in February, 1873, and in August of that year the partnership was dissolved and a mortgage made by Howell to Mrs. Adams to secure the amount of her advances. The plaintiff, as assignee, sought to have this mortgage declared void, as made in contemplation of insolvency. At the time of making the mortgage the business was embarrassed, but the jury found that the mortgage was not made in contemplation of insolvency, and they negatived fraud in the transaction, though they found that the conveyance had had the effect of impeding obstructing and delaying creditors. The Court upheld the conveyance.

Ritchie, E. J., delivered the judgment of the Court:—

The plaintiff is the assignee under the Insolvent Act of 1869, of James B. Howell, and he seeks in this suit to have a mortgage from the insolvent to Maria S. Adams, declared void, and that she may be decreed to reconvey the land comprised therein, and to account to him for all rents, profits, &c., received by her under and by virtue of it, on the ground that it was made in contemplation of insolvency, whereby Mrs. Adams obtained an unjust preference over other creditors, and to impede, obstruct and delay the creditors of the said Howell and his co-partner Stewart in their remedies against them; and also that it was fraudulently and collusively made in order to defraud such creditors, and to withdraw from the business carried on by them the sum of $9500, which of right belongs to the plaintiff as assignee, and to impede, obstruct and delay their creditors, &c., and that such mortgage had that effect.

It appears from the evidence that Howell and Stewart entered into a partnership on the 24th June, 1871, as founders and machine makers, the former being a machinist, and the latter being wholly unskilled in the business, and at the time under the age of twenty-one. By the articles of partnership, which were to continue in operation for ten years, it was among other things stipulated that Howell should give his skill and ability and best attention to the business, and that Stewart should supply the capital to commence with, and purchase stock, &c., to the amount of $4000, and that nothing should be withdrawn till the amount should have increased to $10,000. The net profits were to be divided equally between the parties.

About the time this agreement was entered into a lot of land was purchased from Thomas Mitchell, on which it was proposed to erect the necessary buildings, &c., and to conduct the business, for the sum of $10,000, but no part of the purchase money was paid, the whole amount being secured by a mortgage on the premises, which mortgage still remains unpaid.

The deed was taken in the name of Howell and Mrs. Adams, who is the mother of Stewart, to hold as tenants in common; the moiety conveyed to Mrs. Adams to be held for the benefit of her said son, he to pay her the annual interest on $5000, the consideration for the said moiety. The $4000 was advanced by Mrs. Adams.

Stewart came of age in February 1873, and the partnership continued in operation till August of that year, at which time the business was certainly not in a prosperous state, and Stewart then left it under an arrangement by which his mother, Mrs. Adams, was to receive security for the $4000 and all money which she had advanced, and on the 1st August, 1873, to carry out this arrangement, the mortgage in question was given.

The evidence, it appears to me, leads to the inference that the business was at that time actually insolvent, though, from the unsatisfactory way in which the accounts have been kept it would seem not to have been known to either of the partners. Stewart says positively it was not insolvent, and Howell, that he did not discover it so till afterwards, and that if he had then known the real state of the business, as he subsequently discovered it, he would not have made the arrangement. Certain issues were submitted to a jury which with the findings are as follows:

1st.—Did Maria S. Adams hold the moiety of the land purchased by herself and James B. Howell from Thomas Mitchell, in trust for her son, William Stewart?

A. Maria S. Adams did not hold the moiety of the land purchased by herself and James B. Howell from Thomas Mitchell, in trust for her son, William Stewart, otherwise than as expressed in the deed.

2nd.—Were the moneys advanced for the erection of buildings and machinery on the above land so advanced in discharge of Stewart's agreement in the articles of co-partnership to pay into the concern $4000?

A. The moneys advanced for the erection of buildings and machinery on the above land were advanced in discharge of Stewart's agreement in the articles of co-partnership, to pay into the concern $4000, but it was to be repaid to the said Maria S. Adams.

3rd.—Was the mortgage made in contemplation of insolvency?

A. The mortgage was not made in contemplation of insolvency.

4th.—Did Maria S. Adams thereby obtain, or will she obtain an unjust preference over the other creditors of the insolvent?

A. Maria S. Adams did not thereby obtain an unjust preference over other creditors of the insolvent.

5th.—Was the mortgage given by the insolvent with the intent to defraud his other creditors? Was it given with intent fraudulently to impede, obstruct, or delay his creditors in their remedies against him, with intent to defraud them? Was it so given and intended with knowledge of Maria S. Adams? Did the giving of the mortgage have the effect of impeding, obstructing or delaying the creditors of the insolvent in their remedies, or of injuring them or any of them?

A. The mortgage was not given with intent to defraud the other creditors. The mortgage was not given with the intent to impede, delay, or obstruct his creditors in their remedies against him, with intent to defraud them, nor was it so given with the knowledge of Maria S. Adams. Giving the mortgage had the effect of impeding, obstructing, and delaying the creditors of the insolvent.

It appears to me that the evidence justifies the conclusions at which the jury have arrived. The plaintiff, to succeed, must establish his case as stated in his writ, and this I think he has not done.

The partnership referred to was entered into by Howell with an infant, who had no capital himself and was to obtain it from his mother; it was to continue for ten years, but after it had been in operation about two years, and a few months after Stewart came of age, difficulties occurred and differences arose between the partners, when it was mutually agreed that Stewart should retire and leave the business to Howell, on condition that Mrs. Adams should be secured the advances she had made which had gone into the business, and the mortgage was given by Howell, he believing at the time he gave it that he could carry on the business, and thinking, as he says in his evidence, that as it was established, it was fair enough to give Stewart the money he had advanced to start it.

It was much relied on at the argument that the advances made by Mrs. Adams were made to her son, who alone was responsible to her for repayment; but on referring to the evidence it is far from clear that this was the case. Howell indeed says that it was never contemplated by him that the partnership was to repay the money, but he admits that before Stewart came of age and before it would appear that any difficulties had arisen in the business, this was the subject of controversy between the partners, and that on one occasion, in reference to the subject, he said something about Stewart waiting till he came of age; and the infancy of Stewart is an element not to be forgotten in considering this question. Mrs. Adams says she always from the first expected to get the mortgage as security for the money she advanced. But the testimony of Mitchell, a witness produced on the part of the plaintiff, is the most important. It was through him the money was advanced. He says Mrs. Adams was to put $4000 in the business, to get interest for it and security. Howell was to secure it as Stewart was a minor; so Mrs. Adams said. He proceeds to say, "I said go to Howell, he did not understand it so, he contended it was put in on account of the partnership, he did not say whether it was to be paid back,—all he said was that the $4000 was to be in the firm without paying any interest." And again, "I gave Howell to understand the money advanced was Mrs. Adams'. Before the arrangement was fully made, I gave Howell to understand that he was to pay interest on the money Mrs. Adams advanced."

Can it be said that there is *no evidence* that these advances were to be repaid by the partnership? There is, I think, nothing in the argument that this view is not sustained by the language of the contract of partnership. With the terms of that contract Mrs. Adams has nothing to do; she is no party to it, and according to her evidence, she never saw it; her rights can in no respect be affected by it. I do not wish it to be assumed, however, if the advance had been made as the plaintiff's counsel contended it was, that, under the circumstances of this case, the mortgage would have been rendered inoperative.

I cannot see that any of the grounds relied on by the plaintiff in his writ have been sustained by the evidence. Admitting that at the time the mortgage was given the partnership was really insolvent, if that were unknown to all parties connected with the instrument, it was not made in contemplation of insolvency, and cannot be said to have been made with intent fraudulently to impede, obstruct, or delay creditors so as to invalidate the mortgage in question under the Insolvent Act. Assuming, as I think I am bound to do under the evidence, that when the mortgage was given none of the parties considered the partnership insolvent, however insolvent it might have been, there was no fraud, and the parties were carrying out in good faith what they all deemed to be a fair and reasonable arrangement; and in my opinion, the defendant is entitled to judgment, with costs.

This case was argued upon the assumption that the whole lot purchased from Mitchell was comprised in the mortgage to Mrs. Adams, but such on reference to the deeds in evidence appears not to be the case. Mitchell conveyed the whole lot to Howell and Mrs. Adams, to be held by them as tenants in common; Mrs. Adams conveyed her half to Howell, and he mortgaged that half to her,—so that his title to the other half is not affected by the mortgage.

THE CAPE BRETON COMPANY, LIMITED, *v.* GISBORNE.

The plaintiffs sought in this suit discovery of facts necessary to enable them to plead to an action at law brought against them by the defendant, and the writ contained a prayer for relief in respect of the matters of which discovery was sought. On taking out the writ, plaintiffs obtained an order restraining defendant from further action in the common law suit, and defendant, having filed his answer, sought to have the restraining order discharged. *Held*, that the plaintiff Company having sought relief in this Court, had elected this tribunal, and could not at the same time make the matters referred to in their writ the subject of pleas to the action at law; that the evidence sought for was, therefore, not pertinent to the defence in the action at law, and that the restraining order having been granted solely on the ground that discovery was necessary, must be discharged, irrespective of the sufficiency of the defendant's answer; that the present suit, although it could not be treated as a suit for discovery, still continued as a suit for relief, but that plaintiffs might discontinue the suit and plead the facts set out in their writ as a defence to the action at law.

RITCHIE, E. J., now, (April 30th, 1877), delivered the judgment of the Court:—

In this suit discovery is sought to enable the Company to plead to and defend an action at law brought against them by the defendant Gisborne, such discovery being, as alleged, necessary to enable them to defend the action, as many, if not all of the facts of which discovery is sought are not otherwise susceptible of proof than by such discovery. After setting out specifically in the writ the matters on which discovery is sought, they pray that the defendant should make full discovery of them, and that they should have the benefit thereof in the said action; and they go on to pray that the defendant should be decreed to pay all such sums of money to them in relation to which the discovery is sought, and that the said action at law should be restrained, and that they should have such further and other relief as might be deemed just.

The writ alleges that the action at law was brought to recover from the Company $144,286.17, of which $100,000 is claimed for damages for the non-fulfilment of a contract, and $2433.33 is claimed by him for having resigned the office of Manager of the Company, and the balance for work done by him for them. The Company assert that Gisborne resigned the office of manager on his being charged with fraudulent conduct, and, though he asked to have the sum above mentioned allowed him in consequence of his having so resigned it, that they refused to do so; that they have overpaid him for all work done under the contract and otherwise, while the defendant has not performed his part of the contract, and, in consequence, the Company have instituted an action against

10 f

him and his sureties in the High Court of Justice in England for damages for the non-completion of the said contract, to which they have appeared and pleaded, which action is still pending and undetermined; and they further assert that the defendant has fraudulently retained a very large sum of money belonging to the Company, and has been guilty of other fraudulent conduct in relation to contracts made by him while manager of the Company, and that a large sum of money is due from him to the Company on the accounts between them as they now stand, the amounts and particulars of all of which the defendant is asked to disclose on oath.

On taking out the writ the Company applied for and obtained an order of this Court restraining defendant from taking any further step or proceeding in the action at law until the further order of this Court, and the defendant, having filed his answer, now seeks to have this order discharged. This is resisted mainly on the ground that the answer does not make full and sufficient discovery. The defendant, on the other hand, contends that he has fully answered everything that affects the defence in the action at law and is material to the issues which can be raised in it, either on legal or equitable grounds, and that on that account the order should be discharged; and he further contends that, inasmuch as the plaintiff's writ seeks relief as well as discovery, in having prayed that the defendant should pay all sums of money to which they were entitled in relation to the matters set out in the writ, and that he should be restrained from proceeding with the action, it cannot be treated as a suit for discovery, and therefore the restraining order should not have been taken. The restraining order was granted solely on the ground that discovery was necessary to enable them to plead to and defend the action at law, and that in the meantime it was necessary to restrain the defendant from proceeding in that action by marking a default, or otherwise compromising their right till the discovery should be afforded. If this suit is not to be deemed a suit for discovery, they cannot maintain the order. In *Kerr on Injunction*, 29, it is laid down that a bill which prays for discovery should not contain a prayer for general relief; and if such prayer be added it cannot be treated as a bill for discovery. See also *Daniel's Ch. Pr.*, 1410, *Angel* v. *Westcome*, 6 Sim., 30, and *James* v. *Herriott*, Id. 428.

And it has been held that if a bill contains a prayer for an injunction to restrain the defendant from all proceedings in an action at law against the plaintiff, it is fatal to the bill as a bill for discovery, as that is a prayer for relief; *Andrews* v. *Layton*, 13 L. J., Ch., 201; so any special prayer which will require the cause to be brought to a hearing will be deemed a prayer for relief. *Vaughan* v. *Fitzgerald*, 1 Sch. & Le Fr., 316.

The plaintiffs, having sought relief in relation to the matters set out in the writ, have elected to proceed against the defend- ant in this Court, and they cannot, I think, seek redress here and set up the same matters as a defence in the action at law. If they wished to set up an equitable defence to that action it was open to them to do so, and the Common Law Court has not only the right of adjudicating on equitable defences, but also of compelling discovery. This jurisdiction, which has been conferred by statutes, does not, it is true, take away the right of coming to this Court, but if a party proceeds in this Court to enforce an equitable right he cannot at the same time set up that equitable right to defeat a legal right the enforce- ment of which is sought in an action at law; nor can he, when he has set up an equitable defence to an action at law, proceed for the same in this Court. See *Daniel's Ch. Pr.*, 1473. In *Walker* v. *Micklethwait*, 1 Dr. & Sm., 54, the Vice Chancellor said, "where application is made to this Court to restrain an action, and the defendant at law has pleaded an equitable plea, he has made his choice and elected his Court, but if he has not so pleaded there is nothing to prevent him from coming to this Court;" and in *Waterlow* v. *Bacon*, L. R., 2 Eq., 514, KINDERSLEY, V. C., said, "if a defendant in an action thinks fit to plead an equitable plea, he cannot come to this Court for an injunction to restrain the action on the very ground that he has made the subject of his equitable plea, provided the case is of such a nature that the Court of Law can give such relief on the equitable plea as this Court will give.

This writ is framed on the principle of obtaining discovery to enable the plaintiff to plead to and defend the action at law, and yet it seeks full relief and asks for a decree in respect.

of all the matters of which discovery is sought. If they intended to have set up these matters as a defence to the defendant's action at law, they should have prayed for discovery alone, but, having sought full relief here, they have elected this tribunal for the enforcement of their equitable rights, and they cannot, therefore, by injunction or otherwise, stay the defendant from enforcing his legal rights in the common law court. And under these circumstances, as they cannot make the matters referred to in their writ the subject of pleas to the defendant's action, the evidence sought for in this suit will not be material or pertinent to their defence, and it is incumbent on the plaintiff to show that the discovery sought is material, and such as could be used on the trial of the action at law.

There appears to me to be much unnecessary expense incurred in this litigation. The subject matter is in controversy in the High Court of Justice in England, in an action at law in Cape Breton, and in this Court. I cannot but think that the plaintiffs in this suit could have obtained every advantage in the Court of common law which they can hope to gain here. That Court, doubtless, would have ordered the plaintiff in that action to have answered interrogatories seeking the necessary discovery, if application had been made to it; and, if it had deemed the discovery necessary to enable them to plead, would have given them time to plead till the interrogatories were answered. The only question at present before the Court is whether the restraining order shall or shall not be discharged, and I think the defendant is entitled to have it discharged on the ground that the suit in this Court must be held to be a suit for relief, and cannot be treated as a suit for discovery. In all other respects the suit continues and the parties may proceed to proof, but it will be for the plaintiffs to decide whether to do so and seek the decree they pray for, or to discontinue and plead the facts set out in the writ in the action at law if they consider that they constitute a defence to the claim of Gisborne, either on legal or equitable grounds.

In the view I have taken of the case, that the restraining order should be discharged irrespective of the sufficiency or insufficiency of the defendant's answer, it is not necessary at this stage of the case to say more than that in some particulars it does not give as full and explicit answers as the plaintiffs are entitled to, and if they shall elect to prosecute their suit in this Court for relief, the subject can be brought before me, and I will decide on the exceptions and on what points the plaintiffs are entitled to a further and better answer.

WICKWIRE v. GOULD.

The Wickwire dyke, being outside of and affording protection to the Grand Pre dyke constructed many years before, the proprietors of the Wickwire marsh, acting under the provisions of the statute then in force, (see R. S. Cap. 40, s. 27) took proceedings to settle what proportion of the expense of the maintenance and repair of the Wickwire dyke should be contributed by the proprietors of the Grand Pre Marsh, which sum so settled was annually paid by the proprietors of the Grand Pre Marsh so long as that marsh received any protection from the outer dyke. In 1869 a heavy gale and unusually high tide broke the outer dyke and submerged the Wickwire marsh, and it was not until 1871 that the dyke was reconstructed.

Held, that the proprietors of the Grand Pre marsh could not be called upon to contribute towards the repair of the Wickwire dyke beyond the annual sum originally settled.

Defendants having contended that they could not be required to contribute at all, as their marsh was only partially enclosed and not protected by the Wickwire dyke; and further, that there had been irregularities in the original proceedings;

Held, that having acquiesced in the annual payments for upwards of twenty-five years they could not now raise such a question, and that the alleged irregularities could only have been taken advantage of by *certiorari.**

RITCHIE, E. J., now, (June 11th, 1877,) delivered the judgment of the Court:—

The marsh known as the Wickwire marsh was reclaimed from the sea and enclosed by a dyke many years ago. This dyke enclosed land outside the Grand Pre marsh, which had been reclaimed from the sea previously, and was then protected by a dyke which now divides the two marshes. Some time after the erection of the dyke by the proprietors of the Wickwire marsh, the latter, acting under the provisions of a statute

---

* This decision was confirmed on appeal to the full Court. See reports for 1878-9.

then and still in force, took proceedings to settle and declare
what proportion or degree of benefit had accrued or was likely
to accrue to the Grand Pre marsh from the dyke erected by
them outside of it, and what proportion of expense the proprietors of the Grand Pre marsh should annually contribute
and be assessed for towards the maintenance and repair of the
Wickwire dyke; and a sum to be annually paid was accordingly settled, which the proprietors of the Grand Pre marsh
paid and continued to pay as long as that marsh received any
protection from the Wickwire dyke, and are still willing to
pay.

In the year 1869 a heavy gale and an unusually high tide
broke the outer dyke and the Wickwire marsh was submerged.
The damage thus occasioned was so great that it became questionable whether it would be worth while to repair or recon-
struct it, or whether it would not be better to let the land
remain as salt marsh; and it was not until 1871 that it was
repaired or reconstructed. The evidence shows that the injury
to the dyke was very extensive, but it cannot be said to have
been wholly destroyed, as is asserted by the plaintiffs; and
the damage was increased by the delay which took place in
repairing it.

A question is raised, and it is in my opinion that on which
the whole case turns, whether the proprietors of the outer
marsh can, whenever their dyke sustains damage and requires
repairs, it may be to an unusual extent as in this case, seek an
increased assessment and contribution from the proprietors of
the inner marsh, as the plaintiffs contend, from time to time,
or whether, as the defendants contend, the amount being once
fixed on the erection of the dyke, that is to remain thereafter
without alteration. This depends upon the enactments on the
subject, and the enactments which were in force when the
amount to be paid by the proprietors of the Grand Pre marsh
was first settled and declared have been ever since and are
still in force.

The provisions of the Statute are to the effect that where any
lands enclosed by dykes shall by other dykes erected outside
the same be enclosed and protected, the commissioners in
charge of the lands enclosed by the outer dyke shall call a

meeting of the proprietors of the whole level, &c., &c., &c., who shall elect not less than three nor more than five disinterested freeholders, who, being sworn before a Justice, shall determine what proportion or degree of benefit *has accrued* or *is likely to accrue* to the old or inner dyke and the land lying within the same from the new or outer dyke, and shall settle and declare the proportion of expense the proprietors within the old dykes ought annually to contribute and be assessed towards the maintenance and repair of the new dyke, &c., &c. If such outer dyke shall at any time cease in whole or in part to protect such inner dykes, the lands within the inner dykes shall not for such time contribute or be assessed to the support or repair of the outer dyke.

If, at any time, two-thirds in interest of the proprietors of the lands within the inner dykes shall be apprehensive that the outer dyke is unsafe or out of repair, two-thirds in interest of the whole level may call upon one or more commissioners to examine the outer dyke, and, if it should appear to require repair, he or they, with the assent of two-thirds in interest of the proprietors of the whole level, shall forthwith cause the same to be repaired, or otherwise, with the like consent, put the inner dykes in a state of repair as shall seem most advisable. If the inner dyke be repaired, then the proprietors of the lands enclosed thereby shall bear the expense.

Those who erected a dyke outside a marsh which had been already dyked, but for the provisions of the statute, would have had to repair and keep it in repair at their sole expense. The intention of the Legislature, it appears to me, was that on the completion of the outer dyke resort should be had to the statute to ascertain and determine, taking one year with another, what would be a reasonable sum for the proprietors of the inner marsh to contribute annually for the benefit which they derived from it, and with that amount so contributed by them the proprietors of the outer marsh were annually to assess themselves for whatever might be necessary to keep it in proper repair for the security of both marshes.

Many years ago the sum of £19 was settled under the provisions of the statute as the sum to be so annually contributed, which, up to 1869, has been annually paid, and which the defendants are willing and have offered to pay.

Doubtless during the long period which has elapsed since this contribution was awarded the amount required to keep the dyke in repair in different years must have varied much; in some it would probably be more than they ought to contribute towards it, in others less.

If the Legislature had intended that they should pay a certain proportion of each year's repairs, they would have so enacted. There is nothing in the statutes which indicates that applications for contribution were to be made under it from time to time, or that the contribution was to be increased when extensive repairs should become necessary, whether from the inattention or negligence of the proprietors of the outer marsh, or from their not choosing to expend the funds necessary to keep the dyke in proper order to resist the influx of the tide or to prevent injury from gales of wind or extraordinarily high tides.

After giving the subject my best consideration I am led to the conclusion that persons who reclaim lands outside of lands previously reclaimed and dyked can only call in operation the statute once and have no right to do so on every occasion that serious damage is done to their dyke calling for extraordinary repairs, however occasioned.

The proprietors of the Grand Pre marsh had no right to interfere and compel the owners of the Wickwire marsh to repair the dyke when it sustained damage in 1869, but they had to take care during the time that they chose to leave their marsh submerged that their own dyke was put and kept in order so as to exclude the sea from their marsh.

It was contended on the part of the defendants that the proprietors of the Wickwire marsh had no right to ask for any contribution from them, as, from the evidence, it appeared that their dyke only partially enclosed, and, in itself, did not protect the Grand Pre marsh, so that the statute did not apply; and, also, that there had been irregularities in the course pursued by them in calling and conducting the meeting of the proprietors. But it is too late, I think, now to raise the question whether they are or are not liable to contribute under the statute, as that has been settled years ago and acquiesced in and the annual payments made for many years, certainly upwards of twenty-five years; and any irregularity in the proceedings under the statute could only be taken advantage of by bringing them up to the Supreme Court by *certiorari*.

Though I have arrived at the conclusion that the defendants are entitled to a decree in their favor with costs, I have not done so without much hesitation; and it is satisfactory to me to know that if I have put an erroneous construction on the statute, which is not very clear and explicit in its terms, the plaintiffs are not without remedy.

THE ATTORNEY-GENERAL *v.* BULLOCK ET AL.

A testator bequeathed £2,500, to be invested in stocks, &c., the interest on £1000 to be paid to certain clergymen to provide fuel for the poor of their flocks during the winter ; the interest on £500 to be paid to the National School, and a like sum to the Acadian School, on condition of their each teaching at least twelve poor children; and the interest on £500 to be paid to the Institution for the Deaf and Dumb to assist in educating the poor who might be thus afflicted. The Acadian and National Schools were afterwards superseded by the Free Schools established under the Act and supported by taxation. The Master to whom it was referred to report a scheme to carry out testator's intention reported that the sum bequeathed to the schools so superseded should be paid to the School Commissioners towards the erection of a High School in Halifax, under the Act of 1877, Cap. 39.

Held, that as *the poor* were the objects of testator's bounty, his intentions would not be carried out by the scheme proposed, which would simply relieve the citizens generally of taxation, but that the bequest in question should be divided between the Institution for the Deaf and Dumb, and the Asylum for the Blind, (an analogous institution, but one not in operation when testator made his will), to assist in educating the poor inmates of those institutions.

RITCHIE, E. J., now, (Dec. 4th, 1877), delivered the judgment of the Court:—

William K. Reynolds, late of Halifax, merchant, by his will made the following bequest: "It is my wish, as soon as it can conveniently be done after my wife's decease, that all my real estate be sold for the most that can be obtained, and the proceeds applied as hereinafter named; from said proceeds I give the sum of two thousand five hundred pounds for objects of charity, this sum to be invested in some safe stock or mortgage security, under the name and title of the Reynolds Fund, the interest to be paid annually as hereinafter named; the interest of £1000 to be paid to the officiating clergymen of St. Paul's, St. Luke's, and St. Matthew's Churches, to be equally divided, to enable those persons to give fuel to the poor of their respective flocks during the winter season; the interest of £500 to be given to the trustees of the National School, for which they are to teach at least twelve poor children, and a like sum to the trustees of the the Acadian School, subject to the same conditions. I give to the trustees or superintendent of the School for the Deaf and Dumb, to assist in educating the poor who may be thus afflicted, the interest of £500."

The widow of Mr. Reynolds has since died, but, previous to her death, the National and Acadian Schools ceased to be in operation, having been superseded by the free schools established in Halifax and throughout the Province, and supported by taxation; the schools referred to having been supported by private contributions and the fees paid by certain of the scholars, the poor and destitute receiving their instruction gratuitously.

The object of the present proceedings by the Attorney General is to obtain from the Court a decree whereby the charitable intentions of the testator may be carried out as nearly as possible, and to direct Mr. Bullock, the trustee, to pay the funds in his hands to such purposes as shall be best suited to give effect to the will of the testator, the schools named by him having ceased to exist, and the poor being provided with instruction at the public expense.

On its having been referred to a master to report a scheme best calculated to effect this object, he has reported that the charitable intentions of the testator will be most nearly carried out by the transfer to the Board of School Commissioners for the City of Halifax of the moneys devised by him to the National and Acadian Schools, to be appropriated and used in the erection of a building for the use of the High School establishment in Halifax, under the Provincial Act of 1877, Cap. 39.

If the encouragement of education in the City of Halifax had been the main object which Mr. Reynolds had in view in making the bequest, the scheme reported would be very well suited to carry it out. But such is not the case; the objects of his bounty are declared to be *the poor*. He first provides that a portion of the fund he sets apart for charitable purposes shall be applied in providing fuel for certain of the poor of the city during the winter season, and the remainder he applies to the education of the poor in the schools referred to, and to the school for the deaf and dumb, to assist in educating *the poor* who may be thus afflicted.

Though the charitable intention of the testator will not be defeated merely because the mode of carrying it out has been defeated by subsequent circumstances which render it impracticable, if the object he had in view can be obtained by another mode; yet the charity must be the same or of an analogous character, and it is indispensable that it be charitable. Any scheme, therefore, to be adopted by this Court must have in view not simply education, but education for *the poor*.

The testator has expressly declared that his object in making the bequests was charity, and the scheme reported is not in any respect such. The sole effect of it would be to relieve the citizens generally of the expense of building a school house which the law has imposed upon them, the greater part of which would necessarily fall on the more wealthy class.

The primary object of the testator being to provide for the education of the poor, the question naturally arises whether there exists any class of poor requiring education who are unable to take advantage of the free schools now established by law. If so, it appears to me that his object will be attained by appropriating the fund to their support. The general intention will thus be carried out substantially, though not in the mode pointed out by the will.

There are two institutions in the city at which such poor persons may receive instruction,—one for the deaf and dumb, and one for the blind. The inmates of these institutions are not able to receive instruction at the public schools, and no provision has been made for their education by the Legislature. The Asylum for the Blind was not in operation when the testator made his will, the other was, and it was one of those which the testator selected as the object of his bounty ; and it is not improbable that the other would have been selected if it had been then in operation.   If the Institution for the Deaf and Dumb had not been mentioned in Mr. Reynolds' will I should have considered that applying the fund to the education of the poor there, and at that for the blind, would have carried out the charitable intention of the testator as nearly as possible under the circumstances, but his having made provision for the education of the poor at the Institution for the Deaf and Dumb points to it and to its kindred institution for the blind, as those most suitable for the application of the fund by this Court.

In the *Attorney General* v. *The Iron Mongers' Company*, 2 Beav., 313, LORD LANGDALE indicated that, in seeking for a charity on which to bestow a fund *cy pres*, reference could be had to other analogous objects of the testator's bounty ; and LORD COTTENHAM in the same case on appeal, *Cr. & Ph.*, 208, says, " it is obviously true that if several charities be named in a will and one fail for want of objects, one of the others may be found to be *cy pres* to that which has failed." He goes on to say that such other charity ought not, as he conceives, to be preferred to some other more nearly resembling that which has failed ; and he protects himself against the inference that because the testator has made a charitable bequest in favor of one institution analogous to that which has failed, therefore the whole should go to it, if there should be others having equal claims.   It is to be looked to only as a guide to what the testator would probably have done himself.   His language is ; " in considering the manner in which such benefit should be conferred, it is very reasonable and proper to look to other provisions of the will in order to see whether the testator has indicated any preference to any particular mode of administering charity.   If the testator had given part of his property to support hospitals for leprosy, in any part of England, and another part to a particular hospital, it would be reasonable to adopt the support of hospitals as the mode of applying the disposable funds; but there would not be any ground for giving the whole to the particular hospital." He subsequently says: " I think the most reasonable course to be adopted is to look at the second gift as indicative of the kind of charity preferred by the testator, but making it as general in its application as the first was intended to be, that is, open to all which might stand in need of its assistance."

I think I am adopting this view of the law by decreeing that the interest of the fund set apart by the testator for the National and Acadian schools be equally divided between the Asylum for the Deaf and Dumb and the Asylum for the Blind, to assist in educating the poor inmates of those institutions, who, from their affliction, are shut out of the free schools provided for the instruction of all other classes of the community.

ATTORNEY GENERAL v. AVERY, ET AL.

Testator, who died in 1850, devised property to the Kirk Sessions of St. Matthew's Church, in trust to fit it up for a school under the charge of the Sessions. The property went into the possession of the devisees, but no steps were taken to carry out testator's intentions. Proceedings were instituted in the name of the Attorney General to obtain a decree authorizing the adoption of a scheme to carry out testator's intentions, the devisees and the heir-at-law being made parties. None of the defendants appeared and a default was entered. On application being made for reference to a Master the Court allowed the defendants to raise the question whether, the devisees having taken no proceedings, the property did not revert to the heir-at-law, who then appeared by counsel and had a day appointed for the argument, but on the day appointed for argument none of the defendants appeared and the cause was referred to a Master, who reported that the funds should be appropriated towards the erection of a High School building in Halifax, the Kirk Sesions to have the power of nominating two free scholars, having concurred in the recommendation with that condition. No opposition being made to this report, and no counter scheme being suggested, the report was confirmed and the scheme adopted.

RITCHIE, E. J., now, (Dec. 4th, 1877,) delivered the judgment of the Court:—

James Dechman died in the year 1850, having shortly before made his will, in which, after reciting that he was

desirous that a school should be established under the superin-
tendence and charge of the Kirk Sessions of St. Matthew's
Church, in the City of Halifax, to be used either as a normal
or training school, wherein the principles of sound morality
and religion, as inculcated in the parochial schools of the Church
of Scotland, might be taught, he made the following devise;
(His LORDSHIP here read the clauses of the will as set out in
the writ, devising the property in question to certain members
of St. Matthew's Church, composing the Kirk Sessions, upon
trust that, as soon as convenient after obtaining possession of
the property and raising a fund by voluntary subscription or
in pursuance of a vote of the congregation, they should fit up
and prepare the house for a public school, in connection with
the said church, such school to remain continually under the
supervision and care of the elders of the church from time to
time composing the Kirk Sessions, and to be opened on each
anniversary of the testator's birth-day with certain prescribed
devotional exercises.) The property so devised, on the death
of Dechman, went into the possession of the devisees, and
the rents from time to time have been received by them, but
no appropriation of them has been made, and no steps have
been taken to carry out the intentions of the testator.

The parties who have now the possession of the property
and funds have been made parties to these proceedings, the
object of which is to obtain a decree of this Court, authorizing
the adoption of some scheme whereby the property devised
may be utilized so that the charitable intentions of the testator
may be carried out as nearly as possible; and that the Court
may direct them to sell the lands and premises, and to pay
the proceeds thereof, together with the accumulation of rent
in their hands, to such purposes as this Court should determine
best suited to carry out such scheme. Jas. Dechman, the son
and heir-at-law of the testator. was also made a party. None
of the defendants have appeared and answered, and a default
was entered against them.

An application having been made for a reference to a master
to report a suitable scheme to carry out the testator's intention, I told the counsel acting on behalf of the Attorney
General, that I entertained doubts whether this was a case for

the application of the doctrine of *cy pres*, as it was questionable whether the property did not revert to the heir-at-law of the testator on the failure of the donees to perform the conditions required of them by the terms of the devise. I, at the same time, informed him that, though the defendants had made no defence, and had allowed judgment by default to be entered against them, I would allow the question to be raised and hear it argued, if it should be desired; and, notice to that effect having been given to them, *Mr. Motton* appeared as counsel for Mr. Dechman, the heir-at-law, who had a day appointed for the argument, but on that day no person appeared on behalf either of Mr. Dechman or the other defendant, and no objection having been raised either to the granting of the prayer of the writ or to a reference to a master, a reference was made to Mr. Twining, who subsequently reported as follows; (His LORDSHIP here read the report of the master, to the effect that the intentions of the testator would be best carried out by handing over the property to the Commissioners of Schools for the City of Halifax, towards the erection of a High School under the Act of 1877, c. 39, the Kirk Session to have the power to nominate two free scholars to the school; the Sessions having concurred in that recommendation, on condition of their being allowed to so nominate two free scholars.)

No opposition is now made to this report, nor has any counter scheme been suggested to the Court as better calculated to carry out the testator's intentions. The report will therefore be confirmed and the scheme adopted.

LONGWORTH ET AL., *v.* MERCHANTS' BANK OF HALIFAX, ET AL.

Plaintiffs, as assignees under the Insolvent Act, sought to have certain mortgages decreed to be void, which were made by the defendant Smith, within thirty days of demand made on him to assign, followed by an assignment. The evidence was conflicting, but the Court drew from it the inference that Smith, finding himself in difficulties, applied to the Bank for $3,000, in the belief that, if obtained, it would enable him to arrange with his more pressing creditors and avert the insolvency which must otherwise ensue; that the agent of the Bank first led him to believe that the advance would be made, but the directors refused, and, instead of making the advance, required the mortgages to secure existing liabilities; that defendant consented to make them, encouraged by the agent to believe that if he did so further accommodation would be afforded, but the Bank, having secured itself and considering that further accommodation could not safely be afforded, declined to make any further advance and insolvency ensued, as Smith had anticipated. At the time the mortgages were given, the insolvent's paper was lying overdue in the Bank, and the agent of the Bank, on the execution of the mortgage, told him that he could not expect an advance till after the expiration of thirty days. Plaintiffs having sought relief first, on the ground that the mortgages were made in consideration that the Bank would advance $8000, which would have prevented insolvency, and secondly, that they were given in contemplation of insolvency, and with intent fraudulently to impede and delay creditors, *Held*, as to the first ground that the consideration must be ascertained from the language of the instruments, which referred to existing indebtedness and not advances, and that Smith could not be heard to allege differently; but that on the second ground the mortgages must be decreed to be void as against the plaintiffs and creditors of the insolvent.

Objection was taken that the requisition upon Smith to assign was informally made, the affidavit on which it was based being liable to a technical objection. But, an assignment having taken place under it, and no objection having been made to it in the Insolvent Court, which had proceeded to settle the estate, *Held*, that it was not for a third party in a different Court to call in question the regularity of its proceedings.

Semble. Even before the amendment of sec. 133 of the Insolvent Act of 1875, by the insertion of the words *prima facie*, (Cap. 41 of 1877,) the presumption of fraud could be rebutted.

RITCHIE, E. J., (now December 4th, 1877,) delivered the judgment of the Court :—

This suit was brought by Israel Longworth and Lucius Dickson, the former the assignee of the defendant Robert Smith, the latter the assignee of Smith & Crow, insolvents, praying the Court to declare two mortgages made by Smith to the Merchants' Bank, fraudulent and void, as against the plaintiffs, and to order them to be delivered up and cancelled. Subsequently, the Halifax Banking Company became a defendant, as being interested in the result.

The mortgages in question bear date the 31st December, 1875, and contain recitals that Smith, in the course of his business, had become indebted to the Bank in the sum of $10,000 on certain bills and notes discounted for him, part of which were then overdue and the remainder were then maturing, and that he had, at the request of the Bank, agreed to give mortgages on his real estate as collateral security for the re-payment of these liabilities; and the consideration is therein alleged to be this indebtedness and the nominal consideration of one dollar. Very soon after, an arrangement was entered into between the Merchants' Bank and Smith with the Halifax Banking Company, that the latter, to which Smith was also indebted, should participate *pro-rata* with the Merchants' Bank in the benefit of the security of the mortgages, and an instru-ment to that effect was executed by them, bearing date the 22nd January, 1876.

On the 7th February, 1876, Smith made an assignment under the Insolvent Act to the Official Assignee, having been required to do so by one of his creditors in writing to that effect on the 27th January previous, on which day an affidavit of his insolvency was filed with the Registrar of the Court of Probate and Insolvency. The plaintiffs in their writ seek relief on two grounds; the one is that the consideration stated in the mortgages was not the real consideration, but that they were given and received in consideration that the Bank would, upon the execution of them by Smith, advance to him the sum of $3,000, which sum, if it had been paid to Smith, would have enabled him to meet pressing liabilities and continue his busi-ness, and thereby his insolvency would have been prevented, but which, after having obtained the mortgages, the Bank refused to pay him. The other is that the mortgages were given in contemplation of insolvency, or with intent fraudu-lently to impede, obstruct or delay the creditors of Smith.

The only evidence in support of the first ground is that of Smith, the insolvent, who says that during the summer of 1875 he had difficulty in meeting his obligations, and was obliged to renew a large amount of his notes in full; that he applied to the Merchants' Bank for a loan of $3,000, for which he offered security on his real estate to the amount of $10,000; that Mr. Dickie, the agent of the Bank, told him he would consult the Bank authorities, and a day or two afterwards he told him he thought his request would be considered favorably; that he then gave Mr. Dickie, in writing, what he wanted, with

10 *g*

a memorandum of the properties he proposed as security, and of the amount of claims on them; that on his getting the $3,000, the mortgages were to stand as security for it, and as a collateral security for the notes then in the Bank; that at the next interview Smith had with the agent Dickie, he was informed by him that the Bank had agreed to advance him the $3000, and on the 3rd or 5th of January 1876, the mortgages were executed.

After this, on his calling for money, Mr. Dickie told him he could not give any till the mortgages had been recorded *thirty days;* he never did get the money. He states that he gave the mortgages solely for the purpose of getting the $3000, otherwise he would not have given them; that by obtaining $3000 on the mortgages he thought he would benefit his other creditors, though he then knew he was unable to meet his engagements, and would be insolvent unless he received the advance of $3000. This evidence of Smith's, which is inconsistent with the recitals in the mortgages, is not confirmed by Mr. Dickie, though his statement on the subject is by no means satisfactory, and is distinctly and positively contradicted by Mr. McLean, the Cashier of the Merchants' Bank. The inference that I am led to draw from the tenor of the whole evidence is that Smith, finding himself in serious difficulties, applied to the Bank for the $3000, in the belief that if he obtained it he would be enabled to arrange.with his more pressing creditors and avoid insolvency, which he believed would ensue if he did not receive it; that the Agent of the Bank, in the first instance, led him to think that the advance would be made, but on the directors being applied to they refused, and, instead of giving him the advance, they required him to give the Bank the mortgages to secure his existing liabilities, and this he consented to do, having been encouraged by the Agent, (Dickie,) to believe that, if he did so, further accommodation would be afforded him in his business; but the Bank having secured itself, and having been led to the belief that Smith's affairs were in such a deranged state that such further accommodation could not be safely afforded him, refused it and insolvency ensued, as Smith anticipated would be the case.

Whatever negotiations may have taken place before the

execution of the mortgages, we can only look to the language of those instruments to ascertain what was the real agreement between the parties and Mr. Smith cannot be heard to allege that the terms were different.

Assuming, as we must, that the mortgages were given to secure the debt then due to the Bank, and that no intention, certainly no binding agreement, existed on the part of the Bank to make Smith any further advances, how does the case stand on the second ground taken by the plaintiffs? It is quite clear that Smith was then unable to meet his engagements, and he knew that the only hope he had of avoiding insolvency was his obtaining the advance he asked for, and when, instead of giving the advance, the Bank asked for and obtained the mortgages to secure their existing debt, and, having obtained them, refused all further accommodation and closed their dealings with him, Smith must have known that insolvency would ensue, and the Bank could not but have had reason to doubt his solvency and to believe that its debt was being secured and a preference obtained at the expense of the other creditors. His paper was lying overdue at the Bank, and the Cashier says that he knew that certain of his creditors were pressing him and that he had need of the $3000, for which he effected the mortgages, to meet them. This, too, was well known to Dickie, the Agent of the Bank at Truro, who, if he did not promise the advance asked for, induced him to believe that he would get it; and his language is emphatic and capable of but one construction when he told Smith, on the execution of the mortgages, that he must not expect an advance from the Bank till after the expiration of thirty days from the time the papers were recorded; and this statement of his is not denied.

The Halifax Banking Company considered that the mortgages were given in violation of the Insolvent Act, and insisted on being allowed to participate in the security or they would dispute their validity, and this the Merchants' Bank consented to rather than to have their validity called in question.

It is to be borne in mind that the mortgages, having been made within thirty days from the time that a demand was made on Smith to assign under the Insolvent Act, are presumed to have been made in contemplation of insolvency; and the evidence adduced by the defendant, to my mind, is far from rebutting that presumption. And as the effect of them is to give to the Bank an unjust preference over the creditors of Smith, and to defeat the intention of the Act by preventing a rateable distribution of his assets among them, they should be decreed to be void against the plaintiffs and creditors of the Insolvent.

The claim of the Halifax Banking Company falls, of course, with that of the Merchants' Bank. It is difficult, indeed, to see how, in any case, it could be sustained, as the security was taken for Smith's debt to them when they knew he was insolvent, and was only obtained on a threat to put him in insolvency and to attack the mortgages as taken in violation of the Insolvent Act if the Merchants' Bank would not allow them to participate in the security.

Perhaps I ought not to omit to refer to an objection on the part of the Merchants' Bank, that the requisition on Smith to assign was informally made, the affidavit on which it was based being liable to a technical objection. But an assignment took place under it and no objection was made to it in the Insolvent Court, which has proceeded to settle the estate and distribute the assets, and it is not for a third party in a different court to call in question the regularity of its proceedings. And I cannot concur in the contention on the part of the plaintiffs that the presumption of contemplation of insolvency raised by the Act from the deeds having been executed within thirty days of the insolvency, before the amendment by the insertion of the words "*prima facie,*" was conclusive and incapable of rebuttal. The words inserted seem to me to be declaratory and to have been inserted to remove a doubt which arose from a difference of opinion on the construction of the section among the Judges of one of the courts in Ontario. The language of the section would have been different if the Legislature had intended otherwise; it would have declared that instruments of transfer made within thirty days of insolvency should be void, and there is nothing to indicate that the presumption was to be conclusive and operate as an estoppel as was observed by HEATH, J., in

Jayne v. *Price*, 5 Taunt., 326. Speaking of presumptions in general, nothing can be clearer than this; that a presumption may be rebutted by a contrary and stronger presumption.

The plaintiffs will be entitled to their costs.

TUCKER, Assignee, *v.* CREIGHTON, Assignee, et al.

Parker & Grant having recovered a verdict against Fairbanks, a rule *nisi* was taken out to set it aside. T. & E. DeWolf & Co. became sureties to respond the final judgment and took a mortgage from Fairbanks to secure them from loss on account of their bond, and also to secure the amount of an existing indebtedness. The rule *nisi* having been discharged and judgment entered up against Fairbanks, an execution was issued under which he was arrested and placed in custody. While he was in custody, and after the present suit was brought by plaintiff as assignee of DeWolf & Co. against Fairbanks, to foreclose the mortgage, and after said Fairbanks had answered, his estate was placed in insolvency, and Creighton, his assignee, intervened and became a party. Parker & Grant also became parties as interested in the subject matter. *Held*, first, that the insolvency of Fairbanks did not prevent the plaintiff from proceeding with the foreclosure, and, secondly, that Parker & Grant had not lost their lien on the mortgaged property in consequence of their having arrested Fairbanks under the judgment.[*]

RITCHIE, E. J., (1877) delivered the judgment of the Court:—

This suit was commenced by Tucker, as assignee of John E. DeWolf and John W. DeWolf, who traded under the name of T. & E. DeWolf & Co., insolvents, against Lewis P. Fairbanks to foreclose a mortgage given to them to secure the payment of $2500. Subsequently Francis G. Parker and John N. Grant applied and obtained leave to become parties to the suit as being interested in the subject matter of it, and at a later stage, Fairbanks having become insolvent, Creighton, his assignee, also intervened and became a party.

The facts of the case are not in any essential particular in dispute. Parker and Grant had instituted proceedings at law against Fairbanks which resulted in a verdict against him for $900 and costs; application was made to set aside this verdict,

---

[*]The appeal from this decision to the full Court was dismissed, by judgment of the Court, per SMITH, J., (Dec. 10th, 1878.)

which was refused, and Fairbanks thereupon took out a rule *nisi* under the statute enabling him to do so, giving security to respond the judgment in case the verdict should be sustained. In order to obtain the security he applied to Messrs. DeWolf to become bail. They at first refused, but subsequently consented on his promising to give a mortgage on his property at Nine Mile River to secure them against any liability or loss they might incur by becoming such bail, and also to secure a debt which he owed them. Fairbanks thereupon prepared and executed the mortgage in question, and on delivering it to them the following memorandum was given to him by them: "Lewis P. Fairbanks having delivered to us a mortgage, dated at Halifax the first day of December, 1874, the consideration therein stated to be $2500, secured on a certain tract of land containing 3123 acres, situate in the County of Hants, in order to secure to us the re-payment of $1335, due to us by him on the 22nd September last past, with interest thereon, being two notes of hand for $900 and $435 respectively, and also to secure us from any loss on payments which we may be obliged to pay in consequence of our becoming bound in a bond for $900, to answer a verdict for $900, and costs $200, in favor of Messrs. Parker & Grant against Lewis P. Fairbanks, a rule having been obtained to set the verdict aside on security being given under the law. Halifax, December 1874.   T. & E. DeWolf & Co."

The application to set aside the verdict proved unsuccessful and the rule *nisi* was discharged, after which judgment was entered on it for $950.67 debt and costs, and a writ of execution was taken out under which Fairbanks was arrested. While he was in custody under it, since the commencement of this suit and after he had answered, his estate was placed in insolvency under the Insolvent Act of 1875, and he was subsequently discharged from custody by an order of the Judge of Insolvency. Neither Tucker nor Parker & Grant have made any claim on the insolvent estate, but they look solely to the mortgage as a security for their debts. At the hearing, Mr. Thompson, who appeared for Mr. Creighton, contended that the plaintiff could not proceed with the foreclosure in this court, his only remedy for any claim he might have being under the provisions of the Insolvent Act.

This position is in my opinion untenable; all that passed to the assignee on the insolvency of Fairbanks was the interest and right the insolvent had in property of every kind, but the property comprised in the mortgage had been previously conveyed to Tucker, leaving but an equity of redemption in the insolvents; and that and that alone passed to his assignee.

The sections of the Insolvent Act referred to at the hearing, are not applicable to a case like this. Had Tucker or Parker & Grant made a claim on the estate for a dividend from the assets, considering the mortgage as inadequate security for their debts, there are provisions of the act which would apply to such a case; but even under such circumstances there would be nothing to justify the most unreasonable demand made by the assignee on those parties under date of 24th March, 1877.* A mortgagee cannot be deprived of his security against his will; the assignee may redeem by paying him the amount due him, or may sell the equity of redemption, but his powers extend no farther, so long as he makes no claim on the assets of the insolvent estate, and does not seek to be repaid any part of his debt out of them. See *Doria on Bankruptcy*, 740; and *in re Hurst*, 31 U. C. R., Q. B., 116; *ex parte Peake*, L. R., 2 Ch. A., 458.

Another objection taken on behalf of Mr. Creighton was that as regards Parker & Grant, they had lost their lien on the mortgaged property in consequence of their having arrested Fairbanks under their judgment. But this objection cannot prevail; the arrest of a defendant on execution is not an extinguishment of the debt, nor does it destroy the creditor's lien. See *Woodward* v. *Pell*, L. R., 4 Q. B., 55, and the cases there referred to.

In a case like this where a debtor is in custody under a judgment at the suit of one creditor, and he is forced into insolvency at the instance of another, it appears to me preposterous that the debtor should not only thereby obtain his release from custody, but that the judgment creditor should lose his right

---

* This was a demand made by Creighton, as assignee, upon Parker & Grant, to assign to him their judgment against Fairbanks, and to prove the same and file their claim as provided by Section 84 of the Insolvent Act of 1875.

to participate in the assets of the insolvent with the other creditors. This Mr. Thompson was hardly prepared to contend for, and yet it would be the result if we were to hold that the arrest was an extinguishment of the debt, which he did contend for. No authority was cited to shew that by the arrest under the judgment the creditor lost all right to look to the property on which he held a mortgage. A mortgagee may, as a general rule, pursue all his remedies at the same time both legal and equitable. He may sue on his bond or covenant at law and foreclose in equity, and he may arrest a defendant pending a suit in equity for a foreclosure. *Burnell* v. *Martin,* Dougl., 417; and *Davis* v. *Battine,* 2 R. & My., 76, are authorities for the position that after taking the body of his debtor on execution for the mortgage debt, the mortgagee is, notwithstanding, entitled to the benefit of his mortgage security. In the first case Lord MANSFIELD said it had been settled over and over again, and in the latter the Master of the Rolls said he did not remember to have heard it ever suggested that a mortgagee by proceeding to execution against the body of his debtor, released his interest in the land mortgaged.

These were the only points raised on behalf of the assignee at the hearing, and as, in my opinion, he has entirely failed in making out any defence to the plaintiff's claim, the decree must be against him with costs. I have not adverted to the peculiar nature of Parker & Grant's claim under the mortgage, because it was conceded that if the insolvency did not preclude the plaintiff from proceeding with foreclosure in this court and the arrest by Parker & Grant did not stop them from claiming under the mortgage, they would be entitled to participate with the plaintiff in the benefit of it.

CASES

DETERMINED IN THE

SUPREME COURT OF NOVA SCOTIA,

IN EQUITY.

FROM JANUARY 1, 1878, TO DECEMBER 31, 1878.

N. S. SALT & EXPLORATION CO. *v.* THE HALIFAX AND CAPE BRETON RAILWAY AND COAL CO.

The defendant company was incorporated by cap. 74 of the acts of 1876, sec. 13 of which provided that whenever it should be necessary for the construction &c. of the Company's works &c., that the Company should be invested with any lands, and no agreement could be made for the purchase thereof, the Company might apply by petition to a judge of the Supreme Court, who, if satisfied that the lands were necessary, should direct an appraisement; and by sec. 14, it was provided that, on payment or tender of the compensation awarded, the land should vest in the company with right of immediate possession. By the 86th section the provisions of chapter 70 R.S., (3rd series) were made applicable to the line or lines of railway to be built by the Company, " as far as the same may be applicable," certain sections of said cap. 70 being excepted, among which was section 24, (q.v.) The 11th section of this chapter authorised the Company to take possession of lands required for the track of railways or for stations, and under those provisions the defendant company entered upon and took possession of land of the plaintiff company, (incorporated in 1866), on which borings for salt had been made, and buildings erected with machinery &c. Plaintiffs obtained a rule *nisi* for an injunction, claiming that the defendant company could not resort to the provisions of cap. 70 R.S. (3rd series) to acquire land necessary for their railroad, but must obtain it under the 13th and 14th sections of their own act, under which they were required to tender or pay the appraised value before being entitled to possession. *Held*, that the provisions in the act incorporating the company (sections 13, 14, &c.) related to the obtaining of land for the mining operations contemplated by their act, but that for the purpose of obtaining land for the line of Railway and stations, which was a matter of public interest, they could resort to the provisions of cap. 70 R.S., (3rd series); that no inference against this view could be drawn from the fact that section 24 of cap. 70, making a certain class of damages a county charge, was included among the excepted sections, as that section did not refer to lands required for the track and stations, which were made a county charge by section 52 and following sections of cap. 70 not included among the excepted sections.

The defendant Company, incorporated under chapter 74 of the Acts of 1876, entered upon and took possession of land of the plaintiff company, incorporated by Act of 1866, on which borings for salt had been made and buildings erected with machinery, &c., under the provisions of chapter 70 of the Revised Statutes, 3rd series, (see Appendix to R. S., 4th series, page 27), and proceeded to have the land so taken valued by a jury in the manner pointed out in the chapter last mentioned. The plaintiffs resisted the proceedings and applied to this Court for an injunction to restrain the defendant company, contending that the only mode in which the defendants could enter upon the land was that pointed out in chapter 74 of the Acts of 1876, under which the defendant company was incorporated. The argument arose on the motion to make absolute the rule *nisi* for an injunction.

Thompson, for plaintiffs, says that his principal contention is that chapter 70 of the Revised Statutes (3rd series) under which the defendants have proceeded, is not applicable to the road being constructed by the defendant company.

RITCHIE, E. J., after the reading of the affidavits on which the rule *nisi* is based, and the affidavits in reply, intimates that the Court will not enquire into the amount of damages assessed by the jury, as that is a matter of appeal, nor into the question of the regularity of the proceedings taken by the defendants, as that is a matter which can be reviewed by *certiorari.* He states that there are now just two questions to consider in this cause; 1st, Does the Statute, (chapter 70, 3rd series), apply to the building of this road ? and 2ndly, Is this a case where the Court ought to grant an injunction in the first instance ?

Thompson reviews the several Railway Acts passed by the Provincial Legislature to show that when railways were built under chap. 70 (3rd series), express enactments making the damages a county charge were passed. Sec. 16 of chap. 13 of 1865, made damages a county charge. Chapter 14 of 1866 incorporated the plaintiff company, and the way in which it was to take land was the same as that which the defendant company must pursue. The plaintiffs had thus vested rights prior to the defendants, which must therefore prevail over the latter. Chap. 34 of 1868, incorporating the Windsor and Annapolis Railway Co. provided for an assessment on the county of the damages. Chap. 59 of 1870, incorporating the Eastern Railroad Co., and Chap. 81 of 1870, incorporating the Western Counties Railway, are very much the same as that Act. Chap. 43 of 1873 was an Act to amend this latter Act in regard to the taking of land. ˙ Chap. 12 of 1874 is known as the subsidy Act. All these Acts show that when it is the intention of the Legislature to make railway damages a county charge the Legislature specifically enacts that they shall be such. Chap. 3 of 1876 contains the principle under which defendants represent themselves as acting. Section 6 of this Act, which makes certain sections of Chap. 70, (3rd series,) applicable to the building of this road, is very vague and only re-enacts these sections "as far as the same may be applicable." Quite a number of these sections of Chap. 70 are expressly left out, and notably sec. 24. Chap. 4 of 1876 is a very important act, for it gives to the defendants the benefits of chap. 3 of 1876.

Chapter 74 of 1876 incorporates the Halifax and Cape Breton Railway and Coal Company, and˙ the defendants took advantage of this Act by virtue of chap. 4 of the Acts of the same year. One section of this Act makes tender of amount of damages sufficient to vest the title, and sec. 36 defines the word "company," and re-enacts, "as far as the same may be applicable," certain sections of chap. 70 (3rd series.)

The sections of chap. 70 (3rd series), providing for the taking of land, do not apply to this company, as they are not needed. There is a specific way pointed out in their charter, and they must follow that. There is no provision made for the payment of damages by the Counties. The intention was that money for damages should be assessed by arbitrators and paid by the company. In view of these enactments there is nothing to make damages a county charge, and the proceedings in this˙ case, being on the assumption that they are such, are consequently irregular. Proceedings under sec. 11 of chap. 70 would operate as a dedication of lands to the public, but that could not have been the intention of the Legislature in regard to this company who are to own the road.

Weatherbe, Q. C., (with whom was Graham.) Almost all the

sections cited by plaintiff's counsel are inapplicable. Those which apply are strongly in favor of the rights contended for on behalf of the defendant company. A decision of this court under the act incorporating the Windsor and Annapolis Railway Company is in point. The Windsor and Annapolis Railway is dedicated to the public, and there is a decision of our own Court setting aside an assessment against the company on the ground that the road is a provincial public work. In the case of the Yarmouth road the land is given to the company. Does this Act make provision for making damages a county charge? I think so. Let us look at the Act incorporating the company, viz., chap. 74, of 1876. It is evident that this company was incorporated for two purposes, viz.: first, to open mines, &c., which is its private business; and secondly to build a railroad for public use. My contention is that sec. 13 of chap. 74 of Acts of 1876 refers to the method of taking land when necessary to do so for the private business of this company, and that sec. 36 makes provision for the taking of land for the building of the public railroad.

Section 45, of chap. 70 R. S., 3rd series, provides for the striking of a jury to assess damages, and there are sections of said chapter left unrepealed that provide for certain notices being given to county officers. Section 55 of Chapter 70, (3rd series), is unrepealed, and I rely on that. It provides for the assessment of the county by the Sessions.

I also contend that this is not a case of irreparable injury; *Story's Equity Jurisprudence*, 11th edition, (see pp. 927-928). A very strong case must be made out when an injunction is sought *to stop a railway*. The defendants are in a different position from the plaintiffs in regard to other parties. Our charter is later than theirs.

Section 19 of chap. 1 of Acts of 1854 is section 24 of chap. 70 (3rd series). In chap. 1 of 1854 we have none of the machinery provided by the latter sections of chap. 70, (3rd series), and when these sections were enacted, there was no more need of sec. 19 of chap. 1 of 1854, which was, as I say, incorporated in chap. 70 (3rd series). In that view of the case there was no need of the section, and the repeal of it has no effect. I admit there are mistakes in the charter incorporating this company, and the company have not all the privileges they should have. Our charter, however, is the valid one. The chartered rights of any private company can be modified by the Legislature, and there are authorities to show that no private company has chartered rights as against a railway having legislative power to take a right of way.

The value of the property, moreover, is not such as represented by the affidavit of the plaintiffs. It does not assist the plaintiff company that a large sum of money has been spent. The question is how much is the property *now* worth? The affidavits read by Mr. Graham show that the company never was a successful one.

Again, the plaintiffs are guilty of *laches* in not moving sooner, and Mr. Ross' letter attached to Mr. Gregory's affidavit is a waiver.

Graham.—The plaintiffs can have no vested rights against the defendants. A railway is a public undertaking, and private interests must yield.

By chap. 1 of 1854 no provision was made for assessment by a jury, of damages, made a county charge by sec. 19, but afterwards such provision was made in terms that rendered sec. 19 of chap. 1 of 1854 useless. This section afterwards became sec. 24 of chap 70, (3rd series), but was useless as sec. 55 of chap. 70 is very much more explicit. I think also that sec. 24 of chap. 70 was repealed in 1866 by an amendment, and that the appendix to our Revised Statute was never re-enacted.

The plaintiffs acquiesced in the proceedings of the defendants, as is clear from Mr. Ross' letter in answer to the notice of the company that they were about to enter the lands of the plaintiffs, and in which he asks that an arbitrator may be named. They should have moved sooner and not let the defendants approach the boundaries of their property in both directions before doing anything to let them know that their entry would be resisted. The defendants could not then change the location of the road without a great sacrifice, but they could have done so two months earlier. *High on Injunction*, sec. 387 and 388.

The affidavits of the plaintiffs are misleading, as they do not truly disclose the present state of the property.

RITCHIE, E. J.—If any facts are concealed in regard to the matter as to which an injunction is sought, that is enough of itself to dissolve the injunction.

Graham.—That is just this case.

Further, if there is a question as to the law, the Court will dissolve an injunction.—*Joyce on Injunctions* 910, 816-894.

Thompson in reply.—In regard to Mr. Weatherbe's argument concerning sec. 13 of 1874, I ask could the defendants build a road to-morrow and charge it to the county? According to Mr. Weatherbe's argument they could. The sec. of chap. 70, (3rd series), which defendants seek to apply to this road is only to be applied "as far as applicable." Suppose sec. 24 was not excepted, then the other sections of chap. 70 would be applicable, but without it they are not applicable at all. Sections 391-394 of *High on Injunction* show that injunctions do apply to railways. Moreover, vested rights cannot be taken away by implication and there is no express enactment taking away those of the plaintiffs. Chap. 70 (3rd series), is inconsistent with chap. 74 of 1876 and cannot possibly apply.

RITCHIE, E. J., (now Jan. 7th, 1878,) delivered the judgment of the Court :—

On the 4th of April, 1876, an act of the Provincial Legislature passed incorporating the defendant company for the purpose of constructing, maintaining and operating a railway from some convenient point on the existing railway between Truro and Pictou to a suitable point in the Strait of Canseau, &c., &c.; also for the purpose of acquiring and holding quarries and mines, and opening and working the same, and of manufacturing, working and disposing of the products of the same, and for purchasing, acquiring and holding real estate, mills, etc.

By the 13th sec. it is enacted that whenever it may be necessary for the construction, maintenance, operation, enlargement or other purpose of the company's works or business that the company should be invested with any lands, and no agreement can be made for the purchase thereof, it shall be lawful for the company to apply by petition to any one of the judges of the Supreme Court, who, if satisfied that the lands are required and are not more extensive than necessary, shall direct an appraisement as therein pointed out; and by the 14th section it is enacted that upon payment or tender of the compensation awarded or agreed upon, the title of the land shall vest in the company, with power forthwith to take posession.

By the 36th section, the provisions of chap. 70, of the Revised Statutes, (3rd series), "of Provincial Government Railroads," so far as the same might be applicable, were made applicable to the line or lines of railway to be built under that Act and were thereby incorporated with, and made a part thereof, except certain sections therein specified; the term " Commissioners " or " Contractors," in chap. 70, to include the company, and the term " railway department " to apply to, and include, the company. Under the provisions of another Act of the Provincial Legislature, passed at the same time, a subvention or subsidy in money was given to the company which should construct the road, together with an allotment of crown lands, the class and character of the road to be determined by the Governor in Council to whose approval the route and location of the line of railway are made subject, and provisions were to be made for the regulation of tolls and rates for passengers and freight, and the carrying of provincial property, and generally for guarding the public interest.

The defendant company in the prosecution of its enterprise of constructing the railroad contemplated by its Act, has entered upon and taken possession under the provisions of chap 70 of the Revised Statutes, (3rd series), of the land of the plaintiffs on which borings for salt have been made, and buildings erected with machinery, &c., and has proceeded to have the land so taken, valued by a jury in the mode pointed out by that chapter. The right to do this is resisted by the plaintiffs, who have taken out a rule *nisi* for an injunction to restrain them from removing the buildings and machinery or otherwise interfering with the enjoyment of their property.

The plaintiffs were incorporated by an act of the Legislature, passed in the year 1866, for the purpose of manufacturing salt from brine and exploring for such salt and other minerals, with power to purchase or acquire land, and to construct such rail and tramways or other roads as should be necessary for the transportation of the products of the mines, &c., &c., and to purchase or build wharves, docks, piers, mills, etc. The company was also to have a preferential right to licenses and leases of coals or other minerals which it might discover during its explorations, subject to the power of the Governor in Council to determine the extent of the areas to be so leased. The Act of Incorporation contained a section similar to that in the Act of the defendant company, authorising an application to a Judge of the Supreme Court for acquiring land necessary in the construction and maintenance of the works of the Company where no agreement could be made for its purchase.

The present application to the Court is to make absolute the rule *nisi* for an injunction. The plaintiffs contend that the defendants cannot resort to the provisions of chap. 70 of the Revised Statutes to acquire the land necessary for their railroad, but can only obtain it under the 13th and 14th sections of their Act above referred to, and must pay for it or tender the appraised value before they become entitled to enter upon the possession of it, and that, as the defendant company is a private company like their own, and having the same power of acquiring land for its undertakings, the land of the plaintiff company is not liable to be taken from them by the defendants to carry on their undertaking; that Chap. 70, to which I have referred, can only from its terms apply to land taken for a public undertaking, where the payment of the value of the land taken is made a county charge, and that here it is not made such.

The objects of the defendant company are two-fold, one of which is strictly of a private nature, that of engaging in mining operations; the other is of a very different character, the construction of a public railroad, built under the supervision of the Provincial Government, to the expense of which it has contributed and in which the public is largely interested, which interest is recognized and protected by the law under which it is being constructed.

The act of incorporation contains distinct provisions for carrying out these two objects. Those contained in sections 13, 14, 15 and 16, relating to the mode of acquiring land, are such as are to be found in all acts of incorporation for mining purposes, the policy of the Legislature being to have all such acts uniform in this particular, while the 36th Section can only apply to the construction of the railroad contemplated by the Act, embracing as it does, with certain exceptions, the provisions of chapter 70 of Provincial Government Railroads, so far as the same may be applicable, the very first clause of which enacts that the commissioner or contractor, (by the defendant's Act of Incorporation, made to include "the company"), are authorized to enter upon and take possession of any lands required for the track of the railway and for stations; and they shall lay off the same by metes and bounds, and record a description and plan thereof in the Registry of Deeds for the County in which the lands are situate, and the same shall operate as a dedication to the public of such lands, &c., &c. Subsequent sections point out how a jury shall be drawn, and what course shall be pursued in estimating the value of the lands so taken. Surely these sections would have been excepted if it had not been the intention that they should be acted upon.

Mr. Thompson's contention was that, as a specific mode of acquiring land was pointed out in the Act of Incorporation, that was the only course to be adopted, and that these provisions could only be brought into operation where the payment for the land taken was made a county charge; that the section, 24 of cap. 70, which made the damages a county charge was one of the excepted sections, and that, therefore, the company alone were responsible for them. But it is clear to me that the payment is made a county charge quite independently of this section, which I think was not intended to apply to the land taken *for the line of railway and stations.* The 52nd section, referring to the appraisement of the land taken for the line of railway and stations, by the jury, directs that the amount shall be assessed on the county and levied and paid as soon as possible, and the sections following to 59 point out how they are to be apportioned and collected, and that on failure of the Sessions to perform the duty, the county shall be amerced by the Supreme Court.

As great stress was laid on section 24 being excepted in the

10 *h*

Act of Incorporation, I will now see what effect the exception of that section ought to have.   By the 11th section, to which I have referred, the company was authorized to take possession of land for the line of railway and stations; by the 12th and the several subsequent sections to the 24th the company was authorized to enter upon other land to take soil and other materials from it, and cut trees, etc., for railway purposes, and for obtaining compensation for the damages thus occasioned a different course is pointed out and payment is required to be made in the first instance by the commissioner or contractor; but by the 19th section the county is made liable ultimately to pay them, and it is to these damages that the 24th section has reference, for after the sections referring to these, and to these alone, the section in question follows in these words :— "The moneys payable for *such lands and fencing*, shall form a county charge, but in apportioning the assessment the Sessions shall have respect to the relative benefits derived from the railway by the several sections of the county, and shall apportion the assessment accordingly."   The only object of this section must have been to make the charge apportionable in a particular way in the county, for by the 19th section, they had been expressly made a county charge, so that by excepting the former sections from the defendants' Act of Incorporation, the only effect would be to make the charge assessable over the whole county alike.

The conclusion, therefore, to which I have arrived is that the defendants, if they desire to acquire lands necessary for the mining operations contemplated by their act which they cannot obtain by purchase, must resort to the special provisions therein pointed out; but if land be required for the line of railway or for stations they are to act as they have done in this instance, under the sections of chap. 70 of the Revised Statutes, which have been incorporated in their act.   In this view all parts of the Act are brought into operation without conflict, and carry out, as I think, the intention of the Legislature; and inasmuch as the plaintiff company is in no respect of a public character, but incorporated solely for the pecuniary benefit of the corporators, land held by them may be taken by the defendant company under the powers conferred on them, not to enable them to carry on their mining operations, which are equally of a private character, but for the construction of a public work, undertaken, it is true, by the defendants with a view to profits, but in which the public generally is interested, and to which the public funds have largely contributed.

I have not adverted to the discrepancies in the several affidavits relative to the injury done to the plaintiffs by taking their land and buildings and destroying their enterprise, as these are matters for appeal from the appraisement and do not affect the question now before this court, if the view I have taken of the case be correct.

The rule *nisi* for an injunction must be discharged.

THE ATTORNEY GENERAL *v.* FRASER, ET AL.

A license to search for minerals, other than gold, was granted to the relators under Sec. 86 of Cap. 9, R. S., to expire 21st May, 1874. Previous to its expiration, four other licenses to search over the same area were granted to the relators, which were to expire respectively, 22nd May, 1875; 23rd May, 1876; 26th May, 1877; and 27th May,1878, the area containing only four and a quarter square miles. On the 28th May, 1877, defendants, having a license to search over an area overlying in part the area of the relators, applied for a license, which was afterwards granted, to work one square mile partially overlying and including within its boundaries the area under license to search to the relators. An order *nisi* having been taken to restrain defendants from interfering, *Held* that over the area of four and a quarter miles first above referred to, not more than four valid licenses to search could be granted under R. S. Cap. 9, Sec. 91, that the relators' fifth license to search, which was to expire May 27th, 1878, was invalid, and that on the 28th May, 1877, there was no obstacle to the defendants' obtaining the license to work granted to them.

Obiter dictum; that it was no objection to the license to work that it was taken out in the name of one only of the defendants, Fraser, for their joint benefit; all the defendants having had an interest in the licenses to search, although taken out in the name of Fraser only.

RITCHIE, E. J., now, (Jan'y 28th, 1878), delivered the judgment of the Court:—

An order *nisi* having been taken to restrain the defendants from interfering with the ores, mines and minerals, other than

gold, within and upon a certain area claimed by the relators
under a license to search, from the Commissioner of Mines,
and from removing ores or minerals therefrom, and from interfering with the relators in the enjoyment of their rights under
the license; on motion to have the order made absolute, it was
contended by the defendants that they had obtained from the
Commissioner of Mines, first a license to search, and subsequently a license to work over the area under which they
have been working, and from which the relators now seek to
restrain them.

That the defendants have obtained such licenses is not
denied by the relators, but it is asserted on their behalf that,
when they were granted, they had a valid outstanding license
to search over an area which extended over and embraced that
part of the area from which they now seek to restrain the
defendants from working; the object of this suit being to
obtain a decree that the defendants' license to work so far as
it overlies and includes within its boundaries the area under
license to search to the relators may be declared void, and the
defendants be perpetually enjoined from interfering with the
mines, ores and minerals, within or upon their license.

No fraud, concealment or misrepresentation has been shewn
or attempted to be shewn; the question raised is as to the
right of the Commissioner of Mines to grant the license to
work to the defendants, and that depends upon whether the
relators had, at the time it was granted, an outstanding valid
license to search over it, as, if so, they had acquired such an
interest in it under the statute under which licenses to search
and work were authorized to be granted, as would preclude
the Commissioner of Mines from making the grant to the
defendants, and in that case their license to work would be
deemed to have been improvidently granted, and the relators
would be entitled to the relief sought for.

The 86th sec. of the 9th chapter of the Revised Statutes, "Of
Mines and Minerals," authorized the Commissioner of Mines
to grant licenses to search to be in force for one year from
date of application, to enter upon lands not already under
license or lease, and to dig and explore for minerals other than
gold. By the 87th, no such application shall be valid, unless

accompanied by a payment of $20, and the license to search may cover any single tract of ground not exceeding five square miles in extent, but not more than two and one-half miles in length.

Sec. 90 allows the license to be renewed under special circumstances, subject to approval by the Governor in Council. The 91st sec. provides that when a license to search has been granted, the Commissioner of Mines may grant other licenses to search over the same area, *provided that he shall grant no more licenses than there are areas of one square mile each contained within the area so first licensed;* and after the first licensee has chosen his square mile the others shall select theirs in the order of their licenses, provided that the right of search of the second licensee and his license shall commence immediately after the expiration of the license, or renewed license of the first licensee, or on the selection of his square mile by the first licensee, and so on, till each in order has selected his square mile, and the whole area is disposed of.

The 93rd section enacts that the holder of a license to search may, at any time before the expiration thereof, select from the land covered by such license, an area of one square mile, for the purpose of working the mines and minerals therein, and may make an application in writing to the Commissioner of Mines to work the same, which shall be accompanied by a payment of $50; and the 94th sec. provides that on such application and payment, the Commissioner of Mines shall cause the portion so selected to be surveyed and laid off, &c., &c.

The 96th sec. enacts that upon complying with the requirements of the chapter, the applicant shall be entitled to a license to occupy and work the one square mile applied for.

The applications for licenses to search by the relators were made in the following order: the first on the 20th May, 1872, which expired on the 20th May, 1873; before it had expired, on the 16th April, a second was taken out to go into effect on the expiration of the first; this latter expired on the 21st May, 1874. Previous to the expiration of this license, on the 25th July, 1873, four licenses to search were taken out, which would expire on the 22nd May, 1875, the 23rd May, 1876, the 26th May, 1877, and 27th May, 1878, respectively; so that with the outstanding license there were five licenses to search, granted by the Commissioner of Mines over the same area held by or on behalf of the same people, who, in the month of May 1874, applied for another license, which they renewed from year to year, till the year 1877 ; but these last mentioned applications do not, in my opinion, at all affect the question in dispute.

The applications for licenses to search under which the defendants' claims were made, are as follows : the first on the 20th September, 1872 ; and before its expiration, on the 11th August, 1873, another was made to take effect on the expiration of the first. This license would expire on the 22nd September, 1874, and on the 12th August, 1873, another was taken out, which would expire on the 23rd September, 1875 ; and on the 3rd September, 1873, another license was taken out, which would expire on the 25th September, 1877. While this last license to search was outstanding and in operation, and on the 28th May, 1877, an application was made for a license to work one square mile, which was granted, and it is the validity of this license which is now in dispute between the parties.

It will be seen that at the time the defendants obtained the license to search, under which the license to work was granted, the license to search taken out by the relators on the 25th July 1873, to expire on the 27th May 1878, was in existence, being the fifth right of search over their area when it was granted, and as the area contained in the licenses to search and work, granted to the defendants, overlay and included a part of the area contained in the relator's right of search, it would to that extent be invalid. The question, therefore, is whether this right of search of the relators was a valid one, and its validity is called in question, on the ground that the area described in the relator's application embraced but *four and a quarter* areas, and that over an area of that extent only four valid licenses to search could be granted, and that the fifth was granted illegally and contrary to the express provisions of the act, and was therefore invalid, and could only have been legally granted if there had been *five* square miles in the area.

By the act relating to mines and minerals, as it first passed, no second license to search over an area of five miles could be granted till the previous license had expired. The law as it now stands permits other licenses to be granted over the area, notwithstanding the existence of a prior right of search, such subsequent license not to go into effect till the expiration of those previously granted, so that assuming the area to contain five square miles, each in order becomes entitled to a license to work over one square mile; but it is expressly provided that the Commissioner of Mines shall grant no more licenses to search than there are areas of one square mile each contained in the area first licensed.

That the Commissioner of Mines has granted five licenses to search over an area of four and a quarter miles, is undisputed, and this is, in my opinion, in violation of the terms of the act. I therefore think that the fifth license to search, granted to the relators, is invalid, that no obstacle existed to the defendants' obtaining their right to search and work, and the Commissioner of Mines was justified in granting to them the license to work under which they are now working.

If the relators had no valid right to search, and have now no right to a license to work over any part of the area claimed by the defendants, their application for the injunction must fail. It is hardly, therefore, necessary to advert to the objection raised on their behalf, that the right of search on which the defendants obtained their right to work was taken out in the name of but one of them. It appears that they were interested in the license to search, though it was taken out in the name of Fraser. It was so taken out for their joint benefit, and I can see no objection to the course which has been pursued.

MOSHER *v.* MILLER.

The defendant J. C. S. Miller, mortgaged certain property to W. C. King, whose executors foreclosed the mortgage, J. W. King, the surviving executor of the mortgagee becoming the purchaser at the Sheriff's sale. Defendant remaining in possession of the mortgaged premises, a rule *nisi* was granted for a writ of assistance to put the purchaser in possession. No cause being shown, the rule was made absolute, and a writ issued, under which the property was delivered to J. W. King. Defendant then brought an action of trespass against the Sheriff and J. W. King, whereupon a rule *nisi* was taken for an injunction to restrain the action. Defendant opposed the rule, contending that the property of which he had been in possession was not included in the mortgage; but after a full hearing of the cause, the rule for the injunction was made absolute. J. W. King then put the plaintiff, Mosher, in possession of the land, and the defendant, J. C. S. Miller, brought an action of ejectment, setting up the claim which this Court had previously decided against him, namely, that the lands claimed were not included in the mortgage. The present suit having been instituted to restrain that action, *Held* that the defendant could not resort to the action of ejectment at common law, and there claim the land to which this Court had decreed that he was not entitled, and that the action must be restrained.

RITCHIE, E. J., now, (February 25th, 1878,) delivered the judgment of the Court :—

It appears from the affidavits and the documents referred to in them, that a mortgage was made by one Jacob Miller, and Charlotte his wife, and John C. S. Miller the defendant, and Sarah his wife, to the Rev. William C. King, of all their estate and interest in all that upland farm and marsh lot, or any part thereof, then in the possession and occupation of the said Jacob and John C. S. Miller, which they might have in possession remainder or reversion under and by virtue of the last will and testament of Samuel Miller, deceased, which upland and marsh were more particularly described, and the rights and interest of the said parties respectively, in the said last will on file in the Probate Court of the County of Hants, as would appear by reference thereto.

Some time after, Jacob Miller conveyed to the defendant his interest in the mortgaged premises, and subsequently a suit for the foreclosure of the mortgage was commenced by the executors of Mr. King, who had died in the meantime. No defence was made to this suit by John C. S. Miller, and a decree of foreclosure passed, under which the mortgaged premises were sold, James W. King, the surviving executor of the mortgagee, becoming the purchaser, to whom a deed was executed by the Sheriff, which sale was afterwards confirmed by an order of this Court.

The defendant, at the time of the sale, was in possession of the mortgaged premises, and remained so for some time after, and having refused to deliver up possession, an application was made to this Court for a writ of assistance, and a rule *nisi* was granted, calling upon him to show cause why a writ of assistance should not issue to put James W. King, the purchaser, in possession of that portion of the real estate described in the mortgage of which the defendant was in possession, which passed to him under the Sheriff's deed. A copy of this rule having been served on the defendant, and no cause having been shewn by him why it should not be made absolute, it was made absolute, and a writ of assistance was issued. No proceedings having been taken under it, subsequently, on the 31st August 1876, an *alias* writ of assistance was taken out, under which possession was delivered to James W. King.

On the 28th of November following, the defendant commenced an action of trespass against James M. Geldert, Esq., the Sheriff who executed the writ, and James W. King for what was done thereunder, whereupon a rule *nisi* was taken to show cause why an injunction should not issue to restrain him from proceeding in that action. Mr. Rigby, the then counsel for the defendant, opposed the making of that rule absolute, but after a full hearing of the case it was made absolute, and the injunction granted.*

James W. King having been thus placed in possession by this Court, entered into an agreement with the plaintiff in this suit for the sale of the land to him, and under that agreement put him in possession of the land of which the defendant had been dispossessed, and thereupon the defendant Miller commenced an action of ejectment against him, wherein he claims that he unlawfully withholds from him the possession of the land in question, and this suit having been instituted to restrain him from further prosecuting that action, a rule *nisi* was granted, calling on him to shew cause why the proceedings in that action should not be stayed; and in shewing cause against the rule being made absolute, the defendant claims a right to be repossessed of the land on the same

---

* See the judgment on the motion for injunction, page 284, post.

grounds as those on which this Court has decided against him, viz., that the lands in question are not the same that are embraced within the mortgage. And he contends that notwithstanding such decision he has a right to bring his eject-ment at Common Law, and to try his right to the possession of the land in that tribunal.

This Court having decided that the land in question was comprised in and conveyed under the mortgage and sold under a decree of foreclosure, and the defendant, the mortgagor, having been dispossessed and the purchaser put in possession by the Court, the question now raised is whether the defendant can, without having appealed, resort to an action of ejectment in the Common Law Court, and there claim possession of the land which this Court has decided he is not entitled to, and whether it has the power, and ought to exercise it, of restraining him from proceeding in such action.

That the Court of Common Law is in general the proper tribunal for the trial of titles to land, is unquestionable; but after this Court has been once in possession of a cause in which it has full power to adjudicate and do full justice to the litigating parties, neither of the parties, after a judgment has been given, can resort to another tribunal in respect of the same matter, and after a decree of this Court, neither of them can bring an action at law, which is against the spirit of the decree, or by which it is impeached, directly or indirectly; and the action of ejectment is not, in my opinion, an exception to the rule. In *Walker* v. *Micklethwait,* 1 Dr. & Sm., 51, a sheriff having ejected, under a writ of assistance issued in pursuance of an order of the Court of Chancery, a person from premises which had been sold under an order of the Court, an action of trover against the sheriff was restrained, although the action sought damages for a trespass in taking chattels not included in the order. KINDERSLEY, V. C., said: "The action proceeds on the footing that the Court is entirely wrong, and that the plaintiff is still the owner of the property which has been sold by the order of the Court." The defendant in this suit proceeds in his ejectment on precisely the same footing. *Brennen* v. *Preston,* 10 Hare, 339, is to the same effect. In *Grand Junction Canal Co.* v. *Dimes,* 17 Sim. 301, the Court enjoined Dimes from bringing an action, after decree, inconsistent with it. The Vice Chancellor said that the object of the decree was to settle finally the question between the parties, and that the defendant Dimes, by bringing the action, was reopening the question, and therefore was violating the spirit of the decree.

It is difficult to understand why the principle of these cases should not apply to an action of ejectment, being simply a proceeding to put the party bringing it into possession of the land. This Court has decided, after argument, that the defendant in this suit is not entitled to the possession of the land in question, but that King, the purchaser under the order of this Court, is entitled to possession, and has delivered possession to him. Under these circumstances, to allow an ejectment to be brought by Miller against King, or one placed on the land by him, would be inconsistent with the order of this Court which he has not thought proper to question in the only legitimate manner by an appeal. And in *Selby* v. *Selby*, 2 Dick., 678, the Court having decreed that the plaintiff was entitled to the estates in question, and having ordered that he should be put in possession of them, he was accordingly put in possession, and the defendant, having afterwards brought ejectment to recover possession of the estates, the plaintiff filed his bill and prayed for a perpetual injunction. The Lord Chancellor, THURLOW, said, "the Court will not permit any person to impede the execution of a decree so long as the decree remains unappealed," and he ordered a perpetual injunction. The same doctrine is recognized in the United States Courts. In *McKay* v. *Blackett*, 9 Paige, 437, it was held that the Court would not permit its orders to be rescinded or its jurisdiction to be questioned,—its orders to be rescinded indirectly and not by the Supreme Court of Appeal, and its jurisdiction to be questioned by courts of co-ordinate or inferior authority. The rule will be made absolute with costs.

The following is the judgment of His Lordship the Judge in Equity on the motion to make absolute the rule for injunction in KING *v.* MILLER, referred to *ante* p. 281.

On argument of the rule *nisi* for an injunction to restrain the defendant J. C. Sherbrooke Miller from prosecuting the action at law referred to therein, it was admitted that, under the authorities cited in support of the rule, an injunction could be granted if it clearly appeared that the land of which the defendant was dispossessed under the writ of assistance was the same land as that comprised in the mortgage under foreclosure, and indeed it is unquestionable that redress must be sought in this Court and not elsewhere for what may have occurred in the execution of its process. But Mr. Rigby contended that the Court must be satisfied on the point, and that, if a doubt existed as to the identity of the land, it would not interfere by injunction, but would leave the party to his remedy at law. The mortgage conveys all that upland farm now in the possession of Jacob Miller and J. C. S. Miller, which they may have in possession, remainder or reversion, under and by virtue of the last will and testament of Samuel Miller, deceased, which is particularly described therein.

In the will of Samuel Miller there is devised to Jacob Miller for life, and after his decease to his son J. C. S. Miller, and his daughter Sophia, "one hundred acres of upland, lying and being situate as follows, viz: Beginning at the west side of the Kennetcook road where my son Jacob has begun to clear, running westerly until it strikes the division line between my land and the lands of Antony Shaw, thence on said line northerly, thence across easterly *till it strikes the line between my land and Mr. Dimock's*, thence southerly on said line so far, thence westerly till it strikes the first named boundary on the Kennetcook road, to be laid out by a surveyor."

It appears from the affidavit of Levi Dimock, now the husband of Sophia, that, previous to the death of the tenant for life, the brother and sister made a division of the land to the possession of which they would become entitled on the death of Jacob Miller, whereby the Kennetcook road was made the division line, the piece to the southward of the road to belong to Sophia, and that to the northeast to J. C. S. Miller, and that each party acquiesced accordingly as so assigned. Subsequently in the year 1865, and after Sophia had intermarried with Levi Dimock, he, the said Levi Dimock, though he was aware that a division had taken place, being unable to procure the instrument by which it was effected, was desirous to have it ratified by another instrument to secure to his wife the title to her portion, and an agreement was accordingly executed by and between the brother and sister, whereby the piece on the westerly side of the road was confirmed to Sophia, and the remainder of the lot to J. C. S. Miller,—the parties then being in possession of the respective portions.

The affidavit of J. C. S. Miller, in answer to this of Dimock which is clear, circumstantial and explicit, is most vague and unsatisfactory in every respect. It is difficult to understand what he means by saying that the devise was so indefinite that the land could not be ascertained, and if ascertained could not be divided. He claims no title to the land he occupied other than that of possession, but asserts a right to it merely by possession, and his account of the deed executed by himself and his sister is most lame. True, he confirmed to her, he says, the part to the west of the road, but no tract was then fixed or agreed on as her share. The equivocation is apparent; the lot was a lot of 100 acres; he confirms to his sister the part to the west of the road, and she confirms to him the remainder of the lot of which he had been previously and was then in possession, i. e. the lot in controversy. If we are to take his version we are to infer that nothing passed under the mortgage, or there were no means of ascertaining what it was. But the affidavit of Harvie, adduced by J. C. S. Miller, seems to me to set the matter at rest, as he has annexed a plan of the land which shows clearly, not only that the land in question was part of the land devised to Samuel Miller for life and to J. C. S. Miller and his sister Sophia in remainder, but was the part assigned to the former under the agreement. Taking the plan and commencing at the point I have marked in pencil B., on the west side of the road which is self-evidently the starting point, and following the description in the will, we proceed westerly to Shaw's land, then on the line of that land,

running northerly, thence across easterly till it strikes the
Dimock land, thence southerly on line of said land so far
thence until it strikes the first named boundary on the Kennetcook road. How the mortgagor, Mr. Harvie, with this description before him, and with the plan representing the land and
the lands adjacent, could venture to say that the piece to the
eastward of the road was not comprised in the devise is past
my comprehension. How could he have run the lot devised,
so as to have bounded it on Shaw's land on the west, and
Dimock's on the east, having Kennetcook road running
through it without including in the lot that part which is
now in controversy to the east of the road? He might have
said, with all propriety, that to have run it out without
including that part would have been impossible.

There is a statement in Miller's affidavit which one would
hope has arisen from ignorance on his part of the description
in the will; he says the 100 acres devised to himself and
Sophia was so indefinite, *except that it was known to be on the
west side of Kennetcook road,* the locality of which has never
since been changed, that it was impossible to lay off and define
the same. Now the land devised lay part to the west and part
to the east of the road, and just as it was devised so it has been
divided and possessed and enjoyed by the two devisees; one
taking the west and the other the east; and no matter whether
the testator had or had not a title to the east half, Miller
mortgaged it and is estopped from controverting the title of
the mortgagee,—not that any question has been raised as to
the testator's title.

Has not the question been already before the Court? The
rule *nisi* for the writ of assistance was granted on the affidavit
of Dimock, to which I have referred, setting forth all the facts
of the case, and that rule was to show cause why the writ
should not issue to put Miller, the defendant, out of that
portion of the real estate described in the mortgage foreclosed,
of which he was then in possession, and of which he wrongfully
withheld possession; and it was this piece now in controversy
of which he was then in possession, and of which he withheld
possession. No cause was shewn and the rule was made
absolute. If Miller had intended to contest the plaintiff's

right to the possession of that part, he should have then shewn cause why he should not be dispossessed.

The present rule must be made absolute with costs.

WINDSOR & ANNAPOLIS RAILWAY v. WESTERN COUNTY RAILWAY.

Plaintiffs' bill set out the Act of the Legislature of Nova Scotia (1865 c. 13) providing for the construction of the Windsor and Annapolis Railway; the agreement of November 22, 1866, between the Commissioner of Railways for Nova Scotia and Messrs. Punchard, Barry & Clark for its construction, containing a stipulation that prior to the opening of the road a traffic arrangement should be made between the parties for the mutual use by the Province and the Company of their respective lines of railway from Halifax to Windsor, and from Windsor to Annapolis; the Act of the Provincial Legislature incorporating the Company (1867 c. 36) of which the Act first mentioned and the agreement in pursuance thereof were made a part; the agreement of the Government of Canada, (successor to that of Nova Scotia in relation to the line from Halifax to Windsor), with the plaintiffs made September 22nd, 1871, providing that the Company should, with exceptions not touching the matter in hand, have the exclusive use of the Windsor Branch with station accommodation, etc., and the use, so far as required, of the Trunk Line from Windsor Junction to Halifax, the Company to pay over to the Government monthly one-third of the gross earnings of the Government lines, the agreement to continue twenty-one years, then renewable, but to terminate in the event of the Company failing to operate the Railways between Halifax and Annapolis. Plaintiffs alleged that, having certain equitable claims against the Government of Canada, they allowed their payments due under the agreement of September, 1871, to fall in arrear, but paid them off in November, 1872, after which under similar circumstances they again allowed them to fall in arrear, in consequence of which the Government threatened to resume possession of the road, unless payment was made on or before October 1st, 1873, which period was afterwards extended to November 1st, 1873; that on the 22nd October, 1873, a Minute of the Privy Council of Canada was passed, of which no notice, official or otherwise was given to the Plaintiffs, by or on behalf of the Government, reciting that the Company owed the Government $30,000, and had failed to operate the Windsor Branch, and recommending that the Government should immediately proceed to operate the road between Halifax and Windsor; that afterwards on the 20th June 1875, an agreement was entered into between Her Majesty the Queen, represented by the Minister of Public Works, and the plaintiff Company, whereby the Company agreed to change the gauge of their Railway and release all claims against the Government to July 1st, 1875, and in consideration thereof the debts alleged to be due to the Government by the Company up to January 1st, 1875, were extinguished, and it was declared that the agreement under which the Company held and worked the Branch Line continued in full force and effect, except as thus modified. Plaintiffs alleged that they had continued in possession of said Windsor Branch until August 1877, when the Superintendent of Government Railways took forcible possession and prevented them from using the branch. The road was afterwards transferred by the Dominion Government to the defendants on the 24th September, 1877, such transfer being based on the authority of the Dominion Act of 1874, c. 16. (q. v.) Defendants having demurred to this writ;

Held, That by the agreement of September 1871, the Windsor Branch was in fact leased to the plaintiffs for twenty-one years, that the only event upon which the Government was authorized to re-enter was a failure to operate the road between Halifax and Annapolis; that the statement in the Minute of Council that plaintiffs had failed to operate the road could be controverted in this suit,—and that without making the Crown or the Government, represented by the Attorney General of Canada, a party to the suit,—and having been denied by the plaintiffs. must be taken for the purpose of the argument on the demurrer to be untrue; that, independently of the Act of 1874, the only interest that could be transferred to the defendants by the Government was their reversionary interest in the road, subject to the plaintiffs' lease; that the Act of 1874 did not directly and in terms divest the plaintiffs of their rights, and must be held as intended simply to sanction the transfer to the defendants of such interest as the Government itself had in the road; that the plaintiffs had no adequate remedy at Law, by *scire facias* or petition of right, as they did not seek redress against the Crown, or the Government of Canada, and it was not in the power of the Government of Canada or the Crown to give them the relief sought for,—nor by ejectment, because, assuming that ejectment would lie in respect to the rights claimed by plaintiffs to operate the railway under the agreement of 1871, plaintiffs could not by that action obtain any relief in respect to the original agreement with the Provincial Government as to running powers, and this ground of demurrer being to the whole writ, even if applicable to part of the writ, must be overruled, as it could not be good in part and bad in part.

RITCHIE, E. J., now, (March 11th, 1878,) delivered the judgment of the Court:—

The defendants having demured to the writ of the plaintiffs instead of answering it, the facts stated in it, so far as regards the argument, must be assumed to be true. From the statements therein it appears that on the 2nd of May, 1865, the Legislature of Nova Scotia passed an Act providing for the construction of a Railway from Windsor to Annapolis, and on the 22nd November, 1866, under the authority of that Act, the Commissioner of Railways for that Province entered into an agreement with Messrs. Punchard, Barry & Clark, of London, G. B., for its construction, which contained, among other things, the following stipulation: "And it is hereby mutually agreed that prior to the opening of the railroad, a traffic arrangement shall be made between the parties for the mutual use and employment of their respective lines of railway between Halifax and Windsor, and Windsor and Annapolis, including running powers, or for the joint operation thereof, on equitable terms, to be settled by two arbitrators to be chosen by the said parties in the usual way in case of difference."

On the 7th May, 1867, the members of the firm of Punchard, Barry & Clarke were, by an Act of this Province, constituted a body corporate by the name of, "The Windsor and Annapolis Railway Company," and by the act of incorporation, the act first above referred to and the said agreement were incorporated with and made part of the act of incorporation.

On the 22nd September, 1871, the Government of Canada, which became successor of that of Nova Scotia in relation to the line of Railway between Halifax and Windsor, in pursuance of the power and authority of the said act of incorporation, entered into the following agreement with the plaintiffs :—

"Agreement between the Windsor and Annapolis Railway Company, limited, and the Government of Canada, (approved and ratified by His Excellency the Governor General of Canada, in Council, on the 22nd day of September, A. D., 1871.)

"The several expressions hereinafter referred to shall, when used in this agreement, have the signification and meaning following: "The Company",—the Windsor and Annapolis Railway Company, limited.

"The Authorities,"—the Department of the Government of Canada which for the time being shall have the command or control of the Nova Scotia Railways.

"The Trunk Line,"—so much of the Nova Scotia Railway, with the branches, appurtenances, buildings and conveniences thereto belonging or attached, as lies between the said Windsor Junction and the Junction of such Railway with the Windsor and Annapolis Railway, at or near Windsor.*

---

* The above is the definition given in the writ, but it is in fact the definition of the "Windsor Branch," the "Trunk" being the line between Halifax city and the Windsor Junction. The writ was afterwards amended.

"The Superintendent,"—the Superintendent or other officer for the time being managing the Nova Scotia Railways.

"The Manager,"—the General Manager or other officer for the time being, managing the Windsor and Annapolis Railway.

" 2.—The Company," (meaning the plaintiffs), " shall, except for the purpose of the authorities," (meaning the Government of Canada), " in maintaining the Railway and Works, have the exclusive use of the Windsor Branch, with all station accommodation, engine sheds and other conveniencies, (but not including rolling-stock and tools for repairs), now in use thereon.

" 3.—The Company shall also use, to the extent required for its traffic, the Trunk Line, with the station accommodation thereon, including engine shed, accommodation for five engines, water supply, fuel stages, turntables, signals, telegraphs, wharves, sidings and other conveniences, but not including machine shops and other shops, buildings and appliances for repair of rolling-stock.

" 4.—The Company shall run every day, Sundays excepted, not less than two trains each way, carrying passengers, and shall adopt the same tolls as at present levied, or such other tolls as may from time to time be approved of by the Governor in Council, and shall furnish and maintain its own rolling-stock.

" 5.—The authorities shall maintain in workable condition the Windsor Branch and the Trunk Line, including all the station accommodation and other conveniences thereon.

"6.—The Company shall, on the Windsor Branch, employ their own station agents, booking clerks, watchmen, porters, signalmen, switchmen and other servants, for the management of the traffic.

" 7.—The authorities shall, on the Trunk Line, employ all station agents, booking clerks, watchmen, signalmen, switch-men and other servants, not provided by the Company under clause 17.

"8.—The Company shall not, except with the concurrence of the authorities, carry any local traffic between stations on the Trunk Line, but if so carried they shall charge the same tolls as may be charged by the authorities.

"9.—The Company shall keep and render to the Superintendent an exact detailed account of all traffic carried by them over the Windsor Branch and Trunk Line.

" 10.—The Company shall pay to the authorities monthly one-third of the gross earnings from all traffic carried by them over the Windsor Branch and Trunk Line.

" 11.—All accounts between the authorities and the Company under this arrangement shall be adjusted regularly at the end of each calendar month, and the balance struck and paid over in cash, not later than twenty-one days after the end of each month.

" 12.—The Authorities and the Company respectively, shall, at all reasonable times, have access to and be allowed to inspect all such books, papers and vouchers in possession of the other of them, as have reference to the accounts between them.

" 13.—All regular trains on the Windsor Branch and Trunk Line shall be run in the usual way by time-table, which time-table shall, in respect to the Trunk Line, be prepared by the Superintendent, on consultation with the Manager. The Superintendent shall arrange for the arrival and departure of the trains of the Company at the times desired by the Manager, or as near thereto as practicable; and in this respect, and in every other respect, the Superintendent, the officers and servants of the authorities shall conduct the business and work the traffic of the Company and of the authorities with perfect impartiality and fairness.

" 14.—With respect to special and irregular trains, in order to ensure public safety, the Company shall use the Trunk Line in strict accordance with such rules and regulations as are now in use, or as may hereafter be adopted and enforced by the Manager on the Windsor Branch, so far as necessary, for the guidance of officers and men engaged in maintenance of the Railway.

" 15.—The speed of the Company's trains on the Trunk Line and Windsor Branch shall not exceed the speed adopted by similar trains on the Government Railways in Nova Scotia.

" 16.—The Station Agents and other servants of the authorities at Windsor Junction shall receive, and, as far as practicable, carry out the instructions of the Manager in regard to the arrival, departure and working of the Company's trains, from or to the Windsor Branch; and he or they shall record in a book, to be kept for that purpose, the numbers and particulars of all engines, carriages, truck cars or other vehicles passing through such junction, and shall make a return of the same daily to their respective owners.

"17·—The Company shall employ on the Trunk Line their own Booking Clerks, Carting Agents, Carting Staff or such other staff as they may deem necessary for the booking, collecting, checking, invoicing, receiving, delivering or forwarding their own traffic; and the authorities shall, so far as practicable, provide suitable and convenient accommodation for such servants, and for the accommodation of such business.

"18·—The Company, in using the Trunk Line, shall at all times observe the Regulations and Bye-Laws for the time being in force thereon; and the authorities in using the Windsor Branch for the purpose of repairing and maintaining it, shall at all times observe the Regulations and Bye-Laws, for the time being in force thereon.

"19.—In the event of the Company failing to operate the Railways between Halifax and Annapolis, then this agreement shall terminate, and the authorities may immediately proceed to operate the railway between Halifax and Windsor as they may deem proper and expedient.

"20.—The termination of this agreement under the preceding clause is not to prejudice any rights which the Company may now have.

"21·—This agreement shall take effect on the 1st day of January, 1872, and continue for twenty-one years, and be then renewed on the same conditions or such other conditions as may be mutually agreed on."

The writ proceeds to state that the said agreement had never been broken by the Plaintiffs, except as to non-payment of rent as thereinafter mentioned.

The Plaintiffs began accordingly to operate the said Windsor Branch Railway in connection with the Windsor and Annapolis Railway, and to exercise the running powers over the said Trunk Line into Halifax, and at the same time necessarily increased their rolling-stock, in order to perform the additional service rendered incumbent by such an extension of their operations, and the Plaintiffs continued fully to operate the whole line between Halifax and Annapolis up to the 1st August last, and never failed to operate the same at any time, according to the said agreement.

On the 23rd May, A. D. 1873, the Parliament of Canada passed a resolution authorizing the Government to enter into negotiations for the transfer of the Windsor Branch Railway to reliable parties who would construct a railway between Annapolis and Yarmouth.

The Plaintiffs having certain equitable claims against the Government of Canada, allowed a certain amount of the one-third tolls or earnings reserved under the the agreement of 22nd September, 1871, to fall into arrear, with the hope and to the end that such equitable claims would be allowed to stand as an offset against the said one-third tolls or earnings; but the Government refused, and threatened to resume possession of the said Windsor Branch, and in November, 1872, the Plaintiffs paid the said arrears so due. Under similar circumstances, the said one-third tolls or earnings were again allowed to fall into arrear, and the Minister of Public Works, on behalf of the Government, made several applications to the Plaintiffs to have the balance settled, and finally threatened that unless payment were made on or before the 1st October, 1873, Government would resume possession of the road. The Plaintiffs, being unable to provide the amount within the time stipulated, requested a further delay, and the Minister of Public Works, on behalf of the Government, agreed to take no further action in relation to the arrears, before the 1st November, 1873.

On the 22nd October, 1873, the following Minute of Council was passed by the Privy Council of Canada, but no official or other notice of it was given to the Plaintiffs, either previous or subsequent to its passing by the Government of Canada or by any person or persons on its behalf :—" On a report dated 21st October, 1873, from the Honorable the Minister of Public Works, stating that the Windsor and Annapolis Railway Company have failed to operate the railway known as the Windsor Branch, mentioned in the Order in Council of the 22nd September, 1871, and to comply with the other terms and conditions of that Order in Council, and now owe over $30,000 to the Government of Canada, and, though repeatedly called upon to pay, have failed to do so, and recommending that, inasmuch as the said Company have failed to operate one of the railways between Halifax and Annapolis, the Government of Canada, known as the 'authorities,' by the said Order in Council, do proceed immediately to operate the railway between Halifax and Windsor."

On the 26th May, 1874, an Act passed the Parliament of Canada to authorize the transfer of the Windsor Branch of the Nova Scotia Railways to the Western Counties Railway Company, to the terms and effect of which I shall refer hereafter.

On the 20th day of June, 1875, an agreement was entered into between Her Majesty the Queen, represented by the Minister of Public Works for the Dominion of Canada, and the plaintiffs, which agreement is in the words following :—

"Articles of Agreement made and entered into the twenty-second day of June in the year of our Lord, one thousand eight hundred and seventy-five, between the Windsor and Annapolis Railway Company, (hereinafter called the Company) of the first part, and Her Majesty Queen Victoria, represented herein by the Minister of Public Works, (hereinafter called the Minister), of the second part;

"Whereas the Company was on the 1st day of January last indebted to the Government of Canada in a large sum of money, being one-third of the accrued gross earnings of the Windsor Branch of the Intercolonial Railway, worked and managed by the Company, under an agreement entered into by them with the Government of Canada, dated the 22nd day of September, A. D. 1871, granting the said Branch to the said Company for twenty-one years, from the 1st day of January, 1872;

"And whereas the Company have preferred certain claims against the Government of Canada, by way of set-off to such indebtedness, but which claims have not been recognized or admitted;

"And whereas it is found desirable that the gauge of rails

on the said Branch should be changed from their present 5 feet 6 in. gauge to the standard gauge of 4 feet 8½ in.;

" These presents witness that the said Company, for the consideration hereinafter named, do hereby contract and agree to and with Her Majesty, represented as aforesaid, that the Company shall and will, at their own cost and charge, on or before the 1st day of July now next, in a proper, substantial and workmanlike manner, but subject to the approval of the Minister or officer appointed by him, change the gauge of the Windsor and Annapolis Railway, and make it conform to the present standard gauge above named, and deliver over to the said Minister or whom he may appoint for that purpose, at such place or places as may be fixed, 9 broad gauge locomotive engines, 14 sets of broad gauge passenger-car trucks, and 145 sets of broad gauge freight-car trucks, and also execute and deliver a release of all claims and demands whatsoever against Her Majesty, or the Government of Canada, up to the 1st day of July, 1875 ;

" In consideration whereof her said Majesty, represented as aforesaid, doth promise and agree to and with the said Company;

" That upon the said change of gauge being effected, in the manner hereinbefore described, all debts and liabilities accrued, due by the Company to the Government of Canada, in manner aforesaid up to the first day of January last past shall be discharged and extinguished;

" That the Minister will deliver to the said Company, at Windsor Junction, 9 standard gauge locomotive engines, (3 new and 6 converted ones,) 14 sets of standard gauge passenger-car trucks and 145 sets of standard gauge freight-car trucks ;

" That the said nine standard gauge engines shall be and remain the property of the Government of Canada, and in no way liable for the debts and liabilities of the said Company.

" And it is hereby distinctly understood and agreed between the parties hereto, that nothing herein shall in any wise, (except as to discharging the indebtedness and claims herein above named), alter, vary or interfere with the terms of the agreement under which the said Company hold the said Branch Line; but that all moneys accrued due, as being one-

'third of the gross earnings of the said Branch, from the 1st day of January last, shall be paid by the Company to the credit of the Receiver-General of Canada, on or before the 31st day of July next, and thereafter those accruing shall be paid monthly, as provided in the said agreement under which the Company hold and work the Branch as aforesaid, which, except as aforesaid, is hereby declared in full force and effect."

This last mentioned agreement was prepared under the direction of the Minister of Justice of Canada, executed by the Minister of Public Works, and accepted and acted upon by the Government of Canada and by the plaintiffs, and the Plaintiffs, in accordance with the said last-mentioned agreement, and on the faith of the same, changed the gauge of rails on their railway and delivered up to the Minister of Public Works 14 sets of passenger-car trucks, 9 broad gauge engines, and 145 sets of broad gauge freight-car trucks, and incurred very large expense in making arrangements to carry out the said agreement on their part.

The plaintiffs continued in exclusive and undisturbed possession of the said Windsor Branch, and continued to operate the same and paid the rent as hereinbefore set forth, until the 1st August, 1877, when the Superintendent of the Government Railways, without the consent of the Plaintiffs, and against their will, took forcible possession of the said Windsor Branch, and removed their trains therefrom, and prevented them from using the said Branch or the said Trunk Line, and from running any train thereon, and the Windsor Branch and Trunk Line continued to be operated by the said Superintendent and his subordinates, until the 24th September last, when the Windsor Branch was formally transferred to the defendants, who took possession and continue to hold and operate the same.

On the day last mentioned, the Solicitor of the Plaintiffs demanded on behalf of the Plaintiffs possession of the line of Railway between Windsor and Windsor Junction, known as the Windsor Branch.

No answer having been received, on the 2nd October last their solicitor addressed the following letter to the Secretary of the Western Counties Railway Company :—

" *Sir*,—As the solicitor and attorney of the Windsor and
Annapolis Railway Company, and on their behalf, I hereby
demand the privilege of running trains over the Windsor
Branch Railway, of which the Western Counties Railway
Company is now improperly in possession. You are hereby
notified that, unless in the meantime provisional arrangement
is made, granting the privilege to the Windsor and Annapolis
Railway Company, the said last-mentioned Company will run
an engine over the said Branch line, from Windsor to Windsor
Junction, on Tuesday next, the ninth instant. This demand
is made only for provisional running powers, and is not
intended to waive the rights of the Windsor and Annapolis
Railway Company to the exclusive possession of the said
Branch Railway, to which they are entitled under their lease."

To this letter no reply was given, and on the 9th October an
attempt was made by the Plaintiffs to run an engine from
Windsor towards Windsor Junction, but they were forcibly
prevented from doing so by the defendants. The plaintiffs in
their writ charge that the agreement of the 22nd September,
1871, has never been legally cancelled, and is still in force, and
that they are entitled to operate the said Windsor Branch
Railway under it; that the Act of 26th May, 1874, was not
intended to transfer, and did not in fact transfer to the
defendants any rights save such as were held by the Government of Canada subordinately to the rights of the plaintiffs
under the agreement; that if that Act purports to interfere
with or cancel any of the plaintiffs' rights, it is *ultra vires*
of the Parliament of Canada; that if it is *intra vires* of the
Parliament of Canada, and can be held to take away any of
the rights of the plaintiffs under the agreement, the right of
the plaintiffs to running powers over the said Windsor Branch
and Trunk Line still remains.

The defendants have demurred to the plaintiffs' writ on the
five grounds following :—

First—That as to so much of the writ as seeks to controvert
the truth of the Order in Council, they say that it is not
competent for the plaintiffs, in this Court and in this form of
action, to call in question the truth of the Order in Council,

or of any of the allegations therein, nor is it in the power of
the Court to try or inquire into the truth of such allegations;
and if such power existed, it could only do so in a case where
the Crown or the Government of Canada, by its Attorney-
General or otherwise, was a party, or was otherwise represented
in such suit; and because said Order in Council was an act of
State and a part of the public policy of the then Government
of Canada, and it is not competent for this Court to inquire
into, adjudicate upon, or review such act of State, and even if
the Order in Council were void, the same has been ratified by
the Act passed on the 26th May, 1874, and the ratification
thereof by that Act gives the said Order the full force and
effect of a statute; and by virtue of such ratification, the order
has the same force, validity and effect as if it had been passed
in pursuance of a previous statute authorizing it.

Secondly—That as to the agreement of the 23rd of June,
1875, the defendants say that the Minister of Public Works
had no power to make any agreement in anywise affecting the
defendants' title to the Windsor Branch, and that it is null and
void, and is contrary to the Act of 26th May, 1874.

Thirdly—That as to that part of the writ which alleges that
that Act was *ultra vires*, or that any right was reserved to
the plaintiffs, they say that the Act was not *ultra vires*, and
that it will not bear the construction put upon it by plaintiffs,
and that under it the Windsor Branch became absolutely
vested in the defendants, free from any incumbrances whatever, or claim on the part of the plaintiffs.

Fourthly—That as regards the plaintiffs' claim to running
powers over the Windsor Branch, the agreement of the twenty-
second day of November, 1866, and the legislation thereon did
not give to or create in favor of the plaintiffs any lien or
incumbrance upon the Windsor Branch, and there is nothing
in the arrgement or legislation which interfered with or
restricted the Parliament of Canada from passing the Act
transferring it to the defendants, free from the operation of the
said agreement as to running powers; and the plaintiffs' claim,
if any, is a claim for breach of contract against the Government
of Nova Scotia, or the Government of Canada.

Fifthly—That as to the *whole* bill, including the grounds above mentioned, the defendants allege that the writ does not contain any Equity whereon this Court can ground any decree or give the plaintiffs relief; because they have a plain and adequate remedy at law, by ejectment against the defendants, by *scire facias*, or petition of right to the Crown, and because that Her Majesty the Queen, or the Government of Canada, represented by the Attorney General of Canada, is a necessary party to the suit.

We are to assume then for the purposes of this argument, that, the Legislature of Nova Scotia having by an Act provided for the construction of a railway from Windsor to Annapolis, an agreement under the authority of that Act was entered into on behalf of the Government with Messrs. Punchard, Barry & Clarke for the construction of it, in which it was mutually agreed that prior to the opening of the road a traffic arrangement should be made between them for the mutual use of their respective lines of railway between Halifax and Windsor, and Windsor and Annapolis, including running powers, &c., and that at the following session of the Legislature an Act was passed incorporating the members of the firm of Punchard, Barry & Clarke, by the name of the Windsor and Annapolis Railway Company, the now plaintiffs, which Act referred to the agreement so made, and declared that it should be incorporated into and become part of the act of incorporation, so that the plaintiffs entered upon their undertaking on the faith of the Province being pledged to them that such an arrangement should exist; and, subsequently, when the Government of Canada assumed the proprietorship of the Halifax and Windsor Branch, the arrangement was carried out by the agreement of 22nd September, 1871, the effect of which was to give to the plaintiffs all the rights and privileges which they claim to possess in this suit, for the period of 21 years from the 1st January, 1872, subject to certain stipulations on the part of the plaintiffs, and among them, that they should monthly account for and pay the Government one-third of all the gross earnings of all traffic carried over the Windsor Branch and Trunk Line. By this agreement the Windsor Branch was in fact leased to the plaintiffs for 21 years, after which it was to be subject to renewal. The only stipulation the failure to perform which authorized the Government to re-enter was a failure on the part of the plaintiffs to operate the railway between Halifax and Annapolis. It is alleged and to be assumed that the plaintiffs continued to operate the whole line between Halifax and Annapolis up to the 1st August last and never failed to operate the same, and except as regards the payment of the rent, none of the stipulations contained in the agreement were broken by them, so that the only question open under the agreement, supposing it to have been a valid and binding one, is whether the non-payment of the rent, according to the terms of it, and what has since taken place in regard to it, entitled the Government to re-enter and re-possess itself of the railway, as has been done.

The rent was allowed to fall into arrear in 1872, but there can be no pretence for the Government claiming a forfeiture of the lease or a right to re-enter in respect of that, as in November of that year the arrears were all paid and the parties continued to act under the agreement, and thus a forfeiture, if any occurred, was waived. And in 1873 further arrears accrued due, when the Government threatend to resume possession of the Windsor Branch if the amount was not paid on or before the 1st October of that year, but on the plaintiffs asking for an extension of the time, the Minister of Public Works, on behalf of the Government, agreed to take no further action in relation to the arrears before the 1st November of that year; but on 23rd October the order in Council of that date was passed on the report of the Minister of Public Works, and notwithstanding the statements in that order, which we must at present assume to be all untrue, with the exception of that relating to the non-payment of rent, unless an order in Council is of such a character that whatever is stated in it must be taken by the Court to be true, whether it be so or not, as the defendants contend is the case; (to this, however, I shall refer hereafter;—as regards the waiver of the forfeiture, if any, I would refer to the late case of *Davenport* v. *the Queen,* 3 Appeal Cases, 131); in June 1875, this agreement of September 1871, was confirmed by the Government of Canada in the most emphatic manner, by the last clause, and an arrangement made for liquidating the debt then due by the plaintiffs, they undertaking to alter the gauge of their railway and to perform other stipulations, involving a large outlay on their part, on fulfilling which all debts due by, and liabilities of the plaintiffs to the Government of Canada, up to the preceding 1st January, should be extinguished. After entering into this last-mentioned agreement the plaintiffs continued in possession and paid their rent till they were dispossessed, the Government thus again waiving any claim they might have to a forfeiture for non-payment of rent.

That the taking possession of the Windsor Branch with force, in violation of the lease and agreements entered into with the plaintiffs and ratified by the Dominion Government in the most solemn manner, was unjustifiable, cannot, I think, be questioned, if they are to be considered valid, assuming, as I am at present bound to do, that the plaintiffs have fulfilled all the conditions on their part; and the law recognizes no distinction between the violation of a contract like this by the department of a Government and by a private individual.

But the question before the Court is not between the plaintiffs and the Dominion Government, but between two contending companies both claiming from the Government, and the defendants contend that previous to the agreement of the 20th June, 1875, the Government of Canada had divested itself of the Windsor Branch, and that they had acquired a right to it by virtue of the Act of the Parliament of Canada, passed 26th May, 1874, so that nothing done by the Government after that could affect their title, and that the Act conferred on them an absolute title to the railway, free from all claim or incumbrance on the part of the plaintiffs, whose rights, if they had any, were divested by the Act. If this contention can be sustained it destroys all right of action by them against the defendants, however unjustifiable the acts of the Government may have been.

There are two schedules connected with the Act, and forming part of it. From these it appears that a proposal was made by the defendants to the Dominion Government, in which, after reciting the resolution of the House of Commons of the 23rd May, 1873, above referred to, and that they had undertaken to build the road from Annapolis to Yarmouth in view of the provisions of the resolution, and were desirious of having the Windsor Branch transferred to them, they proposed the following terms: "1st—The Company will undertake to receive the railway and appurtenances on the 1st December, 1873, and from that date to work it efficiently and keep it in repair at their own cost and charges, collecting, receiving and appropriating to their own use all the tolls and earnings of the same. 2ndly— That on the completion of the Western Counties Railway from Yarmouth to Annapolis, then in progress of construction, the said railway and appurtenances from Windsor to the Trunk Line shall be and become absolutely the property of the Western Counties Railway Company. 3rdly—That in consideration of the premises, the said Company engage to prosecute the work of building the railway from Yarmouth to Annapolis, and complete the same with reasonable despatch." The schedule also contained a statement that on the following day a committee of the Privy Council advised that the proposal be adopted, as recommended by the Minister of Public Works, subject to the approval of Parliament. The other schedule is the copy of a report of a committee of the Privy Council, approved in Council on the 30th October, 1873, on a memo. from the Minister of Public Works, dated the 29th October, that he had received from the Western Counties Railway Company, through their President, a proposal to the following effect: "1st—That the Western Counties Railway Company shall carry free of charge all passengers holding Government tickets on all their passenger trains running between Halifax and Windsor Junction. 2ndly —That the Company, or their agents or assigns, shall have running powers over the Intercolonial Railway, between Halifax and Windsor Junction, with such privileges as have been hitherto granted in the agreement with the Windsor and Annapolis Railway." The committee on the recommendation of the Minister of Public Works, advised that the terms of this proposal be approved. After referring to these schedules, it is enacted as follows: "1st—The agreements hereinbefore referred to and set forth in Schedules A and B to this Act, being such as were adopted by the orders of the Governor in Council of the 22nd and 30th of October, 1873, and all matters and things therein contained are hereby approved and declared to

be *as effectual to all intents and purposes as if the said agree-*
ments had been entered into in pursuance of sufficient authority
in that behalf, given before the adoption of such agreements by
Act of Parliament of Canada. 2ndly—Until arrangements are
completed for giving possession to the Western Counties
Railway Company of the said Windsor Branch Railway, for the
purpose of operating it until the completion of their line from
Annapolis to Yarmouth, as provided in the agreement or
proposal hereinafter recited, it shall be competent for the
Government to make such other arrangement as may be
necessary, by continuing the working of the same by the
Windsor and Annapolis Railway or otherwise."

We are now to consider what effect, if any, this legislation
had on the rights of the plaintiffs, who, when it passed, and
when the resolutions on which it was founded were passed by the
Privy Council, were in possession of the Windsor Branch under
an unexpired lease with a right to running powers over it and
the Trunk Line to Halifax. It is obvious that the Dominion
Government had no right in itself to convey more than the
interest it possessed in the Railroad, which was a reversionary
interest with a right to rent and the performance of covenants.
That interest it had unquestionably a right to convey, and a
conveyance of anything beyond, independently of the Act,
would be wholly inoperative. Now the Act in question does
not directly and in terms divest the plaintiffs of their rights.
The first section assumes that the Government has entered into
an agreement without due authority, and it thereby approves
and declares that it shall be as effectual as if it had been
entered into with sufficient authority.

Where statutes interfere with the property or rights of
parties for the benefit of others they are to be construed more
strictly than any other enactments. Courts take notice that
they are obtained on the application of their promoters, and are
in effect contracts between those persons and the Legislature.
Their language is therefore treated as the language of their
promoters, and when doubt arises as to the construction of
that language, the maxim ordinarily inapplicable to the interpretation of Statutes, that *verba cartarum fortius accipiuntur*
contra proferentem, that words are to be understood most

strongly against him who uses them, is justly applied. The
benefit of the doubt is to be given to those who might be prejudiced by the exercise of the powers which the enactment
grants and against those who claim to exercise it. See *Maxwell on Stat.*, 269. And again, that auther says, "So the
Legislature in granting away in effect the ordinary rights of
the subject should be understood as granting no more than
passes by *necessary and unavoidable construction.*

It is difficult to imagine a case where the very strictest construction would be more applicable than where, of the two parties to the contract, treating the Act as a contract, the one is to
give and the other to take what belongs to a third party. It is
impossible to believe that the Legislature ever intended to do
such an injustice; all that the Legislature could have intended
was that, an agreement having been made by the Government
with the defendants to dispose off what belonged to the Government without legislative authority, that authority should
be conferred *nunc pro tunc,* and the terms of the first section
extend so far and no farther; and the second section in no
part goes farther than, assuming that the agreement is a valid
one, and one which the Governor in Council could legally
make, to provide for the operating of the line till its delivery to
the defendants. To put any other construction on the Act,
and to hold that there existed a deliberate intention of violating their contract with one party, to enable them to enter into
a contract with another, would be derogatory to the character
of the Government and of the Legislature, and as I believe
that no such intention existed, so I believe that the words used
do not necessarily indicate such an intention. I hold that any
act which infringes upon the legal rights of the subject must
be so expressed beyond all reasonable doubt, and the enjoyment of his property cannot be trenched upon by an Act, unless
the intention of the Legislature is shown by clear words or
necessary implication; all that the Legislature intended was to
sanction the transfer of their property, *not the property of the
plaintiffs.* In *Ward v. Scott,* 3 Campb. 284, because the Stat.
33 Geo. 3 c. 80 authorized the Grand Junction Canal Co. to
buy land for making the Canal, and to resell such parts as
were not used for that purpose, and declared that such sales,,

conveyances, &c., should be *valid and effective at Law to all intents and purposes whatsoever, any law, statute, usage or custom to the contrary notwithstanding*, it was insisted that sales and purchases of land by that Company, according to the provisions of that statute, were valid and effectual, and the title could not be objected to, but Lord ELLENBOROUGH said; "I must suppose the words relied on refer only to the mode of conveyance without having any operation upon the title to the subject matter conveyed. A contrary construction would be alarming to every land-owner in the Kingdom." So in this case nothing was in contemplation but the sanctioning of the conveyance of the interest of the Government in the railroad in question. In *Dawson* v. *Paver*, 5 Hare, 415, the Vice Ch., WIGRAM, says, "where an Act of Parliament in express terms or by necessary implication empowers an individual to take or interfere with the property or rights of another, and upon a sound construction of the act it appears to the court that such was the intention of the Legislature, it may well be the duty of the court to give effect to the decree of the Legislature so expressed, but where an act merely enables an individual to deal with property of his own for his own benefit, and does not in terms or by necessary implication empower him to take or interfere with the property or rights of others, questions of a very different character arise. Here the distinction between public and private acts becomes material. By a private act I do not mean merely private estate acts, but local and personal, as distinguished from general public acts. Public acts bind all the Queen's subjects, but private acts do not bind strangers unless by express words or necessary implication. The intention of the Legislature to affect the rights of strangers is apparent; that the defendants' act is a local, personal, and in that sense a private one, does not admit of dispute. It is local as confined to a particular place, and personal as being expressed to be for the benefit of individuals named in it, and not for the benefit of all Her Majesty's subjects; however all may be benefited by that which improves the particular district." So in *Scales* v. *Pickering*, 4 Bing., 448; the Chief Justice said; " If the words of a statute on which a party relies to justify

10 *j*

his entry on the land of another are ambiguous, every presumption is to be made against the party in favor of private
property. If such a construction were not adopted acts would
be framed ambiguously in order to lull parties into security."
In *Webb* v. *Manchester and Leeds Railway Company*, 4 My. &
C., 116, the defendants claimed to make a cutting through
the plaintiff's field, and Lord Ch. COTTENHAM said; "The
powers conferred on the defendants are large, and it may be
necessary for the benefit of the public, but they are so large
and so injurious to the interest of the individuals that I think
it the duty of the Court to keep them most strictly within
those powers, and if there be any reasonable doubt as to the
extent of the powers they must go elsewhere and get enlarged
powers, but they will not get them from me by way of construction of the Act of Parliament." In *Stockton and Darl-
ington Railway Company* v. *Barrett*, 7 M. & G., 879 ; Lord Ch.
LYNDHURST said; "In giving judgment it must be observed
that *in dubio* you are always to lean against the construction
which imposes a burden," And Lord BROUGHAM on the
argument of the appeal before the House of Lords repeated
the observation.

If in cases like these a strict construction is resorted to that
injury may not be done to private individuals, surely where it
is contended that an act takes from one class of individuals
their interest in a property, and conveys it to another without
any compensation, the contention must be supported by such
clear and explicit wording of the act as to leave no doubt on
the mind that no other meaning can be given to it. As I
believe a more reasonable construction can be put upon it, I
am disposed to adopt it and thus avoid the very great injustice
which would be done to the plaintiffs by the construction contended for. Let a statute be ever so charitable, said Lord
HOLT, (*Calladay* v. *Pilkinton*, 12 Mod,. 513,) yet if it takes
away the property of the subject it ought not to be counte-
nanced.

Having taken this view of the construction to be put upon
the act, it is not perhaps so necessary that I should enter upon
the question whether the Parliament of Canada had the power
of passing such a statute. It was argued on behalf of the de-

fendant that it possessed the power, as it related to a railroad and one which belonged to the Dominion. If the Dominion had no title to the railroad it could hardly be contended that the Parliament of Canada could legislate as to the proprietorship of it, merely because it was a railroad, being, as it is, wholly within the Province, and it could only be dealt with by the Local Legislature, like other property situate within the Province not belonging to the Dominion. But it is said that, being public property of the Dominion, it comes within the powers conferred on the Parliament of Canada. That body has unquestionably the right to legislate as to and to dispose of any property belonging to the Dominion, but only to dispose of the interest it may have in such property. If, for instance, when the Windsor Railroad was originally made over to the Dominion the right to the use of it at a rent had been reserved to the Province of Nova Scotia for a period of years, could the Dominion Government dispose of the interest so reserved to the Province? Clearly not, and, if not, neither could they dispose of the interest of their lessee which was so reserved. While property of the Dominion is one of the subjects over which the Parliament of Canada has the power of legislating, private property and civil rights were placed within the powers of the Local Legislature, and private property and civil rights are both invaded by this act if the right to the possession of the railroad in question belongs, under this agreement, to the plaintiffs.

Another ground of demurrer urged at the argument was that the allegations in the Order in Council are to be taken as true, and that whether they are so or not, the plaintiffs are estopped from adducing proof of their untruthfulness. This appeared to me a startling proposition, and I waited with some curiosity to see upon what reasoning or authority it could be supported, but no further argument was adduced than a statement of the proposition, as in the demurrer, and the cases cited, do not, in my opinion, bear upon the question. If such a doctrine could be sustained it leads to this, that a company or private individual, a party to a contract with the Government, is to be bound by a statement of facts made by one of the contracting parties, which is to destroy the rights of the other, not made under oath, of the truth of which the party making the statement has no personal knowledge, and yet the other contracting party, whose rights are affected by it, is not to be allowed to rebut it by evidence. A short reference to the cases cited in support of the defendants' contention will shew that they have no resemblance or analogy to this. *Gossett* v. *Howard*, 10 Q., B. 457, was the case of a warrant of the Speaker of the House of Commons, to which validity was given as to a writ of the highest Court, and the statement that a contempt had been committed could not be gainsaid, of which the House itself was the judge. In the *Secretary of State* v. *Kamachee Boye Sahaba*, 13 Moore P. C., 56, the property claimed by the respondent had been seized by the British Government, acting as a sovereign power through its delegate, the East India Company, and it was held that the act so done, with its consequences, was an Act of State, over which the Supreme Court of Madras had no jurisdiction. So in *Elphinstone* v. *Bedreechund*, 1 Knapp, 316, the transaction complained of was that of a hostile seizure, made, if not *flagrante*, yet *nondum cessante bello*, and consequently it was held that the Municipal Court had no jurisdiction over it.

A proclamation of the Sovereign, which is more an Act of State than this Order in Council, in a controversy between individuals in a Court of law, would not be entitled to the consideration contended for, and evidence would be received, that the facts stated in it were unfounded. See *Rex* v. *Sutton*, 4 M. & S., 549. Nor would a litigant party be precluded from adducing proof to shew that the statements in the recitals of a statute, the language of all the branches of the Legislature, are without foundation in fact. In *Reg.* v. *Haughton*, 1 E. & B. 501, the Court so held and decided that such a recital, either of fact or of law, was not conclusive. The contention of the defendant on this point is, in my opinion, wholly untenable.

Another ground taken is that if the Court possessed the power of receiving evidence as to the truth of the statements in the Order in Council, it could only do so in a case where the Crown or the Government of Canada was represented by the Attorney-General and that that officer should have been made a party in this suit. The controversy here is merely between the plaintiffs and defendants, each, it is true, claiming under the Dominion Government, but that by no means involves the necessity of making that Government or any of its officers a party, any more than that in the case of two individual litigants claiming under a grantor or lessor being also a private individual, there would be a necessity of making such grantor or lessor a party. Throughout the argument, it seemed to be assumed on the part of the defendants that they stood in a different position and had other and different rights from what they would have had if they had claimed from a private person having the same title that the Government had. Independently of the Act above referred to, they stand, in my opinion, in no other or better position. The Crown has never been deemed a necessary party to the suit in which grantees from the Crown contend, as to the validity of their respective grants, where they conflict, and if a second grant should issue of the same tract of land, on the assumption that the former had been liable to forfeiture for the non-performance of its conditions, the grantee could shew that no forfeiture had in fact been incurred, or no escheat had taken place or inquest of office, and that, therefore, the second grant was inoperative, and in such suit the Crown need be no party. And I see no reason why, in this case, a different principle should be applied.

As regards the plaintiffs' claim for running powers over the Windsor Branch, the defendants demur on the ground that the agreement of the 22nd November, 1866, did not, nor did the legislation thereon give them any lien or encumbrance thereon. But the right of the plaintiffs to these powers is even stronger than their right to operate it under their lease. It was on the faith of a stipulation to that effect that the Windsor and Annapolis Railway was built, and the plaintiffs became the proprietors of it. Their Act of Incorporation confirms to them the privilege, and the Government under which the defendants claim, took the road, subject to that right, which is recognized and confirmed by the agreement of the 22nd September, 1871.

There is but one other ground of demurrer, which is made to apply to the whole writ, viz., that it does not contain any matter of Equity whereon the Court can ground a decree or give the plaintiffs relief against the defendants, and that the plaintiffs are not entitled to the relief prayed for, because they have a plain and adequate remedy at law, by action of ejectment, by writ of *scire facias* against the Crown, or petition of right. The plaintiffs seek no redress against the Crown or the Dominion of Canada; all the right to the railroad in controversy which was ever vested in them has passed from them, and, if the defendants have a valid title to it, it is not in the power of the Government of Canada or the Crown to give to the plaintiffs the relief sought for in this suit, nor could they obtain it under a decree against either of them. And if the defendants have, as they assert, a right to the railroad, to operate it exclusively and to prevent the plaintiffs from exercising running powers over it, they can seek the relief prayed for from them alone.

It is quite true that resort cannot be had to a Court of Equity, where a plain, adequate and complete remedy can be had at law; but the remedy must be so in all respects. If it be doubtful or obscure, or inadequate or falls short in any respect of what the party is entitled to, and does not secure to him the full rights which he seeks, he may come to a Court of Equity for relief. The remedy by ejectment would not give the plaintiffs adequate and full relief, for the object of this suit is twofold; they claim to have running powers over the road under the original agreement made with the Provincial Government, and they claim to operate the railway under the subsequent agreement, and both of these rights, have been interfered with. Now assuming that an action of ejectment would lie as respects the latter, it certainly would not as respects the former; for that the plaintiffs could obtain no adequate relief, except in a Court of Equity; and this demurrer, being, as it is, to the whole writ, cannot prevail, the plaintiffs appearing by it to have a claim which can only be adequately enforced in this Court. A demurrer cannot be good in part and bad in part, so that if the demurrer is general to the whole, and there is a part to which the defendant ought to put in an answer, the demurrer must be overruled. See *Dan. Ch., Pr.* 500.

Having arrived at the conclusion that the defendants have failed to sustain their several grounds of demurrer, they must be overruled with costs.

BLACK *v.* MURRAY, ET AL., EXECUTORS.

Defendants' testator mortgaged certain property to plaintiff who afterwards foreclosed and the property was offered for sale April 10th, 1876, and bid in by John McDonald, who paid a deposit of $300, but failed to complete the purchase. The property was again offered for sale November 19th, 1877, and realized a sum which with the deposit paid on the first sale satisfied the plaintiffs' mortgage, and left a surplus of $322.29. Upon this surplus a claim was made under R. S. cap. 21, sec. 81, for taxes due by testator for 1874-5-6-7. McDonald, who had bid in the property at the first sale, held a second mortgage upon it to more than the amount remaining in the Sheriff's hands. *Held*, that the statute was not applicable to the case, as the sale referred to in the first branch of the section was a sale by the person owing the rates at the time of the sale, whereas the testator had conveyed the property by the mortgages before the rates had become due, and the property had not been taken under any "process of law" within the meaning of the words in the latter part of the section.

RITCHIE, E. J., now, (March 25th, 1878,) delivered the judgment of the Court:—

This suit was brought to foreclose a mortgage made by Nathan Utley to the plaintiff, and, under an order of foreclosure, the mortgaged premises were offered for sale by the Sheriff of Yarmouth on the 10th April, 1876, and were bid in by John McDonald for $4,476, who then paid a deposit of $300, but he having failed to complete the purchase, the deposit became forfeited, and the mortgaged premises were again offered for sale on the 19th November, 1877, when they were sold and conveyed to Benjamin Hilton by the Sheriff, for the sum of $4,833.42. Out of the amount in his hands, $5133.42, the Sheriff paid to the plaintiff the amount of his mortgage with interest and costs, leaving a balance of $322.29.

Utley, the mortgagor, died sometime since, and there was due by his estate for poor, township and county rates, at the time of the first sale of the mortgaged premises under the order of the Court, the sum of $75.89 for the year 1874, $76.26 for 1875 and $36.10 for 1876; and previous to the last sale, there became due for 1877, the further sum of $42.80, thus making $231.05 then due by the estate of Utley. For this amount, a claim is made for payment out of the surplus proceeds in the hands of the Sheriff. The claim is made under

the provisions of section 81, of chapter 21 of the Revised Statutes. There was a second mortgage on the property to John
McDonald, the person who bid it in at the first sale and forfeited his deposit by not completing the purchase.

The section referred to is as follows; "In case of any
transfer of property, the assessment shall be payable by the
assignee or occupier; and in case of property taken under
execution or any other process of law, the same shall be first
liable for any assessment which shall be due and payable
thereon, and payment thereof enforced, and the sheriff or other
officer shall be bound first to pay such assessment out of the
proceeds of the sale." The previous section had enacted that
the warrant of distress for county rates might be levied and
enforced on any property owned by the delinquent in any
district of the county. The section embraces two objects, one
of them is that if a person owns property and is indebted for
rates, he should not by selling it deprive the county of the
right to resort to it for payment, but that the purchaser should
take it subject to the rates; the other, that if property of such
a person is taken under execution or any other process of law,
it should be first liable for any assessment due thereon. The
section is confined to these classes of cases and cannot be
extended beyond them.

The sale referred to in the section is a sale by the person
owing the rates at the time of the sale, but Utley conveyed
this property when he made the mortgages before the rates in
question became due; all that remained to him was a right to
redeem it, and this suit is brought merely to foreclose that
right of redemption, he not having paid the amount due by
him. The Court having decreed a foreclosure ordered a sale
so that the mortgage might be paid, and if more was produced
than was sufficient to pay the amount due it might enure for
the benefit of subsequent incumbrancers, and if none, for the
mortgagor. The amount produced by this sale has not proven
sufficient to pay off the two mortgages, thus showing that the
property had been mortgaged beyond its value, and that the
interest which remained in it to Utley, viz., the equity of
redemption, was of no value.

A distinction was attempted to be made between the amount

forfeited on the first sale and the surplus which arose on the second; but they stand on the same footing, and must be deemed the proceeds of the mortgaged premises to be applied in payment of the mortgages. Mr. Harrington contended that, but for this claim, the forfeited deposit would be payable to the estate of Utley. I think not. In ordinary cases of a sale it is the seller who becomes entitled to a forfeited deposit. When in money it is considered as a part payment of the purchase money, and not merely as a pledge, and, if not returned to the party making it, it would go to those entitled to the proceeds of the sale of the land. I cannot understand upon what principle Utley's representatives can claim to be entitled to it as against the mortgagees. This sale was by order of the Court for the benefit in the first instance of the parties holding the securities on the property, and they are primarily entitled to whatever is the result of the sale.

There can, I think, be no pretence for sustaining the claim now set up under the latter part of the section referred to, for the mortgaged premises have not been taken under execution or any process of law, and it cannot in any way be brought within its terms.

The rule *nisi* must be discharged.

PATTERSON, Assignee, et al. *v.* ARCHIBALD et al.

McDonald & Baker having a lien on property of the insolvent defendant, under a recorded judgment, a suit was brought by them as co-plaintiffs with the assignee to set aside a judgment next previous to theirs, alleged to have been fraudulently obtained. *Held* on demurrer, that said McDonald and Baker had been properly made parties to the suit, and that although under the Insolvent Act (1875) the assignee had the exclusive right to sue for the rescinding of instruments made in fraud of creditors generally, and should then be the only plaintiff in the suit, it was otherwise where the instrument was made in fraud of certain individuals irrespective of the other creditors.

Patterson, as assignee of the insolvent Merriam, and the other plaintiffs McDonald and Baker as judgment creditors of the insolvent, brought a suit to set aside a judgment alleged to

have been fraudulently entered up against said insolvent, and
recorded against his property next preceding the recorded judgment of the plaintiffs McDonald and Baker.   Next after the
judgment sought to be set aside followed a judgment of the
Bank of British North America, also duly recorded.   The writ
was demurred to on the grounds, first, that the assignee, under
the Insolvent Act of 1875, had the exclusive right to bring a
suit to set aside the judgment in question as obtained in contravention of the Insolvent Act, and that the other plaintiffs
should not have been joined; secondly, that said assignee had
no interest in enforcing the lien of the plaintiffs McDonald
and Baker, or the lien of the Bank of British North America;
thirdly, that, the defendants having abandoned their lien by
filing claims without reference to the said judgment, as in the
bill alleged, the assignee could not ask for the relief sought
for in respect to such judgment; fourthly, that defendants
having no interest in that part of the suit relating to the Bank
of British North America, all the prayer except that part of it
to set aside said judgment was improper; fifthly, that said
McDonald and Baker had no interest in enforcing the lien of
the Bank of British North America.

RITCHIE, E. J., now, (June, 1878), delivered the judgment of
the Court:—

The object of this suit is to set aside a judgment alleged to
have been fraudulently and illegally entered up, which, while
outstanding, forms an encumbrance on the property of the
insolvent Merriam to the injury of those who have valid claims
on it.   According to the statements in the writ, the plaintiffs
McDonald and Baker have a lien on all the estate of Merriam,
situate in the county of Colchester, under a judgment duly
recorded next to the judgment sought to be set aside.   Then
follows the judgment of the Bank of British North America,
also duly recorded, and after that and subject to both liens the
plaintiff Patterson is entitled to all the real estate of the
insolvents as their assignee, and while the first judgment
stands recorded as a valid lien on the property, it materially
affects its saleable value and so renders it less available to all

who have valid claims upon it. All of the parties against whom the demurrer points are directly interested in the result aimed at in the suit; they have a community of interest in having the judgment in question set aside, and if any of them had been omitted it might with reason have been objected that all the proper parties were not before the Court. It is the aim of this Court in any suit before it to settle as far as possible the rights of all parties interested in the subject-matter of it and thus prevent future litigation, and to effect this all such parties should be represented. Lord HARDWICKE in *Poor* v. *Clark*, 2 Atk., 515, says; "You must have all the parties before the Court who will be necessary to make the determination complete and quiet the question." And in *Wilkins* v. *Fry*, 1 Mer., 262, Sir WILLIAM GRANT said; "In equity, all parties interested in the subject of the suit should be before the Court, either in the shape of plaintiffs or defendants." The case of *Brinkerhoff* v. *Brown*, 6 John. Ch. R., 150, bears directly on the question involved in this. The Court there held that different judgment creditors might unite in one bill the object of which was to set aside impediments to their remedies at law created by the fraud of their common debtor, and to have his estate distributed among them according to the priority of their respective liens. The Chancellor (KENT) said; "The plaintiffs are judgment creditors at law seeking the aid of this Court to render their judgments and executions available against fraudulent arts affecting all of them. * * * * There is no sound reason for requiring judgment creditors to separate in their suits when they have a common object in view, which in fact governs the whole case. * * Their rights are already established, and the subject in dispute may be said to be joint as between the plaintiffs on the one hand and the defendants on the other, charged with a combination to delay, hinder and defraud the creditors. If each judgment creditor was to be obliged to file his separate bill, it would be bringing the same question of fraud into repeated discussion, which would exhaust the fund and be productive of all the mischief and oppression attending a multiplicity of suits. It appears to me, therefore, that the judgment creditors, in case of fraud in the original debtor, have a right to unite in one bill to defeat and suppress that fraud, and to have the debtor's fund distributed according to the priority of their respective liens, or rateably as the case may be." Every word of this is directly applicable to the case before us, as much so as it was to that of which the learned judge was speaking.

It was urged that under the terms of the Insolvent Act, the assignee has the exclusive right to sue for the rescinding of instruments made in fraud of creditors. Where the instrument is made in fraud of the creditors generally he alone should be the party to prosecute the suit, but where it is made in fraud of certain individuals irrespective of the other creditors, they should be parties, or the Court would not be in a position to do complete justice. The assignee takes the property of the insolvent subject to the legal and equitable claims of others, who are not precluded by the act from making their claims available, if in so doing, they do not interfere with the rights of the creditors generally, as represented by the assignee. Here the assignee and the other plaintiffs have a community of interest, and are acting in unison in their endeavour to set aside a fraudulent judgment injuriously affecting all of them, and I see no objection whatever to the course which has been pursued, nor can I see any objection to the assignee recognizing the validity of the judgments of McDonald and Baker and of the Bank of British North America, if he deems them to be valid, and asserting his right to the real estate bound by them subject to the prior liens on it. If the defendants who have demurred have practically abandoned their claim under their judgment, as they assume, by claiming on the estate of the insolvent, without placing a value on their security, the plaintiffs are entitled to have the judgment declared void by a decree of the Court, and the recorded encumbrance on the property removed. Instead of demurring, they should have answered, consenting to the prayer of the writ, or, which would have been still more to the purpose, have given the release when it was demanded before the commencement of the suit. The interest of the Bank of British North America is the same in character as that of the plaintiffs McDonald and Baker, though subordinate as being a subsequent encumbrance on the

property of the insolvent, and I see no part of the prayer of
the writ which is not justified by the facts stated in it, so that,
in my opinion, none of the grounds of the demurrer can be
sustained.

I have made no reference to the defendant, Payzant, as no
objection was raised to his having been made a defendant.

The demurrer is overruled with costs.

BARCLAY v. PROAS.

An agreement for the sale of lands good under the Statute of Frauds may be
rescinded before breach of it by parol, provided there is a total abandonment of
the whole contract, and not merely a partial waiver of some of its terms; nor does
the validity of such rescission depend on the existence of a consideration.

RITCHIE, E. J., now, (July 8th, 1878), delivered the judgment
of the Court:—

The plaintiff seeks specific performance of an agreement
entered into between himself and the defendant on the 9th of
November last, whereby the latter agreed to purchase from
him certain real estate, one of the conditions of which was
that he should receive possession on the 21st of that month.
The agreement is admitted, but the defendant asserts that
shortly after it was entered into, and before the commencement
of this suit, it was rescinded, and the plaintiff by a writing
under his hand discharged him from all liability thereunder,
and that he was not put in possession under the terms of the
agreement, and was never tendered with a deed of the property. As regards the document relied on as rescinding the
contract, the plaintiff has replied that it was obtained by
fraud and misrepresentation, that it was signed by him while
intoxicated, that there was no consideration expressed in it,
nor did any consideration exist, and he contends that it was
therefore invalid.

That the plaintiff signed the document in question is clearly
proved by the defendant, and his testimony is corroborated by

that of two other witnesses. The evidence of the plaintiff is far from contradicting their statements, nor is there anything in the evidence to support the statement that there was any fraud or misrepresentation on the part of the defendant, and those who were present when the document was signed say that they saw nothing to induce them to believe that he was at the time in a state of intoxication. Indeed the plaintiff himself does not say so in his evidence, nor does he assert that he was induced to drink by the plaintiff, or that he had been drinking any intoxicating liquor. It is impossible to hold the document invalid on these grounds.

The only other grounds on which the plaintiff contends that it is invalid are, that it is *nudum pactum*, and being an agreement to rescind a purchase of land, it comes within the terms of the Statute of Frauds. But whatever opinions may have been held on this subject, it is now well established that an agreement for the sale of lands, good under the Statute of Frauds, may be rescinded before breach of it by parol, provided there is a total abandonment of the whole contract, and not a partial waiver of some of its terms; nor does the validity of such rescission depend on the existence of a consideration. See *Smith's, L. C.*, (7th ed.) 351. In *Davis* v. *Symonds*, 1 Cox-Cases, 406, the Chief Baron said; "It is contended that though the agreement did take place, yet it was afterwards waived, and that such waiver may be by parol; and it certainly may be so. The waiver is in its nature subsequent to and necessarily collateral to the agreement, and therefore cannot bear any relation to the rule of evidence that a written agreement cannot be varied by parol. There might indeed have been another rule that a written instrument shall not be waived by parol, but Courts of Equity do not consider themselves bound by any such rule, and it is now clear that a written agreement may be so waived." And again; "when it is said that parol evidence shall not affect written instruments, the vice of the argument turns upon the use of the word 'affect', for if it means to vary it, it is true; if it is to be carried beyond that meaning it is not true. There is nothing so clear as the jurisdiction of this Court to affect a written contract by parol testimony." And in *Robinson* v. *Page*, 3

Russ., 119, the Master of the Rolls said: "unquestionably, waiver even by parol would be a sufficient answer to the plaintiff's case. It must be established with clearness and precision, and must amount to a total dissolution of the contract." "It is, says Parke B., in *Foster* v. *Dawber*, 6 Exch., 839, 851, "competent for both parties to an executory contract, by mutual agreement without any satisfaction, to discharge the obligations of that contract." In *Broom's, L. M.*, 889, it is laid down that, "although a contract which is required to be in writing cannot be varied by a subsequent verbal agreement, it seems that neither the 4th nor the 17th section of the Statute of Frauds can apply to prevent a verbal waiver or abandonment of a contract within its operation from being set up as a good defence to an action upon the contract." And inasmuch as the decreeing of specific performance is in the discretion of Courts of Equity, whatever remedy a party may have at law he can hardly expect that such discretion will be exercised in his favor, when he has agreed to abandon his claim to the performance of the contract. Deciding the case on this point, it is not necessary to advert to the other grounds taken by the defendant. I would merely remark that giving the plaintiff to understand that he relied on his waiver of the contract by the plaintiff, and not being prepared to pay the portion of the purchase money payable in cash, he had no right to the possession of the property, nor to have a deed tendered to him. On the other ground, however, the defendant is entitled to a decree in his favor with costs.

THE CITY OF HALIFAX *v.* THE CITY RAILWAY CO.

The defendant Company obtained an Act enabling it to maintain a line of horse-cars in the City, but requiring it to provide rails of the most improved pattern, and lay them even with the surface of the streets, so as not to interfere with the passage of vehicles, and to keep the roadway in repair within the track and three feet on each side. Defendants having ceased to operate the line, the roads fell out of repair and the rails protruded. After the commencement of this suit, which was for a mandamus to compel the defendants to have the rails laid even with the surface, and to put the roads in repair as required by the Act, the City authorities in many instances covered the streets on which the rails were laid, with stones. *Held*, that the City had a right to proceed by mandamus, and was not obliged to resort to an indictment of the nuisance, or to proceedings to fine the defendants under the Act of 1870, Cap. 99, for violation of the provisions of their Act of Incorporation, neither of these courses presenting a remedy as beneficial as the proceeding by mandamus, but that the mandamus must be limited in its operation to those streets on which the railway had not been covered by the the City authorities, as the action of the City in this respect had imposed an unreasonable burden upon the Company in removing the stones.

RITCHIE, E. J., (Aug. 7th, 1878) delivered the judgment of the Court :—

The act which incorporated the City Railway Company and gave it authority, with the consent of the City Council and subject to the regulations imposed by the act, to construct and maintain a line of railway on certain streets of the City, and to use horse-cars thereon for the accommodation of the public, provided that the rails should be of the most approved pattern, and should be laid even with the surface of the pavement or street in such manner as not to interfere with the passage of vehicles, and that the pavement or other surface of the roadway should be kept always in thorough repair by the Company within the track and three feet on each side thereof, under the direction of such competent authority as the City Council might designate.

The Company, having constructed the railway under the act, ran cars thereon for several years, but have ceased to do so for several years past on certain of the streets, and since June 1876, no cars have run on any part of the line. At the time the company ceased altogether to operate the railway the road was in a bad condition, and had been more or less so for two or three years previously, notwithstanding repeated applications were made to the Company to repair it by Mr. Keating, the City Engineer, who had been appointed by the City Council to see that the provisions of the act were complied with.

In the year 1876, from January to the time when this suit was commenced, applications to have the road put in order were made without success, and in the latter part of May, when the attention of the Company was called to the dangerous condition of the streets from the rails protruding above the surface, and reference was made to the legal liability of the Company. Mr. Keating was referred to the solicitor of the Company, who would accept service of any process which might be issued at the instance of the City.

At the argument it was not denied that the Company had violated the terms of the act of incorporation by allowing the rails of their road to protrude above the surface of the streets through which they were laid, or that they had not kept the roadway in repair as required by the act, but it was contended that the City was not entitled to a writ of mandamus inasmuch as it possessed a legal remedy independently of it to which it must resort, and that its course was either to proceed against the Company by indictment, or under the provisions of Chap. 99 of the Acts of 1870, which imposed a penalty of from $10 to $20 for a violation of the provisions of its act of incorporation.

The object of the present suit is not to punish the Company for the neglect of its duty, but to compel a compliance with the terms on which it was allowed the privilege of laying rails in the streets of the city, so that traffic and travel should not be obstructed. All that could be effected by an indictment would be the imposition of a fine, and there might be no property upon which even that might be levied, and as the undertaking would seem to have been abandoned since 1876, it is not unreasonable to assume the probability of this being the case. But whether it be so or not, the Company could not by indictment be compelled to perform the duty imposed on it by the Legislature. The same observations apply to the proceedings under the Act of 1870; neither proceeding would afford the relief prayed in this suit, and a mandamus is only refused on the ground that the party seeking it had another legal remedy when such remedy is in all respects as beneficial and effectual, and affords the specific relief sought for.

This writ does not seek, and the counsel acting for the City intimates that there is no desire on the part of the City to compel the Company to resume the running of cars. He says that no objection would be raised to the removal of the rails

10 _k._

altogether and the replacing of the streets in the state in which they were before the rails were laid; but it is contended on the part of the Company that having ceased to run cars,—in fact, having abandoned the undertaking—no obligation rests on the Company to repair the road or remove the rails.

The corporators, in obtaining the act of incorporation, contemplated a pecuniary benefit, and the Legislature, in allowing the streets to be used to enable them to carry out their object, had in view the benefit which would accrue to the public from the convenience the railway would afford; and it might not unreasonably have been contended that the public had a right to the enjoyment of the railway, and that it was not open to the Company to deprive them of it by abandoning the enterprise. But, whether the rails are used or not, so long as they remain on the streets, the duty imposed on the Company by the act must be performed, so as to prevent their being a nuisance to the City.

The case is somewhat embarrassed by the action of the City authorities in having caused the rails in many of the streets to be covered with stones. This was done after the Company had ceased to use the rails, and since the commencement of this suit. It was urged that to grant a mandamus as prayed for, would involve the expense of removing these stones. The effect of the action of the City is to prevent the Company running cars on the rails, if so disposed, and, at the same time, is an obstruction to its putting the railway in the state required by the act, and I may add that it has removed the obstruction to traffic and travel in those streets. The course was no doubt adopted in the interest of the public which was daily sustaining inconvenience from the continuing of the nuisance. But the delay in obtaining a decision in this suit need not have been great; it was commenced in June, 1876, and the only witnesses examined were those produced by the City, so that there is no reason why the cause might not have been brought to a hearing and judgment given within a few months,—certainly before the end of that year.

The City is entitled to a mandamus but it must be limited in its operation to those parts of the railway which have not been covered by the City authorities, and which now cause obstruc-

ion to traffic and travel. The decree will be that a mandamus
do issue requiring the defendant company to have the rails laid
even with the surface of the pavement or street in such a manner as not to interfere with the passage of vehicles over the
streets, and that the pavement or other surface of the roadway
be put in thorough repair by the defendant company within
the track and three feet on each side thereof under the direction of the City Engineer, Mr. Keating.

The decree will be with costs.

FORD, ASSIGNEE OF MORTON, v. MILES AND OTHERS.

Sylvanus Morton, on the 26th of April, 1873, made a deed of property without
consideration to his daughter, continuing himself in possession of the property
until October, 1875, when he failed. Previous to the date of the deed the Liverpool and Acadia Banks, of one of which Morton was President, and a large shareholder, had suspended; and a firm in which he was concerned had failed two
days before the date of the deed. Previous to the making of the deed the insolvent had admitted to a creditor that if certain proceedings threatened against
him, as President of said Banks, were taken, he would have to assign. And after
the making of the deed he was challenged in reference to it, and said it was all
he could do, under the circumstances, to save his property.

Held, that the deed, having been made at a time when the grantor contemplated
a state of things that might result in insolvency, and which did, in fact, so result,
must be set aside: even had it not been shown that the insolvent continued in
possession, and a few days after making the deed admitted to his creditor that it
was all he could do to save his property.

RITCHIE, E. J., now, (November 1878,) delivered the judgment of the Court:—

The plaintiff, who is the assignee of Sylvanus Morton, an
insolvent, seeks in this suit to have a deed made by the insolvent
to his daughter, Annie S. Miles, set aside, on the ground that
it was fraudulently made, without consideration, and in violation of the rights of creditors.

It is admitted that there was no money consideration, and
Morton alleges that he made the conveyance to his daughter
as an advancement, as he had done to her elder sisters on former occasions. The deed bears date the 26th April, 1873. It

appears, from the evidence, that on the 14th of that month, the Liverpool and the Acadia Banks suspended payment, Morton, the defendant, being the President of the former bank and a large shareholder in it, before which time the firm of Morton, Collie & Spencer were in financial difficulties, and failed on the 24th April, just two days before the making of the deed. Sylvanus Morton being then indebted to the Merchants' Bank of Halifax to the extent of $8,000 or $9,000, of which from $5,000 to $6,000 have not been paid to the present time, and being largely liable to other banks, addressed the following letter to the Cashier, Peter Jack :—

"MILTON, 24th April, 1873.

"*Dear Sir,*—

"By yesterday's mail I received advice that paper to the amount of $2,500 had been protested, and my name is on for $1,600 more. I feel bad about it, but it don't alarm me, if Montreal, Merchants, and B. B. North America will collect all they can from the makers and endorsers and let me pay the balance, or if they give me time. Will you see parties for me, (Duffus & Co. in place of Merchants' Bank,) and let me know the result. I beg of them not to amerce me heavily with damages."

Morton was a partner of the firm of C. & J. Morton & Co., and of that of Morton & Co., but retired from them in January, 1873. At that time C. & J. Morton & Co. were indebted to Cook, one of the witnesses, between $5,000 and $6,000, and in February of that year, Morton admitted to Cook that the firm was in difficulties and required a good deal of money, which if they did not get they must stop ; and on the 22nd April he told him that he had been threatened with proceedings against him, as President of the Liverpool Bank ; that he owed him, and was indorser on the paper of the firms of Morton & Co. and C. & J. Morton & Co., and if the threatened proceedings were taken, he should have to make an assignment ; and when he was challenged a few days after with having made the deed in question, he admitted that he had made it, and said that it was all that he could do, under the circumstances, to save his property. Cook then demanded from him the amount he owed him, and told him that if he could not pay him he should consider the conveyance void. He did not pay, and the debt still remains unpaid; and a month or more after that Morton spoke to Cook about placing his property in trust for the benefit of his creditors, and spoke of Mr. Jack as the trustee. Morton never parted with the possession or use of the property, but remained in possession till October, 1875, when he made an assignment under the provisions of the Insolvent Act of 1875. His assets, as then stated by himself, amounted to $57,000, and the claims against his estate to $130,500. The amount received from the assets has been $10,000, and as. much more is all that is expected to be realized from them. His liabilities to the Bank of Liverpool alone amounted to $34,319, and the claims against the estate embrace large amounts due anterior to the giving of the deed. No evidence was produced on the part of the defendant to show that, notwithstanding all this, he was in fact solvent when the deed was executed.

In order to render such a voluntary conveyance void as against creditors, it is not necessary to prove that the party making it was at the time absolutely insolvent; it is enough to vitiate it if it has been made to appear that, at the time, he contemplated a state of things which *might* result in insolvency, though he may have continued solvent for some time after. See *Mackay* v. *Douglas*, L. R. 14 Eq., 106; *Townsend* v. *Westacott*, 2 Beav., 340, and 4 Beav., 58; *Freeman* v. *Pope*, L. R. 9 Eq., 206, and L. R. 5 Chy., 538; and *Spirett* v. *Willows*, 3 DeG., J. & S. 293.

The language of Lord LANGDALE in his judgment in *Townsend* v. *Westacott*, in which case there was no positive proof of insolvency at the date of the conveyance, but the party making it became insolvent three years after, seems peculiarly applicable. He says: " In the first place, it is alleged on the part of the plaintiff that the deed was executed entirely without consideration; that is admitted. In the next place it is said that the settlor was largely indebted at the time, and of this there is strong evidence. Being largely indebted, he made this voluntary conveyance, and in less than three years afterwards he became absolutely insolvent. On these facts alone, provided they were properly put in issue and proved, I am of opinion that this conveyance ought to be set aside as fraudulent." And again : " It is urged that something amounting to insolvency must be proved to set aside a voluntary conveyance. This is inconsistent with the principle of the Act, (13 Eliz., c. 5,) and the judgment of the most eminent judges."

Morton's deed to his daughter was entirely without consideration ; when he made it he was largely indebted, and the debts remain unpaid at present. In less than three years he made an assignment under the Insolvent Act, and at the very time he made the deed circumstances had occurred which caused his pecuniary embarrassment, which he feared might lead, and which did, in fact, lead to insolvency. To render this deed fraudulent against the creditors, it did not require the additional facts in evidence, that from the time he made the deed to his insolvency, he never parted with the possession of the property, and that a few days after making it, he said to one of his creditors that it was all he could do to save his property.

The decree will be that the deed be declared fraudulent and be set aside with costs.

CAPE BRETON CO. (Limited) *v.* DODD, et al.

Seourity for costs ordered where the insolvent plaintiff Company, though incorporated in the Province, was registered in England, and had its directory and place of business there ; and the parties using the name of the Company in the suit were not in the Province.

Ritchie, E. J., now, (Dec. 1st, 1878) delivered the judgment of the Court :—

The plaintiff Company, though incorporated in this province, had been previously registered in England as a Company limited, under the provisions of the Companies' Acts of 1862, and 1867.

The directory of the Company and its place of business are there, and, having become insolvent, it is now in course of being wound up there by liquidators under those Acts:

The Company is to all intents and purposes an English Company, this Province being merely the locality of their operations in mining and constructing railways; and as not only the Company is shown to be insolvent, but the parties using the name of the Company in this suit are not in the Province, security for costs should be given.

In the *Imperial Bank of China, etc.,* v. *Bank of Hindostan,* L. R. 1 Ch., 437, an order for security was made, on the ground that the plaintiff bank, (being limited), was in course of voluntary liquidation. The application was made under the Companies' Act of 1862, and the only question raised was as to the amount, a larger amount being required under it than under the ordinary practice of the Court. See also *in re Home Assurance Association,* L. R. 12 Eq., 112, where security for costs was ordered.

The rule will be made absolute with costs.

MEAGHER *v.* THE QUEEN'S INSURANCE COMPANY.

Plaintiff brought this suit to compel defendants to deliver to him a policy of insurance for $600, alleging that they had received his premium on the 27th Nov, 1877, and undertaken to insure his house for a year from that date, and to deliver a policy to that effect. The building was destroyed by fire in December, 1877. Defendants alleged that they had been induced to enter into the contract by the misrepresentation of plaintiff, that the Building Society were about to advance $600 on the property, and that they had undertaken to insure it, not for the plaintiff, but for the Society. At the hearing plaintiff's counsel asked for a decree for a policy, and also for the payment of the money.

Held, that, even if such relief could be granted it could only be upon a bill asking for it, whereas plaintiff had in his writ asked only for a policy; and further, that as the evidence was directly in conflict on the point as to misrepresentation, and as to the terms of the contract, plaintiff should be left to his remedy at law.

Bill dismissed without costs.

RITCHIE, E. J., now, (December 16th, 1878,) delivered the judgment of the Court :—

The suit is brought to compel the defendants to make and deliver to the plaintiff a policy of insurance against fire. He alleges that they undertook and agreed to insure his house for $600 for one year from the 27th November, 1877, on which day he paid them the premium agreed upon, and the price of the policy, and they then agreed to grant and issue to him the policy as soon as the same could be prepared, he having taken from them a receipt for the money in the meantime; that on about the 2nd December following, the house was destroyed by fire, and the plaintiff having delivered to the defendants under oath a statement of his loss, demanded payment, which was refused. He then demanded from them the policy of insurance; this also was refused, and he now seeks the aid of this Court to obtain it, and he prays that they may be decreed to deliver to him a policy of insurance in the usual form issued by them, as agreed upon by and between them, and that he may have such other relief as is in accordance with equity. The defendants assert that the agreement which they were induced to enter into arose out of false and fraudulent representations made to them by the plaintiff as to the ownership of the property and its value, and that it was never agreed, nor was it contemplated, that the policy was to be made to the plaintiff, but to the Building Society of Halifax, who had, as the plaintiff asserted, agreed to advance to him the sum of $600, whereas the Society, in fact, never agreed to advance, and never have advanced or loaned that or any other sum to him.

At the hearing the plaintiff's counsel not only asked for a decree requiring the defendant to execute and deliver to him the policy of insurance, but, a loss having taken place, they asked that they should be decreed to pay to him the amount of the loss he had sustained. It may be that where a party is compelled to resort to a Court of Equity to compel the granting of a policy, it would, to avoid multiplicity of actions, decree the payment of the loss, and thus afford a complete remedy; but the writ must have contemplated that, and must have been prepared accordingly. The defendants could never have anticipated from this writ that more would be asked than that they should deliver a policy. The defendants were not only entitled to know what facts the plaintiff proposed to prove; they were also entitled to know what relief was sought, and the plaintiff is not entitled to any relief of which the special prayer has not apprised them. The general prayer may cure any slight omission or deficiency in the bill, but it cannot cover relief of a different character from that specifically prayed for.

In this case, however, the plaintiff is met with a difficulty in the way of his obtaining even what is prayed for. To entitle him to succeed he must show, not only that there has been no misrepresentation or concealment on his part, and that his conduct has been fair and just in every respect, but the terms of the agreement sought to be enforced must be clearly and definitively ascertained. Now, the evidence on the part of the plaintiff and defendants, both as regards the alleged representations of the plaintiff and the terms of the contract, is in direct conflict, and, as the plaintiff is not without remedy at law by which he can obtain redress if he can satisfy a jury that he is entitled to it, he should, under the circumstances, be left to resort to it. There are, it appears to me, two courses open to him at law, either to bring an action for the non-delivery of the policy, as was done in *Robertson* v. *Dudman*, where the verdict was sustained after argument, *(1 Russell & Chesley*, 50,) or to bring an action on the agreement to insure, if the agreement to insure was actually made and all that remained to be done was the preparation of the formal document to embody the agreement already entered into. I know of no absolute necessity for a written policy in an insurance of this nature, especially where there has been a payment and receipt of the premium. Notwithstanding these remedies, however, I should have considered the plaintiff entitled to a decree to have a policy delivered to him, if the evidence had satisfactorily established the terms of the contract and his freedom from misrepresentations; and, deciding as I do upon the evidence on these points being contradictory, the writ will be dismissed, but without costs.

ROBINSON ET AL *v.* HENDRY.

A TESTATOR devised land to M. E. R., giving her in terms an estate for life, the property to go at her death to her children then born, whom he designated by name, and to such other children as she might have, and their lawful children, and to their heirs lawfully begotten. In the next clause he declared that it was his will that the property should be entailed upon the direct descendants of his four children and their offspring forever. In the codicil to his will he referred to the estate he had given by his will as an estate for life to his children, (one of whom was M. E. R.,) and stated that he had entailed the property on their children.

Held, that the words defining the persons to take on the expiration of the life estate were intended as a *designatio personarum* and not as words of limitation; that the rule in Shelly's case did not, therefore, apply, and the devisee took only a life estate.

RITCHIE, E. J., (January 20th, 1879,) delivered the judgment of the Court:—

The plaintiffs in this suit seek partition of certain land referred to in their petition, to which the defendant denies their right, they having, as he alleges, no estate or interest in it.

Both the plaintiffs and the defendant claim under the will of Conrad Deal. The former contend that under it Mary Elizabeth Robinson, now deceased, who in her lifetime conveyed the property in question to the defendant, took but a life estate, and that at her death the plaintiffs became entitled to it, while the contention of the defendant is that she became tenant-in-tail, and, by virtue of the statute abolishing estates tail, became tenant in fee-simple, and that he, under his deed, is absolute and sole owner of it.

The clauses of Deal's will which were referred to at the hearing as alone affecting the question, were the fourth, sixth, seventh, and ninth, and the codicil. By the first of these the estate given to Mary Elizabeth Robinson is in terms an estate for life, and at her death the property is to go to her children then born, *who are designated by name,* and to such other children as she might have, *and their lawful children, and to their heirs lawfully begotten.* The next clause declares that it is his will that the property should be entailed upon the direct descendants of his four children and their off-spring forever. The other two clauses were obviously merely inserted to indicate the locality of the respective shares, without reference to the estate to be taken ; and the same remark applies to the codicil. In that, however, he refers to the estate he had given by his will as an estate for life to his children, one of whom was Mrs. Robinson, and states that he had entailed the property on their children.

Nothing can be more explicit than the terms in which the testator has limited the estate he gave Mrs. Robinson to a life estate; yet, notwithstanding an estate for life was given in the most emphatic manner, if there had been a limitation afterwards to her heirs or the heirs of her body, or by some such words, such a limitation would have given her an estate in fee-simple or fee-tail, but the words used must be words of limitation and not words of purchase; and wherever the words used are intended as a *designatio personæ*, the person indicated takes as a purchaser, and the rule in *Shelly's* case does not apply. That rule will not apply if there are words referring not merely to the mode of succession, but to the objects of succession, indicating them to be individuals other than the persons who are simply to take as heirs. Here the persons to take at the expiration of the life estate are designated by name and the limitation is not to the heirs of the tenant for life lawfully begotten, but to those of the children named; nor are there any words annexed to the tenant for life which can be held to be words of limitation. Indeed, if the children of Mrs. Robinson had not been designated by name, and the word "children" only had been used, that being a word of purchase and not of limitation, I should have held that the rule did not apply, especially as the children were in existence, and the words which limit the estate-tail are not annexed to the tenant for life. I never heard of a case where, after an estate for life was given, and there was a limitation over to persons named and to their heirs or the heirs of their body, the first estate was ever enlarged beyond the estate given. This I intimated at the hearing, for I then entertained no doubt on the question, but, in deference to the Attorney General who referred me to some authorities which he thought bore on the subject in favour of his client, I deferred giving judgment till I should have looked into them. This I have done, but they do not appear to me to conflict with, but rather to sustain the view I have taken of the case.

The plaintiffs are entitled to a decree for partition, with costs.

McKAY v. SUTHERLAND ET AL.

INJUNCTION dissolved on the ground, *inter alía*, that all the material allegations on which the writ was granted were denied by defendants.

RITCHIE, E. J., (March 3rd, 1879,) delivered the judgment of the Court :—

The plaintiff and defendants are tenants in common of the lot of land on which the defendants have cut timber, the removal of which the plaintiff seeks to restrain by an injunction. He also seeks to restrain them from cutting other timber on it. The land is wilderness land chiefly valuable for its timber. After reading the affidavit and papers on which the injunction was obtained, and those on which the rule *nisi* to dissolve it was granted, I cannot infer that what can be termed waste has been committed by the defendants,—certainly nothing like malicious or wanton destruction of the property; what they have done was putting the land to its legitimate use. But whatever inference to the contrary could have been drawn from the plaintiff's writ has been denied by the defendants in their answer and the affidavits they have produced; and they have alleged that they have not appropriated more of the timber than they could justly take, as tenants in common with the plaintiff.

One tenant in common has not a right to an injunction against his co-tenant for waste unless it is made to appear that the party committing it is incapable of compensating the other for the injury done him. The evidence in this case is far from going to that extent, for though the defendants became insolvent a compromise was effected under the Insolvent Act, whereby they were to pay their debts by instalments which they have so far carried out; and they have shewn that they have funds more than sufficient to pay all the instalments.

Where a tenant in common has reason to fear that his co-tenant is taking, or is about to take, more than his share of timber on land such as this he can apply for a partition, and, pending the proceedings to obtain it, this Court can, if it appear proper, enjoin both parties from cutting or taking timber until partition is made; but under ordinary circumstances each tenant has the right to the use and enjoyment of the property, and, unless he can cut and remove timber from such land as this, he can have no enjoyment of it.

In the present case the rule *nisi* to dissolve the injunction should be made absolute, independently of anything else, on the ground that all the material allegations on which the writ was granted have been denied.

THE NOVA SCOTIA SALT WORKS AND EXPLORATION CO. *v.* THE HALIFAX AND CAPE BRETON RAILWAY AND COAL CO.

PLAINTIFFS applied to amend their writ by adding a defendant on the ground that a defect existed in the organization of the defendant company and in order that, in the event of failure against the defendant company, they might have relief against the defendants whom they ought to add.

Held, that the amendment could not be allowed.

RITCHIE, E. J., (March 15th, 1879,) delivered the judgment of the Court :—

This application is made to amend the writ by adding one Harry Abbott as a defendant, on the ground that it has come to the knowledge of the plaintiff company that a defect exists in the organization of the defendant company and they wish Mr. Abbott to be made a defendant so that, in case of failure against the defendants, they may have relief against him as a corporator and a party interested in the proceedings of the company. Such an amendment could not, I think, be allowed, and if the writ had been so framed in the first instance, or if the amendment to it were now made, it would be demurrable. This I intimated at the argument, and the

view I then took I find supported by authority in *Clark*
v. *Lord Rivers*, L. R.. 5 Eq., 91. The Vice-Chancellor
remarked that he had never seen a bill so framed before, and
he did not believe any one in Court had ever done so, and
in his judgment, he said, "I proceed on the broad grounds
that I do not believe it is within the jurisdiction of the Court
to entertain a bill in this alternative form; you may pray
alternate relief against the same defendant or defendants, but
you cannot bring different sets of defendants and say,—' If I
am not entitled to relief against A, I am entitled to relief
against B;' you must make up your mind against whom you
are entitled to relief."

But, independently of this difficulty, amendments are not
allowed which involve an entirely new case, and, as against
Mr. Abbott, individually, this amendment would necessarily
be such.

HOGAN *v.* HOGAN.

PLAINTIFF instructed his brother to purchase certain land for him, the deed
to be taken in the brother's name, but in trust for the plaintiff for life, after his
death for his children, and in case of his death and the death of his children, in
trust for his wife. The land was purchased and plaintiff paid the amount of the
purchase money, but the deed was made out to the brother in trust to pay the
proceeds to plaintiff's son, then living, and in the event of his death to other sons,
&c. Plaintiff went into possession and lived on the premises without any
intimation that he had not a right to do so, and did not discover the omission of
the trust for his own life till after the death of his brother, being an illiterate man
and not having ever learned the contents of the deed. His evidence as to the
intention was uncorroborated and uncontradicted.

Held, that the plaintiff was entitled to have the deed rectified.

RITCHIE, E. J., (May 17th, 1879,) delivered the judgment
of the Court :—

It appears from the evidence that the plaintiff instructed
his brother, John Hogan, to make a purchase for him of the
property mentioned in the writ, intending to have the deed
made to his brother, but in trust for the plaintiff during his
life, and after his death for his children; and in case of the
death of himself and his children, for his wife during her
life. At this time he had but one child, John. The property
was purchased and the plaintiff paid the amount of the pur-

chase money; but, instead of his intentions being carried out, the deed was made to John Hogan, the brother, in trust to hold the land and premises and collect and receive the rents and profits, and to pay and apply them to the maintenance, education, and support of John Hogan, the plaintiff's son, until he should attain the age of twenty-one, and on his attaining that age, in trust, to convey the same to him in fee-simple; and in case he should die before attaining that age, then in trust to hold the same for whichever child of the plaintiff should first attain the age of twenty-one years, and if all of them should die before attaining that age then in trust for Mrs. Hogan, the wife of the plaintiff, to allow her to collect and receive the rents and profits, free from the debts and control of her husband, and at her death for the executors, administrators and assigns. The plaintiff is an illiterate man who can neither read nor write, and he never knew the contents of the deed, which was never read or communicated to him till after the death of his brother; and as soon as he ascertained them, he instructed his solicitor to have the deed rectified. After the purchase the plaintiff went into possession of the premises and has since lived there, and no intimation ever was given him that he was not entitled to do so. John, the son of the plaintiff, named in the deed, died an infant. The plaintiff has now four children, all infants, of whom the defendant is the eldest, and the plaintiff, under these circumstances, asks the Court to decree that the deed should be reformed by substituting for the trusts contained in it the trusts which he had desired to have inserted in it at the time the purchase was made, and which he believed, until after his brother's death, had been contained in it.

This Court will not hesitate to correct a mistake in such an instrument where it is made to appear, by satisfactory evidence, that the terms of it are not what the party intended. It is clear, from the evidence, that the land was purchased with the funds of the plaintiff, and his wishes as to the trusts to be inserted in the deed should have been carried out. It is true that the only evidence we have of what they were comes from the plaintiff, but his statement is uncontradicted, and we have no reason to doubt its truthfulness. That he,

the father of a young family, should deprive himself of all
interest in and control over a property purchased with his own
funds, and apparently all or the most of the means which he
possessed seems to me unreasonable. That he should have contemplated doing so is most improbable, and such a provision in
such a settlement of property is most unusual. Nor is the
disposition of the whole in favor of one child to the exclusion
of all the rest a course very likely to be adopted by a person
in the circumstances of the plaintiff.

In *Smith* v. *Iliffe*, L. R., 20, Eq., 666, there was, as here,
the sole uncontradicted evidence of the party seeking to have
the settlement rectified. The Vice-Chancellor said,—" In the
present case the wife states positively that it was not her intention that she should be deprived of the control of her property in
the events which have happened, and against that statement
there is not a particle of evidence. Such a state of things as
this must, according to the practice of the Court, have great
weight, and there is abundant ground for holding that the
plaintiff is entitled to have the settlement rectified in such a
way as that, in the events that have happened, the property
may be hers absolutely." He had previously quoted the
language of Vice-Chancellor HALL, in *Re Best's Settlement*,
L. R., 18 Eq., 686, " that nothing can be more improbable
than that a lady, in making a settlement of her own property,
should intend to put it beyond her own control in the event
of the husband dying, and there being no child of the marriage."
And in *De la Touche's Settlement*, L. R., 10 Eq., 599,
it was contended that rectification could only proceed on
admission by all parties of the fact of a common mistake, and
the counsel appearing for an infant asserted that he could not
admit the existence of any mistake, but the court nevertheless
decreed that a mistake did exist, and made the decree in
accordance with the correction of it.

In this case there is, I think, ample evidence to shew that
the plaintiff's intentions as to the trust to be inserted in the
deed to his brother were not carried out, whether from misunderstanding or otherwise, and the plaintiff is entitled to
have the deed rectified by inserting in it the trusts which he
contemplated having in it when he made the purchase. The
costs will be paid out of the trust property.

WOODWORTH *v.* WOODWORTH.

PLAINTIFF, as administratrix, sought to foreclose a mortgage for £200 made by defendant ; who, in his answer, set out a series of transactions with the deceased in regard to the mortgage, and further alleged that deceased mortgagee had delivered to him a memorandum, signed by him, as follows :—"·The mortgage which I hold of W. J. W., bearing date, (&c.), for £200, is not payable to my heirs, executors or administrators after my death.—I. W. W." The memorandum was not produced, but on proof of loss, secondary evidence was given, which the Judge considered of a suspicious character.

Held, that the memorandum, even if there were no suspicious circumstances about it, would not operate as a release of the mortgage, either at law or in equity, and that plaintiff was entitled to a decree.

RITCHIE, E. J., (May 17th, 1879,) delivered the judgment of the Court :—

The plaintiff seeks to foreclose a mortgage made by the defendant to Ingram W. Woodworth to secure the payment of £200 with interest. The defendant in his answer admits the making of the mortgage and alleges that he purchased the mortgaged premises from Ingram W. Woodworth, for which he was to give £50 in cash, an annuity of six pounds a year during the life of Ingram W. Woodworth, and this mortgage for £200 ; and, for the fulfilment of these terms, one Asael B. Woodworth became security ; that the £50 was then paid, and he, the defendant, paid the annuity and interest on the mortgage till the winter of 1868, when Asael left the province. He goes on to state that the defendant offered to procure other security, but, instead of accepting such offer, Ingram proposed that the defendant should pay him £100 and an annuity of £12, the same to be in full discharge of the mortgage for £200 and annuity of six pounds, and thereupon the defendant gave him two promissory notes for the £100, which he subsequently paid, that he also paid the annuity of £12 up to the death of Ingram, and it was agreed between them that the mortgage should be delivered up to him at Ingram's death, who died on or about the 16th January, 1873. He further alleges that subsequent to the payment of the two notes Ingram delivered to him a memorandum signed by him, as follows : " The mortgage which I hold of William J. Woodworth, bearing date January 25th, 1865, for two hundred pounds, currency, is not payable to my heirs, executors, or administrators after my death.—I. W. Woodworth ;" and he now submits that he is entitled to have the mortgage released and to be relieved from the payment of the amount secured by it.

In support of this defence the defendant himself appears as a witness, and as he, under the statute, is precluded from giving evidence of any transactions or agreements with the deceased mortgagee, or of any statements or acknowledgements made by him, or of any conversations with him, his testimony as to the alleged verbal agreement must be excluded, so that our attention must be confined to the evidence afforded by the written memorandum referred to; and, as there is no other evidence of such an agreement having been made, the whole defence depends upon proof of such a memo. having been made and on its effect.

The memo. itself is not forthcoming. The defendant asserts that his dwelling house was burned and in it this memo.; that he had previously shewn it to the plaintiff, who acknowledged that it was in the handwriting of her husband, *i. e.*, Ingram, except one word, the word *two*, which she said should be *one*, which was a difference of £100. He afterwards said that what he meant by the plaintiff objecting to the word two was because it was blotted; it looked as though it had been spelled wrong and altered, that was his supposition ; he did not know why it was blotted. On his cross-examination a paper was produced which defendant admitted to be in his handwriting, containing a list of the notes of hand and mortgages of Ingram's estate, and among the latter was that of W. J. Woodworth, the defendant, for $800. William Faulkner saw the memo.; he did not remember whether before or after Ingram's death ; it was in Ingram's handwriting; there was disfiguring or blurring of the word " two," as if wrongly spelled and corrected ; it was plain that something had been done ; it was the same ink; the first letter of the word was not altered, it was the word two. Wm. W. Pecking says he saw the memo. in defendant's possession after Ingram's death ; it was in the handwriting of Ingram ; the word " two " was same ink and same writing as the rest. On cross-examination he says the word "two" had something peculiar about it; it was written with a capital "T." and appeared to have been corrected. Lizzie Faulkner says she saw it in defendant's possession before Ingram's death; one of the figures was a little blurred, she thinks the figure two; it was in writing; no difference in the ink or in the writing. Mrs. Nancy Faulkner saw the paper after Ingram's death in defendant's possession; she remembers there was a word blurred; thinks it was the amount; same ink and same handwriting, that of Ingram. The plaintiff in her testimony admits that the memo. which was shewn her was in the handwriting of her husband, Ingram W. Woodworth; she can't speak as to the word "two"; she told the defendant when it was shewn to her that she did not like that spot, meaning the blot on it; referring to the memo. she saw she said the writing above it was torn off, she saw the mark on the paper where some writing had been torn off; she said that the day before the funeral the defendant asked her if she knew that his uncle, i. e., Ingram W. Woodworth, was going to give him £100; she said she did not, but that if he intended doing so it was all right; he did not say to her he intended to give her the farm. She said that some time after the funeral the defendant looked over his private papers; among them he opened the mortgage in question, and a paper fell to the floor; he picked it up and covered it on his knee with his hand, and asked for another paper; that she turned to get it, and when she again turned he was holding up his papers, and she did not see any more of the paper he had picked up. She does not know what paper it was. She afterwards had a conversation with him; she accused him of having taken the paper spoken of and put it up his sleeve; he denied at first and afterwards said he had picked up a piece of paper from the floor which he had afterwards found in his trousers' pocket; that was some weeks after the funeral; she asked why he had not returned it, to which he made no reply; he did not say what the paper was·

Independently of the question as to the legal effect to be given to such a memorandum, it is impossible to view the document otherwise than with suspicion. An important word is admitted to have been altered; its terms are only given from

recollection. It is said by the plaintiff to have had traces of
other writing on it which had been torn off, and this is not
rebutted or explained by the plaintiff himself or any of the
witnesses who saw the paper; nor is he re-called to deny or
explain the statement that he had posseseed himself of some
paper which fell from the mortgage when he was examining
the papers of the estate of the deceased mortgagee, nor the
statement of the plaintiff that he then made no such claim as
he now does, but asserted that the deceased intended to give
him £100. If this could, it certainly should have been done.
One of the witnesses who spoke of having seen the memorandum, and only one of them, testified to having seen the paper
in the defendant's possession before Ingram Woodworth's
death, but she refers to nothing as fixing the time in her
memory, and it is a circumstance in which a witness might be
easily mistaken.

If such a memo. under other circumstances would operate
as a release of the mortgage and discharge the debt, I should
not be prepared to give any such effect to one surrounded
with such suspicion as this is. But in my opinion such a
document has not and ought not to have any such effect if
unquestionably genuine. That at law it can have no such
effect is beyond a doubt. The instrument sought to be
released is under seal and can therefore only be released by
one of as high a nature. It is an old maxim *nihil tam conveni-*
ens est naturali æquitati quam unumquodque dissolvi eo
ligamine quo ligatum est. This being the case in law does a
different rule prevail in equity? In *Cross* v. *Sprigg*, 6 Hare,
552, the Court held that unless there is a consideration or
some equitable ground of distinction, equity in such cases
follows the law. The evidence in that case was that the
testator, at several different times before his decease, told the
witness, a clerk of the firm of which the testator was a
partner, that he never intended the obligee of the bond to pay
the amount of it as he always considered it a gift, and that
the defendant, the widow and administratrix of his estate,
told the witness that her late husband, shortly before his
death, while he was ill in bed, told her that the obligee was
not to be called on for the money in respect of the bond. The

Vice-Chancellor said : "The first question is whether the testator's declaration justified the conclusion that he had abandoned all intention of recovery upon the bond, and, if so, secondly, what were the consequences. As to this I have no hesitation in holding that the debt remained at law, and if at law it must remain in equity, unless some special grounds were laid for a different conclusion." The previous authorities were cited and commented on. In *Peace v. Hains*, 11 Hare, 151, a testator wrote in his account book opposite the entry of two debts owing to him by his brother, one due on mortgage and the other on a promissory note, the words "*not to be enforced.*"   The Vice-Chancellor said :—"The authorities amount to this, that if a person found to be a debtor and seeking to be relieved from the debt on the ground that some act of the deceased creditor, voluntary or otherwise, has put an end to his liability, he must claim that relief in one of two ways; either the act upon which he relies must be one which would have entitled him to relief in this Court as against the creditor in respect of the debt, or it must be such as will operate as a release of the debt at law. There is nothing in the evidence which shews that the debtor is discharged in either of these ways ; there is certainly no release at law, as the debt is secured under seal. 'Not to be enforced' assumes the security to be valid and continuing and capable of being enforced."

On the part of the defendant *Yeomans v. Williams*, L. R., 1 Eq., 184, was cited to shew that *Cross v. Spriggs* was not recognized by the Master of the Rolls as law, but, as I read the case, he recognizes it as such and distinguishes it from the case before him. *Taylor v. Manners*, L. R., 1, Ch. 48, was also cited, but that case had relation to a debt due on an agreement not under seal, and the policy, the subject of the agreement, was given up, and there was an agreement to release for a consideration, though a small one. It was heard by two Judges only, who differed in opinion. One of them, KNIGHT BRUCE, L. J., remarked: "I am not satisfied, therefore, that from its nature the transaction is capable of being supported without valuable consideration," and "I am not satisfied that there was valuable consideration, whether, in fact, the payment amounted to anything more than a payment by a debtor to his creditor of a less amount than the sum due."

That the mortgagee here had no intention of giving up the debt or releasing the mortgage when he made the memorandum is evident; he not only retained the mortgage in his possession, but received the interest on it as interest up to the time of his death, and we find this interest charged in an account book of his, subsequently to the making of the memorandum and the statement signed by the defendant; and if the document was intended to take effect only at his death it would assume the character of a testamentary instrument, and, as such, would be inoperative, not having been duly attested.

Though there has been no release at law nor anything that amounted to a release in equity, yet if the position of the defendant has been injuriously affected by the act of the mortgagee this Court might not allow him to enforce his security; but this has not been the case, and a party cannot establish in equity a release or forgiveness of a debt by merely shewing an expressed intention to release the debt if there has been nothing which amounted to a release at law. The plaintiff, therefore, is, in my opinion, entitled to a decree of foreclosure with costs.

McKINNON *v.* McDOUGALL.

PLAINTIFF, in his writ, sought to have a judgment, entered against him in the County Court upon a confession signed by him when under the age of twenty-one, declared null and void, and moved for an injunction to restrain a sale under execution, upon affidavits verifying the statement contained in the writ, that the warrant of confession on which the judgment was entered had been procured from him by deceit and imposition. No foundation was shown for this statement.

Held, that the defendant could not be restrained, first, because of the falsity of the material statements on which the injunction was moved for; secondly, because there was an adequate remedy at law by setting the judgment aside; and, thirdly, because the injunction was not specifically prayed for, and could not be granted under the general prayer for relief.

RITCHIE, E. J., (June 23rd, 1879,) delivered the judgment of the Court :—

The plaintiff in his writ asks this Court to declare a judgment entered against him by the defendant in the County

Court at Port Hood to be null and void, and to set it aside with costs, on the ground that when he gave the warrant to confess judgment he had not attained the age of twenty-one years by some months, and that the warrant was obtained from him by fraud, deceit and imposition.

The warrant was given by the plaintiff on the 6th February, 1878, for $40.77, and judgment entered on the 9th February for that sum and $9.85 costs ; and on the 6th of May last the plaintiff took a rule *nisi* for an injunction to restrain the defendant from selling real estate levied on and advertized for sale under an execution issued on the judgment, on affidavits verifying the statements contained in the writ.

Though the plaintiff, in his writ, has made the positive statement that the warrant of confession was obtained from him by fraud, deceit and imposition, and has made an affidavit that the statements so made are true, it is now obvious from the affidavits before the Court that there is no foundation for the charge so made against the defendant. The statement I have referred to is important,—so much so, that if it had been true the plaintiff would have been entitled to an injunction ; but his having made so serious a charge without any foundation for it would of itself deprive him of a right to an ·injunction, and if the writ had been granted would have been a good ground for dissolving it. Another serious objection to the plaintiff's application is that he has at law as full and complete a remedy as he seeks from this Court, by application to the Court in which the judgment is entered to have it set aside if it has been improperly obtained, the Judge of which would have power to stay the execution in the meantime, and this, in my opinion, was the proper course for him to have adopted. Courts of equity may be resorted to and judgments at law impeached where they have been obtained by fraud, but they have never set aside such judgments for irregularity, and it is not the practice to declare the judgment of a Court of competent jurisdiction void and set it aside. What they do is to restrain the party by injunction from enforcing it on a proper case being made for their interference ; and, in all cases, before a court of equity will restrain proceedings at law, the party seeking its aid must shew that his own conduct

has been fair and equitable, and he cannot expect to obtain it
if he has by his own conduct brought about the state of things
of which he complains, for the Court will not allow itself to
be made an instrument of injustice.

There is still another objection to the plaintiff's succeeding
in his application ; that the writ contains no prayer for an
injunction, and it should be specifically prayed for unless in
some very exceptional cases, and the plaintiff is not allowed
to move for the writ under the prayer for general relief. See
Kerr on Injunctions, 607. The rule *nisi* for an injunction
must for the reasons I have given be discharged.

BLIGH *v.* KENNY ET AL.

PLAINTIFF, as official assignee of M., took proceedings to recover back money
paid to defendants in fraud of creditors. Subsequently the creditors' assignee, on
being appointed, obtained a rule *nisi* calling on defendants to shew cause why he
should not be allowed to file a supplemental bill and become plaintiff.

Held, that the plaintiff was entitled to file a supplemental bill.

RITCHIE, E. J., (June 23rd, 1879,) delivered the judgment
of the Court :—

This suit was instituted by Harris Bligh, official assignee
under the Insolvent Act of 1875, by authority from the Judge
of the County Court to take proceedings for the protection of
the estate of Edward Morrison, an insolvent, and to commence
the suit with the view of preventing the claim against the
defendants being barred by the Statute of Limitations.
Subsequently, Francis G. Parker, having been appointed
assignee of the estate, obtained a rule *nisi* calling on the
defendants to shew cause why he should not be allowed to file
a supplemental bill and become plaintiff.

On the part of the defendants the motion to make the
rule absolute is resisted on the ground that the official assignee
was not authorized to bring such a suit, and the Judge of the
County Court had no power to make the order under which it
was instituted, and a distinction was attempted to be shewn

between such a suit as this, which the insolvent himself could not have brought, and a suit for the recovery of a debt due to the insolvent, and it was contended that the 16th section of the act, under which this suit was brought, applied only to the latter class of cases, and that such a suit as this could only be brought under the 39th section. I see no ground for any such distinction. If the Judge of the County Court has power to authorize the official assignee to institute a suit against a debtor of the insolvent whose debt was on the eve of being barred by the Statute of Limitations, I see no reason why he had not the same power to authorize a suit to recover back money alleged to have been paid in fraud of creditors. It was urged that by the terms of the 39th section the right to do so was vested *exclusively* in the creditors' assignee, but by that section no distinction is made between such a suit and one for the recovery of a debt due to the insolvent, the right to sue for which is also vested exclusively in the *creditors' assignee.*

The 16th section vested in the official assignee all the rights and interest which the insolvent had in and to any property, to hold the same for the benefit of the insolvent and his creditors, subject to the order of the Court or Judge, who may upon such order, and before any meeting of the creditors, institute any conservatory process or any proceedings that may be necessary for the protection of the estate. I cannot think that the Judge was wrong in considering this suit a proceeding necessary for the protection of the estate and making the order he did.

There is an apparent repugnance in the authority given by that section to the official assignee to bring the suit and the terms of the 39th section, which declares that the right to institute such a suit shall be exclusively vested in the creditors' assignee ; but in construing a statute the language of every part must be construed as far as possible so as to be consistent with every other part and to give effect to all. This can be done by assuming what I think was the intention of the Legislature, that *on the appointment of the creditors' assignee* he should have the exclusive right to bring the suit referred to in the latter section, which, as regards the insolvent estate,

10 *m*

would come into operation on his appointment, leaving the former section in full operation between the insolvency and his appointment.

Though this question was fully argued and my decision on it invited, the only judgment now is that the rule *nisi* for leave to file a supplemental bill be made absolute, leaving open the question as to the effect that the bringing of the suit by the official assignee should have as regards the Statute of Limitations. I wish this to be understood, so that the defendants, if dissatisfied with the decision of this Court on this point, may not be deprived of an appeal, which would be the case where the decision involved a mere question of practice.

McKENZIE *v.* ÆTNA INSURANCE COMPANY.

PLAINTIFF mortgaged certain property to C. for $434.50, and covenanted in the mortgage to keep it insured for $500 in the name and for the benefit of the mortgagee. Subsequently, plaintiff effected insurance to the amount of $570 on his own account, without reference to the mortgagee, $180 of which was on the personal property, not covered by the mortgage. After loss by fire the mortgagee, finding that the insurance was not in his name, demanded an assignment of the policy, offering to secure to plaintiff the amount due him, and upon his refusal, claimed the amount from the company. Defendants paid the $180 and, upon action brought for the balance, an interpleader order was made.

Held, that the insurance enured to the benefit of the mortgagee, and that he was entitled to interplead, although the claim of the mortgagee was an equitable claim, and the Company was under a contractual obligation to the plaintiff, and although the claim of the mortgagee was smaller than the amount insured.

RITCHIE, E. J., (August 18th, 1879,) delivered the judgment of the Court:—

This action was brought at common law to recover the amount due on a policy of insurance against fire made by the defendant company in favor of the plaintiff. The company admit their liability for the loss under the policy, but in consequence of a claim made by James Crowdis, who asserts that he is the party really entitled to recover the amount due on the policy, an order was made calling upon Crowdis to shew cause why he should not appear and state the nature and particulars of his claim, and maintain or relinquish it, in accordance with which order he did appear and set forth the particulars of his claim, and as it involved questions of equitable jurisdiction, the case was transferred to this Court.

The facts as they now appear are as follows :—McKenzie, the plaintiff, was the owner of a lot of land on which was the dwelling house covered by the policy, which, on the 13th November, 1876, he mortgaged to Crowdis for $434.50, and in the mortgage he covenanted that he would insure and keep insured the buildings then erected or thereafter to be erected on the mortgaged lot against loss or damage by fire in one or more of the fire insurance offices in Halifax for the sum of $500, at the option, by the direction, in the name of, and for the benefit of Crowdis, his executors, &c., and would from time to time and at all times thereafter deliver the policy or policies of insurance, and all receipts for premiums, and all renewal receipts to him.

Subsequently the plaintiff effected insurance to the amount of $570, but on his own account, and not in the name of or for the benefit of Crowdis, there being no reference to him in the policy. While this insurance was in force the dwelling house on the mortgaged premises was destroyed by fire. Shortly after the loss had occurred, finding that the insurance had not been effected in his name, as he had supposed was the case, Crowdis demanded an assignment of the policy, offering to secure plaintiff the balance due on it after deducting his claim. The plaintiff refused and said that he was not aware that the building was insured, whereupon Crowdis gave notice of his claim to the defendant company.

The policy taken by the plaintiff covered insurance on furniture to the amount of $180, but, there being no dispute as to that, it was paid to the plaintiff before the action was commenced against the company. What is now in controversy relates solely to the insurance on the building.

The plaintiff's counsel contests the right of Crowdis to interplead. While he admits that he may have an action against the plaintiff for breach of his covenant, he contends he has no right to interfere with him in his action against the company on the policy and that no interpleader should be allowed where one claim, as that of the plaintiff against the company, is legal, and the other, as that of Crowdis, is equitable ; and that the defendant company, having entered into an agreement with the plaintiff and thereby incurred personal responsibility to him, have no right to ask for an interpleader.   The further objection was raised that the insurance effected was for a larger amount than the covenant stipulated and covered other property.   Cases are to be found to support the position that to entitle the party to an interpleader the claims should be legal as distinguished from equitable, and that the applicant should not be under a special obligation to either claimant; but these rules which once prevailed have been relaxed by later decisions.   In *Rusden* v. *Pope*, L. R., 3 Exch., 269, which was an action brought by the plaintiff, a mortgagee of a vessel, for freight under the charter-party, which was claimed by the creditors' assignee of the mortgagors, it was contended that the plaintiff could not have maintained an action against the charterers, the charter-party being a personal contract not passing to the assignees of the vessel, and the question being one at common law the plaintiff could not recover. CHANNEL, B.: " I cannot agree that the only question we can determine is whether the plaintiff is entitled to maintain this action.   The charterer, claiming no right in the freight, had a clear right to interplead in equity, and it would be a narrow view of the interpleader acts to hold that it was not intended to confer upon the Court a jurisdiction to determine equitable rights." KELLY, C.B., and MARTIN, B., concurred, BRAMWELL, B., dissenting.

In *Duncan* v. *Cashin*, L. R., 10 C. P., 558, BRETT, J., said: " It was formerly supposed that the Courts of law in dealing with questions arising under the Interpleader Act could not take notice of equitable claims, and there is the strong authority of BRAMWELL, B., that it is so, but the rest of the Court thought otherwise." So in *Engelback* v. *Nixon*, L. R., 10 C. P., p. 654, the Court held in the case of an interpleader that it was now settled that a Court of law would recognize equitable claims.   These are decisions at common law and courts of equity recognize the same doctrine in the case of bills of interpleader.   In *Desborough* v. *Harris*, 5 D. M. & G., 455, the Lord Chancellor said: " The foundation of a right to file a bill of interpleader is that there is a conflict between two or more persons claiming the same debt or obligation. Where such a state of things exists, and where that double claim has not been occasioned by the conduct of the person who is liable to discharge the debt or obligation, he may obtain the assistance of this Court, and, upon bringing into Court the amount of debt in dispute, the Court will relieve him and put the conflicting claimants to litigate their rights between one another. I guard myself thus in saying that where the liability is not occasioned by the act of the person liable, for otherwise there is no interpleader." In *Hamilton* v. *Marks*, 5 De. G. & Sm., 638, the same view was taken, and that case meets the objection taken that the sum in the hands of the defendant company exceeded the amount claimed by Crowdis. There the claim of one of the contending parties was legal and the other merely equitable, and limited to an amount that did not exhaust the whole fund. The objections were taken and overruled, the Vice-Chancellor saying that it was as clear a case of interpleader as he had ever seen.

That the rule which was once acted upon that the applicant for an interpleader should not be under a special obligation to either party in respect of the subject in controversy does not now prevail is evident from the later decisions. On the part of the plaintiff in *Tanner* v. *The European Bank*, L. R., 1 Ex., 261, it was urged that the defendants were under special contractual obligation to him who declared upon that contract, and that therefore an interpleader order could not be made, and it was impossible that the rights involved in the contract between the plaintiff and defendants could be settled in a trial with another person who was no party to the contract. But an interpleader order having been made by BRAMWELL, B., it was confirmed by the Court. In *Attenborough* v. *The London and St. Katherine's Dock Company*, 3 C. P. D., 450, on appeal one of the points taken was that the defendants had entered into relations with the plaintiffs and were not entitled to an interpleader. The Court held otherwise, and BAGGALLY, L. J., referring to *Crawshay* v. *Thornton*, 2 My. & Cr, 1, said: " Now it is quite true that that case was decided in the year 1831, when the Interpleader Act was passed, and that Lord COTTENHAM'S judgment proceeded upon the principle that where the person seeking to interplead had entered into any special obligation with either of the parties claiming he was not entitled to be relieved in equity. The same principle was to some extent adopted in the courts of common law, and as to this I may refer to *James* v. *Pritchard*, 7 M. & W., 216, which was mentioned in *Meynell* v. *Angell*, decided by the present Lord BLACKBURN. But these decisions were prior to the passing of the Common Law Procedure Act, 1860, section 12, and I have strong reason to believe that this clause was enacted in order to prevent the further application of the principle laid down in *Crawshay* v. *Thornton*." And BRETT, J. said : " As to the authorities, in my opinion *Best* v. *Hayes*, 1 H. & C., 718, and *Tanner* v. *European Bank* are direct authorities against the authorities put forward on behalf of the plaintiffs. In the latter there was most certainly a contract between the plaintiffs and defendants, and in the former, if the claimant had not intervened it would have been difficult for the defendant to shew that he was not liable upon a contract made with him as auctioneer. But in each case the question as to the property in dispute was directed to be tried between the rival claimants; and I cannot agree that in order to entitle a defendant to interplead the remedy of the plaintiff against the claimant must be co-extensive with the remedy against him."

If ever there was a case where the granting of leave to interplead was just and reasonable, and calculated to do justice and settle the matters in controversy, and where the opposition, raised as it is by the plaintiff, is unjust and unreasonable. it is this. The defendant company is content to stand between the two contending parties as a stakeholder claiming no interest in the amount in controversy, ready to pay to whichever of the parties the Court shall decide is entitled to it. The claim of the plaintiff on the defendant company is a strictly legal one; but for him to insist on recovering the amount and retaining it for his own use would be most inequitable. He undertook to insure for the benefit of Crowdis, and, in violation of his agreement, insured for his own benefit ; under these circumstances Crowdis may be considered as having an equitable lien on the amount insured. Cases in equity are numerous where a party undertaking to do an act for another does it for himself and it enures for the benefit of the former, as where one enters into an agreement to buy a property for another and buys it for himself. So where a party has expressly agreed to purchase and settle property, and buys but neglects to make a settlement, he will be taken to have bought it in performance of his agreement. Equity will assume that a party intended to do what he covenanted to do, and a contract to make a mortgage may create a lien on an estate. If in this case there had been simply a covenant in the mortgage that the plaintiff should insure, with no reference to its being for the benefit of Crowdis, he would have had no right to interfere with the receipt of the money by the plaintiff. That was the case in *Lees* v. *Whitely*, L. R., 2 Eq., 143, cited by Mr. Tupper at the argument. Another case cited on the part of the plaintiff, that of *Livingstone* v. *The Western Insurance Company*, reported in 14 Grant's Ch. R., 461 and 16 Grant's Ch. R., 9, has, in my opinion, no bearing on the question. There the loss would have been payable to the mortgagee but for the violation of a condition by the mortgagor whereby the policy was avoided. So in *Carpenter* v. *Providence Washington Insurance Company*, 16 Peters, 506, the party making the claim on the insurers was not only a stranger unreferred to in the policy, but there was no agreement between the mortgagor and mortgagee that the insurance should be exclusively for the mortgagee, and great stress was laid on that fact. Here the plaintiff, having covenanted to insure for Crowdis's benefit, and having wrongfully insured for his own, it enures for the benefit of Crowdis, and the plaintiff's attempt to claim the money is fraudulent, the former having a claim on it which a court of equity would enforce.

Assuming equitable claims to be within the purview of the Interpleader Act, this case comes within the very words of that act, which provide that if the defendant shews that he claims no interest in the subject matter of the suit, but that the right thereto is claimed or supposed to belong to some third party who has sued or is expected to sue for the same, &c., the interpleader order may be made. I can see no reason why the rule *nisi* for an interpleader in this case should not be made absolute.

DIOCESAN SYNOD NOVA SCOTIA *v.* O'BRIEN ET AL.

UNDER an order of foreclosure and sale, plaintiffs advertized for sale "all the estate, right, title, interest and equity of redemption" of the defendants. At the sale one M. became the purchaser, and paid down the ten per cent. deposit required under the terms of the sale, but refused to complete the purchase, on the ground that a good title in fee simple could not be given. An order for a resale was made and the property was sold for an amount less than the amount of the mortgage. Plaintiffs applied to the Court for an order for the payment to them of the deposit on the first sale. M. showed cause, contending that he was entitled to the return of the deposit as a good title could not be given.

Held, that, as the plaintiffs had only professed to sell the title of the defendants, such as it was, and had not been guilty of fraud or misrepresentation, and the purchaser would, under his purchase, have acquired all that he bid for, he was not entitled to a return of the deposit.

RITCHIE, E. J., (December 8th, 1879,) delivered the judgment of the Court:—

Under the order of foreclosure and sale in this cause, all the estate, right, title, interest and equity of redemption of the defendants, John A. O'Brien, Bridget O'Brien and Catherine Hayden, and of all persons claiming by, through or under them, of, in or to the lot of land described in the mortgage sought to be foreclosed, was advertized by the Sheriff to be sold ; the terms of sale expressed in the advertizement being ten per cent. deposit at the time of sale, remainder on delivery of the deed. On the day specified the sale took place, and Samuel A. Marshall, being the highest bidder, became the purchaser for the sum of $3,025, who thereupon paid a deposit of $300 and signed an agreement in these words : " I hereby consent to become the purchaser of the property described in the annexed handbill for the sum of $3,025. Samuel A. Marshall, for Margaret Jane Marshall, Mary Marshall, Isabel Marshall." The Sheriff subsequently tendered to him a deed and demanded the balance of the purchase money, but he would neither accept the deed nor pay the money, and thereupon an application was made on behalf of the plaintiffs for an order on Marshall to compel him to complete the purchase by payment of the balance of the purchase money. This was resisted on the ground that the purchaser would not acquire a perfect title in fee simple to the land. For the reason thus assigned the Court declined to make the order, but at the plaintiff's instance an order was made for a re-sale, which subsequently took place, when James W. Hutt became the purchaser for $2,005, being less than the amount due on the mortgages foreclosed. The plaintiffs then applied to the Court for an order on the Sheriff requiring him to pay the $300 deposit on the first sale to him, and, an order *nisi* to that effect having been granted, cause was shewn against the rule on the part of Marshall, his counsel contending that, as a perfect title could not be given to him, the deposit should be returned to him.

Where an agreement is made for the sale of land, the purchaser has a right to require a good title from the vendors, but, while this is the case in general, there is nothing to prevent the vendor offering for sale and selling his right and title to the land, whatever they may be, and, if a purchaser agrees to make such a purchase he will be bound to fulfil his agreement and cannot be relieved on the ground that he will not acquire a perfect title to the land, provided he has not been misled by fraud or misrepresentation on the part of the vendor; but it must clearly appear that the right and title of the vendor to the land and no more was to be disposed of. As there is no pretence that anything was done to mislead the purchaser in this case, we have only to see what the bargain was. All that was advertized was the estate and interest of the defendants and all persons claiming under them. This alone was offered for sale by the Sheriff and bid for by Marshall. He may have supposed that their estate was an absolute fee simple, but there was nothing done to lead him to that conclusion.

There is nothing to prevent a vendor from restricting the purchaser's right by the conditions of sale, and the purchaser may be bound by them. *Leake on Contracts*, 829 ; *Sugden, V. & P.*, 337. In *Freme et al.* v. *Wright*, 4 Madd., 365, the estate was purchased by the defendant for £500, who refused to complete the sale for want of good title, and brought an action for the deposit. The Court restrained him from proceeding. The Vice-Chancellor said : " Every person who offers an estate for sale without qualification asserts in fact that it is his to sell, and consequently that he has a good title ; but a vendor, if he thinks fit may stipulate for the sale of an estate with such title only as he happens to have, and the question is whether these particulars of sale import that the vendors asserted a good title to the estate or meant only to sell such title as the bankrupt had." And in suits for specific performance the Court will not direct an enquiry into title where the vendor only contracts to sell such interest as he has. *Fry on Specific Performance,* sections 830 and 571. In *Tweed* v. *Mills,* L. R., 1 C. P., 39, where a tenant from year to year agreed to let all his right, title and interest in the premises for £1,000, BYLES, J., said : " It seems now to be well established that on the sale of a lease there is an implied contract on the part of the vendor that he will shew a good title, but that may be dispensed with, and the first words of this agreement shew that that was not the intention here. The defendant agreed to let to the plaintiff all his right, title and interest in the premises, such as they were ; the rule therefore does not apply to this case." *Clare* v. *Lamb,* L. R., 10 C. P., 334, is to the same effect ; so is *Hume* v. *Pocock,* L. R., 1 Ch., 379, affirming the decree of the Vice-Chancellor, and that was a suit for specific performance of the contract. *Ex parte Barrel,* L. R., 10 Ch., 512, and *Thomas* v. *Brown,* 1 Q. B. Div., 714, shew that where a contract for sale goes off by default of the purchaser the vendor is entitled to the deposit.

This, it will be remembered, is not a case where the purchaser would acquire no estate or interest in the land. The defendants and those claiming under them had an interest in it, and he would acquire a beneficial present interest which may result in an absolute fee simple. Inasmuch as the terms of sale are clear and unambiguous, and the purchaser by paying the balance of the purchase money could have got all that he bid for and agreed to buy, he cannot recover back the deposit, the vendor being willing to convey to him all that was offered for sale.

THE WINDSOR AND ANNAPOLIS RAILWAY CO.

v.

THE WESTERN COUNTIES RAILWAY CO.

DEFENDANTS demurred to plaintiffs' writ, on the ground, among others, that the Attorney-General had not been made a party. The demurrer was overruled by the Judge in Equity, whose decision was sustained by the Court *in banco* on appeal, from which decision an appeal was taken to the Supreme Court of Canada, where the appeal was dismissed on the ground that the Court had no jurisdiction as the decision was not final. Plaintiffs then sought to amend the writ by adding the Attorney-General, to which the defendants objected, on the ground of delay. The defendants were in possession of the property, taken from the plaintiffs, in respect of which the suit was brought, and were enjoying the whole profits of it, so that the delay was prejudicial to the plaintiffs rather than to them.

Held, that the plaintiffs were entitled to the amendment applied for as they had not been remiss in the prosecution of the cause.

RITCHIE, E. J., (December 8th, 1879,) delivered the judgment of the Court :—

Two rules *nisi* have been taken in this case, one at the instance of the defendants either to have the cause set down for a hearing, or, in the alternative, that the plaintiffs speed the cause ; the other at the instance of the plaintiffs that they should have leave to add the Attorney-General of Canada as a defendant and that the writ and pleadings should be amended accordingly. On motion to make these rules absolute they were argued together.

The defendants demurred to the plaintiffs' writ on several grounds, one of which was that the Attorney-General had not been made a party. The demurrer was overruled by the Judge in Equity, and on appeal to the whole Court his judgment was affirmed. An appeal from this latter judgment was taken to the Supreme Court of Canada, but that Court, considering the judgment on the demurrer not a final judgment, held that the case did not come within its jurisdiction. As no stay of proceedings was ordered, the evidence was taken pending the demurrer and completed about the month of March last, and before the Supreme Court of Canada had given any decision. The defendants object to the amendment asked for on the ground of delay, which they say will be prejudicial to them. This may possibly be the case to some extent. It is not likely that the amendment will involve the taking any further evidence, and if it should it could be taken during the vacation just commencing, so that the cause could be heard soon after its termination, in which case there would be no delay, and I do not think the plaintiffs up to this time have been remiss in prosecuting their cause. It would have been most injudicious on their part to have brought it on to a hearing until the ultimate decision on the demurrer, and that has but lately taken place; and it is to be borne in mind that the defendants are in possession of the railway, the subject of the suit, and are enjoying the whole profits of it, the possession of it having been forcibly taken from the plaintiffs, to whom the delay must be more prejudicial than to the defendants. The only question is whether by the practice of the Court such an amendment can be made in this stage of the case.

If the Supreme Court of Canada had entertained the appeal, the plaintiffs' difficulty on this point would have been removed. If it had affirmed the judgment of the Courts of this province the question would have been set at rest, and the joining of the Attorney-General held not to be necessary by the Court of ultimate resort. If, on the other hand, that judgment had been reversed and the demurrer upheld, the plaintiffs would, as a matter of course, have had a right to make the amendment now sought. The present application is made under the idea that the Supreme Court may come to that conclusion, and I see no good reason for refusing it. If at the hearing of the cause the Court should be of opinion that the Attorney-General was a necessary party, it could and I feel sure would direct his being called in, and would permit the case to stand over till it was done, and not dismiss the bill in consequence of his not having been made a party in the first instance, which would occasion greater delay than if the amendment were made now. If the Court should not at the hearing interfere and order the calling in of the Attorney-General before being in a position to make a decree, and the defendants should, notwithstanding the judgment on the demurrer on the point, ultimately take the objection on an appeal to the Supreme Court of Canada, if the case should again be before that tribunal, and there the Atty. General be deemed a necessary party, it would be most unreasonable that the plaintiffs should be shut out of an amendment which they would have been entitled to but for the judgment of our Supreme Court in his favor on the demurrer. If the defendants had undertaken not again to raise the objection there would have been more reason in their opposition.

Great latitude is allowed to a plaintiff in making amendments, and this is especially the case with respect to the adding of parties. The Court will, on grounds shewn for it, allow parties to be added at any time before hearing and at the hearing, and sometimes even after a decree and before its enrolment. See *Harrison's Common Law Practice*, 39. In *Goodwin* v. *Goodwin*, 3 Atk., 370, the objection was taken that the plaintiff had amended his bill after publication and cause set down. The Lord Chancellor held that after publication and cause set down he could amend his bill by adding parties. *Brattle* v. *Waterman*, 4 Sim., 125; *Forbes* v. *Stevens*, 3 N. R., 386; *Bryen* v. *Wetsall*, Kay Appendix, 43, shew that it is all but a matter of course to make such an amendment as this now asked for, and in *2 Atk.* 15 Anon., Lord HARDWICKE said a bill is never dismissed for want of parties, but stands over on paying the costs of the day. A decree of Sir JOSEPH JEKYLL in a cause at the Rolls dismissing a bill for want of parties was reversed afterwards for that reason, and a decree of the same nature in the Court of Exchequer was reversed likewise in the House of Lords.

With reference to the delay complained of in making this application, I may remark that it could not have been made till the appeal to the Supreme Court of Canada was disposed of. In *Ainslie* v. *Sims*, 17 Beav., 174, the plaintiff, pending an appeal, without stating the fact, applied for the common order to amend. The Master of the Rolls said: " Here a bill is filed to which the defendant demurs. Until the demurrer is heard the defendant may obtain an order, of course, to amend. The Court at the hearing of the demurrer either allows it with leave to amend or overrules it, but in either case the parties have a right to appeal. The plaintiff had distinct notice of the appeal being set down before he obtained the common order to amend ; pending the appeal he could not get it." The plaintiffs' application to add the Attorney-

General of Canada as a party to the suit should be granted on
payment of costs to the defendants if any are occasioned by
the amendment. This decision disposes of the rule *nisi*
obtained by the defendants to speed the cause.

GREGORY *v.* CANADA IMPROVEMENT CO. ET AL.

PLAINTIFF claimed to be entitled to $80,000 bonds on the Eastern Extension
Railway, to be secured upon the Pictou Branch road in the event of its being transferred to the defendant Company as a subvention in aid of the construction of Eastern Extension. The defendants were applying for legislation which should provide
that in the event of the road not being operated to the satisfaction of the Governor-
in-Council of the Province, it should become the property of the Province free
from incumbrance. Plaintiff, contending that this would invalidate his bonds
and was a breach of a compromise made with him, sought to restrain the
defendants from applying for such legislation.

Held, that, as the purpose of the concession was to secure the construction and
continued operation of the road, and the proposed legislation contained a proviso
that the trustees of the bondholders should have notice before any forfeiture of
the road, that was all that they had a right to expect, and the plaintiff was not
entitled to the injunction prayed for.

RITCHIE, E. J., (March 15th, 1879,) delivered the judgment of the Court:—

This suit is brought against the Canada Improvement
Company, the Halifax and Cape Breton Railway and Coal
Company, Harry Abbott, the Honorable J. J. C. Abbott, Sir
Hugh Allan, the Honorable John Hamilton, and the Honorable
Samuel Creelman, Commissioner of Public Works and Mines
of Nova Scotia, and the plaintiff prays that the defendants
may be restrained from entering into a contract or agreement
to carry out a preliminary agreement made between the two
companies and the Governments of Nova Scotia and the
Dominion of Canada in fraud of a settlement and compromise
made between the companies and the plaintiff, whereby it was
provided that the Pictou Branch Railway was to be held by
the Dominion Government until the railway extension to the
Strait of Canso and the steam ferry across the Strait are
finished to the satisfaction of the Nova Scotia Government,
when the said branch railway was to be transferred to the

Halifax and Cape Breton Railway and Coal Company, upon
condition that the branch railway and railway extension and
ferry shall be operated to the satisfaction of the Lieutenant-
Governor-and-Council of Nova Scotia, and in the event of
failure so to operate, then the same should become the property
of the Nova Scotia Government, free from encumbrances;
which preliminary agreement, it was stipulated, should
thereafter be embodied in a formal contract, and that the said
companies should apply for the necessary legislation to enable
the same to be carried into effect; and the plaintiff prayed
that the defendants should be restrained from carrying out or
acting upon any agreement theretofore made in violation of
the said settlement or compromise, or from applying for,
encouraging or adopting any legislation by which the value
of the bonds which, by that settlement or compromise, were
to be delivered to the plaintiff, might be depreciated, or the
property on which the same was to be secured might in any
event cease to be the property of the said Railway and Coal
Company, free from liability on account of such bonds.

The Attorney-General, who appeared on behalf of the
Commissioner of Public Works and Mines of Nova Scotia,
produced an affidavit of Mr. Creelman, stating that the formal
contract embodying the terms of the preliminary agreement
had been executed by him before he was served with the writ
in this cause or the notice of motion for an injunction, and
.before he had any knowledge of the application for an
injunction; and Mr. Graham, who appeared for the Halifax
and Cape Breton Railway and Coal Company and Harry
Abbott, produced the affidavit of the latter, in which, among
other things, he alleges that the said agreement had been
executed by him before he had any notice of the plaintiff's
claim for an injunction, and, as he had been informed and
verily believed, was executed by the said company, and by
Sir Hugh Allan and the Honorable J. J. C. Abbott before the
service of the writ on them, or notice of the motion for
injunction. Under these circumstances, that part of the
plaintiff's prayer which asks the Court to restrain the
defendants from executing this agreement is necessarily
unavailing, and the plaintiff is confined to that part which

asks that the defendants should be enjoined from applying for or adopting any legislation by which the value of the bonds which he claims he is entitled to under the settlement or compromise, as set out in his writ, may be depreciated, or the property on which the same is secured may, in any event, cease to be the property of the said railway company, free from liability on account of such bonds.

At the time of the compromise or settlement set out in the plaintiff's writ it was known to all the parties to it that, as the law then stood, it did not permit the issue of the $80,000 bonds and the delivery of them to the plaintiff, nor was there any legislation then existing by which mortgage bonds could be made to attach to the Pictou Branch Railway. It was therefore provided that the Canada Improvement Company would deliver to the plaintiff, *as soon as the same could be legally issued,* to which end the two companies agreed to use every diligence, $80,000 in good, sufficient, legal and available first mortgage bonds of the Halifax and Cape Breton Railway and Coal Company, and *which should, so far as the said companies could make them do so,* attach and be a first lien upon the Truro and Pictou Branch Railway, which was to be handed over by the Government of the Dominion to the Halifax and Cape Breton Railway and Coal Company, as a subsidy towards the construction of the Eastern Railway Extension, *provided always that such branch railway should be so handed over,* and also upon the said Eastern Railway Extension and the said company, and the property, rights and privileges set forth in section 32 of the Act incorporating the company; that the bonds should be free from unusual clauses and conditions by which the holders or trustees might be precluded from selling the property upon which they were to constitute a lien, or foreclosing the mortgage, or otherwise realizing the bonds in case of non-payment; and it was further provided that the Canada Improvement Company would deliver to the plaintiff the said bonds, and that the Halifax and Cape Breton Railway and Coal Company would, if it should prove necessary to do so, apply for and endeavour to procure at the earliest opportunity such legislation as would remedy any alleged defects, if any existed, in their organization.

All parties to the arrangement seem carefully to have guarded themselves from undertaking to perform what it was not in their power to do, and the undertakings of the companies to give a lien on the Pictou Branch were strictly conditional on its delivery over by the Dominion Government and the terms on which it should be delivered. The plaintiff has no grounds for complaining that the Pictou Branch is to be held as the property of the Dominion Government until the Eastern Extension Railway to the Strait and the steam ferry are finished to the satisfaction of the Nova Scotia Government. It could not be reasonably expected that it would be handed over to the Halifax and Cape Breton Railway and Coal Company until then. What was mainly urged at the argument was that the terms were unjust to the bond holders and the bonds rendered less valuable to the plaintiff by the provision that a forfeiture was to be incurred if the railway and ferry were not duly operated. The object of the two governments was not only to have the railway to the Strait of Canso built, but to have it and the ferry put and kept in operation, and it is for this that they agreed to contribute to its construction out of the public funds. This much all parties concerned were aware of, and nothing seems more reasonable in the interest of the public than that, if the Halifax and Cape Breton Railway Company should fail to perform their contract by operating the roads, they should revert to the government, in order that they might be kept in operation. But this provision, it was urged, might be very prejudicial to the interest of the plaintiff as a bond holder, as he might lose his security by the non-performance of the contract by the mortgagor company, without any fault on the part of the mortgagee, and without his being able to prevent a forfeiture. But the Court has now before it the contract entered into in accordance with the preliminary agreement set out in the plaintiff's writ, and from it it appears that the absolute right of property in the Pictou Branch is to be conveyed to the company on the terms that the company is to forfeit all right to it in the event of a failure to operate the railways and ferry efficiently and continuously for a period of six months after notice, and provision is to be made for a

10n

reference to arbitration in case of a dispute arising as to the forfeiture. There is, however, no protection to the bond-holders, and it did occur to me that it would be unreasonable that their security should be liable to be destroyed without notice and without their being able to prevent the forfeiture and protect their interests. But even then if the Dominion Government would not consent to hand over the Pictou Branch on any other terms, I do not see what redress the plaintiff would have. I was glad to find, however, from the Attorney-General, (Mr. Thompson,) that the bill which had been prepared for submission to the legislature, the draft of which he had and read from, contained a clause requiring that notice of intended forfeiture should be given to the trustees for the bond-holders, who might save the forfeiture by their undertaking to perform the duty of keeping the roads and the ferry in operation. This is all that in my opinion they have a right to expect. The road was built and the subvention granted on the stipulation that it should be kept in operation by the company, and any persons claiming through the company, by mortgage or otherwise, could only take subject to that stipulation.

The plaintiff, therefore, is not, in my opinion, entitled to the injunction he has prayed for.

ALMON ET AL. *v.* BUSCH.

DEFENDANT, a member of the Nova Scotia Building Society, obtained an advance, and gave his mortgage and bond; after which he sold his equity of redemption, and a suit was brought to foreclose the mortgage, without making him a party or giving him notice. The land was bought in by the Society for a sum less than the costs in the foreclosure suit. An action was then brought against the defendant on his bond. An equitable plea was pleaded, under which defendant gave evidence that the Secretary of the Society, upon defendant asking for a release of his bond, replied that it would be a good deal of expense add nothing would ever come against him, and no application was therafter made to him for dues or fines, the notices being sent to the purchaser.

Held, that the Secretary had no power to make the arrangement alleged, to which the Directors had not assented, and that the defendant, being a member of the Society, was bound to know the limits of the Secretary's authority; that, although the rules of the Society restricted them to the advancing of money upon real estate security, there was nothing to prevent them from taking the defendant's bond in addition, even if they could not take the bond of a stranger; that the fact of a sale under foreclosure did not prevent the Society from sueing on the bond, so long as they held the land; that the decree against the defendant could not include the costs of the foreclosure suit, to which he was not a party, but that he was not entitled to credit for the proceeds of the foreclosure sale, as they did not amount to the costs in that suit; and that the trustees were the proper plaintiffs.

RITCHIE, E. J., (October, 1879,) delivered the judgment of the Court:—

The plaintiffs seek to recover on a bond given to the Trustees of the Society, for the time being, by the defendant, on his becoming a member and obtaining an advance from the society of $212.64, for which he also gave a mortgage on certain real estate. Equitable pleas having been put in, the case was referred to this Court.

The defendant contends that the trustees were not authorized to take such a bond under the rules of the society, or the act under which it operates, but were restricted to taking security on real estate alone for advances. And for defence on equitable grounds, he alleges that, with the consent of the society, he conveyed the mortgaged property to one Mary Lahy, subject to the mortgage, and she was adopted as its debtor, in place of the defendant, after which this arrangement was acted upon, and the society applying to her and receiving from her the dues, fines, &c., which became due in respect of the advance, released the defendant from his bond, and agreed to give the same up to him, and not to look to him further to perform its conditions, and no application was afterwards made to him, and the plaintiffs subsequently instituted a suit against Mary Lahy, to foreclose the mortgage, without notice to him, or making him a party.

From the evidence, which was taken before the case was transferred to this Court, it appears that the defendant conveyed to Mary Lahy his equity of redemption in the mortgaged premises about five years ago, and, if the statement of the defendant and Thomas Lahy are to be credited, Mr. Burton, the Secretary and Treasurer of the Society, was informed of it, and was told that her father would, in future, make the payments to the society; that the defendant asked for a release and was told by Mr. Burton that it would be a good deal of expense and nothing would ever come against him;

to which he replied that as long as he was clear of it, and
nothing would ever come against him, he would make no
objection; that after this no application was made to him, and
the notices, &c., for dues, &c., were sent to Lahy. Mr. Burton
has no recollection of such a conversation or arrangement,
though he says that after the conveyance of the land to Miss
Lahy the notices were directed and sent to her, and he would
not undertake to contradict the statements made by the
defendant and Lahy. He does say that no *formal* application
was made and no *formal* steps were taken to relieve the
defendant, by which, I presume, he means that no application
was made to the directors, nor any actual release obtained,
which would be quite consistent with the plaintiff's statement,
as is his assertion that the directors never consented to take
Miss Lahy instead of the defendant; that he did not, and
had not the power of doing so, and that she never was a
member of the society. Taking the whole evidence together,
I infer that the defendant, from what took place, considered
himself relieved from all liability to the Society, and he would
be confirmed in this belief by the Society ceasing to treat
him as a member and debtor by dealing with Miss Lahy, as
such, until after the foreclosure and sale of the property.
On the other hand, Mr. Burton must have known that he had
no power to substitute Miss Lahy for the defendant, and release
him from his engagements. All that he intended to convey
to the defendant probably was that, the mortgage being deemed
a good security for the debt, he need not fear being called
upon for any further payment, and that he might consider
himself practically relieved from responsibility under his bond.

But, assuming that Mr. Burton did consent to release the
defendant from all liability to the Society and to take Miss
Lahy as a member in his place, it would. not avail the
defendant if unconfirmed by the directors, who alone had the
power of doing it. The duties of Mr. Burton, as Secretary
and Treasurer of the Society, are specified by the rules, and
his power and authority are strictly limited. He is vested
with no power to release the defendant from his responsibility,
or to transfer it to another, and the defendant, as a member
of the society, was bound to make himself acquainted with

its rules. If, therefore, such an arrangement as that testified to by the defendant and Lahy had been made with Mr. Burton it would be nugatory.

It was contended that the society had no authority to take a bond from the defendant, as it was restricted to taking security on real estate for an advance to a member ; but I cannot see any good reason why, having given a member the amount of his share in advance, it should not be repaid, though the mortgage might turn out an ineffectual security, either from depreciation in the value of the land mortgaged or defect of title, and, if so, why he could not be asked to bind himself to make good the deficiency. The case of the *Canada Permanent Building Society* v. *Lewis et al.*, 8 U. C. Com. Pleas R. 352, was cited as an authority for the contention, but upon turning to it, it will be found more opposed to than in favor of it. There the Society had taken a bond from a member and *another person*, to secure an advance to the former. The Court held that it could not take collateral security *from a stranger* for the security of a loan upon real property. The Chief Justice, in giving his judgment, said ; " A member may, I presume, besides giving his mortgage, give his covenant also, and if his covenant, his bond, the real security being indispensable."

It was also contended that, having foreclosed the mortgage and purchased in the property, the society lost its right to resort to its bond. As a general rule, a mortgagee has a right to enforce all his remedies. If he proceeds on his bond in the first instance, and thereby obtains only a part of his debt, he may foreclose his mortgage for what remains due. But if he forecloses first and sues on his bond for a deficiency, this equity will only allow by his giving the mortgagor a new right to redeem, which he cannot do if the mortgaged property has been sold to a stranger. In this case the property is vested in the society, and the defendant, if he wishes, can acquire a title to it again by paying the amount due on the mortgage. Under these circumstances, the foreclosure only extinguishes the mortgage debt to the extent of the value of the property, and the society is entitled to resort to its bond for the deficiency.

The plaintiffs, in their particulars, claim from the defendants $212.64, being $121.85, the amount due on the advance made the defendant, and $90.79, the costs of the suit against Miss Lahy on the foreclosure, giving no credit whatever for the amount for which the land was sold. This amount, it is obvious, cannot be recovered. The decree can only be for $121.87. The defendant is not chargeable with the costs of the foreclosure ; but, as the amount for which the land was purchased did not exceed the costs incurred in the foreclosure suit, the defendant is not entitled to any credit from that source.

There is no ground for the objection to the plaintiffs as parties. They are the only persons who, in my opinion, could bring the action. The society is a *quasi* corporation, and the trustees for the time being are alone authorized to sue for the society.

The decree will be for $121.87 and costs.

BARTON ET AL. *v.* BALDWIN.

PLAINTIFFS purchased certain real estate, subject to a mortgage held by W., as Guardian, for $5,840, and sold a portion to defendant, who was aware of the mortgage, for $7,000. Defendant paid $1,400 in cash, and received a deed, with an absolute warranty and covenants for title, without reference to the mortgage. On the same day plaintiffs gave a mortgage of the whole property to K., for $3,760, of which defendant had no knowledge when he made his purchase, and which was recorded before plaintiffs' deed. Defendant gave plaintiffs a mortgage for the balance of the purchase money. The mortgage to W. was foreclosed, and the property sold by the Sheriff, and defendant was obliged, in order to protect himself, to become the purchaser, paying for the whole property included in the mortgage $8,850, which was applied to the payment of the amount due on the two mortgages to W. and K., and to a judgment recorded against the property. Plaintiffs then brought an action against the defendant on the covenant in his mortgage.

Held, that they had no equitable right to call for payment of the purchase money until they had cleared the defendant's title ; that defendant was entitled in equity to pay off the mortgages, and had in effect done so, and to recover from the plaintiffs the amount so paid, over and above the purchase money, and that before plaintiffs could re-possess themselves of the portion not included in the conveyance to defendant, they would be obliged to pay him the difference between the amount at which he had purchased and the amount he had been obliged to pay.

Q. Whether the defendant could be compelled to convey even on the terms mentioned.

Ritchie, E. J., (October, 1879,) delivered the judgment of the Court :—

The case, which is a simple one, is complicated by the pleadings, which are confused and prolix and full of needless repetitions. The plaintiffs seek to recover the sum of $3,600 on a bond and covenant in a mortgage given by the defendant. The action was originally brought on the common law side of the Court and, the defendant having put in equitable pleas, it was sent here for adjudication.

From the evidence it appears that the plaintiffs became the purchasers of certain real estate in Halifax, from one James King, in the year 1873, which was then subject to a mortgage held by one Walker, Guardian of McCara, for $5,840 and interest. On the 1st May of that year the plaintiff sold a portion of it to the defendant for $7,000. The existence of the McCara mortgage was known to the defendant. He paid $1,400, and received a deed, with an absolute warranty of title and covenants from the plaintiffs that they had a good, indefeasible title in fee simple, and a right to convey, and for quiet enjoyment, without reference to any encumbrance existing on the property. On the same day the plaintiffs gave a mortgage on the whole property, including that sold to the defendant, to King, for $3,760, which was put on record before the plaintiffs' deed. Of this mortgage the defendant had no knowledge when he made his purchase and got his deed. This mortgage to King was transferred, a few days after it was given, to Mr. Joseph Northup. The defendant gave the plaintiffs a mortgage for the balance of the purchase money. Some time after, the plaintiff, Barton, conveyed to his co-plaintiff, McLellan, his interest in the defendant's mortgage, for the consideration of $1, and is, therefore, but a nominal plaintiff.

The amount due on the McCara mortgage was not paid, and in June, 1874, a suit for the foreclosure of it was commenced, and, a decree of foreclosure and sale having been obtained, the mortgaged property was, on the 24th of October following, offered at public sale by the Sheriff of Halifax, when the defendant, in order to protect the part of the property which he had purchased, was under the necessity of

becoming the purchaser, for $8,850, being the highest sum
offered for it at the sale, and he obtained from the Sheriff a
deed of it. The amount then due on the McCara mortgage
was $6,464.11. The balance in the Sheriff's hands after
paying this was $2,384.88, which was by him paid to the
Accountant-general of this Court. Subsequently, an application
was made on behalf of the estate of Northup for the amount
due on the mortgage which had been assigned to him, it
being the next encumbrance on the property sold, and an
order was made for the payment of the amount due, which
was $2,189.88; after which an application was made by one
James K. Munnis, to be paid out of the balance in the hands
of the accountant-general the sum of $108.78, due on a
judgment obtained by him against the plaintiff, McLellan,
and recorded to bind real estate, as being the next encumbrance, and he obtained an order to that effect.

    The counsel for the plaintiffs contends that no effect should
be given to the agreement set out in the defendant's pleas,
and referred to in the evidence, referring, as it does, to land,
it being verbal and inconsistent with the terms of the deeds;
and this view I am disposed to adopt. He further contends
that he is entitled to recover in this suit on the defendant's
bond, and on the covenant contained in his mortgage, and that
if the defendant has any remedy against the plaintiffs on the
covenants and warranty in his deed, it must be sought in a
cross-action, and that such an equitable defence as is attempted
to be set up cannot be entertained. In this view I do not
concur. The defendant, when he received his deed, and gave his
bond and mortgage for the balance of the purchase money,
was entitled to have the McCara mortgage released, so far as
it affected the part he had purchased, and to have the mortgage
the plaintiffs had wrongfully given to King removed from it,
and till this was done, plaintiff had no equitable right to call on
the defendant to pay the amount due on his mortgage It is
a recognized rule in equity that a purchaser has a right to
apply the unpaid purchase money to pay off encumbrances on
the land he has purchased. Before, therefore, the plaintiff
would have an equitable right to call on the defendant for
payment of the purchase money he should have cleared the

defendant's title by obtaining a release of the encumbrances on the land he had sold him and of which he had warranted the title; and if he failed to do this, the defendant was at liberty to pay the amounts due on them and take an assignment of them, and by so doing he would have paid the amount due on his bond and covenant and could claim on the plaintiffs for the amount he thus paid beyond what he owed them. Now this, in fact, is what the defendant has done. The property was sold on a foreclosure suit against the plaintiffs. They would not protect the title of the defendant or their own and the defendant was compelled to purchase, and his money has paid the encumbrances on the plaintiffs' property, which they were bound themselves to pay.

Mr. Bligh, to support his position, was forced to contend that if the defendant had been dispossessed of the property he purchased, as he would have been if he had not purchased at the Sheriff's sale, he could still be compelled to pay the plaintiffs' mortgage. Surely Mr. Bligh must have forgotten that he was in a Court of Equity, where there is no necessity for the defendant to resort to a cross-action. The whole matter in controversy and all the parties interested in it are before the Court, which acts, as far as possible, with a view of avoiding circuity and multiplicity of suits; and the statute relating to procedure in equity provides that in the final decision of cases the Court shall give judgment according as the very right of the cause and matter in law shall appear, so as to afford to the parties a complete remedy upon the principles which prevail in equity.

The defendant has paid, in the first instance, in cash, $1,400, and, subsequently, $424, and to the Sheriff $8,850, in all $10.675, and, having acquired a legal title to the whole lot, if the plaintiffs wish to re-possess themselves of the part not conveyed by them to the defendant, they cannot reasonably expect to do so without paying him the difference between his purchase, $7,000, and the amount he has paid, $10,674, that is, $3,675. Whether he could be compelled to accept that sum and convey the lot to the plaintiffs it is not necessary to decide, as he has offered before suit, and is still willing, to take a less sum, and make the conveyance to them. The plaintiffs' charge against the defendant of fraud is unwarranted by anything in the evidence and should not have been made. While the plaintiffs' claim is, in my opinion, most unreasonable and unjust, the effect of it, if allowed, would be to make the defendant pay $5,600 in addition to what he has already paid, $10,675, for the property; that is upwards of $4,000 more than the whole property originally cost the plaintiffs. Coming into a Court of Equity, they should have shewn a disposition to do equity, and they have shewn no disposition, and have failed in establishing any case entitling them to a decree in their favor.

The defendant will be entitled to a decree with costs.

CAFFERY *v.* CAMERON ET AL.

THE defendant, Cameron, agreed to sell to plaintiff a farm in Charlotteburg, Ontario, for $45,000, subject to a mortgage for $14,000. The plaintiff, in consideration, was to assume the $14,000 mortgage, and convey certain gold mining areas and other property to defendant, at the price of $20,000, and for the balance of $11,000 he was to convey to defendant his dwelling house at Truro. The defendant obtained a transfer of the areas under circumstances as to which the affidavits were contradictory; but it was uncontradicted that the title to the real estate which he was to convey to plaintiff was encumbered to the extent of upwards of $15,000 more than had been represented. Plaintiff having obtained an injunction to restrain defendant from working the areas,

Held, that, assuming the statements of the defendant to be true as to the way n which he obtained the transfer, there was a serious question to be submitted to the Court, whether the defendant was justified in recording it and claiming the areas, and that the injunction could not be dissolved.

Held, further, that the injunction would not be disturbed on account of misrepresentations in the affidavits on which it was obtained, unless the case were such that if the facts had been stated accurately, the injunction would have been refused.

RITCHIE, E. J., (October, 1879,) delivered the judgment of the Court :—

The question at present before the Court is simply whether the injunction restraining the defendant, Cameron, from disposing of or in any way encumbering the title to the gold mining areas should be dissolved or remain in force until the hearing. The object and effect of the injunction is merely to preserve the property in dispute *in statu quo* till the case is ready to be heard; and if it is made to appear that there is a real and substantial question to be tried, and that the property ought to be preserved in the meantime, the injunction should continue.

Many of the statements made on the part of the plaintiff have been contradicted on the part of the defendant, Cameron. To these I shall not at present advert; but there are others, and those by no means unimportant, which are uncontradicted. The agreements set out in the writ are admitted, and by them Cameron agreed to sell and convey to the plaintiff his farm at Charlotteburg, in the Province of Ontario, subject to a mortgage of about $14,000, held by one Allan Gilmore, with all the household furniture and effects, (linen, pianoforte, family pictures, and personal wear only excepted,) agricultural implements, and chattels of that nature on the farm, the cows, heifers, bulls and calves, (in all nineteen,) two span of horses and harness, oats, hay, straw, and fodder, potatoes, and pigs, for $45,000. The plaintiff, in consideration, was to assume the Gilmore mortgage, at $14,000, in part payment, and to convey to Cameron the gold mining areas in question, and all tools, apparatus, engines, boilers, crushers, and everything belonging to the plaintiff at the mines, together with the stock of goods in the store there at $20,000, and for the balance of $11,000 he was to convey to the defendant, Cameron, his dwelling house and a lot of land at Truro, with all the furniture, live stock, and effects on the premises, (linen, family pictures, and personal wear only excepted,) and the parties became bound, each to the other, to procure all titles and documents necessary to furnish incontestable titles to the properties agreed to be sold, free and clear of all charges, mortgages, and encumbrances, except as therein referred to, the whole to be finally concluded and ended on or before the 1st October then next, so that all should be settled, titles passed, possession given, and finally concluded before that date. The first of the agreements bore date the 5th September, 1878; the other, which modified or supplied an omission, the 21st of the same month.

There is a contradiction as to the circumstances under which the document to transfer the gold mining areas got into the possession of Cameron, after it had been executed by the plaintiff ; but the former admits that, having obtained it, he caused it to be registered at the Department of Works and Mines, at Halifax, and claims title to them, though he had not performed his terms of agreement in any respect. nor offered to perform them, nor does it appear that he was then, or has since been in a position to do so. The title to the real estate which he undertook to convey to the plaintiff was not only subject to the mortgage to Gilmore, referred to in the agreement, but to a mortgage to the Quebec Bank, for $10,000, and to another to William Ramsay, for $5,000 ; while the personal property which he agreed to convey had been previously conveyed to William Ramsay, in security for $5,000, and shortly before the making of the agreement with the plaintiff, had been mortgaged to Daniel A. Cameron, for $1,200. In addition to this there was, in the hands of the Sheriff, an execution against Cameron at the suit of Ramsay by which any property owned by him was bound. This being the state of the property, real and personal, which the defendant, Cameron, had agreed to convey to the plaintiff in consideration of the transfer of the gold mining areas, there is, in my opinion, a serious question to be submitted to the Court, whether the defendant, Cameron, assuming his statement to be true as to the mode in which he obtained possession of the transfer, was justified in having it recorded, and now claiming to hold the areas as his property, and whether therefore the injunction should remain in force, so as to preserve the property until the ultimate adjudication of the case.

I have not failed to consider the points raised by Cameron's counsel that the injunction should be dissolved on account of the misrepresentation and suppression of material facts by the plaintiff, and that the attempt is now made to sustain it on different grounds from those contained in his writ. The only misrepresentation is a statement of the plaintiff, in his writ, that, up to the time of the preparation of the agreements, Lighthall was an entire stranger to him, though he now admits that such was not the case and asserts that the statement in his writ to that effect was a mistake of his solicitor, arising from the plaintiff's deafness. This may or may not have been the case, yet if a party has obtained an injunction on a mis-statement or suppression of fact, it will on that ground alone be dissolved; but the mis-statement or suppression must be material, presenting a case different from that on which the injunction was granted, where it would not have been granted if a more accurate statement had been made. See *Kerr on Injunctions*, 628. This mistake or mis-statement does not appear to me to be of that character, nor do the grounds on which the plaintiff seeks to sustain his injunction appear to me to be substantially different from those on which it was obtained. It is true that in his writ he asks relief on the ground that a fraudulent representation had been made to him respecting Cameron's title to the properties he undertook to convey to him, but he also stated that as soon as he became aware of the encumbrances on them, he, on that ground, objected to Cameron having possession of the transfer of the mining areas, and to its being recorded and acted upon. There may have been no fraudulent conduct on the part of Lighthall or Hawkes; as to that the evidence is contradictory, and I shall at present pass no opinion upon it, but it is a question open for discussion whether, under the facts admitted, the act of Cameron, in putting the instrument on record when he did, and his now insisting on his right to retain the areas, is not a fraudulent proceeding on his part, and that, and not the fraud of Lighthall or Hawkes, is the material question.

PERLEY ET AL. *v.* SNOW ET AL.

A TESTATOR, by his will, devised and bequeathed his real and personal estate to his wife and another, as executrix and executor, in trust to sell the same and invest the proceeds in the best securities they could obtain, and, upon the coming of age of the testator's children, to divide the money among the children and the widow, in specified proportions. The executor, with the consent and acquiescence of the widow and executrix, loaned a part of the trust funds to merchants engaged in ship-building, who afterwards became insolvent and unable to re-pay the money.

Held, that the trustees were not justified in investing the money on personal security, and must make good the loss to the children; but that the widow could not make her co-trustee liable to her for the loss she might sustain, having acquiesced in the investment.

RITCHIE, E. J., (October, 1879,) delivered the judgment of the Court :—

James E. Perley, by his will, appointed the defendant, Jabesh Snow, and his wife, Emma C. Perley, the executor and executrix, and devised and bequeathed to them all his real and personal estate, in trust to sell the same, and to invest the proceeds *in the best securities they could obtain*, and to pay and apply the interest for the maintenance of his wife and children and the education of the latter; and, on his youngest child attaining the age of twenty-one, in trust to divide the money or securities into three equal shares, and to divide two-thirds among his children, the present plaintiffs, share and share alike; the other share of such money or securities to be held by his said wife to her own use absolutely.

After the death of the testator, the business of his estate was principally managed by Mr. Snow, but not without consultation, from time to time, with Mrs. Perley, all the funds of the estate having been received by him, and the investments made by him, with the exception of about $420 of the principal money, which was received by Mrs. Perley. Whatever interest has been received it is admitted has been faithfully paid over by him in accordance with the trust.

Mr. Snow, in his answer, admits that in the month of July, 1864, he, with the consent of his co-trustee, loaned to Lewis A. Sponagle and Stephen E. Tupper, merchants of Liverpool, on their joint and several note, the sum of $1,600, part of the trust fund. These persons were then in good credit, but in 1873 they became embarrassed in their business, and, when called on to pay the amount due, they were unable to do so, and the only security Mr. Snow could then get was the mortgage of a vessel, which turned out valueless. Both Sponagle and Tupper then were, and have ever since been insolvent, and so much of the trust fund has been lost, which the plaintiffs contend the defendants are liable to make good, so far as they are interested in it.

At the time this suit was commenced, Mr. Snow had in his hands, belonging to the trust, $95.20 in cash, and he was indebted to the fund $1,211.10,—a note of hand then held by his co-trustee. These sums have since been paid into Court, by an order of the Court; in addition to which there were two other investments made by Mr. Snow, for which he must be held liable,—and, indeed, he has recognized his liability for them,—one of them to Albert Graves, for $188.33, the other to John Hogan, for $184.69. Neither of the defendants can be held liable for the amount due the estate by A. G. Campbell. It was a debt incurred in the testator's lifetime, and since his death Campbell has been insolvent.

The investment of the trust fund on the promissory note of Sponagle and Tupper was not justifiable. It should not have been made on personal security at all, and unquestionably should not have been loaned without security to persons engaged in trade, and ship building. The loan was made in the first instance with the concurrence of Mrs. Perley. It is obvious from the correspondence in evidence that she felt it was not a satisfactory investment, and it ought to have been called in long before the parties to the note became insolvent. Previously to the loan the money had been invested on bond and mortgage, and it is not to be credited that such an investment of the money could not have been made between 1864 and 1873 ; and however available the answer of Mr. Snow to Mrs. Perley may be, that she consented to the investment remaining rather than incur the risk of losing interest while remaining uninvested, it can avail nothing as regards the plaintiffs. Mr. Snow seems to have been under the impression that if he obtained the consent of his co-trustee, he was relieved from responsibility. This, at most, could be only as respects her own interest in the fund.

If the will of Mr. Perley had been altogether silent as to the investments and it had been so left to the discretion of the trustees, such a loan as that in question would have been unjustifiable. Here they were required to invest the funds *in the best securities they could obtain*, and there was no reason why they should confine themselves to Liverpool. Investments on good security, by bond and mortgage, are constantly obtainable elsewhere on landed property in town and country.

It may be taken as a general rule that trustees are not justified in lending trust money on personal security unless they have an express authority to do so, and mere general expressions giving a discretionary power as to the investments to be made will not be sufficient. The amount of the trust fund to which the plaintiffs will become entitled on the youngest of them attaining the age of twenty-one must be made good, and, as the defendant, Snow, has, in his answer, expressed his willingness to relinquish his trust, and that another or other trustees should be appointed, and the other defendant has made no defence, the decree will be that the defendants pay into Court such sum as, with that now paid in, will amount to two-thirds of the whole trust fund which came to their hands, and that one or more trustees be appointed in place of the present trustees, by whom the amount shall be invested, in accordance with the terms of the will of James E. Perley, deceased, in trust, to divide the same among his children, the plaintiffs, share and share alike, on the youngest attaining the age of twenty-one, and, in the meantime, to pay and apply the interest arising from such investments for the maintenance of his wife and children and the education of his children as specified in his will. The plaintiffs are entitled to their costs.

The judgment I have just given embraces all that was directly before the Court in this suit, but as I am requested, on the part of the defendants, in order to prevent further litigation, to give my opinion as to the liability of Mr. Snow to make good to his co-trustee, Mrs. Perley, the loss occasioned to her by the loan to Sponagle and Tupper, and the parties have agreed to the necessary amendment of the pleading, I will do so. The evidence shows that Mrs. Perley was consulted as to the investment in the first instance and allowed it to be made, and, though apparently doubtful of its propriety, consented to its continuance. She cannot now make her co-trustee liable for the loss she may sustain by it. It has been settled by a series of decisions that where a *cestui que trust, sui juris*, acquiesces in an improper investment, he cannot afterwards call it in question. *Brice* v. *Stokes*, 11 Ves., 319, is a leading case on the question. Lord ELDON there held that if a particular *cestui que trust* has authorized an investment on personal security and permitted it to continue, in a question between him and the trustee the latter will not be held responsible to him for a loss, so far as his interest in the fund is concerned. In *Booth* v. *Booth*, 1 Beav., 130, the Master of the Rolls said ; " I am of opinion, on the authorities and on the established rule of this Court, that a trustee who stands by and sees a breach of trust committed by his co-trustee, becomes responsible for that breach of trust." And again in *Walker* v. *Symonds*, 3 Swans., 64, the Lord Chancellor said ; " It is established by all the cases that if the *cestui que trust* joins with the trustee in that which is a breach of trust, knowing the circumstances, such a *cestui que trust* can never complain of such a breach of trust. I go further, and agree that either concurrence or acquiescence without original concurrence will release the trustee." In this case Mrs. Perley's control over the trust fund was the same as Mr. Snow's and she could have prevented the loss if she had refused her sanction to the loan, or had subsequently required the money to be called in before the failure of Sponagle and Tupper.

FAWSON *v.* NOONAN.

PLAINTIFF and defendant entered into a contract to fish, each in a distinct berth, and each party finding his own seine, boat, and fishing gear. The evidence was conflicting as to the contemplated duration of the agreement, but the Court arrived at the conclusion that it was confined to the taking of a school of fish in each berth. Evidence was given as to the meaning of the term school, as used in such contracts, but it was vague and contradictory and such as to oblige the Court to construe the agreement independently of any alleged usage. Defendant caught fourteen barrels of mackerel in his berth of which he gave plaintiff seven, and plaintiff, shortly after, caught ten barrels in his berth of which he gave defendant five. Plaintiff then abandoned his berth and went elsewhere to fish, and never returned to it. Defendant, in his berth, caught two hundred and fifty barrels, of which plaintiff claimed half.

Held, that the plaintiff was not entitled to participate in the defendant's catch of fish.

RITCHIE, E. J., (December, 1879,) delivered the judgment of the Court :—

The plaintiff, in his writ, sets out that the defendant, in the fishing season of 1875, had the exclusive right to fish, in turn with certain other fishermen, at Prospect, in two berths on that coast, which right was to last until he had caught not less than twenty barrels in each of the berths; and the plaintiff was the proprietor of a seine or net, and was an experienced fisherman, accustomed to fish in such berths, and it was agreed between them that they should enter into partnership and combine their skill and experience during the time the defendant had the right to fish in the berths, and that the plaintiff should, with his seine, fish one of the berths known as that back of Duck Island Point, and the defendant the berth known as Reef Redmond's Island berth, and that all fish caught by each of them should be divided equally between them as they were taken; that they proceeded to fish according to this arrangement, and soon the defendant caught fourteen barrels of mackerel in the berth fished by him seven of which he at once delivered to the plaintiff, and, on or about the same time, the plaintiff caught ten barrels in his berth, five of which he at once delivered to the defendant; that no other fish were caught by either of them until early in the month of October, when the defendant caught, in his berth, about two hundred and sixty barrels of mackerel, of which the defendant has refused to give the plaintiff his share; and he prays that defendant may be decreed to deliver to the plaintiff his share of the fish, or to account therefor, and that he should in the meantime be enjoined from disposing of them.

The defendant, in his answer, denies that there was an agreement between himself and the plaintiff to enter into such a partnership as stated by the plaintiff, and says that the only agreement entered into between them was an agreement made in the month of August in the terms following, viz., that the plaintiff and defendant should employ their respective seines, and seine boats, and other fishing gear in the two berths; that the plaintiff, with his seine and boat, should occupy, watch, and fish the berth at the back of Duck Island Point, and the defendant should occupy, watch, and fish the other berth at Redmond Reef, and all fish caught by and at the two berths should be equally divided between them, and that the venture should exist and continue till one school of fish should be caught by the plaintiff at the berth occupied by him, and until the defendant should take one school at that occupied by him, and no longer; in pursuance of which agreement each party occupied his respective berth, and, almost immediately after, each of them caught a school of fish in their respective berths, being the catches of fourteen and ten barrels referred to in the plaintiff's writ, which were divided, as there alleged, and thereupon their agreement was fulfilled, and the venture between them ceased. And the defendant, in his answer, further alleges that after the two catches were made the plaintiff left the berth at Duck Island Point, and, with his seine boat, seine, and other fishing gear, went to Lower Prospect, and allowed others to fish in that berth and made arrangements with another party to fish with his seine at Lower Prospect and subsequently, on his return to Prospect, entered into an agreement with two other men to go with them on a fishing venture, with his seine boat, seine, and fishing gear to Halifax Bay, which was carried out, and that after his return from that venture, he, in conjunction with another person, caught upwards of forty barrels of fish, none of which he offered to divide with the defendant; and that from the time the plaintiff left the berth at Duck Island Point he never returned there but purposely ceased and abstained from fishing or watching the berth; that it is true that plaintiff did make a catch of about two hundred and fifty barrels of mackerel, but the whole of it was made with the assistance of one Thomas Noonan after the agreement between the plaintiff and defendant had been fulfilled, and the defendant submits that even if the agreement had been as set out in the plaintiff's writ, the latter had failed to carry out the terms of it on his part, and would, therefore, not be entitled to the relief he seeks.

The evidence as to the terms of the agreement is somewhat contradictory. The plaintiff, in his evidence, says; " The defendant and I agreed on a partnership. We were partners *in the first two schools of fish, one on his berth and one on mine.* Each of us had the berth till twenty barrels were hauled. When that quantity was hauled it put us out of the berth. Any over two barrels is a school, as I believe. I am not quite sure. The partnership was entered into in the presence of defendant's brother, Thomas Noonan, and the crews of the two boats. Stephen Shea and John Mosher were my crew." In his cross-examination he said; " When we draw for berths the fishing regulations are that the berth is retained until twenty barrels are caught, *no matter how many schools they are got in.*" Shea's evidence is that "defendant asked plaintiff if he would join him. He said, 'yes.' Defendant said: '*For two schools;*' and he told plaintiff to tell him *till two berths were put out. Plaintiff asked if it would be till the two berths were put out, and defendant said,* '*yes.*' He said he was sharesman with plaintiff, and had an interest in his success. Both he and Mosher have an interest. Plaintiff owned a seine. They both joined him for the whole season."

The defendant, in his evidence, states that he and plaintiff made an arrangement about fishing in the fall of 1875, he having two tickets for fishing berths. Plaintiff was to watch the berth at Duck Island, and he was to watch that at Reef of Redmond Island. He said to plaintiff; "*Jim, the joining is to be only for two schools.*" *Plaintiff said*; "*All right.*" His brother, Tom, then spoke up, and said ; "Jim, you have to watch the berth at Duck Island, and Timothy has to watch that at Redmond Reef." Then they parted. The defendant and his brother Tom fished together on shares. Thomas Noonan says that the bargain was that the plaintiff should watch the berth at Duck Island, and the defendant that at Redmond Reef. *They agreed upon that for two schools.* The defendant said ; "*For two schools, Jim.*" *The plaintiff said ;* "*All right.*" John Noonan, another brother of the defendant, says that he was present at the agreement, and that plaintiff was to tend the berth at Duck Island, and defendant that at Redmond Reef, *only for two schools.*"

I have no hesitation in coming to the conclusion that the agreement entered into between the parties was confined to taking a school of fish in each berth. The plaintiff himself says that was the language used, though the inference he said he drew was that the agreement was to be in force as long as the defendant's right to the berths lasted. An attempt was made to show that among the fishermen of the neighbourhood all that could be taken from a berth until the right was exhausted was known as a school, and what was the construction put upon such agreements by them. A contract may be affected by proof of the existence of a custom or usage, as where words used by the parties have, by known usage, by local custom, or among particular classes, acquired a meaning different from the general one, such evidence may be resorted to in order to ascertain their intention. Or if there has been a recognized practice with reference to the transaction out of which the contract arose in such cases the parties may be supposed to have assumed the existence of the practice and to have used the words as understood in the locality. But the usage and practice must be general and certain, not depending on the judgment and opinion of witnesses, but the fact of their existence must be clearly established, so that both parties must be presumed to have been cognizant of them, and to have made their contract with reference to them. It is enough to say that there is no such evidence here. All that we have on the subject is vague, uncertain, contradictory and unsatisfactory; the general effect of it being that no such usage or practice existed. The contract, therefore, must be viewed independently of any usage or practice, and, taking the language used in making it in its natural meaning, it had ceased to be in operation before the defendant had taken the two hundred and fifty barrels, and therefore the plaintiff can have no right to any part of them. I may remark that a " school of fish " is not a term merely in use at Prospect or its neighbourhood. It, or a shoal of fish, is in use generally among fishermen as indicating a multitude or an undefined quantity of fish together. This meaning the plaintiff must have attached to the term when he said that he considered two or more barrels constituted, in his judgment, a school, and it does appear to me that, by his abandoning the berth and going elsewhere to fish with other men, taking with him his seine-boat, and fishing gear, after the two schools of fish had been taken in the berths, the plaintiff shewed that, in his view, his contract with the defendant was at an end. If, however, the contract had been as contended for by the plaintiff, I do not see how he could hope to succeed, as he had failed to perform his part of the agreement. It was assumed that by the contract the plaintiff and defendant were to be partners,—to be governed by the law relating to partnership. I do not know that if they were to be considered as such it would make much difference. I cannot think, however, that they were, properly speaking, partners. Under the agreement each had to find his own boat, seine, and crew, and whatever fishing gear was required, at his own expense, for which the other was in no way responsible. If no fish were caught he was to bear his own loss, irrespective of the other ; and, in performing his part of the agreement, he became entitled to have delivered to him one-half of the fish caught in each berth. Such an arrangement comes under no definition of a partnership that I am aware of.

That the plaintiff failed to perfect his part of such an agreement as he contends existed is clear from the evidence on both sides ; for, from whatever cause, whether from considering the contract at an end, or from thinking his prospect of getting fish there no sufficient inducement for him to persevere, he left his berth and never returned to it, having entered into other arrangements, with other parties, to engage in fishing in other bays, taking with him all his fishing gear, seine, &c., and, having thus failed to perform his part of the bargain, with what reason can he ask the Court to decree that the defendant should be held to be bound by it, so as to enable him to participate in fish taken by the defendant after he himself had openly abandoned the performance of the contract ? Such a contract may be rescinded by mutual consent or by such a breach of it by one party as entitles the other to rescind or treat is as rescinded. If this suit had been brought at common law,—and it appears to me that would have been the proper tribunal,—the plaintiff would have had to aver in his pleadings, and shew by evidence that he had performed his part of the agreement, before he could succeed.

That he was not entitled to participate in the catch of fish taken by the defendant after he had left his berth, the plaintiff, it seems to me, well knew, for he was present when the two hundred and fifty barrels were enclosed in the defendant's seine, and, though they were in jeopardy from the weakness of it so as to require the use of another seine to secure them, he neither offered his own services, nor the use of his own seine, but allowed another man to furnish a seine and afford the necessary assistance without objection, and, at the time, neither indicated by word nor by act that he had any interest in the catch or concern in having them secured. I cannot but think that his subsequent claim to participate in the fish taken was an afterthought to which he was tempted by the large number of fish taken.

In every view that can be taken of the case the plaintiff has, I think, failed to shew a right to the relief he seeks. The decree must therefore be for the defendant, with costs.

THE WINDSOR AND ANNAPOLIS RAILWAY CO.

v.

THE WESTERN COUNTIES RAILWAY CO.

On the hearing of this cause on the evidence, an objection was taken on behalf of the Attorney General, of Canada, that the agreement of September, 1871, *(ante* p. 287) was not binding on the Dominion Government, because the railroad from Halifax to Windsor was a Provincial public work, and as such passed to the Dominion Government under the B. N. A. Act, not as ordinary Government property, but subject to a trust which the Government was bound strictly to fulfil and which required that it should be worked for the public benefit, in accordance with the terms of the Act under which it was built and subject to the engagements which had been entered into by the Provincial Government and Legislature; and that the terms of the agreement did not carry out this trust, as by the provisions of the Provincial Act of 1867, embodying the contract between the Government and the promoters of the plaintiff company, it was mutually agreed that, prior to the opening of the road, a traffic arrangement should be made for the mutual use by the Government and the Company of their respective lines, which stipulation had not been carried out in the agreement, as there was no provision in it for a traffic arrangement.

Held, that the agreement embodied all the essential provisions of the original contract, and that the Government not having insisted on having running powers over plaintiffs' road was no reason why plaintiffs should be deprived of running powers over the Halifax and Windsor line; but, that, on the other hand, the ground stated applied with great force to the action of the Dominion Legislature, under the Act of 1874, inasmuch as the Dominion Government having taken the road, under the provisions of an Imperial Act, clothed with a trust, the Dominion Legislature was thereby restrained from acting in violation of that trust.

RITCHIE, E. J., (March 1st, 1880,) delivered the judgment of the Court :—

When this cause was argued on the demurrer the statements in the plaintiffs' writ were assumed to be true, and, judgment having been then given for the plaintiffs, it is for the defendants to shew that the facts, as they now appear in evidence, lead to a different conclusion.

The defendants' counsel contend that the evidence shews such an acquiescence on the part of the plaintiffs in the action of the government in the cancellation of the agreement of 22nd September, 1871, that they are now estopped from raising any objection to it. After carefully considering the evidence, I can see nothing to lead to such an inference. What is relied on in support of this contention is that, after the first indication of an intention on the part of the government to transfer the Windsor Branch in October, 1873, negotiations took place between parties connected with the two companies for an amicable arrangement of the difficulty which had arisen.

Mr. Killam, Mr. Doane and Mr. Bingay testify as to what took place between them and defendants, and Mr. Killam speaks of conferences he had with the directors of the plaintiff company in London. In none of these interviews is it alleged that the plaintiffs, or Mr. DePass on their behalf, assuming that he had authority to do so, abandoned their legal rights under their agreement with the government otherwise than by their endeavour to effect an amicable arrangement with the defendant company.

Mr. Reynolds, who, at the time of the passing of the order-in-council of 22nd October, 1873, was acting for the plaintiff company, and the only person then authorized to act for them, stated to the Minister of Public Works that the company would oppose the transfer of the Windsor Branch to the defendant company in every possible way; and he alleges that he never, in any manner, acquiesced in the action of the government, nor admitted the right of the government to make the order, and that, under instructions from the company, he, through Mr. Mackenzie, presented a petition to the Governor-General on the subject on the 10th December following. Indeed, all the authority Mr. Reynolds had with respect to the transfer of the line was to oppose and protest against it.

In June, 1874, Mr. DePass was appointed the agent of the company to negotiate with the government or the defendant company, with no authority to settle anything definitely, as whatever he did was to be subject to the approval of the board of directors ; and he states positively that he never did acquiesce in the cancellation of the agreemcnt of September, 1871, that he had no power to do so, and that the plaintiff company never, to his knowledge, acquiesced, but, on the contrary, always opposed it ; and Mr. Killam does not pretend that, in his interviews with the directors of the company, they recognizcd the cancellation of the agreement.

Up to June, 1875, when the new agreement was entered into with the government, it is obvious from the evidence that the plaintiff company were seeking to be re-invested in their rights, either through the action of the government or by an arrangement with the defendant company, and, if that object were attained, it would be unimportant to them through which of them. Both Mr. Langevin and Mr. Mackenzie, while Ministers of Public Works, advised them to arrange the difficulty, if possible, with the defendant company, and this advice, it appears to me, it was judicious for them to follow, and it could be followed, in my opinion, without its affecting their legal rights in case of failure. The attempt did fail, and in June, 1875, the new agreement was entered into, in which, among other things, the validity of the previous agreement was recognized by the government.

. There was an objection taken by Mr. Lash, on behalf of the Attorney-General of Canada, now a party to the suit, which was much relied on by him, and which, as it had not been urged before, should be referred to. He contended that the agreement of September, 1871, was not binding on the Dominion Government,—was, in fact, invalid,—and the plaintiff company acquired no rights under it. It is somewhat remarkable that such an objection should emanate from the government, as that agreement is admitted to have been made in good faith, to have been executed on behalf of Her Majesty and approved and ratified by the Governor-Generalin-Council, under no misapprehension, and acted upon by both parties, and its validity was never called in question till now. The ground of this objection is that the railroad from Halifax to Windsor was a public provincial work, and as such passed to the Dominion Government, under the terms of the British North America Act, not as ordinary government property, but subject to a trust, which it was bound strictly to fulfil, which required that it should be worked for the public benefit in accordance with the terms of the act under which it was built and subject to the engagements which had been entered into by the Provincial Government and Legislature. And the contention of the learned counsel is that the terms of the agreement do not carry out the trust, inasmuch as by the provisions of the Provincial Act of 1867, which incorporated the plaintiff company and confirmed the contract which had been entered into between the Provincial Government and the promoters of the company, it was mutually agreed that, prior to the opening of the road, a traffic arrangement should be made *for the mutual use and employment of their respective lines of railway between Windsor and Halifax and Windsor and Annapolis, including running powers for the joint operation thereof on equitable terms*, which stipulation, it was contended, had not been carried out in the agreement, because there was no provision in it for a traffic arrangement over both lines or for the mutual use of the respective lines.

When the agreement of 1865 was entered into, it was with a view of encouraging the construction of the railroad from Windsor to Annapolis. The government might or might not insist on having running powers over the plaintiffs' road, but this not having been required was no reason why the plaintiffs should be deprived of running powers over the Halifax and Windsor line. The original agreement was a pledge that if they would build the road certain privileges should be conceded to them, and the pledge so given by the Local Legislature was recognized and carried out by the Dominion Government in this agreement to the satisfaction of all parties; and it appears to me it embraced all the essential provisions of the original contract. The carriage of Her Majesty's troops and mails had been provided for; an arrangement had been made for traffic over the government road, and the company engaged to pay one-third of the gross earnings over it, while the interests of the public were subserved by the stipulation that the company should run every day, except Sunday, not less than two trains over it, and that tolls should not be increased without the sanction of the government. I think, therefore, that this objection cannot be sustained. But while such an objection ought not, for these reasons, to avail the government as regards the agreement of 1871, the ground on which it was attempted to be sustained applies with great force to the action of the Dominion Legislature in passing the Act of 1874, and to the order-in-council referred to in it, for, as the Dominion Government took the railroad from the Provincial Government under the British North America Act, clothed with a trust which the former was bound to carry out, the Dominion Legislature was restrained from acting in violation of it. Mr. Lash argued that the power of the Dominion Legislature was supreme in the matter, but the contract, so to speak, between the Dominion and the Province, under which the transfer took place, was by the Act of the Imperial Parliament, to which both the Dominion and Local Legislatures are subordinate, and if a limited right only was conferred by that Act on the Dominion Government, the Dominion Legislature cannot enlarge it.

All the other arguments relied on were the same as those adduced at the hearing of the demurrer and were referred to rather than repeated, and as they are dealt with in the judgments already given, which have since been reported, (ante p. 287) to which I still adhere, it is not necessary for me to do more than refer to those reports, as shewing the grounds of my judgment on the points there taken. While Mr. Mackenzie, in his evidence, recognizes the fact that the agreement of 1871 was ratified by that of 1875, he asserts that it was done through inadvertence on his part. But the plaintiffs had no reason to assume that this was the case, and the latter agreement gave no more than they had been all along contending for, and, to affect the validity of the agreement, the mistake must have been shewn to have been mutual. It now appears from the evidence that what was assumed to be true on the argument of the demurrer, that there was no foundation for the statement in the Minute of Council of 22nd October, 1873, that the plaintiffs had failed to operate the Windsor Branch, and which was made the ground of divesting them of it, was in fact so. The Minister of Public Works who made the report to the government to that effect must have been misinformed, and this, we may reasonably conclude, has led to all the difficulty which has arisen.

After having given the fullest consideration to the whole case, I am of opinion that the plaintiffs are entitled to the judgment of the Court in their favor, with costs.

GRANT *v.* WHEELER ET AL.

DEFENDANTS, being added parties, resisted a proceeding taken by plaintiff, as assignee of a mortgage, to foreclose the same, on the ground that the mortgage was made in contemplation of insolvency, and was void under the Insolvent Act,—the mortgagee having afterwards become insolvent and assigned under the Act.

Held, that, defendants, seeking as creditors of the insolvent, to impeach the mortgage, solely on the ground that it was in contravention of the Insolvent Act, should have called on the assignee to take proceedings to set it aside, and, upon his refusal, should have applied to the Judge for leave to proceed in his name; and, further, that defendants should have proved their claims in order to entitle them so to proceed.

Q. Whether the defendants could contest the validity of the mortgage at all, without bringing a cross action.

RITCHIE, E. J., (September 20th, 1880,) delivered the judgment of the Court :—

This suit was brought to foreclose a mortgage made by Edwin W. Wheeler, Franklin McLeod, and James Burkett, and their wives, to Robert Taylor, to secure the payment of $12,000. Subsequently the mortgagors, Wheeler, McLeod, and Burkett, became insolvent, and Taylor was appointed assignee of their estate and effects, and the mortgage was by him assigned to the plaintiff. The mortgage bore date the 25th of August, 1873, and was recorded on the 28th of the same month. The defendants did not appear to defend the suit, and judgment by default was entered against them. Thereupon the following persons applied to be made parties, defendants, and to defend the suit, as they were interested as judgment creditors, whose judgments were recorded, and formed a lien on the land sought to be foreclosed, viz., James Robertson, The S. A. Wood Manufacturing Company, John Stewart, and Charles and Willoughby Anderson. And in their answer they admit the making of the mortgage by the original defendants, and the registration of it, as set out in the writ, but they aver that they were traders under the name of E. W. Wheeler & Co., and, the firm being indebted to the added defendants, as well as to numerous other parties, and among the rest to Robert Taylor, Peter Grant, and Rumsey, Ruel & Co., the mortgage was made to Robert Taylor, but for the benefit of himself and Peter Grant and Rumsey, Ruel & Co.; the property comprised in the mortgage being all the real estate possessed by the firm, and including the premises whereon their mills and other buildings were erected, the same being subject to certain judgments entered and recorded, as set out in the plaintiff's writ, and that when the mortgage was so given they were unable to meet their liabilities and were insolvent within the meaning of the insolvent law, and that the mortgage was made in contemplation of insolvency, by way of security for payment to Taylor, Grant, and Rumsey Ruel & Co., who will thereby obtain an unjust preference over the other creditors of E. W. Wheeler & Co., and that the mortgage is therefore void and contrary to the provisions of the Insolvent Act of 1869, and that the mortgage was so made with intent fraudulently to impede, obstruct, and delay the creditors of E. W. Wheeler & Co., in their remedies against them, or with intent to defraud their other creditors, and was so done and intended with the knowledge of Taylor, Grant, and Rumsey, Ruel & Co., and it has had that effect, by reason of which the mortgage is void. And they aver that the assignment of the mortgage to the plaintiff was without consideration, and that they are judgment creditors of E. W. Wheeler & Co., whose judgments were duly registered to bind their land, but were so registered subsequent to their assignment under the Insolvent Act of 1869. And they pray that the mortgage, and the assignment of it, may be decreed to be null and void, and that Taylor do execute a release of it, and that the plaintiff's bill be dismissed, with costs.

It occurred to me at the hearing, and I then suggested to the counsel, that if a mortgage was liable to be impeached on such grounds, the proper course was to have instituted a cross suit, and not to attempt to impeach it as defendants in a foreclosure suit; but whether this course was open to these

defendants or not, they are certainly in no better position
than if they had proceeded by bill as plaintiffs.

The defendants call in question the validity of the mortgage
solely on the ground that it was made in violation of the
Insolvent Act and in contravention of the rights of the
creditors of the insolvents, and the allegations in their answer
are such as would have been contained in a bill to set it aside
by the assignee of the insolvent, and their prayer is the same.
It is objected on the part of the plaintiff that no right exists
in the defendants, or in any of the creditors of the insolvents,
either directly or indirectly, to call in question the validity of
the mortgage, or to seek to invalidate it, as the Insolvent Act
provides that the assignee, in his own name, as such, shall
have the exclusive right to sue for the rescinding of deeds
made in fraud of creditors, who is also authorized to intervene
and represent the insolvent in any suits brought by or against
him. In no case can a creditor take any proceedings to effect
such an object in his own name, and only when the asssignee
refuses to take proceedings which creditors think would be
for the benefit of the estate, may they do so on their obtaining
an order of that Judge to that effect. But even then they must
be taken in the name of the assignee, though for the benefit and
at the expense of such creditors. If, therefore, these defendants
are creditors under the Insolvent Act, they should have called
on the assignee to take steps to have the mortgage set aside,
and, if he had refused, should have applied to the Judge for
leave to proceed in his name for their benefit. If they were
not creditors under the act, they had no right to call into
operation any of its provisions. The definition of a creditor
given in the act is *a person to whom the insolvent is liable,
who shall have proved his claim against the estate of the
insolvent in the manner provided by the act.* And none of
these defendants have proved their claims; so that they can
insist on no other grounds for setting aside the mortgage than
such, if any, as are independent of the Insolvent Act, and none
other than those under the act have been suggested. As this
objection must, I think, prevail, I have not thought it advisable
to consider or give any opinion whether or not the provisions
of the Insolvent Act have been violated. And as regards the

right of parties, defendants in a foreclosure suit, to seek to invalidate the mortgage, I would refer to *Eddleston* v. *Collins*, 3 D. M. & G., 16 ; and *Jacobs* v. *Richards*, 18 Beav., 300. In the former Lord Justice TURNER said; " The applicants attempted to impeach the security upon the evidence taken in the cause, but they are defendants, and I feel great doubt whether it is competent to them to do so. The plaintiff's security I must now assume well created by deed, and I rather apprehend that such a security, if impeached at all, must be impeached by cross bill. The security is good till impeached, and to allow the defendant to impeach it by her answer would be to make a decree in favor of the defendant upon the application of the plaintiff. The objection to decreeing relief upon the answers of defendants is perhaps founded on deeper reasons than may, at first sight, appear." In the latter the defence was that the mortgage was invalid, having been executed by a lunatic. The Master of the Rolls said ; " Where a deed, *prima facie* good at law, is brought before this Court, it acts upon it till it is set aside, and it does not give to *a defendant* active relief." Both were cases of foreclosure. And the Courts of the United States appear to have taken the same view. It is distinctly laid down in *Story's Eq. Pl.*, section 394, 8th edition, that a mortgage will not be reformed upon the answer of the defendants. It can only be done upon a cross bill. If, indeed, a mortgage could be shewn to have been void as between the parties to it, so as in fact not to have been the deed of the mortgagor, it would be a good ground for refusing a foreclosure and sale of the property.

In the present case, however, my judgment is based on the ground that the parties defending have entirely failed in establishing a right to the relief they ask for in their answer, and they would have been equally disentitled to the relief if they had sought it as plaintiffs in a cross bill.

The decree will be for the plaintiff for foreclosure, with costs.

BARTON ET AL. *v.* BALDWIN.

In January, 1879, plaintiffs obtained a rule setting aside defendant's demurrer with costs, and in July of that year the suit terminated by a decree in favor of defendant, with costs. Previous to this decree the defendant became entitled, on the common law side of the Court, to a bill of costs against McClelland, who was the real party in this suit, the other plaintiff being merely a nominal party to the suit. The costs on the decree in favor of the defendant in the suit first mentioned were paid in full by McClelland, who did not apply to have the costs due him on the rule set off or deducted, and, McClelland having died, plaintiffs' attorney entered a suggestion and issued execution for the bill of costs on the rule to set aside the demurrer.

Held, that defendant was entitled to have the costs in the common law suit set off against the costs on the rule, although there was a nominal party in the suit brought in this Court who was not a party in the common law suit.

Q. Whether the cause of action survived to the nominal plaintiff, within the meaning of R. S., cap. 94, sec. 103.

RITCHIE, E. J., (September 20th, 1880,) delivered the judgment of the Court :—

On the 17th May last the defendant obtained a rule *nisi* to set aside a suggestion of the death of McClelland, one of the plaintiffs, and an execution taken out by the plaintiffs' attorney to recover the amount of a bill of costs due on a rule of this Court, made on the 27th January, 1879, setting aside a demurrer of the defendant. On the 14th July of that year the suit terminated by a decree in favor of the defendant, with costs; and, though the costs on the rule setting aside the demurrer were unpaid, McClelland, who was the real plaintiff in the suit, paid the costs on the decree in full. Some time after McClelland died, and on the 6th April last, Mr. Bligh, the plaintiffs' attorney, filed the suggestion and issued the execution.

Previous to the decree in this suit, the defendant, in a cause on the common law side of the Court, became entitled to costs against McClelland, which have never been paid. These costs were taxed at $62.15; those on the first-mentioned rule at $61.95.

When McClelland paid the costs to the defendant on the decree, he made no application to have the costs due him on the rule set off or deducted, and no application was made for payment by McClelland in his lifetime.

In support of the rule *nisi* the defendant contends that the bill of costs for $61.95 due by the defendant should be set off against the amount due him by McClelland, and that Mr. Bligh had no right to file the suggestion and take out the execution, and, at all events, not without the leave of the Court.

Mr. Ervin, the attorney of the defendant, in his affidavit, says that it was agreed between Mr. Bligh and himself that these bills of costs should be set off, the one against the other, and that, at his suggestion, he applied for and obtained from McClelland the costs on the decree, and heard nothing of any claim for payment of the costs on the rule till after the death of McClelland; that he was informed by Barton, the other plaintiff, that he had not instructed the execution to be issued, and that he was not aware of its having been issued, and had a full release and discharge from Mr. Bligh for any costs in respect of this suit; that Barton was a mere nominal party to the suit, having no interest whatever in the result. Mr. Bligh, in his affidavit in answer to that of Mr. Ervin, denies that any such agreement was made by him. But he does not deny that the only real party plaintiff in the suit was McClelland, as, indeed, was shewn clearly to be the case by the evidence. Nor does he assert that he had any authority for taking the proceedings sought to be set aside.

Mr. Bligh having positively denied the existence of any agreement, the question arises whether, independently of any agreement, he was justified in taking those proceedings, and whether the defendant has the right, as he now claims, of having the bill of costs due by McClelland set off against that due him by McClelland.

It was conceded that where costs are payable and receivable by the same party, the Court would, as a general rule, direct them to be set off one against the other, but that this would not be done where the costs were incurred in different actions in different Courts, or in suits where the parties were not identical, or where the effect would be to deprive the attorney of his recourse on the defendant.

It cannot be said that these costs have become payable in different courts. The Supreme Court embraces both a common

10*p*

law and equity side, and this cause, though finally decided on the equity side, was originally brought on the common law side, and was transferred at the instance of the plaintiffs, on the ground that equitable issues were raised by the pleadings and that it would conduce to the ends of justice that it should be heard here. And the statute regulating the procedure in equity provides that the common law practice, so far as it is applicable, shall be observed in equity suits. A long course of decisions has established that costs in one suit may be set off against costs due in another, even though it may enure to the injury of the attorney. I will only refer to one or two of the cases more immediately applicable. In *Emdin* v. *Darby*, 1 B. & P., (N. R.,) 22, application was made to set off costs in that action, in which the plaintiff had been nonsuited, against certain costs due from the defendant to the plaintiff, incurred by the former in removing an indictment preferred against him by the latter from the Quarter Sessions to the King's Bench, in which the defendant was not convicted. Opposition was made on the ground that the attorney would lose the only security he had for the payment of his costs in the action. But the Court observed that such a circumstance could not be allowed to interfere with the equitable arrangement of costs between the parties, and that, as the attorney acts upon the credit of his client, and has his personal security for his costs, the Courts always allowed applications of that kind. *Bourne* v. *Bennett*, 4 Bing., 432, shews that it is by no means necessary that the parties in the several suits should be identical. I cannot, however, view the parties in these suits as other than identical. Barton had no interest whatever in the suit in which he was made a party, or in the subject matter of it, and the benefit in the case of success would have enured solely to McClelland. I do not wish it to be understood that where costs are incurred in different Courts, a set-off would necessarily, on that account, be disallowed,—this Court following, as it does, the common law practice. In *Webb* v. *Nicholas*, 4 Bing., 16, costs in a suit in equity were allowed to be set off against costs of an action at common law. But that question does not, in my opinion, arise in the present case.

Having arrived at the conclusion that the defendant has a right to have the costs due him set off against those due by him to McClelland, it is hardly necessary to consider whether the course adopted by Mr. Bligh in filing the suggestion and taking out the execution was regular. Mr. Bligh relies on the 103rd section of the Practice Act, which enacts that if there be two or more plaintiffs or defendants, and one or more of them die, *if the cause of such action shall survive to the surviving plaintiff or plaintiffs*, the action shall not be thereby abated but such death being suggested on the record the action shall proceed at the suit of the surviving plaintiff or plaintiffs. But the cause of action in this case could not survive to Barton. He neither had nor did he claim to have any interest whatever in the suit. Whatever interest he might have had in the subject matter of it, he had, before the suit was commenced, transferred and assigned to McClelland, in whose favor alone a decree could have been made if the suit had been successful. And if McClelland had died before the decree, there would have been no pretence for asking for a decree in favor of Barton as surviving plaintiff.

The suit having terminated, if an execution could have been taken out, the 189th section of the act directs the course to be pursued where it becomes necessary, by lapse of time, or from a change by death, or otherwise of the party entitled or liable to execution. The party desiring the execution may obtain leave to enter a suggestion, but there is no authority for his making the suggestion without leave, and such leave is not granted as a matter of course nor *ex parte*. The suggestion and execution must therefore be set aside, as having been made and issued irregularly, with costs.

LYNCH *v.* O'BRIEN.

A CAUSE was referred to a Master to ascertain what amount was due on a judgment upon which plaintiff had issued execution, directing the Sheriff to levy for $454. The Master reported only $62 due, and exceptions being taken to the report, it was, after argument, confirmed.

Held, that defendant was entitled to the costs of the reference, although plaintiff did not, at the time of issuing the execution, know what amount was due, in consequence of payments having been made to his attorney, who had left the province.

The plaintiff obtained a judgment against the defendant, and issued an execution, after a number of payments had been made. The defendant denied that the amount for which the sheriff was directed to levy was due, and the matter was referred to a Master to report. Exception was taken to the report of the Master, and on June 14th, 1880, RITCHIE, E. J., delivered judgment, as follows :—

The only exception taken to the report of the Master is that, in consequence of the uncertainty of the evidence as to the time some of the payments were made by the defendant, he computed the interest on what he considered was a fair average, and in my opinion he was justified in doing so. I have carefully considered the evidence, and it appears to me that the average taken by the Master is more favorable to the plaintiff than to the defendant. The only evidence as to the times of payments making up the $1,200, which is the only amount to which the exception relates, is that of the defendant. He says the first payment was in January, 1874, of $140 or $150; the second about the first of April, of $250; the next about the last of April or first of May; and the last payment of the $1,200 was made about the first of June. He does not remember the exact dates of these payments but states them according to his recollection, and there were no better data for the Master to go by; and if he had computed the interest on the basis of these times of payment, as he would have been justified in doing, the amount to which the plaintiff would have been entitled would be less than the sum reported to be due him by the Master. The exception must, therefore, be overruled, and the report confirmed.

The question of costs, not having been determined, was afterwards argued.

RITCHIE, E. J., (October 25th, 1880,) delivered the judgment of the Court :—

The plaintiff, having obtained a judgment against the defendant, on which several payments had been made, issued an execution, with directions to levy for $454.50 and sheriff's fees. The defendant denied that there was then so much due and it was referred to Mr. William Twining to ascertain and report what amount, if any, was due beyond the sum then in the hands of the sheriff, the costs of the motion and reference to abide the order of the Court, or a Judge thereof; the $250 in the hands of the sheriff to be paid to Messrs. Meagher and Chisholm, acting for the plaintiff; $100 to be held by them to abide the result of the reference, and subject to the order of the Court or a Judge.

Mr. Twining, the Master, reported that on the 9th March last there was due $62.30. Exceptions having been taken to this report by the plaintiff, it was, after argument, confirmed, the only question remaining undecided being the costs. And as the reference became necessary from the plaintiff having issued execution and directed a levy for more than was due on the judgment, the costs of the reference should be paid by him. It is objected that he did not know how much was due, as money had been paid to his attorney, Coombes, who had not paid it over, and had left the province. That was his misfortune, but did not justify his demanding from the defendant more than the balance due by him. The defendant having failed in sustaining his exceptions to the report, the plaintiff is entitled to his costs in respect to them.

Mr. Meagher contended that the examination of the plaintiff in the United States was rendered necessary by the defendant having given evidence that he had agreed to forego interest on the judgment, and that having failed in that particular, he should pay the costs of the commission, &c. But I see no such evidence by the defendant, and in his statement of what he considered due he specifies interest as making up the balance.

SPINNEY *v.* PUGSLEY.

PLAINTIFF brought action to redeem a mortgage, setting out an agreement in writing by the defendant to release it on being paid one-half of the principal of the mortgage and interest in twelve months, plaintiff agreeing to give up certain claims against the defendant. The Master construed the agreement, according to plaintiff's contention, as requiring payment of one-half the balance due at the time of the agreement, while defendant contended that it meant one-half the original principal. Evidence was given in support of both constructions.

Held, that, independently of any evidence, the Master's view of the agreement was incorrect, and that there was no necessity of referring the case back to the Master, as the Court had the materials for ascertaining the amount due.

RITCHIE, E. J., (October 25th, 1880,) delivered the judgment of the Court :—

The Master to whom it was referred to ascertain what amount, if any, was due on the mortgage which the plaintiff seeks in this case to redeem, has reported that the plaintiff has overpaid the defendant the sum of $81.85, which he is entitled to be repaid, with interest. This results from the construction which the Master has put upon an agreement entered into between the parties.

The agreement is set out in the plaintiff's writ. It is dated the 1st July, 1875. By it the defendant agreed to release the mortgage and give up the promissory notes of the plaintiff which he held with the mortgage, on being paid *one-half of the principal of the mortgage and interest* in twelve months, which amount the plaintiff agreed to pay and to give up all claim against the defendant respecting a schooner called the " Ebro," and the defendant agreed to indemnify the plaintiff against all claims that Joseph Priest might make against him on account of her. The mortgage was given 7th April, 1878.

The construction contended for by the plaintiff and adopted by the Master is that the amount to be paid by him under the agreement is, not the half of the principal secured by the mortgage, but the half of the balance due when the agreement was entered into, and he alleges that, previous to the settlement when the agreement was entered into, a payment of $100 had been made on account. If this construction is the correct one and the $100 has been actually paid, the Master is right in the report he has made.

The defendant, on the other hand, contends that the proper construction is that that the amount to be paid him was half of the sum for which the mortgage was originally given, viz., $345.74, and the terms of the agreement, it appears to me, sustain this contention. The plaintiff's undertaking is to pay one-half of the principal of the mortgage, and not one-half of the balance of the principal then due. I think this to be the proper construction to be put upon the instrument, and I am of opinion that such was the intention of the parties when the arrangement was made and the agreement executed.

The defendant, in his evidence, states that he, on the settlement, agreed to take $172.87, being half of the consideration of the mortgage, and that the plaintiff never disputed that this was the agreement between them. Neither Mr. Townshend, the plaintiff's attorney, who wrote the agreement and was present at the settlement, nor the plaintiff himself contradicts this statement. All that Mr. Townshend says on the subject is that he does not remember *any amount being specified* other than in the agreement. He says nothing which would lead to the conclusion that the real intention of the parties was other than that alleged by the defendant. He says it was a year after the agreement, that is, in 1876, that he had paid to the defendant for the plaintiff the last payment of $70, he being then overpaid on the plaintiff's construction of the agreement, and that defendant always claimed a balance. And the plaintiff admits that he never pretended to defendant that he had overpaid him till last winter. Subsequently he said he never asked the defendant to pay him the balance he now claims. I cannot but think that the interpretation now attempted to be put on the agreement was an after-thought which first suggested itself last winter, when the statement was made at Parrsboro by Mr. McGillivray.

Mr. Townshend, on behalf of the plaintiff, objected that no evidence should be received of what took place when the agreement was entered into, as shewing the intention of the parties. If that evidence tended to vary the terms of this instrument under the hands and seals of the parties, certainly not, but this evidence is not at variance but in accordance with its terms. There is no ground for contending that the agreement will not bear the construction contended for by the defendant, and if it will also bear that contended for by the plaintiff, the ambiguity is latent. Now, while evidence cannot be given to explain a patent ambiguity, it may, where it is latent, in order to ascertain the intention of the parties, though not to vary the contract. Quite independently, however, of any such evidence in this case, I am of opinion that the Master took an incorrect view of the case, and that the report cannot be confirmed.

There is no necessity to refer the matter back to the Master, as the Court has now the materials for ascertaining the balance due on the mortgage.

KAULBACK *v.* TAYLOR ET AL.

BENJAMIN, FREEMAN & CALDER purchased certain lands, subject to a subsisting mortgage, each of them receiving a deed of one undivided third part. They had formed a partnership for milling and lumbering, and Calder borrowed $2,000 for the purpose of erecting a mill, for which he gave a confession of judgment to the plaintiff, which was duly recorded. The partnership, becoming embarrassed, assigned all their property to Taylor and others, as trustees, and afterwards assigned, under the Insolvent Act, to Taylor, who procured the mortgage to be foreclosed and bought in the property, which he afterwards sold to Benjamin. The plaintiff was not made a defendant in the foreclosure suit, and received no notice of the sale, although Taylor was aware of the fact that the plaintiff held a judgment, and that it was recorded in the county where the land lay, and Benjamin, when he took the deed, was aware of the facts.

Held, that plaintiff was entitled to a re-sale, with notice, and that the plaintiff's lien under his judgment must have priority over the deed in trust.

RITCHIE, E. J., (October 25th, 1880,) delivered the judgment of the Court :—

The plaintiff, in his writ, alleges that one W. J. Gates, being the owner of the land therein mentioned, mortgaged it to one J. M. Bishop; after which Stephen P. Benjamin, Augustus Freeman, and William R. Calder purchased it, subject to the mortgage, each of them receiving a deed of one undivided third part, and these parties, having formed a partnership under the name of Benjamin, Calder & Co., erected a large and expensive gang mill thereon; that in order to enable William R. Calder to raise money to assist in erecting the mill, he borrowed from the plaintiff the sum of $2,000, and gave him a confession of judgment for the amount, which was duly recorded, some time after which Stephen P. Benjamin retired from the firm, the other partners continuing to do business under the name of Calder, Freeman & Co., who, subsequently getting into pecuniary difficulties, assigned all their property to Robert Taylor, Peter Grant, John S. Brown, and Joseph Hea, defendants herein, in trust for the benefit of their creditors; that some time after, the firm having become insolvent, Taylor became assignee under the provisions of the Insolvent Act of 1869; that after the insolvency, Taylor, as assignee, offered a part of the land subject to the plaintiff's judgment for sale at auction, and the plaintiff attended at the time and place of sale, with the intention of bidding thereat to cover the amount of his judgment; and before and at the sale he notified Taylor of his judgment, and of its having been recorded, when Taylor agreed with him to assume and pay the plaintiff the amount due on his judgment,—about $1,800,— in order that he might give a good title, and the plaintiff thereupon refrained from bidding; that the property was knocked down to one McDonald, but, as the plaintiff afterwards discovered, it was bid in by him as the agent, and for the benefit of, Taylor, who, when called upon after the sale by plaintiff to fulfil his agreement by paying him the amount due on his judgment, promised to do so, and Taylor, as he alleges, held the land, subject to the judgment and in trust to pay the same.

And the plaintiff further alleges that Taylor, being a large creditor of Calder, Freeman & Co., procured an assignment of the mortgage above referred to to himself, Peter Grant, John S. Brown and Joseph Hea, with the fraudulent intent of selling the property under the mortgage, in such a manner as to deprive the plaintiff of the benefit of his judgment by keeping him in ignorance of the sale, and in pursuance of such purpose he proceeded to foreclose it in the name of himself and his co-trustees, as plaintiffs, and himself, as sole defend-ant, and procured a certificate from the Registrar of Deeds for the County of Kings of the encumbrances on the mortgaged premises, which certificate did not contain any reference to

the plaintiff's judgment as having been recorded, the same
having been inadvertently omitted by the Registrar, and
though the plaintiffs in the foreclosure suit and Robert
Taylor well knew of the judgment and of the recording
thereof, and of the omission of the same in the certificate by
the Registrar, the certificate so known by them to be false
was presented to the Court as a correct statement of the
encumbrances on the land, and an order of foreclosure was
made, and the property sold thereunder on the 1st February,
1878, to Robert Taylor, for $1,200, the true value being about
$7,000 at least, and Taylor instructed the Sheriff to make
out a deed of the land to one Charles R. Thompson, a defendant
herein, who held the same for Taylor; that the sale was
only advertized in the " Western Chronicle," an obscure paper,
having little or no circulation in Lunenburg, where the plaintiff
resides; that he received no notice of the sale, nor any
knowledge thereof, and that if he had been made aware of it,
he would have attended and bid up the property so as to
cover the amount due on his judgment and costs, as the
property was well worth that amount; that after the
plaintiff became aware of the sale having taken place, Taylor
again promised the plaintiff to settle the amount due on his
judgment, who, relying on such promise, took no steps to set
aside the sale until he was informed that Taylor was
negotiating a sale of the property to the defendant, Stephen
P. Benjamin, when he notified the latter of the facts above set
forth, and of his intention to file a bill to set aside the sale
under the foreclosure, after which the sale to Benjamin was
carried into effect, and a deed given, under the directions of
Taylor, by Charles R. Thompson, for a sum largely in advance
of what Taylor had paid for it, and Benjamin, to secure the
purchase money, gave a mortgage to Taylor for the amount.
And the plaintiff prays that the sale under the foreclosure,
and the subsequent conveyance to Benjamin be set aside, and
that a re-sale may take place under the foreclosure, after
notice to the plaintiff, and that any balance on that sale over
and above the amount due on the mortgage be applied to the
payment of the amount due on the plaintiff's judgment; or
that Taylor be decreed to pay the plaintiff the amount due on

his judgment, in accordance with his promise and agreement; or that Taylor be decreed to account for the difference between the sum paid by him on the sale under the foreclosure and the amount for which he sold the property to Benjamin, and that the amount of such difference be applied towards the payment of his judgment.

Neither Benjamin nor any of the other defendants except Taylor have appeared or made any defence to the suit, and judgment by default has been entered against them. Taylor, in his evidence, says that the property mentioned in the mortgage was purchased by Calder, Freeman, and Benjamin for the use of the firm, with the intent that it should be held in trust as co-partnership property. He admits the recording of the judgment of the plaintiff in Kings County, but alleges that it was so recorded in violation of the express agreement with Calder that it should not be recorded in that county. I may here remark that there is nothing whatever in the evidence to lead to the inference that any such agreement ever existed. And with reference to the sale referred to in the writ as made by him he says he does not know whether the plaintiff was present at it with the intention of bidding up said property to cover his judgment, but he has been informed that such was the case. He denies that at the time of the said sale, and before he proceeded to sell, the plaintiff notified him and those present that he had a judgment recorded against the property for about $1,800, or that he, the defendant, agreed to assume and pay the judgment and says he did no act and uttered no words of that character, that just before the sale, W. H. Owen, attorney-at-law, professing to act for the plaintiff, forbade the sale, alleging that the plaintiff held a judgment for some $1,800, duly recorded against the property, and the defendant having then no evidence of the authority of Owen, and no evidence nor any knowledge of the existence of the judgment, except the bald assertion of Owen, then neither admitted nor denied the right of Owen to interfere with the progress of the sale, but declared that a good title would be given to the property in the event of a sale being effected; that no sale was really effected, as the land was knocked down to McDonald, for the benefit of the estate of

Calder, Freeman & Co., the prices offered being insufficient to warrant the defendant in selling the property. He denies that after the sale he promised to pay the judgment to the plaintiff, or acknowledged that he held the land subject to the agreement, but says he has at all times refused to recognize the plaintiff's claim on the land; and he alleges that he obtained an assignment of the mortgage to prevent a threatened foreclosure and sacrifice of the property, and not with a view of foreclosing it in such a manner as to prevent the plaintiff being aware of the sale, and thus depriving him of the benefit of his judgment, but the foreclosure took place by him in the ordinary way; that the assignment of the mortgage was procured by him long before he had any notice of the judgment, either directly or indirectly; that the usual certificate of the Registrar of Deeds of the encumbrances on the land was obtained and presented to the Court in good faith, without any knowledge that the same was false or incorrect, and all encumbrancers of the land referred to in that certificate were duly notified of the sale under the foreclosure. And he denies that he well knew of the judgment and the registry thereof, and says that Thompson was one of the defendants, to whom the deed was made by the sheriff, under his, (Taylor's,) instructions solely for the benefit of the creditors of Calder, Freeman & Co. And he denies that after the sale under the foreclosure he ever promised to settle the amount due on the judgment, but says that shortly after the sale, on the application of Mr. Owen, he distinctly repudiated all liability in respect of it, and that subsequently thereto no steps were taken to re-open the sale, and he therefore sold the property to Benjamin, and at his instance Thompson has given him a deed of it.

As regards what took place at the sale by Taylor in April, 1877, the evidence is most conflicting, but as that sale fell through, whether, as Taylor says, from the property having been bid in by him for the trustees, or, as McDonald, who actually bid it in, says, for a company to be formed which never was formed, it remained under Taylor's control as before, so that the evidence is not important unless it be that which relates to Taylor's knowledge of the existence of the plaintiff's judgment and to the certificate of the registry of it previous to that sale, and that only because it bears on the subsequent sale under the foreclosure. The evidence clearly establishes the fact that Taylor well knew, certainly the morning before the sale took place, if not a considerable time previously, not only that the plaintiff had the judgment and that it was recorded in Kings County, but that a certificate had been obtained from the Registrar of Deeds to that effect. His own witnesses, R. M. King, Frederick Brown, and McDonald, distinctly prove this to have been the case.

It was after this sale fell through that Taylor had a suit instituted by the trustees against himself to foreclose the mortgage above referred to, and an order of sale was obtained and a sale made under it, at which Taylor became the purchaser, without the plaintiff being made a party to the suit, or having any notice of the sale.

Though subsequent encumbrancers are not necessary parties to a foreclosure suit, the Court, under the statute regulating the procedure in equity, requires for the protection of their interests that notice shall be given of the time and place of sale a specified time before it is to take place ; and the plaintiff in the suit is required, through his attorney, to obtain from the Registrar of Deeds and file a certificate setting forth all encumbrances on the land sought to be foreclosed, in order that it may be made to appear to the Court that the required notice has been given. The certificate produced and filed was that in which all reference to the plaintiff's judgment was omitted.

Messrs. Barss & King were the attorneys employed by Taylor to foreclose the mortgage, neither of whom has been examined, but Taylor says that they told him that they had received two certificates, and Mr. Barss told him that neither of them contained the plaintiff's judgment. Now, from the evidence it appears that but two certificates were obtained from the Registrar of Deeds, and one of them did embrace it, and that had been obtained by Mr. Hunt for Taylor. If his attorneys had two certificates from the Registrar of Deeds they must have been aware of the plaintiff's judgment, and that, therefore, notice should have been given to him, and if they were not aware of it, Taylor, with the information he possessed, was bound to communicate to them the fact of its existence.

Not only did the plaintiff or his attorney not receive the notice which the practice of the Court under the statute required, but it is too apparent that Taylor did not desire that they should have it. The sheriff, by whom the property was sold, says that Taylor was present at the sale and bid in the property, and it was knocked down to him. After the sale he requested that the deed should be made out to one Thompson. Taylor said that he himself was actually the purchaser and would pay him his fee, which he did then and there. Taylor also told him he wanted the deed made out to Thompson, because there was a party had a judgment against the property, and ought to have been aware of the sale, and he wanted to prevent him from coming in and getting his share. This was the reason he gave when he, (the sheriff,) asked him why he wanted the deed made out to Thompson. The Sheriff says he has a distinct recollection of what Taylor said to him, though he may be mistaken as to his having paid him his fee,—his attorney may have paid it. I cannot do otherwise than accept this statement of Mr. Caldwell, (the sheriff,) as correct. He is a public officer, unconnected with either party, and entirely disinterested.

It was especially incumbent on Taylor in this case to see that the plaintiff, (Kaulback,) received due notice of the sale under the foreclosure. Taylor was one of the plaintiffs and the only defendant. He was the person who had the suit instituted. He accepted service of the writ and gave a confession, and not only knew of the plaintiff's judgment, but was well aware that he was contending for his rights under it ; and as the law and the practice of the Court require that, instead of being made a party, a subsequent encumbrancer is to have due notice of the sale, if such notice is not given to him he has the same right to object to the validity of the sale as if in such a suit a subsequent encumbrancer were a necessary party, and he had not been made such. I think, therefore, that the plaintiff's right under his judgment cannot be affected by this sale, but must remain as if it had never taken place.

A question has been raised by the defendant, (Taylor,) which requires consideration. He contends that the land under foreclosure, though held in the name of Calder, was really partnership property of the firm of Calder, Freeman & Co., and that the plaintiff had no lien on it under his judgment against Calder; at any rate, not until the creditors of Calder, Freeman & Co. were all paid.

Where real estate has been purchased, with partnership funds, for the partnership business, and conveyed to the partners, it will be treated as personal property. And though this land cannot be said to have been purchased with partnership funds, and was held by the parties under separate deeds, yet it was obviously purchased for the purpose of erecting on it the mills wherein the business of the partnership was to be conducted. As regards the partners and their creditors, it must, I think, be deemed part of the common stock. It is, however, in equity alone that real estate held by partners for partnership purposes is treated as partnership property. Courts of law can only view it in its legal aspect, and if the legal title is vested in one partner a *bona fide* purchaser from him, having no previous notice of its being partnership property, will be entitled to hold it free from any claim of the partnership or its creditors.

When the deed was given by Calder & Freeman to Taylor and others of the land in question, the plaintiff's judgment had been recorded, and by section 22, chapter 79 of the Revised Statutes it is enacted that, "a judgment duly recorded and docketed shall bind the lands of the party against whom it shall have passed from and after the registry thereof, &c., *as effectually as a mortgage*, whether such lands shall have been acquired before or after the registering of such judgment, and deeds or mortgages of such lands duly executed but not registered shall be void against the judgment creditor who shall first register his judgment." At law, the lien of the plaintiff under this enactment is unquestionable. It was out of his own funds that Calder paid for the land conveyed to him. He procured the amount, he says, from the plaintiff, to enable him to make the purchase, and he gave the judgment to secure the re-payment. The loan was not made to the

firm, and when the money was received from the plaintiff it
was his own property.   Now if, instead of giving a judgment
to secure the re-payment of the amount borrowed, he had
given a mortgage of the land to the plaintiff, I cannot but
think he would have acquired a lien on the land, in equity as
well as at law.

When the trustees took the conveyance from Calder, they
knew, or must be presumed to have known, of this recorded
judgment of the plaintiff; and, looking at the conveyance to
Calder, there was nothing to lead to the inference but that he
held the land under it as his individual property.   And where
an encumbrancer has no knowledge of the equitable rights of
third parties he has a right to have his lien, whether by
mortgage or judgment, satisfied according to priority upon
the records.   In *4 Kent's Com.*, 173, it is said ; " There is
much good sense, as well as simplicity and certainty in the
proposition that every encumbrance, whether it be a registered
deed or docketed judgment, should in cases free from fraud be
satisfied according to the priority of the lien upon the record
which is open for public inspection."

Though I have expressed an opinion that the land in
question, so far as regards the partners and their creditors, is
to be considered partnership property, and to be treated as
personal property, yet, as to this, there is room for doubt.
In *White & Tudor's Leading Cases*, 4th edition, 193, after
referring to the cases which establish the doctrine that land
purchased with partnership means for the purposes of the
partnership is to be held and treated as personal property,
the editors go on to say ; " It seems, however, that where
real estate belonged to the partners at the time of their
entering into the partnership, or has been subsequently
acquired by them out of their own private moneys, or by gift,
conversion will not, unless by express agreement, take place,
although the real estate has been used for the partnership
purposes in trade."

If, however, this land was in fact partnership property,
and as such liable in the first instance to the payment of the
debts of the firm, yet the plaintiff, as a judgment creditor of
Calder, would have a lien on it, subject to the payment of

those debts, and therefore was entitled to notice of the sale under the foreclosure, so that he might have an opportunity of protecting his interest by bidding, if likely to be sacrificed, as indeed it is evident he contemplated doing. I therefore think that the prayer of the plaintiff's writ should be granted, that the sale under the foreclosure should be set aside, and that a re-sale should take place of the mortgaged premises, of which due notice shall be given to the plaintiff, and that, as in my opinion, the lien obtained by the plaintiff under his judgment duly recorded is entitled to priority over that of the defendants under the deed in trust, after payment of the amount due on the mortgage, the balance, if any, shall, in the first instance, be applied towards the payment of the plaintiff's judgment.

As Benjamin took his deed from Taylor with a full knowledge of all the facts he can stand in no better position than Taylor himself. Indeed, he has put in no defence to the suit, and the same is the case with the other defendants who were plaintiffs in the foreclosure suit.

I have passed no opinion on the claim made by the plaintiff that Taylor should pay him the amount due on his judgment, in accordance with a promise to that effect, in consideration of his withdrawing his protest against the sale in 1879, in support of which much evidence was adduced, for if that agreement constituted a ground of action, it should have been brought in a common law Court.

The plaintiff is entitled to the costs.

KNOWLAN *v.* DUNN.

PLAINTIFF brought a suit to obtain from defendant a reconveyance on plaintiff's paying him the amount that should be found due upon an accounting, for
which he prayed. Defendant set up a defence which was not sustained, and insisted
on payment of $400.00, of which the master allowed $29.00. Exceptions were
taken to the report, some of which were allowed and others disallowed.

Held, that the plaintiff was entitled to the costs of the suit, but that the costs
arising out of the exceptions should not be allowed to either party.

RITCHIE, E. J., (October 25th, 1880,) delivered the judgment of the Court :—

The report of the Master is excepted to on the grounds
that the amount allowed for the occupation of the farm by
Dunn, viz., $120, is too much, and also that $20 for damage
to barn, and $12 for poles taken by him should not have been
allowed.

The first exception ought not to be allowed. The amount
reported due for rent is reasonable under the circumstances.
By the order of reference the Master was directed to report
what sum was due on the agreement referred to in the plaintiff's
writ as the condition upon which the land referred to was
conveyed to the defendant ; and secondly, what sum should
be paid by the defendant as rent while he was in possession
of the land. To these questions he was confined, and while
the defendant has, in my opinion, no good grounds of
objection to the amount reported due on the agreement as for
rent, the exceptions to the allowance for damage to the barn,
and for poles taken must be allowed, as not being within the
reference, nor are these subjects made a ground of complaint
against the defendant in the writ.

As regards the costs. The suit was brought to obtain from
the defendant a re-conveyance of the land in question on the
plaintiff's paying to him the amount, if any, that should be
found due to him on an accounting which he prayed might
take place. The statements of the plaintiff in his writ have
been supported by the evidence, and if the defendant had not
set up a defence which he has failed to sustain, he would not
have subjected himself to costs if any amount had been
found due to him on the reference prayed for by the plaintiff,

but the controversy arose and the costs have been occasioned by his setting up a claim which has been disallowed, and he insisted on being paid upwaids of $400 before he would consent to re-convey the land, while the amount reported by the Master, after the deduction of the items disallowed, is but $29.35. Under these circumstances the plaintiff, having succeeded in all the questions in controversy, is entitled to the costs ; but as to the costs arising from the exceptions to the report, as some of the exceptions have been allowed and some disallowed, there should be no costs to either the plaintiff or defendant.

SAUNDERS *v.* HOLDSWORTH ET AL.

PLAINTIFF was joint-owner with defendants of a vessel engaged in fishing voyages, plaintiff being master of the vessel. In his writ plaintiff claimed an amount due, but the master reported an amount due by plaintiff to the defendants, arising out of notes of hand given by plaintiff and defendants jointly for the purchase of the vessel, which notes defendants' had retired, and an order received by plaintiff for money in which all the parties were interested.

Held, that the amounts were properly allowed.

A claim for wages made by plaintiff was disallowed under the evidence.

RITCHIE, E. J., (November 22nd, 1880,) delivered the judgment of the Court :—

It having been referred to a Master to take evidence and report what amount, if any, is due by either party in the suit to the other, he has reported that $22.64 are due by the plaintiff to the defendant, and has returned the evidence taken by him on which he has based his report.

To this report the plaintiff has excepted on the ground that the Master should not have taken into consideration and inserted in his report the account of the owners of the vessel with John G. Hall & Co. for the purchase of the vessel, and that he has wrongfully charged the plaintiff with $30, being three-fourths of an order on M. H. Ives for $40.

I think neither of these exceptions can be allowed. The plaintiff and defendants were joint owners of the vessel referred to in the plaintiff's writ, and he says there is an amount due to him, and he prays that the defendants may fully disclose the condition of the accounts of the vessel during the joint ownership. The defendants, in their answer, allege that they have overpaid the plaintiff, and have fully accounted with him in respect of the vessel. On the purchase of the vessel notes of hand were made by the plaintiff and defendants, whereby they made themselves jointly and severally liable to J. G. Hall & Co. for the amount due. Surely, if these notes were taken up by the defendants and the plaintiff relieved from liability on them, no settlement could be made between the plaintiff and defendants without those notes being taken into account. Any amount paid by the defendants on these notes for the plaintiff could be set off against any claim he could have against them in respect of the vessel.

The exception is not that there is no proof that the notes were paid, but simply that they ought not to have been taken into consideration. Mr. Harrington did orally make the objection, but in the first instance the plaintiff does not pretend that he paid them, and from the evidence it appears that the plaintiff has been relieved of all responsibility, and no better evidence can be adduced of this than that they have taken them up, and they are now in their hands.

As regards the other exception, I do not see how the Master could have done otherwise than charge the plaintiff with the $30. He admits that he received an order on Ives for $40, with which all the four owners were to be credited. He has neither paid the money nor returned the order, and though he has admitted his having so received the order, he does not assert that he did not receive the money, and the inference is irresistible that he did receive it.

Though these are the only exceptions taken by the plaintiff's attorney in writing and served on the defendants' attorney, and to which I think he should be confined, yet an additional exception was taken at the hearing by Mr. Harrington, viz., that the Master ought to have allowed the plaintiff wages in addition to the share of fish to which he was entitled on the fishing voyage in which the vessel was engaged while he was master; but, assuming the exception to

have been correctly taken, it would not, I think, prevail. No
evidence of the plaintiff is receivable of what took place
between himself and Stephen Saunders, since deceased. The
plaintiff says he went master of the vessel two seasons of five
months each; that he charged £8 a month; that masters are
paid £8 10s. 12d. and sometimes £15 a month, according to
the size of the vessel, and there is no evidence of any promise
by the other owners of the vessel to pay him wages. Notwithstanding this, under ordinary circumstances he would be
entitled to wages and a promise to pay them would be
inferred; but this was a fishing voyage, and the owners and
crew were to participate in the profits of the voyage, so that
the plaintiff would have his share as part owner and also as
master. Agreements relating to such voyages have been
subject to legislative regulations, and both master and crew,
under such regulations, were to become sharesmen and to
receive their stipulated shares in lieu of wages in money.
The evidence, I think, clearly shews that the plaintiff, as
master, was to receive his share as such, and the share to
which he was entitled as owner. Both Holdsworth and
Dakin, the other part owners, deny that they ever promised
to pay him wages, and say that they would not have employed
him if he had demanded wages; that they had a settlement
with him in 1877, when he rendered an account which is
produced receipted, and no charge for wages was then made.
That, they say, was a full settlement of everything coming to
plaintiff at that time with the exception of Hall's notes and
accounts. There was a settlement again in 1879, and no
charge was then made for wages on the fishing voyage. The
account he produced on that occasion is in evidence, and
while there is no charge for wages on these voyages, there is
a charge for wages on a voyage to the West Indies and for
a trip to Lockeport. Making these charges and omitting
any charge for the first voyage are in the highest degree
confirmatory of the defendants' evidence that no charges
were to be made for these latter voyages. This last exception
must also be overruled, The report of the Master, therefore,
will be confirmed with costs.

THE ALLIANCE SOCIETY OF LONDON *v.* CHISHOLM.

THE plaintiff company was registered under the Imperial Act, 25 and 26 Vic., cap. 89, and claimed to do business in Canada under 37 Vic., cap. 49. The object of the Society was expressed to be to advance money in various sums to such members as were desirous of receiving it, the repayment to be secured on real or other security ; and in the article of the constitution entitled, Foreclosure and Redemption, it was provided that if any member should desire to pay in advance all or any portion of an appropriation or premium, he shall be at liberty to do so, and shall be entitled to such discount as the actuary may recommend. The writ alleged that, the mortgagee having become a member of the Society, £300 was advanced to him at a premium of £379 6*s.* 8*d.*, the advance and premium to be repayable in quarterly instalments in twenty years ; and that, according to the regulations of the Society, if any instalment or fine remained in arrears for three months, the whole sum advanced, together with the premium, should become due. The proviso and covenants in the mortgage were to this effect, and the plaintiff claimed £675 7*s.* 8*d.*, although the mortgagor had only had the sum of £300 for nine months.

Held, that the plaintiffs were only entitled to the quarterly instalments up to the time of foreclosure and sale, and that the amount of principal due should be ascertained by computing how much of the quarterly payments represented principal, and how much interest.

Matterson v. *Elderfield,* L. R., 4 Ch., 207, distinguished.

RITCHIE, E. J., (February 7th, 1881,) delivered the judgment of the Court :—

On the foreclosure of the mortgage set out in the plaintiffs' writ they claim to be entitled to the sum of £674 7s. 8d. sterling, equal in Dominion currency to $3,282.

The mortgage was made by John A. Stewart to the society on the 11th October, 1878. The amount received by him was £300 sterling. The writ alleges that, having become a member of the society, that sum was advanced to him at a premium of £379 6s. 8d. sterling, the advance and premium being re-payable by quarterly instalments of £8 9s. 10d. sterling each, during the term of twenty years, and that, according to the constitution and regulations of the society, if any instalment or fine should remain in arrears for three calendar months the whole amount of the sum advanced and premium should be at once due, and that proceedings might be taken to recover both advance and premium, and to realize the securities held by the society. The proviso in the mortgage is to that effect, with the further proviso that the mortgaged premises should be kept insured by Stewart for

£300 sterling for the benefit of the society. The mortgage also contained covenants for the payment of the sum advanced and premium. The writ further alleges that the instalments have remained in arrears for more than three months, whereby the whole sum advanced and premium have become due, together with an amount paid for premiums of insurance, and that the defendant, (Chisholm,) became the purchaser of the mortgaged premises at sheriff's sale under a judgment against Stewart. The claim is thus stated :—

	£.	s.	d.
Amount advanced	300	0	0
Premium	379	6	8
Premiums of Insurance	13	0	8
	692	7	4
Less two instalments of £8 9s. d. Dec. 1878, and March, 1879..	16	19	8
Amount claimed.................	675	7	8

The society is a body corporate, registered under the Imperial Act, 25 & 26 Vic., chapter 89, and claims to do business here under the Dominion Act, 37 Vic., chapter 49, which authorizes the Secretary of State for Canada to grant a license to a company duly incorporated under the laws of Great Britain and Ireland for the purpose of lending to transact business in the Dominion.

The agreement thus entered into, so far as the society was to receive at the expiration of twenty years the sum of £679 6. 8d. for a present advance of £300, payable by quarterly instalments of £8 9s. 10d., was not unreasonable. At the expiration of the twenty years, if the instalments were paid up, the society would have been re-paid the amount loaned with, under the circumstances, not an unreasonable amount of interest. It is obvious that what is designated as premium is merely the interest computed on the sum lent for the time when the debt and interest would be paid up by the instalments, and it does appear to me unreasonable, in the highest degree that having had the use of £300 for nine months, and having paid £16 19s. 8d., much more than legal interest, on it, the mortgagor should be required to pay £675 7s. 8d.   This may be highly satisfactory to those members who may have no occasion to become borrowers, and not unsatisfactory to those who have the ability to pay their instalments as they fall due, but to those who unfortunately become unable to do so the enforcement of such a claim would work a grievious hardship.   The case on which the plaintiff's counsel relied was *Matterson* v. *Elderfield*, L. R. 4 Ch., 207, and it would seem at first sight to support the claim, but there the object of that society, as expressed in its rules, was to raise a fund by monthly subscription to enable its members to receive out of the funds of the society the *amount or value of their shares* wherewith to erect or purchase dwelling houses.   Not so this society ; its object is expressed to be *to advance money in various sums to such members as are desirous of receiving it, the re-payment to be secured on real or other security*; and this difference is adverted to in the case I shall refer to. There is an article in the constitution of this society, the 13th, headed, " Foreclosure and Redemption," the first section of which is that under which this claim is made, which is followed by this section ; " If any member desire to pay in advance all or any portion of an appropriation or premium, he shall be at liberty to do so, and *shall be entitled* to such discount as the actuary may recommend the directors to allow."   Any intending borrower reading this would be led to infer that when the money was re-paid in advance, whether at the desire of the mortgagor or by sale of the mortgaged premises, he would become entitled as of right to such a discount.   The case of *In Re Goldsmith*, L. R. 10 Ch., 41, is more like the present than any I have met with.   Goldsmith, the borrower, obtained an advance of £600 from a building society, payable by equal monthly instalments of £9 13s. for which he gave a mortgage, in which it was stipulated that in default of the payment of the instalments the trustees of the society might sell the mortgaged property, and it was agreed that, in case any such sale should take place, all the moneys which would at any time afterwards become due according to the rules of the society should be considered as immediately due and payable.   Goldsmith paid only two instalments and afterwards became bankrupt; the trustees went into possession and sold the mortgaged premises, and they claimed to retain the whole amount of the monthly instalments of £9 13s. to the end of the seven years, together with fines in arrears down to the sale; and in support of that it was urged that the contract was not to pay the principal and interest in the ordinary way, but to pay certain monthly subscriptions for seven years. The Registrar in the first instance sustained the claim, but on appeal this decision was reversed. Lord Chancellor CAIRNS said; " It is clear that for the purpose of this mortgage Goldsmith was treated as if he had' received an advance of £600 at 5 per cent. The way this was done was that it was agreed that the re-payment should be spread over seven years by monthly instalments to be made up by a portion of interest and principal. If that be so, one would, in the absence of any stipulation to the contrary, suppose that if default was made in the payment of any instalment and the property was sold, all that was due for monthly instalments and fines was to be paid out of the proceeds of the sale, but that with regard to the future so much of the principal sum as remained unpaid having been paid off there would be nothing in respect of which interest could accrue. Interest implies forbearance, and therefore when the whole is paid there can be no interest. It is provided that the trustees, after payment of the expenses of the sale, shall retain all such subscriptions, fines, and other sums of money and payments which shall be then due or which would afterwards become due in respect of the shares during the then remainder of the period of seven years, it being agreed that all the moneys which would at any time after become due from Goldsmith in respect of the shares according to the rates of the association shall be considered as being immediately due and payable. With regard to the future you cannot include under, ' *moneys which would at any time afterwards become due*' any *fines;* no more can you include payments in respect of interest, for interest can only arise in respect of a principal sum remaining outstanding forborne. Therefore my conclusion is that everything due in respect of monthly instalments and fines at the time of sale must be retained, and then it must be ascertained how much of the monthly payments represented principal and how much interest, and it will then appear how much of the principal remains unpaid, and that will conclude the transaction." Lord Justices JAMES and MELLISH concurred; the latter Lord Justice said; "According to the rules of this society this was not strictly an advance in anticipation of the sum eventually payable to the member in respect of his shares, as it was in other cases which had been before the courts;" alluding, no doubt, to cases like that of *Matterson* v. *Elderfield*, of which we cannot suppose the Lords Justices and the counsel engaged were ignorant.

Under the authority of this case the claim of the plaintiff society to the extent made cannot, I think, be allowed.

It was objected on the part of the defendant that the society had no authority under its constitution to do business out of the United Kingdom. Though no special authority to do so is given, for the 3rd and 4th sub-sections of article 103, relied on by Mr. Parsons, can have no such effect, yet, as I find nothing which prohibits the society from doing business here if authorized by the law of the Dominion, the objection cannot be sustained. It was also objected that the Dominion Act, under which the license was given to transact business here, provided that the rate of interest to be charged on any loan should not exceed the rate permissible by the acts incorporating similar societies in the several provinces of the Dominion, and that no such society exists in this province which would exact so large an interest as is claimed in this suit; that by chapter 71 of the Acts of 1873 no greater amount than seven per cent. interest can be taken, directly or indirectly, on a loan secured as this is on real estate in Nova Scotia. The Dominion Act under which the society is licensed would appear from its terms to contemplate the licensing of companies to make loans of money generally rather than of such as merely lend to their members, but it clearly provides that, while a society licensed under it may take mortgages, &c., on the security of which it may lend its money, any such loan must be at a rate of interest not exceeding the rate of interest permissible on such securities by the acts incorporating similar companies in the several provinces. The only society referred to as of a cognate character in operation in this province was the Nova Scotia Benefit Building Society and Savings' Fund.   There a shareholder may obtain the amount of his share in advance, and this may be at a premium or bonus, which is deducted from the amount he would otherwise receive, and for which the security is taken.   On one occasion a claim somewhat similar to this was made; see *Slayter* v. *Johnston et al.*, Oldright's Reports, 502.   The Court there held that, under the rules, read in the light of the tables given to elucidate them, the society could not claim the whole amount of the instalments unpaid by the mortgagor, but that he was entitled to a discount.

The intention of the Dominion Legislature was to protect a borrower from the payment of exorbitant interest.   The operations of this society, if carried out as they desire, would amount to this, that for a loan of £300, at the expiration of nine months, in consequence of the inability of the debtor to meet the payment of his next instalment, the society would receive their £300 with interest at the rate of upwards of one hundred and fifty per cent. per annum, and this would be exacted from the poor man on account of his poverty for the benefit of the wealthier members.

In this case, as in that of *In Re Goldsmith*, the plaintiff society are only entitled to the quarterly instalments up to the time of the foreclosure and sale of the land mortgaged, and then the amount of principal due will be ascertained by computing how much of the quarterly payments represented principal and how much interest.

DOGERTY et al *v.* POWER et al.

PLAINTIFFS claimed to be entitled to fish in a certain berth, under regulations made by the Sessions on the authority of an Act of the Legislature.   Under the evidence, the Court inferred that defendants were authorized by the plaintiffs to shoot their seine,—plaintiffs to have half the fish caught,—and having done so the defendants secured a catch of fish, of which plaintiffs claimed half under the agreement.

Held, that the plaintiffs were entitled to half the fish caught, and that the relief which they sought, namely, that defendants should deliver to them their share of the proceeds or account to them, and in the meantime should be restrained from selling, &c., was properly sought in this Court.

RITCHIE, E. J., (July 11th, 1881,) delivered the judgment of the Court :—

The plaintiffs claim to be entitled to half of a catch of fish, taken in a seine of the defendants, on the ground that they were the holders of a ticket drawn under the fishery regulations, made by the Court of Sessions under the authority of the Legislature, which entitled them to fish in turn in a fish berth at Duck Island, in Upper Prospect, called "The Potato berth"—and being entitled to the first turn they went there with their boat and seine to watch for and secure any fish that might appear in the berth ; at their entering it they found the defendants with their boat and seine in it, and immediately asserted their right and required them to leave ; their right was recognized, and the defendants prepared at once to leave. Soon after, and while they were so preparing to leave, fish appeared in the berth, and then, as the plaintiffs say, Coolen, who was in charge of their boat, called out to Buchanan, who was in charge of the defendants' boat, and whose seine was then partly down, to shoot the seine and divide the fish ; this he did and secured one hundred and twenty barrels of mackerel or thereabout, and having done so refused to divide them, but claimed and retained the whole.

The defendants admit the plaintiffs' sole and exclusive right to fish in the berth on their arrival there, and they claim that they are entitled to the fish, not on the ground that they had any right to take them, except under the authority of Coolen, but because he told Buchanan to shoot his seine, saying nothing about division of the fish till they had been taken.

That the plaintiffs should have unconditionally permitted the defendants to take the fish is highly improbable, as they thereby would not only have lost at least the chance of taking them, but would also have deprived themselves of their right to the berth which, under the regulations, would have passed to the person who had the next turn. The more probable story is that of the plaintiffs, that, both parties being on the spot, when the fish appeared, they feared that by shooting their seine inside of that of the defendants they might possibly drive the fish away, and therefore authorized the defendants to shoot their seine, on condition of getting half the catch, which was a very reasonable arrangement under the circumstances.

The evidence given by the plaintiffs and defendants as to what took place is conflicting; the latter do not assert that anything was said which gave them an unconditional right to take the fish, In fact they say that nothing was said by the plaintiffs, but that they acquiesced in silence in their taking the fish. The evidence of Coolen is that their boat being in the berth ready to catch the fish as they rose, on their rising he told Buchanan to catch them and give them half; he did not hear Buchanan reply, but he caught the fish. James Dogerty, one of Coolen's boat's crew, a son of Dogerty the plaintiff, says, "our skipper was the first man to hollow about the fish—he hollowed to Buchanan to catch the fish and give us half; I did not hear Buchanan say anything, and when he went round the fish we got out of his way to allow him to come up to his laying-off arm." The defendant Delong says their boat was in the berth ready to catch mackerel before any rose, just as those in defendants' boat were preparing to leave the fish loose, when Coolen shouted to catch them and give them half. The account given by Buchanan and Barbour, the two of the defendants who have been examined, is that they were about leaving the berth on the plaintiffs having claimed it; that nothing was said by the plaintiffs or any of them on the fish appearing, and that no claim was made for any part of the catch till after they had been secured; that it was Buchanan who called Coolen's attention to the fish having risen; that neither he nor any in his boat made any remark whatever, but allowed him without objection to take them. Two disinterested witnesses were examined on each side, William Christian and Martin Murphy for the plaintiffs, and Martin Duggan and Edward Walsh for the defendants. The evidence of the two latter is in no way confirmatory of the defendants. Walsh was too far off to hear what was said by the parties, as he gave no attention to them. Duggan says he did not hear Buchanan speak; he could not make out what Coolen said to Buchanan; when the latter was shooting Coolen just kept out of his way. While the evidence of Christian and Murphy sustains that of the plaintiffs', the former says he remembers Coolen rowing into the Potato Berth and demanding his berth, telling Buchanan that they had the first shot there, and to haul up his seine, who got under way to do so; he heard Coolen call out,— "there are the mackerel;" he said something more but he did not know what, as he was looking out for the fish to come to him; he did not hear Buchanan make any answer, but he just shot round the fish. The evidence of Murphy is more directly to the point. He says, that when the plaintiffs' boat went into the Potato Berth, he•heard Coolen call to Buchanan, and say that he owned the berth and to haul up his seine; when the defendants began to put on their oil clothes and get ready to haul it up, he did not see the fish rise, but he heard Coolen shout loudly to Buchanan to catch the fish and give them half; after he called out Buchanan shot his seine and caught the fish; he did not hear Buchanan say anything. At his cross-examination he said the exact words Coolen used were,— "Shoot ashore and give me half the fish." The evidence of the plaintiffs being thus corroborated, and being, as I think, by far the most probable account of the transaction, I give credit to it, and infer that the defendants accepted the terms offered by Coolen, and the fish were taken on those terms, the defendants shooting their seine as they were authorized to do, and the plaintiffs refraining from any attempt to catch the fish or interfere with them.

Mr. Tupper contended that no exclusive right to catch fish in the sea or on its shores could exist in any individual, and cited cases to that effect. As a general rule all have a right to do so, but the right of the public may be restricted, and an individual may, by prescription, acquire an exclusive right to fish in coves or arms of the sea, where otherwise every subject would have a right to fish. See *Carter et al.* v. *Murcott et al.*, 4 Burr., 2163. This is recognised in later cases ; See *Woolrych on Waters*, 80, and I do not think it has ever been questioned but that the legislature of a country has the power of making regulations respecting the fishery on its coasts, and unless regulations were in force on our coasts, where net and seine fishery is carried on, endless disputes and contention would continually arise to the injury of all engaged in it.

It was also objected at the hearing that this suit should have been brought, if at all, on the common law side of the Court for damages for breach of contract. Such an objection comes late at the close of the proceedings and after all the costs and expenses of the suit have been incurred. If intended to be insisted on it should have been raised at the earliest stage. There is no demurrer nor does the answer refer to it, but however or whenever taken it could not, I think, prevail. The object of the suit is not to obtain damages. The prayer of the bill is that the defendants should deliver up to the plaintiffs their share of the fish or account to them for it, and they ask that a receiver may be appointed to take possession and dispose of them and to hold the proceeds to answer the final decree of the Court, and that in the meantime the defendants should be restrained from selling or otherwise disposing of the fish ; and if the plaintiffs are entitled to the relief they seek it can only be obtained in this Court. I think that they are entitled to such relief and that a decree should pass declaring them entitled to one-half of the fish or the net proceeds thereof, with costs.

RAYMOND ET AL. v. RICHARDS.

THE defendant, holding a mortgage on certain real estate which was duly recorded, assigned the same to the plaintiffs, after which defendant purchased the equity of redemption, and the deed was duly recorded. Attachments were then issued against the defendant as an absconding debtor and the attachments, as well as the judgments entered thereon, were placed on record before the assignment of the mortgage. The attaching creditors claimed, under Revised Statutes, cap. 79, secs. 19 and 22, to have priority, as against the assignee of the mortgage.

Held, that the mortgage remained a lien on the property, whether the assignment was recorded or not, and that the attaching creditors had not the priority claimed.

RITCHIE, E. J., (July 11th, 1881,) delivered the judgment of the Court :—

The property comprised in the mortgage sought to be foreclosed in this suit was originally conveyed to the defendant by one Joseph Raymond, after which it was conveyed to one George Minse, who gave a mortgage to the defendant to secure part of the purchase money. These instruments were duly recorded. Subsequently, in the year 1876, the defendant assigned this mortgage to the plaintiffs, and afterwards, in the year 1878, Minse conveyed to the defendant his equity of redemption, which was also duly recorded. In the month of October, 1880, writs of attachment were taken out against the defendant by William F. Turnbull, Eben Turnbull, and R. S. FitzRandolph. These were then recorded, and in April following judgments were obtained in the two first-mentioned suits, which were then recorded. The assignment of the mortgage to the plaintiffs was not recorded till the month of May, 1881.

The parties, who have issued their attachments and had them recorded so as to become a lien on any property of the defendant, who had absconded from the province, claim that, inasmuch as the assignment of the mortgage to the plaintiffs was not on record when they took out their writs, which they were induced to do from finding, from what appeared on the books of registry, that the title to the land in question was vested absolutely in the defendant, they are, under the Registry Act, entitled to priority, and should be paid the amount due them in the first instance out of the proceeds of the sale.

The sections of the act relied on by Mr. Ritchie in support of this claim are the 19th and 22nd. The former is to the effect that deeds or mortgages of land, duly executed, but not registered, shall be void against any subsequent purchaser or mortgagee for valuable consideration who shall first register his deed or mortgage; and by the 22nd it is provided that a judgment duly recorded and docketed shall bind the lands of the party against whom the judgment shall have passed from and after the registry thereof as effectually as a mortgage, and deeds and mortgages of such lands, duly executed but not recorded, shall be void against the judgment creditor who shall first register his judgment.

The nineteenth section, it appears to me, has no application to this case, as it has reference only to the case of a purchaser or mortgagee. It is under the twenty-second section that the efficacy is given to a recorded judgment over subsequently recorded deeds and mortgages, and it is placed on the same footing as a mortgage. Now the mortgage under foreclosure in this suit was duly recorded previous to the judgment, and was held by a *bona fide* assignee for valuable consideration. Is the assignee to lose his priority of claim on the property from not having recorded the assignment to him? The only object to be attained by the recording of the assignment of a mortgage would be the protection of the assignee against a subsequent assignment by the mortgagee; the mortgage remains a lien on the property whether the assignment be recorded or not. It is true that from the records, as they stood when the judgment was recorded, the inference would have been that the mortgagee, having taken a conveyance of the equity of redemption, had acquired an absolute title to the land; and if one had purchased from him for valuable consideration, and without knowledge of the assignment of the mortgage, he might have reason to complain of being misled by its not having been recorded;—even then, if there was no actual merger, he would be remediless;—but a judgment creditor stands in a different position. He did not advance money on the property or on the title to it appearing on the records. The only ground upon which the present claimants can obtain priority over the mortgage is by shewing that not only was there an apparent merger but an actual merger of the estate in the defendant, the original mortgagee, and it is clear that this was not the case, for there is merger only when two estates in land coincide and meet in one and the same person without any intermediate estate. Here, when the equity of redemption was conveyed to the defendant, the legal estate in the land was vested in the plaintiffs. Had there been no assignment of the mortgage, and only then, would there have been a merger of the whole estate in the defendant. It is laid down in *Jones on Mortgages*, section 872, " that purchasers cannot rely upon the records as shewing merger, inasmuch as merger generally takes place or not according to the actual or presumed intention of the mortgagee. They must go beyond this and ascertain whether there has been a merger in fact, and they act at their peril if they do not require their grantor to produce the mortgage supposed to be merged."

The rule *nisi* taken out by the judgment creditors must be discharged.

ALMON ET AL. *v.* HUTT.

THE City of Halifax has no lien upon real estate for taxes, section 342, of chapter 81, of the Acts of 1864, having reference only to personal property.*

RITCHIE, E. J., (November 22nd, 1881,) delivered the judgment of the Court:—

The real estate of the defendant, mortgaged to the plaintiffs' having been sold under the foreclosure, a surplus remained after payment of the amount due on the mortgage and costs. This surplus is claimed by William C. Silver and others, they having, on the 10th April last, attached the land under a writ issued against the defendant as an absconding debtor, and subsequently obtained a judgment against him, which was recorded on the 14th October last. This claim is opposed by the City of Halifax on the ground that the mortgaged land was assessed on 4th June last for city, school, and poor rates for the current year, which are still due, and section 342 of chapter 81 of the Acts of 1864, " An Act concerning the City of Halifax," was relied on as entitling the city to be paid in the first instance. That section provides that " no property of any party shall be liable to be taken by virtue of any assignment or mortgage, or execution unless the party who holds the assignment or mortgage, or at whose suit the execution is sued out shall, before taking into possession the property or removal of any goods, pay the city rates for the then current year, and the sheriff or his deputy or other officer is required to levy and pay to the city treasurer such rates or assessments, and the assignee, mortgagee, or judgment creditor who takes the property of any debtor or party, if he do not pay such rates within two days after taking possession, shall be liable to an action for the amount in the name of the City of Halifax, or the *goods so taken may be distrained* upon by the city treasurer for such rates or costs."

This section, it appears to me, has no reference to real estate, and is to be read in connection with the next preceding section, which enacts, " that the *personal* property of all persons assessed shall be liable for city rates, notwithstanding

---

*N. B., the date of the decision.

any assignment or other conveyance made by the owner of the property, or any judgment against him, or execution issued to bind the property." The subsequent section was merely intended to carry out this provision.

My attention was not called to any section of the act which gives the city a lien on the real estate of the party assessed, and I can find none. Such a lien can only be acquired by the city, like other creditors, by obtaining a judgment and recording it, or, if the debtor be absent, by attachment under the 371st section, and then the priority of lien would depend upon the time of registry. Indeed, I do not see how otherwise than by a judgment the city could enforce any claim on real estate. The 369th section points out the only mode of obtaining payment in a summary manner, which is by warrant of distraint, and by it goods and chattels are alone subject to be distrained.

Under these circumstances the Messrs. Silver have a prior right to be paid out of the surplus fund arising from the sale of the property, they having acquired a lien on it next after the mortgage foreclosed in this suit.

GRIFFIN ET AL. v. TAYLOR.

INJUNCTION dissolved on the ground of suppression of material facts, and because the case on which it was obtained was fully met by defendant.

RITCHIE, E. J., (July 11th, 1881,) delivered the judgment of the Court :—

The injunction which is now sought to be dissolved was obtained by the plaintiffs on the affidavit of one of them, Patrick J. Griffin. It enjoined the defendant from collecting any debts due to them and from enforcing a certain judgment obtained by him in the County Court at Halifax against one Mark Power. The defendant has fully answered the plaintiffs' writ, and, assuming the statements in his answer and in his affidavit to be true, as I must do so far as regards the dissolution of the injunction, he has shewn that he is entitled to enforce the judgment referred to, and that he never attempted and is not attempting to collect debts due to the plaintiffs, or interfering in any way with their business, and he asserts that the debt due by Mark Power, for which he obtained judgment, was due to him, and that he obtained judgment after a trial had, and the defence set up was an equitable defence, involving the same questions raised by the plaintiffs in this suit, at which trial the whole matter was gone into, and both Norris, the plaintiff, and Mr. Wallace, his attorney in this suit, were examined ; indeed, they were the only witnesses produced to substantiate the defence.

Had the facts within the knowledge of the plaintiff, (Griffin,) been stated by him on his application for the injunction, it would never have been granted, and it must now be dissolved on the ground of the suppression of material facts as well as on the ground that the case made by the plaintiffs on which it was obtained has been fully met by the answer and affidavit of the defendant.

STEEL COMP'Y CANADA, (LIMITED,) *v.* VANCE ET AL.

PLAINTIFFS alleged in their bill that one of the defendants accepted and executed a lease for fourteen years, determinable on six months' notice, that notice was given, but the period had not expired ; that said defendant intended to contest the right of the plaintiffs, and set up a title in the other defendant to defeat the plaintiffs ; that while this litigation was threatened no action could at present be brought, and that the evidence of a certain witness would be necessary and material to enable them to establish this claim ; that he was aged and about to leave the Province, and though they could obtain his evidence now, they might not be able to do so at the time of an action hereafter brought.

Held, that sufficient had been set out to sustain plaintiffs' bill to perpetuate testimony, and the bill was not demurrable.

RITCHIE, E. J., (March 28th, 1881,) delivered the judgment of the Court :—

I do not think that the demurrer in this case can be sustained.

Our statute provides that where a person shall be desirous to perpetuate the testimony of any witness he may issue a writ of summons, which shall set forth briefly his title, claim or interest in or to the subject concerning which he desires to perpetuate the testimony, and the names of the parties interested or supposed to be interested therein, and the names of the witnesses proposed to be examined. All this the plaintiffs have stated in their writ. They have alleged that the defendant, (Vance,) has accepted and executed a lease from them of the land described therein for the term of fourteen years, determinable on six months' notice. This notice has been given, but the period has not yet expired, and she now alleges that she intends to contend that her execution of the lease was obtained from her by the fraud of the plaintiffs, with the view of preventing them from resuming possession of the land at the expiration of the notice, and that it will be attempted to set up the title of the other defendant, (Phillips,) to defeat that of the plaintiffs ; and that while this litigation is in prospect and threatened, no action can at present be instituted, and that the evidence of James Johnson will be necessary and material to enable them to establish their right to the land and to rebut any claim which may be set up by the defendants or either of them ; that he is an aged person and about to leave the province, and, though now they can obtain his evidence, they may not be able to do so at the time of an action which may hereafter be brought. This, it appears to me, fully complies with all the requirements of our statute, and if the same objections could be taken by demurrer under it as could be taken on a bill to perpetuate testimony under the English practice, I should still think that all was stated that is required by that practice. The demurrer must therefore be overruled with costs.

ATTORNEY GENERAL *v.* AXFORD ET AL.

By letters patent in 1796, the school lands in the township of Cornwallis were granted to the then Rector and Wardens, and the Rector and Wardens for the time being of St. John's Church, Cornwallis, in trust for the use of the school or schools in Cornwallis, to have and to hold during their continuance in the said offices, respectively, for the convenience and benefit of all the inhabitants of said township ; and in trust that all schools in the township furnished with teachers qualified agreeably to law, and contracted with for a term not less than a year, should be entitled to an equal portion of the rents and profits, provided such masters should receive, free of expense, such poor children as might be sent to them by the trustees. Down to 1873 the rents and profits were divided among all the schools of the township complying with the terms set out. After that date the funds were allowed to accumulate, until 1879, when the defendants, being trustees, proposed to appropriate the proceeds to the erection of a school-house in a particular school section, on land which did not belong to the township, but of which the trustees expected to get a deed. The section, in which it was proposed to erect the school-house, was twenty miles distant from one end of the township.

Held, that the lands were held subject to a trust for the benefit of all the schools complying with the terms, and that the proceeds must be divided among them all, and that the action was rightly brought in the name of the Attorney General of the Province, and not of the Attorney General of Canada.

RITCHIE, E. J., delivered the judgment of the Court :—

These proceeedings have been instituted in the name of Mr. Thompson, the Attorney-General of Nova Scotia, on the relation of David N. Dickie and others, on behalf of themselves and the rest of the inhabitants and rate-payers of the Township of Cornwallis, against the Reverend Frederick J. Axford, and William Smith, and Henry Zinck, the Rector and Church-wardens of the Church of St. John in that township. In the writ it is alleged that in the grant of the township, dated the 21st July, 1761, a certain portion of the land of the township was granted and set apart for school purposes, which was, by an act of the legislature passed in June, 1766, vested in trustees for the use and support of schools, that in August following trustees were appointed for such purpose, and the land was held by them and their successors in trust for the schools of the township ; that in 1796 the school lands in the township were by letters patent under the great seal of the province granted to the Reverend William Twining, and John Burbridge and Benjamin Belcher, the then Rector and Wardens of the Church of St. John, and the Rector and Wardens of that Church for the time being, in trust for the use of the school or schools in Cornwallis, to have and to hold during their continuance in the said offices respectively, and to the Rector and Wardens of the said Church for the time being, in special trust to and for the use of one or more school or schools, as might be deemed necessary by the said trustees for *the convenience and benefit of all the inhabitants of the said Township of Cornwallis,* and in trust *that all schools in*

*the said township furnished or supplied with masters qualified
agreeably to the law of the province and contracted with for a
term not less than a whole year should be entitled to an equal
share or portion of the rents and profits arising from said
school lands, provided the masters or teachers thereof should
receive and instruct, free of expense, such poor children as
might be sent them by the said trustees;* that the Rector and
Wardens entered into possession of the lands described in the
writ, and have managed them and acted as such trustees to
the present time; that the Township of Cornwallis is about
twenty-five miles in length and twelve in width, and schools
were established in different parts of it for the benefit and
convenience of all the inhabitants, the masters of which
instructed such poor children as were sent to them from time
to time, and the rents and profits of the lands were divided
annually by the trustees among all the schools the masters of
which complied with the terms required until about 1873,
after which, all the schools having become free, the trustees
refused and neglected to apply the rents and profits arising
from them, (which amounted to about $350 annually,) for the
use of the schools of the township, and allowed the same to
accumulate, so that when the defendants became trustees in
1879 they received from their predecessors the sum of $1,218,
and are about to or have appropriated this accumulation to
the erection of a school house in School Section No. 61, in the
township, which will be of no benefit or convenience to the
general inhabitants of the township, and on land which does
not belong to the trust or the trustees of the school section,
so that all money expended thereon will be lost to the trust;
that there are now schools in the township in which all poor
scholars are instructed free of expense, the masters of which
are duly qualified and contracted with for a term of not less
than a whole year, but the defendants refuse to divide the
rents and profits of these lands among them.

In their answer the defendants admit the issue of the
letters patent to the Reverend William Twining, the Rector
of the Church of St. John, and John Burbridge and Benjamin
Belcher, Wardens of that Church, but they submit that the
estate given by the grant was for their joint lives only, and that

the said three trustees departed this life many years ago and long previous to the possession by the defendants of the lands and moneys referred to; and they admit that since they became such Rector and Church Wardens they have been in possession of all the lands described in the plaintiffs' writ, except three lots which they specify, which have never been in their possession or that of their predecessors; that the land of which they are in possession was received by them from their predecessors in their several offices, from whom they also received the sum of $1,249.07 as accumulations of the rents and profits, but that the net annual income from them does not exceed $250. They believe it to be true that their predecessors annually divided among the schools in the township such portion of the rents and profits of the lands as were not used in improving the same until the present system of free school education was introduced by legislation, after which the schools became so numerous that the sum each would receive would be so small as to be of no practical use.

The defendants admit that they have appropriated the money received by them to the erection of a school house in School Section No. 61, but they deny that it would not be of any benefit to the general inhabitants of the township, or that the money so expended will be lost, and they insist that, in exercising the discretion of building the school house, and providing a teacher therefor, open to all the inhabitants of the township who may resort thereto, they are fulfilling the spirit of the alleged trust; and they further allege that under the statements in the writ the plaintiffs are not entitled to relief in this Court, and if so, not the relief sought, and that the suit could not properly be instituted by the Attorney-General of Nova Scotia; that if such a suit could be maintained it could only be legally instituted by the Attorney-General of Canada.

The case is not very much varied by the evidence. Mr. Axford says that the trustees of the school lands propose to obtain a lease of the land from the Rector and Church Wardens on which they have commenced to erect the school house. He admits that neither the vestry nor the parishioners have agreed or consented that such lease should be given;

that a portion of the trust funds, about $200, was applied in support of School Section No. 61, under the control of the district school trustees ; about six children attended the school from other districts who were charged for,—the books shew that five were so charged for. He admits that it is about twenty miles from that school west to the end of the township, and practically that the school is only available for children of that district and those near it. He went to the parish in June, 1879, and was inducted in August following ; there are about sixty school sections in the Township of Cornwallis ; the school house which the trustees, (the defendants,) were erecting was to cost $1,300, and was intended to be a public school open to all, and not in any respect for the private use of the parish. Mr. Axford produced three books relating to these lands and the division of the proceeds of them, viz., a record book commencing in 1802, and two account books. Mr. Robert Starr was also examined. He stated that he was a church warden and trustee of school lands previous to the appointment of Smith and Zinck, and when he went out of office he delivered the books to the present trustees. As trustee he distributed the funds arising from the lands by paying a dividend to all the teachers in the township who had put in a certificate from the trustees of their sections that they had taught according to the law, being yearly teachers ; after 1872 he stopped making these payments. The record book in evidence commenced in 1802, on the appointment of new church wardens, the offices having become vacant by the resignation of John Burbridge and the death of Benjamin Belcher, and in 1806, the Reverend William Twining having removed to another parish, the Reverend Mr. Norris was inducted in his stead, and he and all succeeding Rectors, as well as all church wardens, as they were from time to time appointed, assumed the duties of trustees, and applied the proceeds of the lands in strict accordance with the terms of the trust.

By the grant of 1761 of the Township of Cornwallis the lands intended for schools were reserved for that purpose rather than granted ; it is unnecessary, however, to go beyond the grant of 1796, as, on the passing of that grant, the parties to whom the land was then granted entered into possession and accepted the trust conferred upon them with the acquiescence of the other grantees, the inhabitants of the township, as have their successors in the respective offices of Rector and Church Wardens of St. John's Church from time to time, and all that is now required of the present defendants is that they, being in possession of the land, will carry out the trust as expressed in the grant.

The defendants are wrong in assuming that the parties named in the grant as trustees took a life estate in the lands, for they were to hold them no longer than their tenure of office. Whether they had an estate for life or while they remained in office the present defendants could claim no title through them, the Rector and Church Wardens not being a corporate body. But however imperfect their legal title, it would not necessarily affect the rights of the *cestuis que trustent;* their interest in the land was not to be confined to the time during which the first trustees held office. That appears expressly from the terms of the grant, and it is a principle well recognized in equity that a trust which has been explicitly created shall never fail from want of a trustee. Whether the trustee named was an improper or incapable one, or had died or refused to act, the lapse of the legal estate has no influence on the trust, and, as the persons named as trustees are only the instruments to execute the trust, this Court will supply the want on failure of a trustee. See *Spence on Equity Jurisdiction.* vol. 1, p. 501, vol., 2, p. 51, 876. And if in this case, in consequence of the parties named in the grant as trustees not being a corporate body, so that the title could not vest in their successors, and the legal title should be held to revert to the crown, it would revert subject to the trust created by the crown, and equity would still follow the property and execute the trust by the appointment of new trustees, as where the legal title of land clothed with a trust escheats to the crown from failure of the heirs of the trustees. See *Hughes* v. *Wells,* 9 Hare, 749. For property charged with a trust will in equity be followed into whosesoever hands it comes, unless he is a purchaser for value without notice ; and these defendants, having gone into possession of the land in question aware of the trust, and in the character of trustees, whether they have a good title or not, will, as regards the *cestuis que trustent*, be deemed trustees *de facto*, and if without a title, as an imperfectly appointed trustee in one case was termed, a trustee *de son tort*. As these defendants received the lands from their predecessors, who, while in office, had always recognized and carried out the trust, they could only accept them subject to the trust, or repudiate all connection with the property. Their only defence now can be that the course they were pursuing with respect to it was justified by the terms of the trust, and this involves the simple question whether the benefit intended to be conferred by the Crown was to be enjoyed by the inhabitants of the whole township of Cornwallis, or whether the defendants have a discretionary power of confining it to one school section of the township, and, with the funds in their hands as trustees, erecting a school house on lands not belonging to the section or the township.

The terms of the grant are, in my opinion, so explicit as to preclude any other inference than that all the schools in the township were to participate in the benefit conferred which were supplied with masters legally qualified, who were engaged for a period not less than one year, and who should instruct poor children sent them by the trustees; all such were entitled as of right to an equal share of the rents and profits arising from the lands. Had the terms of the grant been less explicit the natural inference would have been that, when the whole lands of the township were parted with by the crown to the inhabitants, a portion of which was reserved for education; the benefit was intended for all of the inhabitants, and from the passing of the grant of 1796 to 1872 those who acted as trustees under it, the Rector and Church Wardens of the Church of St. John for the time being, exercised no discretion in the matter, but simply carried out the trust in its terms, and in my opinion they pursued the only legal course open to them.

Free schools were established in the province in the year 1865, after which for six or seven years the rents and profits of the lands were distributed among the teachers as theretofore. The only reason for then ceasing to make the distribution given by the defendants is that the amount to each would be too small to be of any use. The new system introduced by the legislature involved the levying of an assessment on the several school sections of the township, for the erection of school houses and the payment of teachers, and the distribution in the terms of the grant was as applicable after as before the change, and was felt to be so by the trustees up to 1872; and as no discretion was given them by the terms of the trust, they were not justified, for the reason they have assigned, not only in ceasing to make a division of the money as directed, but in applying it otherwise than they were authorized by the grant, and if they had a discretion given them of disposing of the money as they should see fit for the benefit of the inhabitants of the township, the exercise of it in the mode proposed would be a most unfair appropriation in expending what was intended for the whole township in the erection of a school house in one section of the township, and that a populous and wealthy one, leaving the other sections of the township to erect their school houses from their own funds. And I cannot think that the defendants would have exercised sound judgment in expending the trust fund on a building erected on land belonging to the parish of St. John's Church, of which the school section or the trustees had no title nor any certainty of obtaining one; but in the view I have taken of the case this is unimportant. On the other ground I think the defendants should be restrained from expending the money in their hands arising from the rents and profits of the lands in question other than as expressed in the grant, and that the mode in which they proposed to expend them, the erection of the school house in section 61, is in violation of the trust.

It remains to be considered whether the proceedings in this case have been properly instituted by the Attorney-General of Nova Scotia. I can see no ground for the contention that the only person who could institute them was the Attorney-General of Canada. The office of Attorney-General for the Province of Nova Scotia is expressly recognized in the British North America Act, and the constitution of the executive authority in the province was to continue as it existed at the union until altered by that act or under its provisions, and the whole subject matter of the suit is of a local nature, so that it appears to me that it would be out of place for the Attorney-General of Canada to interfere in a case like this. The recognition of such an officer as the Attorney-General of Nova Scotia in the British North America Act assumes that he is, at least in certain cases, to represent Her Majesty. He is recognized as representing her in criminal proceedings, over which the Dominion Parliament has legislative control, and surely where the matter is of a purely local nature and in relation to lands held under grant from the crown which originally belonged to the province, though held in the name of the Crown, over which the local legislature has control, if in any case that officer is to represent Her Majesty, it is in such as this, and though a provincial, he is still a Crown officer, with power to act on behalf of the Crown in all provincial matters requiring the intervention of a Crown officer.

With reference to the trust, I may add that if, in the opinion of the trustees, the trust from altered circumstances could not be carried out in its terms, they could have applied to this Court to authorize a mode of disposing of the trust fund so as to carry out as nearly as possible the intention of the grantor.

CREIGHTON v. MERCHANTS' BANK OF HALIFAX.

THE insolvent, T. J. B., being indebted to the Merchants' Bank, instructed the cashier of the Railway Department by letter, dated Oct. 22, to send to G. M., the cashier of the Bank, any cheque coming to him from the Department. On Nov. 7 a cheque for $691.76, payable to the order of the insolvent, was enclosed in a letter, addressed to the insolvent, care of Merchants' Bank. The agreement between the insolvent and the cashier of the Bank, when the letter was written, was, according to the evidence of the former, that the Bank should have $300 of the money, according to cashier's evidence, $350. The cashier opened the letter and endorsed the cheque "T. J. B., per G. M., agent. For Merchants' Bank of Halifax. Guaranteed. G. M., cashier." The writ of attachment against the insolvent was issued January 18, 1879.

Held, that the cashier had no authority to open the letter or endorse the cheque, but that the Bank was entitled to retain the $300 as agreed upon; that this amount could not be recovered by the assignee under the 130th section of the Act, which had no reference to a case like this, nor under the 134th section, as that was confined to payments made within thirty days of the insolvency.

RITCHIE, E. J., delivered the judgment of the Court :—

The plaintiff, as assignee of Thomas J. Bentley, an insolvent, asks this Court to decree that the defendants should refund a sum of money unjustly received and retained in fraud of the insolvent, and of the rights of his other creditors, and of the plaintiff as their assignee. It appears from the evidence that the railway department was indebted to Bentley, and he, being indebted to the bank, promised Maclean, the cashier, to make him a payment from the money to be received from the department, and, at the instance and in the presence of the cashier, he wrote to Thomas Foot, the cashier of the department, the following letter :—

" DEAR SIR,—Please send to George Maclean, cashier, any cheque coming to me from your department.
                                    THOMAS J. BENTLEY."

This letter was dated 22nd October, 1878, and on the 7th November following Foot enclosed a cheque for $691.76 in a letter addressed to T. J. Bentley, Esq., care of Merchants' Bank, Halifax. The cheque was payable to the order of Bentley, and the letter was in these terms ; " Sir,—I beg to send you herewith cheque No. 7017, $691.76, in payment of voucher No. 1129. Please acknowledge on this form and send to me by return of mail ;" and across its face was ; " Received the within cheque." When the letter was written by Bentley the agreement between him and Maclean was, as Bentley says, that Maclean should receive $300 out of the money, as Maclean says, $350, and according to his account, he was to receive the cheque from the department, and on getting it cashed, to keep that sum and pay over to Bentley the balance. This Bentley denies. He asserts that before signing the letter to Foot, Maclean wanted to receive out of the money $350, which he refused to allow, and he said to him ; " Mr. Maclean, you must give me that cheque when it comes ;" to which he replied ; " Certainly." He then makes the following statement, which remains uncontradicted ; " Mr. Maclean, some time after, sent me a note to come and see him. He then said ; ' Before you get that cheque you have got to get all that wood placed in some safe keeping,' (referring to certain hard pine which had been given to the bank as security). I said; 'All right, but I want the cheque.' He replied that I was not going to get it, or something to that effect. I said; 'If I don't get it I will be in trouble; because if I get that money I can pay McNab, and McNab would help me.' He said I could not get it until he was satisfied. I said; 'Give me that cheque, it is no good to you, and if I don't get it I will burst up.' I saw the envelope in which the cheque had been sent, it was addressed to me. I asked him why he had opened it; I don't remember now what he replied to that. I did not endorse that cheque, nor did I give a receipt for it. I was asked by him to endorse it. I refused and said to give me the cheque and I would give the amount I had promised, $300." A month or six weeks after Maclean told him they had got the money and were going to keep it.

Bentley was indebted to the bank in about $1,000, on notes which had been a long time overdue, and Bentley had used the pine on which the bank had security. On the 18th January, 1879, a writ of attachment was taken out against him under the Insolvent Act.

Maclean admits that he opened the letter and received the amount of the cheque from the Bank of Montreal, on which it was drawn, and has received the whole amount. In order to obtain payment of the check, which was made payable to Bentley's order, Maclean endorsed it thus; "Thomas J. Bentley, per George Maclean, Agent. For Merchants' Bank of Halifax. Guaranteed. George Maclean, Cashier." When the money was received by Maclean does not appear, but his letter to Mr. Foot acknowledging the receipt of the cheque is dated the 28th November, up to which time it was evident Bentley had not authorized him to keep the whole of the money. It is in these terms :—

"THOS. FOOT, Esq., MONCTON,

"Dear Sir,—I duly received the check in favor of Bently, which he authorised you to send me, but we have not yet agreed as to my share of it. In the meantime, if you desire it, I will sign the receipt on his behalf. With many thanks,

"I am Sir, yours truly,

"GEO. MACLEAN, Cashier."

Under these circumstances is the Bank entitled to retain the whole or any or what part of the money so obtained by its cashier ?

It is obvious that the reason for having the check sent in a letter, addressed to the care of the cashier of the Bank, instead of being sent to Bently direct, was to ensure to the Bank the receipt of the sum which Bently had promised ; this, under the contradictory statements regarding the amount, I must assume to have been the smaller sum, and Maclean might have been well justified in insisting on holding the letter if Bently had repudiated the agreement, but he had no right whatever to open the letter nor to endorse the check. The evidence clearly shews that he had no authority from Bently to do so. But, notwithstanding the cashier was not justified in the course he pursued, as the Bank, it is admitted, was entitled to the $300, there are no grounds for requiring that this at once should be refunded, unless, as was contended, the receipt of it was in contravention of the insolvent law, in support of which contention the only section of the Insolvent Act specially relied on was the 130th, but that clearly has no reference to a case like this, assuming as we must that Bently was then unable to meet his engagements. The only section applicable to payments made a debtor, under such circumstances, is the 134th, and that is confined to payments made within thirty days next before the demand of an assignment or the issue of an attachment.

On the refusal of Maclean to give up the check to Bently, and his refusing to receive the $300, the latter, in order to obtain it, agreed to procure two notes for $250, one signed by McPherson, the other by Abbott, and also to transfer certain property to the Bank as security. The notes he was unable to procure and that arrangement fell through in consequence. This was much relied on by the defendant's counsel, as enabling the Bank to appropriate the whole proceeds of the check in discharge of the amount due by Bently, but I cannot come to such a conclusion. Heavy pressure was put upon him to induce him to comply with the demand made by the cashier, and he no doubt would have obtained the security stipulated as a condition of his getting what he was entitled to, independently of any such stipulation, if he had been able to do so, but his inability to do it gave the Bank no right to the money; and in the circumstances in which Bently then was, it is clear that if he had yielded to the demand of the Bank, it would have been at the expense of his other creditors whose interest he was bound to regard as well as that of the Bank.

The decree will be in favor of the plaintiff for the balance of the check received by the cashier of the Bank over the $300, with interest and the costs.

HIGGINS v. McLACHLAN.

To a suit brought to foreclose a mortgage, defendant relied chiefly upon two grounds of defence,—first, that, concurrently with the making of the mortgage, plaintiff gave defendant a bond whereby he bound himself to erect a double house on the land within ten months, which defendant contended had not been built in such a manner as contemplated by the agreement; secondly, that the principal was not to become payable until ten years after the date of the mortgage. The number of years was left blank in the mortgage. Defendant swore that it was to be ten years, which plaintiff denied, and there was no other evidence.

Held, that the first defence could not prevail, as, assuming the defendant's statement to be true, it only formed the ground of an action for damages, and that, as to the second, as there was no satisfactory evidence to supply the omission of the number of years, the Court must construe the mortgage as if no time was mentioned, and plaintiff had a right to foreclose.

RITCHIE, E. J., delivered the judgment of the Court :—

This suit is brought to foreclose a mortgage made by the defendant to the plaintiff to secure the re-payment of $1,000 and interest. The defence is that the defendant was to have ten years for the payment of the principal, which period has not yet expired, and that no interest was due when the writ issued, and no interest was to accrue on the mortgage till after the expiration of ten months from its date. He also relies on a defence arising out of two instruments executed concurrently with the mortgage, the one a bond given by the plaintiff to the defendant, whereby he bound himself within ten months to cause to be built upon the mortgaged premises, at a cost of not less than $1,500, a double dwelling house; the other a lease executed by the defendant, whereby, in consideration of

10 *s*

$600, he leased to the plaintiff the north half of the house to be so built for the lives of himself and his wife, which house was built and occupied by the families of plaintiff and defendant until the death of the wife of the latter, who was a daughter of the plaintiff; and the defendant now urges as a defence to this suit that the house was not such a one as was contemplated by their agreement. This, in my opinion forms no ground of defence to this suit, and all the evidence adduced on the subject is irrelevant. If the house was not built according to contract,—and I am far from intimating that from the evidence such appears to have been the case,—the defendant's remedy was by an action for damages. And as to the lease which was given in evidence it is difficult to see why it was introduced, as it has really no bearing whatever on the case. The only questions, therefore, are whether the interest was to accrue from the date of the mortgage or from ten months thereafter, and whether the defendant is entitled to ten years within which to pay the principal.

As regards the interest, even if a verbal agreement to the contrary had been satisfactorily proved, the terms of the mortgage must prevail. In it the defendant bound himself to pay interest from its date, and oral evidence is not receivable to contradict it and shew that it was not to accrue till a later date, but if such evidence had been receivable all we have here is the uncorroborated statement of the defendant met by the positive denial of the plaintiff.

The other question involves a somewhat different principle, for, though parol evidence cannot be admitted to vary or contradict a written instrument, it may be received to supply an omission where, as in this case, a blank has been left for the time of payment; but can we adopt the defendant's view, and fill it up with ten years? Both plaintiff and defendant admit the existence of the blank, and it is evident that time was to be given, but there is no satisfactory evidence of the extent of such time. The defendant swears that ten years was the time agreed upon. This the plaintiff positively denies under his oath, and there is no other evidence on the subject. Had this been a suit to reform the mortgage it must have failed, and the Court must look to the instrument as it now appears and put the same construction on it as if no time was mentioned for the payment; and I am led to the inference that not only was there an omission to fill up the blank in the mortgage before its execution, but that when it was executed the time when the money should become payable had not been definitely agreed upon. Under these circumstances the plaintiff had a right to commence a suit for the foreclosure, and is entitled to a decree.

BOND v. HUTCHINSON ET AL.

R. M. & Co. sought to have surplus proceeds arising out of a sale under foreclosure applied to a recorded judgment held by them against the mortgagor. The judgment was recorded in May, 1874. Plaintiff's mortgage had been recorded in 1869, and a prior mortgage of the same property had been recorded in 1855. Defendant having become insolvent, his assignee, in order to prevent the sacrifice of the property, paid off the mortgage last mentioned and the interest on plaintiff's mortgage, receiving from the holders of the mortgage which he paid an instrument in which, after reciting payment of the principal and interest, it expressed that the bond was delivered up to be cancelled, (which, however, was not cancelled, but was produced with the mortgage,) and that they remised, released, and quitted claim to him, as assignee, the land therein mentioned, and all the right which they had as executors, and all sums mentioned therein, to have and to hold to the said K., as assignee as aforesaid, his successors and assigns.

Held, that this instrument, though inartificially drawn, was open to the construction that it was a satisfaction of the debt as between the executors and the assignee, but conveyed to the latter all their interest in the mortgage as against subsequent incumbrancers; but that, even assuming that it was a release of the mortgage, and not an assignment, the assignee had a prior claim to the surplus proceeds for the amounts he had advanced on the mortgage to prevent foreclosure and sale, subject to a credit for any amounts received by him for rent of the mortgaged premises.

The assignee had also recovered judgment against the sheriff, who had been indemnified by R. M. & Co., and they being entitled to a lien on the land if their judgment against the defendant was established, if not to a dividend out of defendant's estate, it was agreed that they should be relieved of the assignee's judgment against the sheriff, and that the amount should go against their judgment in the event of its being held valid, or if not, then against their dividend.

Held, that the assignee, under this agreement, had also a prior claim on the surplus proceeds for the amount of the judgment against the sheriff, and that R. M. & Co. were entitled only to the balance.

RITCHIE, E. J., delivered the judgment of the Court:—

On the foreclosure and sale of the mortgaged premises in this suit a surplus remains after payment of the amount due the plaintiff, which Ryerson, Moses & Co. seek to have applied in payment to them of the amount due on a judgment against Hutchinson, which was recorded to bind real estate.

At the time Hutchinson became insolvent, besides this judgment, which was recorded the 1st May, 1874, shortly before his insolvency, there was a mortgage on his property to Henry G. Farish for £100, recorded the 15th February, 1855, and the mortgage to Bond for $1,800, recorded the 12th August, 1869. The land was sold under the foreclosure of the latter mortgage on the 12th August, 1878, and the amount of the surplus proceeds subject to the order of the Court is $5,000.

It appears from the affidavits that Kinney, the assignee of Hutchinson, in September, 1876, in order to prevent the foreclosure and sale of the land subject to the mortgages, paid the amount due on the Farish mortgage, $406.87, and the interest due on the mortgage to Bond, $315.36; these sums Kinney contends he is entitled to out of the fund in Court. He also claims to be entitled to the further sum of $2,236.41, which was advanced to Ryerson, Moses & Co., pending a litigation as to the validity of their judgment, which, it was alleged, was entered in violation of the Insolvent Acts.

It is admitted, as regards the sum paid to take up the Farish mortgage, that if Kinney had taken an assignment of it he would have been entitled to the first claim on the fund. It is obvious that Kinney, in taking up that mortgage, did so in the interest of the estate of which he was assignee, to preserve the property from foreclosure and probable sacrifice, and not to better the position of Ryerson, Moses & Co.

If the mortgagor himself should pay off the mortgage on his property, it would enure for the benefit of subsequent encumbrancers, and by his doing so the mortgage so paid would simply be taken out of the way; but Kinney, standing in a different position, and paying off a mortgage which is threatened to be foreclosed, as assignee and with the funds of the estate of the insolvent, ought in justice to be entitled to take the place of the mortgagee. Ryerson, Moses & Co. are in no way prejudiced; they retain the lien to the same extent which they had when they obtained their judgment. It can hardly be contended that the intention of Kinney was to benefit them at the expense of the creditors of the estate, and I think the question is one of intention, whether the payment was made to relieve the property absolutely, or merely to protect it for the benefit of the parties interested, according to their respective rights in it, and Kinney may in that view assert his claim, though he may have taken no assignment of the mortgage. In *Shrewsbury* v. *Shrewsbury*, 1 Ves. Junr., 233, a charge on an estate was paid off, and an instrument was given and accepted, *purporting to be a discharge of the estate absolutely.* The Lord Chancellor held that it could not be raised higher than as a matter of evidence; that the party making the payment could not be intended *prima facie* to discharge the estate, because it would be discharging the estate of another person. There the tenant for life had paid off the charge. And in the late case of *Adams* v. *Angel*, T. R. 3 Ch. D., at page 645, JESSEL, M. R., says; " Now, in a Court of Equity, it has always been held that the mere fact of a charge having been paid off does not decide the question whether it is extinguished. If a charge is paid off by a tenant for life, *without any expression of his intention,* it is well established that he retains the benefit of it against the inheritance, although he has not declared his intention of keeping it alive ; *it is presumed that his intention was to keep it alive, because it is manifestly for his benefit;"* and again ; " It appears to me that the Vice-Chancellor was quite correct in saying that in all these cases the question is one of intention." Kinney tells us with what intention he took up the mortgage, and even if he had not, the only inference to be drawn from his having done so was that it was to benefit the estate of which he was assignee. I have thus far considered the case, assuming that no assignment had been made to him, but, on turning to the instrument executed by the executors of Farish on the receipt of the money, which at the argument was treated as a release and discharge of the mortgage, it appears to partake as much of the nature of an assignment as of a release. It recites that Kinney, as assignee of the estate and effects of Hutchinson, under the Insolvent Acts, paid them the principal and interest due on the mortgage, in consideration whereof and in full satisfaction of the mortgage and of the bond therein mentioned and therewith delivered up to be cancelled,(which, however, was never cancelled, and is produced with the bond and annexed to his affidavit,) they remised, released, and forever quitted claim to him as assignee the land therein mentioned, and all the right, title and interest, both at law and in equity, which they, as executors, had in and to the same, as also the said bond or obligation, and all such sum or sums as are therein mentioned to be paid ; to have and to hold the same to the said Kinney, as assignee as aforesaid, his successors in office and assigns, to his and their own use and behoof forever.   Looking at this instrument in the light of the surrounding circumstances, I consider it as a satisfaction of the mortgage and discharge of the debt as between the executors of Farish and Kinney, and the instrument cancelled so far as they were concerned, but, as regards subsequent encumbrancers and others as conveying to Kinney all the interest which the executors had in the land mortgaged and the bond or obligation, as well as the money secured thereby.   The document is not artificially drawn, but is open to the construction I have put upon it.   I think that Kinney therefore has a right, with respect to the funds in Court, to occupy the position the executors of Farish would have done if the mortgage were still in their hands unsatisfied ; and so with regard to the payment to keep down the interest on Bond's mortgage, made by Kinney, as assignee, he is entitled to a lien on the fund for the amount prior to Ryerson, Moses & Co. on their judgment.   It was suggested that Kinney had, since he became assignee, received rents from the mortgaged premises. If this should hereafter turn out to be the case, such rents must be credited against these claims.

As regards the $2,236.41, Kinney, as assignee, had recovered a judgment against the Sheriff of Yarmouth, who had been indemnified by Ryerson, Moses & Co., and they, being entitled to their lien on the real estate of the insolvent in case their judgment against him should be established, and if such should not be the case, being entitled to a dividend on the amount due them, he, at their instance, consented that they should be relieved from the payment of that sum which was due him on his judgment against the sheriff, which should go either in discharge of the dividend coming to them from the insolvent estate, if their judgment should be set aside, and if it should be held valid, should go to reduce the amount coming to them from the real estate bound by the judgment.

When the judgment was entered and recorded, there being two previous mortgages recorded against the land, the lien of Ryerson, Moses & Co. was subject to their priority, and one of them having been foreclosed and the land sold, leaving a surplus of $5,000, assuming that Kinney is entitled to the amount he paid on the mortgage he took up and the interest he paid on the other, amounting together to $722.23, and adopting, as I do, the account given by Kinney in his affidavit as correct, I think he is entitled to have deducted also the sum of $2,236.41, and the balance only will be payable to Ryerson, Moses & Co., who will have to make their claim for the amount remaining due to them on the assets of the estate of Hutchinson.

TREMAIN ET AL. *v.* MACKINTOSH ET AL.

Held, that an award could not be set aside at the instance of one of the defendants on the ground of a claim being improperly allowed against the plaintiffs.

Held, further, that where one of the objects of the suit was to require defendants to submit their differences to arbitration under an agreement to do so, and by the rule of reference all matters in difference in the suit were submitted to their award, the award could not be set aside because the arbitrators awarded damages to the plaintiffs.

Held, further, that where all the parties and the arbitrators themselves admitted that a mistake had been made in requiring one of the defendants, as part of the award, to pay off a certain mortgage, which should not have been required, the evidence of the arbitrators was receivable as to such a point, as well as on the point of their having taken into consideration matters not within their jurisdiction, and that, as the arbitrators had inadvertently made a mistake with reference to the mortgage, the award should be sent back to them to be corrected.

RITCHIE, E. J., delivered the judgment of the Court:—

This is an application made on behalf of two of the defendants, James C. Mackintosh and Mather B. Almon, to set aside an award made in the cause under a rule of Court. All of the arbitrators have concurred in awarding that James Jack, as assignee of Robert B. Mackintosh, on a final settlement is indebted to the plaintiffs in the sum of $34.85 ; that there is nothing due by the plaintiffs to J. C. Mackintosh and M. B. Almon, and nothing is due by the plaintiffs to them and James Jack, jointly or severally, and that the plaintiffs are entitled to have assigned to them by Robert B. Mackintosh certain plant, stock, &c., and that J. C. Mackintosh and M. B. Almon shall execute and deliver to Richard Tremain a conveyance of the lands and premises referred to in the plaintiffs' writ, free from encumbrances, and shall also release to him the mortgage made to W. B. Reynolds, there being nothing due to Robert B. Mackintosh or his assignee, or to J. C. Mackintosh and M. B. Almon.

The submission was of all matters of difference in the suit between the plaintiffs and defendants, and the plaintiffs and any one or more of the defendants, and it was ordered that the arbitrators should also settle and adjust the accounts between the plaintiffs and the defendant, Jack, assignee, and between the plaintiffs and defendants, Almon and J. C. Mackintosh and Jack, as such assignee, jointly, and should decide separately on each account.

In the rule *nisi* to set aside the award fifteen grounds are stated. Those relied on at the argument were that the arbitrators had exceeded their authority, inasmuch as they awarded damages against Robert B. Mackintosh for breach of his agreement with the plaintiff, Stewart Tremain, set out in the writ; that as this Court could not decree damages in the suit the arbitrators could not award them under the rule of reference; that they have included in their award matters which occurred subsequent to the commencement of the suit ; that they have awarded that Almon & Mackintosh should convey to the plaintiff, R. Tremain, the land referred to in the writ, free from all encumbrances, which is a gross mistake on the part of the arbitrators, as all the parties to the suit admit that, if he should be held entitled to a conveyance from them, it should be subject to a mortgage to the Nova Scotia Benefit Building Society. There is another ground, which, if sustainable by Robert B. Mackintosh or his assignee, is not available to Almon & Mackintosh, on whose behalf alone the rule *nisi* was taken out; that the award is uncertain on the face of it, in awarding certain property as belonging to Robert B.

Mackintosh, and certain other property as belonging to the plaintiffs, without sufficiently particularizing the articles to which each were entitled. It is sufficient, however, to say, as regards this last ground, that I see no uncertainty; what each is to take is, in my opinion, sufficiently defined. None of the other grounds relied on appears on the face of the award, and as the only evidence in regard to them is that of the arbitrators, and the reception of that has been objected to, it is necessary to consider to what extent it is receivable.

When an award has been made and published it must speak for itself, and cannot be explained or varied by extrinsic evidence of the intention of the arbitrators, and if good on the face of it it is final, and there is no appeal from it unless there is corruption or misconduct on the part of the arbitrators, or there has been an excess of jurisdiction, or there has been a mistake admitted to be such by the arbitrators. While, therefore, arbitrators are precluded from giving evidence as to the composition of their award or the elements which entered into their consideration in making it, if, as in this case, not only the arbitrators but all parties admit there has been a mistake in requiring Almon & Mackintosh to pay off the mortgage to the Nova Scotia Building Society, it would be discreditable to the administration of justice if there was no remedy. On such a point the arbitrators may be examined. So also may they if they have taken into consideration any matter not included in the reference to them, and therefore out of their jurisdiction. If this were not so there would be no means of ascertaining the fact. From the affidavits it appears that the arbitrators estimated damages occasioned to the plaintiffs by reason of the defendant, Robert B. Mackintosh, having failed to perform the conditions of his agreement referred to in the writ, and they have deducted them from the amount he would otherwise have been entitled to receive, and have taken into account money received from sales connected with the business since the commencement of the suit. This, however, consisted of a claim made and allowed *against* Tremain, and the allowance of it reduced the amount coming to him. It is evident that the arbitrators never intended that the defendants, Almon & Mackintosh, should relieve the land referred to from the mortgage to the Nova Scotia Benefit Building Society, and if the award bears that construction it is admitted that a mistake has been inadvertently made.

If the defendant, Robert B. Mackintosh, violated the terms of his agreement, it must be conceded that damages might be awarded against him on an ordinary reference, and I see no force in the contention that these arbitrators are precluded from awarding them because, by the rule of reference, all matters in difference *in the suit* were submitted to their award, and that as the Court could not award damages in the suit, so neither could they. But it was overlooked that one of the objects of the suit was to require the defendants to submit their differences to arbitration under an agreement to do so, and they having consented to the reference contended for by the plaintiffs in their writ, such reference took place just as if it had been entered upon without a suit, and in this view they would be justified in considering matters in relation to the differences between the parties in relation to the agreements referred to in the suit up to the time of making their award, and certainly it is no ground for setting aside the award that a claim of the defendants made by them *against the plaintiffs* is allowed.

Courts are always reluctant to interfere with the award of arbitrators who are judges selected by the parties, and, indeed, have no power to do so if they act within the scope of the submission when no improper motive or misconduct is imputed to them, and there has been no irregularity in their proceedings; for, having been constituted judges of the law and facts, their decision is final, subject to no appeal. And in this case the arbitrators are men experienced in business and well qualified for the office, and against whom no charge is made of improper motive or conduct. The award, therefore, must stand, except as regards the payment to Almon & Mackintosh of the mortgage to the Nova Scotia Benefit Building Society, which is admitted to be an error, not only by the arbitrators, but by the plaintiffs themselves. As regards that, the award will be remitted to the arbitrators to have it corrected.

MATHERS *v.* STAYNER ET AL.

PLAINTIFF set out an assignment to him of logs, which, when sawed, the assignors, in contravention of the assignment, shipped to Stayner ; an agreement with Stayner to indemnify him from loss and account for the proceeds in the same manner as if the lumber had been shipped to plaintiff under the assignment ; a receipt by Stayner of money on account of the lumber for which he refused to account. Defendant denied the allegations in the writ, but the Court sustained the plaintiff's view of the case on the evidence.

Held, that plaintiff was entitled to an account, and that the proceedings were properly instituted in the Equity Court.

RITCHIE, E. J., delivered the judgment of the Court :—

The plaintiff set out in his writ that Stephen P. Benjamin and Joseph M. Wentzell assigned to him a quantity of logs in the LaHave River, which they were to convert into lumber, of which he was to take delivery to meet advances theretofore made or thereafter to be made by the plaintiff to them, the lumber so delivered to be credited at certain prices therein specified ; that after the logs, or a large part of them, had been manufactured into lumber, and when there was due the plaintiff upwards of $4,009, or thereabout, a part of the lumber was shipped to the defendants, whereupon the plaintiff informed the defendants of his assignment, and forbade them receiving more of the lumber, and demanded from them what had been received, when it was agreed between the plaintiff and defendants that, in consideration of the plaintiff allowing them to receive the lumber and sell it, and to return what had been previously received, the defendants agreed to keep the plaintiff harmless from loss, and to protect him from loss in respect of the debt and advances secured by the assignment or bill of sale as fully and to the same extent as if he held and continued to hold the lumber under the same. In accordance with this agreement the plaintiff authorized the delivery of the remainder of the lumber to the defendants, who sold and received the proceeds of it, more than sufficient to pay the balance due to the plaintiff in respect of the advances made by him ; and though they had paid him $1,500 on account, they have refused to pay him the balance of his claim, amounting to $1,905.50, or to account for the amount produced by the sale of the lumber. And he prays that an account may be taken of what is due to the plaintiff under the said assignment or bill of sale, and of the quantity and value of the lumber and boards which have been received by the defendants, which were covered by the said assignment, and that they should be decreed to pay to him the amount due to him, with interest, being $1,905.59, with interest.

The defendants, in their answer, deny that they entered into the agreement as set out in the writ, and that they received the balance on the condition there stated. They deny that they received the proceeds, and say the $1,500 was obtained by misrepresentation, and they believe that, on a true accounting, nothing will be found to be due to the plaintiff in respect of the assignment or bill of sale from Benjamin and Wentzell to the plaintiff; and they deny that they are responsible for the advances made to them by the plaintiff.

The evidence, in my opinion, sustains the statements in the plaintiff's writ as regards the transfer to him of the logs by Benjamin and Wentzell, and the agreement between the plaintiff and defendants, and also the delivery of the lumber to them under it, and I find nothing which leads me to believe that the $1,500 was paid under any misrepresentation by the plaintiff. It was paid in pursuance of the agreement on account of the lumber received by them under it. Even under the evidence given by the defendants, it was incumbent on them to have given an account of all the lumber received by them, and the value of it, and in no view of the case can the contention in their answer prevail that the suit should be dismissed on the ground that proceedings should not be in a Court of Equity. It appears to me it is just such a case as can only be properly dealt with in this Court. The prayer of the writ will be granted and account taken as prayer for.

McLELLAN *v.* FULMORE.

DEFENDANT, in his answer to a suit for foreclosure of a mortgage, set out that the mortgage had been given to secure the payment of a note from defendant to plaintiff for £68 10s., and an advance of $200 to be made by plaintiff to defendant, which was made and re-paid by the defendant before the foreclosure suit was brought by plaintiff, as executor of the mortgagee. In his evidence defendant made an entirely different case,—that the note had been re-paid before the execution of the mortgage, and that the $200 paid by plaintiff to defendant was soon after returned, in the very same money that had been received, having been only intended to strengthen the transaction; defendant contending that the mortgage had been given without any *bona fide* consideration, but merely to protect his property from a claim of W. & G. A jury to whom issues were submitted, found, 1st, that the object of the mortgage was to evade payment of the debt to W. & G.; that the mortgagee was aware of that fact when he received the mortgage, and that the mortgage was given without consideration.

Held, that notwithstanding these findings, the plaintiff was entitled to a decree of foreclosure.

RITCHIE, E. J., delivered the judgment of the Court :—

The plaintiff has brought this suit as the executor of Thomas McLellan, deceased, to foreclose a mortgage made by the defendant to the testator, which is therein stated to have been made in consideration of and for securing the re-payment of £150 in five years from its date, on payment of which sum, with interest, the mortgage, as well as three promissory notes given by the defendant to the testator for the said sum and interest, should all become void ; two of the notes being, as therein stated, of even date with the mortgage, and the third being dated the 29th April, 1856. The mortgage bears date 16th June, 1857.

The facts on which the defendant relies in his pleas as his defence to the suit are that he was indebted to parties in Portland, N. B., Messrs. Whidden & Gwynne, who had placed their accounts in the hands of an attorney for collection and were pushing for payment by a suit; that defendant had dealings with McLellan, who then held a note of his for £68 10s., dated 29th April, 1856, and that McLellan proposed to him that he should give him a mortgage for the sum of £150, which would secure the amount to him, and prevent Whidden & Gwynne from turning him out of house and home, and defendant accordingly did execute the mortgage sought to be foreclosed; that some time thereafter McLellan paid defendant, on account of the said mortgage, $200, and there was no other consideration for the said mortgage, and defendant has, since the date of the mortgage, paid off and discharged the note above mentioned, and also the said $200; and he states that McLellan, in his lifetime, repeatedly offered to release the mortgage, but defendant declined to take a release, as he was indebted to several persons who, he feared, would immediately proceed against the property if this mortgage were released. By the defence thus set up the defendant admits that he owed McLellan a sum of money, to secure which, with a further advance to be made, and which subsequently was made, the mortgage was given.

There is nothing here alleged which could invalidate the mortgage as between the mortgagor and mortgagee, and the only question raised for the Court to decide is whether the amount due on the mortgage has or has not been paid. And the statement of the defendant that, in addition to giving security to McLellan, he had in view the protection of the property from his creditors, however discreditable it might be to himself, cannot benefit him in this suit, if he has not re-paid McLellan the amount due him, and if he has paid him, his defence is equally good without the discreditable allegation.

The defendant, in the evidence which he has given, not only does not support these statements, but attempts to make up an entirely different case. He then stated that he had owed the £68 10s., but had paid it *before the mortgage was given*; that McLellan gave him $200 or thereabouts, and he paid it back in the same money he received a short time after; he did not unroll it; the money was paid to strengthen the transaction; he owed nothing to McLellan at the time of his death; the last settlement between them was when the note for £68 10s. was given; the mortgage was never given for a *bona fide* debt; it was a fabrication for the purpose of protecting the property from the claim of Whidden & Gwynne. Can he be permitted to make out a case in evidence inconsistent with his answer? The great object of pleading is to apprise the parties of the specific nature of the question to be tried, and Taylor in his work on *Evidence*, says, p. 2134;

" This object would be defeated if either party were at liberty to prove facts essentially different from those which he has stated on the record as constituting his claim on the one hand, or his defence on the other ;" and Lord CHELMSFORD, in *Malcomson* v. *Clayton*, 13 Moo. P. C. C., 206, says ; " It is a rule, and a most important rule, to be observed in all Courts, that a party complaining of an injury and seeking for redress must recover only *secundum allegata et probata.* There is no hardship in adhering strictly to this rule against the complainant, for he knows the nature of the wrong for which he seeks the remedy, and can easily state it with precision and accuracy ; but great inconvenience would follow to the opposite party unless this strictness was required, because he might constantly be exposed to the disadvantage of having prepared himself to meet one state of facts, and of finding himself suddenly and unexpectedly confronted by a totally different one.   The great object of all Courts ought to be to bring the parties in distinct agreement as to what is in contest between them, and this object would be frustrated if it were competent for either party to place his right to redress on one ground and abandon it at the trial, although the latter ground would originally have given him the right to recover."

It is difficult to imagine a case which would call for the enforcement of the rule more urgently than the one before us, for all the facts on which the defendant relies to establish his defence were specially within his own knowledge, and yet by his own testimony he sets up a defence different from and inconsistent with that which he has stated on the record.   If the defendant were permitted to do this, even then how would the matter stand ?   The case stated by the defendant in his pleading, viz., the existence of an antecedent debt due at the time of making of the mortgage on a promissory note, and an advance then made by McLellan to the defendant, in accordance with what appears on the face of the mortgage, and a payment subsequently made of the whole debt is disproved by the defendant's own testimony.   We have, therefore, to deal only with the case as made out by him in his evidence ; that the mortgage was, as he termed it, a fabrication, was never given for a *bona fide* debt, and no money was paid on account of it,

and no debt was then due by him to McLellan, and that the
sum handed by McLellan to him, and by him handed back to
McLellan, was so done to give a color of reality to the fraud
which he had in view in giving the mortgage. This being the
defence upon which alone he can rely, (indeed, he has
attempted to prove no other,) does it constitute such a defence
as will avail the defendant? In my opinion it does not, for
where a transaction has been entered into between two persons
with a fraudulent purpose as against the creditors of one of
them, though it may be set aside by the latter, it may, nevertheless be binding between the parties; for a man cannot set
up an illegal or fraudulent act in order to avoid his deed. He
is in that case *estopped* by his deed. But if the rule, both at
law and in equity, were not as stringent as it is in this respect,
is the evidence given by the defendant of such a character as
to justify the Court in making a decree in his favor? We
are asked by him to have a deed prepared by himself set
aside on the ground that he executed it with a fraudulent
purpose, and with a view of depriving a creditor to whom he
admits he owed a just debt, of obtaining payment by levying
on his land. He makes one statement in his pleading and an
entirely different one in his evidence, and that evidence
consisting of conversations between himself and McLellan in
his lifetime, he having died before this suit was commenced.
As the law now exists, such evidence would not be received
under the Act of 1869, but this suit, having been commenced
before that time, is not within its provisions.

In England there is no such statute, and yet, on principle,
and independently of any such enactment, courts place little
or no reliance on evidence of that character unless it is
corroborated by less suspicious testimony. In *Hill* v. *Wilson*,
L. R., 8 Ch. App., 900, James, L. J., in giving judgment, said;
" In considering the case it appears to me that the whole of
the conversation alleged to have taken place between Mr. Hill
and Mr. Wilson, on the occasion when the promissory note
was given, must be eliminated entirely. The conversation is
not alleged for the purpose of shewing that there has been
any mistake or fraud in the *preparation* of the document,
but solely for the purpose of shewing that the written

document does not mean what the written document says. The evidence given is the parol evidence of the maker of a promissory note as to the conversation alleged to have taken place between himself and the person to whom the note was given, that person being dead. Even if the evidence be legally admissible for any purpose, the interests of mankind, in my opinion, imperatively require that, unless corroborated, it should be wholly disregarded. Nobody would be safe in respect of his pecuniary transactions if legal documents found in his possession at the time of his death, and endeavoured to be enforced by his executors, could be set aside or varied or altered by the parol evidence of the person who had bound himself. It would be very easy, of course, for anybody who owed a testator a debt to say; ' I met the testator and he promised he would not sue;" ' I met the testatator and I gave him the money;" I met the testator and in consideration of something he agreed to release me.' The interests of justice and the interests of mankind require that such evidence should be wholly disregarded. In the present case such evidence is inadmissible, because it is the rule of law and the rule of this Court also, that parol evidence cannot be tendered for the purpose of altering the terms of a written contract. I therefore entirely lay aside the whole of that conversation."

It may be said that there is some corroboration of the defendant's statement, and the evidence of John Campbell is relied on. He refers to two conversations he had with McLellan, one shortly after the mortgage was taken, and one shortly before his death. On the first occasion he had stated to him that defendant had got into trouble, and they had made arrangements, and he had taken the mortgage to save him being turned out of house and home. This amounts to nothing, for if he owed McLellan, and gave him a mortgage to secure him, there could be no legal objection to it, though it might have the effect of giving a preference to McLellan over other creditors. He told him, he said, in the conversation shortly before his death, that he had been disappointed in getting some money he expected, and he said he wished defendant would come and get his mortgage released, from which the inference would seem to be that at that time there

10 t

was something due on the mortgage which he wished defendant to pay and take a release, connecting it, as he does, with his having occasion for money, and having failed to get it from another source; and there is, I think, nothing in his evidence which can reasonably be held to be at variance with this. There are some singular circumstances connected with this last conversation. McLellan, he says, came to his house at eleven o'clock at night, after he and his wife had retired, both being in bed at the time; there was, as he expressed it, a good deal of romance in it; his wife heard it; she refreshed his memory with words which McLellan said; he may have said his wife knew little about the matter. His wife was not called to give evidence, and this amounts to very little in corroboration of defendant's story,—at least of the important part of it—but it appears to me that there is much in the evidence of the defendant which is calculated to throw doubt and discredit on his statement that he owed nothing to McLellan at the time of his death. He had said he had paid the note specially mentioned in the mortgage, and had got it back before the mortgage was given, and that this note represented all his indebtedness to McLellan when it was given, (29th April, 1856,) which was probably the case. He does not say when he paid it, or under what circumstances, but he did so before the mortgage was given. At that time he was so impoverished that he was fearful of being turned out of house and home, because he was pressed for payment of a debt of £10. He thinks, he says, he had the note for £68 10s. in his possession when the mortgage was given, but is not positive, and in that document it is referred to as unpaid and outstanding. But the most unaccountable part of the defendant's evidence is that which relates to the £90 note found in McLellan's possession at the time of his death, purporting to be made by the defendant to him. He admits the making of this note; the signature is his, and the body of it is in his handwriting. He admits he gave the note, but he has no recollection of anything about it, when, or why, or for what it was given, and he had ample time to refresh his memory on the subject, as it had been presented to him on a former trial, when the same answers were elicited from him in respect to it. This evidence draws largely on our credulity, but assuming it to be true, the defendant's forgetfulness would not invalidate the note or affect it as evidence of a debt due by him to McLellan.

We are deprived by death of the evidence of McLellan, but, from the evidence we have and the *documents* before us, we may, I think, safely infer what the state of matters was between the parties at the time of McLellan's death. I infer then, *as stated in the mortgage*, that at its date there was a debt due by defendant of £150, and that a part of it was represented by the note for £68 10s. then in McLellan's hands ; subsequently that note found its way to the possession of the defendant, and I infer that he paid it and became entitled to it. Two other notes are alluded to in the mortgage as having been given at the date of the mortgage for the balance of the £150. These defendant says were delivered up to him also, and they may have been, for they were not found among McLellan's papers at his death ; but while the two last-mentioned notes were not found, the note for £90 was found, of which the defendant can give us no account. But is there no inference to be drawn from the existence of that note other than that it is the evidence of a debt due by defendant to McLellan of that amount. If defendant's statement be correct that he had no other dealings with McLellan, then it could have referred to no other transaction than the mortgage. McLellan certainly treated it as an available security, for there is a memorandum on it of the interest which had accrued, on it in his handwriting. The defendant tells us that there had been paid on the note for £68 10. the sum of £9 3s. 9d., which was endorsed on it, leaving due on it £59 6s. 3d. If that sum were paid, and the note taken up, there would be due on the mortgage £90 14s. 6d. I have not taken into account the interest, and I do not mean to have it inferred that such was the exact mode in which the amount of £90 was arrived at, for trifling matters of account may have entered into the settlement that might have slightly affected the balance between them ; but the inferences I have drawn seem to be such as the evidence warrants, and are in accordance with all the documents before me, and I have arrived at the conclusion that at the date of that note the parties settled the balance due on the mortgage at £90. The date of the note is October 1st, 1858.

The late Judge in Equity directed certain issues to be submitted to a jury, and they have found ;—1st. That the object for which the mortgage was given was to evade the payment by the defendant of a debt due by him to Whidden & Gwynne, and probably other debts. 2ndly. That Thomas McLellan, as soon as the existence of the mortgage came to his knowledge, became aware that it had been made to him to enable Fulmore to evade the payment of Whidden & Gwynne's debt. 3rdly. That the mortgage was given without consideration. These findings cannot affect the decree in the view I have taken of this case and of the law bearing upon it. The jury have assumed the correctness of the statements made by the defendant in his evidence, but even if his evidence is to be taken as true in every particular, for the reasons I have given, such statements cannot avail him against his own deed, his allegations being at variance with them in his evidence. The issues, though seemingly found for the defendant, are really destructive of his case, and *Simpson v. Holliday*, L. R., 1 H. L., 319, shews that, though all the issues may be found for one party in a suit, the decree may pass in favor of his opponent. The question before the Court is one of law, whether upon that finding the defendant is entitled to a decree. Thinking, as I do, that he is not, it would be absurd to send the case to another jury, as it could lead to no result. The plaintiff is entitled to a decree of foreclosure and costs.

In Re THE WALLACE HUESTIS GREY STONE CO.

PROCEEDINGS were taken under an Act of the Provincial Legislature to wind up the company on the ground that it was heavily embarrassed and could not extricate itself without having recourse to the double liability of the shareholders. The act of incorporation provided that transfers of shares should be valid and effectual for all purposes from the time they were made and entered in the books of the company. Three of the shareholders claimed that they were not contributories on the ground that certificates of stock were never accepted by them, but it appeared that the certificates were issued to them by direction of the former stockholder from whom they were transferred, that this was approved of by the directors, and the certificates were handed to the transferor, and afterwards received by two of the transferees, who were registered as stockholders in the company's books, and never repudiated the transaction. The third transferee was also registered, and was elected a director previous to his repudiating the transaction, which he did not do until after it became apparent that the affairs of the company were embarrassed. Another class of stockholders claimed to be exempt on the ground that they had surrendered their shares to the company. This surrender had been made and accepted by the company, but the parties surrendering knew that the affairs of the company were embarrassed, and it was with a view of escaping liability that the surrenders were made.

Held, that the provisions of the act were within the legislative authority of the provincial legislature, and that neither class of stockholders could be exempted from contribution.

Held, also, that where there was no registration on the books, and the party sought to be made liable had never deemed himself absolute owner or acted as such, there was no liability.

RITCHIE, E. J., delivered the judgment of the Court :—

The application for the winding up of this company is made on behalf of shareholders, on the ground that it has incurred heavy responsibilities, and that it is impossible to extricate itself from its present embarrassment and meet its liabilities without having recourse on its members under the double liability clause of the act under which it is incorporated, and that any attempt to continue its business would result in further loss.

The only objections to the proceedings which have been taken are made by certain persons who deny their liability as contributories; who also insist that, though they should be held to be liable, the proceedings are invalid, inasmuch as the Act of the Provincial Legislature under which they are taken is unconstitutional and *ultra vires,* as dealing with insolvency, a subject over which the Dominion Legislature has alone the power of legislating.

As this last objection lies at the root of the matter, I shall consider it first. The act does not in terms profess to deal with insolvency, nor is it in its character an insolvent law. The object of such a law is to relieve honest debtors who are unable to pay their debts, and to make a fair distribution of their property among their creditors in discharge of their debts The object of this act is to wind up the affairs of companies in general, where a resolution to that effect has been passed by the company, or where the Court may so order it, as in the present case, on the application of a contributor, on its being made to appear that it is just and equitable that it should be done. This may take place though no debts whatever may be due by the company ; and this act, unlike the English act on the same subject, cannot be called into operation by a creditor of the company. Under the act incorporating this company, its members are made liable for double the amount of stock held by them. No more than the subscribed stock has been paid up, and there is nothing to lead to the inference that the amounts for which the members are still liable will not be sufficient to pay all its indebtedness. It is with the view of having these amounts collected and so applied, and thus avoiding insolvency, that these proceedings have been taken. I think, therefore, that the act under which they have been taken does not trench upon the legislative powers of the Dominion Parliament; so that those who rely on this ground alone must be held to be contributories. The other objectors are those who either contend that they never were shareholders, or who have tranferred their shares, or relinquished them to the company. Of the former class are Robert R. Coates, Joseph Black, and Abraham H. Patterson. These all received certificates of stock, but they assert that the shares were never accepted by them, and that no transfer was ever regularly made to them or accepted by the directors. The stock was originally held by Frederick W. Bent, and was taken, in fact, whether regularly transferred or not, by all three of them, as they allege, as security for debts due to each of them. After considering their affidavits and those in reply I have come to the conclusion, as regards Coates and Black, that the certificates of stock were issued to them by the company, by direction of Bent, who gave up his certificates and directed a new issue of stock to different persons, among them Coates and Black, which was approved by the directors. The certificates were handed to Bent, and were afterwards received by Coates and Black, who were registered as stockholders in the company's books and were thereafter treated as stockholders, neither of them having ever repudiated the transaction. As regards Patterson, he admits that he took the stock as security for a debt due him by Bent, and it was not until some months after he received the stock certificate from the company, and after it became apparent that it was largely embarrassed, that he wrote to the secretary that he would not accept the transfer, previous to which he had been elected a director, which was afterwards, on re-consideration avoided in consequence of his living so far away. In the stock book of the company I find Robert Coates entered as holder of two shares, No. 73 to 74 ; Joseph Black as holding four shares, No. 55 to 58 ; and Abram H. Patterson as holding ten shares, No. 41 to 50. That these parties held the certificates of these shares without repudiating them, until they afterwards discovered the embarrassed state of the company, and were considered by the company as stockholders and recorded in its books as such is evident ; and, as the act of incorporation declares that the transfer of shares shall be valid and effectual for all purposes from the time that such transfer is made and entered in the books of the company, and as the transfer has been made so as to divest the former owner of his title to the stock, and the company has recognized them as stockholders, I think the Court must also recognize them as such, and therefore as contributories. The remaining parties who repudiate their liability admit that they were shareholders, but rely on their having transferred or surrendered to the company their shares. The circumstances under which the surrender or transfer was made differ only in some non-essential particulars.

It appears that the paid-up capital of the company having been exhausted, a resolution was passed at a meeting called for the purpose of arranging in some way to meet its liabilities, by which each member was required to advance $50 to $100, in order to raise $3,000 to meet claims immediately, and if each member should not be willing to loan this amount for twelve months upon the company's bonds, that he be requested to return his stock to the company to assist it, because if this was not done the quarry would be sold under the hammer, when each and every member would be subject to the double liability according to law.

That the parties who surrendered their shares knew of the embarrassed state of the company, and made the surrender with a view of incurring no further liability and escaping being called upon under the double liability incurred as share-holders cannot be doubted. Some two or three paid a small sum to induce the company to take their shares, and in the document agreeing to accept the stock it is declared that they shall be relieved from liability for the debts of the company and also from the double liability imposed on shareholders by the act.

By the act of incorporation the capital of the company is $60,000, which amount or the greater part, it appears, had been paid up and expended when the surrenders were made, and debts to a large amount were due which the company was without the means of paying; and though it had no power under the act of incorporation of dealing with its own shares, or accepting surrenders, or reducing its capital, one hundred and forty-six shares, representing $14,600, were surrendered and accepted by the company, which shares were never afterwards issued. If the transaction should be sanctioned by the Court, and the parties making the surrender not held to be liable as shareholders and contributories, the creditors will be deprived of security for their debts to the extent of $14,600. This double liability was imposed on the shareholders solely for the benefit and protection of the creditors of the company, and these shareholders who now seek exemption from liability under it were among those who incurred the debts now due. It would be most unjust that they should be relieved at the expense of their creditors. If there were no creditors in the case such an agreement as that made between those who wished to retire from the company and those who were willing to prosecute the undertaking, would not be subject to the same objection. Under existing circumstances they must be held liable to the debts of the company to the amount of double that of the stock held by them respectively, less the amount paid in on account of such stock. The company as such had no power to accept transfers or surrender of the stock of shareholders. Those who have professed to make them must, in the winding up of the company, be held contributories. There are numerous cases which establish the principle that, where certain members of a company are allowed to retire and relinquish their shares, on the winding up of the company they are held, in the interest of creditors, to be contributories, even though the retirement may have taken place many years before. *Muntz' Case*, 22 Beav., 55; *Daniel's Case*, 22 Beav., 43; *Walter's Case*, 3 DeG. & S., 244; *Stanhope's Case*, 3 DeG. & S., 198.

This disposes of all those named in scheduldes A. and B., annexed to the affidavit of J. Hiram Black to settle the list of contributaries. There yet remain three names in schedule C. These have received stock certificates, but no transfer of the shares has been registered in the books of the company. William Greenfield is the only one of those who has applied to be relieved, and he, I think, is entitled to be as regards those of his shares referred to in that schedule, as from his affidavit he never seems to have deemed himself the absolute owner, and never acted as such, and has done nothing to estop him from taking the objection, and the transfer was never made effectual by registration.

In Re CHRIST CHURCH, DARTMOUTH.

TRUSTEES were sought to be made personally liable for a sum invested on mortgage, on the ground that they had invested on a second mortgage, and on property of which the mortgagor only had title to a part. Before making the investment the trustees had been advised by their solicitor as to the value as well as the title, the solicitor considering it a first-rate security. The whole property was valued at $5,000, the first mortgage amounted to only $1,200, and the mortgagor's interest in the remaining $3,800 was two-thirds, amounting to $2,532, leaving a margin of $1,170 over and above the amount loaned by the trustees.

Held, that, even if the security was not first-class, the trustees, having believed it to be good, could not be held personally liable for deficiency. R. S., Cap. 108, Sec. 24.

RITCHIE, E. J., delivered the judgment of the Court :—

On the reference to a Master to report on securities taken by the Reverend John L. Bell, John P. Mott, and James W. Turner, trustees of a fund for the benefit of the Incumbent or Rector of Christ Church, on their application to be relieved of the trust, he reported that the mortgage of James W. Betcher, for $1,362.67, being the only security objected to, was, when taken in December, 1875, a good and substantial security. His report is excepted to. The grounds of exception relied on are that the mortgagor had a title to but two-thirds of the land ; that there was a previous mortgage on it, and that the value of the property did not warrant the investment of so large a sum on the mortgagor's interest.

There can be no doubt that the trustees, at the time they made the investment, considered that it was a safe one. Mr. Turner himself inspected the property, and their solicitors, Messrs. James & Foster, advised them on the value of the property, as well as on the title. The former, in his evidence, says he took particular pains about the investment, and he looked upon it as a first-rate security. All the witnesses who speak of the value of the property set it at $5,000 when the mortgage was taken. There was a prior mortgage for $1,200 on the whole property. Of the difference, $3,800, the mortgagor's interest was two-thirds, that is $2,532, thus leaving a margin of $1,170 over the sum loaned. It may be considered as a general rule in England that, where the security is otherwise unobjectionable, trustees may safely advance two-thirds of the actual value of the property, and even where they have lent on the security of property of somewhat less value, they have been protected where they have acted honestly and exercised their best dis-cretion. The circumstances that there was a previous mortgage on the property and that the mortgagor's interest embraced only a portion of it, affects the value of the security, but prudent men do make loans on property so circumstanced where the value of the property is sufficiently good, and a second mortgage here does not occupy so unfavorable a position as in England, where the mortgagee has possession of all the muniments of title and may foreclose the mortgagor's interests without a sale.

While I cannot concur in the opinion that the security was a first-rate one, yet, as the money was loaned and the security taken in good faith, the trustees believing it to be good, and the advance made being a very little over one-half of the value of the interest of the mortgagor in the property, it would be unreasonable to make them liable for a loss by the depreciation of such property since the taking of the mortgage; and by chapter 108 of the Revised Statutes, section 24, it is provided that trustees shall not be held answerable for the insufficiency or deficiency of any stocks, funds, or securities, unless the same shall happen through their own wilful default.

I think the exceptions taken to the report must be over-ruled and the report confirmed. The trustees will be entitled to their costs.

STEWART et al. v. BOAK et al.

PLAINTIFFS' claim for relief was based on the charge that a mortgage of a vessel, executed in blank and delivered to one of the defendants to be filled up, had been filled up for a greater number of shares and a larger amount than was warranted, and that the other and real defendant, to whom the mortgage had been transferred, was not a *bona fide* purchaser, and had notice of the fraud. There was no evidence to impeach the *bona fides* of the defendant, and, as to notice, the evidence was such as to lead the Court to the conclusion that when he purchased he had no notice of any adverse claim, or that the title was questionable.

Held, that the plaintiffs were not entitled to relief.

RITCHIE, E. J., delivered the judgment of the Court:—

This suit is brought by James A. Stewart and Donald Stewart against Robert Boak, Robert Burns Boak, Hodgetts F. Worrall, and Neil Stewart.

The plaintiffs in their writ set out that they, with Neil Stewart, agreed to build a vessel in which each was to have an equal interest; she was launched in 1876, requiring only sails, rigging, &c., to complete her; in 1874 James A. Stewart went to reside in California, from whence he remitted the funds necessary to complete his share, and, in consequence of his absence, the vessel was registered in the names of Donald and Neil, the former as owner of forty-three shares, and the latter of twenty-one, that Donald and Neil applied to E. Albro & Co. to supply them with sails, rigging, and the outfits required to make her ready for sea, and agreed, as they say, to secure them by a mortgage on thirty shares ; that after the goods had been ordered the firm sent a blank form of mortgage to be executed and returned, otherwise they would not be forwarded ; it was signed by Donald, and returned to Albro & Co., in blank, containing no description of the vessel, no amount, no time of payment, nor any other details, Donald intending that these should be inserted by Messrs. Albro & Co., according to agreement, who, instead of doing so, fraudulently inserted thirty-seven shares instead of thirty, and the sum of $2,500, which was, as they say, $500 more than the amount due the firm ; that Edward Albro, who constituted the firm of E. Albro & Co., subsequently became insolvent, and the defendant, Worrall, was appointed assignee of his estate, and in April, 1878, he was registered as mortgagee, and subsequently assigned the mortgage to the defendant, Robert Burns Boak ; that in the month of April, 1877, (that is prior to the execution of the mortgage in blank by Donald,) Neil Stewart mortgaged his twenty-one shares to William Boak, which mortgage was afterwards transferred to the defendant, Robert Boak, who subsequently transferred it to Robert Burns Boak, who, in July, 1878, transferred the fifty-eight shares he then held to Robert Boak ; that in December, 1876, Donald mortgaged six shares to William McAllister, of which Robert Boak subsequently obtained an assignment, and on the 4th July, 1878, the existing registry was cancelled, and the vessel was registered in the name of Robert Boak. The plaintiffs go on to say that they believe the sale to Robert Burns Boak, and that from him to Robert Boak not to have been *bona fide*, and that before the sale to them, Robert Boak and Robert Burns Boak were, as they believe, notified of the fraud and illegality connected with the mortgage by Neil Stewart, and that they never were aware that the mortgage embraced more than thirty shares till the month of June, 1878, when they were informed of it by Neil Stewart ; and they pray that the mortgage to Albro, and the transfers of it, and the title held under it, may be decreed to be void, and that seven sixty-fourth parts, now standing in the name of Robert Boak, may be transferred to the plaintiffs, free from encumbrance, and that thirty sixty-fourth parts should be also transferred to the plaintiffs, subject to a lien thereon for the amount due Albro for rigging, &c., of which an account should be taken, or, upon payment of the amount, that an account should be taken of the earnings of the thirty-seven sixty-fourth parts.

It is apparent that the only real defendant in this suit is Robert Boak, he being now the registered owner of the whole vessel, and the relief prayed for is against him alone.

It is not necessary to enter upon the question whether the mortgage was void in consequence of its having been executed in blank, as the plaintiffs do not insist on that in their writ, or seek relief on that ground. What they ask is that it should be treated as a mortgage of thirty sixty-fourths of the vessel for the amount actually due the original mortgagee. Now, assuming that Albro had been guilty of fraud, and had acted in violation of his agreement in inserting thirty-seven instead of thirty shares, (though I think, after carefully considering the evidence, that there are no grounds whatever for such an imputation,) if Mr. Boak is a *bona fide* purchaser for valuable consideration, without notice of the fraud or improper conduct of the mortgagee, his title cannot be impeached, for this Court will not interfere against such a purchaser if he has purchased from one appearing from the documentary title to have been the legal owner. This has been the recognized doctrine in equity from as far back as *Bassitt* v. *Nosworthy*, cases *Temp.* Finch, 102, and has been so held down to the late case of *Heath* v. *Creerlock*, L. R., 10 Ch., 33, in which JAMES, L. J., laid it down as a rule without exception that, from a purchaser for value without notice, a Court of Equity takes nothing away which that purchaser has honestly acquired.

If this be so in general, more especially will it be the case where, as here, the party seeking relief has himself put it in the power of the mortgagee to mislead others by recklessly signing a mortgage in blank for him to fill up. If the confidence so reposed be abused *he* should be the party to suffer by it, and not an innocent party. In *Hunter* v. *Walters*, L. R., 7 Ch., 85, JAMES, L. J., said; "The rule of equity is the rule of common sense, that where a person has, either *through fraud or otherwise*, executed a deed and signed a receipt containing an unmistakeable representation of a matter of fact, the person who has so executed the deed and signed the receipt is to suffer the loss arising from an undue use of them, and not another person who has in the ordinary course of business, without negligence or default of any kind, trusted to the document;" and in *Weldon* v. *Sloper*, 1 Drew., 193, Sir R. KINDERSLEY said; "It is an elementary principle that a party coming into equity is bound to shew that he has not been guilty of such a degree of neglect as to enable another so to deal with that which was the plaintiff's right as to induce an innocent party to assume that he was dealing with his own."

As regards the plaintiff, James A. Stewart, he has, in my opinion, no *locus standi*,—he was not a registered owner, and was not known to be interested in the vessel by Albro, and if Donald held shares in trust for him, he may be answerable to him for a breach of trust in mortgaging them, but a purchaser ignorant of the trust would take the shares from the trustee free from the trust.

There are, therefore, but two questions involved in this case. Did Robert Boak acquire the title to the vessel *bona fide* for a valuable consideration; and did he do so without notice of any defect in the title, that is, assuming that there was a defect arising from misconduct on the part of Albro, and, I have already said, that in my opinion no such misconduct existed.

On the first point there can be no doubt. There is no evidence whatever to impeach the *bona fides* of the purchase by Mr. Boak, and no doubt exists in my mind from the evidence that when he acquired the title he had no notice of any adverse claim or that the title was questionable. The only witness who asserts that notice was given to Robert Burns Boak is Neil Stewart, and he is contradicted by him. And Mr. Worrall, in whose office he says he informed Boak of the objection to the mortgage just before the sale, testifies that

Boak was not present at the conversation he had with him. He also says he informed Mr. Robert Boak of the objection before the purchase. This is positively denied by Mr. Boak, who asserts that, till after his purchase, he knew of no such objection. Neil Stewart does not deny that he was present when the vessel was sold, and then made no objection, and he admits that after Mr. Boak had become the purchaser he accepted from him the situation of master, and took charge of her and brought her to Halifax, and at the instance of Mr. Boak endeavoured to sell her at Newfoundland, for his, (Boak's,) benefit. Neil Stewart is contradicted by other entirely disinterested witnesses on other points. As regards the agreement between him and E. Albro & Co. as to the number of shares to be inserted in the mortgage, his testimony is directly at variance with that of Austen and Twining, and is not consistent with his own letters to that firm, particularly those of the 28th March, and 16th May, 1877, and no doubt is left on my mind that Mr. Robert Boak is a *bona fide* purchaser of the vessel in question for valuable consideration, without notice, and that the plaintiffs have failed to shew that they are entitled to the relief they seek, and the defendants are therefore entitled to a decree in their favor, with costs.

WHITMAN ET AL. *v.* COLP.

B. & E. COLP, being the owners of certain lands, subject a to mortgage of $2,666, and indebted to other parties in the sum of $691, entered into an agreement with J. Hubley and C. A. Whitman, whereby, in consideration of the latter agreeing to liquidate the mortgage and the other debts, the parties first mentioned agreed to deed to them the real estate mentioned in the mortgage. It was further agreed that Hubley, Whitman and B. Colp, the defendant, should carry on a lumbering business on the property. The debts were accordingly paid, and the plaintiffs and defendant conducted the business, but defendant refused to sign the deed of the property, denied that a partnership had been entered into as alleged, and claimed that the agreement had been procured by misrepresentation, which he failed to prove.

Held, that the plaintiffs were entitled to specific performance of the agreement.

RITCHIE, E. J., delivered the judgment of the Court :—

The plaintiffs, in their writ, set out that the defendant and one Edmund Colp were the owners of certain lands described therein, subject to a mortgage held by one Francis Mumford and others, upon which there was then due $2,666.66, which was under foreclosure ; and the defendant and Edmund Colp, carrying on business as lumberers and millers, under the firm of B. & E. Colp, were also indebted to other parties in the sum of $691.34 ; that they, on the 3rd April, 1879, entered into the following agreement with the plaintiffs :—

"This Indenture, made this third day of April, 1879, between Benjamin Colp and Edmund Colp, of St. Margaret's Bay, in the County of Halifax, and Province of Nova Scotia of the one part, and James Hubley and C. A. Whitman, of St. Margaret's Bay, in the county and province aforesaid, of the other part, witnesseth that the said B. & E. Colp, for and in consideration of the sum of three thousand, three hundred and fifty-eight dollars of lawful money of the Dominion of Canada, to be paid for them, as follows, in liquidating debts, viz. ;— 1st. The present claim of F. Mumford & Sons against them of $2,666.66. 2nd. Several other bills to the amount of $691.34,—by the said James Hubley and Charles A. Whitman, when demanded by their creditors, do hereby agree to deed to the said James Hubley and C. A. Whitman all the property and real estate included in the mortgage now held by F. Mumford & Sons subject to said mortgage, together with all the logs which are now on the lakes or in the river claimed by them. It is further agreed by the said James Hubley and C. A. Whitman to admit the aforementioned Benjamin Colp to an equal possession with themselves severally of the above-mentioned property, on condition of his assuming with them an equal share in the above payment of $3,358 for the late firm of B. & E. Colp, or, in other words, the three parties last mentioned are each to hold *one-third* of the property by paying equal shares of its cost.

> BENJAMIN COLP,
> EDMUND COLP,
> JAMES HUBLEY,
> C. H. WHITMAN."

They further allege that it was agreed that the plaintiffs and defendant should enter into a co-partnership under the style of Whitman, Hubley & Co., for the manufacture and sale of lumber, and that each partner should have one-third of the profits resulting from the business; that immediately on the agreement being entered into, the plaintiffs went into the possession of the lands in conjunction with the defendant, and expended a large sum of money, (about $1,500,) in the erection of a lumber mill upon the premises, and satisfied the claim of the Mumfords against the defendant and Edmund Colp, and paid and satisfied the claims against them specified in the agreement, amounting to $691.34, and expended a large sum of money in the business, but the defendant never assumed his share of the payments referred to in the agreement, or paid any part thereof; that the plaintiffs tendered to the defendant and Edmund Colp all necessary receipts and releases of the debts to be paid by them, and at the same time tendered to them for execution a deed of the said lands, which was executed by Edmund Colp, but the defendant refused and still refuses to do so; notwithstanding this the plaintiffs took him in partnership, and permitted him to participate in the profits, and such partnership continued till the commencement of this suit; that the defendant has violated the terms of the partnership, and has attempted to sell, and is in treaty for the sale of logs cut on the lands for his own private use and benefit, and threatens to sell his interest in the lands irrespective of the rights of the plaintiffs, and the plaintiffs pray for a specific performance of the agreement, and that the defendant may be restrained from selling the lands and selling or disposing of the logs cut thereon, or any assets of the firm of Whitman, Hubley & Co., for his own use; that he may be decreed to convey his interest in the lands to the plaintiffs; that the partnership may be declared to be dissolved, and that an account may be taken of the business, and that whatever may be found to be due from the defendant may be decreed to be paid to them.

The defendant, in his answer, asserts that when he signed the agreement set out in the plaintiffs' writ he did not know its contents; that he did not read it, and trusted to the assertion of the plaintiffs that it was a paper wanted to satisfy the Mumfords; that he was willing the plaintiffs should

10 *u*

arrange the mortgage matter for himself and his brother Edmund, and they both signed the paper, believing this to be the case ; that he never intended or agreed to sell his interest in the property, and if the plaintiffs have obtained his signature to an agreement such as that set out in the writ, it was obtained by fraud and misrepresentation on the part of the plaintiffs ; that he never entered into co-partnership with the plaintiffs under the name of Hubley, Whitman & Co., upon the terms and for the purposes stated in the writ. He admits that the plaintiffs have put a small addition to the mill, but not of the value stated by them, and have paid off a portion of the claims against the property, but have not, as he believes, paid off the mortgage on it, and they have received a large amount from the proceeds of the lumber manufactured, and the defendant claims that he is entitled to one-half of the logs cut during the past winter, subject to one-half of the charges, and the same do not belong to any firm composed of the plaintiffs and the defendant ; and he claims a right to dispose of them in any way he pleases, subject to the charges ; that he has always contended that the agreement was inoperative and of no effect ; that he has expended a much larger sum in connection with the mill and property than the plaintiffs, and he denies their right to have the agreement specifically performed, but is willing that the accounts between them should be settled and adjusted, and as regards the logs cut during the last winter, he claims that one-half of them belong to him, and he is prepared to pay his share of the expenses connected therewith as soon as the same is adjusted.

After careful consideration of the evidence I have come to the conclusion that the agreement set out in the plaintiffs' writ was entered into by the defendant with a full knowledge of its contents, and that there is no foundation for his statement that he was induced to execute it by fraud and misrepresentation on the part of the plaintiffs, and that the partnership referred to in the writ was entered into and carried out for a considerable time by the parties ; and as it appears from the evidence that the plaintiffs have, on their part, fulfilled the terms of the agreement, they are entitled to have them carried out by the defendant by his conveying to them the real estate included in the mortgage to the Mumfords, whereupon the plaintiffs shall convey to the defendant one-third thereof, on its being made to appear that he has fulfilled the terms of the agreement which entitle him to such conveyance; but in the first instance it will be referred to a Master to report thereon, who shall take an account of all matters in controversy between the parties in the suit, and of all the dealings and transactions of the partnership, which is declared to be dissolved,—all parties to be at liberty to apply to the Court as there may be occasion. Costs reserved.

In Re THE HALIFAX YACHT CLUB.

THE petitioner, as administratrix, recovered judgment against the Halifax Yacht Club, and issued execution, which was returned unsatisfied, there being no assets. She then resorted to the individual liability of the corporators under Revised Statutes, chapter 53, section 13, but the Supreme Court decided that the section did not apply to such a corporation. Petitioner then applied to have the affairs of the company wound up.

Held, that the Provincial Act in reference to winding up of companies differing from the English Act in that it was expressly made applicable to clubs, could be invoked for the purpose of winding up the Halifax Yacht Club, but that, as there was no individual liability, and it was admitted there were no assets, the prayer of the petition should not be granted, as it would only create needless litigation.

· RITCHIE, E. J., delivered the judgment of the Court:—

The petitioner, Jane Scott, the widow and administratrix of Alexander W. Scott, deceased, alleges that Alexander W. Scott, for many years preceding and at the time of his decease, was a member of the club, which was incorporated by an Act of this Province, and was then and had been for several years previously the secretary of the club; that about a year after his death she commenced an action against the club for an amount due to her as administratrix, and subsequently obtained judgment on an award made in her favor for $2,464.16; that she caused execution to be issued against the club which has been returned unsatisfied, no assets being found on which to levy; that John Pugh, Esquire, is commodore, and Cuthbert C. Vaux is the secretary, and both are members of the club;

that it has ceased to carry on its operations, and it is not intended, as she believes, to resume them ; that when the debt was contracted and the judgment obtained there was and continues to be a large number of members, as she was informed, but she is unable to give the number or state the names ; and she prays that an order may pass for the winding up of the affairs of the club.

The prayer of the petition is opposed on several grounds ; 1st. That the Provincial Act respecting the winding up of incorporated companies does not apply to such a corporation as this ; 2nd. That the petitioner is not entitled under the terms of the act to apply for the winding up of the corporation ; 3rd. That the members of the corporation, as such, are not liable to contribute towards the payment of the debt due to the petitioner, and it is admitted it has no funds. Such a corporation as this would not come under the operation of the English winding-up act, and neither that act nor ours seems as applicable to clubs such as this as to corporations in general ; but the wording of our act differs from the English, and in terms seems to embrace this club. The second section is ; "This Act shall apply to all incorporated companies, associations, *or clubs* incorporated by the Legislature of the Province of Nova Scotia, or under the authority of any Act of this Province," &c., &c. I do not see how, under an act so worded, I could say that this club cannot come within its provisions. In the English act the word "clubs" is omitted. It does not follow because such a corporation *may* be ordered to be wound up, that it necessarily must be. The order to that effect will be made on the application of a contributor, only when, in the opinion of the Court, such a course is just and equitable ; and the act contemplates that the application shall only be made by the company or by a contributory or contributories, and it by no means follows that all the provisions of the act apply alike to all corporations In winding up a company the liability of members as contributories is to be established, or their freedom from liability ascertained from the constitution conferred upon it, and to certain classes of corporations the act, notwithstanding the comprehensiveness of its terms, is wholly inapplicable.

It is objected that the petitioner here is not a member of the corporation or a contributor, and has no right to make the present application. Whether she can be deemed a contributor or not under the act, it is not really in that character that she applies, but as a creditor seeking by this mode to obtain payment of her debt from the members of the club. This is avowedly the object of the application. Now, if the members are really liable to pay this judgment, a very easy mode is pointed out by which payment may be obtained, for by the 13th section of chapter 53 of the Revised Statutes, "in case any execution on any judgment against a corporation shall be returned unsatisfied, the individual property of each member shall be liable to respond the judgment under execution thereon, as if it were a private debt due by the member." This simple course has been resorted to by petitioner, and the Supreme Court has decided that no personal liability exists on the members composing the yacht club to pay this judgment; that is, that, on general principles, no such liability exists on corporators for the debts of the corporation, and that the provisions of chapter 53 of the Revised Statutes, imposing such liability in certain cases, do not apply to such a corporation as this, and to that decision I feel myself bound to conform. It cannot be questioned that without express provisions to the contrary no member of a corporate body is individually liable for its debts, and as it has been thus decided that chapter 53 of the Revised Statutes, by which alone personal liability is imposed on corporators where charters or acts of incorporation are silent on the subject, has no application to this club, and it is admitted by the petitioner that there is no corporate property, and that, in fact, it has ceased to exist, having for some time past ceased operations as a club, with no intention of resuming them, to grant the prayer of the petition and make an order for winding up its affairs would have no other effect than to create a needless expense and be attended with no beneficial result to the petitioner.

MASON ET AL. *v.* SHEDD ET AL.

THE owner of land leased a parcel to plaintiff, for the purpose of erecting a lobster factory, for the term of five years. About a twelvemonth afterwards the defendant, Shedd, applied for a lease of the same land for a similar purpose. Defendant admitted that when he had part of the materials on the ground for the erection of his building plaintiff forbade him to proceed, and asserted his right to the land, and, although it was alleged in the answer, the evidence did not justify the conclusion that plaintiff had ever abandoned his right under the lease or contemplated doing so.

Held, that plaintiff was entitled to have an injunction to restrain defendant from proceeding with the erection of the building, as the remedy at common law was not full and adequate, and it would be impossible for a jury to estimate the damages with accuracy.

RITCHIE, E. J., delivered the judgment of the Court :—

The plaintiffs in this suit seek to restrain the defendants from erecting a lobster factory on land of which they have a lease, and from committing further trespasses upon it.

In December, 1879, William Henderson leased to the plaintiff, Mason, one-half acre on the north side of Savage Beach, so called, and also his interest in Savage Beach for the term of five years, for the sum of $20, to be paid annually, which if not paid the agreement was to be void.

In his answer, the defendant, Shedd, says that, being desirous of obtaining a suitable site for a lobster factory, he applied to Henderson for a lease of Savage Point, and an additional half-acre on the further (*i. e.*, on the north side of Savage Beach,) side of the road from Savage Point, (the two leases were obviously intended to convey the same premises,) and obtained it. This was in September, 1880. He admits that he knew of the lease to Mason and of its terms, but he says he was told by Henderson that he had abandoned and rescinded the agreement, and had no notice that he claimed under it till a month after, and after he commenced building. It also appears from his answer that Mason's object in obtaining his lease had been to erect a lobster factory on the premises ; that he, Shedd, entered into his agreement, and was induced to do so not only because the previous agreement with Mason had been abandoned, but because there was a failure of consideration on his part in not having proceeded in the ensuing spring with the erection of a lobster factory on the premises, as he had promised to do ; and he alleges that the plaintiffs are not entitled to the relief they seek in this Court, as they can obtain a suitable site for erecting a lobster factory elsewhere in the neighbourhood, and that therefore the injury is not irreparable.

The only defence that can avail the defendant is that previous to the lease to him Mason had surrendered his right to the land to Henderson, and that, whether he had done so or not, he has no right to the relief he now seeks in this Court, his only recourse, if any, being at common law ; for even if he had promised to erect a lobster factory by a verbal agreement, as stated, the lease would not be invalidated by his not having done so.

In his evidence Shedd says that he was aware of Mason's assertion of right by notice given before he commenced building. He had part of the materials on the ground and part in transit when Mason forbade him from interfering with him.

After carefully considering the whole evidence, there is nothing, in my opinion, to justify the conclusion that Mason ever abandoned his rights under his lease, or contemplated doing so. Mason himself denies that he did so, either verbally or in writing, and says that when he went to forbid Shedd trespassing on the land, on Henderson being asked what all this meant, instead of saying that Mason had abandoned all right under his agreement, Shedd's reply was, "he had nothing to do with it; that he was clear of it." And when on that occasion he was asked whether he, (Mason,) should take his half-acre along the road or square, he said : "You had better take it square," and it was then surveyed by Mr. Dawson, without remonstrance from him, but with his assent, and on the New Year's Day following Henderson proposed that if he would give up the lease and go in with him they would make a good thing of it, as there would be no trouble in getting two or three hundred dollars each out of Shedd. William McLean was present when Shedd was notified by Mason of his claim. He had gone on the premises with the surveyor to lay off the half-acre lot. He said to Henderson he was surprised,—why did he not wait till the lease expired ? His answer was, not that Mason had given up his claim under it, but that he had nothing to do with it ; he had secured himself. Mason told him he had come to survey his half-acre. Henderson made no objection. Mason asked which way he preferred, length-ways or square. Henderson said he preferred the square. The surveyor then proceeded. Witness told the surveyor and chainman to take care and destroy as little of the grain as possible. Henderson said it was all right. And he goes on to say that from the time they first met Henderson on the beach until the survey was completed not a word was said by him or by any other person about the abandonment of the lease. Mr. Dawson, the surveyor, was employed by Mason, and went with him and McLean to make the survey. He says Henderson was there ; McLean or Mason said they had come to survey the lot they had leased for a lobster factory ; he said he had nothing to do with it now, he had leased it to another company ; McLean asked him how he could do that when he had leased it to Mason; he replied : "The other company know all about your lease, and you must fight it out with them; they know all about Mason's lease, and have taken a lawyer's advice on it." He said it was not his fault, that he told them everything about it ; they pointed out the half-acre supposed to be leased ; "Henderson told me it was bounded on the road ; they told me to lay it off according to the road and the shore. From the time we landed on the beach till the survey was completed we did not hear Henderson say one word about abandoning, on the contrary, he admitted that Mason had paid all he agreed. Before beginning the survey he said : 'I'll go with you, but I have nothing to do with it ; you must settle it among yourselves.'" The only evidence of Mason having relinquished his right under the lease is that given by Henderson himself, Alice Henderson, his wife, and Margaret Henderson, his mother. The former says ; "I remember one conversation about the lobster factory when my wife and my mother were present ; Mason said there was a company of four or five, and the one with the most coppers had gone away, the company scattered, and they would not go ahead with it ; Mr. Mason told me the same thing afterwards, once at least; Shedd then came along, and I entered into negotiations with him." On cross-examination; "When Mason told me that his company broke up, he said he could not go on *next spring*." Alice Henderson, in her evidence, says; "I remember Mason being down in the spring several times; he was talking different times to me and my husband about the factory; one time we asked him if the factory was going on in the spring; he said, 'No, the company is burst up, we have not coppers enough to go on with it *this* spring; I guess we will have to give it up;' and after that I do not think he was down till they made the survey." Margaret Henderson, referring to the same conversation, says; "William, (*i. e.*, her son,) asked Mason if he was going on with the factory; he said the coppers were too scarce, and the company was scattered, and he did not think the factory would go on; this was the only conversation between them that I picked up."

It is obvious that no legal surrender of Mason's lease had taken place when the lease was given to Shedd. That would not be effected by any such conversation between the parties; but independently of the positive denial of Mason I see nothing in the evidence of the Hendersons to lead me to believe that he ever expressed to them any intention of abandoning his right under his lease. Their evidence, in my opinion, merely shews that he was not able to commence operations on the land that spring, and I cannot help coming to the conclusion that Henderson well knew that such was his meaning. His whole conduct with reference to the transaction shews it; and it is singular that in the conversations referred to he should not have ascertained distinctly from him whether he did wish to surrender his lease. The only time he did make any application on the ground that there were other applicants, the answer of Mason was, "Send them to me." So, too, Mr. Shedd, one would suppose, would have ascertained from Mason whether he had or had not surrendered, especially as he went to a lawyer, who would have told him that to destroy the effect of the former lease there must have been a distinct and unequivocal surrender, and that, too, in writing. I cannot say I have been impressed favorably with the conduct of

Henderson in the transaction, nor with the evidence he has
given.   I need not refer now to the latter, for, assuming it all
to be true, I must have arrived at the conclusion that the
granting of the lease to Shedd was unjustifiable, and that it
conveyed no title to him of any of the land comprised in that
to Mason.

It only remains to be considered whether relief is to be
denied to the plaintiffs on the ground that full and adequate
relief could be obtained at common law.

Mr. Henry contended that this Court would not interfere
and grant relief in case of trespass unless the injury done was
irreparable, and such as could not be compensated by damages.

It is no objection to the exercise of its jurisdiction that a
remedy at law exists ; the question is, can the remedy be as
effectual there as here ?   What the Court deems irreparable
injury is, not merely that which cannot possibly be repaired,
but such as cannot be fully and adequately repaired by
damages, and this Court will give redress when the amount of
damage cannot be accurately ascertained in a court of law.

In this case the plaintiffs have the property for a limited
time ; the defendants, by taking possession and erecting
buildings on it, may so restrict them in the enjoyment of the
term as to render it imprudent for them to expend money in
the erection of buildings, for it may be that but a short balance
of the unexpired term may remain after they are enabled to
get possession.   If recourse should be had to an action of
ejectment, and if no action of trespass should be brought, how
could a jury estimate the injury done to the plaintiffs?   If
prospective losses or damages could be given, which they could
not, in my opinion, in such a case as this, there would be no
means of accurately estimating them.   The plaintiffs are
prevented from erecting their factory and carrying on the
business of canning lobsters, for which they obtained the
lease, which might or might not be profitable, and if profitable
to a greater or less extent.   The defendant, indeed, suggests
that they might go elsewhere and seek a site in the neighbourhood, while he is left in possession of their property, whereon
to erect a rival and competing factory,—a cool proposition,
under the circumstances.   It would, I think, be utterly

impossible for a jury to estimate the amount with any degree of accuracy, and in my opinion this Court alone can give the plaintiffs the relief to which they are entitled. I had some doubt with respect to the half-acre lot, but, on consideration. I think that defendants should be enjoined from building on that or the Savage Beach, and that the prayer of the writ, so far as the injunction is asked for, should be granted with costs, and a decree to that effect will pass.

SMITHERS ET AL. *v.* SMITHERS.

INTERLOCUTORY order, to compel executor to pay in to Court the proceeds of sales, in a suit brought to remove the executor from office, refused, the affidavits on which it was founded being answered in every essential particular.
Summary remedy provided by Probate Act recommended.

RITCHIE, E. J., delivered the judgment of the Court :—

In this suit, which was instituted by the plaintiffs, legatees under the will of the late George Smithers, deceased, against the surviving executor of his will, they seek to remove him from that office, and that he be restrained from selling, or attempting to sell, or disposing of, or intermeddling with the assets of the estate, and that a trustee be appointed in his place, and that in the meantime a receiver be appointed to manage the estate. An order *nisi* was obtained, calling on the defendant to shew cause why he should not pay into Court the proceeds of the sale of any property, real or personal, of the estate, which might then or thereafter be sold by him, and that in the meantime he should not appropriate or use any part of such proceeds to any purpose whatever.

In order to sustain an application for such an interlocutory order in such a suit as this, it is incumbent on the parties applying to make it appear that there has been misconduct on the part of the executor, or that the assets of the estate are in danger of being wasted. This has not been done to my satisfaction in the present instance. The case presented by the affidavits on the part of the plaintiffs was not a very strong one, and it has been answered by the defendant in every essential particular. If the plaintiffs considered they had grounds for removing the defendant from the executorship, I cannot help thinking that their more obvious course of proceeding, the whole estate being before the Probate Court, would have been to have applied there, the Judge of that Court having power, on a summary application, if he should think it for the interest of the estate, to order an executor to pay the money of the estate coming into his hands into a chartered bank to the credit of the estate, and, upon due proof that he is wasting the estate, to require him to give security for the due performance of his duty; and if such order be not obeyed, he may cancel the authority and appoint another in his place. Thus all the relief sought for in this suit would be afforded in the mode pointed out by the legislature at comparatively little expense. Without deciding that this Court might not exercise jurisdiction in such a case as this, I do not think that the plaintiffs have shewn sufficient grounds for the interlocutory order they have asked for, as, in my opinion, none of the charges against the defendant have been established. The order *nisi*, therefore, must be discharged with costs.

NEWCOMB *v.* SIMMONDS ET AL.

DEFENDANT, being indebted to various parties, and fearing lest his creditors should resort to his property to obtain payment, conveyed all his land to his son, the other defendant, while at the same time he and his family were to continue to enjoy the benefit of it. In their answer the defendants alleged a debt due by the father to the son, and an agreement by the latter to support his father, but the defendants gave no evidence.

Held, that the answer of the defendants could not be used as evidence at the hearing, and that plaintiff, as creditor of the father, had a right to a decree to set aside the deed.

RITCHIE, E. J., delivered the judgment of the Court :—

The deed sought to be set aside in this case was made and registered on the 17th December, 1878, and by it the defendant, Christopher Simmonds, conveyed to his son, the other defendant, all his real and personal property. The consideration mentioned in the deed is $5,700. No money was in fact paid.

In their answer the defendants allege that the real consideration was wages due to the son by the father and an undertaking on the part of the son to maintain the father and his family, and to supply the funds to pay his debts. They have,however, not been examined themselves, nor have they produced any evidence in support of their case. The deed is absolute and unconditional in its terms.

The plaintiff has shewn that, previous to the execution of the deed, the defendant, Christopher Simmonds, was indebted to him, for the amount of which he subsequently obtained a judgment. It also appears from the evidence that Christopher was indebted to other persons, in all to the extent of about $1,000.

Having heard that the deed had been made whereby he had divested himself of all his property to his son, the plaintiff asked him for security by a joint note of himself and his son. He said he would see his son, and that he and his son would pay the debt as fast as they could. North, a witness, testified that Christopher was indebted to him. He, also, offered to give time for payment if his son would be responsible to him. He replied that if his son became responsible to him he would have to become responsible to others, and would be torn in pieces. He made the same proposal to William, the son, who said he would be willing to do anything his father said. Riley, another witness, who was a tenant of part of the property, says that in June, 1879, he had a settlement of rent with Christopher up to August, 1879, who then said that he expected to go to gaol in a few days, and he wanted things straightened up before he went. And he also said that shortly after he had given the deed to his son, he sent for him and told him his son was sole proprietor there now, and asked if he knew how long a deed had to be on record before it would stand law. He replied he did not know. Christopher said it used to be thirty days. Witness said he heard it ought to be three months. He then said he would try and keep out of sight for three months. If he had to go to gaol he would make a gaol of his own house ; that he was afraid his creditors were going to tear him to pieces. Witness told him the plaintiff had said that he would take his and his son's note for the debt. He said he would not do it, that he had begun and would carry it through. Witness said plaintiff had told him he would not wait five years; he got angry and said it was only a trap to get his marsh out of him; he would stay in the house three months to make the deed good. He said he owed about $1,000 except the mortgage. (There was a mortgage on the real estate for $400.) He asked if he could put into a promissory note for his son to support the family, pay the bills, and pay the balance to him. Witness replied that he did not think that would be a note of hand, it would be an agreement. He said he intended to swear out; they could not keep him, as he had nothing. Witness asked him how he could keep the notes of hand and swear out. He said he would not give the notes up. His wife was present. The only other witness produced was the sister of Mrs. Simmonds. She was only called to prove the age of William, her son, in case an attempt should be made to prove that wages were due by him to his father. His age, according to her statement, was twenty-one on the 24th of October last. All this evidence is entirely uncontradicted, and from it the only conclusion to be drawn is that Christopher, finding himself indebted, and fearing lest his creditors should resort to his property to obtain payment, conveyed it all to his son, in the hope of preventing this being done, while at the same time he and his family were to continue to enjoy the benefit of it. I can characterize his conduct as no other than fraudulent, and the plaintiff is therefore entitled to have the prayer of his writ granted, with costs. Mr. King, on the part of the defendants, seemed to think he was entitled to use the statements in their answers as evidence on the hearing. That, of course, could not be done; but it does appear to me that the statements made there were such as to lead to the same conclusion as that to which I have arrived from the evidence adduced.

OAKES ET AL. *v.* RYERSON ET AL.

PLAINTIFFS claimed to be entitled to a sum paid into Court by Messrs. Ryerson & Co., under an assignment of it from H. M. Oakes. Previously to this assignment Oakes had given an order to Dunn & Vaughan on Ryerson for the amount, which had been presented, and to which no objection was taken. The order was given to Dunn & Vaughan for supplies furnished by them for a vessel, the sale of which by Ryersons had created the fund, and was given in pursuance of a promise when the supplies were furnished, that they should be paid for out of the proceeds of the sale.

Held, that Dunn & Vaughan were entitled to a decree for the amount of the order, with costs against the plaintiffs.

RITCHIE, E. J., delivered the judgment of the Court :—

The plaintiffs claim to be entitled to a certain sum of money paid into Court by the defendants, Ryersons, to which the defendant, H. Melville Oakes, was originally entitled, under an assignment from him made the 16th November, 1874. Messrs. Ryerson declined to pay the money to them under the assignment, assigning as a reason previous claims of others, and referring particularly to that of the defendants, Dunn & Vaughan, who had previously presented to them an order for $2,170.80 from H. Melville Oakes in their favor. This last-mentioned order was given on the 13th November, 1874, and presented to Samuel L. Ryerson the same day, who made no objection. This order had been given to Messrs. Dunn & Vaughan for supplies furnished towards the building of the vessel, the proceeds of the sale of which created the fund in the hands of Messrs. Ryerson, and was given in accordance with a promise made to them when the supplies were given that they should be paid out of the proceeds of her sale.

Though the giving of the assignment to the plaintiffs by H. Melville Oakes, after having given the order in favor of the defendants, Dunn & Vaughan, was a fraud on his part, there is no evidence that the plaintiffs, when they took the assignment, were aware of the existence of the order, and they now contend that the order previously given cannot have the effect of transferring the money to Dunn & Vaughan, and that they are entitled to it under their assignment. This contention cannot, in my opinion, be sustained. Numerous cases have established the principle that an agreement, even a verbal one, if clearly proved, between a debtor and a creditor, that the debt owing shall be paid out of a particular fund coming to the debtor will create an equitable assignment of the money. It is not too much to say that anything done in pursuance of an agreement for valuable consideration, or in consideration of an antecedent debt, to place a fund out of the control of the owner in favor of another amounts to an equitable assignment. Of the numerous cases in which this doctrine is recognized I will only refer to that of *Burr* v. *Carvalto*, 4 My. & Cr., 702, which is strikingly like the present. There an order was given by a debtor to his creditor upon a third person, having in his hands funds of the debtor, to pay the creditor out of those funds, and it was held to operate as a binding equitable assignment, and that it was not necessary in equity that the party receiving the order should agree or consent to hold the funds for the equitable assignee. In *Yates* v. *Groves*, 1 Ves. Jr., 281, the Court held that the order fixed the money the moment it was shewn to the party on whom it was drawn.

The decree in this case must be in favor of Dunn & Vaughan for the amount of their order on Messrs. Ryerson out of the funds in Court, and their costs against the plaintiffs.

KINNEY *v.* RYERSON ET AL.

PLAINTIFF sought to set aside a judgment entered on a confession as made in contemplation of insolvency; but the judgment creditor alleged and it appeared in evidence that the confession was taken only to indemnify the judgment creditor against loss on accommodation endorsements to be thereafter given, which were given.

Held, that, although the judgment debtor was in insolvent circumstances at the time of giving the confession, the judgment could not be impeached, section 89 of the Insolvent Act of 1875 referring only to securities given for pre-existing debts or liabilities.

RITCHIE, E. J., delivered the judgment of the Court :—

The plaintiff seeks to have a judgment entered by the defendants, John K. Ryerson, Nathan Moses, and Samuel M. Ryerson, doing business at Yarmouth, under the name of

Ryerson, Moses & Co. against John T. Hutchinson, for the sum of $6,000 debt, and $15.80 costs of suit, set aside, as having been taken in violation of the Insolvent Act of 1869.

A confession was given to the firm by Hutchinson for $6000 and judgment was entered on the 30th April, 1874, which was registered to bind his real estate on the following day. On the 15th September following proceedings were taken under the Insolvent Act and he was placed in insolvency.

The plaintiff alleges in his writ that Hutchinson was insolvent when he gave the confession, that it was given in contemplation of insolvency with intent to defraud his creditors, and was so done in collusion with Ryerson, Moses & Co.; that he was not indebted to them in $6000, his indebtedness, if any, not exceeding the sum of $400; that the judgment was obtained and registered by them collusively and in fraud of the just rights of the creditors of the insolvent and with the knowledge that Hutchinson was insolvent, with intent fraudulently to defeat, impede, and delay his creditors in their remedies against him, and to deprive them and the plaintiff, as assignee of the insolvent, of every claim on him or his real estate.

The defendants in their answer deny that Hutchinson was insolvent and unable to meet his engagements when he gave the confession, and say that previously to his giving it he applied to the firm to become accommodation endorsers for him to the extent of $6000, and the firm consented to do so, provided he would give the security of a judgment for that amount to indemnify them for any amount they might be obliged to pay on account of such indorsement; that in pursuance of this agreement the confession was given and the judgment entered and recorded, and on the faith and security of the judgment the firm carried out the agreement and became accommodation endorsers on certain bills of exchange and promissory notes, and became liable to pay and have paid as such endorsers large sums of money, and that at the commencement of this suit there was due the firm the sum of $3875.72 after crediting the sum of $2236 on account of the judgment.

10 *v*

That Hutchinson was in insolvent circumstances and unable
to meet his liabilities when he gave the confession is evident
from his own testimony. He then owed money the payment of
which was repeatedly demanded which he could not then pay
and has not since paid. He had been sustained in his business
up to that time by the use of accommodation notes, and the
firm on whom he relied having failed, he was compelled to
resort to other parties to afford him accommodation to enable
him, as he says, to continue his business, and it was on that
account that he applied to Ryerson, Moses & Co. Though
Hutchinson was at the time unable to meet his engagements
there is no evidence leading to the inference that this was
known to Ryerson, Moses & Co. or that the arrangement entered into was made otherwise than in good faith on their
part. Under these circumstances I fail to see that any of the
provisions of the Insolvent Act have been violated. The
only section which can be relied on by the plaintiff is the
89th, but that section has reference to the pledge of property
made in contemplation of insolvency by way of *security for
payment to any creditor*, or *to the giving of property by way
of payment to any creditor* whereby such creditor will obtain
an unjust preference, etc. Now, without determining whether
Hutchinson gave the confession in contemplation of insolvency
or not, it was not given to secure *a debt due at the time* to
Ryerson, Moses & Co. or by way of payment of a debt due
to them, and if he had been indebted to them or they were
liable as indorsers of his paper the judgment according to the
testimony of himself and Samuel M. Ryerson, the only member of the firm who was cognizant of the transaction, was
only to have a prospective operation and be a security for
liabilities which the firm should thereafter incur on his behalf.
It is true that Eakins says that Ryerson told him he would
indorse for Hutchinson if he would give security for liabilities
already incurred and for future liabilities, but it is not alleged
that this was communicated to Hutchinson, and both he and
Ryerson assert that the security was given to cover liabilities
subsequently to be incurred. The whole tenor of the
evidence goes to show that the object Hutchinson had in
view was obtaining *future* accommodation and this was the

substantial inducement for him to give the confession. The section I have reference to could only have been applied, if, assuming the judgment to have been given in contemplation of insolvency, it had been given to secure a pre-existing debt or liability, and Ryerson, Moses & Co. stand in no worse position than they would if, instead of undertaking to incur liability by indorsing the bills and notes of Hutchinson, they had agreed, as a consideration for giving the judgment to advance money to him from time to time thereafter and had subsequently made the advances in good faith on their part to enable him to carry on his business.

BROWN *v.* PEARMAN.

PLAINTIFF, as creditors' assignee, sought to set aside a judgment given by confession by two alleged co-partners, as made in contemplation of insolvency. Defendant denied that plaintiff was assignee, and it appeared that at the meeting of creditors there was only one person who had filed a claim, and his claim was without a voucher, yet, instead of abandoning the meeting as a failure and calling another, giving due notice, the meeting adjourned to another day, on which the plaintiff was appointed assignee.

Held, that the appointment was invalid, that the proceedings could be impugned without going into the Insolvency Court, and that the defendant's denial that plaintiff was assignee as alleged obliged him to prove it.*

Beulair v. *Gilliott*, (referred to in 1 R. & C. 264,) questioned.

RITCHIE, E. J., delivered the judgment of the Court:—

The object of this suit is to set aside a judgment entered by the defendant against Wm. A. and Joshua Reed, insolvents, as having been obtained in violation of the provisions of the Insolvent Act of 1875. The insolvent, Joshua Reed, on the 10th December, 1878, gave to the defendant a warrant of confession for $1400 on which judgment was entered for $1109.69 debt and costs, which was recorded on the following day and became a lien on certain real estate belonging to him in the County of Kings; and at the same time William A. Reed, the other insolvent, gave him a warrant of confession on which judgment was entered for $1109.75 and recorded

---

* There was also a question whether a partnership existed, the decision of which turned on the evidence.

so as to become a lien on certain property owned by him in the same county. On the day on which these judgments were recorded, viz., the 11th December, 1878, a writ of attachment under the Insolvent Act was issued against both the Reeds and recorded the same day.

The plaintiff alleges in his writ that on the 1st February, 1879, he was duly appointed assignee at a meeting of the creditors of the insolvents, and that the warrants of confession were given by the insolvents in contemplation of insolvency and were so given voluntarily and gratuitously with the intention of defrauding other creditors, and that this was done with the knowledge of the defendant who knew that they were insolvent and had probable cause for believing such to be the case.

The defendant in his answer alleges that Joshua and William A. Reed were never partners in business, and that the former was not a trader within the meaning of the Insolvent Act and was not liable to have his estate placed in liquidation, and that so far as his estate is concerned the proceedings in the insolvent court are inoperative; that the plaintiff was never duly appointed assignee under the Insolvent Act. And, as regards Joshua Reed, he contends that his judgment is valid and binding and forms a legal lien on his land in Kings County, but as regards William A. Reed, as he believes he was a trader liable to the provisions of the Insolvent Act, he is willing to release his judgment for the general benefit of his creditors.

Unless Joshua Reed were a partner in the business carried on by William A. Reed there is no pretence for making him liable as a trader under the terms of the Insolvent Act. The plaintiff in his writ does not assert that the insolvents were partners and up to the time of the issuing of the attachment and while the business was being carried on he had no reason to suppose that any partnership existed between them unless from the fact that Joshua, the father of William A. Reed, was occasionally at the brickyard where the business was carried on, took an interest in what was going on, and occasionally gave instructions to the men employed, and in one or two instances gave assistance. Brown, the plaintiff, says that he had a conversation with Joshua just before the attachment was taken out when he said to him, referring to the brick-making business, " you know that you expected to share in the profits of that concern ;" he said he could not deny it that he expected to share in the profits and expected to make money. But though these parties both owed the plaintiff he never saw any note or paper or other document signed by William A. and Joshua Reed and never heard of the name of the firm till after the insolvency.

That Joshua was interested in the brick-making business is clear; he was so as the father of William in whose name it was carried on. He was also as assisting him by endorsing his paper to enable him to carry it on, and he was also interested as the lessor of the brick-yard, under the lease of which he was to receive a sum for every thousand of brick he manu-factured there. This accounts in my opinion for all the interest he took in what was going on there, and after the most care-ful consideration I cannot infer from the evidence that any partnership ever existed between the two.

There is another objection taken by the defendant that, even if the partnership had been established, the plaintiff was not in a position to institute this suit inasmuch as he had never been legally appointed assignee.

A meeting of the creditors was called for the 27th Jan'y., 1879. From the minutes of that meeting, signed by the plaintiff as chairman and Edward J. Cogswell the official assignee, acting as secretary, the only person present who had filed a claim was Irad Benjamin and his claim was without a voucher so that neither the chairman nor any other person was qualified to take part in the proceedings; but instead of considering the meeting a failure and calling another by giving the notices required by the Insolvent Act, a motion was made and carried to adjourn that meeting till the follow-ing Saturday, February 1st, when the plaintiff was elected creditors' assignee. It is clear that this meeting was not constituted under the terms of the Insolvent Act, but it is contended on behalf of the plaintiff that the validity of the meeting and its proceedings cannot be called in question in this court and could only be impugned in the Insolvent

Court, or by appeal, and the case of *Beulair* v. *Gilliott*,[*]
decided on the common law side of the court was cited, which
certainly would seem somewhat to sustain that contention.
There, however, what was in controversy was the validity of
the discharge of the insolvent, a subject specially within the
jurisdiction of the Insolvent Court, though the court went a long
way in holding that it could not be shewn that it had no jurisdiction on account of the party not having been a trader.   Here
the action is brought by the plaintiff against a defendant, no
party to the insolvency proceedings, to set aside a judgment
entered against the alleged insolvent.   Had no creditors'
assignee been appointed the official assignee could have done
so, but a creditors' assignee must, where his appointment is
denied, shew that he has been duly appointed.   This is established by both English and Canadian cases.   In *Butler* v.
Hobson, 4 Bing., N. C. 290, which was trover by the assignee
of a bankrupt it was held that a plea that he was not
assignee put in issue that fact and required the plaintiff to
show that he was regularly appointed.   So in *Buckton* v.
Frost, 5 A. & E., 844; also trover by assignee of a bankrupt,
a plea denying that they were such.   In *Grove* v. *McArdle*,
33 U. C. Q. B. 252, the same view is taken and the very
terms of the Act indicate the same, for the 144th section
declares that the authenticated copy of the record of the
appointment of the assignee shall be but *prima facie* evidence
of the appointment and of the regularity of the proceedings.
The plaintiff in this case has given evidence of his appointment, but from that evidence it is manifest that the appointment took place at a meeting called without the notice
required by the Insolvent Act, and is, therefore, invalid.

---

[*] This case is referred to by McDONALD, J., in *Godkin* v. *Beech*, 1 R. & C., 264.

BIGELOW ET AL. *v.* RAND ET AL.

A VESSEL was built and registered,—twenty shares in the name of E. V. Crandall, a plaintiff, twenty in the name of H. V. Crandall, a defendant, twelve in the joint names of E. Bigelow, Sons & Co., plaintiffs. The outfits were purchased by E. Bigelow, Sons & Co., and E. V. and H. V. Crandall, composing the firm of Crandall Bros., under an alleged agreement that they should be paid for out of the first earnings, before any division was made among the owners. The shares of Crandall Bros. were afterwards transferred to J. E. & E. Rand, who claimed a right to divide the earnings before paying for the outfits. The evidence was contradictory, both as to the original agreement and as to the knowledge of it on the part of the Rands, but the Court drew from the evidence the inference that there was such an agreement, and that the Rands were aware of it, and decreed an accounting as prayed for.

RITCHIE, E. J., delivered the judgment of the Court :—

A vessel called the *Canning* was built in or about the year 1874, and was registered, twenty shares in the name of the plaintiff, Ebenezer V. Crandall, twelve shares in the joint names of the plaintiffs, members of the firm of E. Bigelow, Sons & Co., twelve shares in the name of Thomas E. Kenny, and twenty shares in the name of the defendant, Henry V. Crandall. Soon after Thomas E. Kenny transferred his shares to E. Bigelow, Sons & Co.

The outfits of the vessel were purchased by the plaintiffs, E. Bigelow, Sons & Co. and Crandall Brothers, of which latter firm the two Crandalls were the members, from the firm of T. & E. Kenny. These amounted to $13,000, for which they gave promissory notes. Subsequently the plaintiff, Alonzo Michner, purchased from Ebenezer V. Crandall two shares of the vessel, and from Henry V. Crandall two shares, and was appointed master of her. Henry V. Crandall was appointed managing owner and ship's husband. On the part of the plaintiffs it is asserted that an agreement was entered into by and between these owners that the whole of the earnings of the vessel should be applied in the first instance to the payment of her outfits, for which some of them had made themselves liable, and that no part should be divided till they were actually paid for. That any such agreement was entered into is denied on the part of the defendants.

The plaintiffs allege that the firm of Crandall Brothers became indebted to the firm of J. E. & E. Rand, of which the defendants, Rands, were the members, in the sum of $3,100, and in order to secure the payment of the amount, Ebenezer V. Crandall conveyed his remaining eighteen shares to James E. Rand, and Henry V. Crandall conveyed his eighteen shares to Ebenezer Rand, the thirty-six shares to be held in trust until the earnings of the vessel should, in the first place, pay off the balance due T. & E. Kenny for her outfits, which then amounted to $7,600, and in the next place should pay the indebtedness of Crandall Brothers to J. E. & E. Rand, and that until then the earnings of the vessel should be applied to no other purpose.

The defendants, Rands, deny that they knew of the indebtedness to T. & E. Kenny, for outfits, until after the thirty-six shares had been transferred to them, and say they knew nothing of the alleged agreement between the original owners till they saw the statement to that effect in the plaintiffs' writ.   They allege that the firm of J. E. & E. Rand had endorsed notes for Crandall Brothers, which were outstanding when the transfers were made, and that Ebenezer Crandall, for the purpose of securing the firm of J. & E. Rand, by bill of sale dated 7th December, 1874, transferred to James E. Rand his eighteen shares, in trust to secure them, and for no other purpose, and that Henry V. Crandall, on or about the 9th September, 1875, by bill of sale, transferred his eighteen shares to Ebenezer Rand, to secure to him the payment of a debt due to him personally from Henry V. Crandall, and upon no other trust, and that about the end of the year 1876 Henry V. Crandall, finding himself unable to pay the debt, requested him to accept the shares absolutely, which he agreed to do. This was a verbal arrangement. The defendant, Henry V. Crandall, has not appeared or answered. He has, however, been tendered by the defendants, Rands, as a witness. On all the essential points of the case the only witnesses examined are parties to the suit, and I regret to say that upon all these points there is a direct conflict between the evidence of the plaintiffs and that of the defendants, and on this account the case requires the most careful consideration.

That such an agreement as I have referred to was entered into by the original owners of the vessel is proved by Ebenezer Bigelow, John E. Bigelow, and Ebenezer Crandall; and Michner says that when he purchased his shares from the Crandalls, he did so subject to that agreement. The only evidence at variance with it is that of Henry V. Crandall, and his evidence, at variance as it is with his utterances and conduct, is not entitled to much consideration. In his direct evidence he says; "There was not any positive agreement made with my consent that the earnings of the *Canning* should go first to pay for her outfits." In his cross-examination he is more guarded. He then says; "I do not think there was any agreement to that effect." But in a letter from Crandall Brothers to E. Bigelow, Sons & Co., under date 31st January, 1874, *in the handwriting of this Henry V. Crandall*, they say; "We would like the outfits procured on as long time as can be reasonably had, and insured down there, for one year at least, on our proportion, and then if we want to pay cash we can do so, and take any advantages of discount, so that we can have a choice. Sometimes it is best for a vessel to pay her own outfits in this way." On the 4th March of the same year E. Bigelow, Sons & Co. wrote to Crandall Brothers; "We have been some time answering yours of the 13th January, on account of an arrangement for outfits for the barquentine with parties in Halifax by the name of T. & E. Kenny, who take an interest of three-sixteenths, and agree to furnish the outfits at cash first cost, including expenses from England in a vessel direct, &c., &c., for which we have agreed to allow them five per cent. on their money so advanced *when they shall have received their money from the first earnings of the vessel*. This agreement fulfilled must certainly lessen the cost of outfits very much, instead of getting them from parties in St. John or in Halifax, who expect their pay from the first earnings of the vessel on the back of their profits."

To this letter Crandall Brothers, on the 27th of the same month, reply; "Yours of the 21st is to hand, and contents noted. The arrangement that you have made about the outfits we think a very good one and satisfactory; the firm of T. & E. Kenny is a very good house, and it will be our policy to keep the vessel free of all encumbrances. It will be our object to first apply all the vessel's earnings to pay for her outfits. This is always understood when outfits are procured on time, and also to be insured for the parties furnishing." This letter also is *in the handwriting of Henry V. Crandall.* And in August, 1876, after the tranfers had been made to the Rands, Henry V. Crandall, who had been appointed to act as agent in the management of the vessel, in writing to the master, says; " Crandall Brothers used about $8,000 of the *Canning's* money which should have gone to pay her outfits." And again in the same letter; " All the money that you remit to Messrs. Rand will go to pay outfits and insurance, which will be due soon. The firm of Crandall Brothers is dissolved." On the 19th September following he writes; " I stated before all the money that you remit them, (the Rands,) goes to pay insurance and note due on outfits next month." And on the 30th October he writes; " Want you to send every dollar you can to J. E. & E. Rand to pay note on outfits due November 4th, $3,745 and insurance note in Halifax, $1,201, part due October 28.' This language of Henry V. Crandall, so consistent with the testimony of the Bigelows, his brother, Ebenezer V. Crandall, and Michner, and so inconsistent with his denial of the agreement, leads me to put full confidence in the evidence of the existence of such an agreement.

In order to shew how little the evidence of Henry V. Crandall could be relied on, the plaintiffs produced an affidavit made by him in this cause on the 26th February, 1878, in which is this passage; " I say it is not true, as stated in the plaintiffs' bill herein, that the firm of E. Bigelow, Sons & Co. and the said plaintiff, Crandall, and the said defendant, Crandall, purchased the outfits for said ship or vessel, the *Canning,* from the firm of T. & E. Kenny ; that I had nothing to do with the purchase of said outfits, which were purchased, I believe, solely by said firm of E. Bigelow, Sons & Co. ; that no agreement was at any time made by and between all the owners of said vessel that the whole of her earnings should be appropriated in the first instance to the payment of her outfits; and that no part of their earnings or income should be divided until said outfits were wholly paid for, as alleged in said bill that if any such agreement was ever made, I had no notice or knowledge thereof, nor was the same made with my consent." One cannot, under the circumstances, but feel surprised that such a statement should have been made under oath, especially when we find, among the vouchers in evidence, a promissory note dated the 31st December, 1874, to the firm of T. & E. Kenny, for $3,300, "for outfits of *Canning*," signed by E. Bigelow, Sons & Co. and Crandall Brothers, *the latter signature in the handwriting of Henry V. Crandall.* This was one of the original notes given. The four notes then given all were dated 31st December, 1874, and were all signed in the same way, as testified to by Ebenezer Bigelow, and his statement on this point is not denied.

It still remains to be seen whether this agreement relative to the payments of the outfits was known to the defendants, Rands, when they took the transfers or was recognized or adopted by them. In this respect also the evidence is contradictory. Ebenezer V. Crandall says that he came to Nova Scotia in 1874 relative to the building of the vessel, when the agreement was first talked over as to the mode of payment for the outfits, that he then saw and conversed with the Rands on the subject. He told James E. Rand, the father-in-law of Henry V. Crandall, the circumstances under which the outfits were to be purchased; that they were bought at eighteen months from T. & E. Kenny, and were to be paid for in the usual way by the first earnings of the vessel; that he had also a conversation with Ebenezer Rand to the same effect. Though all knowledge of this agreement is denied by the Rands and Henry V. Crandall, it is clear from the letter of the latter to the master, a year after the transfers had been made, that an arrangement to that effect then existed, which the Rands recognized and were carrying out, Henry V. Crandall then acting as agent and ship's husband, under the appointment of the Rands, as holding a majority interest in the vessel, and that the Rands themselves were cognizant of this, for in February, 1877, we find the signatures, "J. E. & E. Rand," and "H. V. Crandall, Agent," to the following note; "Capt. A. Michner,—Sir,—You will please remit all your freight, after deducting disbursements, to Messrs. E. Bigelow,

Sons & Co., or to their order, the same to apply to outfits and bills against the *Canning* until said outfits are paid up and you receive further notice." And on the 11th May of the same year we find the signature of the firm of J. E. & E. Rand in conjunction with that of E. Bigelow, Sons & Co. to a note for $2,000 in favor of T. & E. Kenny, on the face of which is " *Barkt. Canning.*" Before this note was shown to him, J. E. Rand, who had signed the name of the firm to it, had said that he had endorsed notes for the accommodation of the Bigelows, but he did not know that they were used in connection with the vessel. He would not at first admit the signature to be his, or rather refused to say whether he had signed it or not. The signature, he said, resembled his ; it might possibly be his ; he had no recollection of having given such a note ; did not keep an account of all the notes he signed for the Bigelows ; if the signature is his, he does not think it is one of the accommodation notes that he had referred to.

It is not disputed but that the shares of the Crandalls in the vessel, though conveyed to them in severalty, were partnership property, and, this being the case, Henry V. Crandall had no right to convey the eighteen shares held by him, being assets of the firm, to his father-in-law, J. E. Rand, to pay a debt due by himself, nor do I think, in view of the whole evidence on the subject, that he did so. It is evident that these parties were on the most confidential terms. James E. Rand says he did not keep books himself, but is willing to be bound by the entries of Henry V. Crandall in his books ; and, on turning to his entries in the books of Crandall Brothers, we find in the journal C., this entry, June, 1876 ;

" J. & E. Rand, Dr. to cost account barqt. *Canning* for thirty-six sixty-fourth shares of said vessel, sold them Sept. 9th, 1875, and other debts, for $9,463.63."

In ledger A., page 58, is the cost account of the *Canning*, and at the close of it the following entries were made by *Henry Crandall ;* " 1875. Sept. 9. By *J. E. & E. Rand, for thirty-six sixty-fourth* shares, sold them for $9.463.61, and other debts." And on page 432 is the entry of the Rands' account with Crandall Brothers, thus :—

J. E. & E. RAND, DR.

1876.

May 31.	To Capt. Michner.............	$ 336	51
June 30.	To cost account barqt. *Canning*	9463	61

$9830 12

CR.

1876.

March 31.	By cash....................	$3220	50
June 30.	H. V. Crandall..............	757	40
"	Vaughan Bros..............	5713	63
Barqt. Canning.......................		130	53

$9830 12

From these books we find the Crandall Brothers, as a firm, treating their interest in the vessel as partnership property, and dealing with it as such, and transferring it to the Rands *as property of the firm of J. E. & E. Rand.* In his evidence, H. V. Crandall says he "made the above entries in the spring of 1876; cannot say whether before or after 6th June; the credit of March 31, 1876, $3,220.50, represented the endorsements that Rand had to take up; the same entry on page 341 of the journal was made in June; the debit entry of May 31, 1876, $366.51, represents the balance of Captain Mitchner's shares in the vessel, which we paid Rands; the next debt, 30th June, 1876, cost account, $9463.61, represents the cost account of the *thirty-six shares* of the *Canning*; it is entered in page 350 of the journal, and was made in June, 1876.' These entries are utterly at variance with the account given of the transaction by the defendants, and though Henry V. Crandall had every opportunity to explain these entries he fails to give any account of them consistent with the evidence he had given.

That the bill of sale to James E. Rand was an invalid instrument at the time it was recorded cannot, I think, be questioned. There is said to have been the signature of Ebenezer V. Crandall to the paper, but Henry V. Crandall made it a bill of sale by filling up the blanks, and either he or Ebenezer Rand, being aware that it required to be executed in the presence of a subscribing witness, the latter was induced to put his name to the paper, though he admits he never saw it executed. Henry V. Crandall says he did this in consequence of a telegram and letter he received from his brother. The telegram was on the 6th September, 1875, to this effect :—

"Sent bill of sale Saturday. Act quick. Impossible to go further. Two Howards gone back, Don't ship plaster. No sale.   CRANDALL BROS."

He says the letter enclosed the blank bill of sale, and requested him to fill it up and give it to J. E. Rand. This letter, unfortunately, is not forthcoming, but it is obvious that when Ebenezer Crandall heard from his brother what had been done, he did not consider his instructions had been complied with. Henry V. Crandall, on the same day that he filled up the bill of sale from Ebenezer V. Crandall to James E. Rand, made the bill of sale from himself to Ebenezer Rand, and both were registered *on the same day and hour*, and Henry V. Crandall says he gave his bill of sale in consequence of the telegram and letter, as then he first became aware that they could not go on in business. It is somewhat remarkable that Ebenezer Rand should in his evidence assert that when he sent his bill of sale to be registered, with a declaration of ownership, he did not send his brother's, and did not know whether his brother had got his bill of sale or not at that time, and yet they were both executed the same day, the 9th September, 1875, and were both entered for registry at the same time, nine o'clock A. M. of the 10th September, he himself having put his name to his brother's as a witness in order that it might be registered. In December, 1876, the Rands, having reason to believe that Ebenezer V. Crandall intended to dispute the validity of the bill of sale to James E. Rand, Ebenezer Rand, at his request, met Ebenezer V. Crandall and Henry V. Crandall, at St. John, and a negotiation took place which resulted in an agreement on the part of Ebenezer V. Crandall to confirm the bill of sale on receiving from Ebenezer Rand a bond which was given, the condition of which was that Ebenezer Rand should re-convey to Ebenezer V. Crandall the eighteen shares *when and after the ship should, after deducting all necessary disbursements, have* *by her earnings paid off the two notes for $7,600, and when the thirty-six shares should have paid off the indebtedness of $3,100 ; the earnings of the ship would not be appropriated to any other purpose in the meantime.* This arrangement must be considered that of all the parties interested, and yet a month after the Rands insisted on dividing the freight received instead of applying it or any part of it to the payment for the outfits. It was urged that the Bigelows had received, without objection or protest, their share of the earnings when offered to them. This they positively deny, and the two plaintiffs, who were present, assert in their evidence that they protested and remonstrated against the money being divided, claiming that it should be applied to the payment of the outfits ; and here again, as has been so often the case, there is corroborative evidence of the correctness of the plaintiffs' statements and none of those of the defendants. In James E. Rand's letter to Ebenezer Crandall, under date of August, 1877, he says ; " At the rate of the *Canning's* earnings for the past year, it will take all of her earnings for ten years to pay those bills, referring to the outfits, &c., with interest and premiums of insurance. The Messrs. Bigelow were not satisfied with their proportion of the balance my brother received of the charter up the Mediterranean, *but wanted the whole of it.*" Now there is no pretence that the Bigelows ever claimed the whole, or ever made any claim whatever for the whole or any part of the earnings of the vessel for their own use. When they claimed the whole of the freight which had been received by Ebenezer Rand, it was that the whole should go towards payment of the outfits, as they stated in their evidence.

After having given the most careful consideration to the whole evidence, replete as it is with contradictory statements, and taken into account the conduct of the parties, both before and after the transfers to the defendants, Rands, and the documents produced, I can draw no other inference from them than that the *Canning* was partnership property of Crandall Brothers, and that the transfer of her was made by the members of the firm to the members of the firm of J. E. & E. Rand, to secure that firm for liabilities incurred for them at a time when their insolvency was anticipated or

feared, and that the Messrs. Rand were aware of and recognized
the agreement which originally existed that the liability
incurred for the outfits of the vessel should be paid out of her
first earnings, and took subject to the agreement. I have
avoided expressing any opinion on the accounts. They will
be for future consideration, and in case additional evidence is
offered, it can be heard by the Court, or there can be a reference
to a Master. The plaintiffs, in their bill, ask that an account
may be taken of all dealings and transactions between the
parties touching the vessel, and the defendants, Rands, in their
several answers also pray that an account may be taken, and
they also pray that the shares in the vessel registered in their
respective names may be sold, and the proceeds appropriated
to the payment of the liabilities on them in their regular order.

In taking the account reference will be had to the suits at
common law brought by James E. and Ebenezer Rand against
Bigelow and others, which, by an order of that Court, have
been transferred to this Court, and the subject matter of them
brought into the accounting.

KNOLAN *v.* DUNN et al.

PLAINTIFF, being indebted to several persons, conveyed property to his son,
under an agreement that the son should liquidate the debts, and the plaintiff
should have six years to pay him such amounts as he should advance, plaintiff to
remain in possession in the meantime ; and if he failed to re-pay the amounts, the
land should become absolutely the property of the son, who, contemporaneously
with the execution of the deed, delivered a bond conditioned for the fulfilment of
the agreement. The son afterwards conveyed the property to Dunn, who was
aware of the terms of the agreement.

Held, that the transaction was in effect a mortgage, and that Dunn could not
claim to hold the land as security for an alleged claim against the plaintiff which
he had discharged, and which was not mentioned in the original agreement, but
should re-convey the land on payment of the amount due on the agreement
between plaintiff and his son, less any income derived by Dunn from the land.

RITCHIE, E. J., delivered the judgment of the Court :—

The plaintiff, in his writ, sets out that, being indebted to
several persons, he agreed with his son, the defendant, John
E. Knolan, that if he would assume the payment of these
debts, he would convey to him the land described in the writ,

on the special agreement that he should have six years to re-pay to him such sums of money as he should expend in paying such debts, and that he, the plaintiff, should remain in possession of such land during that period, and if he failed in re-payment during the period the land should become the property of the son ; and that in accordance with that agreement, he executed and delivered to him a deed of the land ; that though the deed was absolute in its terms, it was to operate only as a mortgage, and that, contemporaneously with the execution of the deed by the plaintiff, John E. Knolan executed and delivered to the plaintiff a bond binding himself to fulfil the terms of the agreement. The bill also sets out that the other defendant, Daniel Dunn, was well aware of the agreement at the time it was entered into, and was a subscribing witness to the deed, yet he has taken an absolute deed of the land from his co-defendant, and, though the plaintiff was then in possession, and John E. Knolan had failed in the payment of the debts of the plaintiff, which he undertook to pay, the defendant, Dunn, during the temporary absence of the plaintiff, fraudulently entered upon the land and took possession, and has since withheld from him the possession of it ; and he prays that Dunn may be decreed to convey the land to him on his paying all that may be due by him on the agreement entered into with his son, John E. Knolan, and that an account may be taken of the profits of the land received by Dunn since he entered into possession of it.

Dunn alone has appeared and made defence. In his answer he admits in effect the agreement set out in the plaintiff's writ, and his knowledge of it ; he specifies the debts which John E. Knolan agreed to pay for his father, amounting together to $220, and that John E. Knolan agreed with the plaintiff that if the latter should re-pay him that sum within six years, together with interest, yearly, he would then re-convey the land to the plaintiff, otherwise he should be released from the ageeement. In his evidence he values the land at $400. He states that the deed to John E. Knolan was executed in his store and that he was a subscribing witness to it, that it was given to him to be recorded, and that he was also witness to the bond which was given at the same

10 w

time, and that he then understood from the conversation
between the parties, and it was in the bond, that the plaintiff
was to have six years to pay the *principal,* $220, and the
annual *interest,* as it grew due thereon. And further on in his
evidence he says ; " In addition to what I have stated about
the bond, the land was to become John's if plaintiff did not
pay the *principal at the end of ten years and the annual
interest* as it grew due thereon ;" that on the 18th August,
1877, he purchased the land from John E. Knolan, and paid
him, and took a receipt, which is produced, and is in the
following terms :—

"KENNETCOOK, the 18th August, 1877.

"Received in full of all dues, debts, and demands up to
this date from Daniel Dunn, Senr., but twenty dollars, which
he agrees to pay to my mother, in goods out of his store,
whenever she calls upon him for the same.

JOHN KNOLAN.

"Signed in presence of W. J. DUNN."

At this time one of the debts which John E. Knolan had
agreed to pay, that of Patterson, who held a mortgage on the
land, was unpaid, though a release of the mortgage had been
obtained. He had previously said that on the execution of
the deed by the plaintiff to his son, the release of Cochran's
judgment and that of Patterson's mortgage was handed to him
to be recorded. Now, at that time, Cochran had given no
release, nor did he execute any till several months after, and
while the deed was registered in February, 1876, Cochran's
release was not recorded till the following June. Notes were
given by John E. Knolan for these debts, and when the note
to Patterson became due he was arrested under a capias, and
his father having become bail for him, and he having absconded,
the latter was compelled to pay the debt by giving him a
pair of oxen valued at $80. John E. Knolan gave to Cochran
a joint note of himself and one McLean for the amount of his
debt, and about a year after, Knolan, not being able to pay it,
plaintiff gave his son a pair of cattle to pay it, and $14 he
owed his son. The value of the cattle was $60.

With reference to the conveyance of the plaintiff to his
son, and the agreement on which it was given, I have confined

myself to the evidence of the defendant, Dunn, as that which
is the least favorable to the plaintiff, whose case is established
satisfactorily by that of this defendant. The contention on
the part of Dunn is that the conveyance to John E. Knolan
vested the land in him absolutely, and that all the right his
father had was the privilege of re-purchasing it at the
expiration of six years, on his paying the money which had
been advanced for him, and the interest annually in the
meantime. If this were the effect of the agreement entered
into between the parties, and the plaintiff had failed to fulfil
the terms of it, the Court could give him no redress, but I
cannot see that he has failed in any respect. The term limited
for the re-payment of the principal has not yet expired, and
the payments he has made on account of his son have far
exceeded the interest which has accrued on it. I cannot,
however, view the deed and agreement as operating otherwise
than as a mortgage. All the circumstances connected with
the transaction, it appears to me, go to shew that the conveyance was intended merely as a security, and are inconsistent
with the idea of its being intended to operate as an absolute
conveyance. The plaintiff remained in possession after the
conveyance as before, John E. Knolan never pretending to
have a right to it, and according to Dunn's estimate, the
amount agreed to be advanced to John E. Knolan was little
more than half the value of the land. What Dunn gave on
his obtaining a deed of it his own evidence leaves in doubt.
The question involved is, did the parties contemplate a sale
and purchase of the land with the right of the plaintiff to
re-purchase, or was the deed given merely as a security for the
re-payment of money? And Dunn, in his evidence, clearly
indicates that they looked upon the transaction as a security
for a sum of money advanced, or to be advanced. His language
is; "John E. Knolan agreed to pay for his father debts
amounting to $220, and if the latter should *re-pay him* that
sum *with yearly interest* within six years, he would re-convey
the land, otherwise not." And again; "The plaintiff was to
have six years to pay *the principal* and the annual interest
as it grew due;" and "*the land was to become John's if the
plaintiff did not pay the principal at the end of six years,*

and the annual interest." Now, it is a recognized principle that where two instruments are made and delivered at the same time by the parties relating to the same matter, they will be regarded as parts of one instrument and be construed together, and in that view the usual proviso contained in a mortgage expresses the terms of the agreement in this case; "Provided, nevertheless, that if the plaintiff shall pay to John E. Knolan $220, with interest, in six years, the deed to be void." It was contended that there was no undertaking on the part of the plaintiff to re-pay the money to John E. Knolan, and that in the absence of such an undertaking the conveyance to the latter could not be held to be a mortgage. This circumstance, no doubt, is an important element in the consideration of the question, yet it does not follow that it is essential to constitute it a mortgage that there should be such an undertaking if the evidence satisfies the Court that the parties only intended a mortgage security. There must, indeed, be the evidence of the existence of a debt between the grantor and grantee. Here the language used by all the witnesses refers to the existence of a debt between them. They speak of principal to be re-paid, and interest till so re-paid, and Dunn says it was distinctly agreed that the interest should be paid annually. And though the non-existence of an obligation to re-pay the money in many of the English cases is a circumstance much dwelt upon by the Court, as leading to the inference that the conveyance was not intended to operate as a mortgage, it is by no means conclusive. *Goodman* v. *Grierson,* 2 Ball & B., 274; *King* v. *King,* 3 P. Wm., 358; *Floyer* v. *Lavington,* 1 P. Wm., 268; *Eaton* v. *Graves,* 1 Ven., 138.

The case of *Murphy* v. *Colley,* 1 Allen, 107, is almost identical with this, except that there there was no special reference to re-payment of principal and interest as such. That was a suit to redeem mortgaged premises. An absolute deed was taken, and an agreement from the grantee binding himself to re-convey the premises to the grantor whenever within five years, he should re-pay $1,000 to him, and if he should not do so the agreement to be void and the deed to be absolute. The Chief Justice, in giving the judgment of the

Court, said; "The terms of the agreement clearly indicate that the parties only intended to create a mortgage interest. It was urged by the counsel that there was no collateral undertaking to pay the money, but this is by no means conclusive of the nature of the transaction; it is only one circumstance to be regarded, but it cannot operate with any force where, as in the present case, the intent of the parties to make a mortgage is clear." Whether, therefore, the deed given by the plaintiff to his son, in the case before us, be considered as a mortgage or as an absolute sale and conveyance, with a collateral agreement for a re-purchase on the payment of the amount advanced for him by the latter, he is now entitled to a re-conveyance on his paying such amount. Dunn, in his answer, states his willingness to give such re-conveyance upon payment to him of $220, and interest thereon since the date of the release of the mortgage of Patterson and the judgment of Cochran, and a further sum of $192.35, and interest thereon since September, 1877, which last-mentioned sum was, as he alleged, due on a judgment of Thomas C. Haliburton against the plaintiff, and formed a lien on the property, which he had paid. There was, in fact, no such judgment, or none of any validity. A docket was produced signed by the Prothonotary, bearing date the 13th June, 1864, for $92.45 debt, and $15.60 costs, of which a certificate was recorded on the 16th June of the same year, but there is no record of any such judgment, nor can any record ever be made of it, nor anything be now done to give it validity, as no writ was ever taken out in the case, nor any bill of costs taxed; no execution was ever issued, nor any attempt ever made to enforce it, and the plaintiff is now dead. Dunn alleges that he made some settlement with Mr. Blanchard, who had been Mr. Haliburton's attorney. What that settlement was Dunn is unwilling to tell. He must have known, and if he had not recollected, Mr. Blanchard, who is now his attorney, could have informed him if he had desired to tell. The receipt given by Mr. Blanchard would lead to the inference, and Dunn intended that the inference should be drawn, that $192.30 was paid, that is $108.05, and thirteen years' interest, (six years' only could be claimed,) $84.28; and this sum of

$192.30, with interest from the day of the alleged settlement, is what he claims in his answer he is entitled to in addition to the $220. In his answer Dunn says he settled and paid this judgment. In his evidence, after much prevarication, he admits that he paid less than $90. This judgment, or what purports to be a judgment, has not been assigned, but Mr. Blanchard has undertaken to procure for Dunn an assignment *if possible*. Mr. Blanchard does not appear to have possessed the least authority to receive money on account, or to make any settlement of it. Dunn says he was authorized by the plaintiff to make the settlement. I give credit to the statement of the plaintiff that he never requested or authorized him to pay or settle it. If he had acted as the agent of the plaintiff all he could have asked to be paid him would have been the $80 or thereabouts that he now says he paid Blanchard, instead of the $192.30 which he claims from him. The inference that I am led to is that he made the settlement and obtained the promise of an assignment of the judgment to strengthen his claim on the property, on which, from all I can gather, even from his own evidence, he had previously paid but $50, thirty to John E. Knolan, and twenty to his mother. At any rate, however, whatever his claim may be on the plaintiff in respect of the payment made to Mr. Blanchard, he has no right to insist on requiring that the plaintiff shall pay him as a condition of his getting a re-conveyance of the property conveyed by him to his son, as it formed no element of the agreement entered into between them when the deed was given. The defendant, Dunn, will be decreed to re-convey the land to the plaintiff on payment by the latter of the amount due by him on the agreement entered into between him and his son, John E. Knolan, less any income and profits derived by Dunn from the property during the time he has been in possession of it, and that an account be taken of the amount so due by the plaintiff under the agreement, and of the income and profits so derived by Dunn from the possession of the land, as prayed for by the plaintiff in his writ. The question of costs is reserved.

METZLER *v.* SPENCER ET AL.

PLAINTIFF, as administrator, complained in his writ that defendant wrongfully caused a vessel to be condemned and sold, and received the proceeds, and appropriated them to his own use, refusing to account to him therefor. The bill was dismissed with costs, as to two of the defendants, as there was no evidence of their having received anything. As to another defendant, the Master reported that he had received upwards of $400, but that he had disbursed a greater amount. Exceptions were taken by plaintiff to this report, which the Court held to be sustained by the evidence, and the decree was for plaintiff, with costs.

RITCHIE, E. J., delivered the judgment of the Court :—

The defendants in this suit are Samuel Spencer, George McLellan, James Loughead, William Watt, and Robert Hunter, who, with Edwin Metzler, deceased, were owners of a vessel called the *W. A. Black,* Spencer being the owner of sixteen sixty-fourth shares, McLellan of twenty-four sixty-fourths, Loughead, Watt and Hunter each of four sixty-fourths, and Edwin Metzler of twelve sixty-fourth shares ; and the plaintiff sues as administrator of the last-named, who died in November, 1867.

The plaintiff complains that the defendants wrongfully and contrary to equity and good faith caused the vessel to be condemned and sold in the port of St. Thomas, and received the proceeds, and converted them to their own use, and have refused to account to him therefor, and he prays that each of them may be ordered to account for the money so received by him.

There is no foundation whatever for the allegation that the defendants had caused the vessel to be wrongfully condemned at St. Thomas. It was the act of the person acting as master, with which they had nothing whatever to do. The only defendants who have appeared and answered are Spencer, Loughead, and McLellan, and there is no evidence whatever that either of the two former has received any part of the money arising from the sale of the vessel or from the insurance that was on her, and it is admitted that the plaintiff can have no decree against them. As to them, therefore, the bill must be dismissed with costs. There was no reason that they should be made parties, assuming that the other defendants had received money to which the plaintiff was entitled as administrator, and for which they were bound to account.

It is in evidence that $394.35 were received by McLellan from the proceeds of the sale of the vessel, and that $80 were received by him from the insurance which was on her, and the Master has so reported; but he has also reported that at the time of the sale of the vessel at St. Thomas, McLellan had made payments and disbursements on account of her to such an amount that nothing was coming to the plaintiff on account of Edwin Metzler's share. The plaintiff excepts to the report of the Master on the ground that, since the receipt of the $394.35, McLellan made no disbursements on account of the vessel out of it, and that his previous disbursements had been more than re-paid by his previous receipts. 2nd. That by his admission, and that of Spencer and Loughead, $100 at least was due him. 3rd. That, as Watt had been paid $100 as his share, the plaintiff was entitled to a proportionate share. 4th. Because McLellan has not been debited with the money received by him on account of the vessel.

There is no evidence of any admission that $100 or any amount was due the plaintiff by McLellan. The plaintiff himself admits that. What is relied on is that Spencer, who it is admitted received none of the money arising from the sale of the vessel or her insurance, said he would give $100 *to stop the suit.* The offer was not accepted, and it was withdrawn. This offer, if it·had been made by McLellan, could only be considered an offer to buy his peace, and not as an acknowledgement of a debt, especially as he, at the very time, was repudiating all liability.

A large part of the evidence taken before the Master was objected to, and is not receivable to affect the defendants who have appeared and answered, as, for instance, all that Watt told the witness, John W. Metzler, and the plaintiff; also the whole of the evidence of Dimock. This evidence must, therefore, be eliminated from the case. As regards the payment to Watt, it was not made by McLellan. He received the amount from Spencer, who says he received nothing from the vessel since 1865; that the $100 paid to Watt was paid out of his own pocket; that, as Watt had purchased his shares in the vessel from him, and as the insurance money had been expended to pay previous claims against her, Watt made a claim on her, and he paid him that sum in settlement; that the claim was not against the owners, only against him.

The only money shewn to have been received by McLellan in respect of the last voyage of the vessel, or the proceeds of the sale of her, or from her insurance, for which alone this suit is brought, are the two sums of $394.35 and $80 referred to in the Master's report. The reception of the evidence of McLellan, as against the estate of Edwin Metzler, deceased, might have been open to objection, but as no objection was made, either before the Master or at the hearing, and he was cross-examined on the part of the plaintiff, if the evidence was open to objection it has been received. He allows that, instead of his owing anything to the other part-owners, they are indebted to him about $1,300. He was the first managing owner, then Spencer, and then he again became so. Watt says that he was master from 1864 to 1866, and while he sailed the vessel the earnings were all paid to Spencer. McLellan, when he first ceased to be managing owner and Spencer took charge, closed his account. The last item on the credit side is £74 or $296 cash from the insurance office. This would make the balance against him, but for the last entries on the debit side of last-paid dividends to the several owners, including himself, amounting to £79 19s. 4½d. It is unaccountable that, at the time of his ceasing to have the management of the vessel, after which her earnings were to be paid to another, he should have divided among the owners upwards of $160 more than he had received, and never called on them to refund. The balance then due him was largely increased, he says, so that in 1867 or 1868 it amounted to about $1,300, for which, from that time to this, he has never presented an account to the other owners, Spencer, Loughead, Watt, and Hunter, nor required payment, nor ever pretended to have a claim against the estate of Metzler, till threatened with this suit years after. Though he has now produced an account, he has adduced no proof of the several items. The account itself is unsatisfactory, and when asked for explanations, they are equally so. Some of his statements are inconsistent with others, and are vague and uncertain. He says the $296 received in 1864 was the last money he received on account of the vessel; he has since made disbursements for the vessel; he cannot tell how much; the money he sent to Watt for the vessel's use in 1866, £125 3s. 9d., must have been sent out of insurance money, at least he believes so; if he got the money it would be credited in his account; he did not recollect whether he got the money or not; it is a long time ago; he knew he paid premium notes, but he would not swear that he paid them except from his books. Referring to a charge in his account of £100 paid to Black Bros., he says; "I won't swear it was not $100 instead of £100; if £100 is marked in my book as paid, then I paid it; I don't recollect the date at which I made the charge in my book; I won't swear that Black Bros.' account, now shewn to me, is wrong; I might have paid $100 on the 27th January, 1865; I won't swear that I did not receive, on 30th April, 1867, $60 from Black Bros.; if I had received it I should likely enter it in my account; if I marked the materials for sheathing the vessel in my book, I must have paid it somehow." Mr. Allison, the secretary of the Avon Insurance Company, says that on the 12th May, 1876, he paid McLellan $500.75, the exact sum charged as remitted to Watt by McLellan at that date, and Spencer, in his account, charges against the vessel in 1865 cash paid to McLellan $200 to pay insurance premiums, and $220 retained by Sprague, Lowe & Co. on account of McLellan. No credit is given by McLellan nor explanation afforded, but in July of that year $205.30 is charged as paid to the insurance company. After the total loss of the vessel, Mr. Allison says that on the 24th March, 1868, among other payments on account of the insurance, he paid $80 to McLellan. The evidence of McLellan, so far from establishing his claim, is more calculated to throw discredit on his account. Giving every consideration to the evidence adduced before the Master, I think that it does not justify the conclusion he arrived at, that at the time of the sale of the vessel at St. Thomas, she was indebted for payments and disbursements to McLellan, and therefore that he is accountable to the plaintiff

as administrator of Edwin Metzler for his proportion of the
two sums received by him since her sale, viz., $394.35 and $80
against him. The plaintiff will be entitled to costs.

HARVIE v. WYLDE ET AL.

DODGE & Co., being largely indebted to various creditors, and having notes
lying overdue at the bank to the amount of $7,000, with others maturing, took
from one McPherson four promissory notes, dated October 26th, 1870, for lumber
sold to him, three of which notes, to the aggregate amount of about $4,800, they
endorsed to defendants, to meet a note for $3,000, endorsed by defendants, dated
July 26th, 1870. The notes so transferred were discounted, and the proceeds
applied to the payment of the $3,000 note, leaving a balance of $835, which was
retained by defendants, though nothing was then due them by Dodge & Co., and
was used to retire a note of Dodge & Co. that subsequently became due. One
month after the $3,000 note became due, Dodge & Co., on November 29th, 1870,
made a voluntary assignment, their liabilities being upwards of $100,000. The
jury were instructed that if, when the notes were transferred, Dodge & Co. had
reason to believe and did believe that their affairs were in such a situation that
insolvency would in all probability ensue, though there was a possibility of their
tiding over their difficulties, the transfer would be in contravention of the statute,
(the Insolvent Act of 1869,) and be deemed to be made in contemplation of
insolvency, and was invalid if made to give the defendants a preference over other
creditors. The jury found for the assignee.

Held, that this instruction was correct, and that the statute was applicable,
although defendants were not at the time creditors.

RITCHIE, E. J., delivered the judgment of the Court :—

It appears from the evidence in this case that Dodge & Co.,
having sold lumber to one Daniel McPherson, took from him
four notes for the purchase money, dated the 26th October,
1870, payable in three months, for $1,500, $1,333.75, $1,333.75,
and $1,167.50, and handed over the three last to defendants
in order to meet a note for $3,000, which was made by
Dodge & Co., and endorsed by the defendants, bearing date
the 26th July, 1870, and had been discounted at the Union
Bank, notice of its being about to fall due having been given
by the bank. McPherson's notes were at once discounted, and
with the proceeds the defendants retired the $3,000 note, and
credited the balance of $835 to Dodge & Co., though nothing

was due from them to the defendants except some outstanding notes of theirs which the defendants had endorsed for them; and when one of these outstanding notes subsequently fell due, in November, it was paid in part by the $835 and renewed for the balance.

There can be no doubt that Dodge & Co. were hopelessly insolvent when these notes were transferred to the defendants. Black says that in August, 1870, a note of Dodge & Co. fell due at the ·bank, and lay over dishonoured four weeks, and that about the middle of October another fell due and was dishonoured, for the amount of $4,000 or $5,000; and Dodge says notes of theirs were lying over unpaid at the bank, which they could not meet, a week before the notes were taken from McLellan, to the amount of $7,000, and that other notes of theirs were then maturing at the banks. With these notes of theirs lying dishonoured at the banks, and with no funds to meet them, except what was derived from the sale to McPherson, made after they fell due, they apply no part of it in paying what was then actually due by them, and not only transfer the three notes referred to to the defendants, to take up a note endorsed by them not then due, but place in their hands, and deprive themselves of the use of $835, at a time when they had pressing need of it to pay their debts, which sum is held by the defendants till other notes endorsed by the defendants for them should come to maturity; and just one month after the note for $3,000 became due, the 29th October, they made a voluntary assignment under the Insolvent Act, the 29th November, their liabilities being upwards of $100,000, and yet from the time of the transfer of these notes to the defendants to the time of their assignment, the only available funds to meet their liabilities consisted of the four notes they got from McPherson.

The Courts in England have held, independently of any special enactment to that effect, that, if *a trader* assigned any part of his property, such assignment, though not fraudulent and void *per se*, was deemed so, if made *in contemplation of bankruptcy, and with intent to give a creditor an undue advantage over others*, on the ground that the policy of the Bankrupt Act was thereby contravened. Subsequently there was a statutory provision to the effect that such an assignment constituted an act of bankruptcy, and under the English decisions all that was required to make such an act fraudulent and void was to shew that it was done in *contemplation of bankruptcy, and voluntarily;* so that if the 89th section had been omitted from the Insolvent Act of 1869, by the voluntarily depriving themselves of almost the whole of their then available funds of Dodge & Co. to provide for the payment of a debt not due, when notes were lying dishonoured to a large amount which they had no means of paying, in the light of these decisions we would be justified in coming to the conclusion that their transfer of the notes in question was void against their general creditors as directly in contravention of the policy of the act.

Smith, in his work on *Mercantile Law,* p. 572, 8th edition, says; "An assignment of part of a debtor's effects, even on account of a by-gone and before contracted debt, does not, like an assignment of the whole, carry with it any intrinsic evidence of fraud, since everybody must, in the course of business, have power to make over some parts of his property to creditors, but, though not fraudulent *per se,* yet if made *in contemplation of bankruptcy, and with an intent to give the transferees an undue advantage over other creditors, it is fraudulent and void,* and though not formerly so, is now an act of bankruptcy by the present Bankrupt Act ; and whether an act be or be not of this description, in other words, whether it be or be not a fraudulent preference, must be ascertained by considering whether the transfer, etc., were made *in contemplation of bankruptcy, and voluntarily."* In *Gibson* v. *Bontts,* 3 Scott, 229, the Chief Justice says ; "Where a party is in so hopeless a state of insolvency that he cannot reasonably expect to avoid bankruptcy, though he chooses to fight off as long as possible, I cannot look upon a payment voluntarily made by him to a favored creditor in any other light than as a payment calculated and intended to defeat the bankrupt law."

Two late cases were cited on the part of the defendants from the L. R., 10 Eq., 654, *Ex parte Crane,* and 12 Eq., 363, *Ex parte Blackburn.* These cases had reference to the

construction of the 92nd section of the present English
Bankrupt Act, which differs widely from the 89th section of
our Insolvent Act. It renders void certain transfers made
with a view of giving a creditor a preference over others, and
says *nothing* about the act being done *in contemplation of
bankruptcy*, whereas our act declares that the transfer shall
be void if made *in contemplation* of insolvency, if *thereby*
a creditor obtains or will obtain an unjust preference.
Yet in the former of these cases, BACON says, p. 657;
" In my opinion, the statute now in force has in no respect, so
far as affects the question before me, altered that law in
bankruptcy which had been well established by a long series
of decisions, and was well known before this statute came
into operation. The fraudulent preference which is made
void by the statute is the same fraudulent preference as was
invalid before, for the same reason and under the same
circumstances. The motive or view which may have actuated
the debtor, wholly or partially, is not material, unless it has
also induced him, without pressure or just request from his
creditor, to give him a preference over other creditors." The
only question there was whether the transfer was voluntary
or not. The learned Judge, in alluding to the decisions
anterior to the passing of the Bankrupt Act of 1869, refers
specially to *Marks* v. *Feldman*, L. R., 5 Q. B., 275;
10 B. & S., 371, as the most recent case in which the principle
is adverted to. That was before the Exchequer Chamber on
appeal from the Queen's Bench, and KELLY, C. B., there said,
p. 279; " If a man, at a time when he contemplates bankruptcy, delivers goods or money into the hands of a creditor
whom he intends to benefit, that transaction is perfectly valid
between the parties, but, if bankruptcy supervenes, and there
is an adjudication against the transferor or donor, it is a
fraudulent preference, and invalid as against the assignees,
not under any express provision in the bankrupt laws, but as
contrary to the spirit and principle of those laws;" and
MARTIN, B., p. 284, said; " In my judgment, as far as I can see,
whether the bankruptcy was obtained by a creditor hostilely,
or on the bankrupt's own petition, the law of fraudulent
preference remains the same. If the act is done in contem-

plation of bankruptcy, it has the effect of defeating the law which says that creditors are entitled to all the bankrupt's property, and if a man attempts to defeat that right by voluntarily parting with his goods, in my opinion they are recoverable back ; and whether it is by an action of trover, or an action for money had and received, or any other action, is utterly immaterial; the substance is that the goods or the value may be got back." In a previous part of his judgment, p. 283, he had referred to Lord MANSFIELD'S decision in *Alderson* v. *Temple*, 4 Burr., 2235, as establishing this doctrine.

In this view of the law, the only question in the present instance is whether the transfer of the notes was made *in contemplation of insolvency*, or rather, whether the case was properly submitted to the jury, for that the transfer was voluntary, and that the defendants obtained a preference over other creditors of the insolvent is unquestionable. The question was directly put to them, and they were instructed that if, when they transferred the notes, Dodge & Co. had ·reason to believe, and did believe, that their affairs were in such a situation that insolvency would in all probability ensue, though there was a possibility of their tiding over their difficulties, the transfer would be in contravention of the statute, and be deemed done in contemplation of insolvency, and would invalidate the act if done to secure and give a preference to the defendants over other creditors.

These instructions are, I think, fully justified by the decisions. In *Ex parte Blackburn*, already referred to, BACON, Chief Judge, said ; " The Act of 1869, (the English Bankrupt Act.) is the first statute that contains an express and direct enactment on the subject of fraudulent preference. Before that statute it was necessary, in order to constitute a fraudulent preference, that two things should concur,—the payment must be voluntary, and it must have been in contemplation of bankruptcy. The current of recent decisions has established with regard to the latter that where a man was in such a hopeless state of insolvency as that it was impossible for him to satisfy his creditors or to carry on his business, *he must be held* to have contemplated bankruptcy, and upon these principles it was that juries were directed to consider whether, upon the facts proved, the just inference was that a fraudulent preference had been made or intended by the debtor." That Dodge & Co. were utterly and hopelessly bankrupt when they made the transfer to the defendants the evidence clearly establishes. The learned Chief Justice adverted to the fact that contemplation of bankruptcy is not referred to in the English Act as a test of the validity of a transfer ; and in *Ex parte Norton*, L. R., 16 Eq., 408, the same learned Judge said Courts were formerly often embarrassed about " contemplation of bankruptcy." In this act there is nothing about " contemplation of bankruptcy," so that English decisions on this point under it can have little or no bearing on the construction of this section of our act which we are considering.

We have, however, a decision of high authority, both as regards the Court in which it was given, and the Judge who delivered it, on the clause of an act which *does* contain these words, the Jamaica Insolvent Act, the 67th section of which enacts, " that if any person, *in contemplation of insolvency,* shall transfer any of his estate to any creditor, such transfer shall be deemed fraudulent and void against the official assignees, unless made within six months of such insolvency." Lord WESTBURY, in giving the judgment of the Privy Council in *Nunes* v. *Carter*, L. R., 1 P. C. C., 347, defines a fraudulent preference under that act thus ; " Where a debtor, in contemplation of bankruptcy, that is, knowing his circumstances to be such as that bankruptcy must be or will be the probable result, *though it may not be the inevitable result,* does, *ex mero motu*, make a payment of money or a delivery of property to a creditor, not in the ordinary course of business, and without any pressure and demand on the part of the creditor." And in *Robson on Bankruptcy*, p. 130, the doctrine is recognized that though there might not be *in the mind* of the debtor any actual contemplation of bankruptcy, yet if he were in such a hopeless state of insolvency that he could not reasonably expect to avoid it, a payment voluntarily made would be considered as made in contemplation of bankruptcy ; that *Morgan* v. *Brundrett*, 5 B. & Ad., 296, would seem to have gone too far in holding that actual contemplation of bankruptcy by the debtor was necessary and that the correct interpretation of the words would seem to be that of TINDAL, C. J., in *Gibson* v. *Boutts*. Section 89 of our Insolvent Act makes the contemplation of insolvency the test of the validity of such a transfer, if thereby the creditor obtain an unjust preference over other creditors of the insolvent. It is in these words ; " If any sale, etc., or transfer be made of any property, real or personal, by any person in contemplation of insolvency, by way of security for payment to any creditor, or if any property, goods, effects, or valuable security be given by way of payment by any such person to any creditor, whereby such creditor obtains or will obtain an unjust preference over other creditors, such sale, deposit, transfer or payment shall be null and void, and the subject thereof may be recovered back for the benefit of the estate of the insolvent by the assignee, and if made within thirty days before the execution of a deed of assignment, etc., shall be presumed to have been made in contemplation of insolvency." And in *Adams* v. *McColl*, 25 U. C., Q. B. R., 219, on a clause of the Canadian Insolvent Act of 1864, similar to this, Chief Justice DRAPER said ; " The knowledge by the plaintiff, therefore, of the insolvent's inability to pay his debts, or of a fraudulent intention on his part to impede or obstruct or delay his creditors, is not material to make the transfer null and void, and even the existence of a fraudulent intention is not necessary." It presents, as applicable to this case, no other question than whether the insolvent, *in contemplation of insolvency*, gave the timber by way of payment to the plaintiff, whereby he obtained an unjust preference over other creditors. We take the policy of the act to be to distribute the insolvent's effects rateably among his creditors, and that if any of them obtain payment in full by the means stated in this section, while the others get nothing, it is an unjust preference contrary to its letter and spirit.

If the jury were not misdirected, then, did the evidence justify them in finding a verdict for the assignee ? I confess I do not see how they could have found otherwise. The only conclusion to be drawn from the facts in proof was that Dodge & Co., being utterly unable to meet their engagements,

10 *x*

made the transfer of the notes to defendants, in order to secure them from loss on those notes which they had endorsed for them, and this was done, not in the ordinary course of business, for then Dodge & Co., the makers, would have paid them themselves at maturity to the bank which held them, on receiving the notice that they were about to fall due. Nor was it in the ordinary course of business for the insolvents, when unable to pay their outstanding and dishonoured notes at the bank, to place in the hands of the defendants, and out of their own control, $850 more than sufficient to pay the note of $3,000, to take up which when due it is said the transfer was made, with no particular object, and with no instructions as to its application.

But it was contended that the act did not apply to this case because the defendants were *not creditors* of the insolvents.

If such a position could be maintained it would be at variance with the whole scope and policy of the Insolvent Act. If a person insolvent and contemplating to take the benefit of the Act could, before making his assignment, transfer his assets to such of his friends as might have endorsed notes for his accommodation, to enable them to retire them as they fell due, and leave himself without funds to pay his other creditors who have become such in the ordinary course of business, by purchase of their property or otherwise, the act would be rendered in most cases useless, and the effect of a decision to that effect would be, instead of making a rateable distribution of the assets of the insolvent among all his creditors, to give preference to such as, by endorsing his accommodation paper, had given him a false credit and thereby encouraged and enabled him to contract those debts which would remain unpaid.

A stronger case can hardly be put than the case before us, where the transfer was made to the defendants, and the liabilities were $100,000 and upwards, while notes were lying dishonoured at the bank. The means by which they might have paid some of their debts then due they hand over to an accommodation endorser, and then make their assignment, and have from ten to twenty cents in the dollar for their other creditors. Had they pursued the same course with Mr. Black, who had also endorsed paper to a large amount for their accommodation, and was similarly situated with the defendants, there would have been nothing whatever for what I think may be termed their legitimate creditors. The only case cited in support of this position was *Yates* v. *Hoppe*, 9 C. B., 544, but that is wholly inapplicable, as the jury there found that the payment was not made in contemplation of bankruptcy, and I have found no case to sustain it. There are cases, however, which take an entirely different view of the subject. *Devoe et al., Assignees*, v. *Watts*, Doug., 89, was trover and verdict for the plaintiff. Several bills and notes had been endorsed for the bankrupt by Watts and others, which remained unpaid, and he agreed to assign a lease to secure the payment of the debt. Lord MANSFIELD held that the assignment was fraudulent, as the assignees were preferred to other creditors, and it was void as made in contemplation of insolvency. So in *Hasuls, Assignee*, v. *Simpson*, reported in a note to the foregoing, (p. 92,) an assignment of property was made to defendant, to indemnify him on a bond he had entered into for the bankrupt. It was urged that defendant was not a creditor, and that he did not become such till after the commission of bankruptcy issued. Lord MANSFIELD held the assignment fraudulent, and said it made no difference that Simpson *was not a creditor at the time;* it was a preference to him when he should become a creditor, and the other Judges concurred. *Leah* v. *Young*, 5 El. & B., 955, is to the same effect. The case of *Groom, Assignee*, v. *Watts*, 4 Ex.,727, is very like that before us. In March, 1845, Francis, the bankrupt, and Miss Eiche, as a surety for him, made their joint and several promissory note for £270, payable to Lazarus & Myer. The defendant, in 1846, married Miss Eiche. In June, 1848, Francis became embarrassed, and placed his assets in the hands of one Wood, for the benefit of his creditors. In September of that year the defendant first became aware of the existence of the note, and, by his desire, his wife applied to Francis for money to enable her husband to take up the note, which was in the hands of Lazarus & Myer. Francis gave an order upon Wood for

£270. They refused to receive that amount unless the whole
of Francis' debt was paid to them. He was indebted to them
in a larger amount. The defendant kept the £270 as an
indemnity. On the 10th February, 1849, a fiat of bankruptcy
issued against Francis on his own petition. The learned
Judge told the jury that the plaintiffs were entitled to recover
if Francis, knowing himself to be insolvent and contemplating
insolvency, voluntarily gave defendant the £270, intending to
favor him beyond other creditors. The jury found for the
plaintiff for that sum. Gurney moved for a new trial on the
ground of misdirection, contending that *the defendant was not
a creditor* of the bankrupt, but a mere agent for the conveyance
of the amount of the note to the holder. It was the same as if
the bankrupt had given money to his servant to take it up, (the
very language used to us on the argument by the counsel for
the defendant.) POLLOCK, C. B. ; " This is a totally different
matter ; the money was given to defendant *to protect him.*
A servant is a mere messenger." ALDERSON, B. ; " This was
money had and received by defendant to the use of the
assignee, inasmuch as it was money handed over by the
bankrupt, *under such circumstances that it was against law
that he should retain it ;*" and the rule was refused. I will
refer to one more case, because the circumstances seem
identical with this. In *Churcher* v. *Cousins*, 28 U. C., Q. B. R.,
544, the insolvent sold lumber to Campbell for $300, for
which he gave his note. The note was taken to the bank of
British North America, to be applied to payment of a note
in the bank for $130, *made by the insolvent and endorsed by
the defendant*, and the balance on another note endorsed by
him. The transfer was held *void* under the section of the
Upper Canada Act, similar to ours, and the subject recoverable
back from the defendant for the benefit of the estate.

I have gone the more at large into the reasons which led
me to the conclusion at which I have arrived in this case,
because I have felt the question involved to be one of much
importance to the commercial community ; for, if transfers
made under circumstances like the present are to be upheld,
and an equal distribution of his assets can be so easily
prevented by the insolvent, the beneficial operation of the

insolvent law will be destroyed, and the effect of it will rather be to sanction and legalize such preferences as it was supposed to have been the object of it to prevent.

In Re FRASER & PAINT.

THE following opinions of RITCHIE, E. J., should have been published in 3 R. & C. at p. 16. They were delivered after argument before the full Court of the appeals from his decision as Judge in Equity, reported *ante* p. 68, but did not come into the reporters' hands when 3 R. & C., was going through the press.

RITCHIE, E. J., read the following opinion :—

The opinion which I have expressed in this case remains unchanged. The appellant has, I think, failed to shew sufficient grounds for setting aside the award, but, if it had been open to objection, the delay which took place in making his application would be fatal.

By our Common Law Practice Act, in all cases not otherwise provided for, the practice and proceedings of the Court shall conform, as nearly as may be, to those of the Superior Courts of Common Law in England in force previous to the first year of William IV.; and in the Equity Procedure Act it is provided that the practice of the Supreme Court, as far as applicable, shall be observed on the equity side, except as altered or modified by statute or the rules of the Equity Court. In other cases the practice of the English Chancery shall be adopted.

It was assumed at the argument that if the submission and award had been made a rule of the common law side of the Supreme Court, the objection must have prevailed, in consequence of a full term having intervened between the publication of the award and the application to set it aside ; but it was contended that, inasmuch as the Equity Court is always open, irrespective of terms, the statute of 9 & 10 William IV., chapter 15, and the practice under it, could not apply, and that, therefore, there was no limitation within which the application must be made. There is, in my opinion, no ground for such a contention. In England, the

Court of Chancery, like the Equity Court here, was always open without reference to the law terms, but that Court, nevertheless, adopting the rule in analogy to the statute, would not set aside an award where a term, that is a common law term, had been allowed to pass without any steps having been taken. In *Nichols* v. *Roe*, 3 Myl. & K., 437, the Lord Chancellor held that the application to set aside an award, made under a submission similar in effect to this, must be made before the last day of the term after the publication of the award, and that to allow a party to come to that Court, even by bill to set it aside, would be to render the provisions of the statute wholly nugatory. The same objection was taken there which was urged on us, that the opposite party had not made it a rule of Court within the time, so that a motion to set aside the award could not be made. To this the Lord Chancellor observed that there never was a greater mistake; the party objecting to the award might himself have made it a rule of Court, and then moved.

Lord ROMILLY, in the course of his judgment in *Peek* v. *Gurney*, L. R., 13 Eq., 79, observed that no conduct was more rigidly reprobated in Equity than the system of playing fast and loose. The appellant in this case seems to have done this when, knowing everything connected with the alleged irregularities of the arbitrators of which he now complains, he yet proceeded with the reference without objection, lying by until he should have ascertained whether the award was in his favor or not; and again, after becoming acquainted with the contents of the award, he makes no objection to it, attends the sale under it, and not only makes no protest against it, but, by affording information in relation to the property offered for sale, induces those present to suppose that he sanctioned what was going on, and only objects some time after, when the result of the sale is known, and takes no steps to set aside the award till the expiration of six months, or thereabouts, from the time of its publication.

Surely purchasers at that sale might well contend that the appellant was estopped from objecting to its validity. If, therefore, there had been more in the objections taken to the award than I think there is, and even if injustice had been done to the appellant, of which there is no pretence, I should have been forced to the conclusion that, by the course he has pursued, and by his own laches he has deprived himself of the right to relief from this Court.

On the second appeal His Lordship read the following opinion :—

The only question involved in this case is whether the Court had power to order the deed to be executed by a Master on the neglect or refusal of Paint to execute it, his counsel contending that the statute authorizing such a course relates to *causes* in the Court, and that the proper and only course would have been to proceed against Paint by attachment for disobeying the order of the Court.

The object of making a submission and award a rule of Court is to enable the party in whose favor it is to enforce it, or if by the other party, to enable him to bring them in Court, so as to enable him to set aside the award if he has grounds for so doing. Until the Imperial Act, 1 & 2 Vic., chapter 110, the only mode of enforcing payment of an award which had been made a rule of Court was by attachment for a contempt in not obeying the order of the Court. That statute extends the remedy greatly, and our statute goes still further, and, it appears to me, clearly recognizes the proceedings as a cause in the Court, as it provides that the Court may enforce obedience to any award by directing judgment to be entered and execution to issue for the amount thereof, with costs, *or otherwise* to carry into effect such award. The view I have taken of the case is that a party, seeking to enforce an award in his favor, if he resorts to a common law Court, may, by making it a rule of Court, entitle himself to the remedies of that Court by execution, attachment, etc., or, if to the Court of Equity, to the remedies incident to and belonging to that Court, and among them, in this Court, to the right of having a conveyance executed by a Master when the party who was bound to have executed it has refused or neglected. There is nothing whatever, in my opinion, in the objection that this conveyance can only be made in the case of a suit for specific performance. The clause authorizing a conveyance

by a Master is re-enacted from an old Chancery Act, and is
there wholly unconnected with specific performance. The
argument was that it was grouped with other clauses under
the head of specific performance, etc. The other objection is
equally untenable, that there was an appeal outstanding.
The act regulating procedure in Equity provides that stay of
proceedings shall not be consequent upon appeals unless the
Judge in Equity, upon special application, shall so order, or
unless in special cases the Supreme Court shall interpose to
that effect. In this case no stay of proceedings was ordered
by the Equity or the Appellate Court, and the party was
therefore not precluded from proceeding under the judgment
given, but of course he did so at the peril of his proceedings
being nullified by the reversal of the judgment.

INDEX.

INDEX.

ABSCONDING DEBTOR.

See INSOLVENT ACT, 1.

ACCOUNT.

1. Plaintiff was joint-owner with defendants of a vessel engaged in fishing voyages, plaintiff being master of the vessel. In his writ plaintiff claimed an amount due, but the master reported an amount due by plaintiff to the defendants, arising out of notes of hand given by plaintiffs and defendants conjointly for the purchase of the vessel, which notes defendants had retired, and an order received by plaintiff for money in which all the parties were interested.

    Held, that the amounts were properly allowed.

2. A vessel was built and registered,—twenty shares in the name of E. V. Crandall, a plaintiff, twenty in the name of H. V. Crandall, a defendant, twelve in the joint names of E. Bigelow, Sons & Co., plaintiffs. The outfits were purchased by E. Bigelow, Sons & Co., and E. V. and H. V. Crandall, composing the firm of Crandall Bros., under an alleged agreement that they should be paid for out of the first earnings, before any division was made among the owners. The shares of Crandall Bros. were afterwards transferred to J. E. & E. Rand, who claimed a right to divide the earnings before paying for the outfits. The evidence was contradictory, both as to the original agreement and as to the knowledge of it on the part of the Rands, but the Court drew from the evidence the inference that there was such an agreement, and that the Rands were aware of it, and decreed an accounting as prayed for.

ADMINISTRATION, Discretion of Judge of Probate in granting.

See DISCRETION OF JUDGE.

AGENCY.

Defendant obtained a loan of £200 on mortgage from Cogswell, through a Solicitor doing business at Wolfville, who made a charge of £10 for conveyancing and commissions, and a further charge of £10 for guaranteeing the defendants from loss in case the principal was called for within five years. The mortgage did not authorize the taking of anything beyond the legal rate of interest, was not cognizant of it, and did not participate in it. The rate of interest stipulated for was six per cent., which was all that the mortgagee received. The Solicitor stated, in evidence, that when the defendant applied to him for money he wrote to the mortgagee, who agreed to lend it on the security offered, and sent a sum which, together with an amount already in his hands, made up the £200 ; that he was not the agent of the mortgagee in any case to invest his money, and that in remitting the interest he deducted nothing for commissions. But defendant swore that on the first occasion when he applied to the Solicitor, the latter told him that he had £200 to lend, that he had advertized it, and that it was the mortgagee's money.

Held, that the wrong done to defendant was not done by the mortgagee, but by the Solicitor, not as mortgagee's agent but while acting on his own behalf, and further, that, assuming him to be the agent of the mortgagee, as he was not a *general* agent, but a particular agent, defendant could not assume that he had been authorized to do an illegal act.

See also FORECLOSURE, 2.

ALLIANCE SOCIETY OF LONDON.

The plaintiff company was registered under the Imperial Act, 25 and 26 Vic., cap 8, and claimed to do business in Canada under 37 Vic., cap. 49. The object of the Society was expressed to be to advance money in various sums to such members as were desirous of receiving it, the repayment to be secured on real or other security ; and in the article of the constitution entitled, Foreclosure and Redemption, it was provided that if any member should desire to pay in advance all or any portion of an appropriation or premium, he should be at liberty to do so, and should be entitled to such discount as the actuary might recommend. The writ alleged that, the mortgagee having become a member of the Society, £300 was advanced to him at a premium of £379 6s. 8d., the advance and premium to be repayable in quarterly instalments in twenty years ; and that, according to the regulations of the Society, if any instalment or fine remained in arrears for three months, the whole sum advanced, together with the premium, should become due. The proviso and covenants in the mortgage were to this effect, and the plaintiff claimed £675 7s. 8d., although the mortgagor had only had the sum of £300 for nine months.

Held, that the plaintiffs were only entitled to the quarterly instalments up to the time of the foreclosure and sale, and that the amount of principal due should be ascertained by computing how much of the quarterly payments represented principal, and how much interest.

Matterson v. *Elderfield*, L. R., 4 Ch., 207, distinguished.

APPOINTMENT OF ASSIGNEE.

See INSOLVENT ACT, 10.

ARBITRATION.

1. Fraser and Paint, having terminated their partnership business, referred all their disputes of every description to the award of two arbitrators and such umpire as they should select before entering upon their duties as arbitrators. Authority was given to the arbitrators or any two of them to enlarge the time for making the award, and the two originally appointed extended the time, and after doing so, selected an umpire and entered upon the inquiry. Desiring to obtain all the information possible, the arbitrators, without the request of either party, called before them certain persons, neither of the parties being present, but it appeared that the persons so called had no evidence to give about the matters in controversy, and no objection was taken by the party

moving to set aside the award, who knew that the arbitrators had called such persons before them, but yet continued to attend and conduct the reference on his own behalf. The partnership was indebted to Fraser in the sum of $52,840, and there was due to it by Paint $2624, and the award directed that the assets should be held and managed by Fraser under the inspection of the umpire, and that the sale of the partnership property should be made by him at such times and places as the umpire should approve. The award was made 28th September 1875, and no motion was made to set it aside until March 1876, the objecting party having in the meantime, with knowledge of the facts upon which he based his objections, proceeded with the arbitration, attended the sale of the property, and, at the request of the auctioneer, furnished information as to the boundaries of the land.

Held, that the provision in the award as to the sale of the property by Fraser, under the approval of the Umpire, was not such a delegation of authority as should invalidate the award ; that although the arbitrators had acted unadvisedly in calling persons before them in the absence of the parties, yet as Paint had made no objection, but had afterwards proceeded with the reference, the objection was not, in view of the lapse of time, entitled to much favor ; that the two arbitrators, in extending the time, before appointing an umpire, had not " entered upon their duties as arbitrators " within the meaning of the clause of the submission providing for the selection of an umpire before so entering upon their duties ; that the policy of the Legislature and the practice of the Court required a party desirous of setting aside an award, to move promptly, and that Paint, by his delay in moving as well as by his tacit and active acquiescence in the award, had waived irregularities in the conducting of the arbitration.

2. *Held,* that an award could not be set aside at the instance of one of the defendants on the ground of a claim being improperly allowed against the plaintiffs.

Held, further, that where one of the objects of the suit was to require defendants to submit their differences to arbitration under an agreement to do so, and by the rule of reference all matters in difference in the suit were submitted to their award, the award could not be set aside because the arbitrators awarded damages to the plaintiffs.

Held, further, that where all the parties and the arbitrators themselves admitted that a mistake had been made in requiring one of the defendants, as part of the award, to pay off a certain mortgage, which should not have been required, the evidence of the arbitrators was receivable as to such a point, as well as on the point of their having taken into consideration matters not within their jurisdiction, and that, as the arbitrators had inadvertently made a mistake with reference to the mortgage, the award should be sent back to them to be corrected.

ARREST OF DEFENDANT, Effect of.

Parker & Grant having recovered a verdict against Fairbanks, a rule *nisi* was taken out to set it aside. T. & E. DeWolf & Co. became sureties to respond the final judgment, and took a mortgage from Fairbanks to secure them from loss on account of their bond, and also to secure the amount of an existing indebtedness. The rule *nisi* having been discharged and judgment entered up against Fairbanks, an execution was issued under which he was arrested and placed in custody. While he was in custody, and after the present suit was brought by plaintiff as assignee of DeWolf & Co. against Fairbanks, to foreclose the mortgage, and after said Fairbanks had answered, his estate was placed in insolvency, and Creighton, his assignee, intervened and became a party. Parker & Grant also became parties, as interested in the subject matter. *Held*, first, that the insolvency of Fairbanks did not prevent the plaintiff from proceeding with the foreclosure, and, secondly, that Parker & Grant had not lost their lien on the mortgaged property, in consequence of their having arrested Fairbanks under the judgment.

ASSIGNMENT, Inartificial instrument construed as.

R. M. & Co, sought to have surplus proceeds arising out of a sale under foreclosure applied to a recorded judgment held by them against the mortgagor. The judgment was recorded in May, 1874. Plaintiff's mortgage had been recorded in 1869, and a prior mortgage of the same property had been recorded in 1855. Defendant having become insolvent, his assignee, in order to prevent the sacrifice of the property, paid off the mortgage last mentioned and the interest on plaintiff's mortgage, receiving from the holders of the mortgage which he paid an instrument in which, after reciting the payment of the principal and interest, it expressed that the bond was delivered up to be cancelled, (which, however, was not cancelled, but was produced with the mortgage,) and that they remised, released, and quitted claim to him, as assignee, the land therein mentioned, and all the right which they had as executors, and all sums mentioned therein, to have and to hold to the said K., as assignee as aforesaid, his successors and assigns.

Held, that this instrument, though inartificially drawn, was open to the construction that it was a satisfaction of the debt as between the executors and the assignee, but conveyed to the latter all their interest in the mortgage as against subsequent incumbrancers; but that, even assuming that it was a release of the mortgage, and not an assignment, the assignee had a prior claim to the surplus proceeds for the amounts he had advanced on the mortgage to prevent foreclosure and sale, subject to a credit for any amounts received by him for rent of the mortgaged premises.

See *also* EQUITABLE ASSIGNMENT.

ATTACHMENT.

See INSOLVENT ACT, 1.

AWARD.

See ARBITRATION.

BRITISH NORTH AMERICA ACT.

See ULTRA VIRES.

BUILDING SOCIETY, Nova Scotia.

See FORECLOSURE, 2.

BURDEN OF PROOF.

F. McDonald, deceased, made a mortgage to plaintiff, which plaintiff brought suit to foreclose. Defendants set out an agreement by which plaintiff agreed to release the mortgage on receiving three promissory notes made by one McKinnon, to whom part of the land had been sold by the mortgagor. Plaintiff replied that the notes were only taken as collateral security, to be credited to the mortgagor when paid, and that nothing had been paid an account of them. On the trial of the issue plaintiff proved the mortgage, and defendants produced no evidence whatever. The jury found for defendants. *Held*, that the burden of proof of the issue raised was on the defendants, and that as they had proved nothing, the finding must be set aside.

CITY TAXES.

See TAXES, Lien for.

CONSTRUCTION of Agreement.

Plaintiff brought action to redeem a mortgage, setting out an agreement in writing by the defendant to release it on being paid one-half of the principal of the mortgage and interest in twelve months, plaintiff agreeing to give up certain claims against the defendant. The Master construed the agreement, according to plaintiff's contention, as requiring payment of one-half the balance due at the time of the agreement, while defendant contended that it meant one-half the original principal. Evidence was given in support of both constructions.

Held, that, independently of any evidence, the Master's view of the agreement was incorrect, and that there was no necessity of referring the case back to the Master, as the Court had the material for ascertaining the amount due.

———————— OF INSTRUMENT.

The Insolvent conveyed certain property to Wylde, Hart & Co. by an instrument, reciting that he had agreed to give them security on all his real estate, *plant and machinery*, in the City of Halifax, and after conveying certain lands, he conveyed "all that and those the *machinery, implements and things* specified in the schedule hereto annexed," which schedule was headed, "Plant in the Machine Shop," and was found to contain, not stock on hand or articles manufactured, but only such articles as would come under the designation of machinery, implements and *things of that sort*. A subsequent part of the instrument, provided that all the *machinery, implements and things* which, during the continuance of the security, should be fixed or placed in or about the land described in addition to or substitution of the said machinery, implements and things described in the schedule annexed, should be subject to the trusts, &c. expressed in the instrument. *Held*, that, under the instrument, only the things enumerated in the schedule annexed, or those added to or substituted for them, passed to Wylde, Hart & Co., and that the word "things," could not be held to embrace the general stock in trade, but must be limited to property *ejusdem generis* with that described in the words preceding and connected with it.

The word "plant," defined as applied to a manufactory.

———————— OF STATUTE.

See WINDSOR AND ANNAPOLIS RAILWAY.

CONSTRUCTIVE NOTICE.

See REGISTRY OF DEEDS.

CONTEMPLATION OF INSOLVENCY.

1. Howell and Stewart, in June 1871, entered into co-partnership as founders, &c., the former to give his skill and ability to the business, and the latter, who was a minor, to supply capital and purchase stock to the extent of $4000. At the time of the agreement a lot of land was purchased for $10,000 on which to erect buildings for the business, but nothing was paid on account of the purchase money, which was secured by a mortgage. The deed was taken in the name of Howell and Mrs. Adams, the mother of Stewart, who advanced the $4000 to start the business. Although plaintiff contended that this advance was simply made by Mrs. Adams to her son, there was some evidence to show that it was to be repaid by the partnership. Stewart became of age in February, 1873, and in August of that year the partnership was dissolved and a mortgage made by Howell to Mrs. Adams to secure the amount of her advances. The plaintiff, as assignee, sought to have this mortgage declared void, as made in contemplation of insolvency, and they negatived fraud in the transaction, though they found that the conveyance had had the effect of impeding obstructing and delaying creditors. The Court upheld the conveyance.

2. Sylvanus Morton, on the 26th of April, 1873, made a deed of property without consideration to his daughter, continuing himself in possession of the property until October, 1875, when he failed. Previous to the date of the deed the Liverpool and Acadia Banks, of one of which Morton was President, and a large shareholder, had suspended ; and a firm in which he was concerned had failed two days before the date of the deed. Previous to the making of the deed the insolvent had admitted to a creditor that if certain proceedings threatened against him, as President of said Banks, were taken, he would have to assign. And after the making of the deed he was challenged in reference to it, and said it was all he could do, under the circumstances, to save his property.

Held, that the deed, having been made at a time when the grantor contemplated a state of things that might result in insolvency, and which did, in fact, so result, must be set aside ; even had it not been shown that the insolvent continued in possession, and a few days after making the deed admitted to his creditor that it was all he could do to save his property.

3. Dodge & Co., being largely indebted to various creditors, and having notes lying overdue at the bank to the amount of $7,000, with others maturing, took from one McPherson four promissory notes, dated October 26th, 1870, for lumber sold to him, three of which notes, to the aggregate amount of about $4,800, they endorsed to defendants, to meet a note for $3,000, endorsed by defendants, dated July 26th, 1870. The notes so transferred were discounted, and the proceeds applied to the payment of the $3,000 note, leaving a balance of $835, which was retained by defendants, though nothing was then due them by Dodge & Co., and was used to retire a note of Dodge & Co. that subsequently became due. One month after the $3,000 note became due, Dodge & Co., on November 29th, 1870, made a voluntary assignment, their liabilities being upwards of $100,000. The jury were instructed that if, when the notes were transferred, Dodge & Co. had reason to believe and did believe that their affairs were in such a situation that insolvency would in all probability ensue, though there was a possibility of their tiding over their difficulties, the transfer would be in contravention of the statute, (the Insolvent Act of 1869,) and be deemed to be made in contemplation of insolvency, and was invalid if made to give the defendants a preference over other creditors. The jury found for the assignee

CY-PRES.

no proceedings, the property did not revert to the heir-at-law, who then appeared by counsel and had a day appointed for the argument, but on the day appointed for argument none of the defendants appeared and the cause was referred to a Master, who reported that the funds should be appropriated towards the erection of a High School building in Halifax, the Kirk Sessions to have the power of nominating two free scholars, having concurred in the recommendation with that condition. No opposition being made to this report, and no counter scheme being suggested, the report was confirmed and the scheme adopted.

Attorney-General v. *Avery et al*.. 253

DEED decreed to be mortgage.

See EQUITABLE MORTGAGE.

DEMURRER.

See PRACTICE.

DISCRETION OF JUDGE.

The granting of administration *de bonis non* to the widow of the deceased was appealed from by his daughter, on the ground that the administratix had been guilty of waste on the lands set off to her as dower. It appeared from Respondent's affidavit that, whether her acts amounted to waste or not, she considered herself justified in the course she had pursued.

Held, that as there was nothing to indicate such dishonesty on the part of the widow as should preclude her from all right to the administration, the Court could not control the discretion conferred by the act on the Judge of Probate.

In re the Estate of James W. Roop.................................... 162

DRAINAGE.

See INJUNCTION, 3.

DYKE LANDS.

The Wickwire dyke, being outside of and affording protection to the Grand Pre dyke constructed many years before, the proprietors of the Wickwire marsh, acting under the provision of the statutes then in force, (see R. S. Cap. 40, s. 27) took proceedings to settle what proportion of the expense of the maintenance and repair of the Wickwire dyke should be contributed by the proprietors of the Grand Pre Marsh, which sum so settled was annually paid by the proprietors of the Grand Pre Marsh so long as that marsh received any protection from the outer dyke. In 1869 a heavy gale and unusually high tide broke the outer dyke and submerged the Wickwire marsh, and it was not until 1871 that the dyke was reconstructed.

Held, that the proprietors of the Grand Pre marsh could not be called upon to contribute toward the repair of the Wickwire dyke beyond the annual sum originally settled.

Defendants having contended that they could not be required to contribute at all, as their marsh was only partially enclosed and not protected by the Wickwire dyke ; and further, that their had been irregularities in the original proceedings ;

Held, that having acquiesced in the annual payments for upwards of twenty-five years they could not now raise such a question, and that the alleged irregularities could only have been taken advantage of by *certiorari*.

Wickwire v. *Gould*.. 245

EJECTMENT.

Plaintiff brought action of ejectment, claiming under a deed from one Purdy, but it appeared from uncontradicted parol evidence that Purdy had purchased the land for the benefit of defendant's father, who had paid considerable sums on account of the purchase money. After the death of defendant's father, Purdy agreed to convey the land to plaintiff; and it was in evidence that plaintiff held the land for the benefit of defendant, then in possession of the property, that he was to give him a deed of it when he paid him what he owed him, and that plaintiff was to have the hay and half the pasture for interest; but no writings passed between the parties. Plaintiff received part of the hay and had pasturage on the property, and before action brought defendant tendered to him the principal money. Held, that the equitable defense, based upon the above facts, must prevail.

ELIZABETH, Statutes of.

See INSOLVENT ACT.

See also FRAUDULENT CONVEYANCE.

EQUITABLE ASSIGNMENT.

Plaintiff claimed to be entitled to a sum paid into Court by Messrs. Ryerson & Co., under an assignment of it from H. M. Oakes. Previously to this assignment Oakes had given an order to Dunn & Vaughan on Ryerson for the amount, which had been presented, and to which no objection was taken. The order was given to Dunn & Vaughan for supplies furnished by them for a vessel, the sale of which by Ryersons had created the fund, and was given in pursuance of a promise when the supplies were furnished, that they should be paid for out of the proceeds of the sale.

Held, that Dunn & Vaughan were entitled to a decree for the amount of the order with costs against the plaintiffs.

MORTGAGE.

1. Defendant took a conveyance of land from A. F. LeBlanc in the form of an absolute deed, dated 26th July, 1864, and at the same time executed a bond to re-convey upon re-payment of the consideration money of the deed within two years. At the expiration of that period, defendant asked LeBlanc whether the money would be repaid or he should keep the land, to which LeBlanc replied that he would prefer that defendant should keep that land. The bond was given up to defendant and he took the land, allowing LeBlanc to live on it, but no rent was paid, and neither the principal nor the interest of the money advanced by defendant, who afterwards sold the land for a larger sum than the amount of his advances. LeBlanc afterwards became insolvent, but at the time of his giving up the property he was not indebted to any of the creditors who had claims against him when he went into insolvency. His assignee sought in this action to have the deed decreed to be a mortgage. Decree for defendant with costs.

2. Defendant, in March 22, 1861, conveyed to J. J. Marshall certain real estate, by an instrument in the form of an absolute deed, but which defendant contended was given as a mortgage to secure a debt due Marshall. On January 1, 1862, Marshall signed a memorandum acknowledging the receipt of £78-18-4 from defendant on account of the

property, " leaving a balance of £171-12-11—which when paid to me, and the interest thereon, I bind myself to reconvey the said property, &c.;" and there were other memoranda showing that Marshall had treated the conveyance as a mortgage. In January, 1868, defendant, having continued in possession of the land ever since the execution of the conveyance, became the tenant of Marshall under a lease then entered into. After the death of J. J. Marshall, the plaintiff, claiming under his will, brought an action of ejectment against the defendant. *Held*, (an equitable plea having been pleaded,) that the conveyance from defendant was a mortgage, and that the relation of mortgagor and mortgagee was not altered by the fact of the lease being made in 1868.

3. Plaintiff, being indebted to several persons, conveyed property to his son, under an agreement that the son should liquidate the debts, and the plaintiff should have six years to pay him such amounts as he should advance, plaintiff to remain in possession in the meantime , and if he failed to re-pay the amounts, the land should become absolutely the property of the son, who, contemporaneously with the execution of the deed, delivered a bond conditioned for the fulfilment of the agreement. The son afterwards conveyed the property to Dunn, who was aware of the terms of the agreement.

Held, that the transaction was in effect a mortgage, and that Dunn could not claim to hold the land as security for an alleged claim against the plaintiff which he had discharged, and which was not mentioned in the original agreement, but should re-convey the land on payment of the amount due on the agreement between plaintiff and his son, less any income derived by Dunn from the land.

EQUITABLE PLEA.

Plaintiffs purchased certain real estate, subject to a mortgage held by W., as Guardian, for $5,840, and sold a portion to defendant, who was aware of the mortgage for $7,000. Defendant paid $1,400 in cash, and received a deed, with an absolute warranty and covenants for title, without reference to the mortgage. On the same day plaintiffs gave a mortgage of the whole property to K., for $3,760, of which defendant had no knowledge when he made his purchase, and which was recorded before plaintiffs' deed. Defendant gave plaintiffs a mortgage for the balance of the purchase money. The mortgage to W. was foreclosed, and the property sold by the Sheriff, and defendant was obliged, in order to protect himself, to become the purchaser, paying for the whole property included in the mortgage $8,850, which was applied to the payment of the amount due on the two mortgages to W. and K., and to a judgment recorded against the property. Plaintiffs then brought an action against the defendant on the covenant in his mortgage.

Held, that they had no equitable right to call for payment of the purchase money until they had cleared the defendant's title; that defendant was entitled in equity to pay off the mortgages, and had in effect done so, and to recover from the plaintiffs the amount so paid, over and above the purchase money, and that before plaintiffs could re-possess themselves of the portion not included in the conveyance to defendant, they would be obliged to pay him the difference between the amount at which he had purchased and the amount he had been obliged to pay.

Q. Whether the defendant could be compelled to convey even on the terms mentioned.

See also EJECTMENT.

ESTOPPEL.

Plaintiff brought suit to foreclose a mortgage made by defendant, who alleged in her answer that she had been induced to sign it by the fraud of Thomas S. Fowler. Her testimony as to the imposition alleged to have been practised upon her was contradicted by Fowler, and it was in proof that she had re-executed the instrument in the presence of the clerk of plaintiff's solicitor, who had deferred paying over the money in order to assure himself that defendant understood the transaction. There was also evidence that defendant was aware of the nature of the instrument shortly after signing it, and did not repudiate it, but entered into negotiations to obtain security from Fowler, who had retained the money advanced on the security of the mortgage. The Court, in view of the evidence, concluded that defendant, when she signed the instrument, must have understood its nature, and held that, whether she did or did not understand it, she was estopped, as against plaintiff, from saying that she was not aware of its contents.

See also INSOLVENT ACT, 2, 5.

EVIDENCE.

1. D. made a mortgage to defendants' testator, to secure the payment of three promissory notes. The notes were paid, and handed over to D. upwards of twenty years before this action was brought by D. to compel defendants to execute a release of the mortgage. During the subsequent period no payments were made by D. or demanded of him, and the estate of testator was settled without any reference to the mortgage as an outstanding debt due the estate. After bringing the action D. became insolvent, and made an assignment under the Insolvent Act, and his Assignee intervening, under an order of the Court, became plaintiff in the suit.

   Held, that D., not being a party to the suit when evidence was taken, was not prevented by Section 41 of Chapter 96, R. S., from giving evidence of transactions with defendant's testator.

2. On the trial of issues of fact, an account book was produced, kept by plaintiff, and the attention of the Court was turned to certain entries.

   Held, that, although in going into an accounting every portion of the book could be referred to by both parties, yet on the trial of the issues, only those portions of the book could be commented on to the jury which had been referred to and read.

3. Plaintiff, as administrator, sought to foreclose a mortgage for £200 made by defendant; who, in his answer, set out a series of transactions with the deceased in regard to the mortgage, and further alleged that deceased mortgagee had delivered to him a memorandum, signed by him, as follows :—" The mortgage which I hold of W. J. W., bearing date, (etc.), for £200, is not payable to my heirs, executors or administrators after my death.—I. W. W." The memorandum was not produced, but on proof of loss, secondary evidence was given, which the Judge considered of a suspicious character.

   Held, that the memorandum, even if there were no suspicious circumstances about it, would not operate as a release of the mortgage, either at law or in equity, and that plaintiff was entitled to a decree.

——————— TO SET ASIDE AWARD.

See ARBITRATION, 2

EVIDENCE, Conflicting.

Plaintiff purchased a house from the defendant, the consideration stated in the deed being £250. Defendant had mortgaged the property to the Building Society, and there was a balance due the Society on the mortgage of £210 16s, which plaintiff agreed to assume. The other conditions of the bargain were in controversy, and defendant contended that plaintiff was to pay him all the sums that he had paid to the Society for dues, in addition to the bonus and entrance fee, and the difference between the consideration and the amount due the Building Society on the mortgage, while plaintiff stated that he was only to make good to the defendant the payments he had made in obtaining the loan. The evidence was conflicting, but the plaintiff's statement was corroborated by his wife.

Held, that plaintiff could not be charged with the amounts paid by defendant to the Society as dues.

FISHING VENTURE.

See also **PARTNERSHIP**, 4.

FORECLOSURE.

1. Hon. James Tobin, by his will, devised land to his executors to their use during the natural life of his son, Michael Tobin, upon trust to permit his said son to occupy the said premises and receive the rents, after certain deductions, for his own use and benefit, and from and immediately after the decease of his said son Michael, in trust to convey and assure said premises unto the child or children of his said son Michael, living at the time of the decease of his said son Michael, and to their issue. Defendant, a son of said Michael Tobin, mortgaged his interest to plaintiff, and in answer to the writ of foreclosure, set out the above facts, adding that said Michael Tobin was still living, and that some of his children were married and had lawful issue.

    Held, that defendant, having mortgaged his interest to plaintiff, could not repudiate the transaction, and ask to have the mortgage declared inoperative, while retaining the amount received as consideration for it; and further that plaintiff was not bound to wait until the title of the mortgagor became complete, before foreclosing.

2. Defendant, a member of the Nova Scotia Building Society, obtained an advance, and gave his mortgage and bond; after which he sold his equity of redemption, and a suit was brought to foreclose the mortgage, without making him a party or giving him notice. The land was bought in by the Society for a sum less than the costs in the foreclosure suit. An action was then brought against the defendant on his bond. An equitable plea was pleaded, under which defendant gave evidence that the Secretary of the Society, upon defendant asking for a release of his bond, replied that it would be a good deal of expense and nothing would ever come against him, and no application was thereafter made to him for dues or fines, the notices being sent to the purchaser.

    Held, that the Secretary had no power to make the arrangement alleged, to which the Directors had not assented, and that the defendant, being a member of the Society, was bound to know the limits of the Secretary's authority; that, although the rules of the Society restricted them to the advancing of money upon real estate security, there was nothing to prevent them from taking the defendant's bond in addition, even if they could not take the bond of a stranger; that the fact of a sale under foreclosure did not prevent the Society from suing on the bond, so long as they held the land; that the decree against the defendant could not include the costs of the foreclosure suit, to which he was not a party, but that he was not entitled to credit for the proceeds of the foreclosure sale, as they did not amount to the costs in that suit; and that the trustees were the proper plaintiffs.

3. To a suit brought to foreclose a mortgage defendant relied chiefly upon two grounds of defence,—first, that concurrently with the making of the mortgage plaintiff gave defendant a bond whereby he bound himself to erect a double house on the land within ten months, which defendant contended had not been built in such a manner as contemplated by the agreement; secondly, that the principal was not to become payable until ten years after the date of the mortgage. The number of years was left blank in the mortgage. Defendant swore that it was to be ten years, which plaintiff denied, and there was no other evidence.

Held, that the first defence could not prevail, as, assuming the defendant's statement to be true, it only formed the ground of an action for damages, and that, as to the second, as there was no satisfactory evidence to supply the omission of the number of years, the Court must construe the mortgage as if no time was mentioned, and plaintiff had a right to foreclose.

4. Defendant, in his answer to a suit for foreclosure of a mortgage, set out that the mortgage had been given to secure the payment of a note from defendant to plaintiff for £68 10s., and an advance of $200 to be made by plaintiff to defendant, which was made and re-paid by the defendant before the foreclosure suit was brought by plaintiff, as executor of the mortgagee. In his evidence defendant made an entirely different case,—that the note had been re-paid before the execution of the mortgage, and that the $200 paid by plaintiff to defendant was soon after returned, in the very same money that had been received, having been only intended to strengthen the transaction; defendant contending that the mortgage had been given without any *bona fide* consideration, but merely to protect his property from a claim of W. & G. A jury to whom issues were submitted, found that the object of the mortgage was to evade payment of the debt to W. & G.; that the mortgagee was aware of that fact when he received the mortgage, and that the mortgage was given without consideration.

Held, that notwithstanding these findings, the plaintiff was entitled to a decree of foreclosure.

See also SALE UNDER FORECLOSURE.
See also ALLIANCE SOCIETY OF LONDON.

FORECLOSURE, notice to encumbrancers.

Benjamin, Freeman & Calder purchased certain lands, subject to a subsisting mortgage, each of them receiving a deed of one undivided third part. They had formed a partnership for milling and lumbering, and Calder borrowed $2,000 for the purpose of erecting a mill, for which he gave a confession of judgment to the plaintiff, which was duly recorded. The partnership becoming embarrassed, assigned all their property to Taylor and others, as trustees, and afterwards assigned, under the Insolvent Act, to Taylor, who procured the mortgage to be foreclosed and bought in the property, which he afterwards sold to Benjamin. The plaintiff was not made a defendant in the foreclosure suit, and received no notice of the sale, although Taylor was aware of the fact that the plaintiff held a judgment, and that it was recorded in the county where the land lay, and Benjamin, when he took the deed, was aware of the facts.

FRAUDULENT CONVEYANCE.

1. W. J. C. being indebted to plaintiff, was sued November, 1867, and judgment recovered for $293.52, a docket of which was registed October, 1868. Execution was issued on the judgment, and land of said W. J. C. was bought in by plaintiff, under Sheriff's sale. In May 1866, W. J. C., being so indebted, conveyed all his real estate, (found to have been then worth $850,) to his son, the present defendant, the consideration named in the deed being $300, and this suit was brought to set aside the deed as fraudulent. The jury found that W. J. C. was in possession of the land at the time that he gave the deed to defendant, and continued so for four years afterwards, to May 1870; that he was in possession at the time of Sheriff's sale to plaintiff, and at that time resided in the old homestead; that defendant was in possession, exclusively of W. J. C., from May 1870, under title of conveyance from W. J. C.; that there was no money paid by defendant at the time the deed was given, except two fifty dollar notes of hand; that defendant knew, at the time he got the deed, that W. J. C., was indebted to plaintiff; and that the deed was given by W. J. C. and received by defendant to prevent or impede plaintiff and other creditors of W. J. C. in obtaining payment of their debts.

Held, that under the findings of the jury, which the Court considered warranted by the evidence, the deed from W. J. C. to defendant must be set aside as fraudulent.

2. One R. T. Muir, who died 4th September, 1871, by his will, bequeathed his business, including stock in trade, &c., to A. F. Muir, on certain conditions, among which was the payment or guaranteeing to defendants as trustees for his two sisters, the sum of $4000 each, for which they were to take security upon the stock in trade if they saw necessary, within a convenient time after the death of the testator; and it was also provided by the will that a sum of $2000 should be paid or secured to the defendants personally. A. F. Muir continued trading, collecting the debts of the concern, and disposing of the stock, the money payable to the defendants on their own account and as trustees being left in the business without any security being taken. On the 5th April 1875, A. F. Muir conveyed his stock, then worth about $60,000, to the defendants as security for the payment of the said sums together with a further sum alleged to be due to one of the defendants from the estate of R. T. Muir, and on the 15th June, 1875, defendants took possession of the stock and proceeded to sell it, shortly after which, on the 30th June, A. F. Muir made an assignment under the Insolvent Act. Plaintiff as assignee brought this action to set aside the conveyance to defendants, alleging in his writ that the conveyance had been made to give the defendants a preference over other creditors, and that the defendants knew or had reasonable cause to know and believe that A. F. Muir was unable to meet his liabilities. Defendants in their answer denied that A. F. Muir was insolvent when he made the conveyance to them and asserted that when they received it they believed him to be solvent. They denied all fraud on their part in the transaction, and asserted that they demanded the security in pursuance of the directions of the will of R. T. Muir.

The jury found that, at the time of the conveyance being made, A. F. Muir was embarrassed and unable to meet his engagements, that defendants did not then know and had not reasonable cause to know that such inability existed, that the conveyance was not made by A. F. Muir with intent fraudulently to delay or impede his creditors, and that the original stock had all been disposed of except about $1600 worth of machinery.

Held, that under the findings of the jury the conveyance must stand, and that it was not competent for the plaintiff to contend that, even in the absence of knowledge on the part of the defendants, the conveyance

GENERAL WORDS, Construction of.

See CONSTRUCTION OF INSTRUMENT.

———— AGENT.

See AGENCY.

IMITATION OF LABEL.

See LABEL.

IMPEACHMENT OF WASTE, Devise without.

See WASTE.

INJUNCTION.

1. Sanderson, one of the defendants, had been obtaining discounts from the Bank of Nova Scotia on paper endorsed by one or more persons, and the Agent of the Bank becoming dissatisfied on account of the numerous renewals, and referring to the possibility of the endorsers being called upon to take up the notes, Sanderson, in July, 1879, gave the Bank a judgment for the exact amount then due on the notes. In September, 1860, the plaintiffs recovered judgments against Sanderson, and a number of other judgments were entered up against him by parties who were made defendants in the present suit. Sanderson continued to get notes discounted until 1874, when his affairs became embarrassed, and the Bank ceased to discount his paper. The notes then at the Bank were taken up by the endorsers, and Sanderson ceased to be indebted to the Bank. In 1874 the parties who were then endorsers on Sanderson's paper discounted at the Bank took proceedings to revive the judgment, and issued and delivered to the Sheriff an execution, with instructions to levy on Sanderson's real estate.

    Held, that, the judgment having been taken for a specified sum ascertained at the time to be due the Bank and which had been long since paid, neither the Bank nor the endorsers of Sanderson's paper could make it available for any subsequent labilities.

    Simultaneously with the issuing of the execution at the suit of the Bank, the other defendants whose judgments were subsequent to those of the plaintiffs, had executions placed in the Sheriff's hands by Mr. Grantham, who was the attorney by whom all the executions were issued, with instructions to levy for the amount of them on Sanderson's real estate, and the land was advertized by the Sheriff as one sale, the advertisement being headed in all the causes of the several defendants, including the Bank.

Held, that under the circumstances, the sale being under the direction of Grantham, the attorney in all the causes, the plaintiffs were justified in making the encumbrancers subsequent to the Bank defendants in this suit. Otherwise, possibly, if those subsequent encumbrancers had not connected themselves with the Bank, but had advertized the sale under their respective judgments, subject to prior encumbrances

Injunction to stay the sale until the validity, or otherwise, of the judgment at the suit of the Bank was settled, continued, but only on the condition that the plaintiffs should give an undertaking to bring on the case for trial at the next term of the Supreme Court in the County, or that their bill be dismissed.

Costs decreed against the Bank, but not as against the other defendants.

2. Plaintiff applied for an injunction to restrain defendant from selling or otherwise disposing of lumber of which he claimed to be owner under an alleged purchase from the company, the validity of which was disputed. The injunction was refused, plaintiff having an adequate legal remedy at Common Law by actions for damages.

3. Where the defendant had no drain leading from his premises to the common sewer on the street, and the plaintiff prevented all access to a drain on his own property through which the water might flow to the sewer from defendant's property, but defendant proved no title or right to use such drain, the Court granted an injunction to restrain defendant not only from permitting his waste water to flow on plaintiff's property, but from receiving water from the city water works until a suitable drain was constructed, the evidence showing that the introduction of such supply, in the absence of a suitable drain, occasioned an overflow on plaintiff's premises.

4. Plaintiff, as assignee of E. W. Chipman, under the Insolvent Act, obtained an order to restrain the Sheriff of Annapolis from selling under execution personal property of the insolvent, which he claimed had passed to him under the assignment, said property having been allowed by the assignee to remain in the hands of the insolvent, who had removed it to Annapolis, where it was levied upon. *Held*, that, as the remedy of the assignee by action at law, assuming the levy and proposed sale to be unjustifiable, was complete, the restraining order must be discharged.

5. Where trustees, having power to sell a mining property conveyed to them by way of mortgage to secure the payment of interest on bonds issued by the Mining Company, the principal of which was not yet due, advertised the property for sale, instead of proceeding by way of foreclosure, and the plaintiffs, who had the equity of redemption, although aware of the intention to sell, delayed seeking the information necessary to enable them to prevent a sale to their injury, and applied for an injunction only two days before the day of sale, the Court granted the injunction upon payment by the mortgagors of the interest on the outstanding bonds, and their undertaking to pay the expenses incurred in preparing for the sale.

them their share of the proceeds or account to them, and in the mean. time should be restrained from selling, &c , was properly sought in this Court.

10. The owner of land leased a parcel to plaintiff, for the purpose of erecting a lobster factory, for the term of five years. About a twelve. month afterwards the defendant, Shedd, applied for a lease of the same land for a similar purpose. Defendant admitted that when he had part of the materials on the ground for the erection of his building plaintiff forbade him to proceed, and asserted his right to the land, and, although it was alleged in the answer, the evidence did not justify the conclusion that plaintiff had ever abandoned his right under the lease or contemplated doing so.

Held, that plaintiff was entitled to have an injunction to restrain defendant from proceeding with the erection of the building, as the remedy at common law was not full and adequate, and it would be impossible for a jury to estimate the damages with accuracy.

See also FRAUDULENT CONVEYANCE, 2.

INJUNCTION to restrain action at law.

1. Mitchell sold property to Dodge for $16,000, which plaintiffs purchased from Dodge for $20,000. The property was subject to a mortgage made by Mitchell to Davis, who assigned it to Sterling, and it was agreed between Dodge, Mitchell and the plaintiffs, that Mitchell should take up the mortgage, and that plaintiffs should pay Dodge $5000, give him notes for $2000, and make a mortgage to Mitchell for the balance of $13,000, payable in instalments, for which notes were also given to Mitchell. In the mortgage made by plaintiff to Mitchell it was provided that the latter should pay off the mortgage made by him and assigned to Sterling, and that until it was paid off Mitchell should only receive from plaintiff the difference between the interest on Mitchell's mortgage assigned to Sterling, and that until Sterling's mortgage was paid, plaintiffs should not be liable for anything but the difference between that mortgage and their mortgage to Mitchell. Defendants Wier and White obtained from Mitchell an assignment of plaintiffs' mortgage and notes as security for a debt, after which Mitchell became insolvent, defendant Graham becoming his assignee, and Sterling's mortgage was foreclosed, and the property sold. Wier and White obtained a resale on giving a bond to the assignee to bid the property up to $11,300. Wier and White purchased the property for $8520, and an action was brought on the bond, to which they pleaded that the balance had been credited to Mitchell, by agreement, on account due White. Plaintiffs paid on the mortgage to Mitchell $2250 besides interest, and took up three notes for $750 each, when Wier and White commenced action against them to recover the amount of two other notes for $750 and $500 respectively.

Held, that Wier and White should be restrained from further proceeding in the action to recover the amount of the notes, and from transferring the remaining notes, the difference between plaintiff's mortgage and the mortgage assigned to Sterling being more than covered by the amount paid by plaintiffs, and the amount credited by Wier and White to Mitchell on the purchase at the Sheriff's sale under foreclosure.

2. The defendant J. C. S. Miller, mortgaged certain property to W. C. King, whose executors foreclosed the mortgage, J. W. King, the surviving executor of the mortgagee becoming the purchaser at the Sheriff's sale. Defendant remaining in possession of the mortgaged premises, a rule *nisi* was granted for a writ of assistance to put the purchaser in possession. No cause being shown, the rule was made absolute, and a writ issued, under which the property was delivered to J. W. King. Defendant then brought an action of trespass against the Sheriff and J. W. King, whereupon a rule *nisi* was taken for an injunction to restrain the action. Defendant opposed the rule, contending that the property of which he had been in possession was not included in the mortgage, but after a full hearing of the cause, the rule for the injunction was made absolute. J. W. King then put the plaintiff, Mosher, in possession of the land, and the defendant, J C. S. Miller, brought an action of ejectment, setting up the claim which this Court had previously decided against him, namely, that the lands claimed were not included in the mortgage. The present suit having been instituted to restrain that action.

Held, that the defendant could not resort to the action of ejectment at common law, and there claim the land to which this Court had decreed that he was not entitled, and that the action must be restrained.

See also PRACTICE—Discovery.

INSOLVENT ACT.

1. Writs of attachment against the mortgagor, as an absconding debtor, were issued, and delivered to the Sheriff on May 20. An appraisement of the mortgaged premises was made, and copies of the writ, with the appraisement and description of the land, were registered on May 21. On the same day a writ of attachment, under the Insolvent Act of 1869, was taken out against the mortgagor, but was not delivered to the Sheriff until after he had registered the documents connected with the proceedings under the Absconding Debtor's Act.

Held, that the claim of the Assignee of the estate, to the surplus proceeds, must prevail over that of the attaching creditors.

Section 24 of Chap. 79, R. S., is controlled by the Insolvent Act.

2. J. T. F. & Co., being indebted to the plaintiff, gave, as collateral security, a mortgage which they were to receive on a vessel being built by McK. & V, debtors of theirs in Prince Edward Island. The arrangement was made October 19, 1875, and on the same day J. T. F. & Co. wrote to plaintiffs, enclosing a draft on H. & Co., Liverpool, at ninety days, for £1,000, stating that the same was drawn against proceeds of the vessel, which was to be sold in Liverpool, G. B., by H. & Co., and concluding; "The above vessel is herewith pledged to you for the due payment of said Bill of Exchange, as well as for payment of the obligations of McK. & V." J. T. F. & Co. then proceeded to Prince Edward Island, to obtain the mortgage; but previous to its being delivered to plaintiffs, they had, on the 12th November, caused a demand of assignment to be served on J. T. F. & Co., and the plaintiffs' manager, when the mortgage was afterwards tendered to him, said it should have been made to the Bank, instead of to J. T. F. & Co., and handed it back to J. T. F., who gave it to the Assignee. On the 15th November J. T. F. & Co. made an assignment, under the Insolvent Act, and on the 27th November, the Bill of Exchange, for £1,000, was presented and dishonored. The vessel was sold for more than £1,000, by the Assignee, who retained the proceeds. Plaintiffs claiming to have an equitable lien on the mortgage for the amount of the Bill of Exchange, and of an unpaid note of McK. & V., endorsed by J. T. F. & Co.,

Held, that, although, if the proceedings were between the plaintiffs and J. T. F. & Co. alone, the latter might be estopped from resisting the claim of the plaintiffs, on the ground that they had no title to the vessel at the time they pledged her; yet, under the provisions of the Insolvent Act of 1875, Sec. 118, the pledge or lien, if it could otherwise have been effective, was rendered null and void, a demand of assignment, followed by an asignment, having been served within thirty days after the pledge was given, and the plaintiffs, (upon whom the burden of proof lay under that section,) not having shown that the pledge had not been made in contemplation of insolvency.

3. The Messrs. Pryor, in December 1872, of their own accord, signed and sealed a mortgage, whereby defendant was to be secured from loss on endorsements of their paper; but defendant did not become aware that such a mortgage had been made until some time in 1874, and his information then was not derived from Messrs. Pryor or any person authorized by them. The mortgage was not recorded until March 20, 1875, when the Messrs. Pryor knew they would have to go into bankruptcy, and on March 22, 1875, they made an assignment under the Insolvent Act of 1869.

Held, that the mortgage was void, being made in contemplation of insolvency.

4. Crowe, as judgment creditor of the insolvent McLellan, filed a claim for the full amount of his judgment, stating that he held such judgment as security, but could give no estimate of its value, and ranked on the insolvent estate for the full amount of the judgment. Previous to the insolvency he had assigned the judgment to McDonald & Witt, who acted as his solicitors in the filing of the claim.

Held, that by claiming for the whole amount of the judgment without putting a value upon it as required by Section 60 of the Act, Crowe had practically abandoned his security, and McD. & W. could not succeed in the present application, which was for surplus proceeds on foreclosure and sale.

5. Plaintiffs, as assignees under the Insolvent Act, sought to have certain mortgages decreed to be void, which were made by the defendant Smith, within thirty days of demand made on him to assign, followed by an assignment. The evidence was conflicting, but the Court drew from it the inference that Smith, finding himself in difficulties, applied to the Bank for $3000, in the belief that, if obtained, it would enable him to arrange with his more pressing creditors and avert the insolvency which must otherwise ensue; that the agent of the Bank first led him to believe that the advance would be made, but the directors refused, and, instead of making the advance, required the mortgages to secure existing liabilities; that defendant consented to make them, encouraged by the agent to believe that if he did so further accommodation would be afforded, but the Bank, having secured itself and considering that further accommodation could not safely be afforded, declined to make any further advance and insolvency ensued, as Smith had anticipated. At the time the mortgages were given, the insolvent's paper was lying overdue in the Bank, and the agent of the Bank, on the execution of the mortgage, told him that he could not expect an advance till after the expiration of thirty days. Plaintiffs having sought relief, first, on the ground that the mortgages were made in consideration that the Bank would advance $3000, which would have prevented insolvency, and secondly, that they were given in contemplation of insolvency, and with intent fraudulently to impede and delay creditors;

Held, as to the first ground, that the consideration must be obtained from the language of the instruments, which referred to existing indebtedness and not advances, and that Smith could not be heard to allege differently; but that on the second ground the mortgages must be decreed to be void as against the plaintiffs and creditors of the insolvent.

Objection was taken that the requisition upon Smith to assign was informally made, the affidavit on which it was based being liable to a technical objection. But, an assignment having taken place under it, and no objection having been made to it in the Insolvent Court, which had proceeded to settle the estate;

Held, that it was not for a third party in a different Court to call in question the regularity of its proceedings.

Semble. Even before the amendment of sec. 133 of the Insolvent Act of 1875, by the insertion of the words *prima facie,* (Cap. 41 of 1877,) the presumption of fraud could be rebutted.

6. Parker & Grant having recovered a verdict against Fairbanks, a rule *nisi* was taken out to set it aside. T. & E. DeWolf & Co. became sureties to respond the final judgment and took a mortgage from Fairbanks to secure them from loss on account of their bond, and also to secure the amount of an existing indebtedness. The rule *nisi* having been discharged and judgment entered up against Fairbanks, an execution was issued under which he was arrested and placed in custody. While he was in custody, and after the present suit was brought by plaintiff as assignee of De Wolf & Co. against Fairbanks, to foreclose the mortgage, and after said Fairbanks had answered, his estate was placed in insolvency, and Creighton, his assignee, intervened and became a party. Parker & Grant also became parties as interested in the subject matter.

Held, first, that the insolvency of Fairbanks did not prevent the plaintiff from proceeding with the foreclosure, and, secondly, that Parker & Grant had not lost their lien on the mortgaged property, in consequence of their having arrested Fairbanks under the judgment.

7. The insolvent, T. J. B., being indebted to the Merchants' Bank, instructed the cashier of the Railway Department, by letter, dated Oct. 22nd, to send to G. M., the cashier of the Bank, any cheque coming to him from the Department. On Nov. 7 a cheque for $691.76, payable to the order of the insolvent, was enclosed in a letter, addressed to the insolvent, care of Merchants' Bank. The agreement between the insolvent and the cashier of the Bank, when the letter was written, was, according to the evidence of the former, that the Bank should have $300 of the money, according to cashier's evidence, $350. The cashier opened the letter and endorsed the cheque, "T. J B., per G. M., agent. For Merchants' Bank of Halifax. Guaranteed. G. M., cashier." The writ of attachment against the insolvent was issued January 18, 1879.

Held, that the cashier had no authority to open the letter or endorse the cheque, but that the Bank was entitled to retain the $300 as agreed upon; that this amount could not be recovered by the assignee under the 130th section of the Act, which had no reference to a case like this, nor under the 134th section, as that was confined to payments made within thirty days of the insolvency.

8. Plaintiff sought to set aside a judgment entered on a confession as made in contemplation of insolvency; but the judgment creditor alleged and it appeared in evidence that the confession was taken only to indemnify the judgment creditor against loss on accommodation endorsements to be thereafter given, which were given.

Held, that, although the judgment debtor was in insolvent circumstances at the time of giving the confession, the judgment could not be impeached, section 89 of the Insolvent Act of 1875 referring only to securities given for pre-existing debts or liabilities.

9. Plaintiff, as creditors' assignee, sought to set aside a judgment given by confession by two alleged co-partners, as made in contemplation of

insolvency. Defendant denied that plaintiff was assignee, and it appeared that at a meeting of creditors there was only one person who had filed a claim, and his claim was without a voucher, yet, instead of abandoning the meeting as a failure and calling another, giving due notice, the meeting adjourned to another day, on which the plaintiff was appointed assignee.

Held, that the appointment was invalid, that the proceedings could be impugned without going into the Insolvency Court, and that the defendant's denial that plaintiff was assignee as alleged obliged him to prove it.

Beulair v. *Gilliott,* (referred to in 1 R. & C., 264,) questioned.
Brown v. *Pearman* 491

See also PARTIES.

See also PRACTICE—Supplemental Bill.

INSURANCE, MARINE.

1. Plaintiff, a member of the firm of Black Bros & Co., took a mortgage of a vessel which was given by defendants for outfits supplied by that firm, and a policy of insurance was effected to secure the payment for the outfits. The vessel was lost and plaintiff received the insurance, which he credited in account with one Malcolm, to whom he had agreed to sell 36-64 shares in the vessel.

Held, that the amount received from the insurers must go to the credit of the mortgage.
Troop v. *Mosier et al* 189

2. Plaintiff filled up an application for a policy of marine insurance, describing the risk thus : " Voyage at and from Block House Mines to Montreal; vessel arrived at Sydney 2nd August; on chartered freight $3000." The defendants being authorized to effect the insurance, inserted in the policy without plaintiffs' privity the words, " beginning the adventure upon said freight from and immediately following the loading thereof on board." The vessel was lost at Block House Mines before she commenced taking her cargo on board, and plaintiff first became aware of the insertion of the last recited words in the policy on being informed that the Company did not hold themselves liable.

Held, an action having been brought to reform the policy, that the plaintiffs had a right to assume that the Company in preparing the policy would strictly adhere to the terms in the memorandum, that had the policy been so prepared, the plaintiff would have had a right to recover under it, and that it must therefore be reformed accordingly.
Wylde et al. v. *Union Marine Insurance Co* 203

3. Joseph Banks, one of the plaintiffs, applied for a policy of insurance on the Brigantine *Sophia* by filling up a printed form. "J. Banks and others " were entered as owners, and the " hull and materials " filled in as what was to be insured ; and the application, after the printed words "effect the above on account of," was signed, "Joseph Banks." The policy issued by the Company purported that Joseph Banks did make assurance, &c., but the words, " or whom it may concern," were not inserted in the policy. The vessel being lost the plaintiffs, as owners, brought action on the policy, the claim being resisted on the ground that there was not a total loss, but on the trial the objection was raised for the first time by the defendant's counsel, that the policy covered only the interest of Joseph Banks. Plaintiffs then brought suit in the Equity Court to have the policy reformed on the ground of mistake, and issues were settled by the Equity Judge and tried by a jury, who found that there was a mutual understanding between the parties which the policy, as executed, did not carry out, and that, to do so, it would require to be altered by inserting the names of the other registered owners ; which finding there was evidence to justify.

Held, that the policy must be reformed so as to cover the interests of all the owners.
Banks et al. v. *Wilson* 210

10z

ISSUES, Practice on Trial of.

See PRACTICE—New Trial.

JOINT STOCK COMPANIES.

1. Proceedings were taken under an Act of the Provincial Legislature to wind up the company on the ground that it was heavily embarrassed and could not extricate itself without having recourse to the double liability of the shareholders. The act of incorporation provided that transfers of shares should be valid and effectual for all purposes from the time they were made and entered in the books of the company. Three of the shareholders claimed that they were not contributories on the ground that certificates of stock were never accepted by them, but it appeared that the certificates were issued to them by direction of the former stockholder from whom they were transferred, that this was approved of by the directors, and the certificates were handed to the transferor, and afterwards received by two of the transferees, who were registered as stockholders in the company's books, and never repudiated the transaction. The third transferee was also registered, and was elected a director previous to his repudiating the transaction, which he did not do until after it became apparent that the affairs of the company were embarrassed. Another class of stockholders claimed to be exempt on the ground that they had surrendered their shares to the company. This surrender had been made and accepted by the company, but the parties surrendering knew that the affairs of the company were embarrassed, and it was with a view of escaping liability that the surrenders were made.

Held, that the provisions of the act were within the legislative authority of the provincial legislature, and that neither class of stockholders could be exempted from contribution.

Held, also, that where there was no registration on the books, and the party sought to be made liable had never deemed himself absolute owner or acted as such, there was no liability.

In re The Wallace Huestis Grey Stone Co............................ 461

2. The petitioner, as administratrix, recovered judgment against the Halifax Yacht Club, and issued execution, which was returned unsatisfied, there being no assets. She then resorted to the individual liability of the corporators under Revised Statutes, chapter 53, section 13, but the Supreme Court decided that the section did not apply to such a corporation. Petitioner then applied to have the affairs of the company wound up.

Held, that the Provincial Act in reference to the winding up of companies, differing from the English Act in that it was made expressly applicable to clubs, could be invoked for the purpose of winding up the Halifax Yacht Club, but that, as there was no individual liability, and it was admitted there were no assets, the prayer of the petition should not be granted, as it would only create needless litigation.

In re The Halifax Yacht Club.................................... 475

JURY, Finding of ignored.

See FORECLOSURE, 4.

LABEL.

The imitation of labels and wrappers whereby the public are misled and the plaintiff injured will be restrained as a fraud upon him, and though an imitation will be deemed colorable if it be such that a careful inspection is required to distinguish it, yet a Court will not interfere when ordinary attention would enable a person to discriminate. It is not enough that a careless, inattentive or illiterate purchaser might be deceived by the resemblance.

Johnson et al. v. Parr.. 98

LAND, Sale of.

LEGISLATIVE AUTHORITY.

LICENSES TO SEARCH.

LIEN FOR RENT.

LIMITATIONS, Statute of.

1. Allan McKav conveyed property to plaintiff by a deed, absolute in its terms, but admitted to have been given as security for a debt. Nothing was paid on account of principal or interest by the mortgagor or his heirs, for a period of over twenty years before suit to foreclose, but within that period an action of ejectment had been brought to recover possession, in which a judgment was obtained, a record filed and a writ of *hab. fac. pos.* issued but not executed.

   Held, that these proceedings prevented the statute of limitations from operating except from the judgment.

2. Plaintiff brought action in 1873 to enforce payment of $400 and interest for land alleged to have been purchased by defendant, the deed being made out to defendant's brother and left with a third party, to be delivered to defendant on his handing him a note for the purchase money signed by himself and his brother. Defendant, in his answer, contradicted all the statements in the writ, and set out that the sale was made directly to his brother, though he admitted that he would have assisted him by joining a note for the purchase money. The evidence was conflicting, but the alleged agreement having been made in 1876, the Court held that the delay in sueing was itself a bar to the action, if, as plaintiff contended, the agreement was to be considered as the original undertaking of the defendant, while, on the other hand, if it was to be viewed as a guarantee, the statute of frauds prevented a recovery.

MANDAMUS.

The defendant Company obtained an Act enabling it to maintain a line of horsecars in the City, but requiring it to provide rails of the most improved pattern, and lay them even with the surface of the streets, so as not to interfere with the passage of vehicles, and to keep the roadway in repair within the track and three feet on each side. Defendants having ceased to operate the line, the roads fell out of repair and the rails protruded. After the commencement of this suit, which was for a mandamus to compel the defendants to have the rails laid even with the surface, and to put the roads in repair as required by the Act, the City authorities in many instances covered the streets on which the rails were laid with stones.

Held, that the City had a right to proceed by mandamus, and was not obliged to resort to an indictment of the nuisance, or to proceedings to

fine the defendants under the Act of 1870, Cap. 99, for violation of the
provisions of their Act of Incorporation, neither of these courses presenting a remedy as beneficial as the proceeding by mandamus, but that
the mandamus must be limited in its operation to those streets on which
the railway had not been covered by the City authorities, as the action
of the City in this respect had imposed an unreasonable burden upon the
Company in removing the stones.

MINES AND MINERALS.

A license to search for minerals other than gold, was granted to the
relators under Sec. 86 of Cap. 9, R. S., to expire 21st May, 1874. Previously to its expiration, four other licenses to search over the same area
were granted to the relators, which were to expire respectively, 22nd
May, 1875 ; 23rd May, 1876 ; 26th May, 1877 ; and 27th May, 1878, the
area containing only four and a quarter square miles. On the 28th May,
1877, defendants, having a license to search over an area overlying in part
the area of the relators, applied for a license, which was afterwards
granted, to work one square mile partially overlying and including
within its boundaries the area under license to search to the relators. An
order *nisi* having been taken to restrain defendants from interfering.

Held, that over the area of four and a quarter miles first above referred to, not more than four valid licenses to search could be granted under
R. S. Cap. 9, Sec. 91, that the relators' fifth license to search, which was
to expire May 27th, 1878, was invalid, and that on the 28th May, 1877,
there was no obstacle to the defendants' obtaining the license to work
granted to them.

Obiter dictum ; that it was no objection to the license to work that it
was taken out in the name of only one of the defendants, Fraser, for their
joint benefit; all the defendants having had an interest in the license to
search, although taken out in the name of Fraser only.

MINING VENTURE, Partnership in.

See PARTNERSHIP, 1, 2.

MISTAKE.

1. Plaintiff and defendant, in settling their affairs on dissolution of their
co-partnership, entered into an accounting by which it was shown that
plaintiff had drawn $318.86 from the partnership funds in excess of the
sum drawn by defendant, which defendant contended was due from
plaintiff to him, but which plaintiff insisted was due to the partnership,
so that only half the amount was due to defendant. Plaintiff finally
yielded to defendant's contention, and paid over the money. Becoming
satisfied afterwards that his own view was correct, he brought action,
after the lapse of about a year, to recover the amount improperly paid
over. *Held*, that having paid over the money with full knowledge of the
facts, the very point now in controversy having been discussed at the
settlement, the plaintiff could not, after the lapse of a year, during which
he had carried out in all respects the settlement agreed upon, apply to
have the mistake corrected.

2. Plaintiff instructed his brother to purchase certain land for him, the
deed to be taken in the brother's name, but in trust for the plaintiff for
life, after his death for his children, and in case of his death and the
death of his children, in trust for his wife. The land was purchased and
plaintiff paid the amount of the purchase money, but the deed was made
out to the brother in trust to pay the proceeds to plaintiff's son, then
living, and in the event of his death to other sons, &c. Plaintiff went

into possession and lived on the premises without any intimation that he had not a right to do so, and did not discover the omission of the trust for his own life till after the death of his brother, being an illiterate man and not having ever learned the contents of the deed. His evidence as to the intention was uncorroborated and uncontradicted.

Held, that the plaintiff was entitled to have the deed rectified.

See also FORECLOSURE.

MISTAKE in Award.

See ARBITRATION, 2.

MONEY RECEIVED to use of Plaintiff.

Plaintiff set out an assignment to him of logs, which, when sawed, the assignors, in contravention of the assignment, shipped to Stayner; an agreement with Stayner to indemnify him from loss and account for the proceeds in the same manner as if the lumber had been shipped to plaintiff under the assignment; a receipt by Stayner of money on account of the lumber for which he refused to account. Defendant denied the allegations in the writ, but the Court sustained the plaintiff's view of the case on the evidence.

Held, that plaintiff was entitled to an account, and that the proceedings were properly instituted in the Equity Court.

MORTGAGE of ungranted Crown Lands.

Thomas and John Archibald mortgaged to plaintiff two third parts of several lots of ungranted crown lands applied for and paid for by Ellerhausen and others the right to receive which was by them transferrred to the St. Croix Manufacturing Company, (said Archibalds having become interested to the extent of two third parts.) Before the grants were taken out the Archibalds became insolvent, and defendants, as trustees for the creditors, procured said grants of lands based on the original application, but they selected the lots in localities somewhat different from those indicated in such application.

Held, that plaintiff had a lien on two-thirds of the land comprised in the grants for the debt intended to be secured by the mortgage, and that an order must pass that the amount thereof should be paid to him, otherwise said two thirds of the land to be sold to satisfy plaintiff's claim.

MORTGAGEE, Insurance for benefit of.

Plaintiff mortgaged certain property to C. for $434.50, and covenanted in the mortgage to keep it insured for $500 in the name and for the benefit of the mortgagee. Subsequently, plaintiff effected insurance to the amount of $570 on his own account, without reference to the mortgagee, $180 of which was on the personal property, not covered by the mortgage. After loss by fire the mortgagee, finding that the insurance was not in his name, demanded an assignment of the policy, offering to secure to plaintiff the amount due him, and upon his refusal, claimed the amount from the company. Defendant paid the $180 and, upon action brought for the balance, an interpleader order was made.

Held, that the insurance enured to the benefit of the mortgagee, and that he was entitled to interplead, although the claim of the mortgagee was an equitable claim, and the company was under a contractual obligation to the plaintiff, and although the claim of the mortgagee was smaller than the amount insured.

NEW TRIAL.

F. McDonald, deceased, made a mortgage to plaintiff which plaintiff brought suit to foreclose. Defendants set out an agreement by which plaintiff agreed to release the mortgage on receiving three promissory notes made by one McKinnon, to whom part of the land had been sold by the mortgagor. Plaintiff replied that the notes were only taken as collateral security, to be credited to the mortgagor when paid, and that nothing had been paid on account of them. On the trial of the issue, plaintiff proved the mortgage, and defendants produced no evidence whatever. The jury found for defendants.

Held, that the burden of proof of the issue raised was on the defendants, and that as they had proved nothing, the finding must be set aside.
See also PRACTICE—New Trial.

NUISANCE.

See MANDAMUS.

PARTIES.

1. Plaintiff in his writ, set out among other things, that defendant and himself were engaged in a co-partnership as Attorneys, &c., from September 1866, to December 1871, that in 1867 one Kirby informed them that a certain coal area would be vacant, and asked them to join with him in applying for it, as he anticipated trouble in getting it, and wanted assistance, to which they agreed, the license to search being taken in the name of the defendant, who held it for the benefit of said Kirby and the said firm (the respective proportions being set out in the writ) ; that afterwards defendant obtained with the same consent, and for the benefit of the same parties, a license to work, the fee therefor being paid out of the partnership funds ; that a renewal of the license to work was afterwards obtained by defendant, and before the expiration of the renewal, and after the dissolution of the co-partnership, defendant, without consulting plaintiff, and without his knowledge, obtained a lease of the area in conjunction with said Kirby, and refused to recognize plaintiff's claim to any interest therein.

Held, on demurrer, that it was not necessary that the agreement in respect to said area be alleged in the writ to have been in writing ; that Kirby mentioned in the writ was not a necessary party, as no complaint had been made against him, no relief was sought from him, and no decree could be made against him ; and that the facts set out constituted a good ground for the relief sought for by plaintiff, as, assuming the statements in the writ to be true, the defendant was a trustee for the plaintiff to the extent of plaintiff's interest in the area.

2. Objection having been taken that certain proceedings (*see* case cited *infra*) should have been by information in the name of the Attorney General,

Held, that the plaintiffs had rightly proceeded by the writ substituted in this Court by statute for the bill in Chancery, and that although the writ stated that plaintiffs were acting on behalf of all the Presbyterian members of the congregation, even that was not necessary, as they might under R. S. Cap. 95, Sec. 19, have maintained the suit on their own behalf alone.

The statement was made in two writs that by certain legislation the title to certain lands in question was vested in the Presbyterian Church of Canada, but the legislation referred to did not affect the title to the property in question in the suits. Defendants not having demurred to the writ.

Held, that they could not reasonably ask to have plaintiffs turned out of Court because the Presbyterian Church was not a party to the suits when the Court was satisfied that it could not be made a party, and that the proper parties were before the Court.

PARTIES, Objection for want of.

See PRACTICE—Waiver of Objection.

PARTNERSHIP.

working the mine, as they became due from month to month, were paid by the defendant, George Hamilton, and only a small portion being refunded, the latter wrote to plaintiff that if his indebtedness was not paid by a day named, he would consider that he intended to withdraw from the adventure. Receiving no reply, he afterwards wrote to plaintiff, enclosing the amount received from him on account of his contributions, to which plaintiff replied, accepting the money, and concluding, "now that I am no participator with you in the tribute, let your mind rest quiet, and let the past *requiescat in pace.*" The mine having subsequently turned out well, plaintiff, claiming to be a partner, brought action for an account, &c., which was dismissed with costs.

Distinction between mining and ordinary trading partnerships as to *delectus personae.*

3. Plaintiff, the widow of Chas. S. Silver, was entitled to certain property, placed in trust among other things for the payment of rents,&c. free from the control of her husband and not subject to his debts. She directed her trustees to pay over to her husband the income for certain years. Her husband was at that time in partnership with William C. Silver, carrying on a business in Halifax which was conducted by Chas. S. Silver alone, Wm. C. Silver having withdrawn from the management of it, and taking no oversight of its affairs. When plaintiff directed the money to be paid to her husband she knew he was in embarrassed circumstances, and he had then and long before exhausted his capital and become indebted to the firm, his family being meanwhile supported from the funds of the firm. In those circumstances he had ordered the money paid over to him by his wife's trustees to be paid to creditors of the firm, and opened an account on the firm books, charging the firm and crediting Mrs. Silver with the money so paid. Chas. S. Silver died insolvent in 1870, when Wm. C Silver first became aware of the course pursued by his co-partner. Plaintiff in this suit claimed from Wm. C. Silver, as surviving partner, the re-payment of the money so received by the firm, and credited to her.

Held, that Chas S. Silver was not justified in crediting such moneys to plaintiff without her concurrence or that of Wm. C. Silver, and that the latter was not liable.

4. Plaintiff and defendant entered into a contract to fish, each in a distinct berth, and each party finding his own seine, boat, and fishing gear. The evidence was conflicting as to the contemplated duration of the agreement, but the Court arrived at the conclusion that it was confined to the taking of a school of fish in each berth. Evidence was given as to the meaning of the term school, as used in such contracts, but it was vague and contradictory, and such as to oblige the Court to construe the agreement independently of any alleged usage. Defendant caught fourteen barrels of mackerel in his berth, of which he gave plaintiff seven, and plaintiff, shortly after, caught ten barrels in his berth, of which he gave defendant five. Plaintiff then abandoned his berth and went elsewhere to fish, and never returned to it. Defendant, in his berth, caught two hundred and fifty barrels, of which plaintiff claimed half.

Held, that the plaintiff was not entitled to participate in the defendant's catch of fish.

PREFERENCE.

See CONTEMPLATION OF INSOLVENCY.
See also FRAUDULENT CONVEYANCE.
See also INSOLVENT ACT.

POLICY OF INSURANCE, Action to reform.

PRACTICE.

Amendment of Writ.

1. Plaintiff brought action against the defendants for a mandamus to compel them to provide for a debt due him by the trustees of a school section. The writ was against the detendants personally, but contained a statement that they were trustees, &c., and that defendant, D., was secretary. Evidence was taken as to the existence of the debt, and the case came on for hearing under the pleadings and evidence

   Held, that the trustees could only be sued in their corporate name; and that the amendment to that effect, asked for by plaintiff at the hearing, could not be permitted.

2. Plaintiffs applied to amend their writ by adding a defendant on the ground that a defect existed in the organization of the defendant company and in order that, in the event of failure against the defendant company, they might have relief against the defendants whom they sought to add.

   Held, that the amendment could not be allowed.

3. Defendants demurred to plaintiffs' writ, on the ground, among others, that the Attorney-General had not been made a party. The demurrer was overruled by the Judge in Equity, whose decision was sustained by the Court *in banco* on appeal, from which decision an appeal was taken to the Supreme Court of Canada, where the appeal was dismissed on the ground that the Court had no jurisdiction as the decision was not final. Plaintiffs then sought to amend the writ by adding the Attorney-General, to which the defendants objected, on the ground of delay. The defendants were in possession of the property, taken from the plaintiffs, in respect of which the suit was brought, and were enjoying the whole profits of it, so that the delay was prejudicial to the plaintiffs rather than to them.

   Held, that the plaintiffs were entitled to the amendment applied for as they had not been remiss in the prosecution of the cause.

Answer of Defendants not Evidence at Hearing.

Defendant, being indebted to various parties, and fearing lest his creditors should resort to his property to obtain payment, conveyed all his land to his son, the other defendant, while at the same time he and his family were to continue to enjoy the benefit of it. In their answer the defendants alleged a debt due by the father to the son, and an agreement by the latter to support his father, but the defendants gave no evidence.

Held, that the answer of the defendants could not be used as evidence at the hearing, and that plaintiff, as creditor of the father, had a right to a decree to set aside the deed.

PRACTICE.

ANSWER TO AMENDED WRIT.

Plaintiffs having amended their writ, served it on defendant, with a notice, endorsed, requiring him to answer within fourteen days, otherwise, plaintiffs to be at liberty to sign final judgment by default, and have the writ taken *pro confesso.* Defendant, who had duly put in his answer to the original writ, did not within the time limited in the notice, answer the amendment, and plaintiffs obtained a rule *nisi,* calling upon him to shew cause why the writ should not be taken *pro confesso,* etc., before the argument of which rule defendant put in an answer, not denying the statements in the amendment, but leaving the proof of them to the plaintiffs.

Held, that the rule *nisi* be must discharged with costs, defendant having a right to put in his answer at any time before the marking of a default.

APPEAL FROM PROBATE COURT.

The Court will not consider other grounds of appeal than those contained in the statement filed in the registry of the Probate Court.

COSTS.

1. D. made a mortgage to defendant's testator, to secure the payment of three promissory notes. The notes were paid, and handed over to D. upwards of twenty years before this action was brought by D., to compel defendants to execute a release of the mortgage. During the subsequent period no payments were made by D. or demanded of him, and the Estate of the testator was settled without any reference to the mortgage as an outstanding debt due the Estate. After bringing the action, D. became insolvent, and made an assignment under the Insolvent Act, and his Assignee intervening, under an order of the Court, became plaintiff in the suit.

Held, that defendants must be decreed to execute a release of the mortgage, though without costs, they not having opposed the proceedings of plaintiff.

2. Where plaintiff prayed for an account on the dissolution of co-partnership between himself and defendant, alleging that a balance was due him, but the Master's report, showing a large balance to be due to defendant, was sustained, except as to a comparatively small item.

Held, that the defendant was not entitled to a decree *with costs* as the plaintiff had succeeded in establishing his right to one half interest in a mill, which was disputed.

3. Plaintiffs having amended their writ, served it on defendant. with a notice, endorsed, requiring him to answer within fourteen days, otherwise, plaintiffs to be at liberty to sign final judgment by default, and have the writ taken *pro confesso.* Defendant, who had duly put in his answer to the original writ, did not within the time limited in the notice, answer the amendment, and plaintiffs obtained a rule *nisi,* calling upon him to shew cause why the writ should not be taken *pro confesso,* etc., before the argument of which rule defendant put in an answer, not denying the statements in the amendment, but leaving the proof of them to the plaintiffs.

Held, that the rule *nisi* must be discharged with costs, defendant having a right to put in his answer at any time before the marking of a default.

4. H. & M. McDonald made a bill of sale of personal property, dated July 5th, 1876, conditioned for the payment of $400 on the 5th July, 1877, and became insolvent 24th April, 1877. On the 8th June, 1877, to avoid leaving the property on the premises as a lien for rent, which accrued on the 12th of June, the insolvent's assignee and the holder of the bill of sale, after each advertising a sale of the property to which the other objected, agreed that it should be sold, reserving the proceeds for the adjudication of the Court.

Held, that the holder of the bill of sale was entitled to the proceeds, which were less than the amount due him, but that the decree should be without costs, as the controversy had arisen out of an asserted right to sell which did not exist in either party.

5. A cause was referred to a Master to ascertain what amount was due on a judgment upon which plaintiff had issued execution, directing the Sheriff to levy for $454. The Master reported only $62 due, and exceptions being taken to the report, it was, after argument, confirmed.

Held, that defendant was entitled to the costs of the reference, although plaintiff did not, at the time of issuing the execution, know what amount was due, in consequence of payments having been made to his attorney, who had left the province.

6. Plaintiff brought a suit to obtain from defendant a reconveyance on plaintiff's paying him the amount that should be found due upon an accounting, for which he prayed. Defendant set up a defence which was not sustained, and insisted on payment of $400, of which the Master allowed $29. Exceptions were taken to the report, some of which were allowed and others disallowed.

Held, that the plaintiff was entitled to the costs of the suit, but that the costs arising out of the exceptions should not be allowed to either party.

PRACTICE.

DEFAULT, Effect of.

Plaintiff brought suit against defendants as administrators of the estate of John Beaton to recover an amount due on an account stated and interest, and obtained judgment by default, no answer having been put in; after which it was referred to a master to ascertain the amount due. At the investigation all the parties were represented by their respective attorneys, and the master reported a sum due by defendant. Some of the defendants having objected to the report, on the ground that many of the charges comprised in the settlement had been originally entered against another party, and that no right of action existed against John Beaton's estate;

Held, that the objection was not now open, but should have been taken in an answer to the writ.

DEMURRER.

Where the demurrer is to the whole writ, if there is any part of it which entitles the plaintiff to relief, the demurrer must be over-ruled.

See also WINDSOR AND ANNAPOLIS RAILWAY.

PRACTICE.

DISCOVERY.

The plaintiffs sought in this suit discovery of facts necessary to enable them to plead to an action at law brought against them by the defendant, and the writ contained a prayer for relief in respect of the matters of which discovery was sought. On taking out the writ, plaintiffs obtained an order restraining defendant from further action in the common law suit, and defendant, having filed his answer, sought to have the restraining order discharged.

Held, that the plaintiff Company having sought relief in this Court, had elected this tribunal, and could not at the same time make the matters referred to in their writ the subject of pleas to the action at law; that the evidence sought for was, therefore, not pertinent to the defence in the action at law, and that the restraining order having been granted solely on the ground that discovery was necessary, must be discharged, irrespective of the sufficiency of the defendant's answer; that the present suit, although it could not be treated as a suit for discovery, still continued as a suit for relief, but the plaintiffs might discontinue the suit and plead the facts set out in their writ as a defence to the action at law.

INJUNCTION.

An injunction must be specifically prayed for, and will not be granted under the general prayer for relief.

INSOLVENT ACT.

Defendants, being added parties, resisted a proceeding taken by plaintiff, as assignee of a mortgage, to foreclose the same, on the ground that the mortgage was made in contemplation of insolvency, and was void under the Insolvent Act,—the mortgagee having afterwards become insolvent and assigned under the Act.

Held, that defendants, seeking as creditors of the insolvent to impeach the mortgage, solely on the ground that it was in contravention of the Insolvent Act, should have called on the assignee to take proceedings to set it aside, and, upon his refusal, should have applied to the Judge for leave to proceed in his name; and, further, that defendants should have proved their claims in order to entitle them so to proceed.

Q. Whether the defendants could contest the validity of the mortgage at all.

INTERLOCUTORY ORDER.

Interlocutory order, to compel executor to pay into Court the proceeds of sales, in a suit brought to remove the executor from office, refused, the affidavits on which it was founded being answered in every essential particular.

Summary remedy provided by Probate Act recommended.

PRACTICE.

INTERPLEADER.

Plaintiff mortgaged certain property to C. for $434.50, and covenanted in the mortgage to keep it insured for $500 in the name and for the benefit of the mortgagee. Subsequently, plaintiff effected insurance to the amount of $570 on his own account, without reference to the mortgagee, $180 of which was on the personal property, not covered by the mortgage. After loss by fire the mortgagee, finding that the insurance was not in his name, demanded an assignment of the policy, offering to secure to plaintiff the amount due him, and, upon his refusal, claimed the amount from the Company. Defendants paid the $180 and, upon action brought for the balance, an interpleader order was made.

Held, that the insurance enured to the benefit of the mortgagee, and that he was entitled to interplead, although the claim of the mortgagee was an equitable claim, and the Company was under a contractual obligation to the plaintiff, and although the claim of the mortgagee was smaller than the amount insured.

NEW TRIAL.

1. The practice of the Supreme Court on the common law side, in relation to setting aside verdicts and granting new trials, is peculiarly applicable to the trial of issues in Equity, on circuit, and a party dissatisfied with a verdict in an equity suit, tried on circuit, should apply to the Judge before whom it was tried for a rule *nisi*, or, in the event of his refusing a rule, should take it out under the statute, and cannot, having ignored that practice, move the Equity Court at Halifax to set aside the verdict.

2. Where the trial took place at Halifax before the Judge in Equity, and the verdict was found on September 25th, and the rule, having been refused by the Judge, was not taken out until October 30th,

Held, that, assuming the plaintiff to have had a right to take out a rule under the statute, he had allowed too much time to elapse, and had by the delay lost his right to do so.

PERPETUATING TESTIMONY.

Plaintiffs alleged in their bill that one of the defendants accepted and executed a lease for fourteen years, determinable on six months' notice, that notice was given, but the period had not expired ; that said defendant intended to contest the right of the plaintiffs, and set up a title in the other defendant to defeat the plaintiffs ; that while this litigation was threatened no action could at present be brought, and that the evidence of a certain witness would be necessary and material to enable them to establish their claim ; that he was aged and about to leave the Province, and though they could obtain his evidence now, they might not be able to do so at the time of an action hereafter brought.

Held, that sufficient had been set out to sustain plaintiffs' bill to perpetuate testimony, and the bill was not demurrable.

PRACTICE.

SECURITY FOR COSTS.

Security for costs ordered where the insolvent plaintiff company, though incorporated in the Province, was registered in England, and had its directory and place of business there ; and the parties using the name of the company in the suit were not in the Province.

SETTING ASIDE AWARD.

See ARBITRATION.

SETTING OFF COSTS.

In January, 1879, plaintiffs obtained a rule setting aside defendant's demurrer with costs, and in July of that year the suit terminated by a decree in favor of defendant, with costs. Previous to this decree the defendant became entitled, on the common law side of the Court, to a bill of costs against McClelland, who was the real party in this suit, the other plaintiff being merely a nominal party to the suit. The costs on the decree in favor of the defendant in the suit first mentioned were paid in full by McClelland, who did not apply to have the costs due him on the rule set off or deducted, and McClelland having died, plaintiffs' attorney entered a suggestion and issued execution for the bill of costs on the rule to set aside the demurrer.

Held, that defendant was entitled to have the costs in the common law suit set off against the costs on the rule, although there was a nominal party in the suit brought in this Court who was not a party in the common law suit.

Q. Whether the cause of action survived to the nominal plaintiff, within the meaning of R. S., cap. 94, sec. 103.

SUPPLEMENTAL BILL.

Plaintiff, as official assignee of M., took proceedings to recover back money paid to defendants in fraud of creditors Subsequently, the creditors' assignee, on being appointed, obtained a rule *nisi* calling on defendants to shew cause why he should not be allowed to file a supplemental bill and become plaintiff.

Held, that the plaintiff was entitled to file a supplemental bill.

WAIVER OF OBJECTION.

The original plaintiff died after writ issued and before answer, and the suit was revived by her executor. Defendants, in their answer, did not call in question the death of the original plaintiff, or the appointment of the present plaintiff as her executor, and raised no objection to his not being the proper person to revive the suit. But after the issues raised by their answer were found against them, the objection was taken at the hearing that other parties should have been before the Court as plaintiffs

Held, that the objection should have been raised by demurrer or plea, or defendants should have insisted on it in their answer, and that, although such an objection might be taken at the hearing, if it were made to appear that the rights of other parties not before the Court would be prejudiced by the decree sought for, yet if the Court could make a decree which would do justice to all parties, it would not allow the objection then to prevail.

RAILWAY ACT, PROVINCIAL, Construction of.

The defendant company was incorporated by cap. 74 of the acts of 1876, sec. 13 of which provided that whenever it should be necessary for the construction, &c. of the company's works, &c., that the company should be invested with any lands, and no agreement could be made for the purchase thereof, the company might apply by petition to a Judge of the Supreme Court, who, if satisfied that the lands were necessary, should direct an appraisement ; and by sec. 14 it was provided that. on payment or tender of the compensation awarded, the land should vest in the company with right of immediate possession. By the 36th section the provisions of chapter 70 R S., (3rd Series) were made applicable to the line or lines of railway to be built by the company, " as far as the same may be applicable, certain sections of said cap. 70 being excepted, among which was section 24, (q v). The 11th section of this chapter authorized the company to take possession of lands required for the track of railways or for stations, and under those provisions the defendant company entered upon and took possession of land of the plaintiff company, (incorporated in 1866), on which borings for salt had been made, and buildings erected with machinery, &c. Plaintiffs obtained a rule *nisi* for an injunction, claiming that the defendant company could not resort to the provisions of cap. 70 R. S , (3rd series,) to acquire land necessary for their railroad, but must obtain it under the 13th and 14th sections of their own act, under which they were required to tender or pay the appraised value before being entitled to possession.

Held, that the provisions in the act incorporating the company (secs. 13, 14, &c.) related to the obtaining of land for the mining operations contemplated by their act, but that for the purpose of obtaining land for the line of railway and stations, which was a matter of public interest, they could resort to the provisions of cap. 70 R. S., (3rd series) ; that no inference against this view could be drawn from the fact that section 24 of cap. 70, making a certain class of damages a county charge, was included among the excepted sections, as that section did not refer to lands required for the track and stations, which were made a county charge by section 52 and following sections of cap. 70 not included among the excepted sections.

N. S. Salt & Exploration Co. v. *Halifax & C. B. Railway & Coal Co...* 265

REFERENCE.

See ARBITRATION.

REFORMING DEED.

See MISTAKE, 2.

See also INSURANCE, Marine, 2.

REGISTRY OF DEEDS.

Mitchell, who had been the owner of three lots upon which the plaintiff held mortgages foreclosed in the present suit, conveyed one of the lots, known as the Chebucto Foundry lot, to Montgomery and Budd, by deed registered in 1866. In 1871, Budd became insolvent, and his assignee conveyed his interest in the lot to Montgomery, by deed registered in 1871, after which, in October, 1872, a mortgage was made by Montgomery to Stairs, which was recorded in November, 1872. Previously to Budd's failure, Montgomery and Budd entered into an agreement with Mitchell, reciting that plaintiff held mortgages on certain property of Mitchell, on which there was due $16,000, that Montgomery and Budd had purchased part of said property, and as part of the consideration therefor agreed to assume the said mortgages and relieve Mitchell therefrom, and the instrument contained covenants to indemnify Mitchell, his heirs, &c., from all actions which might arise in consequence of the said mortgages covering more land than that purchased from him, or in consequence of the bonds given with the said mortgages. This agreement was registered, previously to the mortgage to Stairs, but was unknown to him and to Wylde, Hart & Co., who were interested with him in the mortgage, until after the mortgage was recorded. The Master, reporting as to the disposal of the surplus proceeds, treated Stairs as the first encumbrancer, after the plaintiff, on the property over which his mortgage extended, and exception was taken to the report on the ground that effect had not been given to the agreement registered previously.

Held, that,—although Montgomery, if he had not given the mortgage, and those claiming under him with a knowledge of the existence of the agreement when they took the conveyance from him, would have been deprived of any right to the surplus funds, the agreement in question was not an instrument the registration of which was contemplated by the Registry Act, and therefore the registration of it could not be deemed to be notice of its existence and contents to a party claiming under a deed or mortgage for valuable consideration, and that Stairs and those claiming with him, not having received actual or constructive notice of its existence when the mortgage was taken, were to be considered as *bona fide* mortgagees, unaffected by it.

REGISTRY OF ASSIGNMENT.

The defendant, holding a mortgage on certain real estate, which was duly recorded, assigned the same to the plaintiffs, after which defendant purchased the equity of redemption, and the deed was duly recorded. Attachments were then issued against the defendant as an absconding debtor, and the attachments, as well as the judgments entered thereon, were placed on record before the assignment of the mortgage. The attaching creditors claimed, under Revised Statutes, cap. 79, secs. 19 and 22, to have priority, as against the assignee of the mortgage.

Held, that the mortgage remained a lien on the property, whether the assignment was recorded or not, and that the attaching creditors had not the priority claimed.

RELEASE, Decree to Execute.
See PRACTICE—COSTS.

———— BY AGENT WITHOUT AUTHORITY.

Defendant, D. McD., being part owner, with plaintiff and the other defendants, of a barque, was authorized by the other owners to sell her, and did so, depositing plaintiff's share of the proceeds to his own credit, in the Pictou Bank. Plaintiff wrote to one S. C. in these terms : " I want you to put my share of the money in the bank, to my credit. I have written D., (meaning D McD.,) stating that I have authorized you to do so." S. C. had, before this letter came to him, drawn the money from the bank, the manager having advanced it to him on his own check; but defendant, D. McD., upon the letter being shewn to him by S. C., signed a release to the bank from any claim on account of the payment of the money to S. C.

Held, that D. McD., was not justified in releasing the bank; that in doing so, he assumed the liability which the bank had incurred by the unwarrantable payment to S. C. of the money placed to his (McD.'s) credit, and that plaintiff was entitled to a decree for the amount of his share, deposited in the bank.

RE–SALE under proceedings to foreclose.

See FORECLOSURE, RE–SALE, &c.

SALE UNDER FORECLOSURE.

Under an order of foreclosure and sale, plaintiffs advertized for sale "all the estate, right, title, interest and equity of redemption" of the defendants. At the sale one M. became the purchaser, and paid down the ten per cent. deposit required under the terms of the sale, but refused to complete the purchase, on the ground that a good title in fee simple could not be given. An order for a re-sale was made and the property was sold for an amount less than the amount of the mortgage. Plaintiffs applied to the Court for an order for the payment to them of the deposit on the first sale. M. showed cause, contending that he was entitled to the return of the deposit as a good title could not be given.

Held, that, as the plaintiffs had only professed to sell the title of the defendants, such as it was, and had not been guilty of fraud or misrepresentation, and the purchaser would, under his purchase, have acquired all that he bid for, he was not entitled to a return of the deposit.

Diocesan Synod N. S. v. O'Brien et al............................... 352

SHELLY'S CASE, Rule in.

A testator devised land to M. E. R., giving her in terms an estate for life, the property to go at her death to her children then born, whom he designated by name, and to such other children as she might have, and their lawful children, and to their heirs lawfully begotten. In the next clause he declared that it was his will that the property should be entailed upon the direct descendants of his four children and their offspring forever. In the codicil to his will he referred to the estate he had given by his will as an estate for life to his children, (one of whom was M. E. R.,) and stated that he had entailed the property on their children.

Held, that the words defining the persons to take on the expiration of the life estate were intended as a *designatio personarum* and not as words of limitation; that the rule in Shelly's case did not, therefore, apply, and the devisee took only a life estate.

Robinson et al v. Hendry.. 330

SPECIFIC PERFORMANCE.

1. Plaintiff brought suit to compel the performance by defendant of a contract in writing for the purchase of a house. During the negotiations defendant asked expressly as to the drainage, which plaintiff assured him was perfect, but which in fact was seriously defective. It appeared that the representations had been made by the plaintiff in good faith and in ignorance of the facts, and, the house being occupied, defendant could not inspect it for himself. Nothing was said about the matter in the written contract.

   Held, that in the suit for specific performance the verbal representations made previous to the written contract must be taken into consideration, and that, being material representations on the faith of which defendant entered into the contract, they constituted a defence, although plaintiff did not know them to be untrue

   Thomson v. Longard........ 181

2. Plaintiff brought this suit to compel defendants to deliver to him a policy of insurance for $600, alleging that they had received his premium on the 27th November, 1877, and undertaken to insure his

house for a year from that date, and to deliver a policy to that effect. The building was destroyed by fire in December, 1877. Defendants alleged that they had been induced to enter into the contract by the misrepresentation of plaintiff that the Building Society were about to advance $600 on the property, and that they had undertaken to insure it, not for the plaintiff, but for the Society. At the hearing plaintiff's counsel asked for a decree for a policy, and also for the payment of the money.

Held, that, even if such relief could be granted, it could only be upon a bill asking for it, whereas plaintiff had in his writ asked only for a policy ; and further, that as the evidence was directly in conflict on the point as to misrepresentation, and as to the terms of the contract, plaintiff should be left to his remedy at law.

Bill dismissed without costs.

3. B & E. Colp, being the owners of certain lands, subject to a mortgage of $2,666, and indebted to other parties in the sum of $691, entered into an agreement with J. Hubley and C. A. Whitman, whereby, in consideration of the latter agreeing to liquidate the mortgage and the other debts, the parties first mentioned agreed to deed to them the real estate mentioned in the mortgage. It was further agreed that Hubley, Whitman and B. Colp, the defendant, should carry on a lumbering business on the property. The debts were accordingly paid, and the plaintiffs and defendant conducted the business, but defendant refused to sign the deed of the property, denied that a partnership had been entered into as alleged, and claimed that the agreement had been procured by misrepresentation, which he failed to prove.

Held, that the plaintiffs were entitled to specific performance of the agreement.

STATUTES OF ELIZABETH.
See ELIZABETH, STATUTES OF.

———— OF FRAUDS.
See FRAUDS, STATUTE OF.

———— OF LIMITATIONS.
See LIMITATIONS, STATUTE OF.

SURPLUS PROCEEDS.

R. M. & Co sought to have surplus proceeds arising out of a sale under foreclosure applied to a recorded judgment held by them against the mortgagor. The judgment was recorded in May, 1874. Plaintiff's mortgage had been recorded in 1869, and a prior mortgage of the same property had been recorded in 1855. Defendant having become insolvent, his assignee, in order to prevent the sacrifice of the property, paid off the mortgage last mentioned and the interest on plaintiff's mortgage, receiving from the holders of the mortgage which he paid an instrument in which, after reciting payment of the principal and interest, it expressed that the bond was delivered up to be cancelled, (which, however, was not cancelled, but was produced with the mortgage,) and that they remised, released, and quitted claim to him, as assignee, the land therein mentioned, and all the right which they had as executors, and all sums mentioned therein, to have and to hold to the said K., as assignee as aforesaid, his successors and assigns.

Held, that this instrument, though inartificially drawn, was open to the construction that it was a satisfaction of the debt as between the executors and the assignee, but conveyed to the latter all their interest in the mortgage as against subsequent incumbrancers; but that, even assuming that it was a release of the mortgage, and not an assignment, the assignee had a prior claim to the surplus proceeds for the amounts he had advanced on the mortgage to prevent foreclosure and sale, subject to a credit for any amounts received by him for rent of the mortgaged premises.

The assignee had also recovered judgment against the sheriff, who had been indemnified by R. M. & Co., and they being entitled to a lien on the land if their judgment against the defendant was established, if not to a dividend out of defendant's estate, it was agreed that they should be relieved of the assignee's judgment against the sheriff, and that the amount should go against their judgment in the event of its being held valid, or if not, then against their dividend.

Held, that the assignee, under this agreement, had also a prior claim on the surplus proceeds for the amount of the judgment against the sheriff, and that R. M. & Co. were entitled only to the balance.

TAXES, Lien for.

1. Defendants' testator mortgaged certain property to plaintiff who afterwards foreclosed and the property was offered for sale April 10th, 1876, and bid in by John McDonald, who paid a deposit of $300, but failed to complete the purchase. The property was again offered for sale November 19th, 1877, and realized a sum which, with the deposit paid on the first sale, satisfied the plaintiffs' mortgage, and left a surplus of $322.29. Upon this surplus a claim was made under R. S. cap. 21, sec. 81, for taxes due by testator for 1874-5-6-7. McDonald, who had bid in the property at the first sale, held a second mortgage upon it to more than the amount remaining in the Sheriff's hands.

Held, that the statute was not applicable to the case, as the sale referred to in the first branch of the section was a sale by the person owing the rates at the time of the sale, whereas the testator had conveyed the property to the mortgagee before the rates had become due, and the property had not been taken under any "process of law" within the meaning of the words in the latter part of the section.

2. The City of Halifax has no lien upon real estate for taxes, sec. 342 of chap. 81 of the Acts of 1864, having reference only to personal property.

TRADE MARK.

See LABEL.

TRAFFIC ARRANGEMENT.

See WINDSOR AND ANNAPOLIS RAILWAY CO.

TRUST.

1. Thos. S. Crow, an ordained Presbyterian minister, and David and Jacob Frieze, Presbyterians and members of his congregation, purchased a lot of land in 1853 for the purpose of building a house of worship, and for a burial place for that part of the congregation residing in its neighborhood, and having erected at their own cost a place of worship, and fenced in the land, conveyed the land and building in 1854 to W.

McDonald and other persons, thirty in number, by deed, in which it was recited that the land had been purchased for a Presbyterian Church and Cemetery, and that the grantors had agreed to sell the land and church on the same terms and for the same use as they held them. The deed proceeded to convey to the said thirty persons in fee simple thirty-eight forty-fifths of the land and buildings (reserving seven forty-fifths to the grantors) to be held in common by the grantees, but as separate and sole owners of the pews on which their names were recorded on a plan annexed. The persons to whom the deed was given were then Presbyterians, and Mr. Crow was a minister of that Church, and after he ceased to officiate, a Mr. McLellan, who had been his colleague and succeeded him, officiated there until 1871. He was a regularly ordained minister of the Presbyterian Church, but about that time charges were preferred against him by his congregation. He first appealed to the Synod at Truro, but afterwards intimated that he had joined the Congregationalists, and was thereupon deposed, some of the congregation seceding with him The plaintiffs, (as Presbyterians,) and the defendants, (as Congregationalists,) each party claiming the exclusive right to the lot of land and building;

Held, that the intention of the parties being clear and unequivocal, that the house of worship was to be for the use of Presbyterians, the Court must carry out that intention and could not recognize the right of the defendants, even if comprising a majority of the congregation to defeat such intention, though it might be otherwise if the congregation were unanimous.

2. Caleb Putnam conveyed a lot of land to the persons named in the deed for the purpose of building a Presbyterian Church and for a burial ground, to hold to the said grantees for aforesaid purpose only.

Held, that even should the grantees unanimously concur in changing the use of the property from that of a Presbyterian Church, &c., such change could not be effected, but the property on being applied to other uses than those for which it had been conveyed, would revert.

3. By letters patent in 1796, the school lands in the township of Cornwallis were granted to the then Rector and Wardens, and the Rector and Wardens for the time being of St. John's Church, Cornwallis, in trust for the use of the school or schools in Cornwallis, to have and to hold during their continuance in the said offices, respectively, for the convenience and benefit of all the inhabitants of said township; and in trust that all schools in the township furnished with teachers qualified agreeably to law, and contracted with for a term not less than a year, should be entitled to an equal portion of the rents and profits, provided such masters should receive, free of expense, such poor children as might be sent to them by the trustees. Down to 1873 the rents and profits were divided among all the schools of the township complying with the terms set out. After that date the funds were allowed to accumulate, until 1879, when the defendants, being trustees, proposed to appropriate the proceeds to the erection of a school house in a particular school section, on land which did not belong to the township, but of which the trustees expected to get a deed. The section, in which it was proposed to erect the school house, was twenty miles distant from one end of the township.

Held, that the lands were held subject to a trust for the benefit of all the schools complying with the terms, and that the proceeds must be divided among them all, and that the action was rightly brought in the name of the Attorney-General of the Province, and not of the Attorney-General of Canada.

TRUSTEE, Liability of.

Provision in a will that defendant should hold land, &c., in trust to cultivate, demise, let and manage the same to the best advantage for testator's daughter, without impeachment of waste, held not to exonerate the trustee from responsibility for wasting the trust property, but simply to empower him to do "such acts as he could do if a tenant who was not accountable for waste."

Held, further, that the trustee under such devise was not obliged to work a mill on the trust property; and that if the trustee was unable to procure a suitable tenant, he ought not to be held answerable for the unproductiveness of the property.

Held, further, that the defendant, in selling the grass uncut at auction, instead of making it into hay and storing or disposing of it as such, had pursued a course which he was, under the circumstances, at liberty to adopt.

——————— LIABILITY OF, FOR INVESTMENT.

1. A testator, by his will, devised and bequeated his real and personal estate to his wife and another, as executrix and executor, in trust to sell the same and invest the proceeds in the best securities they could obtain, and, upon the coming of age of the testator's children, to divide the money among the children and the widow, in specified proportions. The executor, with the consent and acquiescence of the widow and executrix, loaned a part of the trust funds to merchants engaged in ship-building, who afterwards became insolvent and unable to re-pay the money.

    Held, that the trustees were not justified in investing the money on personal security, and must make good the loss to the children; but that the widow could not make her co-trustee liable to her for the loss she might sustain, having acquiesced in the investment.

2. Trustees were sought to be made personally liable for a sum invested on mortgage, on the ground that they had invested on a second mortgage, and on property of which the mortgagor only had title to a part. Before making the investment the trustees had been advised by their solicitor as to the value as well as the title, the solicitor considering it a first-rate security. The whole property was valued at $5,000, the first mortgage amounted to only $1 200, and the mortgagor's interest in the remaining $3,800 was two-thirds, amounting to $2,532, leaving a margin of $1,170 over and above the amount loaned by the trustees.

    Held, that, even if the security was not first-class, the trustees, having believed it to be good, could not be held personally liable for deficiency. R. S., Cap. 108, Sec. 24.

TRUSTEES OF SCHOOLS, Corporate character of.

Plaintiff brought action against the defendants for a mandamus to compel them to provide for a debt due him by the trustees of a school section. The writ was against the defendants personally, but contained a statement that they were trustees, &c., and that defendant D., was secretary. Evidence was taken as to the existence of the debt, and the case came on for hearing under the pleadings and evidence.

Held, that the trustees could only be sued in their corporate name; and that the amendment to that effect, asked for by the plaintiff at the hearing, could not be permitted.

ULTRA VIRES.

Plaintiffs had security on the undertaking of the defendant company, future calls on shares, and all tolls and money arising from the undertaking, for £200,000 as a first lien. Messrs. Roberts, Lubbuck & Co., an English firm, had a lien on the rolling stock for £25,000, and there were about £70,000 due to unsecured creditors. Defendants, under Chapter 104 of the Acts of 1874, of the Legislature of Nova Scotia, entitled, "An Act to facilitate arrangements between Railway Companies and their creditors," filed a scheme, whereby preferential stock to the extent of £75,000 was to be created, to be a first charge on both the undertaking, calls, tolls, &c., and the rolling-stock, and this, or the money coming from it, was to be applied to the payment in full of Messrs. Roberts, Lubbuck & Co, and certain other unsecured debts specified; stock to the extent of £350,000 was then to be created, to be a subsequent charge on the undertaking, &c., and rolling-stock. and to be issued at par to the existing debenture holders in lieu of the debentures they then held, which were to be delivered up to be cancelled. Plaintiff obtained an order for the appointment of a receiver, which defendants obtained a rule *nisi* to rescind The Court, considering that the Act was *ultra vires*, as it dealt with the subject of insolvency, and further, that the scheme filed was unreasonable, as its object was to secure other creditors at the expense of debenture holders having a first lien, discharged the last rule *nisi*, but, in view of the possible reversal of the judgment on appeal, offered to modify the order appointing the receiver, by directing him to pay the amount to be received to the Receiver-General, to abide the further order of the Court.

Murdoch v. *W. & A. Railway Co* 137

See also JOINT STOCK COMPANIES, 1.

UMPIRE.

See ARBITRATION, 1.

VERBAL REPRESENTATIONS, Effect of upon written contract.

See SPECIFIC PERFORMANCE, 1.

VERDICT, Setting aside.

See PRACTICE—NEW TRIAL.

WAIVER of irregularities in proceedings for dyke rates.

Defendants having contended that they could not be required to contribute to the maintenance of a dyke, as there had been irregularities in the proceedings to assess the rate.

Held, that having acquiesced in the annual payments for upwards of twenty-five years, they could not now raise such a question, and that the alleged irregularities could only have been taken advantage of by *certiorari*.

Wickwire v. *Gould* 245

——— OF OBJECTION.

Plaintiff brought suit against defendants, as administrators of the estate of John Beaton, to recover an amount due on an account stated and interest, and obtained judgment by default, no answer having been put in ; after which it was referred to a master to ascertain the amount due. At the investigation all the parties were represented by their respective attorneys, and the master reported a sum due by defendant. Some of the defendants having objected to the report, on the ground that many of the charges comprised in the settlement had been originally entered against another party, and that no right of action existed against John Beaton's estate.

Held, that the objection was not now open, but should have been taken in an answer to the writ.

McNeil v. *Beaton et al* 144

See also ARBITRATION, 1.

WASTE, Without impeachment of.

Provision in a will that defendant should hold land, &c., in trust to cultivate, demise, let and manage the same to the best advantage for testator's daughter, without impeachment of waste, held not to exonerate the trustee from responsibility for wasting the trust property, but simply to empower him to do " such acts as he could do if a tenant who was not accountable for waste."

Held, further, that the trustee under such devise was not obliged to work a mill on the trust property ; and that if the trustee was unable to procure a suitable tenant, he ought not to be held answerable for the unproductiveness of the property.

Held, further, that the defendant, in selling the grass uncut at auction, instead of making it into hay and storing or disposing of it as such, had pursued a course which, he was, under the circumstances, at liberty to adopt.

Vernon et al v. *Seaman* 190

WILL, Construction of.

1. J. W., by his last will, among other things, devised all his real estate to trustees, to let it during the natural life of his wife, or, in case she should die before his youngest surviving child should attain the age of twenty-one years, then until such child should attain that age, to receive the rents and, after paying a certain annuity and charges, to divide all balances equally among *all his before-mentioned children*, and such further child or children as might be born. The testator, in another part of his will, clearly indicated his intention that upon the decease of his wife or upon his youngest surviving child attaining the age of twenty-one years, whichever event should last happen, the real estate should be sold and the proceeds divided equally among his *surviving* children.

During the life of the widow a daughter died, leaving children, who claimed the daughter's share of the rents.

Held, that they were entitled to such share.

Daniel et al. v. *Veith et al* 46

2. G. E. Bisset, by his will, bequeated to his daughter, Maria Matheson, £2,000, " for herself and her children, issue of her marriage, now or hereafter living, to be exempt from any debts or liabilities of her husband, Donald Matheson, should he from accident or misfortune hereafter become embarrassed, with power in his executors to invest the same at her desire in good securities with interest for her and her children's benefit," subject to a deduction of £870 due the testator by Donald Matheson. The plaintiff, together with Matheson, testator's widow, and another, were appointed executors. Testator died in 1861, there being at that time and at the time of the making of the will,

WINDING UP.

See JOINT STOCK COMPANY'S ACT.

WINDSOR & ANNAPOLIS RAILWAY CO.

1. Plaintiff's bill set out the Act of the Legislature of Nova Scotia
(1865 c. 13) providing for the construction of the Windsor and Annapolis Railway ; the agreement of November 22, 1866, between the Commissioner of Railways for Nova Scotia and Messrs. Punchard, Barry
& Clark for its construction, containing a stipulation that prior to the
opening of the road a traffic arrangement should be made between the
parties for the mutual use by the Province and the Company of their
respective lines of railway from Halifax to Windsor, and from Windsor
to Annapolis ; the Act of the Provincial Legislature incorporating the
Company (1867 c. 36) of which the Act first mentioned and the agreement in pursuance thereof were made a part ; the agreement of the Government of Canada (successor to that of Nova Scotia in relation to the
line from Halifax to Windsor), with the plaintiffs, made September 22nd,
1871, providing that the Company should, with exceptions not touching
the matter in hand, have the exclusive use of the Windsor Branch with
station accommodation, etc., and the use, so far as required, of the
Trunk Line from Windsor Junction to Halifax, the Company to pay
over to the Government monthly one-third of the gross earnings of the
Government lines, the agreement to continue twenty-one years, then
renewable, but to terminate in the event of the Company failing to operate the Railways between Halifax and Annapolis. Plaintiffs alleged
that, having certain equitable claims against the Government of Canada, they allowed their payments due under the agreement of
September, 1871, to fall in arrear, but paid them off in November, 1872,
after which under similar circumstances they again allowed them to fall
in arrear, in consequence of which the Government threatened to resume
possession of the road, unless payment was made on or before October
1st, 1873, which period was afterwards extended to November 1st, 1873 ;
that on the 22nd October, 1873, a Minute of the Privy Council of Can-

ada was passed, of which no notice, official or otherwise, was given to the Plaintiffs, by or on behalf of the Government, reciting that the Company owed the Government $30,000, and had failed to operate the Windsor Branch, and recommending that the Government should immediately proceed to operate the road between Halifax and Windsor; that afterwards on the 20th June, 1875, an agreement was entered into between Her Majesty the Queen, represented by the Minister of Public Works, and the plaintiff Company, whereby the Company agreed to change the gauge of their Railway and release all claims against the Government to July 1st, 1875, and in consideration thereof the debts alleged to be due to the Government by the Company up to January 1st, 1875, were extinguished, and it was declared that the agreement under which the Company held and worked the Branch Line continued in full force and effect, except as thus modified. Plaintiffs alleged that they had continued in possession of said Windsor Branch until August, 1877, when the Superintendent of Government Railways took forcible possession and prevented them from using the branch. The road was afterwards transferred by the Dominion Government to the defendants on the 24th September, 1877, such transfer being based on the Dominion Act of 1874, c. 16. (q. v.) Defendants having demurred to this writ:

Held, That by the agreement of September 1871, the Windsor Branch was in fact leased to the plaintiffs for twenty-one years, that the only event upon which the Government was authorized to re-enter was a failure to operate the road between Halifax and Annapolis; that the statement in the Minute of Council that plaintiffs had failed to operate the road could be controverted in this suit,—and could be so controverted without making the Crown or the Government, represented by the Attorney General of Canada, a party to the suit,—and having been denied by the plaintiffs, must be taken for the purpose of the argument on the demurrer to be untrue; that, independently of the Act of 1874, the only interest that could be transferred to the defendants by the Government was their reversionary interest in the road, subject to the plaintiffs' lease; that the Act of 1873 did not directly and in terms divest the plaintiffs of their rights, and must be held as intended simply to sanction the transfer to the defendants of such interest as the Government itself had in the road; that the plaintiffs had no adequate remedy at Law, by *scire facias* or petition of right, as they did not seek redress against the Crown, or the Government of Canada, as it was not in the power of the Government of Canada or the Crown to give them the relief sought for,—nor by ejectment, because, assuming that ejectment would lie in respect to the rights claimed by plaintiffs to operate the railway under the agreement of 1871, plaintiffs could not by that action obtain any relief in respect to the original agreement with the Provincial Government as to running powers, and this ground of demurrer being to the whole writ, even if applicable to part of the writ, must be overruled, as it could not be good in part and bad in part.

2.   On the hearing of this cause on the evidence, an objection was taken on behalf of the Attorney General of Canada, that the agreement of September, 1871, (*ante* p. 287) was not binding on the Dominion Government, because the railroad from Halifax to Windsor was a Provincial public work, and as such passed to the Dominion Government under the B. N. A. Act, not as ordinary Government property, but subject to a trust which the Government was bound strictly to fulfil and which required that it should be worked for the public benefit, in acordance with the terms of the Act under which it was built, and subject to the engagements which had been entered into by the Provincial Government and Legislature; and that the terms of the agreement did not carry out this trust, as by the provisions of the Provincial Act of 1867, embodying the contract between the Government and the promoters of the plaintiff company, it was mutually agreed that, prior to the opening of the road, a traffic arrangement should be made for the mutual use

by the Government and the Company of their respective lines, which stipulation had not been carried out in the agreement, as there was no provision in it for a traffic arrangement.

Held, that the agreement embodied all the essential provisions of the original contract, and that the Government not having insisted on having running powers over plaintiffs' road was no reason why plaintiffs should be deprived of running powers over the Halifax and Windsor line; but that, on the other hand, the ground stated applied with great force to the action of the Dominion Legislature, under the Act of 1874, inasmuch as the Dominion Government having taken the road, under the provisions of an Imperial Act, clothed with a trust, the Dominion Legislature was thereby restrained from acting in violation of that trust.

See also ULTRA VIRES.

WRITTEN CONTRACT affected by verbal representations.

Lightning Source UK Ltd.
Milton Keynes UK
UKHW020738251118
332796UK00002B/280/P